HANDBOOK OF
BUSINESS PRACTICES AND
GROWTH IN
EMERGING MARKETS

HANDBOOK OF BUSINESS PRACTICES AND GROWTH IN EMERGING MARKETS

edited by

Satyendra Singh

University of Winnipeg, Canada

World Scientific

NEW JERSEY · LONDON · SINGAPORE · BEIJING · SHANGHAI · HONG KONG · TAIPEI · CHENNAI

Published by

World Scientific Publishing Co. Pte. Ltd.

5 Toh Tuck Link, Singapore 596224

USA office: 27 Warren Street, Suite 401-402, Hackensack, NJ 07601

UK office: 57 Shelton Street, Covent Garden, London WC2H 9HE

British Library Cataloguing-in-Publication Data
A catalogue record for this book is available from the British Library.

HANDBOOK OF BUSINESS PRACTICES AND GROWTH IN EMERGING MARTKETS

ISBN-13 978-981-279-177-1
ISBN-10 981-279-177-9

Typeset by Stallion Press
Email: enquiries@stallionpress.com

Printed in Singapore by B & JO Enterprise

CONTENTS

v

ACKNOWLEDGMENTS

I gratefully acknowledge the support of Centre for Emerging Markets, Faculty of Business and Economics and Global College, University of Winnipeg in providing the Centre's Grant (# 0-60-7199-61020-000) and Discretionary Grant (# 0-60-7133-61020-000) for editing this handbook. I am particularly thankful to Professor Dr Michael Benarroch, Dean, Faculty of Business and Economics for supporting the Centre and its mission to conduct research in emerging markets, which are under-represented in literature. This handbook fills this gap. I would also like to thank Yury Eskin and Jenna Buckley for their editorial assistance, and my wife Dr Meera Kaur for being supportive of this project. My thanks are also due to the authors, reviewers, collaborators, and the publishing team; without their support, this Handbook would not have been produced.

FOREWORD

This is the first book that focuses on examining such a wide range of business issues across emerging markets with an eye on providing recommendations to enhance and improve decision making and organizational efficiency. This book considers a wide range of issues such as finance, marketing, international business, economic development, the environment, information technology, etc. and relates them to issues arising in emerging markets. While the chapters contained within the handbook are diverse in terms of their subject matter and approach, this book provides valuable insights into the prevailing best business practices in emerging markets across the world. Dr Singh has brought together a collection of studies from some of the world's leading academics on emerging markets. This book is written in a manner that is accessible to senior undergraduate students, graduate students, and managers. It should be a standard reference for researchers and practitioners interested in business issues relating to emerging markets.

Professor Michael Benarroch
Dean, Faculty of Business and Economics,
University of Winnipeg,
Canada

NOTE ON EDITOR

Satyendra Singh is a Director of Centre for Emerging Markets and associate professor of Marketing and International Business in the Faculty of Business and Economics, University of Winnipeg, Canada. He has published several articles in reputed journals such *as Thunderbird International Business Review, Industrial Marketing Management, Service Industries Journal, International Journal of Nonprofit and Voluntary Sector Marketing, Journal of Services Marketing,* among others. He has authored two books titled *Market Orientation, Corporate Culture and Business Performance* (Ashgate, UK, 2004), and *Business Practices in Emerging and Re-emerging Markets* (Palgrave Macmillan, USA, 2008). He is also Editor-in-Chief of *International Journal of Business and Emerging Markets.* He can be reached at s.singh@uwinnipeg.ca

NOTES ON CONTRIBUTORS

1. Mohammed Alam

Mohammed Nurul Alam, who obtained his Doctoral Degree on "Small Business Finance by Islamic Banks" from "Lund University", Lund, Sweden, is basically a teacher in various commerce subjects like financial accounting, international accounting, managerial accounting and auditing. He worked with the United Nations under UNDP Umbrella Project as "Lecturer in Accounting and Finance" at Kenya Institute of Administration (KIA) Nairobi, Kenya, from 1979 to 1985. He worked as an Assistant Professor in Accounting at the Islamic University, Bangladesh from 1987 to 1989. At Lund University, he worked as a research fellow from 1996 to 2000 and taught different subjects like international marketing and banking to the students of the Master's program on South East Asian Studies. From 2000 to 2003, Dr Alam worked with the BMC in Mississuga, Canada, as a coordinator of a so-called "Fresh Start" program (Small Business Training for women), funded by the Ontario Trillium Foundation. Since February 2004, Dr Alam has been teaching accounting subjects in the Department of Accounting at the Sultan Qaboos University in Oman. Since 2006, he has been teaching PhD students as a visiting professor, in the department of Islamic Economics and Finance at Trisakti University, Jakarta, Indonesia. E-mail: mna5@rogers.com

2. Denise Chaves Carvalho Barbosa

Denise Chaves Carvalho Barbosa graduated in Business Administration by Faculdades Integradas Anglo Americano, 1993; master in Administration by Faculdades IBMEC-RJ, 2007. He has been working since 1982 in a multinational company, involved with IT activities for the last six years. Has scientific papers published in Revista Eletrônica de Sistemas da Informação (Information Systems Electronic Magazine) — RESI. Participates as a presenter in the second encounter of scientific initiation, September 2007, representing Faculdades Integradas IBMEC-RJ. E-mail: denise_ccb@yahoo. com.br

3. John Branch

John Branch is currently a Lecturer of Marketing and Strategy at the Stephen M. Ross School of Business at the University of Michigan, where he teaches marketing and international business courses at the undergraduate, MBA, and executive levels. He also serves as Director of Educational Outreach at the William Davidson Institute (a University institute which focuses on emerging economies), and holds a Faculty Associate position at the Center for Russian and East European Studies. John teaches and consults regularly in emerging economies around the world, and is a visiting professor at several international business schools, including the Stockholm School of Economics in Riga, Latvia, and the Zagreb School of Economics and Management in Zagreb, Croatia, where he also helps manage the master of marketing program. He earned his PhD in marketing from the University of Cambridge. E-mail: jdbranch@bus.umich.edu

4. Luciano Thome e Castro

Luciano Thome e Castro is MSc and is currently pursuing PhD at the University of Sao Paulo, Brazil. E-mail: ltcastro@markestrat.org

5. Qimei Chen

Qimei Chen is Chair and Associate Professor of Marketing at the Shidler College of Business, the University of Hawaii at Manoa and an advisory professor at Fudan University, Shanghai, China. She received a bachelor degree from Nanjing Normal University (JiangSu, China) and an MA and a PhD from the University of Minnesota, Twin Cities. Her current research interests include advertising effectiveness, online/offline consumer behavior, and innovation/knowledge. Her research has been published in journals such as *Journal of Advertising, Journal of Advertising Research*, and *Journal of Retailing*. E-mail: qimei@hawaii.edu

6. Gin Chong

Gin Chong, an associate professor and graduate faculty member at the College of Business, Prairie View A&M University (USA), teaches advanced auditing, law and ethics, and managerial accounting courses. Prior to joining Prairie View A&M University, Dr. Chong taught at Southampton Solent University (UK) and was a visiting scholar of many European and Chinese universities. He holds an MBA degree at Bath University (UK) and gained his PhD at Sheffield University (UK). He presents research findings at various international conferences and peer-reviewed refereed journals and has received two separate best paper awards for his research publications. His research interests include performance measurements, materiality and audit risk, auditing in the emerging markets, and voluntary disclosure of financial information. While in the UK, he advised a number of business organizations and was an independent director for a number of business and non-profit organizations. Dr Chong is a chartered certified accountant with more than 10 years of assurance and related exposures. E-mail: hgchong@pvamu.edu

7. Régis Dumoulin

Régis Dumoulin is a Professor of Strategy and Organization Theory at the University of Angers. He belongs to the GRANEM Research team. His research interests and publications focus on the management of complex organizations (networks, JV, alliances...) and on the new approaches to strategy (time pacing, strategic intent, and institutional coordination). He is member of the board of the French Strategic Management Society (AIMS). E-mail: regisdumoulin@tele2.fr

8. Hasan Fauzi

Hasan Fauzi is a Director, Indonesian Center for Social and Environmental Accounting Research and Development (ICSEARD), Faculty of Economics, Sebalas Maret University. He is a committed member of the international research community as journal editor (Issues in Social and Environmental Accounting, editorial board (*International Journal of Accounting and Finance*) and scholarly/research networks such as Global Academy of Business and Economics Research and Center for Social and Environmental Accounting Research (CSEAR). He is a frequent author of international journal articles and international conference contributions. His research agenda consist of various research subjects and has published in areas such as control system and management accounting, social and environmental accounting, business ethics, strategic management and business environment, and sustainable development and organization change. E-mail: hfauzi2003@hotmail.com

9. Christian Felzensztein

Christian Felzensztein, BCom (Hon.), MBA, Universidad Austral de Chile. Pg.D. Local Economic Development, Weitz Center for Development Studies, Rehovot, Israel. MSc and PhD International Marketing, University of Strathclyde, Glasgow, Scotland. He is head of the Graduate School of Business and Assistant Professor of Marketing and International Business in the Faculty of Management and Economics at Universidad Austral de Chile, Valdivia, Chile. He has researched and published in the subjects of country of origin effect in agricultural and aquaculture products as well as in the field of regional clusters, entrepreneurship and innovation. Currently, he is leading a major international research project on natural resource-based clusters. E-mail: cfelzens@uach.cl

10. Eduardo P. Garrovillas

Eduardo P. Garrovillas is a professor and chair of Marketing Department and faculty of MBA Graduate School, Jose Rizal University, the Philippines. E-mail: ed.garrovillas@jru.edu

11. Walter Gassenferth

Walter Gassenferth graduated as Electric Engineer from Universidade Federal Fluminense in 1980; master in Business Administration from Faculdades IBMEC-RJ in 2005; MBA in Business Management from Faculdades IBMEC-RJ in 2003; Specialization in Software Engineering by PUC-Rio (Catholic University) in 1984. Worked for Three Telecom Operators Companies, accumulating 29 years of experience in the areas of business processes management, business planning, business performance control and telecom networks operations, business processes and quality executive manager in TIM (Telecom Italia Mobile, Brasil) since 2006; Consultant-Partner of Quântica Consultoria Empresarial; and Projects Management MBA's teacher in FGV. Responsible for the change management of TIM's Balanced Scorecard deployment project in 2007; Coordinator of EMBRATEL's (Brazilian largest long distance telecom company) Sarbanes–Oxley Project in 2005; Manager of TELEMAR's

(Brazilian largest local telecom company) enterprise transformation and evolution project in 1998; Manager of EMBRATEL's reengineering project in 1997. Member of the Scientific Papers Evaluation Committeé from Computer Science Journals of Elsevier publishing. He has 21 scientific papers published in journals and presented in international conferences, in the areas of management control, controller office, business performance indicators, operational research, e-learning, IT systems usability, and organizational culture; as well a book about *Quantitative Methods Using MS Excel*, being published in 2008, by Cengage Learning. E-mail: wgassenferth@timbrasil.com.br

12. Claire Gauzente

Claire Gauzente is a Professor of Marketing and Organization researching at the University of Angers (GRANEM research team). Her research interests include research methods, franchise research, market orientation, e-marketing, and ethics. She has published several research articles in academic journals such as *Journal of Consumer Marketing*, *Journal of Electronic Commerce Review*, *Academy of Marketing Science Review*, *Forum Qualitative Sozialforschung*, and *Journal of Small Business Management*. E-mail: cg.lj@online.fr

13. Nicholas Grigoriou

Nicholas Grigoriou commenced employment with RMIT University in 1995 as a teacher of marketing subjects. Since then, he has broadened his responsibilities to include management of the staff, students, and curriculum for the Advanced Diploma of Business (Marketing). Prior to entering academia, Nick held sales and marketing roles in the banking, furniture, and petroleum refining industries. Nicholas holds a Bachelor of Business (Marketing) and a Graduate Diploma of International Business (Marketing) both from Monash University. In 2001, he undertook a PhD at Swinburne University in Melbourne, Australia. His area of research interest relates to new product development decisions for consumer goods exported to China. He has published in refereed journal articles in the *International Journal of Marketing Research*, the *Journal of International Marketing, and Exporting* and the *Journal of Social Psychology* and is a member of the IACMR (International Association of Chinese Management Research) as well as the Academy of International Business. In 2004, he published a text book titled *International Marketing: A Practical Approach* (McGraw Hill, Sydney, Australia). E-mail: Nicholas.Grigoriou@college.monash.edu.au

14. Robert Hinson

Robert Hinson is a senior lecturer in the department of marketing at the University of Ghana Business School. His research interests span e-commerce, services marketing, and small business development. He holds an MPhil in marketing from the University of Ghana Business School and has had papers accepted for publication in the *Place Branding Journal, Journal of Business and Industrial Marketing, Journal of Ecommerce in Organizations, Journal of African Business*, and the *International Journal of Healthcare Quality Assurance*. E-mail: rhinson@ug.edu.gh

15. Mostaq Hussain

Mostaq M. Hussain is an Associate Professor of Accounting in the Faculty of Business at the University of New Brunswick-Saint John, Canada. He graduated from the University of Dhaka, Bangladesh, and received his PhD in Accounting from the University of Vaasa, Finland. He worked in Japan, Sweden, Finland, and Oman before he joined UNBSJ in 2006. He is the *Editor-in-Chief* of *International Journal of Accounting and Finance (IJAF)*, and *International Journal of Management Development (IJMD)*. His fields of research are in management accounting practices in organizations, performance management, and measurement in services. He has published a good number of articles in international refereed journals, and received more than two dozens of scholarships/awards from different institutions/foundations in Finland, Sweden, Japan, Norway, and the United Kingdom. He also received Literati Club's "Awards for Excellence," and SQU's "Distinguished Research Award" in 2002 and 2005, respectively. E-mail: mhussain@unb.ca

16. A. Kanagaraj

A. Kanagaraj is presently working as Assistant Professor at IIM, Indore. He has presented number of papers in various national seminars and conferences. His areas of interest include corporate finance, investment management, and international finance. He has done management development programs for leading Indian corporate houses. E-mail: kanagaraj@iimidr.ac.in

17. Angelika Kokkinaki

Angelika Kokkinaki is an Associate Professor in MIS and the Associate Dean of the School of Business at the University of Nicosia, Cyprus. Her research interests include inter- and intra-organizational information systems. She has worked as researcher and lecturer in the United States, the United Kingdom, and the Netherlands. She has participated in many national- and EU-funded programs and has published extensively. She has received her PhD in Computer Science from University of Louisiana at Lafayette (ULL), Lafayette, LA, USA, in 1995, her MSc in Computer Science from Northeastern University, Boston, MA, USA in 1991 and a 5-year curriculum Diploma in Computer Engineering and Informatics from Patras University in 1987. She is a Chartered Engineer (Technical Chamber of Greece, 1987) and an accredited Project Manager (MIT Professional Programs, 1998). E-mail: kokkinaki.a@unic.ac.cy

18. Olga Kuznetsova

Olga Kuznetsova is currently Senior Lecturer at the Manchester Metropolitan Business School. She started her studies of Russian economic processes in the early 1980s. She authored and coauthored papers on different aspects of socioeconomic transformation in Russia, including the emerging of new managerial practices and business culture, corporate governance development, the role of the state, corporate social responsibility and institutional aspects of post-communist transition. E-mail: O.Kuznetsova@mmu.ac.uk

19. Ruby P. Lee

Ruby P. Lee is an Assistant Professor of Marketing at the College of Business, Florida State University. Dr Lee received a bachelor degree with honors from the University of Hong Kong, an MPhil from the Chinese University of Hong Kong, and a PhD from Washington State University. Her current research interests include new product development and introduction, knowledge management, marketing metrics, marketing strategy, and global marketing. Her research has been published in the *Journal of Marketing*, *Journal of the Academy of Marketing Science*, and *Journal of Product Innovation Management*, among others. E-mail: rlee3@fsu.edu

20. Peter Lewa

Peter Lewa has extensive working experience in both the public and private sectors. He has been in research, teaching, and consultancy for 16 years, 12 at university level. He worked with the government of Kenya in senior positions for a total of 16 years. He has considerable experience working with

NGOs, industry, and public corporations in such diverse areas such as public procurement, supplies management, strategic planning, projects management, monitoring and evaluation, food security and policy, and development administration and training. He has worked as a consultant for international agencies and overseas universities and institutions. Lewa has traveled widely and has been to such countries as the United Kingdom, German, United States, South Africa, Indonesia, Malaysia, Austria, Tanzania, Uganda, Zimbabwe, Ethiopia, and Somalia. E-mail: lewapm@usic.ac.ke

21. Susan Lewa

Susan K. Lewa is a Senior Lecturer at the University of Nairobi, Kenya Science Teachers College Campus. She is an Adjunct Faculty at USIU and KEMU. In the past, Susan worked in middle-level colleges and high Schools in Kenya. She is a qualified and experienced counseling psychologist. She is also an experienced management consultant and is a Director of Consultancy, Research & Training Associates Ltd, a consulting firm in Kenya. Susan has interests in psychology, communication, management, human resources management, and ethics. E-mail: sklewa@usiu.ac.ke

22. Chunhui Liu

Chunhui Liu received her PhD in 2003 from National University of Singapore. She is currently an assistant professor in the University of Winnipeg, Canada. Her research topics include international accounting, emerging markets, ecommerce, and computer-user interface. Her research paper has been published in internationally refereed journal such as *International Journal of Human Computer Studies*. E-mail: m.liu@uwinnipeg.ca

23. Maria Augusta Soares Machado

Maria Augusta S. Machado graduated in mathematics from Universidade Santa Úrsula in 1972; Master in mathematics from Universidade Federal Fluminense in 1978; Doctorate in Electrical Engineering from PUC-Rio (Catholic University) in 2000. Worked for Brazilian enterprises in the areas of mathematical models, statistical validations of experiments, and logistics. Teacher in Faculdades IBMEC-RJ since 2000, giving classes of mathematics, statistics, quantitative methods, forecast methods and applied computational intelligence, for administration graduation and masters courses. Coordinator of Scientific Initiation Project (PIBIC) through a partnership with Brazilian Research Center (CNPq) in 2005; coordinator of the logistic project in EL PASO, 2003, and 2005; and coordinator of the spare parts optimization in ENDESA, 2007. Member of publishing committee of Pesquisa Naval Magazine, RESI Electronic Magazine, member of scientific papers evaluation committee of IBIMA, SEGET, SIMEP, SIMPOI, ANPAD conferences. Member of scientific papers evaluation committee of CONTEXTUS, BM&F, ERA e Gestão e Produção Journals. Also evaluates after graduation researches in production engineering, UFF. Has books and scientific papers are published in the areas of mathematics, statistics, operational research and applied computational intelligence. E-mail: mmachado@ibmecrj.br

24. Nnamdi O. Madichie

Nnamdi O. Madichie is a senior lecturer at the Business School, University of East London, the United Kingdom. His research interests include marketing and entrepreneurship in the small business sector as well as international business — especially in the context of emerging markets. He is an Associate Editor of the *African Journal of Buisness Management* as well as Book Review Editor for *Management Decision* (Emerald). He is a member of leading professional bodies such as the Academy of International Business, Institute for Small Business & Entrepreneurship and the International Academy of African Business & Development (VP membership, 2004/2007). E-mail: madichie@googlemail.com

25. Maja Martinović

Maja Martinović is an assistant professor at the Zagreb School of Economics and Management, Marketing Department, where she teaches principles of marketing, marketing management, and product and brand management. She also conducts seminars on brand building and marketing communications for executives of leading companies from East Europe. She has edited several books in the field of marketing, including an *MBA book of Strategic Marketing Management*. Prior to joining ZSEM, she worked as a marketing and sales manager for over 10 years, mostly with Matrix Croatica, the largest and oldest Croatian publishing company. Today, she consults to Croatian and foreign companies, helping to draw up business plans, conduct feasibility studies and market research projects, and develop brand identities. Maja received both her MSc and PhD from the Faculty of Economics, Zagreb.

She also completed the International Faculty Development Program at IESE Business School, Barcelona. E-mail: mmartino@zsem.hr

26. Ehab Mohamed

Ehab K. A. Mohamed is the assistant dean for Undergraduate Studies at the College of Commerce & Economics, Sultan Qaboos University, Muscat, Oman. He is also the Head of the Department of Accounting at the college. He graduated from Cairo University and received both his Masters and PhD from the Department of Accounting and Finance, City University Business School (Cass), London, the United Kingdom. He was formerly on the faculties of the City University Business School (Cass) in London. He is a Fellow of the Institute of Internal Auditors, the United Kingdom and Ireland. He is also a member of the American, British, and European Accounting Associations. His areas of research are in auditing, fraud, performance measurement, business education, financial reporting, banking regulations, and corporate governance. He has published a number of articles in international refereed journals and presented research papers at numerous international conferences. He has published two books on financial accounting and auditing standards. He holds leading consulting positions with international accounting bodies. E-mail: ehab@squ.edu.om

27. Brent McKenzie

Brent McKenzie is an assistant professor in the Department of Marketing and Consumer Studies, in the College of Management and Economics, at the University of Guelph, in Guelph, Ontario, Canada. Dr McKenzie's research interests are in the area of retail service quality in transition economies, particularly the Baltic States, as well as cross-cultural service issues. Dr McKenzie has presented his research at a number of Canadian and international venues, and has been a visiting professor at the Estonian Business School, and the Stockholm School of Economics in Riga. His research has been published in such academic and practitioner publications as the *Journal of Business Research*, *Management Decision, the Baltic Journal of Management*, and the *European Retail Digest*. Prior to entering academia, Dr McKenzie worked in various management positions with large Canadian companies such as the Royal Bank of Canada, Nortel, and Canadian Tire Corporation. Dr McKenzie also operates his own consulting practice in the areas of business analysis, project management, and operational improvement. E-mail: bmckenzi@uoguelph.ca

28. Marcos Fava Neves

Marcos Fava Neves is a professor of Marketing and Strategy at the School of Economics and Business of the University of Sao Paulo (USP), Brazil. He is also leader of the Agribusiness Program of USP. E-mail: mfaneves@usp.br

29. Adnan Priyanto

Adnan A. Priyanto is a researcher at the Indonesian Center for Social and Environmental Accounting Research and Development, Faculty of Economics, Sebelas Maret University, Indonesia. E-mail: ahmad_maksi@yahoo.co.id

30. Kofi Poku Quan-Baffour

Kofi Poku Quan-Baffour is a senior lecturer at Institute for Adult Basic Education and Training, University of South Africa, Pretoria, Republic of South Africa. He is a teacher and adult educator and a development practitioner. He has taught in many schools, colleges, and universities in Ghana, Lesotho, Botswana, and South Africa. He loves teaching and research especially in adult education and development issues. Dr Quan-Baffour coordinates the BEd Honors program at the Institute for Adult Basic Education and Training. He lectures development studies for education and training practitioners which covers small business development and management and tourism issues. Dr Quan-Baffour has published over 12 articles in international peer-reviewed journals in his field. He has passion for learner support and education for development. He believes in development through education. Dr Quan-Baffour has a DEd and three masters degrees in adult/distance education, development studies, and education management. E-mail: Quanbkp@unisa.ac.za

31. Azhar Rahman

Azhar Abudul Rahman is an associate professor at College of Business, Northern University of Malaysia. He is a committed member of the international research community as editorial board (Issues in Social and Environmental Accounting). He is a regular author of international journal articles and international conference contributions. His research agenda consists of various research subjects and has published in areas such as financial reporting, accounting education, Islamic accounting, and corporate social responsibility. E-mail: azhar258@uum.edu.my

32. C. P. Rao

C. P. Rao is currently a professor of Marketing and Director of Case Research and Teaching Unit at the College of Business Administration, Kuwait University, Kuwait. He held distinguished academic position at the Old Dominion University as Eminent Scholar and at the University of Arkansas (Fayetteville) as University Professor and Walton Lecturer in Strategic Marketing. He was elected as Senior Fellow of the Academy of Marketing Science (1991). He is a frequent contributor to various academic and professional journals in marketing and international business. He also held leadership positions in the Academy of Marketing Science and the Academy of International Business. He was a visiting professor at many overseas universities in several countries including: Nigeria, India, Singapore, Norway, Malaysia, Taiwan, Australia, New Zealand, South Africa, Peru, the Netherlands and the UK. E-mail: cprao@cba.edu.kw

33. S. V. Ramana Rao

S. V. Ramana Rao has obtained MBA, MPhil and PhD. He has almost 15 years of experience in teaching courses like financial management, financial derivatives, and management accounting. Dr Rao's last assignment was with a premier business school in India, based at Manipal. He has published papers in reputed journals and presented papers in various conferences in India. E-mail: sindhe_rao@yahoo.co.in

34. Ravinder Rena

Ravinder Rena obtained his PhD from the Department of Economics, Osmania University, Hyderabad, India, with an achievement of University Gold Medal (for the best PhD candidates/thesis in the field of Economics/Commerce/Business Management). All in all he has earned six degrees. He has authored nine books and the recent book includes: "*Eritrean Educational Reforms — Issues, Perspectives and Policy Implications,*" published by The ICFAI University Press in 2008. He has over 170 articles to his credit many of them have been published in refereed journals in different countries of the world. He has widely written in the areas of economics of education, globalization, development aid, and food security strategies. Dr Rena is an *Editor-in-Chief of International Journal of Education Economics and Development (IJEED)*. He has worked in Eritrea for more than a decade and he is currently working as the Head of Economics, Department of Business Studies, the Papua New Guinea University of Technology, Papua New Guinea. E-mail: drravinderrena@gmail.com

35. Zubeiru Salifu

Zubeiru Salifu is a research and teaching assistant at the Department of Finance of the University of Ghana Business School. His research interests include private equity and venture capital financing, electronic banking; risk management; investment and fund management; international trade finance and foreign direct investment among others. He holds an MPhil in finance from the University of Ghana Business School and has previously had a paper accepted for publication in the *Journal of Risk Finance*. E-mail: zubeiru@fidelitycapitalpartners.com

36. Alkis Thrassou

Alkis Thrassou is an associate professor of marketing in the School of Business at the University of Nicosia, Cyprus. Dr Thrassou obtained a BEng (Hons.) degree in Engineering with Management and a PhD in strategic marketing management from the University of Leeds (United Kingdom). From 1996 until 2002, he worked as a business and project manager for an engineering and management firm in Cyprus, leading teams of professionals through many projects of varying sizes and nature. In 2002, he joined the marketing department of the University of Nicosia, Cyprus, involving himself in various scholarly activities, lecturing on marketing-related subjects to both under-graduate and post-graduate students, and undertaking research in the fields of services, consumer behavior, and marketing communications. He has an extensive publication's record and retains strong ties with the industry, acting also as a consultant. E-mail: thrassou.a@unic.ac.cy

37. Naliniprava Tripathy

Naliniprava Tripathy is currently working at Indian Institute of Management, Shillong. Prior to joining IIM Shillong, she has served as an associate professor at the Indian Institute of Management Indore. She holds PhD and DLitt degree in management. She is having 17 years of experience in teaching, consulting, and research. Her research papers have appeared in internationally refereed journals, conferences, books, and leading business periodicals. She has written four textbooks. She is teaching corporate finance, financial services, investment banking, financial modeling, and empirical finance. Prof. Tripathy has offered professional services and management development programs to many leading Indian corporate and business schools. E-mail: nalini_prava@yahoo.co.in

38. Demetris Vrontis

Demetris Vrontis is a professor in marketing and the Dean of the School of Business at the University of Nicosia, Cyprus. He is also a visiting teaching faculty for Henley School of Management in the United Kingdom, a visiting professor for Vorarlberg University in Austria, a visiting research fellow at Manchester Metropolitan University in the United Kingdom, a visiting fellow at Leeds Metropolitan University in the United Kingdom and an external examiner for Cape Peninsula Technological University in South Africa and Nottingham Trent University in the United Kingdom. His prime research interests are on international marketing, marketing planning, branding and marketing communications, areas that he has widely published in over 50 refereed journal articles, contributed chapters and cases in books/edited books and presented papers to conferences on a global basis. Dr Vrontis is also the author of eight books mainly in the areas of international marketing and marketing planning. He is also the founder and editor of the *EuroMed Journal of Business* and the founder and executive chairman of the EuroMed Research Business Institute. E-mail: vrontis.d@unic.ac.cy

39. Kwok Kee Wei

Kwok Kee Wei is dean and chair professor of information systems in the Faculty of Business at the City University of Hong Kong. He is fellow of the Association of Information Systems (AIS) and was the president of that association in 2003/4. Dr Wei is serving on the Series Editorial Advisory Board of Idea Group Publishing/Information Science Publishing and on the editorial boards of a good number of international journals including the *IEEE Transactions on Engineering Management*. He has served as senior editor of *MIS Quarterly* and associate editor of *Information Systems Research*. He has also played major roles in ICIS and PACIS. Dr Wei has published more than 140 journal and conference papers. He is actively pursuing research on e-commerce, knowledge management, and virtual communities. E-mail: isweikk@cityu.edu.hk

40. Steven White

Steven White is an associate professor of management at the China Europe International Business School (CEIBS) in Shanghai. He has two research streams related to the broad issue of fit. The first is focused on the process of achieving and maintaining strategic fit, with a particular focus on the challenges of innovation and internationalization. The second focuses on relational fit between alliance partners and how to create cooperative advantage that increases the value of relationships. His teaching covers strategic management, M&A and alliances, leadership and cross-cultural management. After completing his PhD at MIT's Sloan School of Management and before joining CEIBS, he taught at INSEAD, the Chinese University of Hong Kong, and Hong Kong University of Science and Technology. His work has appeared in *Strategic Management Journal, Academy of Management Journal, Organization Studies, Journal of Management, Asia Pacific Journal of Management*, and the *International Journal of Technology Management*. E-mail: stevenwhite@ceibs.edu

41. Wei Xie

Wei Xie is an associate professor in the Department of Innovation and Entrepreneurship, School of Economics and Management, Tsinghua University, Beijing, China. He received his BS in automotive engineering and PhD in the Management of Technology. He has held visiting scholar positions at MIT/Sloan and United Nations University (INTECH). His research focuses on innovation management and competitive strategies of latecomer firms, with two projects currently underway in the auto and electronics industries. Currently, he has been the associate editor of *Journal of Technology Management in China*. Prior work includes his contribution to China's Innovation and Learning Capabilities. Before it joins the WTO, as a background paper for UNIDO's the annual World Industrial Development Report 2002/2003, articles in Research Policy, R&D Management, Technovation, *International Journal of Technology Management, Journal of Technology Management in China and Industry and Innovation*, etc. E-mail: xiew@sem.tsinghua.edu.cn

42. Hamid Yeganeh

Hamid Yeganeh is a professor of international management at Winona State University in Minnesota, USA. Dr Yeganeh holds a PhD in international management, a Master of Science (MS), and a Master of Business (MBA) from Université Laval in Quebec, Canada. Dr Yeganeh is a multilingual, multicultural person affected by Persian, French, German, and American heritage. Professor Yeganeh is author/coauthor of numerous articles in scientific journals. His research interests focus on international management, cross cultural management, organization, and international strategies. E-mail: hyeganeh@winona.edu

Chapter 1

INTRODUCTION

SATYENDRA SINGH

Background to Emerging Markets

An emerging market generally refers to a developing market economy with low-to-middle per capita income. Countries in this category are usually undertaking a process of economic development and reform. The vast majority of countries in the world fall in this category. An important feature of most emerging markets is that they are in the process of moving from closed economies to more open economies. As part of this process, emerging countries generally experience rapid growth in both local and foreign investment. For foreign investors, the emerging market is an opportunity to expand its production and revenue. From the perspective of the emerging market, it gains access to new employment opportunities, transfers of skills and technology, and a source of economic growth.

In the last decade, many developing countries have been adjusting their economies through economic reform policies to attract a greater share of global foreign investment. The impact of these reforms on both domestic markets and consumers is significant; for example, in recent years, the fastest-growing countries such as Brazil, China, India, and Eastern European countries have attracted the most foreign investment, followed by promising emerging markets of the Middle East and Africa. While increased foreign investments bring much-needed jobs to the emerging markets, local firms that previously faced little competition are now forced to compete with the international firms that take advantage of relatively low investment costs.

Purpose of this Book

Growth in business developments has created germane grounds for conducting research with respect to emerging markets. Thus, this *Handbook of Business*

Practices and Growth in Emerging Markets aims to generate and disseminate knowledge by commissioning a series of chapters in one volume that describe the current business environment, organizational culture, consumer behavior, financial investments, and examples of best prevailing practices in emerging markets. Specifically, the goal of this research-based book is to provide a comprehensive guidance for business managers and students by discussing a range of issues from the diverse emerging markets, enabling them to develop a strategic thinking, and a market-oriented culture. This handbook contributes to four major areas of business: (1) marketing, (2) strategy, (3) operations, and (4) finance. Given changing business dynamics, government policies, and demands in the industry, this book is both timely and topical.

Why Another Book?

This is not a typical *how to* style conventional handbook, rather the objective of this handbook is to guide the readers into a new strategic thinking. To achieve this objective, and to stand out from existing publications, the focus of this handbook in each chapter is on the identification of different business issues in different emerging markets (e.g., Asia, Africa, and South America), and on the implementation of a proposed set of recommendations. Further, as several leading practitioners and experts in the areas of their expertise contribute to this handbook, the text is rich in its contents and has a balance of academic rigor and managerial implications.

Benefits to the Readers

This handbook is truly global in its scope and thus an ideal companion for business managers and an essential reference for business students. The carefully selected chapters make use of both qualitative and quantitative techniques to assist in decision making and in improving efficiency and effectiveness in organizations operating in emerging markets that are now exposed to global forces, stiff competition, and vast markets. Further, the readers will appreciate the easy-to-read style of writing, and a multidimensional view of financial and non-financial performance measurement of businesses. In fact, 26 diverse chapters, authored by 42 professors and managers in 18 emerging markets and supplemented by diagrams and case studies, cover the major areas of business in this handbook.

Key Features of this Book

This handbook has four key features: (1) it reviews current business practices relevant to current challenges in emerging markets; (2) it covers all the continents, and thus has a global representation of emerging markets; (3) it covers all the major functional areas of business such as marketing, strategy, operations and finance; and (4) it includes case studies and sections on implications for managers and policy makers in addition to empirical articles for a balance of academic and managerial implications.

Overview of Chapters

This handbook is divided in six parts representing six regions of the emerging markets: China, Commonwealth of Independent States, Latin America, Africa, Middle East, and Asia. Table 1.1 reports name of contributing authors, brief description of the chapters, nature of the study, and function of business and country.

Part 1: China

In Chapter 2, Grigoriou focuses on the factors that an international product planner needs to consider in researching, developing, and marketing consumer goods in emerging markets. With growing incomes and a greater awareness of foreign-branded goods, consumers in emerging markets are increasingly seeking such goods to satisfy their needs. In this backdrop, this chapter recommends international marketers the new ways to target emerging market consumers.

In Chapter 3, Xie and White address the question of how latecomers in emerging markets may compete against incumbent multinationals. This chapter proposes a generic process model for analyzing competition dynamics between latecomers and multinationals, examines the competition between local and foreign firms in China's handset manufacturing industry, and highlights the contingencies that may determine the likelihood that latecomer firms will emerge as initial and then sustained competitors vis-à-vis incumbent multinationals.

In Chapter 4, Liu and Wei examine resource management trends of top fortune global multinational enterprises from emerging markets. Drawing on the resource- and competence-based strategic management theories, it is

Table 1.1. Overview of chapters.

Chapter	Authors	Description of the chapter	Nature of the study	Business function	Country
Part I: China					
1.	Singh	Introduction			
2.	Grigoriou	New product development	Theoretical	Strategy	China
3.	Xie & White	Competing with multinationals: entry and evolution of latecomer firms	Theoretical	Strategy	China
4.	Liu and Wei	Current Business practices of top fortune global emerging multinationals	Empirical	Finance	Emerging markets
5.	Lee and Chen	Link between information system integration and performance	Empirical	Strategy	Emerging markets
6.	Chong	Legal cases and auditing practices	Theoretical	Finance	China
Part II: Commonwealth of independent states					
7.	Kuznetsova	CSR: business accountability and legitimacy	Theoretical	Strategy	Russia
8.	Kuznetsova	Corporate governance system: promises and realities	Theoretical	Strategy	Russia
9.	Martinovic and Branch	Brand management: the role of private labels	Case study	Marketing	Croatia
10.	McKenzie	Retail trade and shopping behavior	Theoretical	Marketing	Baltic

(Continued)

Table 1.1. (*Continued*)

Chapter	Authors	Description of the chapter	Nature of the study	Business function	Country
Part III: Latin America					
11.	Barbosa, Gassenferth, and Machado	Data mining as a decision tool for materials procurement management	Empirical	Operations	Brazil
12.	Felzensztein	Importance of natural resources-based industry clusters	Case study	Strategy	Chile
13.	Neves and Castro	Inserting small holders in the supply chain management	Case study	Strategy	Brazil
14.	Gauzente and Dumoulin	Franchise as an efficient mode of entry: the legitimacy point of view	Theoretical	Strategy	Emerging markets
Part IV: Africa					
15.	Lewa and Lewa	Public procurement reform	Case study	Operations	Kenya
16.	Quan-Baffour	Rural tourism	Case study	Marketing	S. Africa
17.	Alam and Hussain	Interest-free microfinance and Islamic banking	Case study	Finance	Sudan
18.	Madichie, Hinson, and Salifu	Challenges of Internet adoption of banks	Case study	Marketing	Ghana

(*Continued*)

Table 1.1. (*Continued*)

Chapter	Authors	Description of the chapter	Nature of the study	Business function	Country
Part V: Middle East					
19.	Mohamed and Hussain	Impact of religious nature of organization on firm performance	Theoretical	Marketing	Gulf
20.	Rao	Challenges and opportunities for international marketers	Review	General	Kuwait
21.	Yeganeh	Society and management	Review	General	Iran
22.	Thrassou, Vrontis, and Kokkinaki	Internet consumer behavior	Empirical	Marketing	Cyprus
Part VI. Asia					
23.	Fauzi, Rahman, Hussain and Priyanto	Corporate social performance of state-owned and private companies	Empirical	Strategy	Indonesia
24.	Tripathy, Rao, and Kanagaraj	Individual stock futures and stock market volatility	Empirical	Finance	India
25.	Garrovillas	Business opportunities and strategic marketing in the twenty-first century	Review	General	The Philippines
26.	Rena	Challenges and prospects in the South Pacific	Review	General	Papua New Guinea (PNG)
27.	Singh	Conclusion			

argued that firms that best manage their resources and possess hard-to-copy resources are likely to have a competitive advantage. Data from Fortune Global multinational enterprises operating in emerging markets show a trend toward spending more on research and development, registering more new patents, and better usage of assets from 2002 to 2007.

In Chapter 5, Lee and Chen test the link between informational technology (IT) and firm performance and argue that knowledge codification, a deliberate learning mechanism, must be developed for a firm to take advantage of its IT resources. Further, to what extent the firm can translate knowledge and information into performance outcomes depends on its ability to respond to the market. Drawing on the dynamic capabilities perspective and its extensions, the authors develop a conceptual model to examine the missing links — knowledge codification and market responsiveness — between information system integration and firm performance.

In Chapter 6, Chong reviews audit environment and legal cases in China, assesses the extent of audit changes in China based on the audit reports issued by the National Audit Office in 2005, and recommends the need for further improvement. These recommendations have implications for the policy makers, audit professionals, and users of the audit reports.

Part II: Commonwealth of Independent States

In Chapter 7, Kuznetsova explores corporate social responsibility (CSR) as business practice within the context of market transformation in Russia. This chapter introduces historic circumstances surrounding the development of CSR in the emerging market economy, and outlines particularities of CSR in the country and its potential to contribute to the socioeconomic development.

In Chapter 8, Kuznetsova scrutinizes the development of corporate governance within the emerging institutional context of the market economy of Russia, and looks at the forces that have determined the shape and performance of the corporate governance system in the period following the collapse of the centrally planned economy. This chapter is instrumental in formulating strategy for investors considering doing businesses in transitional, emerging, and developing economies.

In Chapter 9, Martinovic and Branch provide a brief overview of brand management and private labels in emerging markets, outline the evolution of private labels in Croatian grocery retailing, and present the case of Dona Trgovina D.O.O., one of the leading Croatian manufacturers of private grocery labels. Certainly, brand management has become challenging in emerging markets that have attracted multinationals with their established brands. Private labels — sometimes called house branding — are a form of brand management which have their own peculiarities and which, in emerging markets, are racing to catch up to that of the developed world.

In Chapter 10, McKenzie presents an overview of the retail sector in the Baltic States of Estonia, Latvia, and Lithuania, and examines the retail sector from an historic perspective, including a discussion of the role of retail trade in these countries during the Soviet communist period through re-independence in 1991 and accession to the European Union in 2004. Although retailers may wish to view the region as a single market, there are significant differences in how consumers perceive retail service delivery, and thus these differences need to be taken into account for a superior retail performance.

Part III: Latin America

In Chapter 11, Barbosa, Gassenferth, and Machado recommend data mining as a decision tool for materials procurement in a multinational company based in Brazil. This chapter reviews decision making, data warehouse, and data mining relating to IT, analyzes the results, and suggests the use of data mining as a tool to obtain information that supports the decision-making process and develops business strategy in the procurement area. This chapter is useful for procurement managers.

In Chapter 12, Felzensztein discusses the importance of natural resource-based industry and explores the role of marketing and practices in clusters of three key natural resource-based industries in Chile. This chapter reviews the literature relating to geographic, location, social networking, and regional innovation from a Latin-American perspective.

In Chapter 13, Neves and Castro identify four fundamental dimensions of agribusiness that governments and development agencies use to attract the right investments: the technical and economical viability; the organizational aspects — the players' ability to efficiently coordinate their transactions; business competitiveness; and the environment sustainability. This chapter illustrates implementation of the dimensions through a project completed by PENSA (Agribusiness Intelligence Center) and CODEVASF (Sao Francisco and Parnaíba Rivers Valleys Development Agency) in Brazil.

In Chapter 14, Gauzente and Dumoulin explain why franchise as an efficient mode of entry can be a successful strategy in emerging markets, delineate the different suboptions within the franchise option, and introduce the concept of legitimacy as a critical success factor. Based on the institutionalism theoretical framework, this chapter discusses different types of legitimacy — coercive, normative, and cognitive — in the light of emerging markets' characteristics.

Part IV: Africa

In Chapter 15, Lewa and Lewa examine the reform of public procurement in the emerging markets of Kenya. Based on the literature review on procurement, this chapter recommends that institutional and regulatory frameworks need to be revised and harmonized with the laws; suppliers need to be empowered; training of procurement staff need to be given a priority; a better system of remuneration be developed; political and other interests' need to be addressed, and key stakeholders must be allowed to play an important role in public procurement.

In Chapter 16, Quan-Baffour focuses on rural tourism in South Africa by discussing the case of two countryside destinations — Damdoryn and Bufflespoort. This chapter finds that rural tourism is a function of socioeconomic factors. Although South Africa is naturally endowed with beautiful geographical features, game parks, and historical sites, most of these attractive tourism sites were exclusive to the Westerners before the democratic dispensation in 1994. This chapter explains the cause of the rapid growth of these tourist destinations and presents implications for managers.

In Chapter 17, Alam and Hussain explore the partnership mode of Islamic banking; that is, how and to what extent Islamic banking finance contributes to eliminating poverty and creating job opportunities for unemployed people in rural areas. Using the "Institutional-Network" theoretical approach, the findings suggest that the partnership mode of Islamic banking finance may work effectively in developing countries because lenders and borrowers join in a particular venture and develop a unique lender–borrower network relationship.

In Chapter 18, Madichie, Hinson, and Salifu highlight the challenges of the Internet adoption of banks in Ghana and the opportunities provided by IT for the development of competitiveness in banks. Given that IT has been largely adopted on a commercial basis by businesses across the globe, this chapter should be particulalry useful for bank managers operating in emerging markets.

Part V: Middle East

In Chapter 19, Mohamed and Hussain state that the objective of Islamic Financial Service Industry (FSI) is not only to maximize a profit, but also to improve the socioeconomic condition of the community while complying with the principles of Shariah, which actively advocate non-profit activities that support the needy and poor, and promote welfare programs that may or may not be financially viable. This chapter reveals that management accounting plays a moderate role in measuring both financial and non-financial performances in the Islamic FSI in Gulf countries, and that the nature and characteristics of organization (Islamic FSI) do not have a great impact on performance measurement practices, though it is generally held belief that Islamic FSI should conform to the principles of Shariah.

In Chapter 20, Rao presents an overview of the country's business environment, highlights the growth trends of the country's gross domestic product and the overall contributions of oil and non-oil sectors of the economy, and discusses Kuwait's business environment, demographics, and marketing conditions. In the light of the implementation of WTO regime in 2005, this chapter reviews challenges and opportunities for international marketers.

In Chapter 21, Yeganeh sheds light on some aspects of society and management in Iran. This chapter is organized in two parts: the first part examines the Iranian social context by taking into account demographic, economic, religious, political, and cultural factors; and the second part analyzes management practices in Iranian organizations and presents recommendations for managers willing to enter in Iranian market.

In Chapter 22, Thrassou, Vrontis, and Kokkinaki investigate the relationship of Cypriots with the Internet, comprehend their consumer behavior, and identify a set of critical factors influencing the behavior. Critical factors affecting Internet purchases include product variety, quality, and price.

Part VI: Asia

In Chapter 23, Fauzi, Rahman, Hussain, and Priyanto analyze the difference in corporate social performance between State-owned companies (SOCs) and private-owned companies (POCs) in Indonesia, and test the link between the corporate social performance and the corporate performance. The chapter indicates no significant difference in corporate social performance between SOCs and POCs, and no association between corporation social performance and financial performance both in SOCs and POCs.

In Chapter 24, Tripathy, Rao, and Kanagaraj test the impact of the introduction of stock derivatives trading on the underlying stocks volatility in India by applying both GARCH and ARCH model for a period from June 1999 to

July 2006. This chapter indicates that stock future derivatives are not responsible for an increase or decrease in spot market volatility and that other market factors contribute to increasing the stock market volatility.

In Chapter 25, Garrovillas explores business opportunities in the Philippines and studies its history, sociopolitical system, business environment, and economic indicators. Given the Philippines' affiliation with the ASEAN and WTO, this chapter offers a useful guide for business investors and marketers, as well as for the international business scholars and educators.

In Chapter 26, Rena examines the challenges in the PNG economy, explores the prospects for the future development of its economy, and highlights the recent economic trends in PNG. This chapter suggests that a prudent macroeconomic policy and favorable terms of trade trends have helped PNG maintain macroeconomic stability, strong external balances, and solid economic growth over the past 5 years. The country, however, faces difficult developmental challenges such as weaknesses in governance, infrastructure, human development, the business climate, public financial management, security, and service delivery.

In concluding chapter, Satyendra Singh gives an overview of the chapters' recommendations for managers for growth in the emerging markets.

Part I

CHINA

Chapter 2

NEW PRODUCT DEVELOPMENT IN EMERGING MARKETS

NICHOLAS GRIGORIOU

Abstract

With growing incomes and a greater awareness of foreign branded goods, consumers in emerging markets are increasingly seeking such goods to satisfy their needs. In this backdrop, international marketers and their research and development teams are looking for new ways to target emerging market consumers. This chapter focuses on some of the factors that an international product planner needs to consider in researching, developing, and marketing consumer goods to emerging markets.

Introduction

With established domestic and international markets becoming increasingly saturated, international marketers are increasingly looking to emerging markets for sales, profit, and product development growth (London and Hart, 2004). These markets present international marketers with tremendous opportunities and unique challenges. Indeed, potential lower production and labor costs, a growing number of affluent consumers, and growing gross domestic product (GPD) rates make these markets increasingly attractive to multinationals and smaller organizations alike. Further, many such economies are opening their borders to freer trade and joining regional trading blocs to further maintain their economic growth (Hoskisson *et al.*, 2000). Therefore, any consumer product development strategy aimed at emerging markets requires, in most cases, an adjusted strategic approach to that of the home or more developed international markets (Hoskisson *et al.*, 2000).

15

Indeed, success in emerging markets may require innovative goods that are then often sold into mature international markets or even the organization's domestic market(s). By doing so, the international marketing organization extends its product life cycle, since planned obsolescence occurs more quickly in mature markets than it traditionally has in the past (Cordero, 1991; Griffin, 1993).

Emerging markets on a purchasing power of parity basis (PPP) now total 44% of the world's economy. Furthermore, between 1989 and 1999, emerging markets were responsible for two-thirds of the world's economic growth (Gingrich, 1999). Indeed, the five largest emerging economies (China, India, Brazil, Indonesia, and Mexico) now have a combined purchasing power already half that of the Group of Seven nations. However, as Prahalad and Hammond (2002) warn, 65% of the world's total population still earns less than US$2,00 each year. That equates to approximately 4 billion people, who may be the emerging markets of the future.

There are two primary forces that have enhanced the attractiveness of emerging markets. First, as a result of economic growth in these countries, an identifiable target market has emerged exhibiting higher disposable incomes. Second, the Internet has made it possible for small- and medium-sized organizations to reach emerging market consumers that would not have been possible prior to the current technological revolution since the time and costs of establishing either a manufacturing base or traditional distribution channels would be out of the financial reach of most small- to medium-sized enterprises (Arnold and Quelch, 1998).

The primary concern facing these international marketers then is knowing which aspects of their research, development, and marketing to adjust, in what way, and to what extent. The main focus of this chapter is to consider these issues from a marketing, product branding, and product development perspective whilst acknowledging the role of research and development in the entire strategic business process. This commences with an understanding of emerging markets consumers.

Starved for choice for many years, consumers in emerging markets are seeking consumer goods of a better quality and, and as a result of rising middle classes in many such economies, are ready to spend their incomes on such goods to replace poor quality manufactured goods from domestic producers (Gingrich, 1999; Prahalad and Lieberthal, 1998). Indeed, foreign branded goods provide opportunities for such consumers to differentiate themselves from other consumers in the same market (Dhillon, 2005; Jin *et al.*, 2006). Consumer goods marketers targeting emerging markets consumers must first understand that these consumers whilst enjoying increased incomes are still relatively poor compared to Western standards. This is where Prahalad and Hammond (2002) suggest that international consumer goods marketers take a closer look. It is true to assume that emerging market consumers are still too poor to fulfill anything other than their basic needs; however, these consumer often do buy luxury items. This is because in many cases, emerging market consumers cannot afford to buy their homes so they allocate their disposable income to relative luxury goods such as household appliances.

Another attractive characteristic of consumers in emerging markets is that they tend to live in large, often over population centers such as Mumbai in India, Johannesburg in South Africa, and Chongqing in China, making it easier for consumer goods exporters to reach these consumers with their product and their promotional message.

The New Product Development Process for Emerging Markets

New product success or failure depends on selecting the correct development process and then adapting that process where necessary to the chosen emerging market(s) (Mahajan and Wind, 1992; Griffin and Page, 1993). Simply having an attractive market for the new product, one that is large enough to sustain long-term growth amid weak competition does not guarantee new product success. Product developers for emerging markets must choose a comprehensive new product development process and carefully follow each step in the process to increase the likelihood of success.

To generate and sustain profits in an emerging economy, the international marketer must successfully commercialize products in the local market(s). According to Isobe *et al.* (2000), the marketing organization can consider two strategic alternatives to achieve this objective. First, they can transfer superior technological knowledge from the home country (or another international market), or to build technological leadership in the emerging market. This strategic choice will impact on the products the marketing organization chooses to sell in the emerging markets (Dawar and Chattopadhyay, 2002) as well as the level of resources they are prepared to commit to the project (Child and Tse, 2001; Child and Tsai, 2005).

An understanding of the influences on managerial decisions related to product development for emerging markets is an important element in international marketing. Increasingly, managers are being urged to increase the organization's geographic scope to increase its competitiveness and profitability (Delios and Beamish, 1999; Li and Ogunmokun, 2003). How managers reach strategic decisions related to the development and marketing of products into export markets and how those decisions subsequently affect the performance of that product in those markets assists in the development of successful products for emerging markets.

Whilst there are several ways in which new products can be developed, Cooper and Kleinschmidt (1986) suggest a new product developers adopt a comprehensive 13-step approach. This process is described in Table 2.1.

Once international product developers have selected and implemented their preferred approach to new product development for emerging markets, their next responsibility is to agree to an approach for measuring new product success or failure. In most cases, this measurement goes beyond using profit or sales as the sole determinants. Given the amount of time, effort, and financial resources associated with introducing new consumer products into emerging markets (Child and Tse, 2001; Child and Tsai, 2005; Peng *et al.*, 2008) and the inherent risk associated with such a project, a more integrative approach is required. Rogers *et al.* (2005) suggest a framework for measuring international new product projects. Their approach is illustrated in Fig. 2.1.

The Rogers, Ghauri, and Pawar model addresses the managerial process and the organizational mechanisms through which NPD is performed and its link to organizational performance and success. It provides new product developers and business managers with the necessary variables by which to consider their new product success or failure.

Alternate Models of New Product Development

When an organization sets out to develop a new product, its primary objective is to attract new consumers through need satisfaction and to do so profitably (Coughlan and Wood, 1992). This often leads to a misconception about emerging market economies, namely that the goods already sold in these markets are cheap, thus leaving no room for new competition and difficulties in generating profits (Prahalad and Hammond, 2002). It is important to know that many emerging markets have a growing middle class of consumers who are looking for superior, often imported and products and are willing and can afford to pay higher prices.

Developing a desired product or product range for emerging market consumers begins with an understanding of the different ways in which organizations make such product-related design decisions. Product strategy involves decisions about an organization's target market, product mix,

Table 2.1. The 13-step approach to product development.

Activity	Description	Implications for emerging markets
1. Initial screening	The initial go or no-go decision where it was decided to allocate funds for the new product	Requires top management commitment to the project; predicated on sound market knowledge rather than intuitive feel
2. Preliminary market assessment	Initial, preliminary, non-scientific market assessment	Involves visits to the market and meetings with possible distributors and supply chain partners
3. Preliminary technical assessment	Initial appraisal of the technical merits of the project	Ensuring the emerging market has the technical capabilities to support the project
4. Detailed market research	Selection of research methodology, data collection techniques, and selection of sample size	Use of a professional international marketing research organization to assist with the market research; cultural implications of collecting data from lesser-developed nations
5. Business analysis	Formal financial analysis leading to a go or no-go decision	If money is borrowed from emerging market to finance the project currency and exchange rate implications need examination; financial stability of project partners
6. Product development	Actual design and development of the product	Location of product development (Home market? Emerging market? Both?)

(Continued)

Table 2.1. (*Continued*)

Activity	Description	Implications for emerging markets
7. In-house product testing	Testing the product under laboratory conditions	Involvement of raw materials suppliers? Location of such suppliers?
8. Customer tests of product	Testing the product under market conditions	Duration of test; selection of geographic locations in the emerging markets;
9. Test marketing	Selling the product to a limited set of potential consumers	Selection of distributors and retailers should mimic the actual distributors and retailers on full-scale launch; price should mimic intended selling price; small-scale promotional campaign needed
10. Trial production	Aimed at testing the production facilities	Location(s) of production should be in close proximity to supply chain partners
11. Pre-launch business analysis	Final chance to adjust the financials associated with the development and launch of the product	Independent auditing of budgets and forecasts to ensure sufficient funds for project; contingency plans may need to be greater than developed markets due to greater uncertainty of success
12. Production startup	Commencing full-scale production	Finalization of contractual arrangements with supply chain partners and distributors
13. Market launch	The full launch of the product into the chosen market	Careful timing to coincide with promotional campaigns

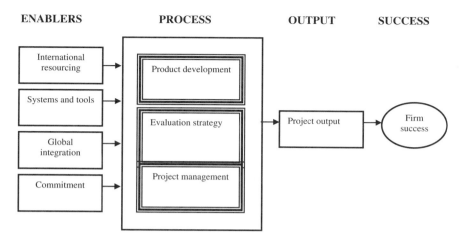

Figure 2.1. Factors influencing NPD process evaluation.

resource allocation, and technology selection (Krishnan and Ulrich, 2001). These are important considerations given the frequency with which new products fail and the associated reasons for new product failure (Wheelwright and Sasser, 1989). Further, organizations face pressure from key stakeholders to produce short-term financial performance with new product offerings as well as producing highly creative and distinctive offerings that the market desires (Moorman and Miner, 1997; Adams and Lacugna, 1994). Ideally, a new product can establish industry standards. These standards become a competitor's barriers to market entry and could even open up additional segments in the emerging market (Wheelwright and Sasser, 1989). Let us now consider some of the different approaches to designing new products for emerging markets.

Localization

One model of new product development proposed by Dawar and Chattopadhyay (2002) and Khanna *et al.* (2005) is to localize or adapt the entire marketing program to the local conditions. This may involve manufacturing the product in the emerging market using raw materials from that market or sourced from the home country or a third country market. The authors' rationale for such strategic choice centers around the availability of cheap(er) resources (especially labor and raw materials) in the emerging market possibly leading to a cost advantage over other competitors. They also add that there are sufficient consumers in most emerging markets to warrant such a strategy, that is, the costs inherent with a localization strategy can be offset by spreading the cost over much larger volumes of demand for the product, or product range.

Front end focus

Focusing on the "front end" is an approach to new product development suggested by Khurana and Rosenthal (1998) that at its core emphasizes getting the phases prior to the initial screening phase (suggested by Cooper and Kleinschmidt, 1986 as being the starting point of new product development) and corrects, before moving on to the next phases that require larger commitments in corporate resources. The essence of Khurana and Rosenthal's model is that the "front end" emphasis in an ongoing commitment to new product development and never actually ceases. They refer to this as the pre-phase in the new product development process. Therefore, unlike the Cooper and Kleinschmidt (1986) model, it is not as linear (notwithstanding the similarities between the two models). The Khurana and Rosenthal (1998) model is illustrated Fig. 2.2.

The unique aspect of the Khurana and Rosenthal model in relation to its relevance to product planning for emerging markets is the emphasis that it places in the pre-product concept phase. Essentially, it forces international product planners for emerging makets to give additional consideration to the

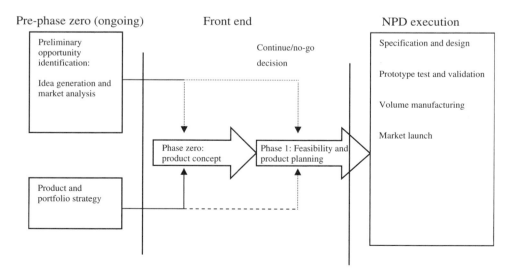

Figure 2.2.   A stylized model of the front end of new product development.

unique and dynamic markets that they are considering entering and by doing so may prevent costly mistakes.

Core capabilities focus

Capabilities are considered core if they differentiate a company strategically (Leonard-Barton, 1992). For capabilities to be relevant to product development, they need to be *unique, distinctive, difficult to imitate*, or *superior to that of the competition*. The starting point in understanding this new product development framework is for the marketing organization to determine what its product-related core competencies are in its domestic market. They then need to determine how many of these can be re-developed, refined, or transplanted into its emerging markets. As Zucker (1977) suggests, core capabilities are *institutionalized* in that they are part of the organization's taken-for-granted reality. Leonard-Barton (1992) identifies four dimensions to this reality: *knowledge and skills, technical systems, managerial systems*, and *values and norms*. These are illustrated in Fig. 2.3.

Let us now consider each of these product development dimensions individually.

Managerial systems: This includes incentives for innovative activities such as new product suggestions, invention of new product research, and development capabilities. International marketers should consider the extension of these incentives to staff, retailers, distributors, or suppliers in the emerging markets prior to the new product development process where possible.

Norms and values: This includes empowering new product development project members for championing new products or processes. It differs from incentives in that it is longer term and provides key new product development

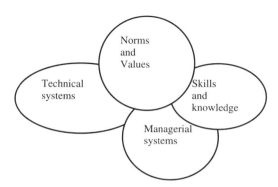

Figure 2.3.   The four dimensions of a core capability.

personnel with delegated authority to commence new product development or product line extension development. Typically, this takes longer to implement in emerging markets, where staff are developed over time and are usually required to work as part of project teams first prior to being given such authority.

Skills and knowledge: This dimension centers on management identifying skills shortages in research and development areas of new product development and bridging those skills gaps through education and training. An example might be to temporarily relocate on skilled product developer from the head office base to the emerging market to train local staff, retailers, or distributors on the technical aspects of a product or the appropriate installation and use of a newly developed product.

Technical systems: This dimension centers on investing in ongoing technical expertise and mechanics that enable continuous improvement in new product development processes. Over time, these systems might be located or colocated in one or more of the organization's emerging markets.

Product mapping

Product mapping is a new product development approach proposed by Wheelwright and Sasser (1989). Mapping allows product developers to see the evolution of new products from "where we are" to "where we need to be." This approach not only allows product developers to consider each international market with different focal lens. Mapping also provides a basis for sharing new product development information among the functional groups associated with product development. In its simplest form, new product development mapping has seven components. These are illustrated in Fig. 2.4.

The *core* product refers to the standard product, possibly found in the domestic market and/or one or more of the organizations international markets. The *hybrid* product is developed out of two core products; it can usually be developed relatively quickly based on the basic product development infrastructure already exists, and is often developed to embrace new market opportunities quickly. The *cost reduced* product refers to a "stripped down" product that has many of its features removed if they are deemed unnecessary to the needs of a particular market and enables the organization to market them at a lower price to price sensitive markets (Nowlis and Simonson, 1996). *Customized products* represent "top of the line" products aimed at wealthier consumers who want extra features and benefits

Increasing

functionality, price

value

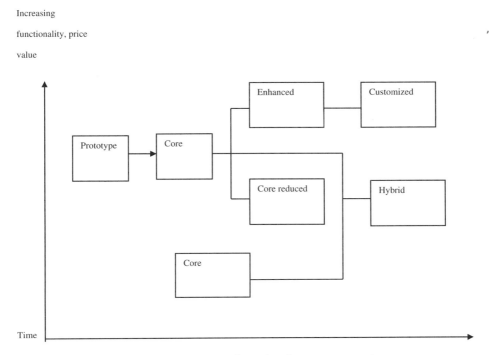

Figure 2.4. New product development mapping.

and are willing to pay for the these extras. Finally, *enhanced products* are developed from the core product with a few added features for more discerning consumers.

The implications of the mapping approach to new product development for emerging markets are that such a map helps focus product development projects and limits them in their scope, therefore making them more manageable. It also provides a process for planning that avoids too much detail (like budgeting).

Consumer Ethnocentrism in Emerging Markets and Its Role in New Product Development

Globalization presents considerable challenges and opportunities for international marketers. The relaxation of trade policies has provided consumers with more foreign product choices than ever before. Consequently, their attitudes toward products originating from foreign countries have been of interest to international business and consumer behavior researchers for decades

(Wang and Chen, 2004). Products may be linked to a country because of its location, weather, and natural resources or because of traditional manufacturing expertise (Usunier and Cestre, 2007). In addition, products may be linked to countries because of the particular country is known for its (product) innovation and development (Usunier and Cestre, 2007). To help us understand the effects *of consumer ethnocentrism* on product choice in emerging markets, it is useful to consider a couple of definitions of ethnocentrism.

Klein and Ettenson (1999) define consumer ethnocentrism as

> the belief among consumers that it is inappropriate, or even immoral, to purchase foreign products because to do so is damaging the domestic economy, costs domestic jobs, and is unpatriotic. (p. 6)

Pecotich and Rosenthal (2001) offer:

> ...ethnocentric consumers believe that the purchase of imported goods is wrong because it results in damage to the domestic economy and is unpatriotic. (p. 34)

Previous studies in consumer ethnocentrism have suggested a positive correlation between the evaluations of domestic products and a nation's level of economic development (Toyne and Walters, 1989; Wang and Lamb, 1983). Consumers tend to purchase products made in a technologically advanced nation if they judge its quality as better than that of a good produced in a less developed country. Moreover, a product's country of origin often serves as a cue activating a consumer's ethnocentric tendency (Huddleston *et al.*, 2001). As such willingness to buy domestic or foreign-made products is influenced by both ethnocentrism and quality judgment (Wang and Chen, 2004). These influences may, of course, be contrary to each other.

Consumers' intentions to purchase domestic versus foreign products will be influenced by *perceived quality* (Wang and Chen, 2004). Previous research into consumers' behavior toward foreign-made goods suggests that *quality perception* is treated as a multidimensional construct including *appearance, color and design, fashion, durability, function, reliability, texture, prestige, value for money, technical advancement*, and *workmanship* (Schutz and Wahl, 1981; Darling and Arnold, 1988; Darling and Wood, 1990; Imran, 1999). The effect of visual sensations should not be underestimated. Human perception of quality is dependent on visual image (Hetherington and MacDougall, 1992). All of these constructs have implications in terms of product design decisions for emerging markets. These constructs, if deemed relevant by emerging market consumers for a specific product (or product range), become embedded in the organization's new product development process.

The globalization of markets means that researchers and practitioners need to better understand the factors that influence consumer attitudes toward foreign products. "Consumer ethnocentrism" suggests that nationalistic emotions affect attitudes about products and purchase intentions (Usunier and Cestre, 2007). In particular, consumer ethnocentrism implies that purchasing imported products is wrong, because not only it is unpatriotic, but also because it is harmful to the economy and results in loss of jobs in industries threatened by imports (Kaynak and Kara, 2002). Highly ethnocentric consumers are probably most prone to biased judgment by being more inclined to adopt the positive aspects of domestic products and to discount the virtues of foreign-made products (Kasper, 1999; p. 155, Klein and Ettenson, 1999). Gaedeke (1973) found that attitudes toward a specific product or brand could be substantially changed, both favorably and unfavorably, when the country of origin of the product or brand was revealed to the consumer.

Herche (1994) looked at ethnocentric tendencies and their affect on marketing strategy and consumer behavior. His research study stems from the idea that product origin bias represents a challenge for product developers because an added dimension of complexity must be factored into the development and implementation of plans to achieve and maintain competitive advantage. Hereche's work has important implications for product planners targeting emerging market consumers. The first consideration facing product planners in their product design decisions for emerging markets is how or how much to vary their product based on domestic market purchase behavior versus emerging market purchase behavior. Marketing research is critical to answer this question. Second, to what degree are the purchase intentions of emerging market consumers based on ethnocentric tendencies and to what degree are they based on the organization's overall marketing strategy?

International product developers are concerned with the effects of consumer ethnocentrism because emerging market consumers may evaluate a product based on their perception of the product's country of origin. As new foreign markets emerge, knowledge about consumer ethnocentrism images in those markets will enable product designers to make wiser decisions.

New Product Development Teams

Group interactions have always been important to the effective working of organizations, and with the proliferation of product design and development teams in business today, it has become increasingly important to understand how teams function best and what antecedent factors lead to the effective function of new product development teams.

Organizations rely on teams to make decisions that are critical to their viability and effectiveness. When these teams are encouraged to think in new ways, previously undetected patterns among market phenomena are recognized and perceived market opportunities increase (Senge, 1990). Teams are expected to produce decisions of higher quality with greater acceptance by their members (Vroom, 1969) while finding resolution to the differences of opinions that occur among members of the team.

Selecting new product development team members

Research on developing organizational teams has shown that the individual characteristics of the team members play a crucial in the success of a project (Katz, 1982; Keller, 1986; Gupta and Wilemon, 1990; McDonough, 1993).

When team members are selected on the basis of their experience and expertise and aspire to working together to achieve outstanding results, organizations and their stakeholders prosper. To this end, Larson and LaFasto's (1989) *standards of excellence* and *competent team members* are crucial for the international product designer. Product-related decisions for emerging markets are only as good as the people who made those decisions. This creates a challenge for emerging market product developers because it forces them to carefully consider the composition of the product design team, and it requires them to identify and set a benchmark for achieving the emerging market product the organization can produce. This raises a number of questions for the organization's management:

Who will lead the group?
Where will the team members be based (emerging market, home country, or another location)?
What are the selection criteria of the team members?
Is the team permanent or temporary? (That is, has the team been development to design and produce a specific product for the emerging market and then disbanded, or is it a permanent team?)
What are the benchmarks for achieving the ideal emerging market product or product range?
How many team members are required?
Can this product development team be used for more than one project, that is, can this team design and develop a product for more than one

emerging market or is it necessary to develop a new team for a different market?

The list of questions above is not exhaustive, yet the answers to the questions are critical to new product development success in emerging markets.

Managing product development teams

As an international marketing organization expands its presence in emerging markets, it increasingly finds that some of its new product development team members are based in the emerging market and others in the domestic market. One challenge facing new product development team leaders is the challenge of managing team members, who may reside in different geographic locations, specifically, in different nations. This possibility raises several subchallenges such as managing team conflict, when that conflict exists between team members from different cultures. For instance, Chinese people with their collectivist values have been thought to be particularly sensitive to how conflict is dealt with in interpersonal and team settings (Tjosvold *et al.*, 2006), and indeed to avoid conflict because it disrupts relationship harmony (Jehn and Weldon, 1992). The value of conflict as well as theories to analyze team conflict as portrayed in the extant previous cannot be assumed to apply to a collectivist nation like China (Hofstede, 1993; Liu *et al.*, 2005; Tjosvold *et al.*, 2006). A competitive approach favored in Western cultures may be communicating aggressiveness and disrespect in Chinese culture.

To assist the export decision maker manage cross-cultural team conflict Triandis (1995) notes that *attitudes* are sound predictors of team behavior in individualist cultures while *social norms* are better predictors of behavior in collectivist cultures. On a related topic, Jehn and Wendon (1997) found that when managing conflicts, American managers focus on the task, while Chinese managers focus on the social and relational aspects of the conflict. These findings have significant implications for new product development teams are management. As an organization grows its presence in emerging markets, it must also employ leaders to manage new product development teams with the requisite cultural sensitivities.

Level of compromise in new product development teams

It is important that team members have confidence in the team's procedures and decisions rather mere grudging acceptance. Team members who merely comply with product-related development decisions may begin to distance themselves from the group during the decision implementation phase (Verzberger, 1994). A key ingredient to team decision making is the degree of compromise associated with the decision being made. Hinsz (1999) proposes that group team processes related to quantities involve compromise and are characteristically different from the consensus processes that occur for discrete choices. Hinsz's work emanates from social decision research that has previously demonstrated that the decision process associated with group outcomes varies as a function of the context in which the decision is made.

To illustrate his position, Hinsz builds on the earlier work of Gigone and Hastie (1997) who suggest that discrete responses involve *choices* whereas quantitative responses involve *judgments*. Hinsz posits that the consensus processes that have been used to describe team decision processes with categorical responses may be inadequate or inappropriate for predicting team decision processes of a quantitative nature. Since quantitative judgments will rarely have more than one team member favoring a single value, majority and plurality decision process are not as likely to exist for quantities as they are for nominal response categories (Gigone and Hastie, 1997). Using Hinsz's work to understand product decisions for overseas markets raises some questions. Do international product design and development decisions represent *choices* or *judgments*? Are these decisions compromised and if so, in what way? The answers to these questions may be specific to individual organization, products, or emerging markets. Whilst the questions are not necessarily simple to answer, the answers are important to the success development of targeted emerging market products.

As organizations contemplate the composition of their new product development teams, an adjunct consideration that should be addressed is the location of these teams. We consider this in the next section.

Location of New Product Development Teams: An Introduction to Virtual Teams

Virtual teams, in which members use technology to interact with one another across *geographic, organizational,* and *other boundaries,* are becoming common in organizations (Gibson and Cohen, 2003). Contrasted against face-to-face teams, members of virtual teams are not constrained to one physical location and can be located throughout the world (Montoya-Weiss *et al.*, 2001). Virtual teams are conceptualized as having a more fluid membership such that specific expertise can be added or removed as tasks change (Alge *et al.*, 2003). Additionally, researchers have noted the tendency for virtual teams to possess a shorter lifecycle as compared to face-to-face teams (Jarvenpaa and Leidner, 1999). A proposed benefit of virtual teams is that they can bring together individuals with the needed key success factors regardless of their location (Blackburn *et al.*, 2003).

As organizations increase the number of international markets they enter, virtual teams may assist the managers to improve the quality of the decisions they make by drawing on knowledge and experience from team members located in the nations in which the export products is manufactured and the nations in which it is sold. Arguably, the better the decision, the better the product. As Zigurs (2003) suggests, members of virtual teams are drawn from different organizations by outsourcing or through joint ventures among service providers who work across organizational boundaries.

One idea that organizations targeting emerging markets with new products that stem from Zigur's research is that team members need not belong to the one organization, that is, some of the new product development functions (e.g., research and development) can be outsourced. If we couple this with the idea that new product development teams for emerging markets can be physically located together or operated as virtual teams, we can illustrate these two concepts in one framework that is illustrated in Table 2.2.

The framework illustrated in Table 2.2 gives the organization developing new products for emerging markets 12 discreet choices in forming their new product development team. Whilst these choices do appear discrete, they can actually be used in a more dynamic, temporal, and directive sense. For instance, an organization can start off in the top left hand quadrant (that is, employing their own new product design and developer team based in their

Table 2.2. Employer-location paradigm in forming new product development teams for emerging markets.

Product manufacturer in home country market only	3rd party contractor in home country market only	Product manufacturer and 3rd party contractor in home country market only
Product manufacturer in emerging market only	3rd party contractor in emerging market only	Product manufacturer and 3rd party contractor in emerging market only
Product manufacturer in both home country and emerging market (physical location)	3rd party contractor in both home and emerging market (physical location)	Product manufacturer and 3rd party contractor in both home country market (physical location)
Product manufacturer using virtual teams	3rd party contractor using virtual teams	Product manufacturer and 3rd party contractor using virtual teams

Table 2.3. Employer-location paradigm in forming new product development teams for emerging markets — temporal shifts caused by environmental factors.

Product manufacturer in home country market only	3rd party contractor in home country market only	Product manufacturer and 3rd party contractor in home country market only
Product manufacturer in emerging market only	3rd party contractor in emerging market only	Product manufacturer and 3rd party contractor in emerging market only
Product manufacturer in both home country and emerging market (physical location)	3rd party contractor in both home and emerging market (physical location)	Product manufacturer and 3rd party contractor in both home country market (physical location)
Product manufacturer using virtual teams	3rd party contractor using virtual teams	Product manufacturer and 3rd party contractor using virtual teams

own (home) country, and over time gradually move to different quadrants as the environmental forces require this to happen. An example of this is illustrated in Table 2.3.

Regardless of the location and composition of the new product development teams, one consideration they should consider when developing new products for emerging markets is determining the right branding strategy for the emerging market product. We consider this in the next section.

Product Branding for Emerging Markets

The idea of a brand has previously been associated with product strategy (Dickson and Ginter, 1987). Kotler (2003) defines a brand as "a promise that is made about customers about the quality and value of the product or service they purchase." Inherent in Kotler's definition is the idea that product planners and designers know what consumers see as being value in a given product and how consumers perceive quality in a product. These value and quality perceptions differ from market to market and in some cases from market segment to segment within a market. The starting point for product planners and designers is to ascertain, usually through market(ing) research, the value perceptions that emerging market consumers hold for a given product and the elements of that product that create the impression of that product's quality.

A product's branding is one of the more visible aspects of that product in the eyes of a consumer. It provides the product and its developer with a reputation that can be used as leverage to develop and introduce new products (brands) into existing and emerging markets (Ni and Wan, 2008). Indeed, Ni and Wan (2008) suggest that an organization's competitive advantage in a market depends on the extent to which they can coalign their brand with the market conditions. A simple example of market conditions is that in India consumers prefer to buy local and global branded consumer goods whereas in China consumers prefer to buy branded goods from the United States, European, and Japanese consumers (Khanna *et al.*, 2005).

One difficulty in branding consumer goods for sale into emerging markets is the fact that in many such markets consumers have not been exposed to brands for long time and in some cases are not sure how to interpret them (Eckhardt and Cayla, 2003). In such cases the perceptions, attitudes, and behavior of consumers toward specific product categories that are considered foreign or new are based on the product category, not the specific brand (Eckhardt and Cayla, 2003).

Previous research in product branding for emerging markets has tended to support the idea that, as international marketers are attracted to the size and growth of consumer markets in emerging economies like China's, they have largely overlooked the diversity among indigenous consumers (Cui and Liu, 2000). Although many consumers in emerging markets desire brands international brands and associate them with superior quality, rosy forecasts of macroeconomic statistics and higher consumer expectations have not translated easily into soaring demand and actionable strategies for multinational companies (Cui and Liu, 2001). This often results in international organizations seeking access to emerging economies assume a huge market with homogeneous consumers. This often leads to difficulties in assessing demand for consumer goods and services, and difficulties in devising effective marketing strategies (Cui and Liu, 2001). One such strategy is the decision to market standardized (domestic) products into China or to adapt/customize the domestic product for export. Thus, as Batra (1997) and Swanson (1996) suggest, understanding the diversity among consumer groups and its implications for marketing strategies is essential for success in emerging markets. To compete effectively, organizations need to define the consumers of emerging markets. Regional disparities in consumer purchasing power in countries like China, Indonesia, and India often pose significant barriers for exporting organizations to adopt uniform strategies in this market (Batra, 1997). We conclude from this that emerging markets should not been seen as one homogeneous consumer goods and services market, rather several regional markets. This understanding may be important for product planners during the product branding process.

To better understand product branding in emerging markets, let us look at three intertwined branding issues, namely, *brand name*, *brand image*, and *brand origin*.

Brand name

Consumers in emerging markets often experience low familiarity with foreign-made and foreign-branded products. According to Park and Lessig (1981), consumers who have low familiarity with foreign made products tend to select extrinsic cues such as brand name as the only product attribute of significance. This creates one potential problem for emerging market product developers. Many emerging markets have low literacy rates making it difficult for many consumers to read the product's packaging. This problem may be overcome through promotional campaigns using audio media such as radio advertising, where consumers can listen rather than having to read brand names.

Whilst the Park and Lessig (1981) study is of use to emerging market product planners, its findings differ from those of a study undertaken by Forsythe, Kim, and Petee (1995) that found that product design is an attribute that impacts on consumer evaluations and purchase intentions for Chinese consumers. Brand name was not a strong cue in product evaluations for Chinese consumers, although it was significant predictor of value perceptions. One challenge facing product designers is to link their preferred value perceptions of a brand in a particular emerging market to that product's brand name. The careful development and implementation of a promotional campaign are important in this effort.

A study by Pan and Schmitt (1995) hypothesized that the way a brand name is written should be a more important predictor of brand name attitudes in Chinese than English. Another study found that Chinese consumers use high profile brand names to provide security because of their limited experience with a modern free market system (Eckhardt and Houston, 1998). Since the ideographic nature of Chinese characters (i.e., the Chinese alphabet), Pan and Schmitt also predicted that a Chinese word is more likely than an English word to be associated with mental imagery. They found support for both of their hypotheses. Thus, the work of Pan and Schmitt (1995) has important implications for product planners and designers. For international marketers looking to adapt their product for China, the brand name chosen for that product in China influences the likelihood of that product being accepted by Chinese consumer, hence it has potentially positive influence on product success.

Henessey *et al.* (2005) posit that a product's brand name has implications for word recognition and thus has practical implications for product development. Their research is supported by a recent study that showed the phonetic properties of a brand name could influence consumer judgment (Yorkston and Menon, 2004). Finally, Harris *et al.* (1994) found that a product's brand name and image may be a proxy for country of origin cues. For example, brands like Ford, Nestle, and Samsung may automatically activate origin cues among consumer segments, even though the name of the country of origin does not appear in the brand name. This leads us to the next section.

Brand origin

Thakor and Kholi (1996, p. 27) define *brand origin* as the "place, region, or country, where a brand is perceived among its target consumers."

Thakor's definition of brand origin has one major implication for product managers. It is based on consumer perception. What most international marketing organizations are interested in are outcomes that are within the power of consumers to dispense, for example, selecting one brand over another. Hence, the actual place that the brand originates from may be irrelevant, even if it were possible in an era of globalization where corporations have dispersed their functions across national borders to identify such a place.

Thakor and Kohli recognize that *brand origin* may be more salient for some brands more than others, in that some brands may not have an especially distinct personality and/or may rely on appeals founded on other bases than origin. They consider brand origin to be a demographic variable, and part of a brand's personality, in the sense that brands can be described in terms of their origins. However, they also recognizes that brands that seek to associate themselves with favorable country or regional images may render themselves vulnerable to counter attack if their claims, even implicit, can be shown to be false. For instance, a Mazda motor vehicle manufactured in the United States may still be thought of as a Japanese car. The brand (name) origin is Japanese. The country of origin is the United States. To American consumers, is Mazda a Japanese or American car? Furthermore, Audi is quintessentially a German brand regardless of where the product is manufactured. This issue that product managers face is that dominant associations between products and their country of origin is to make the most of the country of origin association, where those associations are perceived by consumers as being positive. Underpinning this thinking is robust marketing research into the associations that emerging market consumers have to a product, its origin, and its brand name.

To assist with the conceptualization of brand origin, Thakor and Lavack (2003) propose a model of antecedents and consequences of *brand origin*. This model assists export decision makers to plan strategic responses to the antecedents of brand origin based on the consequences in the Thakor and Lacack (2003). In addition, Thakor and Lavack (2003) demonstrate that the place where a product is made is not important compared to the origin of the brand and the components of the product. Their model is illustrated in Fig. 2.5.

Thakor and Kohli's (1996) research raises an interesting challenge for emerging market product designers, namely, how to manage the differences between country of origin and brand origin. Country of origin is primarily concerned with determining the effects of consumers' perceptions of countries and their ratings on products' quality and choice processes. Brand origin refers to the "integration of origin cues within the brand image, in recognition of the reality that this is by far the most common way in which origin cues are utilized by marketers."

There seems to be a consensus among authors that brand image and country image are inextricably linked (Johansson *et al.*, 1985; Thakor and Katsanis, 1997; D' Astous and Ahmed, 1999). In the next section we consider brand image.

Brand image

The globalization of business enterprises has reached a point where it is sometimes difficult to determine with certainty the country of origin of a

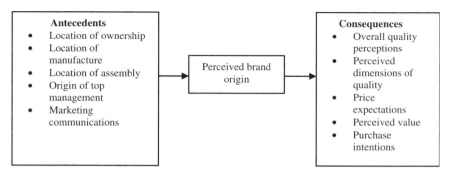

Figure 2.5. A model of the antecedents and consequences of brand origin.

brand. Despite this reality, most previous research into country of origin effects primarily addressed consumers' reactions to brands that are foreign made and foreign branded versus those which are domestically produced and domestically branded. Further, despite the strategic importance of brand image, Roth (1995) found surprisingly little is known about the effects of brand image strategies across international markets, whilst Seitz (1998) suggested that all individuals regardless of their ethnic background prefer to buy the majority of self-image type brands in stores. In addition, cultural, economic, social, and other differences make it difficult to identify single brand image strategies that have global appeal (Madden *et al.*, 2000).

To assist international product marketers to better understand brand image, Biel (1993) defines brand image as a "cluster of attributes and associations that consumers connect with a brand name." In this backdrop, Paswan and Sharma (2004) argue that consumer knowledge of a brand's country is crucial for the transfer of the country of origin image to the brand image, while other researchers (e.g., Chung Koo, 1995) suggest that through familiarity with products from different countries, consumers develop countries images that have considerable impact on their evaluation of those products.

So, how do organizations targeting emerging market consumers use previous research to develop a favorable brand image for the product? Roth (1995) recommends starting with an idea of the ideal brand image before focusing on marketing mix (that is, product, placement, promotion, and price). He argues that having a specific brand image in mind can assist with the rest of the product development challenges. On the other hand, Park *et al.* (1986) have proposed a useful model of brand image strategies, suggesting that international product managers should base their images on a particular consumer need, that is, develop a brand image that relates to a functional, social, or sensory need. Needs for any consumer good may differ globally. This raises several important questions for product planners. How does this affect the need to customize some aspect of the brand (e.g., image) to meet the needs of the emerging market? What form might this customization take? What elements of the product's physical form are affected in the customization?

To assist product planners even further, Roth (1995) studied the relationship between brand image, brand performance, and market conditions. He found that although international marketing organizations consider some cultural and socioeconomic conditions of foreign countries in forming their international brand image strategies and those conditions moderate the market share effects of their brand image strategies, international product managers could enhance brand performance by broadening the information they use in making global brand image strategy decisions. An organization's choice and use of marketing communications (promotional) strategies in the emerging market are important in achieving this important goal.

Summary

To effectively compete in emerging markets, organizations must develop products that are carefully targeted to the needs of the consumer. As the emerging market grows toward a more industrialized economy, these needs will change over time. To successfully compete in emerging markets, Duarte de Abreu Filho *et al.* (2003) and London and Hart (2004) suggest that new product developers should consider multiple products for each emerging market. Their reason for such a suggestion is that as emerging market economies grow, there is a greater income disparity among its consumers. Therefore, the organization should develop high-end products for the growing middle class consumers found in emerging markets (Hart and Millstein, 1999). This enables the international marketing organization to peruse consistent brand-building strategies. A second "stripped down" product should also be developed for the middle class of consumer of tomorrow, in other words for consumer who today cannot afford a high-end version of the product but may be able to do so in the future.

Another important aspect of developing products for emerging markets is not to consider these markets as homogeneous patterns of economic development in which all markets are evolving toward Western style business environment (London and Hart, 2004). This is due to the fact that while the emerging market economies are growing, the vast majority of consumers in these markets find it difficult to afford foreign-branded consumer goods. In many cases, such purchases are considered luxuries.

Regardless of how many or what types of products international marketing organizations consider for their emerging market consumers, conformance of those products to local laws regarding products standards, product quality, packaging, and labeling must be adhered to. Products often fail in international markets because of non-conformance to local laws. The difficulty facing new product developers in this regard is that in many emerging markets such laws are unclear, always changing, and at times difficult to interpret. This as well as many other product-related considerations must form part of the marketing organization's marketing research into the emerging market prior to new product development.

References

Adams, M and J Lacugna (1994). *And Now for Something Completely Different: 'Really' New Products*. Cambridge, MA: Marketing Science Institute.

Alge, BJ, C Wietlof, and HJ Klein (2003). When does the medium matter? Knowledge building experiences and opportunities in decision-making teams. *Organisational Behaviour and Human Decision Process*, 91, 26–37.

Arnold, D and JA Quelch (1998). New strategies in emerging markets. *Sloan Management Review*, 40(1), 7–20.

Batra, R (1997). Executive insights: Marketing issues and challenges in transitional economies. *Journal of International Marketing*, 5(4), 95–114.

Biel, AL (1993). Converting image into equity. In *Brand Equity and Advertising*, Aaker, DA and AL Biel (eds.), Hillsdale, NJ: Laurence Erlbaum and Associates.

Blackburn, R, SA Furst, and B Rosen (2003). *Building a winning virtual term: KSA's, selections, training, and evaluation*. In *Virtual teams that work: Creating conditions for virtual team effectiveness*. Gibson, CB and SG Coren (eds.), San Franscisco: Jossey–Bass.

Child, J and DK Tse (2001). China's transition and its implications for international business. *Journal of International Business Studies*, 32(1), 5–21.

Child, J and T Tsai (2005). The dynamic between firms' environmental strategies and institutional constraints in emerging economies: Evidence from China and Taiwan. *Journal of Management Studies*, 42(1), 95–125.

Chung Koo, K (1995). Brand popularity and country image in the formation of consumer product perceptions. *Journal of Product and Brand Management*, 4(5), 21–33.

Cooper, R and E Kleinschmidt (1996). An investigation into the new product process: Steps, deficiencies, and impact. *Journal of Product Innovation Management*, 3, 71–85.

Cordero, R (1991). Managing for speed to avoid planned obsolescence. *Journal of Product Innovation Management*, 8, 283–294.

Coughlan, P and A Wood (1992). Getting product designs right. *Business Quarterly*, 56(4), 63–69.

Cui, G and Q Liu (2000). Regional market segments of China: Opportunities and barriers in a big emerging market. *Journal of Consumer Marketing*, 17(1), 55–72.

Cui, G and Q Liu (2001). Emerging marketing segmentation in a transitional economy: A study of urban consumers in China. *Journal of International Marketing*, 8(1), 84–106.

d' Astous, A and A Sadrudin (1999). The Importance of country images in the formation of consumer product perceptions. *International Marketing Review*, 16(2), 108–125.

Darling, JR and DR Arnold (1988). The competitive position abroad of products and marketing practices of the United States, Japan, and selected European countries. *Journal of Consumer Marketing*, 5, 61–68.

Darling, JR and VR Wood (1990). A longitudinal study comparing perceptions of US and Japanese consumer products in a third/neutral country: Finland 1975 to 1985. *Journal of International Business Studies*, 21(3), 427–450.

Dawar, N and A Chattopadhyay (2002). Re-thinking marketing programs for emerging markets. *Long Range Planning*, 35, 457–474.

Delios, A and B Paul (1999). Geographic scope, product diversification, and the corporate performance of Japanese firms. *Strategic Management Journal*, 20(8), 711–725.

Dhillon, A (3 April 2005). India's new rich go on a spending spree. *The Sunday Times*.

Dickson, PR and JL Ginter (1987). Market segmentation, product differentiation, and marketing strategy. *Journal of Marketing*, 51(2), 1–10.

Duarte, de Abreu Filho, G and N Calicchio (2003). Brand building in emerging markets. *The McKinsey Quarterly* (June), 1–6.

Eckhardt, GM and MJ Houston (1998). Consumption as self presentation in a collectivist society. In *Asia Pacific Advances in Consumer Research*, Hung, K and KB Monroe (eds.), pp. 52–58. Provo, UT: Association for Consumer Research.

Eckhardt, G and J Cayla (2003). Branding strategies in emerging markets. *AGSM Magazine*, 3, 1–6.

Forsythe, S, JO Kim, and T Petee (1999). Product cue usage in two Asian markets: A cross-cultural comparison. *The Pacific Journal of Management*, 16(2), 275–292.

Gaedeke, R (1973). Consumer attitudes towards products "Made in" developing countries. *Journal of Retailing*, 49(2), 13–24.

Gibson, CB and SG Cohen (2003). *Virtual teams that work: Creating conditions for virtual term effectiveness.* San Francisco: Jossey–Bass.

Gigone, D and R Hastie (1997). The impact of information on small group choice. *Personality and Social Psychology*, 72(1), 132–140.

Gingrich, J (1999). Five rules for winning emerging market consumers. In *Best Practices in International Business*, Czinkota, M and I Ronkainen (eds.), pp. 327–338. Forth Worth Tx: Harcourt College Publishers.

Griffin, A (1993). Metrics for measuring new product success. *Journal of Innovation and Management*, 10(2), 112–125.

Griffin, A and A Page (1993). An interim report on measuring product development success and failure. *Journal of Innovation and Management*, 10(4), 291–308.

Griffin, A and A Page (1993). PDMA success measurement project: Recommended measures for product development success and failure. *Journal of Innovation and Management*, 13(6), 478–496.

Gupta, AK and DL Wilemon (1990). Accelerating the development of technology based new products. *California Management Review*, 32(2), 24–44.

Harris, RJ, B Garner-Earl, SJ Sprick, and C Carroll (1994). Effects of foreign product names and country of origin attributions and advertisement evaluations. *Psychology and Marketing*, 11(22), 129–144.

Hart, SL and MB Millstein (1999). Global sustainability and the creative destruction of industries. *Sloan Management Review*, 41(1), 23–33.

Hennessey, JE, TS Bell, and RJ Kwortnik (2005). Lexical references in semantic processing of simple words: Implications for brand names. *Psychology and Marketing*, 22(1), 51–69.

Herche, J (1994). Ethnocentric tendencies, marketing strategy and import purchase behavior. *International Marketing Review*, 11(3), 4–16.

Hetherington, MJ and DB MacDougall (1992). Visual and instrumental attribute models of fruit juices and milk. *Food Quality and Preferences*, 3, 165–174.

Hinsz, VB (1999). Group decision making with responses of a quantitative nature: The theory of social decisions schemes for quantities. *Organizational Behavior and Human Decision Process*, 80(1), 28–49.

Hofstede, G (1993). Cultural constraints in management theories. *Academy of Management Executive*, 7(1), 81–94.

Hoskisson, RE. *et al.* (2000). Strategy in emerging economies. *Academy of Management Journal*, 43(3), 249–267.

Huddleston, P, LK Good, and L Stoel (2001). Consumer ethnocentrism, product necessity and polish consumers' perceptions of quality. *International Journal of Retail and Distribution Management*, 29(5), 236–246.

Imran, N (1999). The role of visual cues in consumer perception and acceptance of a product. *Nutrition and Food Science*, 995, 224–228.

Isobe, T, S Makino, and DB Montgomery (2000). Resource commitment, entry timing, and market performance of foreign direct investments in emerging economies: The case of Japanese international joint ventures. *Academy of Management Journal*, 43(3), 468–484.

Jarvenpaa, SL and DE Leichner (1999). Communication and trust in global teams. *Organization Science*, 10(6), 791–815.

Jehn, KA and E Weldon (1992). A comparative study of managerial attitudes towards conflict in the United States and the People's Republic of China: Issues of theory and measurement. *Academy of Management*, Las Vegas, NV.

Jehn, KA and E Weldon (1997). Managerial attitudes towards conflict: Cross cultural differences in resolution styles. *Journal of International Management*, 3, 291–321.

Jin, Z, B Chansarkar, and NM Kondap (2006). Brand origin in an emerging market: Perceptions of Indian consumers. *Asia Pacific Journal of Marketing and Logistics*, 18(4), 283–302.

Johansson, JK, SP Douglas, and I Nonaka (1985). Assessing the impact of country of origin on product evaluations: A new methodological perspective. *Journal of Marketing Research*, 22, 388–396.

Kasper, H (1999). *Services Marketing Management: An International Perspective*. New York, NY: John Wiley & Sons.

Katz, R (1982). Three effects of group longevity on project communication and performance. *Administrative Science Quarterly*, 27(1), 81–104.

Kaynak, E and K Ali (2002). Consumer perceptions of foreign products. An analysis of product-country images and ethnocentrism. *European Journal of Marketing*, 36(7/8), 928–949.

Keller, R (1986). Predictors on the performance of project groups in R&D organizations. *Academy of Management Journal*, 29(4), 715–726.

Khanna, T, KG Palepu, and J Sinha (2005). Strategies that fit emerging markets. *Harvard Business Review*, 83(6), 63–76.

Khurana, A and SR Rosenthal (1998). Towards holistic "front ends" in new product development. *Journal of Product Innovation Management*, 15(1), 57–74.

Klein, JG, R Ettenson, and MD Morris (1999). Consumer animosity and consumer ethnocentrism: An analysis of unique antecedents. *Journal of International Consumer Marketing*, 11(4), 5–24.

Kotler, P (2003). *Marketing Management*. Harlow: Prentice Hall.

Krishnan, V and T Ulrich (2001). Product development decisions: A review of the literature. *Management Science*, 47(1), 1–21.

Larson, C and F LaFasto (1989). *Teamwork: What Must Go Right/What Can Go Wrong*. Newberry Park: Sage.

Leonard-Barton, D (1992). Core capabilities and core rigidities: A paradox in managing new product development. *Strategic Management Journal*, 13(Summer), 111–125.

Li, L and G Ogunmokun (2003). Effective marketing control on export venture performance: The moderating role of relationship intensity and market dynamism. *Journal of Global Marketing*, 16(3), 5–29.

Liu, LA, RA Friedman, and SC Chi (2005). Ren Qing versus Big Five: The role of culturally sensitive measures of individual difference in distributive negotiations. *Management and Organization Review*, 1(2), 225–247.

London, T and SL Hart (2004). Reinventing strategies for emerging markets: Beyond the transnational model. *Journal of International Business Studies*, 35(5), 1–21.

London, T and SL Hart (2004). Reinventing strategies for emerging markets: Beyond the transnational model. *Journal of International Business Studies*, 35, 350–370.

Madden, TJ, K Hewett, and MS Roth (2000). Managing images in different cultures: A cross-national study of color meanings and preferences. *Journal of International Marketing*, 8(4), 90–107.

Mahajan, V and J Wind (1992). New product models: Practice, shortcomings and desired improvements. *Journal of Innovation Management*, 9(2), 128–139.

McDonough EF, III (1993). Faster new product development: Investigating the effects of technology and characteristics of the project leader and team. *Journal of Product Innovation Management*, 10(2), 241–250.

Montoya-Weiss, M, A Massey, and M Song (2001). Getting it together: Temporal coordination and conflict management in global virtual teams. *The Academy of Management Journal*, 44(6), 1251–1262.

Moorman, C and AS Miner (1997). The impact of organizational memory on new product performance and creativity. *Journal of Marketing Research*, 34(1), 91–106.

Ni, N and F Wan (2008). A configurational perspective of branding capabilities development in emerging economies: The case of the Chinese cellular phone industry. *Journal of Brand Management*, 15(6), 433–451.

Nowlis, S and I Simonson (1996). The effect of new product features on brand choice. *Journal of Marketing Research*, 33(1), 36–46.

Pan, Y and BH Schmitt (1995). What's in a name? An empirical comparison of Chinese and Western brand names. *Asian Journal of Marketing* (December), 7–16.

Park, CW and VP Lessig (1981). Familiarity and its impact on consumer decision biases and heuristics. *Journal of Consumer Research*, 8(2), 223–230.

Park, CW, BJ Jaworski, and DJ MacInnes (1986). Strategic brand concept image management. *Journal of Marketing*, 50, 135–145.

Paswan, AK and D Sharma (2004). Brand-country of origin (Coo) knowledge and Coo image: Investigation in an emerging franchise market. *Journal of Product and Brand Management*, 13(3), 144–155.

Pecotich, A and M Rosenthal (2001). Country of origin, quality, brand and consumer ethnocentrism. *Journal of Global Marketing*, 15(2), 31–60.

Peng, M, YL Wang, and Y Jiang (2008). An institution-based view of international business strategy: A focus on emerging economies. *Journal of International Business Studies*, 39(April), 920–936.

Prahalad, CK and K Lieberthal (1998). The end of corporate imperialism. *Harvard Business Review*, 80(9), 48–57.

Prahalad, CK and A Hammond (2002). Serving the world's poor, profitably. *Harvard Business Review*, 80(9), 48–57.

Rogers, H, P Ghauri, and KS Pawar (2005). Measuring international NPD projects: An evaluation process. *Journal of Business and Industrial Marketing*, 20(2), 79–87.

Roth, MS (1995). Effects of global market conditions on brand image customization and brand performance. *Journal of Advertising*, 24(4), 55–75.

Schutz, HG and DL Wahl (1981). Consumer acceptance of the relative importance of appearance. *Criteria Perception of the Relative Importance Symposium Proceedings*, 97–116.

Seitz, V (1998). Acculturation and direct purchasing behavior among ethnic groups in the US: Implications for business practitioners. *Journal of Consumer Marketing*, 15(1), 23–31.

Senge, P (1990). *The Fifth Discipline: The Art and Practice of the Learning Organisation.* New York, NY: Doubleday.

Sengupta, K and A Chattopadhyay (2006). Importance of appropriate marketing strategies for sustainability of small business in a developing country. *Asia Pacific Journal of Marketing and Logistics*, 18(4), 328–341.

Swanson, LA (1996). 1.19850+ billion mouths to feed: Food linguistics and cross-cultural, cross-national food consumption habits in China. *British Food Journal*, 98(6), 33–44.

Thakor, MV and CS Kohli (1996). Brand origin: Conceptualization and review. *Journal of Consumer Marketing*, 13(3), 27–38.

Thakor, MV and LP Katsanis (1997). A model of brand and country effects on quality dimensions: Issues and implications. *Journal of International Consumer Marketing*, 9(3), 79–100.

Thakor, MV and AM Lavack (2003). Effect of perceived brand origin associations on consumer perceptions of quality. *Journal of Product and Brand Management*, 12(6), 399–407.

Tjosvold, D, KS Law, and H Sun (2006). Effectiveness of Chinese teams: The role of conflict types and conflict management approaches. *Management and Organization Review*, 2(2), 231–252.

Toyne, B and P Walters (1989). *Global Marketing Management: A Strategic Perspective.* Boston, MA: Allyn and Bacon.

Triandis, HC (1995). *Individualism and Collectivism.* Boulder, Co: Westview Press.

Usunier, JC and G Cestre (2007). Product ethnicity: Revisiting the match between products and countries. *Journal of International Marketing*, 15(3), 32–72.

Verzberger, YYI (1994). Collective risk taking: The decision making group and organization. In *35th Annual Convention of the International Studies Association*, Washington DC.

Vroom, VH (1969). *Industrial Social Psychology, Handbook of Social Psychology*, 2nd edn., Vol. 5, G Lindzey and E Aronson (eds.).

Wang, C-K and CW Lamb (1983). The impact of selected environmental forces upon consumers' willingness to buy foreign products. *Journal of the Academy of Marketing Science*, 11(2), 71–84.

Wang, CL and ZX Chen (2004). Consumer ethnocentrism and willingness to buy domestic products in a developing country setting: Testing moderating effects. *Journal of Consumer Marketing*, 21(6), 391–400.

Wheelwright, SC and WE Sasser (1989). The new product development map. *Harvard Business Review*, 67(3), 112–125.

Yorkston, E and G Menon (2004). A sound idea: Phonetic effects of brand names in consumer judgments. *Journal of Consumer Research*, 31(1), 43–52.

Zigurs, I (2003). Leading in virtual teams: Oxymoron or opportunity? *Organizational Dynamics*, 31, 339–351.

Zucker, LG (1977). The role of institutionalization in cultural persistence. *American Sociological Review*, 42, 726–743.

Chapter 3

COMPETING WITH MULTINATIONALS: ENTRY AND EVOLUTION OF LATECOMER FIRMS IN CHINA'S HANDSET INDUSTRY

WEI XIE AND STEVEN WHITE

Abstract

The question of how latecomer firms in emerging markets may compete against incumbent multinationals is significant to both types of firms as well as governments of host countries. Based on previous studies on this topic, this chapter proposes a generic process model for analyzing competition dynamics between latecomers and multinationals. Through examining the competition between local and foreign firms in China's handset manufacturing industry, this chapter highlights the series of contingencies that help determine the likelihood that latecomer firms will emerge as initial and then sustained competitors vis-à-vis incumbent multinationals.

Introduction

The question of how latecomer firms in emerging markets may compete with incumbent multinationals is significant to both types of firms as well as governments of host countries. Managers of latecomer firms need guidance about how to meet the challenges as they first enter and then attempt to grow and ultimately compete with larger, more experienced multinationals. At the same time, multinationals may have entered emerging markets like China and India and faced little or no local competition, but over time found themselves facing aggressive and increasingly successful local firms both in the host country market and later in third markets.

They need to have a better understanding of the potential of firms who, in the beginning, they may feel warrant no serious attention. Finally, development-oriented governments are concerned that multinationals will dominate entire industries and leave little potential for homegrown firms to emerge and grow.

Four characteristics discussed by Matthews (2002) are useful in describing latecomer firms in this context. First, they are entering the industry late by historical necessity, not choice. In other words, they did not have the option of being first-movers in the focal market and industry. Second, in the beginning they lack key resources, including technology and market access. Third, their primary strategic intent is to catch-up with the incumbent firms. Finally, they have some initial advantages vis-à-vis the incumbents; for example, lower costs or local market knowledge.

A number of researchers have approached the issue of latecomer firms and their competitiveness vis-à-vis multinationals with superior scale, resources, and capabilities. Dawar and Frost (1999), for example, describe conditions under which local emerging market firms may not be at a disadvantage; namely, when pressures for globalization in an industry are low and when resources and capabilities are not easily transferred across borders. In such industries, local firms may even have an advantage over multinationals. They also propose four generic strategies emerging market firms may take, depending on the nature of the industry along those two parameters.

Other researchers have focused on the particular disadvantages that latecomer firms must overcome, as well as the advantages that they must exploit. Matthews (2002) focuses on the former, arguing that the core of latecomer firm strategy is to overcome competitive disadvantages through linkages, resource leveraging, and learning. Others have focused primarily on the need to learn in order for firms and industries late-industrializing countries to emerge as competitive with multinationals both in their home countries and in international markets (e.g., Kim, 1997a,b; Amsden, 1989, 2001; Kim and Nelson, 2000).

Complementing this focus on learning, Cho *et al.* (1988) propose that latecomer firms must exploit opportunities arising from entry order effects. Like most other studies of market entry and performance (e.g., Lilien and Yoon, 1990; Kalyanaram and Urban, 1992; Schnaars, 1994; Makadok, 1998), they recognize the advantages associated with first-movers. Benefits include the chance to lock in customers by increasing switching costs, the chance to pre-empt competitors for resources and market opportunities, and superior returns from technological leadership, learning curve effects, and various forms of industry experience. As Shamsie *et al.* (2003, p. 70) points out, these are the same kinds of advantages that lead some previous studies to conclude that "the success of earlier entrants would make it difficult for subsequent entrants to make significant inroads into the market."

However, Cho *et al.* (1988) also propose an alternative set of benefits that latecomers may have vis-à-vis first- or early movers. These include the chance to free ride on the efforts of the first movers (such as in consumer education about new products and services, information spillover, and trial-and-error learning); lower investment risk once dominant designs are established and customer preferences understood; and a greater pool of external knowledge on which they may draw.

In this chapter, we intend to build on this work by integrating the elements of awareness, motivation, and ability to respond that are a focus of studies of competitive dynamics (e.g., Chen, 1996) with prior work in latecomer entry and growth strategies. We propose a generic process model and identify the key contingencies in each stage as latecomer firms in an emerging economy enter an industry dominated by large multinationals (Fig. 3.1). These contingencies represent key challenges and choices at each stage for

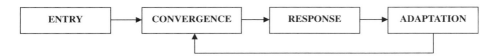

STAGE 1:   ENTRY

Latecomers have the opportunity and ability to enter. No direct competition with incumbents.

   Contingencies: *Is the latecomer allowed to enter (a license to operate)? Is there a market segment ignored or underserved by multinational incumbents? Can the latecomer acquire the resources and capabilities necessary to enter the industry?*

STAGE 2:   CONVERGENCE

Latecomers exploit advantages and compete more directly with incumbents. Market and resource overlap increases.

   Contingencies: *Does the latecomer pursue markets dominated by incumbent multinationals? Can the latecomer exploit or extend its resources and capabilities to enter markets dominated by multinationals?*

STAGE 3:   RESPONSE

Incumbents see latecomers as a threat and respond with tactical and/or strategic initiatives.

   Contingencies: *Has the basis of competition shifted as a result of the incumbents' response? Have the value of the latecomers' resources and capabilities changed as a result?*

STAGE 4:   ADAPTATION

Latecomers adapt strategy to achieve new sources of competitive advantage in response to evolution of industry and competitive dynamics.

   Contingencies: *Are latecomers aware and accurately interpret changes on the basis of competition? Are latecomers willing and able to make strategic changes in order to achieve competitive advantage?*

Figure 3.1.   Emergence of latecomer-incumbent competition: key stages and contingencies.

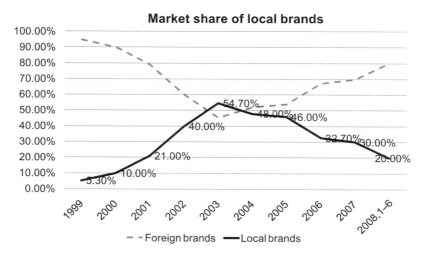

Figure 3.2.   Shares of chinese and foreign firms in china's handset market.

Source: 1999–2003 data are from the *2003 Yearbook of China's Electronics Industry and Ministry of Information Industry*; 2004–2006 data from the 2006–2007 China's IT Industry Map (in Chinese), China Social Science Literature Publisher, Beijing; and 2007–2008 data from an interview with an anonymous analyst of Yiguang Guoji Company on June 10, 2008.

managers of latecomer firms, with significant implications for incumbent multinationals and the evolution of an industry.

The following section introduces this model and illustrates it through a case study of the mobile phone handset industry in China and a firm-level analysis of Ningbo Bird over the period 1999–2008 that saw the rise and decline of local Chinese manufacturers (Fig. 3.2). Chinese firms were extremely successful entrants, with their share of the Chinese market (in terms of units) rising from below 5% in 1999 to over 50% in 2003. However, they were unable to sustain their momentum, and their combined market share dropped to 20% by 2008. We show how they were able to enter and initially converge in competitive terms with incumbent multinationals (Stages 1 and 2 of our model), and then why they lost market share in the face of incumbent response (Stages 3 and 4).

We focus on Bird to illustrate some of the firm-level features that emerged and evolved over this period.[1] Founded in 1992 as a pager manufacturer, Bird only entered the handset industry in 1999, but was manufacturing 700 thousand handsets by 2000 and 12 million by 2003. It was consistently the largest domestic manufacturer since 1999. In 2005 and

---

[1] Interview with Xieli Zhou, Ningbo Bird, 18 August 2004.

2007, however, it posted losses and its future prospects in the industry do not seem attractive.

Model of Latecomer Entry and Competition

The generic model presented in Fig. 3.1 integrates variables and findings from research on successful entry by latecomer firms with those from research on competitive dynamics. It has two important features. First, it is a process model, but is not deterministic. For each stage, we have proposed key contingencies that would increase or decrease the likelihood that a latecomer firm would go through that stage. Whether any particular firm or group of latecomer firms progresses through these stages depends on environmental factors and managerial choice. For example, the initial entry decision depends on latecomer being allowed to enter (surmountable barriers to entry), there being a market opening where it can find a foothold, and it being able to acquire the resources and capabilities required to operate in the industry. If these conditions are not met, there can be no entry. Similarly, convergence will take place if the latecomer pursues markets dominated by the incumbent and develops and exploits resources and capabilities that allow it to compete in those markets. If convergence does not occur, then it is likely that latecomers and incumbents would coexist by serving different markets without moving to the next stage of incumbent response.

Second, to capture the dynamics of competitive rivalry, we have a pathway from *Adaptation* back to *Convergence*. We argue that industry evolution will be characterized by periods of strategic differentiation as firms seek new sources of competitive advantage in response to reduced performance resulting from higher and higher degree of strategic convergence (the "red oceans" described by Kim and Maubourgne, 2005). Convergence will again increase as firms imitate the strategic changes made by firms who emerge as successful, and the cycle will be repeated. Over time, of course, it may not be the incumbent multinationals who initiate a strategic, industry-altering response to convergence. There is no *a priori* reason that firms who entered the industry as latecomers could not become leaders in introducing changes that shift the basis of competition and change the value of particular resources and capabilities.

Rise and fall of Chinese handset manufacturers

In this section, we use this model to frame our analysis of the entry and evolution of Chinese handset manufacturers and the Chinese industry. From this analysis, we are able to identify the combination of managerial choices and industry features that generated the competitive outcomes represented by the reverse of fortunes for multinational incumbents and latecomer Chinese entrants. We find that the Chinese latecomers were able to successfully enter the industry and then converge and initially compete successfully vis-à-vis the multinationals. The multinationals, however, were able to take both tactical and strategic actions to which the Chinese firms have not been willing or able to successfully adapt.

Stage 1: Entry

Latecomers can be expected to enter an industry when barriers to entry are sufficiently low, they are able to acquire the necessary resources and capabilities to enter, and there is an attractive market opportunity that is either ignored or underserved by multinational incumbents. As of the mid-to-late 1990s, there were significant barriers to latecomer entry in China's domestic handset market. First was their already significant presence and operating scale. Six multinationals had established production, marketing, and sales operations during 1993–1996, mostly in the form of Sino-foreign joint ventures, and benefited from economies of scale in component sourcing and production. They also benefited from the cost advantages of undertaking production in China, unlike in many other industries in which foreign firms selling in China were importing products produced in higher-cost locations. These multinationals were also vertically integrated and had long-term supplier relationships, providing them with more reliable supplies of any critical components they did not produce themselves. Nokia, for example, not only built a joint venture assembly base in Beijing, but also enticed ten of its suppliers to establish operations near it (the Beijing Economic and Technical Development Zone) to provide locally made components. Finally, the government had restricted entry by not granting many production licenses.

By 1999, several changes occurred that significantly lowered these barriers to entry. First, the government began to promote the development of a significant domestic industry in handset manufacturing, seeing significant growth prospects in terms of employment and both the domestic and export markets, as well as the benefits of developing domestic capabilities in the related industries of software and electronic components.[2] The Ministry of Information Industry (MII) and the State Planning Commission jointly published "Several Opinions on the Development of China's Mobile Telecommunications," usually referred to simply as Document 5 (see Table 3.1). It set as one goal that Chinese firms would be able to capture 30% of the market by 2003, a goal that was seen as too aggressive at that time. One critical result of this policy

---

[2] Interview with Peigen Shi, Siemens China, 11 June 2004.

Table 3.1. Key policies measures in documents.

Implications	Conditions
Preferential treatment for local handset makers	• Local firms are allowed to sell 100% of their output domestically. • The MII would invest up to RMB 1 billion (about $120 million at former official exchange rate) for domestic handset and telecom equipment manufacturers.
Requirements for foreign-invested enterprises	• With a few exceptions, foreign firms are not allowed to establish wholly owned handset production facilities in China. • Sino-foreign joint ventures are required to export no less than 60% of their output. • The import content of joint venture's product is no more than 50%. • Manufacturers with foreign involvement are required to establish R&D centers in China.
Manufacturing licenses	• Manufacturing license system will be adopted. Only firms granted manufacturing licenses can produce handsets in China.

focus was the granting of many more production licenses. By the end of 1999, production licenses had been granted to 16 Sino-foreign joint ventures, one wholly owned foreign enterprise, and 10 domestic firms. By 2004, there were 30 licensed manufacturers of GSM handsets and 19 for CDMA. While the financial subsidies suggested in the policy document were not implemented, there were other preferential conditions granted to domestic firms. For example, they could more easily obtain licenses, and were allowed to sell all of their production domestically, while Sino-foreign joint ventures had export requirements.

Two related developments in the technological environment of the handset industry coincided with the changes in government policy and also lowered the barriers to entry for latecomer Chinese firms. First, the industry had passed the stage at which the market belonged to firms like Motorola, Nokia, and Ericsson based on their lead in R&D. The technology had matured, and the basis of market competition was shifting from technical sophistication to product design, or the ability to make handsets that were stylish, comfortable to hold, and user-friendly. Competing no longer required expensive in-house R&D.

The second major change in technology was the disintegration of the value chain, resulting in the emergence of independent technology and component suppliers.[3] As the technology supporting the components and subsystems of

---

[3] Interview with Wanmeng Jiang, Wanyan TV Research Institute, 27 January 2003.

handsets became increasingly sophisticated and R&D costs increased accordingly, even the incumbent multinationals could not maintain all of the necessary technical expertise and produce all components internally. This, as well as the pressure to reduce product development cycle time, led to a product development model in the global handset industry based on networks of technology and component suppliers.

Because many of these overseas suppliers — primarily Taiwanese, South Korean, and Japanese — had established production facilities in China, it was possible for new Chinese firms to source standardized components relatively easily. Other firms were even providing entire subsystems, such as Wavecom, a NASDAQ-listed French firm that began to supply WISMO modules commercially in 1997. WISMO modules are specifically designed compact devices for downstream handset assemblers. A module contains all of the digital, base-band and radio frequency hardware and software that assemblers need for a complete wireless solution. Not only does it remove the necessity for an assembler to design and manufacture such modules, but it also reduces product development and field-tests time.

The increasing availability of components from independent suppliers, the removal of the high barriers to entry represented by R&D, product design, and manufacturing expertise made it more attractive for Chinese firms to enter the handset market. This is particularly relevant in the low-end handset market, for which hardware and software requirements are fairly standard. Indeed, this was the basis on which firms such as TCL Mobile Communications, now one of the leading local players in China's handset market, initially entered and grew. TCL relied on WISMO modules and concentrated its resources on external handset design, marketing, and distribution.

The third major factor, which made it possible for latecomer Chinese firms to enter the handset industry, was a significant market segment that was largely ignored by the multinationals. The multinationals and their Level 1 distributors had remained focused on the larger, richer cities. China Postal Mobile Communications Equipment, a Level 1 distributor for Motorola, Nokia, Ericsson, Siemens and other multinationals, in 2000 sold over 8 million handsets and generated RMB 12 billion, almost entirely accounted for by nine major cities including Beijing, Tianjin, Shanghai, Wuhan, Xian, Shengyan, Harbin, and Shenzhen. Penetration rates had reached 50%–70% in those regions, and additional growth would be very slow. As Table 3.2 shows, even in 2001, there was a significant difference in penetration rates among geographic markets. In 1999, as the latecomers were considering their possibilities, the differences were even greater.

Table 3.2. Handset penetration in a sample of provinces and municipalities.

National average	33.97
Highest penetration	
Beijing	62.40
Shanghai	49.60
Guangdong	85.67
Zhejiang	58.18
Fujian	66.94
Jiangsu	37.98
Shandong	31.64
Hunan	40.39
Yunnan	43.13
Lowest penetration	
Henan	17.81
Shanxi	19.74
Xiangjiang	13.72
Gansu	25.97
Shaanxi	15.39

Note: Units: handsets per 100 households.
Source: *2001 China's Statistical Yearbook*, p. 341.
Beijing: China Statistics Publishing Company.

While the multinationals had already established an extremely strong presence and penetration rate in the richest cities, they were almost absent from most markets that had the greatest growth potential, namely, the Tier 3 and lower urban locations and rural areas. Theoretically, the multinationals were represented in some of those markets through their Level 1 distributors and the Level 2 and, under them, Level 3 distributors who served retailers in those markets. However, the additional mark-up as the multinationals' handsets made their way through each layer of the distribution system, combined with a lack of significant incentives to front-line sales people, resulted in the multinationals having almost no presence in these markets.

This lack of effective penetration beyond Tier 2 cities left the largest and potentially fastest growing markets to the latecomers, although these markets were also geographically dispersed. The latecomers were able to enter and grow in these markets for two reasons. First, they introduced low-price models that also had capabilities, such as greater ruggedness and signal reception power, to match the customers in those markets. Second, they created more direct distribution channels to retailers and customers in those markets, both lowering cost and enabling them to provide more incentives to front-line sales people to promote their handsets over those of the multinationals. Much of the unit sales growth by latecomer Chinese firms during these initial few years was in these markets.

Finally, the latecomers marketing strategies included brand-building campaigns that were not focused on technical features or capabilities, for which the multinationals handsets were clearly superior. Instead, they used innovative campaigns featuring popular singers, athletes, and actors to build brand awareness among consumers.

Bird's entry

Ningbo Bird's entry illustrates all of these factors impacting the ability and strategic approach to entering an industry initially dominated by multinationals with greater technological, production, financial, and other resources and capabilities. At the end of 1998, before diversifying from pagers into handset production, Bird undertook an investigation of major handset manufacturers and the domestic consumer market. Bird's managers found that most of the handsets sold in China at that time did not have reception capabilities strong enough to receive signals in the western provinces of China, where base stations were few and the geography limited users' ability to use their phones. From its experience in providing pagers to the same market, Bird saw this type of territory as a niche market in which it could enter relatively easily because there were essentially no competitors, but which could provide a means of gaining initial market share.

Bird, however, had none of the necessary product design and manufacturing know-how, nor none of the critical components for producing handsets. Furthermore, none of the leading multinationals who already had their own manufacturing and sales operations in China were interested in Bird's overtures for a cooperative venture.

Fortunately for Bird, Sagem Electronics of France had not received a handset manufacturing license from the Chinese government and was interested in some kind of partnership that would enable it to participate in the Chinese market's growth. Sagem, at that time the sixth largest handset producer in the world, also supplied RF components to French Mirage fighter jets.

In January 1999, Bird and Sagem signed a cooperative production agreement. Under the terms of the agreement, Bird would import product designs, production equipment, and quality assurance systems from Sagem.

Bird would also import all components from Sagem, from the case, LCD, PCB, antenna, and battery. Essentially, Bird's primary responsibility was to assemble these components and sell the handsets in China.

To do this, however, Bird had to assimilate Sagem's knowledge related to handset assembly and quality assurance. Meanwhile, Sagem's French experts came to Bird to oversee the training and implementation of those processes. Bird also established a quality management committee consisting of sub-groups focused on different quality domains — design, suppliers, production, after-service — and continuous quality improvement. These subgroups coordinate with each other to implement total quality control, as well as achieve improvements in quality performance measures. This system not only enabled Bird to maintain acceptable handset quality, but also led to Bird become the first Chinese handset manufacturer to receive European CE production certification.

At this initial stage, Bird also made the strategic decision not to compete head-on with the multinationals who already had a strong presence in China. Instead, Bird focused its sales and marketing efforts on the western (i.e., non-coastal) regions of China, which had also been the primary market for its pagers. This region is less populated than much of the coastal regions, and multinationals had decided not to allocate their marketing and distribution efforts there. As a result, within a year Bird was able to quickly build up market share in these provinces; for example, over 40% in Xingjiang and over 30% in Gansu and Henan.

Bird's products were all Sagem designs, including the RC818, Mirage RC838, RC838L, MC858, and L968. Bird, however, did draw on its understanding of the customer market in this region to decide which products to offer at what timing. It also linked the product and consumer characteristics with its marketing message. For example, its advertisements featuring pop singer Coco Lee positioned Bird's products as the "fighter of handsets," emphasizing their greater signal reception capability that was particularly important to consumers in these relatively remote and rural areas.

Bird, however, faced a challenge in finding distributors for its products; established distributors showed no interest in Bird's products. Bird had no choice but to establish its own distribution channels, again drawing on its sales and distribution experience in the pager business. By the end of 2000, Bird had a distribution system in place that included 28 province-level sales branches, 30 province-level customer service centers, 400 medium- and small-size city customer service centers, 1,600 county-level consumer service centers and 50,000 retailers selling Bird's products.

Stage 2: Convergence

Although latecomers will typically enter markets ignored or underserved by incumbent multinationals, over time their targets and growth may make them converge increasingly with incumbents in terms of resources or markets. In the case of China's handset industry, latecomers were able to converge with incumbents in terms of market overlap due to differences in their distribution strategies and product development. As already described, the latecomers by necessity had by-passed the Level 1 and often Level 2 distributors, and often had no or only one distributor between them and retailers. This allowed them to keep their prices low and also give the retailer and front-line sales people a higher margin and incentive to promote their handsets over those of multinationals. As the latecomers entered the multinationals' primary markets, this shorter distribution structure became one competitive advantage for them over the multinationals. An increasing proportion of the latecomers' sales was coming from the markets that had been nearly completely controlled by the multinationals.

The latecomers also converged on some market segments with the multinationals as they more aggressively pursued alternative distribution channels, besides differences in geographic coverage and layers in their distribution system. The latecomers were the first to distribute handsets through the emerging retail chain stores, such as Guomei, Suning, and Dazhong. This increased volume as well as improved their cost structure and thereby their competitiveness vis-à-vis multinationals. They also undertook B2C sales to consumers via the Internet.

The product development approaches of the latecomers also led them to converge in terms of market overlap with the multinationals. The latecomers, originally completely focused on the Chinese market, developed handsets and designs expressly for the Chinese consumers. In contrast, multinationals usually launched "global models" and those that had sold well in their other markets. This caused the multinationals to lose some major market opportunities to the latecomers. For example, the clam shell design came to account for nearly 60% of the Chinese market, but the multinationals were very slow (if they did at all) to offer this type of phone because that design had not been as popular in their home markets. TCL specifically targeted market segments dominated by Motorola, Nokia and Siemens, offering clam shell models as well as a wide range of cosmetic design variations that included, for example, faux-diamond studded casings. While the internal technology and capabilities of TCL and other latercomers' handsets were quite standard, they were able to compete in some market segments with the multinationals based on promotion, cost, and design.

Finally, some of the firms were also increasing the technical sophistication of their handsets to further converge with the multinationals in terms of handset capabilities. Bird, for example, extended its original resources and capabilities from simple assembly to module-based manufacturing. It continued to import the module (containing all of the digital, base-band, and radio frequency hardware and software that are central to a handset) from Sagem, but began to source other components such as batteries, microphones, antenna, and so on itself. To be successful, Bird had to develop new capabilities in sourcing, supplier management, and quality assurance. One way it developed these additional capabilities was through alliances with both Chinese and foreign firms. For example, Bird began to work with component suppliers such as BENQ, Quanta, and LG to source and establish procedures for testing and selecting components. It collaborated with Bellware and Mobile Link in R&D to develop new products, and brought in several Korean industrial design houses to develop handset designs. It also collaborated with software and hardware firms to introduce new technical features into its phones, such as its collaboration with TTP to develop handsets with fast Chinese short messaging service (SMS) capabilities.

Stage 3: Response

As latecomers increasingly converge in terms of market and resources with incumbents, incumbents will likely respond. By 2003, when the multinationals saw a dramatic decrease in their market shares (even though unit sales were increasing), they began to see latecomer Chinese firms as significant threats. They then responded rapidly with a series of tactical and strategic moves. First, the multinationals kept tighter control over critical know-how and other strategic information. Domestic firms did not have as easy access as before. Second, the multinationals began to imitate the product design approaches of the successful domestic firms. For example, while the multinationals had laughed at TCL's faux-diamond studded phone casing designs, after 2003 both Samsung and Motorola were offering their own versions. Third, the multinationals adopted the latecomers' marketing strategies that included popular Chinese singers and actors in their advertising campaigns.

Finally, the multinationals began to restructure their distribution channels to be more like the local firms. They began selling some of their production directly to Level 2 regional and provincial distributors, by-passing their national distributors. Nokia led others in providing handsets directly to large specialty retailers, such as electronics and home appliance sellers Guomei and Suning. They also began to extend their geographic coverage beyond Tier 2 cities and introduced a wider variety of handsets that would better match the customers in those geographic markets.

Stage 4: Adaptation

By 2006, the success of the multinationals' responses to the local firms was becoming evident, as the changes in market share show (Fig. 3.2). They had simply adopted many of the relatively straightforward features of the successful domestic latecomers. As a result, while the related resources and capabilities continued to be important in participating in the market, they no longer provided the latecomers with any competitive advantage. Now, the advantage is going to the firms, now all multinationals, who are able to undertake chip-based manufacturing, which is much more knowledge-intensive than module-based manufacturing as it requires more proprietary technology and the integration of components, operating system, and applications. Manufacturing is also more complex, requiring the integrated assembly of the subsystems related to power control and amplification, signal transmission and reception, voice filters, and others.

As of 2008, local firms do not seem to have the willingness or ability to move into the fourth stage, strategic adaptation in response to significant changes in the industry, and sources of competitive advantage. As a group, rather than aggressively develop resources and capabilities related to chip-based manufacturing or seek out new sources of competitive advantage and "blue oceans," the domestic firms continue to focus on the same activities that allowed them to enter and initially challenge the incumbent multinationals; namely, distribution and product design. TCL, for example, was able to challenge Motorola and Nokia in their core markets, the richer Tier 1 and Tier 2 cities, because of their channel management strategies and handset casing design. Those resources and capabilities are still necessary for competing, but they have now become generic and are no longer a source of competitive advantage. TCL, like the others, have not made significant efforts to develop new sources of competitive advantage.

Bird initially seemed to be an exception among the domestic firms when in 2002 it made initial moves to enter chip-based manufacturing. In addition to internal R&D efforts, it established Ningbo Bird Sagem Electronics, a 50–50 joint venture (US$2.5 million) with Sagem, who had been its first partner when it entered the handset industry in 1999. The stated objectives of the joint venture were to develop the skills for chip-based manufacturing of handsets and related components that would help it expand Bird's market share in China and enter the European market.

Despite this initiative, Bird continued to focus most of its resources on distribution and product design, although these were no longer giving it significant competitive advantage.[4] As a result, Bird's core software and non-chip circuitry design capabilities remained far behind those of the multinationals. While continuing to claim a strong focus on handset R&D, in 2007 it invested some of its scarce financial resources into an attempt to diversify into the auto industry, and in March 2008 sold its share in the Ningbo Bird Sagem Electronics joint venture to Sagem.

Conclusion

The analysis of the entry, rise, and decline of China's handset manufacturers illustrates the series of contingencies that help determine the likelihood that latecomer firms will emerge as initial and then sustained competitors vis-à-vis incumbent multinationals. Chinese latecomers were able to successfully enter this industry because (1) barriers to entry were reduced; (2) they were able to acquire the resources and capabilities to operate in the industry, even if below the standard of incumbents and (3) they initially entered markets ignored or underserved by the incumbents. They then began to converge with the multinationals in terms of market overlap by exploiting their capabilities, in particular their distribution strategies and product development focus. The multinationals then came to see these latecomers as significant threats to their growth objectives and initiated a series of tactical and strategic responses that neutralized the latecomers' sources of competitive advantage up to that time. This signaled the beginning of a steady decline in the performance of the latecomers because they have not been willing or able to strategically adapt to this change on the basis of competition. Instead, they have continued to do "more of the same"; that is, focus on distribution and marketing activities and essentially cosmetic product development.

The process model we have used to frame our analysis of these firms' entry, evolution, and performance brings together two usually separate streams of research and analysis; namely, the questions of whether and

---

[4] Aside from slow response to the strategic adjustment of multinationals in China, another reason led to the fall of Bird is that over years some illegal producers have emerged in South China. Telephone interview with an anonymous interviewee in Bird, 2 August, 2008.

how to enter a market dominated by incumbents, on one hand, and competitive dynamics on the other. This has practical implications for latecomer firms, presenting the series of fundamental challenges they will face from entry to growth and more direct competition with incumbents, as well as factors that affect the likelihood that they will move through each stage.

Acknowledgments

The research for this chapter was financially supported by the National Natural Science Foundation of China (Project Reference: 70573060, 70773067 and 70890082) and Humanities and Social Science Foundation of Education Ministry of China (Project Reference: 05JA630030). The authors would like to express their thanks to Mr Dingzhuo, who assisted in collecting information on market information of China's mobile handsets. Mr Zhiping Zhao, Mr Yinen, and Mr Xuanwen Zhao helped with the interviews.

References

Amsden, AH (1989). *Asia Next Giant: South Korea and Late Industrialization.* New York: Oxford University Press.

Amsden, AH (2001). *The Rise of the Rest: Challenges to the West from Late-Industrializing Economies.* New York: Oxford University Press.

Chen, M-J (2001). Competitor analysis and interfirm rivalry: Toward a theoretical integration. *Academy of Management Review*, 21, 100–134.

Cho, D-S, D-J Kim, and D-K Rhee (1998). Latecomer strategies: Evidence from semiconductor industry in Japan and Korea. *Organization Science*, 19, 489–505.

Dawar, N and T Frost (1999). Competing with giants: Survival strategies for local companies in emerging markets. *Harvard Business Review*, 119–129.

Kalyanaram, G and GL Urban (1992). Dynamic effects of the order of entry on market share, trial penetration, and repeat purchases for frequently purchased consumer goods. *Marketing Science*, 11, 235–250.

Kim, CW and R Mauborgne (2005). *Blue Ocean Strategy.* Boston: Harvard Business School Press.

Kim, L and RR Nelson (2000). *Technology, Learning and Innovation: Experiences of Newly Industrializing Economies.* Cambridge: Cambridge University Press.

Kim, L (1997a). The dynamics of Samsung's technological learning in semiconductors. *California Management Review*, 39, 86–100.

Kim, L (1997b). *Imitation to Innovation: the Dynamics of Korea's Technological Learning.* Boston: Harvard Business School Press.

Lilien, GL and E Yoon (1990). The timing of competitive market entry: An exploratory study of new industrial products. *Management Science*, 36, 568–585.

Makadok R (1998). Can first-mover and early-mover advantages be sustained in an industry with low barriers to entry/imitation? *Strategic Management Journal*, 19, 683–696.

Mathews, JA (2002). Competitive advantages of the latecomer firm: A resource-based account of industrial catch-up strategies. *Asia Pacific Journal of Management*, 19, 467–488.

Schnaars, SP (1994). *Managing Imitation Strategy*. New York: Free Press.

Shamsie, J, C Phelps, and J Kuperman (2003). Better late than never: A study of late entrants in household electrical equipment. *Strategic Management Journal*, 25, 69–84.

Chapter 4

CURRENT BUSINESS PRACTICES OF TOP FORTUNE GLOBAL EMERGING MULTINATIONALS

CHUNHUI LIU AND KWOK-KEE WEI

Abstract

This chapter examines resource management trend of top fortune global multinational enterprises from emerging markets. Drawing on the resource-based and competence-based strategic management theories, it is argued that firms that best manage their resources and possess hard-to-copy resources are more likely to have a competitive advantage. Data of top 30 Fortune Global multinational enterprises from emerging markets show a trend toward spending more on research and development, registering more new patents, and better usage of assets from 2002 to 2007. Implication for managers is that they can achieve sustainable competitive advantage through efficient and effective management, of assets, encouragement, and investment in research and development.

Introduction

Emerging markets are the markets in a transitional phase between developing and developed status that have a rapid pace of economic development and boast government policies favoring economic liberalization and a free-market system (Arnold and Quelch, 1998). Good examples are Brazil, Russia, China, and India also known as BRIC countries. These countries are experiencing exponential growth and have a population hungry for new products and services. Emerging markets comprise 80% of the world's population and about 75% of their trade growth in the foreseeable future according to the U.S. Department of Commerce (Alon and McIntyre, 2004). The potential economic growth of emerging markets calls for better understanding of the dynamics of these markets.

Due to great potential of return, the investment into emerging markets has been on the rise. Morgan Stanley estimates that net portfolio inflows into emerging markets is $50.2 billion (U.S.) in 2007, against $15.2 billion in the same period a year ago and $12.5 billion in 2005 (Saft, 2007). Take China as an example, the foreign direct investments from Japan alone have increased from $2,317 million to $6,169 million at 166% during the period from 1996 to 2006 according to the ASEAN–Japan Statistical Pocketbook 2007. In addition, the emerging markets are also believed by many to be the markets of the future (Waggoner, 2007). The recent trend toward investments in emerging markets by multinational enterprises forces local managers to compete with the foreign firms or faces the prospect of extinction (Singh, 2008). Attaining sustained competitive advantage becomes the key for many companies' survival. Despite the volatile character of the future competitive position of organizations, a controlled development of competitive advantage is not impossible. Market orientation (Kohli and Jaworski, 1990), superior quality products and services (Bitner, 1992), ethical corporate values (Singh, 2008, p. 71), and economies of scale (Agarwal and Ramaswani, 1992) among others have been suggested as possible ways of achieving competitive advantages. We propose an alternative to such strategies; that is, achieving sustainable competitive advantage through better resource management based on competence-based/resource-based strategic management theories.

Competence-based or resource-based management explains how organizations can develop competitive advantage in a systematic and structural way. The difference of the mixed available resources between enterprises, the speed with which resources are used and developed, and the costs which are involved is determinative for the realization of the organizations competitive advantage. (Vernhout, 2007).

This study is designed to identify resource management trend of top Fortune Global multinational enterprises from emerging markets for at least three reasons. First, resource management reveals why some firms outperform others according to resource-based view theory, whose prominence is reflected by its dominance in the academic journals and its inclusion in leading strategic texts (Sheehan and Foss, 2007). Second, there are many successful companies in emerging markets like Brazil, Russia, India and China that have become world-spanning multinational enterprises in face of severe competition from well-established multinational enterprises from developed countries. Examples of such companies are everywhere. From

Brazil, Embraer has become a big supplier of regional jets in the airline industry. Russian companies like Gazprom are using Russia's natural resources to leap into the United States and other countries. India is producing powerhouses in technology services like Wipro. In China, Haier is emerging in appliances while Huawei Technologies is competing against Cisco Systems to sell telecommunications equipment around the world. Finally, identifying best practices in resource management of such successful multinational enterprises from emerging markets provides effective benchmarking for other firms in emerging markets as it helps crack through resistance to change by demonstrating other methods of solving problems than the one currently employed, and demonstrating that they work, because they are being used by others.

The purpose of this chapter is to contribute to the literature by revealing recent trends in resource management among top Fortune Global multinational enterprises from emerging markets. Understanding sources of sustained competitive advantage for firms has become a major area of research in the field of strategic management (Barney, 1991). Enterprise strategy in emerging economies is clearly an area of considerable interest to both strategy scholars (Hoskisson *et al.*, 2000) and managers of multinational enterprises in emerging markets.

This chapter first reviews extant research on competence-based management and resource-based management, provides the theoretical foundation for the study, and develops hypotheses. Then, the research findings and their implications for researchers and managers will be presented.

Extant Research

Since the early days of strategic management, researchers and managers have tried to find general rules for developing successful business strategies. Previous studies have explored research questions; for example, why are some competitors more profitable than others or what are successful strategies to outperform a competitor (Grunert and Hildebrandt, 2004). Understanding industry structures was perhaps the primary concern of strategic management theory in the 1970s. Characterizing firms as unique bundles of resources has become an important perspective since the 1980s. Conceptualizing and analyzing the competences of organizations have become a key focus of management thinking since the 1990s (Sanchez, 2004).

Resource-based and competence-based approaches have achieved an increasing popularity in understanding the nature and causes of competitiveness and competitive advantages. In this context, organizations are seen as distinct bundles of resources and competences which have evolved over time (Penrose, 1959). A firm's resources at a given time could be defined as those (tangible and intangible) assets which are tied semi-permanently to the firm (Wernerfelt, 1984). Such resources enable the firm to conceive of and implement strategies that improve its efficiency and effectiveness (Daft, 1983). Competence is the ability to sustain the coordinated usage of assets in ways that help a firm to achieve its goals (Sanchez, 2004). Some competences arise from the static efficiency of a firm — its ability to use current assets in cost-effective ways. Other competences come from a firm's dynamic efficiency — its ability to incur low costs when changing the assets it uses or when changing the uses to which its assets are applied. Moreover, some competences seem to depend on an organization's specific combinations of static and dynamic efficiencies (Black and Boal, 1997).

The central questions addressed by the resource-based view and competence-based view concern why firms differ and how they achieve and sustain competitive advantage. Resource-based theories of strategy assert that firms gain and sustain competitive advantages by deploying valuable resources and capabilities that are inelastic in supply. It argues that valuable and unique resources of the firm, meeting specific criteria like imperfect imitability/substitutability and imperfect mobility, were proposed as the real causal factors of business success and sustained competitive advantage (Peteraf, 1993). Imitability refers to the extent to which rivals can imitate a competence or resource. This stream of research gained momentum in the late 1980s/early 1990s when researchers elaborated on resource-related ideas expressed earlier by Wernerfelt (1984). Penrose (1959) argued that heterogeneous capabilities give each firm its unique character and are the essence of competitive advantage. Wernerfelt (1984) suggested that evaluating firms in terms of their resources could lead to insights different from the traditional industrial/organization (I/O) perspective (Porter, 1980). Barney (1986) suggested that strategic resource factors differ in their tradability and that these factors can be specifically identified and their monetary value determined via a strategic factor market. Barney (1991) indicated that firm resources and capabilities could be differentiated on the basis of value, rareness, inimitability, and substitutability.

Mahoney and Pandain (1992) reminded scholars that a "firm may achieve rents not because it has better resources, but rather the firm's distinctive competence involves making better use of its resources." They continued by suggesting that firms that make the best use of their resources are those that allocate them in such a way that their productivity and/or financial yield are maximized. To do so, they defined a dynamic capability as "the firm's ability to integrate, build, and reconfigure internal and external competences to address rapidly changing environments" (Teece *et al.*, 1997, p. 516). Eisenhardt and Martin (2000) and others have averred that the possession of a valuable, rare, inimitable, non-substitutable resource is a necessary but insufficient condition for explaining a firm's competitive position. These scholars suggest that a resource can only contribute to this end when it is paired with an appropriate dynamic capability or organizing context.

Resources are based in a context and depending on characteristics of that context, a focus on resources could create strategic inflexibility and core rigidities for a firm that would lead to negative returns (Leonard-Barton, 1992). Therefore, resources should be dynamic in response to changes. Given the amount of uncertainty that may be present in a firm's operating environment, it is not surprising that organizational agility has been found to be a key factor in promoting financial and competitive success (Webb and Pettigrew, 1999). The primary aim of dynamic approach of the competence-based management is realizing competitive advantage by constantly improving the existing resources and obtaining new resources. Oliver (1997) analyzed the issue of a firm's sustainable advantage in terms of resource-based and institutional factors and suggested that firms are able to create or develop institutional capital to enhance optimal use of resources. Firms therefore have to manage the social context of their resources and capabilities to generate rents. This idea is also underscored by the work of Miller and Shamsie (1996), who found that the Hollywood film industry provided a context that changed over time and created different strategic assets as changes were made.

Moreover, management thinking has been especially inspired by the work of Prahalad and Hamel (1990). In their paper, the authors called for abandoning the concept of strategic business units as the central planning unit of corporate strategy in favor of company-wide core competencies potentially applicable in diverse industries and for multiple products. For example, developing and sustaining technological competencies are important to continuous innovation in firms. Many recent perspectives of firm behavior suggest that firm competencies are stocks of knowledge (Lev and Sougiannis, 1999) accumulated over time, difficult for competitors to replicate, and are the source of competitive advantage (Reed and DeFillippi, 1990). The competence perspective has brought both significant theoretical extensions and important practical benefits to contemporary management thinking (Sanchez, 2004).

The resource-based view and competence-based view significantly improved the understanding of the origins of company success as evidenced by much supportive empirical evidence. Newbert (2007) indicated that of the 161 tests in which the relationship between a capability and either competitive advantage or performance is analyzed, empirical support is found for 114 (71%) and of the 24 tests in which the relationship between a core competence and performance is analyzed, empirical support is found for 16 (67%). Zahra and Nielsen (2002) find support for 16 (80%) of 20 tests of the relationship between four firm capabilities (internal and external human capabilities and internal and external technological capabilities) and four measures of competitive advantage. De Carolis (2003) finds support for eight (67%) of 12 tests of the relationship between three core competencies (technological, marketing, and regulatory) and four measures of financial performance. Schroeder *et al.* (2002) tested the relationship between learning capabilities and competitive advantage as well as the relationship between competitive advantage and performance and found support for all (100%) three tests conducted. Most of empirical work that develops measures of a firm's resources and capabilities and the extent to which they meet the criteria established in the theoretical literature for generating sustained competitive advantages and then correlates these measures with some measures of firm performance has been consistent with resource-based theory (Barney and Arikan, 2001).

Though the resource-based view of the firm is one of the most widely accepted theoretical perspectives in the strategic management field (Rouse and Daellenbach, 1999) and a dominant theory upon which arguments in academic journals and textbooks alike have been grounded, little research using a resource-based view framework has examined strategy differences in the social context of emerging economies (Hoskisson *et al.*, 2000). Besides, empirical work on dynamic capabilities is still in its infancy (Newbert, 2007). This study contributes to literature relating to resource management in emerging markets.

Research Hypotheses

Resources are those assets that are semi-permanently linked to the firm and are inputs into a firm's production process (Grunert and Hildebrandt, 2004). Resources of a firm include tangible assets such as land and intangible assets such as knowledge (tacit and embedded) (Wernerfelt, 1984). Wernerfelt (1984, p. 171) argued that "resources and products are two sides of the same coin." While a firm's performance is driven directly by its products, it is indirectly driven by the resources that go into their production. Because, the firm is "a collection of productive resources" (Penrose, 1959), and this is justified to consider resources as the "basic units of analysis" (Grant, 1991) of the firm.

Competences arise from a firm's ability to use current assets in cost-effective ways or its ability to incur low costs when changing the assets it uses or when changing the uses to which its assets are applied (Black and Boal, 1997). Dynamic capabilities, the capacity of the organization to renew competences to match the requirements of the changing environment, are critical for sustainable competitive advantages (Teece *et al.*, 1997). Examining dynamic capabilities, such as the ability to learn continuously (Lei *et al.*, 1996), and the knowledge-based view of the firm (Conner and Prahalad, 1996) are critical in the study of emerging markets. Empirical analysis based on longitudinal data and dynamic research is appropriate for examining resource-based theory (Barney, 2001). Therefore, this study takes a dynamic view of companies' efficiency in using assets or resources by comparing their resource management of 2002 against their resource management of 2007.

Both resource-based view and competence-based view argue that sustainable competitive advantages come from efficient usage of companies' assets. As such, top Fortune Global multinational enterprises' success depends on improved efficiency in using their assets. Multinational enterprises often focus on the revenue-generating potential associated with big emerging economies (Hoskisson *et al.*, 2000). Therefore, this study uses two popular financial ratios to measure the enterprises' usage of assets in generating revenue. Asset turnover ratio (revenues/total assets) helps measure the change in efficiency of a company's use of its assets in generating sales revenue or sales income. Return on assets (net income/total assets) helps measure how profitable a company's assets are in generating revenue. Financial measures remain the most popular and widely accepted approach in strategy-performance studies (Geringe *et al.*, 1989). Hence, we propose the following hypotheses:

H1: Asset turnover ratio increased in top Fortune Global multinational enterprises from emerging markets from 2002 to 2007.

H2: Return on assets ratio increased in top Fortune Global multinational enterprises from emerging markets from 2002 to 2007.

Resources can be separated into those that are property-based and those that are knowledge-based (Miller and Shamsie, 1996). Property-based resources normally refer to tangible input resources, whereas knowledge-based resources are the intangible ways in which firms combine and transform these tangible input resources (Galunic and Rodan, 1998). Knowledge-based resources may be particularly important for providing sustainable competitive advantage, because they are inherently difficult to imitate, thus facilitating sustainable differentiation (McEvily and Chakravarthy, 2002). They play an essential role in the firm's ability to be entrepreneurial and improve performance (McGrath *et al.*, 1996). As a result, the firm possessing intangible resources can gain competitive advantage (Cho and Pucik, 2005). Many studies emphasize that a firm should possess certain intangible resources that competitors cannot copy or buy easily (Newbert, 2007). Like most resources that create competitive advantage, resources for competitive advantage in emerging economies are, on the whole, intangible (Hoskinsson *et al.*, 2000). We propose to test the third hypothesis:

H3: Top Fortune Global multinational enterprises from emerging markets have higher ratio of intangible assets to total assets from 2002 to 2007.

A major intangible resource that competitors cannot copy or buy easily is patent. Earlier works have measured knowledge-based resources and have operationalized the stock of knowledge with patent data (De Carolis and Deeds, 1999). Patents are one manifestation of firm knowledge. The learning that occurs to produce the innovation contained in the patent — whether that learning is acquired through combining existing internal knowledge or combining existing internal knowledge with new internal knowledge — is represented on that patent. The ownership of enforceable property rights protects valuable resources from competitive imitation (Lippman and Rumelt, 1982). Such protection help ensure competitive advantage. According to resource-based view and competence-based view, top Fortune Global multinational enterprises from emerging markets' success attribute to intangible knowledge-based resources as manifested in new patents registered each year. Thus, we advance the fourth hypothesis as follows:

H4: Top Fortune Global multinational enterprises from emerging markets have more new patents registered each year from 2002 to 2007.

Internal developed patents come from research and development. Isobe *et al.* (2000) examine whether early movers and technology leaders attain superior performance in emerging economies and find that technology leaders and first movers in Sino-Japanese joint ventures in China do attain superior performance. The resource-based view distinguishes between resources that can be acquired in factor markets and those developed inside the firm. To confer competitive advantage, resources must not be possessed by all competing firms, they must be difficult to imitate or duplicate through other means, and contribute positively to performance (Barney, 1991, p. 107). Therefore, internal research and development are critical for generating inimitable resources. In addition, competence has been operationalized by using financial measures of intensity such as the ratio of research and development to revenue (De Carolis, 2003). Research and development expenses have been used as a proxy for innovation or competence (Hill and Snell, 1988) because more funds committed to research and development may open more chances a firm has to be innovative. Research and development competence reflects a firm's ability to add new technological competences (Danneels, 2002). So, our final hypothesis is

H5: Top Fortune Global multinational enterprises from emerging markets invest more into research and development as reflected in increased ratio of research and development to revenues from 2002 to 2007.

Research Methodology

The variables measured were asset turnover ratio (operating revenues/total assets), percentage of intangible assets in total assets (intangible assets/total assets), number of patents registered in a year, and research and development expense/revenue in a year. Data for the variables were collected from annual reports of individual multinational enterprises for fiscal year 2002 and for fiscal year 2007. Most annual reports were readily downloadable from the enterprises' Web sites. However, not all enterprises provide an online version of annual reports as old as 2002. When annual reports were not available, data were collected from the World'vest Base Inc.'s database. Thirty multinational enterprises from the emerging markets were studied. As Singh (2008) indicated, emerging markets of particular interest to international investors and business managers are those tracked by the Morgan Stanley Capital International (MSCI) and the International Finance Corporation (IFC). Therefore, emerging markets were identified based on the Morgan Stanley Emerging Markets Index as of June 2006. The following markets were identified as emerging markets: Argentina, Brazil, Chile, China, Colombia, Czech Republic, Egypt, Hungary, India, Indonesia, Israel, Jordan, Malaysia, Mexico, Morocco, Pakistan, Peru, the Philippines, Poland, Russia, South Africa, South Korea, Taiwan, Thailand, and Turkey.

Benchmarking works the best only when organizations evaluate various aspects of their processes in relation to the best practices from top performers. Therefore, the sample was chosen enterprises from emerging markets in 2007 Fortune Global 500 list from top down (CNN, 2007). The sample included only listed companies but excluded non-listed or state-owned companies as the annual reports and financial information on listed companies were publicly available. The studied sample enterprises are listed in Table 4.1.

The sample consisted of 17% mining and construction, 27% manufacturing, 20% transportation, communication, and utilities, 7% wholesale and retail trade, and 30% finance, insurance, and real estate enterprises. Enterprises with revenue under $50 m, between $50 m and $100 m, and over $100 m were 73%, 23%, and 1% of the sample, respectively. Enterprises with employees under 5,000, between 5,001 and 50,000, and over 50,000 represented 7%,

Table 4.1.   Sample enterprises studied.

No.	Company name	Rank among 500	Emerging economies
1	Sinopec	17	China
2	Samsung Electronics	46	South Korea
3	Gazprom	52	Russia
4	Petrobras	65	Brazil
5	LG	73	South Korea
6	Hyundai Motor	76	South Korea
7	SK	98	South Korea
8	Lukoil	110	Russia
9	Indian Oil	135	India
10	Hon Hai Precision Industry	154	Taiwan
11	Industrial & Commercial Bank of China	170	China
12	China Mobile Communications	180	China
13	Koç Holding	190	Turkey
14	China Life Insurance	192	China
15	PTT	207	Thailand
16	Bank of China	215	China
17	Banco Bradesco	224	Brazil
18	Korea Electric Power	228	South Korea
19	China Construction Bank	230	China
20	POSCO	244	South Korea
21	Reliance Industries	269	India
22	China Telecommunications	275	China
23	Itaúsa-Investimentos Itaú	288	Brazil
24	Hutchison Whampoa	290	China
25	Banco do Brasil	291	Brazil
26	Sinochem	299	China
27	Sabic	301	Saudi Arabia
28	Rosneft Oil	323	Russia
29	Bharat Petroleum	325	India
30	América Móvil	330	Mexico

33%, and 60% of the sample, respectively. The sample size was determined with considerations of time, cost, and the objectives of this study. The sample size of 30 enterprises out of about 60 listed enterprises from emerging markets in 2007 Fortune Global 500 was deemed to have a good representation of the whole population.

Analysis and Results

Before data were compared between year 2002 and year 2007, skewness and kurtosis were tested to measure the asymmetry and peakedness of the probability distribution of the variables. Table 4.2 presents the results. Neither skewness nor kurtosis of the variables was close to zero. Therefore, none of the variables were normally distributed.

Due to non-normal distribution of the data, the two-tailed, nonparametric, Wilcoxon sign-rank test was used to compare data between 2002 and 2007. Table 4.3 reports the results of the comparisons.

Table 4.2. Probability distributions of variables.

Variables	Mean	Skewness	Kurtosis
2002 asset turnover	0.76	1.32	1.02
2007 asset turnover	0.99	2.30	5.81
2002 return on assets	0.05	1.12	1.49
2007 return on assets	0.11	4.62	23.49
2002 intangible assets/total assets	0.03	3.03	9.96
2007 intangible assets/total assets	0.03	3.05	10.27
2002 patents	46	2.70	7.45
2007 patents	489	2.54	6.66
2002 research and development/revenues	0.01	1.95	3.76
2007 research and development/revenues	0.05	2.28	5.25

Table 4.3. Variable means for 2002 and 2007.

Variables	Mean for 2002	Mean for 2007	Z-Stat
Asset turnover	0.76	0.99	−2.602**
Return on assets	0.05	0.11	−3.013**
Intangible assets/total assets	0.03	0.03	−1.816
New patents registered	46	489	−2.668**
Research and development/revenue	0.01	0.05	−2.201*

*denotes significant difference at $p < 0.05$; ** denote significant difference at $p < 0.01$.

Significant differences were found between 2002 and 2007 for both asset turnover ratio and return on assets ratio. Both ratios reflected higher efficiency and effectiveness in using assets to generate revenue in 2007, suggesting that given $1 invested in assets, more revenue ($0.99 in 2007 vs. $0.76 in 2002) and higher net income ($0.11 in 2007 vs. $0.05 in 2002) on average were generated in 2007 than in 2002. Hence, we accept the hypotheses H1 and H2. Likewise, significant differences were also found for both new patents registered and research and development/revenue variables. 2007 data had a significantly higher mean than that of 2002 indicating that enterprises invested more in research and development ($0.05 in 2007 vs. $0.01 in 2002) and fostered more new patents in 2007 (489 in 2007 vs. 46 in 2002) on average. Therefore, we also accept the hypotheses H4 and H5. However, no significant difference was found between 2002 and 2007 for intangible assets/total assets variable, indicating that intangible assets were relatively constant in regard to its proportion out of total assets (around 3%) from 2002 to 2007. Hence, we reject the hypothesis H3.

Discussion

The purpose of this study was to contribute to the literature by revealing recent trends in resource management among top Fortune Global multinational enterprises from emerging markets. Our findings indicate that these top enterprises had significantly increased their efficiency in resource management by generating higher revenue and net income with their assets, invested more into research and development, and had more patents registered and that there was no significant difference in their possession of intangible assets as a proportion of total assets. Results of this chapter are relevant to business managers as explained in the following section.

Our finding that there was significant increase in resource management efficiency and effectiveness in top Fortune Global 500 enterprises from emerging markets coincides with the competence-based theory. Efficient and effective usage of assets contributes to competences that help companies achieve competitiveness. The finding that significantly more patents were registered in 2007 than in 2002 among these top enterprises matches up with the resource-based management theory. Knowledge-based assets or resources such as patents provide heterogeneous capabilities that give each firm its unique character and are the essence of competitive advantage. Another important finding is that the top enterprises increased their investment in research and development. This finding further confirms the importance of creating valuable, rare, inimitable resources to achieve superior performance as indicated by the resource-based view. Market available resources can be easily bought and copied by other companies, thus contributing little to getting sustainable competitive advantage.

Despite the increase in research and development and new patents registered, no significant change in intangible assets' proportion of total assets was found. There are two possible reasons. On the one hand, dynamic capabilities manifest the organizational capacity to purposefully create or modify the firm's resource base (Moliterno and Wiersema, 2007). Modification of resource base involves not only generation of new resources, but also elimination of old resources. The capacity of the organization to renew competences to match the requirements of the changing environment is critical for sustainable competitive advantages (Teece *et al.*, 1997, p. 516). Old intangible assets may be replaced by new ones resulting in little in the total value. On the other hand, the investment into research and development generally takes a long time to generate productive assets. Therefore, it might take longer than six years to fully identify its impact on intangible assets as whole. This could be evidenced by the fact that an increase in intangible assets/total assets was identified at $p < 0.10$ though it was not significant at $p < 0.05$.

Implication for Managers

The major implication for managers is that effective and efficient usage of assets should be a part of corporate culture despite possible low-cost advantage in natural resources or labor in some emerging markets (Aulakh *et al.*, 2000). This strategic goal is especially important for emerging markets as resources such as financial resources that are valuable in a market context are generally scarce (Filatotchev *et al.*, 1996). In addition, knowledge-based assets should not be ignored just because they are often hard to measure and take a long time to materialize. Patents, for example, embody stocks of accumulated knowledge — not only just from one or two years, but also from many years (De Carolis and Deeds, 1999). Managers should encourage and invest in improving learning and innovating capabilities within the firm. Learning helps produce innovation contained in the patent — whether that learning is acquired through combining existing internal knowledge or combining existing internal knowledge with new internal knowledge. Investing in productive research and development, recruiting, and retaining intelligent people are critical for generating and renewing heterogeneous resources.

Limitations and Direction for Future Study

Applicability of this study's research findings is limited in at least three aspects. First, the small sample size limits the generalizability of the findings. Future research may study the complete population of the emerging market enterprises among Fortune Global 500. Second, this study is limited in that only emerging market enterprises were analyzed. Future study may include Fortune Global 500 enterprises from developed economies to identify similarity and differences between the developed markets and the emerging markets. Finally, this study is also limited in that only patent was studied as representative of knowledge-based resource management. This is far from the whole picture of intangible assets, which is critical for sustainable competitive advantage. Future study may also research important resources such as relationships with governments. In emerging economies, advantages are difficult to establish without good relationships with home governments. Early relationships give tangible benefits, such as access to licenses, whose number is often limited by a government. Diversified business groups have evolved in many emerging economies. Such groups often obtain licensing advantages because of their government relationships (Hoskisson *et al.*, 2000, p. 256). In addition, marketing and human resource management capabilities and resources could also be studied as these two functions are as important as production and general management of resources.

Conclusion

The purpose of this study is to identify trends in resource management among top emerging market multinational enterprises. The findings comply with resource-based and competence-based theory of strategic management. Top enterprises studied showed significant increase in asset management efficiency and effectiveness, research and development investment, and new patents registered from year 2002 to 2007. In general, by better managing company resources, managers can develop sustainable competitiveness.

References

Agarwal, S and SN Ramaswami (1992). Choice of foreign entry mode: Impact of ownership, location and internationalization factors. *Journal of International Business Studies*, 23, 1–27.

Alon, I and JR McIntyre (2004). *Business Education in Emerging Market Economies Perspectives and Best Practices*. New York: Kluwer Academic Publishers.

Arnold, DJ and JA Quelch (1998). New strategies in emerging economies. *Sloan Management Review*, 40, 7–20.

Aulakh, PS, M Kotabe, and H Teegen (2000). Export strategies and performance of firms from emerging economies: Evidence from Brazil, Chile, Mexico. *Academy of Management Journal*, 43, 342–361.

Barney, JB (1986). Strategic factor markets: Expectations, luck and business strategy. *Management Science*, 31, 1231–1241.

Barney, JB (1991). Firm resources and sustained competitive advantage. *Journal of Management*, 17, 99–120.

Barney, JB (2001). Is the resource-based 'view' a useful perspective for strategic management research? Yes. *Academy of Management Review*, 26, 41–56.

Barney, JB and AM Arikan (2001). The resource-based view: Origins and implications. In *Handbook of Strategic Management*, Hitt, MA, RE Freeman and JS. Harrison (eds.), pp. 124–188. Oxford, UK: Blackwell.

Bitner, MJ (1992). Servicescapes: The impact of physical surrounding on customers and employees. *Journal of Marketing*, 56, 57–71.

Black, JA and KB Boal (1997). Assessing the organizational capacity to change. In *Competence-Based Strategic Management*, Heene, A and R Sanchez (eds.), pp. 151–168. Chichester: Wiley.

CNN (2007). http://money.cnn.com/magazines/fortune/global500/2007/full_list/index.html.

Conner, KR and CK Prahalad (1996). A resource-based theory of the firm: Knowledge versus opportunism. *Organization Science*, 7, 477–501.

Cho, H-J and V Pucik (2005). Relationship between innovativeness, quality, growth, profitability, and market value. *Strategic Management Journal*, 26, 555–575.

Daft, RL (1983). *Organization Theory and Design*. New York: West.

Danneels, E (2002). The dynamics of product innovation and firm competences. *Strategic Management Journal*, 23, 1095–1121.

De Carolis, DM (2003). Competencies and imitability in the pharmaceutical industry: An analysis of their relationship with firm performance. *Journal of Management*, 29, 27–50.

De Carolis, DM and DL Deeds (1999). The impact of stocks and flows of organizational knowledge on firm performance: An empirical investigation of the biotechnology industry. *Strategic Management Journal*, 20, 953–968.

Eisenhardt, KM and JA Martin (2000). Dynamic capabilities: What are they? *Strategic Management Journal*, 21, 1105–1121.

Filatotchev, I, RE Hoskisson, T Buck, and M Wright (1996). Corporate restructurings in Russian privatizations: Implications for US investors. *California Management Review*, 38, 87–105.

Galunic, DC and S Rodan (1998). Resource combinations in the firm: Knowledge structures and the potential for schumpeterian innovation. *Strategic Management Journal*, 19, 1193–1201.

Geringer, MJ, PW Beamish, and RC Dacosta (1989). Diversification strategy and internationalization: Implications for MNE performance. *Strategic Management Journal*, 10, 109–119.

Grant, RM (1991). The resource-based theory of competitive advantage: Implications for strategy formulation. *California Management Review*, 33, 114–135.

Grunert, KG and L Hildebrandt (2004). Success factors, competitive advantage and competence development. *Journal of Business Research*, 57, 459–461.

Hill, CWL and SA Snell (1988). External control, corporate strategy and firm performance in research intensive industries. *Strategic Management Journal*, 9, 577–590.

Hoskisson, RE, L Eden, CM Lau, and M Wright (2000). Strategy in emerging economies. *The Academy Of Management Journal*, 43, 249–267.

Isobe, T, S Makino, and DB Montgomery (2000). Resource commitment, entry timing, and market performance of foreign direct investments in emerging economies: The case of Japanese international joint ventures in China. *Academy of Management Journal*, 43, 468–484.

Kohli, AK and BJ Jaworski (1990). Market orientation: The construct, research propositions, and managerial implications. *Journal of Marketing*, 54, 1–8.

Lei, D, MA Hitt, and R Bettis (1996). Dynamic core competences through metalearning and strategic context. *Journal of Management*, 22, 549–569.

Leonard-Barton, D (1992). Core capabilities and core rigidities: A paradox in managing new product development. *Strategic Management Journal*, 13, 111–125.

Lev, B and T Sougiannis (1999). Penetrating the book-to-market black box: The R&D effect. *Journal of Business Finance & Accounting*, 26, 419–449.

Lippman, SA and RP Rumelt (1982). Uncertain imitability: An analysis of interfirm differences in efficiency under competition. *Bell Journal of Economics*, 13, 418–438.

Mahoney, J and R Pandain, Jr (1992). The resource-based view within the conversation of strategic management. *Strategic Management Journal*, 13, 363–380.

McEvily, SK and B Chakravarthy (2002). The persistence of knowledge-based advantage: An empirical test for product performance and technological knowledge. *Strategic Management Journal*, 23, 285–305.

McGrath, RG, M-H Tsai, S Venkataraman and IC MacMillan (1996). Innovation, competitive advantage, and rent. *Management Science*, 42, 389–403.

Miller, D and J Shamsie (1996). The resource-based view of the firm in two environments: The Hollywood film studios from 1936 to 1965. *Academy of Management Journal*, 39, 519–543.

Moliterno, TP and MF Wiersema (2007). Firm performance, rent appropriation, and the strategic resource divestment capability. *Strategic Management Journal*, 28, 1065–1087.

Newbert, SL (2007). Empirical research on the resource based view of the firm: An assessment and suggestions for future research. *Strategic Management Journal*, 28, 121–146.

Oliver, C (1997). Sustainable competitive advantage: Combining institutional and resource-based views. *Strategic Management Journal*, 18, 697–713.

Penrose, ET (1959). *The Theory of the Growth of the Firm*. Oxford: Basil Blackwell.

Peteraf, MA (1993). The cornerstones of competitive advantage: A resource-based view. *Strategic Management Journal*, 14, 179–191.

Porter, ME (1980). *Competitive Strategy*. New York: Free Press.

Prahalad, CK and G Hamel (1990). The core competence of the corporation. *Harvard Business Review*, 68, 79–91.

Reed, R and RJ DeFillippi (1990). Causal ambiguity, barriers to imitation and sustainable competitive advantage. *Academy of Management Review*, 15, 88–112.

Rouse, MJ and US Daellenbach (1999). Rethinking re-search methods for the resource-based perspective: Isolating sources of sustainable competitive advantage. *Strategic Management Journal*, 20, 487–494.

Saft, J (2007). Standing on their own feet. *Toronto Star*, 29 November 2007, Y.2.

Sanchez, R (2004). Understanding competence-based management: Identifying and managing five modes of competence. *Journal of Business Research*, 57, 518–532.

Schroeder, RG, KA Bates, and MA Junttila (2002). A resource-based view of manufacturing strategy and the relationship to manufacturing performance. *Strategic Management Journal*, 23, 105–117.

Sheehan, NT and NJ Foss (2007). Enhancing the prescriptiveness of the resource-based view through porterian activity analysis. *Management Decision*, 45, 450–461.

Singh, S (2008). *Business Practices in Emerging and Re-emerging Markets*. New York: Palgrave Macmillan.

Teece, DJ, G Pisano, and A Shuen (1997). Dynamic capabilities and strategic management. *Strategic Management Journal*, 18, 509–533.

Vernhout, A (2007). Management challenges in the competence-based organization. Working Paper. Available Online November 2007: http://www.competentiedenken.nl/PDF/Management%20challenges%20in%20the%20competence-based%20organization.pdf.

Waggoner, J (2007). Emerging markets have rocked, so now it's time to roll. *USA Today*, 02 November 2007, 03b.

Webb, D and A Pettigrew (1999). The temporal development of strategy: Patterns in the UK insurance industry. *Organization Science*, 10, 601–621.

Wernerfelt, B (1984). A resource-based view of the firm. *Strategic Management Journal*, 5, 171–180.

Zahra, SA and AP Nielsen (2002). Sources of capabilities, integration and technology commercialization. *Strategic Management Journal*, 23, 377–398.

Chapter 5

BETWEEN INFORMATION SYSTEM INTEGRATION AND PERFORMANCE, WHAT ARE THE MISSING LINKS?

RUBY P. LEE AND QIMEI CHEN

Abstract

Although a large body of research has supported that information technology (IT) is critical to firm success, empirical findings on how it affects firm performance remain inconclusive. The authors argue that knowledge codification, a deliberate learning mechanism, must be developed for a firm to take advantage of its IT resources. Further to what extent the firm can translate knowledge and information into performance outcomes depends on its ability to respond to the market. Drawing on the dynamic capabilities perspective and its extensions, the authors develop a conceptual model to examine the missing links, knowledge codification, and market responsiveness, between information system integration and firm performance. Hypotheses are tested on survey data collected from 140 foreign subsidiaries in China. Results indicate that the performance impact of information system integration must work through knowledge codification and market responsiveness.

Introduction

An MNC is characterized by its operations in multiple countries where its headquarters and subsidiaries are located in different geographic boundaries. Because differences in political, economic, and sociocultural factors across various boundaries exist, it becomes particularly challenging and relevant for MNCs when considering knowledge transfer between business units. "In the global arena, the complexities increase in scope as multinational firms grapple with cross-border knowledge transfers and the challenge of renewing organizational skills in various diverse settings" (Inkpen, 1998, p. 69). This underlies the importance of an MNC to use information technology (IT) to enhance communications, coordination, and knowledge sharing between its headquarters and subsidiaries, among other important avenues.

Moreover, as an MNC continues to globalize, institutionalizing information technology that enables its headquarters and subsidiaries to have equal access to real-time knowledge and information within its network boundary is crucial; its outcome, however, remains inconclusive (Brynjolfsson and Hitt, 1996). Notably, the continued growth of IT creates unprecedented challenges for MNCs, making the consequences of learning and knowledge transfer between business units even more erratic. As recent research (Rai *et al.*, 2006) has discovered, the availability of IT does not promise the success of an MNC in multi country markets. Thus, to understand the implications of IT, it is imperative to understand any underlying mechanisms that may affect the efficacy of IT (Johnston and Paladino, 2007).

Against this backdrop, the objective of our study is to enhance our understanding of how IT, specifically, information system integration influences firm performance by examining two mechanisms, knowledge codification and market responsiveness. Recent research in international business has overlooked an important issue as to what mechanism may facilitate an MNC's headquarters and subsidiaries to have equal access to diverse market information and knowledge, and more importantly, what capability is needed to codify and make sense of such knowledge for success (Melville *et al.*, 2004).

Our research attempts to contribute to academia and practitioners in two areas. First, debates on whether IT investments yield significant and positive returns remain (Brynjolfsson and Hitt, 1996). We argue that knowledge codification is the first missing link between information system integration and performance. Although recent literatures have emerged to identify contingency factors to improve our understanding of the driving force behind the success of IT deployment, knowledge codification, as a learning mechanism, remains under-explored. This learning mechanism is critical because it guides the subsidiary to turn the information available on the integrated information system into meanings, offering strategic inputs to increase market responsiveness and firm performance (Zollo and Winter, 2002). Second, although extant research on market responsiveness offers significant theoretical implications, its mediating role, specifically in the context of MNC, and how this dynamic capability works as a mechanism to configure codified knowledge into operant resources to create firm value, is not well documented (Gold *et al.*, 2001). Taken together, this research attempts to add to the literature by suggesting that knowledge codification mediates the impact of information system integration on market responsiveness, and in turn market responsiveness mediates the effect of knowledge codification on firm performance.

The remainder of the chapter is organized as follows. We first review the literatures on dynamic capabilities, learning, and IT, and draw on these literatures to develop our hypotheses. Hypotheses are tested on data collected from 140 foreign subsidiaries in China. Results show that the impact of information system integration on firm performance must sequentially work through knowledge codification and market responsiveness. We close with findings, implications, and conclusions.

Literature Review and Theoretical Framework

The recent advancement of organizational theory has emphasized the importance of organizational learning and knowledge. Researchers suggest that a firm's knowledge can be accumulated through deliberate learning inside (e.g., Tsai, 2001) or outside of a firm (Cohen and Levinthal, 1990). In particular, dynamic capabilities theorists contend that learning can be viewed as both an outcome and a process to shape and turn routines into more generic competencies, which allows a firm to evolve its capabilities from time to time (Teece *et al.*, 1997; Teece, 2007). Consistent with evolutionary theory, learning guides firms to select and retain past behaviors, and thereby accumulating experience to develop firm wisdom (Nelson and Winter, 1982). Learning further enhances a firm's ability to respond to various levels of uncertainty, to build skills to meet new environmental challenges, and to avoid competency rigidities (Leonard-Barton, 1992).

More recently, Zollo and Winter (2002) advance the notion of deliberate learning and further suggest that firms absorb knowledge through articulation and codification to develop dynamic capabilities. In particular, knowledge articulation reflects the process of expressing ideas, confronting different viewpoints, synthesizing collective information, and communicating clearly between firms (Zollo and Winter, 2002). Knowledge can be articulated through discussions and sharing. Knowledge codification, on the other hand, depicts the process of disentangling the link between actions and performance outcomes, and finding ways and logics to uncover what is required to make a firm succeed (Zollo and Winter, 2002). In the context of MNC, knowledge codification reflects a subsidiary's process to identify and establish causal links of market knowledge of different countries and converts such knowledge into its own system. In contrast to knowledge articulation, we focus on knowledge codification, which emphasizes more indepth learning required by a foreign subsidiary to cope with various challenges (Zollo and Winter, 2002).

Market responsiveness, on the other hand, is a higher order form of dynamic capabilities. It reflects the extent to which a subsidiary can respond to the needs of its customers in a timely manner such as by launching new products faster than its competitors (Luo, 2001). Thus, within the context of MNC and from the viewpoint of a foreign subsidiary, dynamic capabilities allow the subsidiary to select and retain knowledge generated by its headquarters and over time, the subsidiary can develop synergies through combining of its own knowledge and information together with the headquarters and other subsidiaries of the MNC (Almeida and Phene, 2004).

Although recent research has studied the effect of IT on performance, findings remain inconclusive, leading to the ongoing debate of the IT-productivity paradox (e.g., Brynjolfsson and Hitt, 1996). We argue that the effect of IT stems from its influence on a firm's ability to deploy IT such that it can enhance its ability to access existing knowledge to generate alternative insights before the firm can respond to market challenges (Luo, 2003). Accordingly, guided by the theory of dynamic capabilities (Teece *et al.*, 1997; Zollo and Winter, 2002), we propose that knowledge codification is a mean to convert integrated information systems into operant resources that influence market responsiveness, and in turn affect firm performance. We summarize our expectation in Fig. 5.1 and detail our theoretical underpinnings below.

Figure 5.1.   Proposed model.

Hypotheses

Effects of information system integration

Information system is a structural mechanism designed to encourage information and knowledge sharing between firms or across business units (Melville *et al.*, 2004). It enables large amounts of information to be stored, shared, and retrieved at real time, which can support decision making (Ross, 2003). Within the context of MNCs, information system integration refers to the extent to which a subsidiary's IT infrastructure pertaining to information and databases is incorporated with its headquarters and other subsidiaries. Thus, an integral information system implies that each of an MNC's business units must use a similar platform such that they can easily transmit, share, retrieve, and integrate data and information each of them possesses in real time (Melville *et al.*, 2004). Without a common and shared platform, it will become challenging, if not impossible, for different MNC units to link sales data, market analyses, etc. of multiple locations, and to remain informed of changes in internal and external environments (Barua *et al.*, 2004).

Further, as opposed to tradition information and communication approaches such as written documents, information system integration allows greater and more accurate sharing across time and geographic locations (Bharadwaj, 2000). For example, using available online databases, the subsidiary can compare target market profiles across countries to improve its product offerings against its competitors and timeliness to the market. In other words, because of increased communication speed and information richness, the subsidiary in which its information system is built in closer with others' is likely to be more informed of differences in social complexities, knowledge structures, etc., making it possible for the subsidiary to establish causal links of knowledge of different countries. As a result, increases in information system integration facilitate knowledge codification to take place. The importance of information system lies in its ability to store and retrieve information and knowledge in a standardized way such that an MNC's headquarters and subsidiaries can access each other's information and data. Integrated information systems allow the headquarters and subsidiaries to easily share, retrieve, and access data. Consequently, this digitally enabled environment enhances the process of codifying multiple sources of information and converting it into one's own system. Thus, we posit:

Hypothesis 1: There exists a positive relationship between information system integration and knowledge codification.

Effects of knowledge codification

As discussed previously, the extent to which IT investments influence firm perform is attributed to the question of whether IT is an asset or resource that can create competitive advantage of itself. According to the resource-based view of the firm, resources must be unique, nonsubstitutable, rare, and inimitable to generate firm value (Barney, 1991). Recent knowledge-based researchers (Grant, 1991; De Luca and Atuahene-Gima, 2007) argue that resources by themselves do not constitute competitive advantage unless they can be deployed, utilized, or integrated with other resources or capabilities to create competitive advantage. In other words, simply having integrated information systems does not guarantee success.

Information system, an IT infrastructure, is digitally enabled technology such as databases that assist in the acquisition, storage, and dissemination of information and data across business units of an MNC. Although the importance of information system integration lies in its ability to store and retrieve information and knowledge in a way that is more standardized (Adams *et al.*, 1992), such information does not speak for itself as to how it may be different from other similar information when taking into consideration of cultural differences across countries. Because information is culturally embedded and can be affected by its social complexities, information and knowledge generated in countries other than the subsidiary's host country may consist of different meanings beyond the subsidiary's knowledge store and understanding. To strive for success, knowledge codification as a deliberate learning mechanism provides a means to convert shared data into meaningful inputs in decision making.

Knowledge codification is a deliberate learning mechanism that reflects a subsidiary's capacity to disentangle causal linkages of knowledge of different countries and converts such knowledge into its own system. Such a learning mechanism that fosters the subsidiary to interpret and establish causal links involves an extensive cognitive appraisal of knowledge and information gathered from various market situations (Zollo and Winter, 2002). Although information of different market conditions may not be identical, if the subsidiary can draw a common thread through its understanding of various social contexts and can convert such understanding into its knowledge store, it enhances its abilities to respond to its host market (Almeida and Phene, 2004).

The process outcome of market responsiveness is influenced by the degree to which the subsidiary codifies knowledge of its headquarters and other subsidiaries specific to its market conditions. Prior literature has shown that cognitive information processing is particularly relevant in dynamic environments (Homburg *et al.*, 2007). Knowledge codification requires significant amounts of cognitive efforts to process and interpret information that should have important consequences on the subsidiary's competence (Zollo and Winter, 2002). In particular, the importance of timing and speed in response to new demands and needs arising from customers of the host country puts pressures on the subsidiary to further evaluate and examine relevant knowledge such as from similar situations faced by other MNC units. Thus, engaging in knowledge codification increases its ability to respond timely and accurately to environmental threats and opportunities. We propose to test the following hypotheses.

Hypothesis 2: There exists a positive relationship between knowledge codification and market responsiveness.

Hypothesis 3: Knowledge codification mediates the relationship between information system integration and market responsiveness.

Effects of market responsiveness

Because knowledge is culturally embedded and can be affected by its social complexities, knowledge and information generated in countries other than the subsidiary's host country may consist of different meanings beyond the subsidiary's knowledge store and understanding. Thus, knowledge codification by itself may not be sufficient to generate superior performance. The effect of knowledge codification on firm performance hinges on the extent to which the firm's abilities to use codified knowledge in response to market needs. Market responsiveness serves as a dynamic capability to configure information into operant resources such that the subsidiary can respond speedier and more efficient to the local market.

In line with recent research that has shown that a firm's responsiveness lies in its awareness of opportunities and threats (Jayachandran and Varadarajan, 2006), we posit that the impact of knowledge codification on subsidiary performance must work through market responsiveness. When the subsidiary is incapable of codifying different knowledge, it would become less informed of any opportunities and solutions presented in the market. When market responsiveness is missing, the direct effects of knowledge codification on firm performance will suppress. Thus, we posit:

Hypothesis 4: Market responsiveness positively influences firm performance.

Hypothesis 5: Market responsiveness mediates the effects of knowledge codification on firm performance.

Methodology

Sample and data collection

Recent research has suggested that understanding how headquarters and their overseas subsidiaries co-create knowledge is a critical issue (e.g., Cui *et al.*, 2005). In this study, we focus particularly on foreign subsidiaries in China. With the saturation of domestic markets, MNCs from developed countries such as the United States and Europe have increasingly expanded to foreign markets through setting up subsidiaries, and financial returns on their expansion specifically in transition economies are proved substantial (Wooster, 2006). China is an enormous market where her culture is distinct largely from Western economies. The foreign subsidiaries in China are very often required to develop their own strategies in response to the local market. Thus, this country provides an appropriate setting to test our theory.

We identified approximately 300 foreign firms operating in Shanghai, China. Of which, 140 completed the survey. Similar to previous studies, we collected the data on-site in China. Among our respondent firms, 53% of their headquarters were located in the United States, 34% in Europe, 10% in Asia, and the rest in other continents. These subsidiaries represented a wide range of high-tech industries including telecommunications, software development, and IT, etc. and had operated for an average of 14 years in China.

Questionnaire design and development

We relied on previous research to generate item pools where appropriate for individual construct operationalizations. For new scales, we followed established procedures to develop our measures (Churchill, 1979). Because the initial questionnaire was constructed in English, we used two bilingual graduate students and followed established procedures to translate the questionnaire in Chinese and back translate it in English. The authors then compared the back-translated questionnaire with the original English version and found no major differences. After academic and industrial experts reviewed the Chinese research instrument, we pretested it on five senior executives who were familiar with their operations in multinational markets in China to ensure that our questions were relevant and that the model was appropriately bounded. The pretest subjects were extensively debriefed following their completion of the survey. The survey instrument was refined based on their comments.

Measures

Information system integration is the extent to which the headquarters and the subsidiaries have the same IT platform to process, integrate, retrieve, and obtain information (Bharadwaj, 2000). We adapted a four-item, seven-point Likert scale from recent IT literatures (Bharadwaj, 2000; Barua *et al.*, 2004). A sample item includes, "data can be shared easily among various internal systems." On the other hand, knowledge codification reflects the degree to which the subsidiary can disentangle the causal ambiguity of the headquarters' knowledge and converts it into its own system (Zollo and Winter, 2002). We based on the literature to develop four new items anchored on a seven-point Likert scale from one, strongly disagree to seven, strongly agree. A sample item includes "we can turn the customer knowledge we have learned from our headquarters into our own system." Market responsiveness depicts the extent to which the subsidiary can respond to the opportunities of its host country in a timely manner. We based on the past research to include four items (e.g., Jaworski and Kohli, 1993; Homburg *et al.*, 2007). A sample item is "when we find our customers are unhappy with the quality of our services/products, we take corrective actions immediately," and is anchored on a seven-point Likert scale from one, strongly disagree to seven, strongly agree. Firm performance is captured by a subsidiary's market performance in relation to its competitors on the areas of product quality, customer satisfaction, and profitability. We detail our measures in the Appendix.

Response bias and validity checks

We verified the validity of our data in two ways. First, we assessed potential non-response bias by comparing non-respondent firms with respondent firms in terms of firm age, sales, and the number of employees. We used our purchased business directory and other sources to acquire the necessary secondary data. Our t-test results suggest no significant difference between respondent and non-respondent firms. Second, we performed a validity check on our key informants' qualification. Respondents were asked in the survey to report on their positions and years employed with their company. Ninety percent of our respondents were senior executives familiar with their local operations and had worked for their company for an average of five years.

To avoid common methods variance, we used several approaches as suggested in recent research (Crampton and Wagner III, 1994; Podsakoff *et al.*, 2003). First, we carefully designed our questionnaire by separating our key constructs into several subsections and by using different formats to reduce simply "straight line" responses by our informants. Second, we used the Hamon's single factor test to assess whether a common method bias exists in our data. Using exploratory factor analysis, we estimated a model that had items for all of the latent constructs. Four eigenvalues exceed 1, ranging from 1.23 to 5.3. The rotated component matrix shows that all of the measurement items, shown in Table 5.1, are loaded onto their respective factors.

Table 5.1.   Constructs and measures.

Constructs and measures	Standardized factor loadings	Average variance extracted	Composite reliability
Subsidiary performance			
Please indicate the level of this subsidiary's performance compared to your major competitors in the past three years in terms of (a 7-point scale from 1 = "low" to 7 = "high." Overall product/service quality Overall profitability Customer satisfaction	0.73–0.91	0.72	0.89
Knowledge codification			
We can turn the competitor knowledge we have learned from our headquarters into our own system. We establish the causal link between the knowledge we have generated from the headquarters and our local customer environment. We establish the causal link between the knowledge we have generated from the headquarters and our local competitive environment.	0.66–0.82	0.55	0.78
Information system integration			
Data can be shared easily among various internal systems (e.g., forecasting, production, manufacturing, shipment, finance, accounting, etc.). Policy changes are automatically reflected in the headquarters' and all other subsidiaries' systems. This subsidiary's systems can easily transmit, integrate, and process data from the headquarters and all other subsidiaries.	0.76–0.85	0.65	0.88

(*Continued*)

Table 5.1.   (*Continued*)

Constructs and measures	Standardized factor loadings	Average variance extracted	Composite reliability
Employees at the headquarters and different subsidiaries can easily retrieve information from various databases for decision support (e.g., cost information, reporting tools).			
Market responsiveness			
When we find that our customers are unhappy with the quality of our services/products, we take corrective actions immediately.	0.76–0.82	0.61	0.86
When we find that our customers would like us to modify a product or service, we are all involved to make concerted efforts to do so.			
We respond to our customer needs in a speedy manner.			
Our entry to new markets is timely.			

Goodness-of-fit indexes: $\chi^2 = 79.319$, d.f. $= 71$, $p = 0.233$, CFI $= 0.992$, NFI $= 0.927$, RMSEA $= 0.029$.

We used AMOS 6.0 to conduct a confirmatory factory analysis to evaluate all items. All latent variables were included in one multifactorial confirmatory factor analysis model. Measurement purification was performed following established procedures (Anderson and Gerbing, 1988). The adjusted overall chi-squared value ($\chi^2 = 79.319$; d.f. $= 71$), root mean square error of approximation (RMSEA $= 0.029$), normed fit index (NFI $= 0.927$), and comparative fit index (CFI $= 0.992$), provide evidence of the overall fit (see Table 5.1). Further, all the items loaded significantly on the expected constructs, indicating convergent and discriminate validity of the measure. Finally, we calculated the average variance extracted and composite reliability of each construct and found all of indicators passed the suggested threshold values (Anderson and Gerbing, 1988; Bagozzi and Yi, 1988; Nunnally and Bernstein, 1994). We summarize our measures and their properties in Table 5.1 and the basic descriptive statistics and the correlation coefficients of our constructs in Table 5.2.

Results

Based on the excellent fit of the structural model, the proposed hypotheses are tested and results are summarized in Table 5.3. Specifically, H1 expects a direct relationship between information system integration and

Table 5.2.   Descriptive statistics and correlation matrix.

	1	2	3	4
1. Information system integration	0.881			
2. Knowledge codification	0.315**	0.779		
3. Market responsiveness	0.273**	0.371**	0.863	
4. Firm performance	0.208*	0.329**	0.542**	0.881
Mean	4.144	4.437	4.974	5.146
Standard deviation	1.255	1.133	1.068	1.022

$^*p < 0.10$, $^{**}p < 0.05$, $^{***}p < 0.01$.

Table 5.3.   SEM results — Main effect tests.

Hypothesis and path direction	Estimate	Conclusion
H1: Information system integration → knowledge codification	0.390***	Supported
H2: Knowledge codification → market responsiveness	0.495***	Supported
H4: Market responsiveness → firm performance	0.655***	Supported

$^{**}p < 0.05$; $^{***}p < 0.01$.

knowledge codification. We find support for it ($b = 0.39$, $p < 0.01$). H2, which posits that knowledge codification affects market responsiveness, is supported ($b = 0.495$, $p < 0.01$). H4 posits a positive impact of market responsiveness on firm performance and we find support for it ($b = 0.655$, $p < 0.01$).

With respect to the mediation hypotheses, H3 and H5, we use the established procedures recommended by Preacher and Hayes (2004) to test the significance of possible mediation effects. Bootstrapping is increasingly popular to test mediation effects since this approach does not require meeting the normality assumption and can effectively apply to smaller sample sizes. We set our bootstrap sample size to 1,000 and examine (H3) the mediating effects of knowledge codification on the link between information system integration and market responsiveness and (H5) the mediating effects of market responsiveness on the link between knowledge codification and firm performance. The results of the mediation analysis are as follows: knowledge codification (direct effect = none; indirect effect = 0.208, $p < 0.01$; total effect = 0.208, $p < 0.01$) and market responsiveness (direct effect = none; indirect effect = 0.149, $p < 0.01$; total effect = 0.149, $p < 0.01$). These findings reported in Table 5.4 support both H3 and H5 that knowledge codification fully

Table 5.4. SEM Bootstrapping results — Mediation effect tests.

	Endogenous variables								
	Knowledge codification			Market responsiveness			Performance		
	Total effects	Direct effects	Indirect effects	Total effects	Direct effects	Indirect effects	Total effects	Direct effects	Indirect effects
Information system integration	0.374** (0.105)	0.374** (0.105)	—	0.306** (0.100)	0.154 (0.107)	0.152** (0.057)	0.230** (0.102)	−0.005 (0.095)	0.235** (0.073)
Knowledge codification	—	—	—	0.407** (0.103)	0.407** (0.103)	—	0.392** (0.109)	0.158 (0.110)	0.234** (0.072)
Market responsiveness	—	—	—	—	—	—	0.575** (0.102)	0.575** (0.102)	—
(SMC) R square		0.152**			0.245**			0.429**	
Fit statistics:	$\chi^2 = 84.315$ (d.f. = 74), χ^2/d.f. = 1.139, CFI = 0.990, GFI = 0.924, TLI = 0.987, RMSEA = 0.032.								

Note: We report standardized coefficients and two-tailed test results; standard errors are in parentheses. The mediation analysis is tested using the bootstrapping method ($N = 1000$).
*** $p < 0.001$, ** $p < 0.01$, * $p < 0.05$, # $p < 0.10$.

mediates the effects of knowledge complementarities and information system integration on market responsiveness.

Competing models analyses

To assess the robustness of our conceptual model, we construct two rival models and their fit indices are reported in Table 5.5. Specifically, we construct Rival Model 1 (Fig. 5.2) by removing knowledge codification from our conceptual model. The overall model fit indexes of Rival Model 1 (χ^2 = 113.884, d.f. = 74, GFI = 0.90, CFI = 0.96, RMSEA = 0.062) are less satisfactory compared with our proposed model. Additionally, we construct Rival Model 2 (Fig. 5.3) to examine whether knowledge codification has a direct

Table 5.5. Fit indices of competing models.

Model	DF	χ^2	p	χ^2/DF	ΔDF	Δχ^2	GFI	CFI	TLI	RMSEA
Proposed	74	84.315	0.193	1.139	1		0.924	0.990	0.987	0.032
Rival 1	74	113.884	0.002	1.539	1	29.569***	0.900	0.960	0.951	0.062
Rival 2	74	114.388	0.002	1.546	1	30.073***	0.900	0.959	0.950	0.063

Figure 5.2. Rival model 1.

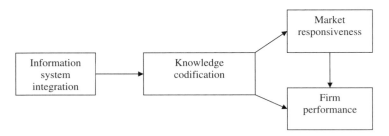

Figure 5.3. Rival model 2.

impact on firm performance. Based on our original model, we add a path from knowledge codification to firm performance. Again, the overall model fit indexes of Rival Model 2 (χ^2 = 114.388, d.f. = 74, GFI = 0.90, CFI = 0.959, RMSEA = 0.063) are less satisfactory than our proposed model.

Discussion and Conclusion

Our research and corresponding findings suggest that a subsidiary's perform-ance relies on its IT infrastructure, learning mechanisms, and responsiveness. By recognizing the sequential impacts of information system integration, knowledge codification, and market responsiveness, the subsidiary can deploy resources appropriately to these different areas. Consistent with recent research (Rai *et al.*, 2006), our results reveal although an integrated informa-tion system is crucial in today's increasingly globalized economy, it does not by itself create superior firm performance. Information system integration is an IT structural mechanism designed to encourage information and knowl-edge sharing between business units (Melville *et al.*, 2004); its effect, however, must go through knowledge codification and market responsiveness to enhance firm performance.

Knowledge codification is a deliberate learning mechanism to establish causal linkages of organizational routines embedded within the firm, which is a critical mediator found in our study. Specifically, the "fit-as-mediation" view alluded in contingency frameworks (Venkatraman, 1989) suggests that a firm is an information processor to convert inputs into outputs such as behaviors (Galbraith, 1974). Thus, knowledge codification is critical as it is a mandated process for learning and establishing linkages of knowledge accumulated in different markets (Zollo and Winter, 2002). In other words, knowledge cod-ification can be viewed as the firm's process to draw insights from information acquired from customers and competitors of multiple markets.

Market responsiveness is the degree to which a subsidiary reacts to the market by introducing and launching new products more and faster than its counterparts in the same host country (Homburg *et al.*, 2007). This outcome variable is particularly relevant. First, consistent with previous marketing lit-erature (Varadarajan and Jayachandran, 1999; Homburg *et al.*, 2007), we find a significant and positive effect on performance. Second, in the context of MNC, because subsidiaries in different countries face different environ-ments, their headquarters may not be able to develop strategies appropriate to the local market. Thus, a subsidiary needs to have internal and external understandings of resources and environments to respond quickly to any threats or opportunities arising from its own host market. Our findings suggest that market responsiveness is a function of knowledge codification and information system integration. Information system integration, in particular, does not constitute operant resources to the subsidiary. Rather, when the subsidiary can turn such information embedded in the information system into market responsiveness, superior firm performance results. Further, the subsidiary that has stronger knowledge codification increases its odds to establish causal linkages of information available in the information system, resulting in higher market responsiveness, and ultimately, firm performance.

Implications for Managers

Setting a context in China, our study provides insights to practitioners as to how to manage their foreign subsidiaries. During the past 20 years or so, China has become a strategically important market for multinational corporations across the globe. International trade has shifted from cross-Atlantic to cross-Pacific, especially China. While successful cases abound, yet many organizations have failed to make any progress in this enormous market. Our study demonstrates the criticality of knowledge management. Specifically, knowledge codification and information system integration are equally important. Because the Chinese market is different from an MNC's home market, having a learning mechanism that can allow managers to understand and convert local knowledge into systems is crucial. Knowledge acquired without understanding of causal ambiguity is of no use to the MNC and its subsidiary, in particular. Alternatively, managers should be encouraged to establish an information system that is compatible to their operations in China. Integrative information system allows managers to share information and knowledge with other foreign operations easier and faster. With quicker responses to the market, superior firm performance likely follows.

Critically, the essence of knowledge management lies perhaps in the identification of appropriate personnel who understands not only the local Chinese market, but also the company's operations. An alignment between local market knowledge and organizational philosophy and management proves to be effective. Connecting to the local market through guanxi or relationship building facilitated by local personnel likely enables the MNC's operations to succeed in China. Ambiguities of market knowledge government regulations and policies can be more correctly interpreted by the use of local employees to enhance the understanding of the Chinese market.

Limitations and Future Research

While we recognize several limitations of our study, they also provide avenues for future research. First, our study, similar to some other organizational research, uses a single informant approach to collect data. Although we used different approaches to reduce common method bias, such a concern remains. Future research may attempt to use multiple informants to enhance reliabilities and eliminate the concern of common method bias.

Second, we have identified two missing links between IT and firm performance. Future research is encouraged to explore any other missing variables that may influence this relationship. For example, environmental factors such as market turbulence may have effects on knowledge codification (Zollo and Winter, 2002) and well as market responsiveness (Jaworski and Kohli, 1993). Taking into account of other factors can improve our understanding of knowledge management practices.

Finally, complementarities of organizational resources and structures are found influencing firm performance (e.g., Sarkar *et al.*, 2001). Nevertheless, our model does not consider similarities in resources, organizational cultures, and management, among others between the subsidiary and its headquarters that may facilitate or hinder the consequences of information system integration, knowledge codification, and market responsiveness. Future research is encouraged to expand our model by including more relevant precursors. We believe that by including more managerial relevant factors into our current model, it should provide a better understanding of how subsidiaries can develop dynamic capabilities created by knowledge codification and supported with information system integration.

Conclusion

This study addresses an important issue of IT impacts on firm performance. We have examined two missing variables, knowledge codification and market responsiveness. Our research looks at knowledge codification as a deliberate learning mechanism to navigate information and data available between the subsidiary and its headquarters. Market responsiveness reflects the subsidiary's dynamic capabilities that are particularly important to navigate businesses in foreign countries. We urge managers to develop an IT platform that allows the subsidiary and the headquarters to have online access to information. By promoting deliberate learning, this should result in increased market responsiveness, and ultimately, firm performance.

References

Adams, DA, RR Nelson, and PA Todd (1992). Perceived usefulness, ease of use, and usage of information technology: A replication. *MIS Quarterly*, 16, 227–250.

Almeida, P and A Phene (2004). Subsidiaries and knowledge creation: The influence of the MNC and host country on innovation. *Strategic Management Journal*, 25, 847–864.

Anderson, JC and DW Gerbing (1988). Some methods for respecifying measurement models to obtain unidimensional construct measurement. *Journal of Marketing*, 19, 453–460.

Bagozzi, RP and Y Yi (1988). On the evaluation of structural equation models. *Journal of the Academy of Marketing Science*, 16, 74–94.

Barney, JB (1991). Firm resources and sustained competitive advantage. *Journal of Management*, 17, 99–120.

Barua, A, P Konana, AB Whinston, and F Yin (2004). An empirical investigation of net-enabled business value. *MIS Quarterly*, 28, 585–620.

Bharadwaj, AS (2000). A resource-based perspective on information technology capability and firm performance: An empirical investigation. *MIS Quarterly*, 24, 169–196.

Brynjolfsson, E and L Hitt (1996). Information technology and productivity. A review of the literature. *Advances in Computers*, 43, 179–214.

Churchill, GA Jr (1979). A paradigm for developing better measures of marketing constructs. *Journal of Marketing Research*, 16, 67–73.

Cohen, WM and DA Levinthal (1990). Absorptive capacity: A new perspective on learning and innovation. *Administrative Science Quarterly*, 35, 128–152.

Crampton, SM and JA Wagner III (1994). Precept–Percept inflation in microorganizational research: An investigation of prevalence and effect. *Journal of Applied Psychology*, 79, 67–76.

Cui, AS, DA Griffith, and S Tamer Cavusgil (2005). The influence of competitive intensity and market dynamism on knowledge management capabilities of multinational corporation subsidiaries. *Journal of International Marketing*, 13, 32–53.

De Luca, LM and K Atuahene-Gima (2007). Market knowledge dimensions and cross-functional collaboration: Examining the different routes to product innovation performance. *Journal of Marketing*, 71, 95–112.

Elville, N, K Kraemer, and V Gurbaxani (2004). Review: Information technology and organizational performance: An integrative model of it business value. *MIS Quarterly*, 28, 283–322.

Galbraith, JR (1974). Organization design: An information processing view. *Interfaces*, 4, 28–36.

Gold, AH, A Malhotra, and AH Segars (2001). Knowledge management: An organizational capabilities perspective. *Journal of Management Information Systems*, 18, 185–214.

Grant, RM (1991). Toward a knowledge-based theory of the firm. *Strategic Management Journal*, 17, 109–122.

Homburg, C, M Grozdanovic, and M Klarmann (2007). Responsiveness to customers and competitors: The role of affective and cognitive organizational systems. *Journal of Marketing*, 71, 18–38.

Inkpen, AC (1998). Learning and knowledge acquisition through international strategic alliances. *Academy of Management Executive*, 12, 69–80.

Jaworski, BJ and AK Kohli (1993). Market orientation: Antecedents and consequences. *Journal of Marketing*, 57, 53–70.

Jayachandran, S and R Varadarajan (2006). Does success diminish competitive responsiveness? Reconciling conflicting perspectives. *Journal of the Academy of Marketing Science*, 34, 284–294.

Johnston, S and A Paladino (2007). Knowledge management and involvement in innovations in MNC subsidiaries. *Management International Review*, 47, 281–302.

Leonard-Barton, D (1992). Core capabilities and core rigidities: A paradox in managing new product development. *Strategic Management Journal*, 13, 111–125.

Luo, Y (2001). Determinants of local responsiveness: Perspectives from foreign subsidiaries in an emerging market. *Journal of Management*, 27, 451–477.

Luo, Y (2003). Market-seeking MNEs in an emerging market: How parent-subsidiary links shape overseas success. *Journal of International Business Studies*, 34, 290–309.

Nelson, RR and SG Winter (1982). *An Evolutionary Theory of Economic Change*. Cambridge, MA: The Belknap Press.

Nunnally, JC and IH Bernstein (1994). *Psychometric Theory*. New York: McGraw-Hill.

Podsakoff, PM, SB MacKenzie, JY Lee, and NP Podsakoff. Common method biases in behavior research: A critical review of the literature and recommended remedies. *Journal of Applied Psychology*, 88, 879–903.

Preacher, KJ and AF Hayes (2004). SPSS and SAS procedures for estimating indirect effects in simple mediation models. *Behavior Research Methods, Instruments, & Computers*, 36, 717–731.

Rai, A, R Patnayakuni and N Seth (2006). Firm performance impacts of digitally enabled supply chain integration capabilities. *MIS Quarterly*, 30, 225–246.

Ross, WT (2003). Creating a strategic IT architecture competency: Learning in stages. *MIS Quarterly Executive*, 2, 31–43.

Sarkar, MB, R Echambadi, S Tamer Cavusgil, and PS Aulakh (2001). The influence of complementarity, compatibility, and relationship capital on alliance performance. *Journal of the Academy of Marketing Science*, 29, 358–373.

Teece, DJ (2007). Explicating dynamic capabilities: The nature and microfoundations of (sustainable) enterprise performance. *Strategic Management Journal*, 28, 1319–1350.

Teece, D, G Pisano, and A Schuen (1997). Dynamic capabilities and strategic management. *Strategic Management Journal*, 18, 509–533.

Tsai, W (2001). Knowledge transfer in intraorganizational networks: Effects of network position and absorptive capacity on business unit innovation and performance. *Academy of Management Journal*, 44, 996–1004.

Varadarajan, PR and S Jayachandran (1999). Marketing strategy: An assessment of the state of the field and outlook. *Journal of the Academy of Marketing Science*, 27, 120–143.

Venkatraman, N (1989). The concept of fit in strategy research: Toward a verbal and statistical correspondence. *Academy of Management Review*, 31, 197–217.

Wooster, RB (2006). US companies in transition economies: Wealth effects from expansion between 1987 and 1999. *Journal of International Business Studies*, 37, 179–195.

Zollo, M and SG Winter (2002). Deliberate learning and the evolution of dynamic capabilities. *Organization Science*, 13, 339–351.

Chapter 6

LEGAL CASES
AND AUDITING IN CHINA

GIN CHONG

Abstract

Over the last decades, the world has witnessed the political and economic revolutions in the People's Republic of China. The administration of the country has constantly called for changes to its directions to continuously boost its economic power, business culture, and accountability. Audit is the tool to help project transparency and identify reliability in the control systems. This chapter assesses the extent of audit changes within the country based on the four audit reports issued by its National Audit Office (NAO) in 2005. The finding shows positive approaches adopted by the administration, in particular the NAO, but there are areas that need further improvements. The recommendations have implications to the policy makers, audit profession, and users of the audit reports.

Introduction

For the last 30 years, the world has witnessed the foundation of the People's Republic of China in 1949 that went through series of major mass political movements. The country has isolated itself from the rest of the world, especially the capitalist world, on trade and labor migration. At the brink of a total economic collapse, China moved from its closed-door policy to an open-door policy in 1978 focusing on economic developments using the market-oriented economic reforms, while emphasizing on social responsibilities. These changes have brought modern approaches to the government and independent auditing systems to replace its outdated monitoring mechanisms

101

of the 1950s (Hao, 1999; Xiao *et al.*, 2000; Chong, 2008). Transformation of a country's political structure will bring along major shifts in its auditing and accounting systems (Chong, 2000). This is evidenced in the Chinese context. The country's political structure can be categorized in three organizational systems: the National People's Congress (NPC) as the supreme legislature; the State Council as the central executive body or central government; and the People's Supreme Council and Court (PSCC) as the legal enforcer. The current top-down system means that once a piece of legislation is being passed by the NPC, it moves to the state, municipal, and then provisional levels for implementations. In rare occasions, the system reverses the order of bottom-up flow of recommending and updating the legislations. Even though the ordinary citizens have shown respect and adapted to the one way hierarchical flow of rules and regulations, the Central Government has strategically placed representatives at various government units and practiced cross-board memberships whereby representatives at the NPC may also sit on the PSCC, the lowest level of the organization, to ensure consistency in the design and implementations of law throughout the systems.

In 1982, the NPC passed a constitution allowing the formation of the National Audit Office (NAO). The NAO becomes a government unit in 1983. The unit is responsible to ensure accountability, transparency, and integrity of the government servants and units in the course of discharging their duties of care. Audit offices were set up by the provincial, municipal, and county governments. The NAO is responsible for designing the audit standards for all its audit offices, while all the audit offices are responsible for conducting audits and report the findings of the state and provisional units, at least annually, to the NAO (Chong and Vinten, 1998). The NAO will then compile and submit these reports to the Congress. Though the regional audit offices have autonomy to conduct the audits, the NAO intercepts in situations where the audit assignments relate to departments dealing with national securities and trade secrets. Regional offices may occasionally request for additional supports and resources, including the required technical skills, manpower and time, from the NAO. Although this audit system has made significant contributions toward the Chinese economic reform, has gained confident from the investors, and has opened its door to the world over the past years (Chinese Auditing System Research Group, 1999; Chong, 2000), it suffers from a lack of audit independence and objectivity in the audit approaches. This is due to its monopoly in the market, its organizational structure, and the decisions of whether to report fraud and omissions remain in the hands of some powerful individuals. These individuals have close connections with the administrations and have remained in power since the inception of the NAO. Further, the main source of financial support comes from the taxpayers, and it is essential for the NAO and its regional offices to please the wealthy and fame to continue for its operations and existence (Yang *et al.*, 2008). Under this system, government departments and officials can, both theoretically and practically, interfere with the government audits, thereby affecting the objectivity, integrity, and fairness of the audits and auditors. Nonetheless, to project the image of care for the people, the congress attaches a significant importance to, and makes increasing use of, the audit reports (Shou and Yam, 1987) to propaganda its achievements and willingness to expose weaknesses in the internal controls, identify the culprits, and surface discrepancies in the budgets. More and more stakeholders, especially the taxpayers, have paid attentions to how their money is used by the authority (Yang *et al.*, 2008). While the NAO's lack of independence has always been a problem ever since its establishment, this problem is creating increasing tensions in the current political setting because of the accountability needs of the legislature and taxpayers.

This chapter looks at the various audit reports published on the web site of the NAO in 2003. Thus far, the site has published four audit reports. The basis of selecting these reports and reasons for delaying publications of these reports remains a myth. Notwithstanding these, the NAO has caused "audit storms" to the government departments with the disclosures of serious illegal acts (Yang *et al.*, 2008). However, although this storm has been useful in drawing attentions to many stakeholders, the level of audit independence remains questionable for only a small percentage among the total number of audit reports were being published. Despite all these, the NAO has made a right move to show its courage and authority of publicizing the needs for accountability, governance, and integrity among the civil servants (Chong and Vinten, 1998). The NAO needs to project a positive image to the public that it is an independent body and capable of exercising its authorities to express the duties of care, due diligence, and efficiency, effectiveness, and economical use of resources (e.g., Yan, 1986; Qin, 1994; Zhang, 1996; DeFond *et al.*, 2000). Yang (1989) and Xiang (2002) find that the NAO needs to constantly project that it has conducted the audits to justify for its existence, capability, and resource allocations. These justifications need to be supported by its audit findings, and extent of wasted resources is being exposed, recovered, and rectified.

Theoretical Background and Literature Review

Research on government auditing in China began when the NAO was first established in 1982. Yan (1986), Li (1998), and Yang (1989) investigate government auditing from the perspective of public accountability. They report that the Chinese auditing system, supposedly to evaluate and report on the government's accountability to the people and to the legislature, should have been set up independent of the government's authority. Qin (1994), Zhang (1996), and Xiang (2002) extend this research on the relationship between public accountability and government auditing and propose the legislature approach. This means that the NAO should, as a body, break away from the central government and become part of the NPC (the parliament of China). Similarly, regional government audit offices would also be transferred from regional governments to regional people's congresses. This change would bring China's government auditing structure in line with the West in particular, the United States and the United Kingdom (Wang, 2001). In the United Kingdom, the Comptroller and Auditor General's (C&AG) independence is achieved, at least in theory, by taking the appointment of the C&AG out of the control of the executive and making the statutory responsibility of the C&AG to report to the House of Commons (Jones and Pendlebury, 2000, p. 233). This independence was strengthened by the 1983 National Audit Act that significantly reduced the influence of the Treasury (part of the executive) over the work of the C&AG. However, the legislative approach relates to a structural reform of the State Council. This requires substantial constitutional amendments and may be challenging to obtain political supports. While there appears a call for the NAO to be independent, at least to be seen to be independent, the move taken by the NAO to publish its audit finding and publish them on the web is a step to project independence, confidence, and objectivities to the stakeholders.

Independence is arguably the hallmark of the public accounting profession (Shockley, 1981; Whittington and Pany, 2001). In the United States, the second general standard of Generally Accepted Auditing Standards (GAAS) states, "In all matters relating to the assignment, an independence in mental attitude is to be maintained by the auditor or auditors" (AICPA, 2001). This statement makes no distinction between audits of public companies and non-public companies. The auditor "must be without bias with respect to the client since otherwise he would lack that impartiality necessary for the dependability of his findings; however, his excellent technical proficiency may be" (AICPA, 2001). One objective of the independence standard is to ensure that users of audited financial statements maintain a level of confidence in the auditor and audited financial statements (Carey and Doherty, 1996). The US Statement on Auditing Standards No. 1 elaborates that "it is of utmost importance to the profession that the general public maintains confidence in the independence of the independent auditors." Public evidence would be impaired by evidence that independence was actually lacking and it might also be impaired by the existence of circumstances, which reasonable people might believe is likely to influence independence. To be independent, the auditors must be intellectually honest and, to be recognized as an independent, they must be free from any obligation or interest in the client, management, or its owners' (AICPA, 2001).

Thus, it is important that auditors appear independent to third parties (Mayhew and Pike, 2004). If auditors ignore users' perceptions and a lack of independence is perceived, then the auditors' reputations may become questionable, the worth of their reports doubtful, and the usefulness of audited financial statements suspect. Because the auditor is hired and paid by the audited company, the auditor cannot be totally independent (AICPA, 1978). This financial dependency on the client has long been considered as built-in anti-independence (Mautz and Sharaf, 1961, p. 211). Nonetheless, the accounting profession has built a reputation of independence in "fact and appearance" when rendering attestation services.

It is also argued that a key theme underlying the debates on reforming corporate financial reporting and auditing practices is of how to define the auditor's responsibility to maintain auditors' independence. A related theoretical issue is whether the profession self-regulation or the public monitoring mechanism could be more effectively prevent the occurrence of corporate reporting and auditing failures, and thus better serve the interests of the stakeholders, in particular the investors. For the developed countries, the self-regulations have long been in place (e.g., AICPA, 1994; Chandler and Edwards, 1996; Carmichael, 2004); however, there remains an expectation gap on the responsibility of the auditors, as the auditing profession in these countries argue that the objectives of independence have long been achieved, and that the audit opinions attested on the financial statements are fairly presented. In principle, the auditors should not be considered as bloodhound against frauds, irregularities, and illegal acts (AICPA, 1994; Carmichael, 1999; Bell and Carcello, 2000). However, users of the auditing services generally believe that the auditors must assume a responsibility beyond examining and attesting the fairness of the financial statements and shoulder a direct obligation to protect the interests of audit beneficiary, who may directly or indirectly depend on the financial statements and on audit reports for decision making (Nelson *et al.*, 1988; Palmore, 1988; Sikka *et al.*, 1998; Dean *et al.*, 2002).

Various theories exist on the causes of an expectation gap. Traditional thought has attributed the gap to a misperception of financial audits by users or the general public. In other words, an expectation gap arises due to the over-expectations of the audit function (Chapman, 1992; Kachelmeier, 1994; Tidewell and Abrams, 1996; Kaudous, 2000; McEnroe and Martens, 2001). However, some argue that the auditors should be blamed for not meeting the minimum users' expectations and needs. To a large extent, the profession's refusal of performing the fraud detection duties had fueled the expectation gap (Levi, 1986; Epstein and Geiger, 1994; Dewing and Russell, 2001). In addition, the expectation gap could be an outcome of the contradiction of minimum government regulation and the profession's self-regulations (Sikka *et al.*, 1992). Thus, the profession's over protection of self-interest might have widened the expectation gap (Chandler and Edwards, 1996; Sikka *et al.*, 1998; Heim, 2002).

Another theory suggests that the auditors' responsibility is "an amalgamation of public policy consideration" (Chung, 1995; Kadous, 2000), which means that as business operations become more complex due to globalizations and restructuring, the investors have increased their tendencies on relying upon the auditors' work to monitor and offer assurance on the reliability of the financial reports. The expectation gap emerged as the profession has failed to react (Francis, 1994; Munter and Ratcliffe, 1998; Power, 1998). Nonetheless, an expectation gap arises due to time lag. This means that the auditors and profession need to react immediately when a gap exists (Kinney and Nelson, 1996; Farrell and Franco, 1998; Sikka *et al.*, 1998; Kadous, 2000; Dewing and Russell, 2001; McEnroe and Martens, 2001), and if possible take proactive steps to ensure these gaps do not exist.

Auditors are expected to provide objective and reliable attestation services (Kinney, 1999). The utility of the audit function depends upon the integrity, objectivity and independence of the auditors (Yost, 1995; Craig, 1997). Auditors' independence is crucial to maintain the integrity of financial reporting and confidence of the capital and financial markets (Cox, 2000; GAO, 2002). Thus, the auditors' independence has been codified in the profession's auditing standards and ethical rules. In particular, the auditors are obligated to maintain impartiality and intellectual honesty, and be free from conflicts of interest in auditing engagements (Falk *et al.*, 1999; Shafer *et al.*, 1999; Marden and Edwards, 2002). In fact, the auditors' independence can be classified as independent of fact and independent in appearance. Both elements are necessary in the course of discharging the duties of care; however,

Craig (1997) and Trackett and Woodlock (1999) report that the auditors tend to place more attentions on independence in appearance. This could be because independence of fact could be relatively easily verified. This means that if an auditor is deemed independent, the individual has complied fully with the rules and regulations specified by the auditing profession and avoids any possible conflict of interests. Despite this, non-audit services may cause the auditors to compromise on the independence on fact (Kleinman and Farrelly, 1996; Sutton, 1997; Hussey and Lan, 2001; Swanger and Chewing, 2001). With the introduction of Sarbanes Oxley Act (SOA) in 2002, the auditing profession is under a much strong pressure and stringent scrutiny to ensure its independence, integrity, and quality of audit reports and services (Reinstein and Coursen, 1999; Melancon, 2000; Firth, 2002; Geiger *et al.*, 2002; Heffes, 2002; Stephens and Schwartz, 2006). However, provisions of SOA do not form part of the auditing standards for the NAO. The provisions of the SOA are meant for listed firms in the United States while NAO remains a government unit within the Central Government. It would be interesting for future research to assess whether SOA has similar impact on the non-listed firms, non-profits organizations, and government units.

Methodology

Source and procedures

The audit reports were downloaded from the official web site maintained by the NAO (2008). The NAO submitted three audit reports. These reports contain four separate audit cases. Apart from these audit cases, the NAO maintains other sections of the web site in English and Chinese. The English section contains a brief history of the NAO, reporting procedures and current events and issues. Having maintained the web in dual languages enhances the image and appeals of the government unit to a wider audience on their roles and responsibilities, rather than confining to the Chinese readers.

For the audit reports, the author translated them into English and then done independently by a native Chinese scholar.[1] Upon completion, we compared both the translated versions for accuracy and completeness, and revisited the Chinese version for any discrepancies and reconciliations. The process was repeated until the translated version reflected the content of the original Chinese version. The process of independent translations and comparisons

---

[1] The translation from Chinese to English was done independently by a graduate student majoring in accounting.

helped eliminate misinterpretations, omissions, ambiguity, and misunderstanding of the original content.

Analysis of the four Audit cases

The four cases are briefly summarized as follows:

Case 1: Construction of nine higher educational establishments in four cities in 2004; report dated May 31, 2005: The NAO reports that (1) in accordance with the local governments' regulations on land usage, anyone who intends to develop more than 35 acres of the existing agricultural land or 70 acres of the non-agricultural land needs approval from the Central Government. This is not for the case of two of the nine educational establishments that were constructed without prior approval of the Central Government despite they were constructed on the allowed acreage limits; (2) about 60% of the source of finance to construct these buildings came from banks. The cost of borrowing is too expensive and the bank charges are too high; (3) the educational establishments are facing financial instability. Despite this, the institutions are reluctant to increase their tuition fees, even though the Department of Education has allowed them to raise the fees limit and (4) some of the new buildings are too lavish and are a waste of the public funding.

Case 2: Earthquake in Yunnan Province in 2003, report dated April 27, 2005: Two separate earthquakes hit Yunnan Province in Kumning state (South West China) on July 21, 2003 and October 16, 2003, with the scale of 6.2 and 6.1, respectively. The Yunnan Provincial government received altogether $366.62 million (US$25.11 million) from various sources, including the Central Government and charities. The NAO reports that (1) The Central Government claimed to have allocated altogether $51.74 million (US$3.54 million) for emergency, but till November 14, 2003, the Treasury of the Central Government has only received $12 million (US$0.82 million); (2) until March 31, 2004, the Yunnan Provisional Finance Department has failed to allocate $5.174 million (US$0.35 million) to the local council for the redevelopment projects; (3) there are 25 claims, altogether $8.68 million (US$0.59 million), filed by two provinces (within Kunming) for compensations, even though they were not affected by the earthquakes; (4) there is a claim for $200,000 (US$13,700) to construct a building for the Ministry of Health, but in fact, the building has already completed in June 2003 (i.e., it has finished before the earthquake); (5) a claim filed by a province in Kunming for $800,000 (US$54,800) to construct houses and buildings but the costs for these buildings were only $179,000 (US$12,260); (6) Others claim for compensations, totaled $41.11 million (US$2.82 million) submitted by province, state, councils, development, and educational and health departments, were without justifications. For example, Chow Ann Chau Agricultural Farm took $17.48 million (US$1.2 million) for refurbishing its buildings, Pein Chuan council used $1.5 million (US$0.1 million) to construct for a social welfare building, the Ministries of Health in Chow Ann Province and Tar Chow Province have each applied for $250,000 (US$17,123) for constructing squatters for their employees, while the Finance Department of Chian Ting and Chow Ann have used $5.65 million (US$0.39 million) and $3.5 million (US$0.24 million) of the fund to balance their books of accounts; (7) there is no fixed formula for allocating the funds, among and within the provinces, to reconstruct the houses. The deviations could vary for more than $100,000 (US$6,849) per house. Based on a sample of 40 houses, the audit reveals that 20 of these do not comply with the local government housing regulations (the regulations were not stipulated in the audit report) and (8) a small number of officers make use of this opportunity to apply for the housing loans for themselves and relations. For example, Mr. Lee, the Deputy Provisional Director of Tai Chow Province, filed false reports to claim for seven houses. Out of these, he retained two for his own private uses, three for his relations and the remaining two were sold. Those five that are still in his possessions are now worth $200,000 (US$13,700). As at April 1, 2004 (date of the audit), it was revealed that another officer of the Province, also Mr. Lee, has defaulted the fund of $290,500 (US$20,000).

Case 3: Amount allocated to the HR department in 2004; report dated November 17, 2004: In 2003, the NAO found that the Human Resources Department uses (1) the surplus fund of the previous year to purchase one medium-sized and two-small-sized vehicles amounting to $930,000 (US$63,700). These items were not included in the budget or the actual expenses for the year ended June 30, 2003. This contravenes the "Procedures to prepare for budgets" (Central Government Notification, 2003) that all items purchased be included in the current year's expenses and (2) $4.4893 million (US$0.31 million) to purchase 16 sets of items for the workers' accommodation. This amount is not included or authorized in the 2003 budget, and not in line with the Government's budget policy.

Case 4: Railway department 2003 budget; report dated November 17, 2004: (1) In 2003, the Railway Department submitted its maintenance expenditure budget to the Ministry of Finance (MoF) and the Central Government. The amount submitted to the MoF was $23.88 billon but the amount submitted to the Central Government was $18.26 billion (US$1.25 billion). There is a discrepancy for $5.62 billion (US$0.38 billion). This contravenes with the guidance set out by the MoF on procedures to prepare for the budgets; (2) the budgeted amount submitted to the MoF for $23.88 billion (US$1.64 billion) was approved and allocated, but it was reflected in the books of the Railway Department for $22.16 billion (US$1.52 billion). There is a discrepancy for $1.72 billion (US$0.12 billion); (3) between 2000 and 2003, the Railway Department Management Center, without prior approval of the Central Government, collected advertising and inquiry fees amounting to $41.49 million (US$2.84 million). Because the department is supposed to exercise its social responsibilities and not permitted to collect fees from the private organizations and the general public, this is not in line with the "Trading and collection of inquiry fees (2000)" broachers issued by the MoF and Central Government Central Committee; (4) between 2000 and 2002, the Railway Department Management Center has collected $10.82 million (US$0.74 million) as management fees. The amount was banked in a private bank accounts rather than the account specified by the MoF. This contradicts the "Dealing with construction and supervision fees" broacher issued by the MoF. NAO suggests that the amount should be properly accounted for and banked in the appropriate accounts approved by the MoF and emphasizes that embezzlement is a serious offence; (5) in August 1995, the Railway Department incorporated and invested in Road Ying Limited (in Shan Shee Provision). Till the end of 2002, total investment was $13.23 million representing 75% of the share capital of the company. In May 2003, without approval of the Valuation and Assets Management Department, the Railway Department transferred $95.6 million worth of shares to Lok Tong Transportation Limited. This contravenes the "transfer of state and federal government's assets" notification issued by the Government Assets Management Department; (6) in 2003, The Railway Department outsourced its transportation and managerial administrative functions for $0.12 billion (US$0.82 million). This expenditure is not included in the budget, and thus is not in line with the Federal Government Budgetary Legislation as "all items of income and expenditure should be properly and accurately included in the budget" and (7) in 2003, without prior approval from the MoF or included in the budget, the Railway Department has spent $8.51 million (US$0.58 million) to construct four architectural and designed blocks as part of its premises. In fact, application for constructing these four blocks was rejected in 2002. In view of the Railway Department, it is not supposed to be a commercial entity. The amount spent is not in line with the provisions of the Central Government Budgetary Legislature.

Analysis of the Reports: Audit Independence

The above four cases show that NAO is critical in its approach and content. The opinions are objective, firm, and independent of the addressees. To some extent, the reports offer details of the cases, including the amount and individuals involved. Fraud, embezzlement, and misappropriation of funds are widespread including an evidence of weaknesses in the internal control, lack of accountability, and social responsibilities of the auditees. The NAO has made the reports transparent, and has successfully projected itself as a body that is deemed to be independent of its addresses. This attempts to project its image of objectivity and integrity in discharging its duties of care and opportunity to arouse audit storms. These storms are intended to stimulate the provisional and federal governments to take firm actions to strengthen their systems of internal controls and punish the fraudsters before bad publicity takes place.

Analysis of the Four Reports: Compliance to the Auditing Standards

These cases have shown varying degrees of compliance with the auditing guidelines. For example, in Case number 1 (construction of nine higher educational establishments), the NAO mentioned the audit procedures, discussed the implications of the case, and put forward its recommendations. However, the recommendations were relatively weak and vague; for example, sentences such as in order to ensure future projects for education, developments and proper usage and management of land, secure proper sources of finance, effective and efficient in the utilization of resources. Thus, it is essential that future projects should comply with the legislation stipulated by the Local and Central Governments, and seek advice from the Ministry of Education. Apart from weak recommendations, the report fails to update the readers on the current situation; that is, whether the NAO has satisfied themselves that all the recommendations have been properly followed up and resolved, and funds have been accounted for and rectified satisfactorily, in particular those projects that are being funded by the external sources have the authorities sorted out the appropriate level interest rates for the loans, and whether the tuition fees have been reviewed and revised. The report should not be confined to those findings but should continue with the follow-up results.

For all the four cases, the NAO does not mention how the audits were conducted, and whether the cases reflect misconducts of the individual officers or weaknesses in the internal control of the respective government units.

Cases of this nature arise due to ignorance or intentions of the responsible officers, and presumably, these individuals should be made aware of the needs to comply with the stipulated rules, accountability, ethical behavior, and social responsibilities. Vagueness in the reports could be because the NAO does not intend to smear the reputations of the individual auditees, while maintaining a sign of warnings to all concerned. This process helps firm up the fragile relationships between the NAO and auditees. The NAO wants to maintain its position as being a watchdog while maintaining the Guanxi and networks with the auditees. Once these relationships and trusts have been broken, it takes a long time and efforts to reconstruct it.

All the responses from the addressees were included in the reports, and have met the 90-day deadline. However, the auditees' responses are vague. For example, in Case number 3 (HR Department), the Minister of HR has personally responded to the NAO and agreed to ensure that "the internal control system will be strengthened." This is a positive gesture from the Ministry, but there remains a lack of illustrations of how and when will these be restored. The respondents seem silent on issues relating to embezzlement of funds and any prosecutions have taken place against those fraudsters. Presumably, these issues would be dealt with separately by the authority. All these suggest that the audit techniques and responses should be made clear in the reports. Without these, the purpose of requesting for specific responses may equate to a waste of time and efforts, and the reports look like merely for a formality, but without much authorities.

Limitations

This study is limited to those cases that are posted on the web site. These cases represent a small selection in comparison to the total audit samples and the full reports that have been submitted to the Congress. The web site does not mention the basis and reasons for posting these reports or whether they were subjected to censorships or editorial reviews before posting on line. All these limitations could seriously affect the results of this research.

Conclusion and Direction for Future Research

It is a step forward by the NAO to post the audit reports on its web site. Even though some reports seem to be vague in details, the NAO has made a right decision on exercising and projecting transparency on its audit reporting and findings. Undoubtedly, the NAO intends to show its sense of authority, impartiality, and objectivity to the public and fund providers; however, these reports need to be much more robust, in particular those relating to follow-up responses from the addressees. The addressees seem complying with the deadlines, but the responses remain vague and ambiguous. The results of this research are the initial steps to share the efforts and achievements of the NAO with the outside world, and to understand the audit procedures adopted by the NAO and independence of this organization. Future research could assess the actual contributions of the NAO by mean of questionnaire surveys and face-to-face interviews. Interviews with officers in charge of the audit would be interesting. This process reveals the actual audit techniques adopted in the processes. If surveys were to be conducted, the respondents should not be confined to those within the NAO but to the fund providers and general public. The results will help build the needed expectation gaps between the actual work done by the NAO and those perceived by the general public. The audit cases are also useful references for the curriculum for the institutions of higher education. Educating the next generation on the shameful events could help organizations establish a proper system of control and reduce the level of fraud and embezzlements.

Based on the contents of the audit reports, the NAO seems to project an image of an independent institution. The actions by the NAO have supported the theory; as independence by fact and appearance increase, expectation gap will decrease. However, it would be interesting to assess whether the NAO's performance is linked to the number and gravity of audit findings that it submitted to the Congress in a particular year. Future studies could include an assessment of the correlations, if any, between the fees allocated to the NAO and volumes of its audit findings. The budget allocations could be a sensitive issue, and thus might pose a challenge to researchers interested to pursue this issue in details in the future.

The NAO should post more audit reports to enable longitudinal evaluations on the magnitude and nature of audit findings. All these could improve a stronger accounting and auditing framework and enhance confidence of the existing and potential fund providers. It will be interesting to compare results of this research with other countries, in particular the emerging economies. The pace of change is swift but the Chinese is coping well. It is certainly worthwhile to revisit the progress of the NAO in view of the changing complexity of the auditing environment. As long as auditing is applied and interpreted in a true sense, it remains a useful tool to anyone who has faith in it.

References

American Institute of Certified Public Accountants (AICPA) (1978). *Report, Conclusions, and Recommendations: Commission on Auditors Responsibilities.* New York, NY: American Institute of Certified Public Accountants, Cohen Commission.

American Institute of Certified Public Accountants (AICPA) (1994). *Strengthening the professionalism of the independent auditors.* New York, NY: American Institute of Certified Public Accountants, Kirk Commission.

American Institute of Certified Public Accountants (AICPA) (2001). *Codification of Statements of Auditing Standards.* New York, NY: American Institute of Certified Public Accountants.

Bell, T and J Carcello (2000). A decision aid for assessing the likelihood of fraudulent financial reporting: A European perspective. *Auditing: A Journal of Theory and Practice*, 19(3), 169–184.

Carey, JL and WO Doherty (1996). The concept of independence review and restatement. *Journal of Accountancy*, 38–47.

Carmichael, DR (1999). In search of concepts of auditor independence. *The CPA Journal*, 69(5), 38–43.

Carmichael, DR (2004). The PCAOB and social responsibilities of the independent auditor. *Accounting Horizons*, 127–133.

Chandler, RA and JR Edwards (1996). Recurring issues in auditing: back to future. *Accounting, Auditing and Accountability Journal*, 9(2), 4–29.

Chapman, B (1992). Limited auditors' liability: Economic analysis and the theory of Tort Law. *Canadian Business Law Journal*, 43(4), 281–285.

Chinese Auditing System Research Group & National Audit Office Institute of Auditing Research (1999). *Research on Chinese Auditing System.* Beijing: China: China Auditing Press.

Chong, G (2000). Auditing framework in the People's Republic of China and the international auditing guidelines: Some comparisons. *Managerial Finance Journal*, 26(5), 12–20.

Chong, G (2008). Auditing in China. *Journal of Corporate Accounting and Finance*, 19(6), 49–54.

Chong, G and G Vinten (1998). Harmonization of government audits in the People's Republic of China. *Managerial Auditing Journal*, 13(3), 159–164.

Craig, JL (1997). Preserving auditor independence. *The CPA Journal*, 67(2), 16–22.

DeFond, M, TJ Wong and S Li (2000). The impact of improved auditor independence on audit market concentration in China. *Journal of Accounting and Economics*, 28, 269–305.

Dewing, I and P Russell (2001). Financial reporting accounting issues: The expectation gap. *Accountancy*, 128(8), 94–98.

Epstein, MJ and MA Geiger (1994). Investor views of auditor assurance: Recent evidence of the expectation gap. *Journal of Accountancy*, 60–64.

Farrell, B and J Franco (1998). The changing role of the auditor: An analysis of view points from the auditors' perspective. *The Mid-Atlantic Journal of Business*, 34(2), 101–124.

Firth, M (2002). Auditor provided consultancy services and their associations with audit fees and audit opinions. *Journal of Business Finance and Accounting*, 34(2), 101–124.

Francis, J (1994). Discussion of lawsuits against auditors. *Journal of Accounting Research*, 32 (Suppl.), 95–102.

Geiger, M, D Lowe and K Pany (2002). Outsourced internal audit services and the perception of audit independence. *The CPA Journal*, 72(4), 20–24.

Hao, Z (1999). Regulation and organization of accountants in China. *Accounting, Auditing and Accountability Journal*, 12, 286–302.

Heffes, E (2002). Special report: Impact of the new regulations on corporate America. *Financial Executive*, 18(6), 73–74.

Hussey, R and G Lan (2001). An examination of auditor independence issues from the perspectives of UK finance directors. *Journal of Business Ethics*, 32(2), 169–178.

Jones, R and M Pendlebury (2000). *Public Sector Accounting*, 5th edn. London: Prentice Hall.

Kachelmeier, S (1994). Discussion of an experimental investigation of alternative damage-sharing liability regimes with an auditing perspective. *Journal of Accounting Research*, 32 (Suppl.), 131–139.

Kadous, K (2000). The effects of audit quality and consequences severity on juror evaluation of auditor responsibility for plaintiff losses. *The Accounting Review*, 75(3), 327–341.

Kinney, WR (1999). Auditor independence: A burdensome constraint or core value. *Accounting Horizons*, 13(1), 69–75.

Kinney, WR and MW Nelson (1996). Outcome information and the expectation gap: The case of loss contingencies. *Journal of Accounting Research*, 34(2), 281–297.

Li, J (1998). China's Governmental Auditing System. *International Journal of Government Auditing*, 25(2), 10–12.

Mautz, RK and HA Sharaf (1961). *The Philosophy of Auditing*. Sarasota, FL: American Accounting Association, Monograph No. 6.

Mayhew, B and J Pike (2004). Does investor selection of auditors enhance auditor independence? *The Accounting Review*, 79, 797–822.

McEnroe, JE and SC Martens (2001). Auditors' and investors' perceptions of the 'expectation gap'. *Accounting Horizons*, 15(4), 345–358.

Melancon, B (2000). The proposed SEC rule on auditor independence and its consequences. *Journal of Accountancy*, 26–28.

Munter, P and TA Ratcliffe (1998). Auditor's responsibility for detection of frauds. *The National Public Accountants*, 43(7), 26–28.

Palmore, Z (1988). An analysis of auditor litigation and audit service quality. *The Accounting Review*, 63(1), 55–73.

Power, M (1998). Auditor liability in context. *Accounting, Organizations and Society*, 23(1), 77–79.

Qin, R (1994). *On accountability*. Dalian: China, Northeastern University of Finance and Economics Press.

Reinstein, A and GA Coursen (1999). Considering the risk of fraud: Understanding the auditors' new requirements. *The National Public Accountants*, 34–38.

Shockley, RA (1981). Perceptions of auditors' independence: An empirical analysis. *The Accounting Review*, 4, 785–800.

Shou, W and SC Yam (1987). Audit profile: People's Republic of China. *International Journal of Government Auditing*, 14(4), 11–12.

Sikka, P, A Puxty, H Willmott, and C Cooper (1992). *Eliminating the Expectation Gap*. London, UK: Association of Chartered Certified Accountants.

Sikka, P, A Puxty, H Willmott and C Cooper (1998). The impossibility of eliminating the expectation gap: Some theory and evidence. *Critical Perspectives on Accounting*, 9, 299–330.

Stephens, L and RG Schwartz (2006). The chilling effect of Sarbanes-Oxley: Myth or reality? *CPA Journal*, 14–18.

Sutton, MH (1997). Auditor independence: The challenge of fact and appearance. *Accounting Horizons*, 11(2), 86–91.

Swanger, SL and EG Chewning (2001). The effect of internal audit outsourcing on financial analysts' perceptions of external auditor independence. *Auditing: A Journal of Practice & Theory*, 20(2), 115–129.

Tidewell, GL and AL Abrams (1996). Auditor's liability and responsibility in finding fraud. *Business and Economic Review*, 42(2), 28–32.

U.S. General Accounting Office (GAO) (2002). *Government Auditing Standards*. Washington, DC: U.S. General Accounting Office.

Wang, JCF (2001). *Contemporary Chinese Politics: An Introduction*, 7th ed., Beijing: China: Prentice Hall.

Whittington, OR and K Pany (2001). *Principles of Auditing*, 13th ed., New York, NY: McGraw Hill.

Xiang, J (2002). *Research on the Legal System of Government Auditing*. Beijing, China: China Modern Economy Press.

Xiao, JZ, Y Zhang and Z Xie (2000). The making of independent auditing standards in China. *Accounting Horizons*, 13, 69–89.

Yan, J (1989). The nature and functions of auditing. *Shanxi Auditing*, 3, 6–11.

Yang, S (1989). The modernization of the Chinese auditing. *The Communication of Accounting and Finance*, 2, 3–8.

Yang, S, J Xiao and M Pendlebury (2008). Government auditing in China: Problems and reform. *Advances in Accounting, Incorporating Advances in International Accounting*, 24, 119–127.

Yost, JA (1995). Auditor independence as a unique equilibrium response. *Journal of Accounting, Auditing and Finance*, 10(1), 81–103.

Zhang, J (1996). *A Study of the Basic Structure of Modern Auditing*. Guangzhou, Guangdong: Guangdong Higher Education Press.

Part II

COMMONWEALTH
OF
INDEPENDENT STATES

Chapter 7

CSR IN THE EMERGING MARKET OF RUSSIA: FINDING THE NEXUS BETWEEN BUSINESS ACCOUNTABILITY, LEGITIMACY, GROWTH AND SOCIETAL RECONCILIATION

OLGA KUZNETSOVA

Abstract

In the full-fledged market economies, it is competition and institutional constraints that create incentives and conditions propitious for various business practices to thrive. But how do such practices develop in evolving markets of which weak institutional environments is a typical feature? This question is central to this chapter, which explores corporate social responsibility as business practice within the context of market transformation in Russia. It introduces historic circumstances surrounding the development of CSR in the emerging market economy, outlines particularities of CSR in the country and its potential to contribute to the socio-economic development.

Introduction

In the past years, corporate social responsibility (CSR) has transformed from a sporadic activity of an altruistic nature of individual charity-minded firms into a business practice increasingly regarded as the core element of modern strategic management. More and more firms see long-term value in developing and projecting a caring image that is critical to the building up of an organization's reputation (Burke and Logsdon, 1996; Key and Popkin, 1998;

Lantos, 2001; McWilliams *et al.*, 2006). There is a growing trend among academics and practitioners to acknowledge CSR as a strategic function tied to general organizational goals such as profitability or strengthening intangible assets. This attitude is motivated by the realization that creating a caring public image is necessary for modern corporations to safeguard some space for the freedom of business action in the pursuit of profit.

In a nutshell, modern CSR is characterized by three major trends (Nelson, 2004): (1) for leading companies, CSR is moving from the corporate margins to the mainstream, to cover not only philanthropy, but rather how a company manages the totality of its impacts on and contributions to society; (2) CSR is moving to greater accountability and transparency to more stakeholders through various forms of stakeholder engagement that include, but go beyond public reporting and (3) corporations leaders in CSR are moving from a compliance-based mindset to asserting CSR as one of their major values.

This implies that although it is not impossible for firms to engage in CSR on largely moral or ethical grounds, modern firms get involved in CSR on an increasing scale because of the business advantages that this practice can offer in the current social climate. This "enlightened self-interest" explanation of CSR has become popular in managerial literature (Mitchell, 1989; Jones, 1995; Mahoney, 1997; Lawrence *et al.*, 2005).

CSR is not just a product of corporate strategists. Societal expectations are a major factor contributing to its development. Corporations have proved themselves as the best wealth-creation machines and modern Western society wants them to continue with their mission: the maximization of profit within the rules set up by a legitimate authority. There are, however, numerous examples of the misuse of corporate power when the narrow interests of corporations, or even influential groupings inside the corporations, are placed ahead of societal interests. It has been the feature of recent years though that such behavior is treated as less and less appropriate. As never before, businesses face the pressure to recognize their role as an agent for the creation of general good for society. There is an increasing support to the claim that corporations should contribute to economic growth that makes possible sustainable, equitable, and democratic development (Stiglitz, 1999; Nellis, 1999; Fox and Heller, 1999). According to Heal (2005), the contribution of CSR to economic performance is that it helps the market to align corporate profits and social costs. In other words, there is a growing appreciation of the social consequences of the activities of the economic agents. There is also an understanding that lasting social change needs a combination of solid governmental support and committed corporate action (Vogel, 2005).

In transitional economies, economic growth is a key issue. However, the rate of growth is not all that matters: modern literature makes a distinction between different qualities of growth depending on the social system of production. The modern system of production involves cooperative structures that build up trust in social organizations among the actors (Sabel and Zeitlin, 1997; Hollingsworth and Boyer, 1997). Such a system has CSR as an integral part, in as much as caring relations are paramount for developing trust. Many transition economies, in particular those developing in post-communist countries, show the signs of low social trust in the conditions of a deficit of manifested concern for public needs both on the side of the state and business. Available provision of social resources is often not sufficient; a modern social safety net is almost nonexistent. This creates disillusionment and tension within the society. The demonstration effect of CSR could help to mend this attitude. CSR also builds up the legitimacy of big business with stakeholders: as literature suggests (Frye, 2006), the private provision of some public goods may increase the legitimacy of capitalism in the eyes of the population and improve economic performance. CSR also increases the legitimacy of big business with the state because socially responsible behavior is normally interpreted by the state as a sign of competence (Gabarro, 1978).

The dynamics of relations between business and society is reflected through various elements of corporate performance that change over time and the practice of CSR is among them. The spread and variety of CSR practices has become wider, their content richer and more flexible. This suggests that there exists a "market for virtue": incentives and conditions propitious for these practices to thrive. In the full-fledged market economy, such conditions are created by the institutional constraints and competition. But, how do business practices develop in emerging markets, in which a weak institutional environment is a typical feature? This question is central to this chapter. It will, first, introduce the historic circumstances that surround the development of CSR practices and demand for them in an emerging market economy, using Russia as a case study. Second, it will outline specific characteristics of CSR in two different groups of Russian companies: the so-called big business, representing "blue-chips" which are well exposed to the scrutiny of the international markets; and large to medium firms that represent the core of the corporate sector in the country, but are not subject to international scrutiny.

Conceptual Framework

CSR is addressed by many disciplines, which bring about a vast number of descriptions and definitions (for overview see Vogel, 2005; Lockett *et al.*, 2006; McWilliams *et al.*, 2006; Blowfield and Murray, 2008). As a result, the necessary point of departure for any CSR-related analysis is to establish its conceptual framework. In her approach to CSR, this author follows a tradition in the literature (McGuire, 1963; Davis, 1973; Carroll, 1979; McWilliams and Siegel 2001; Waldman *et al.*, 2006) that defines CSR as a set of business practices where the firm intentionally goes beyond compliance with the requirements of the law for the benefit of some social or environmental good. Evidently, this definition has its advantages and disadvantages. On the one hand, it focuses attention on what are the essential qualities that distinguish the pursuit of CSR from any other business functions. Rather than describing the social performance of corporations, it provides meaningful criteria for delineating CSR actions: they should be voluntary; they should go beyond existing statutory norms, and they should be beneficial for society. On the other hand, this definition is far from being exhaustive. It leaves the exact position of the dividing line between a CSR and non-CSR activity open for interpretation because it does not fully account for country-specific conditions. In a way, this definition is skewed toward the realities of the developed market economies and may create ambiguity when applied to emerging markets. The reason is that this formula implicitly assumes that public law is fully operational and therefore complying with the law is a necessary requirement that cannot constitute for corporations an act of voluntarily accepted social responsibility. And yet there are countries in the world, some transition and developing countries in particular, where the rule of law is weak and the public regulations are basic. Thus, a case can be made that even when an international company, operating in such an environment, exceeds the requirements of the law this may still not be enough to constitute the act of CSR because her action falls well within the realm of minimal expected norms of behavior in her home country. As Fülöp *et al.* (2000) note, in Hungary, where CSR is a new concept, the understanding of CSR differs from industry to industry and from enterprise to enterprise. Some companies choose to define their social responsibility with respect to the law, some — on a much broader basis; still other show no concern toward public opinion at all. In the countries where the tools, procedures, and structures for CSR have not been established, it is not impossible to dress up as CSR various activities of no strategic importance, such as a routine philanthropy. Thus, a report on Bulgaria concludes that businesses in the country engage in responsible social practices and giving mostly due to emotional reasons and personal pride (Iankova, 2008).

A different but relevant set of conceptual complications emerges from a well-documented fact that many legal norms are vague. This may result in a discrepancy between the letter and the spirit of the law. Indeed, from a formal point of view, acting in accordance with the letter of the relevant regulations is outside the domain of CSR, but what about obeying the spirit of the law? It might well be the case that in order to comply with the latter the firm may need to go beyond statutory requirements, but whether this would represent the act of CSR is open to discussion.

The chosen working definition of CSR, however, provides a good pointer as to where the motivation for CSR comes from. It implies that the corporation has not only economic and legal obligations formalized in laws, regulations, statutes and norms, but also certain responsibilities to the society that extend beyond these normative obligations. In other words, CSR suggests the existence of an implicit social contract in which business is accountable to society's expectations or demands. In this sense, CSR is an instrument which makes company performance meaningful in the eyes of society as it contributes to the development and growth.

Background to CSR in Russia

The importance of the Soviet legacy cannot be overestimated as a path-defining influence that has affected the establishment of CSR practices in all European post-communist countries, but in Russia in particular. During the Soviet period, it was taken for granted that companies would offer social and community benefits to the citizens going well beyond their operational brief. It was common that state-owned enterprises provided health services, recreational facilities, child care, heating and water supply and so on not only to their employees and their households, but also to the local communities. Some of these were available free of charge or on a subsidized basis. As a matter of fact, for many in modern Russia the lowering of the living standards in the post-communist period is related to the inability or reluctance of many industrial enterprises to continue providing social services that once were customary.

Despite an extensive involvement of enterprises in the supply of social services, it is important to realize that this was not corporate social responsibility as understood in the West. To begin with, the element of goodwill was mostly missing as enterprises were forced by the state, who owned them, to deliver these services. The state acted as a topmost manager that assumed responsibilities over defining and protecting the interest of the public and balancing social costs and benefits. The public, however, despite the official rhetoric, was deprived of the means of control over the state, as the state and the party bureaucracy had succeeded in erecting insurmountable barrier between themselves and the people. Consequently, despite its official doctrine, the communist state had never come about to prioritize social and welfare objectives in practical terms. The structure of the economy was such that relatively few resources were made available for the production of services and consumer goods. Instead, resources were deliberately concentrated in heavy industry and military sectors. In turn, state-owned enterprises were expected to cover the shortage of public provisions as many social functions were transferred to the enterprise level, cultivating paternalism in relations between the enterprise and internal and external stakeholders. This system was not flexible, as the allocation of recourses was pre-planned. Nor was it fair: some enterprises belonged to more powerful ministries or had more clout with planning authorities than other and could allocate more resources toward the social sphere. This was yet another cause of inequality in the allegedly egalitarian society.

The socialist legacy has a number of implications for the modern Russian corporate sector. First, many newly privatized firms had found themselves stuck with non-profile assets, which they needed to take care of. Second, when they tried to reduce their engagement in social services, it became clear in many cases that neither the state agencies nor the markets were ready to take over. Among other things, this situation was bound to have, at least initially, an unfavorable impact on the cost of labor, thus aggravating an uneasy economic situation even further. Finally, by distancing themselves from the implementation of certain functions, which the public was accustomed to associate with local enterprises, Russian corporations have created tensions in their relations with many categories of stakeholders. This latter complication was exaggerated by the crisis of public confidence faced by corporations following the biased nature of the Russian model of privatization.

CSR and the legacy of privatization

The circumstances under which corporate ownership came into existence in modern Russia are critical for understanding the situation with CSR in the country. The corporate sector emerged as an outcome of the mass-privatization program of the early 1990s, which had as its side effects a profound disappointment on the part of the vast strata of population, unchecked corruption, and widespread poverty. This program has transferred enterprises previously owned by the state into joint-stock companies by handing out the major part of shares to insiders (workers and managers). Using to own advantage their privileged position within privatized enterprises, the managers were soon able to take full control over privatized firms (Kuznetsov *et al.*, 2008). In the mid-1990s, during the second stage of privatization, the most lucrative enterprises were sold by the state at nominal prices to a selected group of bankers with close personal links to the government of the day, creating the small clique of fabulously rich Russian oligarchs (for details see Yelkina, 2003). Not surprisingly, the way privatization was implemented undermined the legitimacy of private property in the eyes of many Russians. As Miller and Tenev (2007, p. 568) aptly put it, in Russia "privatisation was a wasteful process associated with stealing of state assets and consequently with lack of legitimacy of newly established property rights."

A poll of Russian citizens as late as 2006 revealed that 52% of the respondents wanted the majority of private assets in the country to be nationalized (CEFIR, 2007).[1] These data indicate that the societal acceptance of the market system is still an issue in Russia as corporations have difficulty acquiring the necessary status of legitimacy and respectability with the society at large (Table 7.1).

Table 7.1. The views of Russians on economy and business.

	The share of respondents supporting the statement (%)			
	2003	2004	2005	2006
The results of privatization should be revised (fully or in part)	77	78	77	72
The actions of Russian business tycoons are detrimental to the interests of Russia	49	53	49	44
My attitude toward the people who made fortune in the last 10–15 years is anger, contempt, and hate	28	33	28	29

Source: Compiled from Levada-Centre "Obschestvennoje mnenije (2004). Privatizatsija, vlast' i bizness" (Public Opinion in 2004: Privatisation, Authorities and Business) and "Obschestvennoje mnenije 2006: Privatizatsija, vlast' i bizness" (Public Opinion in 2006: Privatisation, Authorities and Business); http://www.levada.ru/sborniki.html [15 December 2007].

---

[1] This result is not dissimilar from data obtained in other transition economies. A representative survey of citizens in 28 post-communist countries in 2006 found that over 80% of the respondents would like to revise current privatization in some way (EBRD, 2007a,b).

The implementation of privatization program in Russia had multiple consequences at different levels. The most important of them from the point of view of the development of CSR can be summarized as follows: (1) a corporate sector was established in the country, creating opportunities for the development of new business practices; (2) two distinct groups of companies, in terms of their prominence and economic potential, emerged. The first group includes big, assets-rich companies operating in profitable sectors with a proven potential of attracting domestic and foreign investors and propensity to internationalization. In terms of ownership, these companies are closely held by small groups of individuals with controlling power and involve complex cross holding. The second group consists of companies, operating predominantly on the domestic markets. They are usually less profitable than the first group and require restructuring in order to stay afloat or grow. These companies have little potential for internationalization and limited ability to compete internationally. Their shares are not actively traded on the financial markets. This distinction between two groups of enterprises is important from the point of view of the development of the new business patterns and practices in post-communist Russia. As we show later, these two groups of companies have quite a different attitude to the philosophy and practice of social responsibility; (3) newly privatized enterprises have inherited social assets but lost the incentives to remain the providers of public services. In the absence of a social safety net, this naturally created hostility between the population and business and distrust with the authorities that could not compensate for the loss of security and benefits; (4) the state also has acquired the status of a prominent shareholder in some lucrative sectors, such as oil and gas. But it has been slow to use its wealth to enhance the provision of public goods; (5) because of the deterioration of the quality of life of the majority of population and the perceived injustice of privatization, both the state and business have seen their public legitimacy decreasing. As the initial turbulent stages of post-communist transition were over, these two parties have recognized the importance of restoring public trust and started to pay more attention to addressing societal expectation.

Ownership transformation coincided with a period of a profound economic crisis in the country, which further contributed to the corporate legitimacy crisis. Market competition was extremely depressed. At the same time, the atmosphere was charged with the sensation of abounding opportunities for quick and easy enrichment. A direct outcome of these ambiguous circumstances was the disregard of many commonly recognized behavioral rules designed to induce collaborative conduct in the modern society. The moral standards of business deteriorated and the criminalization of economy intensified. Further complications were caused by the fact that, throughout the post-privatization period, shareholding did not bring any real benefits to most of the shareholders as shares had low liquidity and dividends were not paid. On top of that, the capital market was not functioning well. As a result, shareholders-insiders were motivated by their interests as stakeholders-employees, such as maintaining the viability of their organizations and the levels of employment, rather than the optimization of company performance.

The role of the state

Summing up, it can be argued that privatization has created both the supply side and demand side conditions for the emergence of CSR as a form of business practice in modern Russia. Since CSR involves business–society relations, the demand for and the forms of CSR are formed by the interaction of the society and corporations. In post-communist countries, the civil society and the relevant institutions and infrastructures are still under construction (Blanchard and Kremer, 1997; Black *et al.*, 1999; Buck, 2003; Kuznetsov and Kuznetsova, 2003). Consequently, their ability of putting pressure on corporations is relatively weak. A similar situation is with the pressures coming from the market and competition: both are not fully functional yet. These circumstances have allowed the state and state bureaucracy to acquire a far more active economic role than it is usual in a market economy. In fact, it was the state which initiated the public discourse on responsible corporations when in 2003 the president of the country set poverty elimination through economic growth as a priority of the national economic policy and "invited" corporations to make a major contribution to its execution.

The state has been emphasizing the social agenda as a means of achieving some cohesion in a much-divided society. In this context, the interest that the authorities showed in CSR acted as an impetus that in Western countries would normally come from non-governmental organizations, lobbying groups, stockholders, and other. The authorities have made it very clear that they expected Russian business to accept the ideology of CSR and, furthermore, to take part in implementing social programs. At the Congress of the Russian Union of Industrialists and Entrepreneurs (CRUIE) in 2004, the Russian president emphasized once again the importance of the social responsibility of Russian businesses (*RIA Novosti*, 2004). He also noted that the state expected Russian businesses to increase their investments in social projects, science, education, and the development of the so-called "human factor" and that the authorities planed to create the necessary legislative base for partnerships between the state and private businesses. Russian experts summarized these demands in a rather cynical manner: "…companies should invest where the state needs are" (Litovchenko and Korsakov, 2003, p. 62).

On the face of it, state-forced CSR does not meet the requirements of the conceptual framework for CSR outlined earlier on because the freewill component is missing. In fact, the Russian example highlights the thesis that there can be no theory of CSR equally valid for developed and emerging economies. The weakness of institutions in the latter, including the state, implies that complying with the law cannot be taken for granted. Characteristically, in his 2004 address to the CRUIE Russian president, when talking about CSR, was actually urging the business community to pay regular taxes timely and in full. This interpretation of CSR is also unusual in terms of how CSR is described in the West, where the state is normally efficient enough to assure tax collection without relying on the benevolence of the taxpayers. Therefore, because of the low efficiency of the state, in countries like Russia even explicit governmental pressure does not signify that corporations have no choice but to become socially responsible. Ironically, it can be argued, that in a sense, in a weak institutional environment firms have a greater variety of activities, which they can undertake to demonstrate a socially responsible behavior.

The response of Russian firms to the state interference is quite similar to that predicted by the "enlightened self-interest" argument, developed by Western academics. State interventionism encourages Russian companies to seek ways to safeguard some freedom of action in the pursuit of profit. Increasing legitimacy with the state and society is one possible response because greater legitimacy gives the firm assurance that what it does is desirable and proper within the existing system of social norms, values, believes, and definitions. Because the "primal sin of privatization" is still an issue in Russia, "companies are prepared for any form of social responsibility as long as their property is protected" (Denisov and Sitnina, 2005). Firms are also interested in good public image as protection against what Shleifer and Vishny (1999) called the "grabbing hand" of state bureaucracy: the state officials in emerging economies demonstrate a tendency to generate excessive regulations to increase their income through bribes.

Research suggests that if society wants corporate decisions to reflect something more•than just what is best for shareholders, it has to rely on government to define a corporation's responsibilities to society through institution building, "laws and regulations" (Reich, 1998). In this respect, the attempts of the Russian state to focus the attention of corporations on CSR represent a positive development. But the Russian state itself goes through a transitional period. Its relations with other social actors are not straightforward. It does not enjoy much authority in the eyes of public as is evident from

Table 7.2. "Who has power in Russia?" (agency for regional political surveys: survey results, August 2003).

Lawmakers	4%
Big business and oligarchs	37%
Organized crime	19%
President of Russia	15%

Source: Vedomosti, No 153, 27 August 2003.

Table 7.2. Also, there are serious reservations regarding the effects of the state becoming more involved in the development of the institutional framework because of the dangers of the alleged "state capture," a process characterized by oligarchs and selected firms gaining the ability to manipulate policy information and even form upcoming regulations and norms to their own advantage by providing illicit private rewards to public officials (Hellman *et al.*, 2000a,b; Hellman and Schankerman, 2000). As a result, there is a considerable degree of mutual suspicion between the people, big business, and the state in Russia. The people see the so-called oligarchs as usurpers of public wealth and politicians as their accomplices. In turn, politicians are weary of oligarchs' political aspirations while the latter fear state interventionism. When the government tries to fight economic crime, this causes suspicion that they are picking on political opponents; when big business starts to spend money on charitable actions politicians suspect that oligarchs seek to create an alternative political power base. Paternalistic tradition and spread of poverty in the Russian society govern people to expect the state to continue as a provider of public goods and social safety net but the state has neither the infrastructure nor the recourses for such involvement. This all put the state in a position where it needed to regain and confirm its legitimacy in the eyes of the population as much as big business does.

The Specifics of CSR in Russia

It was suggested in the previous sections that the motivation of Russian firms in respect to CSR is very much related to their legitimization agenda. This agenda, however, as pursued by the "blue ship" companies differ from that of other companies. Much depends on the public "visibility" of the firm, its relations with the state, and its aspirations to attract foreign investors. Some corporations, like *Gazprom*, *Norilsk Nickel*, *Russian Aluminium* (*Rusal*) are among the largest firms the world. They are of strategic importance to the national economy and the worlds markets in certain products and, consequently, operate under constant scrutiny at the national and international levels. The majority of firms, however, operate outside the limelight of public attention. The pressure on them to correlate their behavior with societal expectations is lower. Not much is known about CSR commitment of this group of firms, as the level of information transparency in Russia in general is typically very low (*Informatsionnaja otkrytost' sotsialnoj politiki rossijskikh kompanij*, 2004). Companies might hide CSR-related information because it may provoke unhealthy attention from a variety of parties, ranging from self-interested bureaucrats to criminals. The following section discusses the difference in response to CSR demands by these two distinct types of Russian companies.

The case of "strategic" companies

In the last five years, the Russian government has sought to re-build its authority over corporations that control strategic assets to reassure the public that it will make these businesses more mindful of public welfare and strategic policy reasons in view of Russia's international relations. The consequence is that the state attempts to take the initiative of promoting CSR on its own terms. Authorities favor an interpretation of CSR that emphasizes the payment of taxes, job creation or the responsibility of firms over social issues that are traditionally covered by the state. Charity is also encouraged. In 2004, the Russian Minister of Finance officially defined CSR as the direct payment of all taxes (as opposed to through offshore subsidiaries), charity, and, finally, support for political forces interested in the development of the country, a euphemism for political loyalty (*RIA Novosti*, 2004). The efforts of the state are focused on large strategic corporations, which are called upon to put in place CSR policies and become more transparent and accountable to the public and international investors and thus contribute to improving the legitimacy of both the state and these strategic corporations. In this respect, the adoption of Western rhetoric and conceptions of CSR is an important part of this political strategy and is an example of institutional isomorphism.

Other factors are also at work. The largest of Russian firms are seeking listing on international stock markets. They are concerned that international investors may be skeptical about their performance, and the price of their stock may be discounted as a result as non-financial risks are becoming increasingly important for investors. In order to be accepted outside the country, Russian companies have no options but to play according to the international rules of transparency and accountability. At the moment, the lack of transparency is one of the most problematic areas as far as big business in post-communist countries is concerned. In a recent survey, 86% of the respondents from Hungary, the Czech Republic, Ukraine, Poland, and Russia were of the opinion that for stakeholders it was simply not possible to establish the CSR credentials of the big businesses (Litovchenko and Korsakov, 2003). But a better CSR record is an obvious choice for firms looking to improve their position in international financial markets because such records are seen by investors as reduced risks of internal and external social conflicts and environmental sanctions. Characteristically, when the world's biggest aluminum producer *Rusal* started preparation for listing abroad it commissioned a report to compare its corporate responsibility with that of its international peers. Overall, however, according to the CSR Russian Centre, only 40 Russian companies reported on corporate responsibility matters in 2007 (Ethical Corporation, 2008). Of these, 15 reported on corporate responsibility as a separate section in their annual reports; 18 produced social reports; eight reported on sustainable development and four issued separate environmental reports. Some of these documents were prepared in accordance with internationally accepted standards. This could be interpreted as an indication that commitment to CSR as expressed by the firm in Russian conditions is still a product for export rather than a response to internal demand. Not surprisingly, 46% of the Russian citizens deny the business (including international companies) an ability to improve social parameters of their life (*Narod ne ustajot zhdat' kogda gosudarstvo ego nakormit, napoji i deneg dast,* 2003, p. 27).

This may change, however, if the giants of the Russian corporate sector followed the example of Unified Energy System (UES) of Russia, the company that produces 70% of electricity nationwide. For the first time in 2006, the company announced that the ecological component was to become an integral part of its general business concept and made public an account on sustainable development using the brand new third-generation standard GRI-G3. Some experts see this as a critical breakthrough, opening a new stage in the business practices of large Russian corporations (Kostin, 2007).

Skepticism Prevails

Most firms in Russia do not belong to the exclusive club of blue chip stock. They are medium-to-large enterprises, employing between 300 and 5000 workers (*Obzor zanyatosti v Rossii,* 2002, p. 64) They enjoy no exclusivity or any special relations with the state but remain the backbone of the national economy. Yet, preciously little is known about their stance in regard to CSR.

Some light on their position in respect to CSR was thrown by the survey of executive managers of 129 Russian corporations, organized in November 2004 by a group of British academics of which this author was a member. It revealed that almost half of the respondents believed that the conditions were not yet right for their firms to take on more social responsibility. Lack of financial resources was indicated as a major constraint. Managers also blamed the state and the legal system for not providing enough incentives (20% and 24% of the respondents, respectively) The majority of companies reported that they could not afford any degree of transparency, partly because of the inconsistency and ambiguity of the fiscal system. Interestingly, 14.5% of the respondents stated "not enough interest on the part of stakeholders" as a hindrance to enhanced CSR.

The frequency analysis of responses reveals the following picture. First, a considerable number of Russian managers do not regard CSR as topical in modern Russia. As many as 39.53% of the respondents answered negatively to the question "Do you agree that the idea of CSR is consistent with the current socio-economic conditions in Russia?" There is also a belief among managers that for many firms CSR is a slogan rather than a strategy. Two-thirds of the respondents supported the following statement: "In most cases declarations by firms that they adhere to the principles of corporate social responsibility are in fact purely public relation exercises," whilst only 15.65% disagreed.

Among the characteristics that are attributed to the CSR practices by this group of companies, some features are cited more frequently (Table 7.3).

Table 7.3. Characteristics of CSR as perceived by Russian managers.

Rank	Characteristic	Frequency
1	Looking after employees	0.904
2	Protecting the environment	0.760
3	Paying taxes	0.704
4	Being ethical with the stakeholders	0.632
5	Creating jobs	0.608
6	Contributing to charities	0.584
7	Contributing to the welfare of the local community	0.576
8	Obeying laws	0.576
9	Making a profit	0.395
10	Adhering to international standards of ethical business conduct	0.296

Strictly speaking several of them (paying taxes, creating employment, and abiding by the law) should not be there according to the recognized definition of CSR as "activity that goes beyond standard legal requirements and contracts."

Russian managers do not see CSR performance as an important influence determining the public image of the firm; instead financial results are assigned the greatest impact (Table 7.4).

Furthermore, respondents do not believe that active involvement in CSR will result in more freedom from the state: only 6.20% of the respondents think that socially responsible corporate performance will reduce regulatory oversight.

Two results of the survey stand out with particular prominence. First, firms appear to embrace the policies of CSR as a means of legitimization much less willingly than might be expected on the basis of accepted theory. Second, the interpretation of CSR by Russian managers differs in many respects from the Western rhetoric and conceptions of CSR. These responses may be explained by the specific institutional context of the transitional period in the socioeconomic development of Russia. If institutions are firmly in place, they provide the procedures and routines that allow for the resolution of economic conflict and thus offer a solid and cost-effective foundation for market transactions. Under these circumstances, a business has to operate according to accepted norms and this is not regarded as something worthy of special praise. Consequently, activities aimed at increasing legitimacy require proof of an extra effort on the part of the firm that goes beyond statutory requirements and demonstrates its recognition of and commitment to certain social expectations. From this point of view, the popular choices of CSR

Table 7.4. Characteristics of the firm that have the greatest impact on its public image as perceived by Russian managers (1-minimal impact; 5-maximum impact).

Rank	Characteristic	Mean	n
1	Financial results	4.26	121
2	The reputation of the firm	4.26	112
3	The reputation of the brand	4.05	111
4	Identification and pursuit of opportunities	3.95	109
5	The competence of managers	3.89	115
6	Business ethics	3.69	110
7	Labor practices	2.75	116

activity from the study's respondents, such as paying taxes and abiding by the law, look distinctly out of line. They, however, fit well into the picture drawn in the literature that presents Russia as the country with a weak institutional environment, in which laws are abused, rules are either feeble or not enforced, and institutions are incomplete, tendentious, and corrupt (Blanchard and Kremer, 1997; Black *et al.*, 1999; Buck, 2003; Kuznetsov and Kuznetsova, 2003). In this context, CSR is likely to acquire new dimensions compared to a standard Western interpretation.

A recent report on the role of business in the national development in Russia (Managers Association, 2006) that reflects the opinions of analysts and businessmen allows comparing normative approach with the real practical involvement of business. As reported, ideally, business would like to make impacts on the quality of life of the population, development of the economic infrastructure, human factors and capital, private initiative, innovation, globalization, development of the markets and market values, management practices, and culture. What it does in reality goes not much beyond the fundamental purpose of the business. The report cites the provision of employment, improvement of the output quality, creation of value added, fulfillment of the fiscal responsibilities as the parameters that scored high on the scale of CSR related achievements.

Our survey failed to support the proposition on the perceived relationship between CSR activity and the legitimization of large and medium business. On the one hand, 52% of the respondents demonstrated awareness of the fact that the society had certain yet unfulfilled expectations vis-à-vis their firms. On the other hand, they put little value on CSR as both a means to increase the prestige of the firm in the eyes of the public and as an opportunity to earn some freedom of action from the state. This does not mean that these firms do not need to make a legitimization effort. For them, it takes on a different form which reflects their current priorities and that pubic opinion is more tolerant to this group of companies (Table 7.5).

The respondents to our survey have been asked to evaluate the importance of "showing responsibility to society at large." Figure 7.1 shows distribution of the spread of opinions regarding this parameter (the mean of 3.16). This is most likely to happen either when the respondents are unsure about the meaning of the question or there is no prevailing view on the issue, or both. In any case, this pattern of distribution may be interpreted as a sign that managers participating in our survey did not see the development of a policy on CSR as a priority.

Medium to large enterprises in Russia, as the analysis suggests, have not adopted CSR practice as a part of their day-to-day operations and thus are

Table 7.5. Is the activity of (a) and (b) in Russia beneficial or harmful at present? (%).

	(a) Big enterprises	(b) Medium enterprises
Definitely beneficial	9	12
More likely beneficial	34	51
More likely harmful	32	17
Definitely harmful	12	6
No answer	13	14

Source: Opinion survey by Levada Centre (13 September 2006); http://www. levada.ru./prerss/2006091302.html (accessed December 15, 2007).

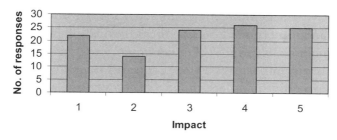

Figure 7.1. The impact of "showing responsibility to society at large" on the public perception of the firm (1-minimal impact; 5-maximum impact).

not accountable to the majority of stakeholders. When the state took the initiative of promoting CSR on its own terms it focused on big strategic corporations. The citizens, on their side, have no means to impose any pressure on the companies. What is more, the society is still confused about what to expect from business. Business environment in Russia not only unable to put any competitive pressures on companies in respect to CSR; it makes it even dangerous for the companies to show any signs of successful performance. It is not surprising for a country, where businesses nominate the quality of produced goods as the main facet of their socially responsible behavior (Managers Association, 2006, p. 18). One probable explanation of the evidence that Russian managers appear to attach less importance to some elements of CSR that are traditionally high on the agenda of Western corporations is that the legitimacy issue in the Russian context has a different focus. Opinion polls demonstrate that the Russian public tends to deny business people such virtues as morality, integrity, talent, or hard work. Instead, many Russians regard dishonesty and connections as the keys for business success in their country (Kuznetsov and Kuznetsova, 2005). In turn, it is not uncommon for members of the business community to maintain that the current economic and institutional set-up in the country precludes honest ways of making money (Latynina, 1999; Managers Association, 2004a). In contrast to other countries, in Russia there is a considerable degree of ambiguity regarding some most fundamental issues including ownership rights, the role of contract, the concept of legality, the notion of business ethics, contributing to the unpopular image of the entrepreneur and businessman. This suggests that the legitimacy challenge for Russian business outside of the largest strategic corporations is very much in establishing a consensus where business can be seen as conducting honorable and acceptable activity that will command respect and support from the wider society. In any case, by not engaging in CSR practices, medium and large enterprises remain insulated from the society, which inadvertently impedes their own contribution to the development and growth.

Conclusion

The attitude to CSR on the part of the Russian medium and large companies contradicts the picture that the government seeks to create: the growth of CSR is a priority for both politicians and corporations. One explanation is that usually CSR in Russia is discussed in relation to the handful of super large firms, operating in lucrative industries. By contrast, our respondents represented the hard core of industrial firms that enjoy no exclusivity. Their attitude signals that the link between CSR, trust, and economic growth as a way out of poverty is not fully recognized in Russia.

Deficit of CSR in Russia should not come as a surprise if looked at through the "strategic approach" lenses. If a strategy does not bring performance or competitive advantages, then we cannot expect that it will be implemented by the company. From this perspective, the near absence of CSR initiatives from the managerial practices in modern Russia is not surprising. Moreover, in a sense it can be seen as an encouraging sign indicating that firms are now tuned up with the market signals and tend to abandon or disregard practices that do not bring adequate rewards even if there is a non-economic pressure to do otherwise. This is a welcome departure from the model of thinking and operating that prevailed during the period of central planning.

Another explanation of the slow take off of CSR in a transitional economy like Russia may be related to the newness of the CSR concept. Many manages are not well informed about CSR, the current academic debate and existing practices or the possible benefits associated with CSR activities.

There are not many training opportunities either. Managers who responded to the surveys conducted by the Managers Association strongly held the opinion that CSR-related information available from various sources was not sufficient. Only few mentioned education establishments were there as providers of relevant knowledge (Litovchenko and Korsakov, 2003). The same respondents indicated that information sources are not decidedly trustworthy. Not surprisingly, only less then a quarter of the surveyed linked CSR with the potential growth of their company's competitiveness. It is possible that commitment to CSR might require more market experience on the side of the Russian management as, according to some studies, Russian managers are still struggling to grasp the very concept of the market in its totality (Holden *et al.*, 2008).

The CSR landscape in Russia is changing as the presence of foreign companies and experience of the Russian companies abroad provide learning opportunities, but it still has its distinctive atmosphere that cannot be understood out of the context of the country's recent history and transitional framework. CSR in Russia is at its earliest stage of development, it brings returns and rewards only on rare occasions (Managers Association, 2004b). The national model of CSR in Russia is still at its tentative sate. The belief that it might spontaneously emerge under contemporary conditions is misplaced (for discussion see Kuznetsov *et al.*, 2007). The government must take the initiative and underwrite and guarantee consistent, fair, and enforceable rules and laws so that firms may follow their inclination toward CSR without fear. In this way, the state may start the "virtuous circle," by showing that some trust may cause reaction that will endorse more trust. The importance of this process cannot be overestimated, also in terms of national competitiveness.

Acknowledgments

The author wishes to express gratitude to Prof. A. Kuznetsov for valuable comments on the earlier draft of this chapter. The author acknowledges financial support received from the British Academy (LRG: 35419).

References

Black, BS, K Reinier, and A Tarasova (1999). Russian privatization and corporate governance: What went wrong? *Working Paper*, 178, Stanford Law School.

Blanchard, O and M Kremer (1997). Disorganization. *Quarterly Journal of Economics*, 112(4), 1091–1126.

Blowfield, M and A Murrey (2008). *Corporate Responsibility: A Critical Introduction*. New York: Oxford University Press Inc.

Buck, T (2003). Modern Russian corporate governance: Convergent forces or product of Russia's history? *Journal of World Business*, 38(4), 299–313.

Burke, L and JM Logsdon (1996). How corporate social responsibility pays off. *Long Range Planning*, 29(4), 495–502.

Carroll, AB (1979). A three dimensional conceptual model of corporate performance. *Academy of Management Review*, 4(4), 05–495.

CEFIR (The Centre for Economic and Financial Research) (2008). *What Russians Think About Transition: Evidence from RLMS Survey*. CEFIR Policy Report, Moscow, CEFIR 2007, http://www.cefir.ru/download.php?id=1232 [06 May 2008].

Davis, K (1973). The case for and against business assumption of social responsibilities. *Academy of Management Journal*, 16(2), 22–312.

Denisov, A and V Sitnina (2005). Dekadans-Kapital. *Vremya Novostei*, 3 February 2005, 17, 7–8.

EBRD (2007a). *Life in transition, a Survey of People's Experiences and Attitudes*. London: EBRD-European Bank for Reconstruction and Development. pp. 88.

EBRD (2007b). *People in Transition. Transition Report*. London: EBRD-European Bank for Reconstruction and Development pp. 216.

Ethical Corporation (2008). Central and Eastern Europe: Russia — springtime for responsible business. Ethical Corporation 10 April 2008; http://www.ethicalcorp.com/content asp?ContentID=5831&rss=ec-main xml [2 May 2008].

Fox, MB and MA Heller (1999). Lessons from fiascoes in Russian corporate governance, *New York University Law Review*, October 1999, http://ssrn.com/abstract=203368 [6 May 2008].

Frye, T (2006). Original sin, good works and property rights in Russia. *World Politics*, 58(4), 479–504.

Fülöp, G, RD Hisrich, and K Szegedi (2000). Business ethics and social responsibility in transition economies. *Journal of Management Development*, 19(1), 5–31.

Gabarro, JJ (1978). The development of trust, influence and expectations. In *Interpersonal Behaviors: Communication and Understanding in Relationships*, Anthony, GA and JJ Gabarro, pp. 290–303. Englewood Cliffs, NJ: Prentice Hall.

Heal, G (2005). Corporate social responsibility — An economic and financial framework. *Paper presented at the Annual Conference of the Monte Paschi Vita in 2005. The Geneva Papers*, 30(3), 387–409.

Hellman, J, G Jones, D Kaufmann, and M Schankerman (2000a). Measuring governance, corruption, and state capture. How firms and bureaucrats shape the business environment in transition economies. *Policy Research* WP 2312. The World Bank World Bank Institute and EBRD.

Hellman, JS, G Jones, and D Kaufmann (2000b). Seize the state, seize the day. State capture, corruption, and influence in transition. *Policy Research Working Paper 2444*, p. 41. The World Bank and European Bank of Reconstruction and Development, WB Institute, Governance, Regulation, and Finance Division, http://www.worldbank.org/wbi/governance/pdf/seize_synth pdf [06 May 2008].

Hellman, J and M Schankerman (2008). Intervention, corruption and capture: The nexus between enterprises and the state. WP#58 (October 2000):3; http://www.ebrd.com/pubs/econo/wp0058.htm [6 May 2008].

Holden, N, O Kuznetsova, and G Fink (2008). Russia's long struggle with Western terms of management and the concepts behind them. In *International management and language*, Tietze, S (ed.), London UK: Routledge.

Hollingsworth, JR and R Boyer (1997). Coordination of economic actors and social systems of production. In *Contemporary Capitalism: the Embededness of Institutions*, Hollingsworth, JR and R Boyer, pp. 1–48. New York: Cambridge University Press.

Iankova, EA (2008). From corporate paternalism to corporate social responsibility in post-communist Europe. *Journal of Corporate Citizenship*, 29, 75–89.

Informatsionnaja otkrytost' sotsialnoj politiki rossijskikh kompanij p. 48. Moscow: Assotsiatsija menedzherov.

Jones, TM (1995). Instrumental stakeholder theory: A synthesis of ethics and economics: A survey. *Academy of Management Review*, 20(2), 37–404.

Key, S and SJ Popkin (1998). Integrating ethics into the strategic management process: Doing well by doing good. *Management Decision*, 36(5), 38–331.

Kostin, A (2007). Russia: The evolving corporate responsibility landscape. *Compact Quarterly*, 1; http://www.enewsbuilder.net/globalcompact/e_article000775164.cfm [22 May 2008].

Kuznetsov, A and O Kuznetsova (2005). Business culture in modern Russia: Deterrents and influences. *Problems and Perspectives in Management*, 2(2), 25–31.

Kuznetsov, A, R Kapelyushnikov, and N Dyomina (2008). Performance of closely held firms in Russia: Evidence from firm-level data. *The European Journal of Finance*, 14(4), 58–337.

Kuznetsov, A and O Kuznetsova (2003). Institutions, business and the state in Russia. *Europe-Asia Studies*, 55(6), 22–907.

Kuznetsov, A, O Kuznetsova, and R Warren (2007). CSR, legitimacy and institutions. *Paper Presented at British Academy of Management (BAM) Conference, Management Research Education and Business Success: Is the Future as Clear as the Past?* Warwick Business School, University of Warwick, Coventry, UK September 11–13, 2007. *British Academy of Management (BAM) 2007 Conference Proceedings* [CD-ROM].

Lantos, GP (2001). The boundaries of strategic corporate social responsibility. *Journal of Consumer Marketing*, 18(7), 595–630.

Latynina, Y (1999). Zapiski iz podpol'ia. *Ekspert*, 3, 3–31.

Lawrence, AT, J Weber, and JE Post (2005). *Business and Society: Stakeholders, Ethics and Public Policy*. Sydney: McGraw-Hill Irwin.

Litovchenko, S and M Korsakov (eds) (2003). Corporativnaja sotsialnaja otvetstvennost': obschestvennye ozhidanija. *Assotsiatsija Menedzherov*, Moscow.

Lockett, A, J Moon, and W Visser (2006). Corporate social responsibility in management research: Focus, nature, salience and sources of influence. *Journal of Management Studies*, 43(1), 36–115.

Mahoney, RJ (1997). Shareholders, stakeholders, and enlightened self-interest. *Business and the Contemporary World*, IX(2), 36–325.

Managers Association (2004a). *Information Bulletin*, 23 April 2004, Managers Association, Moscow, 2004, http://www.amr.ru/pdf/Inf_23apr.pdf [07 May 2008].

Managers Association (2004b). *The report on Social Investments in Russia for 2004: Role of Business in Social Development*, Managers Association, Moscow.

Managers Association (2006). *Natsionalny doklad Biznes i obschestvennoje razvitije Rossii: problemy i perspectivy*, Moscow.

Miller, JB and S Tenev (2007). On the role of government in transition: The experiences of China and Russia compared. *Comparative Economic Studies*, 49(4), 71–543.

Mitchell, NJ (1989). *The Generous Corporation: A Political Analysis of Economic Power*. New Haven, CT: Yale University Press.

McGuire, JW (1963). *Business and Society*. New York: McGraw-Hill.

McWilliams, A and D Siegel (2001). Corporate social responsibility: A theory of the firm perspective. *Academy of Management Review*, 26(1), 27–117.

McWilliams, A, DS Siegel, and PM Wright (2006). Corporate social responsibility: Strategic implications. *Journal of Management Studies*, 43(1), 1–18.

Narod ne ustajot zhdat' kogda gosudarstvo ego nakormit, napoji i deneg dast. *Vestnik assotsiatsiji menedzherov*, 2003, October, 1, 26–28.

Nellis, JR (1999). Time to rethink privatization in transition economies? *Transition*, 10(1), 4–6.

Nelson, J (2004). The public role of private enterprise: Risks, opportunities and new models of engagement. *Working Paper of the Corporate Social Responsibility Initiative, Kennedy School of Government*, Harvard University, Cambridge, MA.

Obzor zanyatosti v Rossiji (2002). *Bureau of Economic Analysis*. Moscow: TEIS.

Reich, R (1998). The new meaning of corporate social responsibility. *California Management Review*, 40(2), 8–17.

RIA Novosti (2004). Social responsibility of Russian businesses. November 29, 2004. Johnson Russia List (JRL) 2004, (8472): No. 20, http://www.cdi.org/russia/johnson/8473-20.cfm [6 May 2008].

Sabel, CF and J Zeitlin (1997). Stories, strategies, structures: Rethinking historical alternatives to mass production. In *World of Possibilities: Flexibility and Mass Production in Western Industrialization*, Sabel Charles, F and J Zeitlin, pp. 1–34. New York: Cambridge University Press.

Shleifer, A and RW Vishny (1999). *The Grabbing Hand: Government Pathologies and their Cures*. Cambridge: Harvard University Press.

Stiglitz, JE (1999). Wither reform? Ten years of transition. Keynote Address, World Bank Annual Bank Conference on Development Economics, Washington DC, April 28–30, 1999, http://ideas.repec.org/a/nos/voprec/1999-07-0500.html [6 May 2008].

Vogel, D (2005). *The Market for Virtue: The Potential and Limits of Corporate Social Responsibility*. Brookings Institution Press.

Waldman, DA, MS de Luque, N Washburn and RJ House (2006). Cultural and leadership predictors of corporate social responsibility values of top management: A GLOBE study of 15 countries. *Journal of International Business Studies*, 37, 37–823.

Yelkina, A (2003). Privatization in Russia: Its past, present, and future. *SAM Advanced Management Journal*, 68(1), 14–21; http://www.allbusiness.com/finance/488332-1.html (accessed on May 8, 2008).

Chapter 8

THE RUSSIAN SYSTEM OF CORPORATE GOVERNANCE: PROMISES AND REALITIES

OLGA KUZNETSOVA

Abstract

This chapter puts under scrutiny the development of corporate governance within the emerging institutional context of the market economy of Russia. It looks at the forces that have determined the shape and performance of the corporate governance system in the period following the collapse of the centrally planned economy in an attempt to evaluate the strengths and weaknesses of this system and its impact on firm management. The reported findings about Russia might be instrumental in choosing strategy by investors considering doing business in transition, emerging, and developing economies.

Introduction

It is known among scholars and representatives of international originations such as the Word Bank that institutional constraints is the most important factor in defining various facets of the outcome of the process of economic development. Research and empirical observations suggest that qualitative parameters of institutional environments in different countries are responsible for conditions that encourage different managerial practices, the speed of economic growth, and the development of international competitiveness. Accordingly, both theory and practice emphasize the significance of institutional complementarity and consistency as factors determining the dynamism of the socioeconomic progress. At the same time, the analysis of the impact of a particular institution in a particular country usually requires a country-specific approach as institutional structures and institutional effectiveness vary from country to country.

There have been attempts to establish the objective limits to the usability of traditional corporate governance mechanisms created in countries with developed market economies, within the context of emerging markets (McCarthy and Puffer, 2003a,b). It is a widely spread view in the literature that transitional countries suffer from the deficiency and poor performance of their market institutions (Berglöf and von Thadden, 2000; Dolgopyatova, 2002; Yakovlev, 2004; Kuznetsov *et al.*, 2006). As far as corporate governance is concerned, literature suggests that countries with a weak institutional setup are more likely to develop the model of corporate governance based on concentrated shareholding (La Porta *et al.*, 1998; Claessens and Djankov 1999). Although the advantages and weaknesses of concentrated shareholding in relation to economic development and growth are well documented (see La Porta *et al.*, 1999 for references), the case of post-communist transition economies such as Russia remains far less researched. Many issues deserve attention. One of them is the prevalence of concentrated ownership and the question of why corporate governance is oriented more toward the protection of shareholders-insiders rather than shareholders in general. This chapter seeks to provide some tentative explanations to the development of this feature in the context of the Russian corporate governance. Analysis is based on a variety of sources. The original data used have been collected in Russia, mostly from the repeated surveys of a representative sample of executive managers of industrial enterprises, agricultural firms, and banks in almost all regions of Russia conducted on a regular basis by the Russian Economic Barometer (REB).

In a modern society, the importance of corporate governance is enormous. It is responsible for reassuring individual investors that the money they invest in a public company will be handled with due care by the management of the company, so that the interests of investors are protected. Ever since their early days, the task of corporations would have been to pull together resources provided by individual investors to deal with projects which they believed were too risky or too expensive to undertake on their own. A system of corporate governance may be defined as the set of processes, customs, policies, laws, and institutions affecting the way a corporation is directed, administered, or controlled. Corporate governance is typically seen as complex system of mechanisms that establishes relations between finance providers and users in publicly held companies ensure their mutual accountability. In this, it institutes the rules in respect of which corporate performance can be evaluated. Seen in this perspective, corporate governance presents itself as one of the fundamental institutes of modern Western democracy and market economy, acting as a guarantor of sustainable economic growth (Sullivan, 2002).

Over time, all industrialized countries of the world have accumulated substantial experience in organizing, running, and controlling corporations that has evolved into a variety of national systems of corporate governance. As it stands, the system of corporate governance of post-communist Russia does not fit comfortably any standard conceptual framework based on the example of other industrialized countries. According to some authors, this should be attributed mainly to the inefficient institutional set-up in the country (McCarthy and Puffer, 2003a; Puffer and McCarthy, 2003; Kuznetsov and Kuznetsova, 2003a, 2004, 2005). As Yakovlev (2004) puts it, the Russian model of corporate governance in its development has shown consistent disregard to the stated objectives of government policy and had as its modus operandi the systematic violation of formal rules. More than 15 years in the making, the Russian system of corporate governance remains a controversial construct as far as its conceptual foundations, features, efficiency, and future are concerned. The practical implications of this situation are considerable. For instance, there is a sizable gap between the real assets of the firms and capitalization,[1] indicating that corporate governance is not a well-established institution and investors are preoccupied with the safety of their money.

This chapter puts under scrutiny the development of corporate governance within the emerging institutional context of the market economy of Russia. It looks at the forces that have determined the development, shape, and performance of the system of corporate governance in Russia in the period following the collapse of the centrally planned economy in an attempt to evaluate the strengths and weaknesses of this system in its current form and its impact on firm management.

---

[1] At its peak before the 1998 collapse, the total stock market capitalization of all Russian industry only reached about $130 billion — less than Intel Corp. (Fox and Heller, 1999). Importantly, analysis by Black (2001a,b) further suggests that firm's corporate governance behavior can have a huge effect on its market value in a country where other constraints on corporate behavior are weak. Black concluded that the market value of large Russian companies could increase manifold by listing on a major international stock exchange where corporate governance requirements are strict.

The Determinants of the Russian Corporate Governance System

When Russia initiated the introduction of the foundations of corporate governance in the early 1990s, it had no own experience to rely upon. This might appear as an insignificant complication considering the amount of experience accumulated by other industrialized countries of the world and available for adaptation. In reality, the challenge of choosing the model has proven to be quite daunting.

To begin with, Western practices have proved more than one model of corporate governance as workable. Two of them are referred to particularly often: the American (also known as Anglo-Saxon or market-oriented) system and the continental (also known as Germanic or network-oriented) system. It is also becoming increasingly common to recognize the importance of some other models these days.[2] An academic debate on comparative advantages of various models (Milgrom and Roberts, 1992; Hart, 1995; Shleifer and Vishny, 1997; Yoshimori, 1995; De Jong, 1997; La Porta *et al.*, 1999) has nominated no clear winner. Every system has its strong sides and weaker aspects but, according to Moerland (1995), it is impossible to say that one system is better than the other on theoretical grounds as the optimization of economic organization leaves room for multiple configurations. This claim is echoed by Rozman (2000) who, having compared the Anglo-Saxon and Germanic systems, reaches the conclusion that both are logical and in harmony within themselves despite being different. Furthermore, none of the forms usually exists in its pure form, so when components of the different corporate governance systems merge a hybrid form might emerge.

Not just the theory but also Western practice confirms that no normative preferences could be given to a particular type of corporate governance system. The important thing to notice here is that the multiplicity of national systems of corporate governance is not so much the result of deliberate action, but rather has evolved in the course of an evolutionary process in

---

[2] De Jong (1997) writes about the Anglo-Saxon, the Germanic and the Latinic types of corporations with the latter represented by firms in France, Italy, and Spain among others. Yoshimori (1995) conducts his discourse in terms of monistic, dualistic, and pluralistic concepts of corporation. The first exists in the United States and the United Kingdom with a focus on shareholders; the second is characteristic of Germany and France and put a premium on the interests of both the shareholder and employees. Japan is the home for the third concept that assumes that the firm belongs to all stakeholders.

response to the requirements of a particular national socioeconomic environment.[3] In post-communist countries the mechanism of corporate governance had no chance to develop while central planning was in place; and yet, in its current form it bears the features that suggest that corporate governance has been influenced by the communist past and still is in captivity of the immediate past. "Bad inheritance" of behavioral legacies and "pervasive failures" have their roots in the deficiencies of the command economy (Brada, 1996). More often than not, "red directors" — the top managers who moved into their positions before the market reforms started, ran newly privatized enterprises. The relevance of their skills to the new business conditions has always been questionable. As a result, self-preservation has become their prevailing motivation, thus narrowing the strategic horizons of the emerging private sector. The interests of small shareholders have been often ignored. It did not help that this category of shareholders had few options to protect their interests as financial markets were in their infancy. For the majority of small investors shareholding was not very meaningful: financial gains were almost non-existent due to low level of dividend payout, stock prices were very artificial and did not convey enough information to allow justified investment decisions.

Another factor that distorted the relations of corporate governance in Russia was that the shares had been distributed between the equity holders charge-free in the process of voucher privatization. As a result, for many people possessing a stock had no or little association with investing, ownership, and rewards expectations. Understandably, corporate governance issues were outside the agenda of the majority of the economic players in Russia until, a few years after mass privatization, a property redistribution wave, inspired by

---

[3] For instance, Potthof (1996) emphasized the historical roots of differences between Anglo-Saxon and Germanic systems. In the 19th century, German banks were looking for ways to convert their short-term assets into long term but they were not interested in managing firms. Thus, the German system stresses supervision of joint-stock companies and not management by banks. By contrast, in Britain and the US capital was scares. Risk-taking individuals wanted more control over their assets and therefore demanded extended authority over managers. Consequently, the system that developed in Britain and the United States put importance on the responsibility of managers before shareholders while in Germany on their responsibility before the law. In turn, La Porta *et al.* (1997) attribute precedence to a legal framework as the cause of variation in corporate systems, establishing a link between market-oriented model of corporate governance and the dominance of common law in Britain and the United States, on the one hand, and the network-oriented model and civil law in continental Europe, on the other.

the activities of the first generation of Russian financial tycoons and emerging interest from foreign investors, has changed the prevailing attitude.

The fact that national systems of corporate governance are products of historical circumstances, that is that they have been influenced by cultural, political, and socioeconomic factors specific to age and nation, has important consequences for countries like Russia. While it is possible to try and import conceptual and statutory underpinnings of corporate governance wholesale from the West, it is not possible to recreate the circumstances under which they emerged. Attempts to transfer Western benchmarks inevitably created a number of unexpected problems related to adaptation and interpretation of practical ideas and the evaluation of the cost of their implementation. The elements of corporate governance that were set in place in Russia during and immediately after privatization were somewhat artificial constructs implanted by the state which at that time was under control of political forces that saw it as their mission to change the economic landscape in the country in such a radical way that the restoration of the Soviet regime would become impossible. As a result, arrangements regarding corporate governance were not a product of a development process prioritizing efficiency, but rather the implementation of a certain political agenda. What followed was that these elements soon found themselves coexisting and sometimes in competition with other elements that were emerging out of the everyday practice of corporate relations as they were evolving in the national economy.

The conflict between the norms and rules imposed from above and the motivation of the economic agents has been increasingly identified as a determining factor of the development of corporate governance and its particular features in Russia (Yakovlev, 2004). Initial attempt to create a widespread base of shareholders failed and the country has been witnessing the solidifying and concentration of equity blocks in the hands of fewer owners, the development of closely held companies run as family firms, unification of ownership and control, corporate governance system unaccountable to the market and deepening of the principle–principle or intra-shareholders conflict (Dharwadkar *et al.*, 2000; Kuznetsova and Kuznetsov, 2001).

The history of corporate governance in post-communist Russia is relatively short. It started technically with mass privatization and clearly showed the dependence on the privatization model that has prompted the adoption of certain forms of governance. During this time, the economic policies favored by the authorities did not purposely encourage the development of the institutional structures adequate and supportive for the advancement of the corporate governance compatible with emerging patterns of ownership structures. As the efficiency of corporate governance refers to control execution, institutional order and relevant legislation are essential for enabling the whole mechanism. The discrepancy between what institutional environment in developing market can provide in order to enable a particular type of corporate governance and the emerging needs of the development of an operational form of corporate governance is very noticeable in Russia. This inconsistency weakens the system of corporate governance and translates into low level of transparency and trust that surrounds business transactions as solutions are often left to the discretions of the circumstances and individuals instead of governing mechanisms. To put it into technological terms, corporations in Russia are still run "manually" rather than "automatically" by relying on a sophisticated ensemble of the established procedures. Following this, the results of the functioning of corporate governance in Russia are not entirely predictable.

Mass privatization that allocated property rights to the citizens formed the background for the development of corporate governance in Russia. It insured the concentration of the majority of corporate shares in the hands of insiders: managers and workers[4] resulting in an asymmetric ownership structure. The reformers favored this model of ownership distribution, as its main advantage was speed and breadth that left beyond the turning point the restoration the socialist system of production. It was expected that widely spread private ownership would intensify market forces and as soon as they took over they would urge more efficient redistribution of ownership through a secondary market (Chubais and Vishnevskaya, 1997). Yet, the bias in the allocation of shares has remained a feature of the Russian corporate system ever since after privatization. According to the data collected by REB, as late as 2005 insiders remained the largest group of shareholders, controlling nearly 47% of all outstanding shares (Table 8.1). This does not mean though that the configuration of shareholding had remained unaltered during this period. In reality, it had experienced some sharp and pronounced changes. Data by the REB indicate that as much as 15% of shares were changing hands between the four categories of shareholders (managers/workers; insiders/outsiders) in a typical Russian firm every year between 1995 and now. The redistribution of shares proceeded in such a way that ownership shifted from workers to managers; from insiders to outsiders; from the state to private owners. Top managers have come out as frontrunners, having secured the keeping on average of 31% of all shares. As the REB data show, already by 2003 in an average industrial firm managers had amassed more shares than the rest of employees, whose original stake was closer to 44% and by 2007 they were expected to

---

[4] Large stakes were initially retained by the state, but the state has never played a notable independent role as a shareholder (Kuznetsova and Kuznetsov, 1999).

Table 8.1. Ownership allocation within Russian firms based on REB survey results.

	1995	1997	1999	2001	2003	2005	2007 (forecast)
Insiders, total	54.8	52.1	46.2	48.2	46.2	46.6	54.0
Managers	11.2	15.1	14.7	21.0	25.6	31.5	40.0
Employees	43.6	37.0	31.5	27.2	21.0	15.1	14.0
Outsiders, total	35.2	38.8	42.4	39.7	44.8	41.0	40.1
Non-financial outsiders, total	25.9	28.5	32.0	32.4	35.6	33.5	29.3
Individual investors	10.9	13.9	18.5	21.1	20.1	18.0	15.0
Other firms	15.0	14.6	13.5	11.3	15.5	15.5	14.3
Financial outsiders, total	9.3	10.3	10.4	7.3	9.2	7.5	9.8
The state	9.1	7.4	7.1	7.9	4.3	7.3	4.1
Other shareholders	0.9	1.7	4.3	4.2	4.9	5.2	2.8
Total	100	100	100	100	100	100	100
Number of firms	136	135	156	154	104	108	71

control 40% of all shares against 14% held by other employees. These figures indicate that increasing managerial shareholding is a distinct feature of the Russian corporate governance. Evidence also suggests that it is matched by increasing managerial control in the Russian companies.

According to the classification[5] proposed by Berglöf and von Thadden (2000), the presence of strong, in some cases omnipotent managers can be typically observed in nearly all corporate governance arrangements apart from closely held firm. However managerial strength has different underpinnings. Thus, widely held firms are controlled by professional and institutionally empowered managers; family firms open opportunity for a particular provision with regard to managerial agreement, while close holding allows strong blockholders to dominate the decision-making process. It was probably inevitable that in the newly privatized Russian enterprises the entrenched managers were to gain very strong positions. First, decision-making process was a legacy of the old authoritative and highly hierarchical operational and organizational model, which could not disappear overnight. The chance to rely on the trusted and tested operational model had some advantages at the

---

[5] This classification includes five categories: widely held firm: strong managers, weak owners; closely held firm: strong blockholders, weak minorities; family firm: strong managers, no outsiders; transition firm: omnipotent managers, little resistance; development firm: strong managers, related investors.

time when other points of institutional reference have disappeared along with the old institutional arrangements now dismantled. Second, the continuity was crucial for survival in a highly volatile environment. Third, networking was a prominent feature of the Russian business practice, so that personal contact was more important for business success than anything else. Therefore, having on board an established well-connected individual could increase a company's survival probability. Finally, the market for professional managers and management did not exist in post-communist Russia (and is hardly significant now), so the newly established "new management" simply inherited functions and, in effect, was not "new." According to the EBRD survey, less than one-third of former managers has been replaced in privatized firms in all post-communist economies. Forty percent of the new executives came from outside, while 60% had been promoted within the same enterprise (EBRD, 1999). The important difference was that "new" mangers were shareholders and in this respect were seemingly at par with other insiders.

As for the outsiders, initially there were only limited opportunities and incentive (such as in the case of the state) for their involvement in corporate governance. Lately, the participation of outsiders has increased but not as much as could have been expected. Currently, according to REB, outsiders on average control 41% of the capital of a typical firm, which is about as much as controlled by insiders. The important feature of the modern ownership structure from the point of view of corporate governance is that industrial firms and individuals represent the majority of outsiders. Individuals tend to be representing poorly protected minority equity holders, while the outsiders represented by industrial firms in reality increase further the control power of the managers-insiders through a complex system of cross holding. The share of banks, financial companies, and investment funds — institutional investors in general — remains stable and low at about 10%. Foreign participation generally is also very low: only one in nine firms has shareholders from abroad. The observations indicate that when there is a stake owned by a foreign party it tends to be rather high at the average figure of 43% of the authorized stock (Dolgopyatova, 2004), reflecting widely held perception about the poor efficiency of the corporate governance mechanism in Russia and high risk of investing under poorly institutionalized environment. Obvious strategy of addressing such risks includes attempts to amplify control over companies through increasing shareholding. As managers happened to be in a more advantageous position in this respect, and legislation did not encourage otherwise, rather naturally Russian corporate governance developed a tendency toward a model that favored strong insiders hold, managerial in particular. The format of corporate governance that emerged under such conditions favored the growing powers of managers-insiders. In this respect, modern Russia provides a peculiar diversion from a well-established trend of separation of ownership and control.

As is evident from the above account, the chosen model of privatization, the ideological framework, and the concepts imported from the West has influenced many aspects of corporate governance in Russia. Equally important was the fact that institute of corporate governance was developing in a virtually institution-free environment and as a result was influenced by the factors endogenous to individual companies. Overall the formation and consequent fine-tuning of the mechanism of corporate governance in Russia has been influenced by a variety of factors that represented the reality of the business environment in the country such as: shareholding scattered among individuals who were employees of the organizations; shareholding conditional (on many occasions) to the employment with a company, so the initial insider holding would not diminish; shareholding comparatively concentrated in the hands of managers; shareholding concentrated in the hands of insiders, as opposed to outsiders; impassive shareholding (there was indifference to the shareholding issues on the part of the employees); predominantly non-investment nature of the insider shareholding (shareholding resulted from shares distribution rather than investment on the part of the owners of capital); unregulated shareholding (there was lack of procedures for corporate control; imposing managerial activism in equity consolidation and gaining control over the companies); state shareholding in strategic industries; insignificant presence of the outsiders shareholding; wide spread of complex cross-holding among different companies; non-functioning financial markets; low level of trust and absence of the market control mechanisms; concentration of control in the hands of companies managers; absence of managerial market. All these features happened to be responsible for the emergence of the internally oriented corporate governance in Russia.

Revolution in Corporate Governance: Unification of Ownership and Control

The task of a system of corporate governance is to create trust based on control between investors and agents that run corporations. No system anywhere in the world is perfect but the level of de facto protection that the Russian system offers to shareholders is extremely low. The Russian variety of corporate governance is built around the prominence of dominant ownership.

In market economies with a mature and sophisticated institutional set-up, the distinction between biggest and dominant ownership is mostly non-existent because domination is based on exercising ownership rights according to the principle "one share-one vote" (DeMarzo, 1993). Under the Anglo-Saxon system, the stake as low as 3–5% can give its owner considerable power; under the continental system concentration of ownership is higher and as result the stake has to be close to 50% to give noticeable influence to a shareholder. In Russia, poor legal protection of shareholder rights, lack of disclosure about the business operations or finances of corporations, the underdeveloped state of the security market and a weak shareholder culture signify that holding even large and very large blocks of shares may result in little or no effective control over the firm.[6] Same conditions favor people who are privy to the firm's management decisions. This category includes primarily senior managers. They have an important advantage because they strengthen the power of shareholding with the power of decision making. As a result, domination can be achieved by simple if unscrupulous means exploiting the situation when other categories of shareholders cannot accurately monitor day-to-day performance of the firm.

In developed economies, concentrated ownership is widely considered as a tool of aligning the interests of principle and agent. In emerging economies, by the contrast, concentrated ownership tends to create a conflict within the camp of principles. In transition economies, where on many occasions the role of a dominant principle converges with that of a manager, the opportunities for expropriation of minorities increase greatly and corporate governance defaults on its role of a democratic institution of governance.

Privatization in ex-communist countries has put senior managers in an exceptionally strong position vis-à-vis employees and outsiders. From the outset, their control of the firms was far in excess of their share of ownership due to advantages inherent in the system. As pre-privatization incumbents, they enjoyed the position of a dominant stakeholder. They had privileged

---

[6] This is the reality that some foreign investors have learnt to own cost. This is how *Fortune* describes the treatment that Khodorkovsky, one of Russia's so-called oligarchs and the one-time CEO and principal owner of *Yukos*, gave to his minority shareholders: "He bought *Yukos* in Russia's infamous "loan for shares" scheme in 1995; got rid of US investor Kenneth Dart, a large minority stakeholder in *Yukos*, via a brazenly massive share dilution; then survived the economic collapse of 1998 by simply stonewalling three big Western institutions whose loans to Khodorkovsky's bank were collateralized by 30% of *Yukos*' shares. Despairing of their ability to prevail legally in a virtually lawless Russia, the Westerners eventually walked, ending up with a fraction of what their stakes would be worth today." (*Fortune* 13.05.2002:32). Another more recent example is a "year 2008 corporate war" within TNK-BP establishment.

access to information, admission to important networks and, at least initially, support of the labor force. Later they developed special tactics intended to uphold and strengthen their position by the way of supplementing it with dominant shareholding, so to keep the affair in the "family." These include, for instance, keeping share registries locked up in their offices; keeping more than one registry; changing entries into the registry at will; threatening to fire workers who sell shares to outsiders; misleading "undesirable" shareholders about dates and venues of the general meetings; refusing to register equity purchases by outsiders; declining to recognize board directors properly elected by minority shareowners, abuse of custodian responsibilities, and others. These tactics bring results; thanks to a low level of corporate transparency and effective law enforcement (Kuznetsov *et al.*, 2008). In 2005, according to some estimates (*ibid*) among firms controlled by top managers as a group, 44% were controlled by their former "red directors" while 56% were controlled by the teams who arrived after privatization. Among firms where the CEO was the largest shareholder the proportion was 36% and 64%. Under such condition, the limits for managerial opportunism is no more an issue.

In the end of the day, however, it was control over financial resources of the firms that solidified the domination of managers. In the economy stricken with shortage of financial resources, institutional chaos has opened an unrivaled opportunity to use corporate resources for illegal personal enrichment. In big firms, the most popular scheme of such enrichment involves creation of a number of small affiliated firms that are put in charge of the cash flows of the big firm. This makes the control of cash flows extremely complicated and allows the organizers of the scheme to transfer money into their personal accounts either directly or through offshore companies and various facade firms. These resources could be used by senior managers for increasing own block of shares and preventing other parties from accumulating more shares. Eventually, the combination of give-away privatization and underdeveloped institutions has brought about the situation in which, in the majority of joint-stock companies, the function of a manager and the function of the biggest owner became united. That turned a big shareholder into a dominant one.

Official sources and data are not too helpful in validating this fact. The secretive nature of the Russian corporate world makes it problematic to quantify the configuration of ownership. Within the sample covered by REB surveys, the proportion of firms that have their senior manager as the largest shareholder increased from 24% to 39% in 1999–2005. It is also typical that the stake of the largest shareholder tends to grow, currently on average it

Table 8.2. Ownership concentration within Russian firms based on REB survey results.

	1999 (%)	2001 (%)	2003 (%)	2005 (%)
The proportion of firms in which the largest shareholder holds				
Fewer than 10% of shares	21	16	9	2
10–25% of shares	28	33	35	15
25–50% of shares	26	26	30	32
More than 50% of shares	25	25	26	51
Total	100	100	100	100
Average stake of the largest shareholder	32.9	34.5	37.2	51.8
Average stake of the second largest shareholder	—	—	17.2	20.3

exceeds 40% of authorized capital (see Table 8.2). According to expert evaluation based on in-depth empirical studies, senior management is in control of no less than 50% of firms because many shareholders-outsiders are just a façade for managers (Sizov, 2004; Dolgopyatova, 2005).

The standard problem of corporate governance, therefore, transforms: it is no longer a conflict between managers and owners, but rather a conflict between different categories of owners of which one has advantages because of its position within the firm, being in management. Such situation is typical for what is considered to represent a family firm (Fama and Jensen, 1983; Shleifer and Vishny, 1997; Burkart *et al.*, 2003). But in the Russian context, the situation took one step further: the position of managers is strengthened by equity ownership concentrated in their hands. Managers in Russian companies have motives to act in a chosen way and have means to exploit their position. Consequently, Russian corporations acquire many features of manager-owned firms before firms reached the point of transition from founder to professional management. Some authors call them the "threshold firms" (Daily and Dalton, 1992). Russian companies, as for now, show no intention of moving toward a modern corporate prototype run by professional managers. Russian model of corporate governance is predominantly internally focused. This can be explained by the fact that it needs to manage a variety of conflicts within the insiders.

It has been noticed that in recent years conflict between insiders, typical for the "threshold firms," has become a dominant feature of the corporate sector in emerging economies. The downside of the "threshold" state is that the intra-shareholders conflict has a tendency to escalate (for more detailed discussion see Young *et al.*, 2008). This conflict has performance-related implications for the companies and consequences for the wider stakeholders as it create conditions for underperforming of the market socio-economic system. More typical performance shortcomings of the corporate governance system affected by the intra-shareholders conflict, as indicated by research, are poor accountability due to asymmetric allocation of control, minority shareholders abuse and expropriation, lower valuation of firms, limited number of listed companies, poor dividend pay record, lack of investment activities and innovation indifference, undersupplied information as signaled by the stock price fluctuation (Young *et al.*, 2008). Research on the current developments in Russia confirms overwhelmingly the presence of all these shortcomings without exceptions.

In most countries of the world, companies with highly concentrated ownership grew and developed as family firms, often from entrepreneurial origins. In Russia where private property of industrial assets has its origins in mass voucher privatization, medium and large firms neither originated with some innovative ideas of the founder-owners, nor could they become a family affair. Nonetheless, the majority of them are tightly held firms: shares are usually concentrated in the hands of very small number of individuals tied by informal links and shared background. Indeed, the owners of such firms usually go back together a long time. Often they knew each other professionally before the market reforms started; they did their first steps as businessmen together and now own comparable stakes in the firm. This model of concentrated ownership, which may be called a "companionship" firm, may be found in the most successful Russian companies. It also facilitates such important feature of the Russian corporate scene as the deliberate complexity of ownership rights with the aim to conceal the identity of true owners. Often this is a reaction to poor protection that the legal system offers to legitimate owners. Indeed, each emerging economy has a corporate governance system that reflects its institutional conditions. Non-transparency of property rights is artificially maintained by the owners of many companies as a barrier against possible interference of the state or a capture by hostile takeovers (Pappe, 2002). Also, in general, the development of the concentrated ownership acts as a mechanism intended to compensate for the deficiency of the existing corporate governance system.

While ersatz mechanisms "may solve some problems, they create other, novel problem in the progress" (Young *et al.*, 2008, p. 199). Others noticed that corporate governance in developing markets might resemble the systems of the developed economies in form but not in substance (Peng, 2004). Russia provides an example of such a case. In terms of concentration of ownership, Russia is no different from the rest of the world, but it is quite different in at least two other respects: first, family ownership is not a predominant feature of the Russian tightly held firms; and second, tightly held firms there are characterized by the entrenchment of managers. Coalitions of shareholders aimed at exercising some of their rights in a predetermined fashion are not an unusual feature in modern corporate systems. What distinguishes the Russian version is the nature of relations between the members of the coalition. The rise of "companionship" capitalism in Russia gives prominence to a number of issues few of which have been thoroughly studied in the literature so far. For example, there are no answers to the questions of whether "companionship" firms are going to be a lasting feature of Russian corporate governance and if it negatively affects the efficiency of Russian firms in a long run. Even if corporate governance based on concentrated ownership might be the most viable alternative for emerging and transforming markets (Young *et al.*, 2008), its net benefit might diminish with advent of more advanced and complex market environment where features such as high level of public and internal accountability, transparency and public disclosure, more formalized relations, institutionalized procedures and enforceable practices will be positively reflected through different aspects of companies' performance, including growing stakeholders democracy.

The progress of corporate governance toward a more conventional modern model is unrealistic without changes in the political, social, and economic realities of Russia in the first place. In other words, the current system of corporate governance is yet another manifestation of an inadequate state of the institutional infrastructure in the country. The paradox is that certain behavioral patterns and business arrangements in Russia bring rewards although they should be a ticket to failure in a market economy as contradicting its rules and institutions. In this context, the idiosyncratic behavior of economic agents determined to by-pass the "legal" market economy is in fact a rational reaction to the uncertainty and challenges caused by institutional distortions. The high perceived cost of acting legally is a fundamental impediment to the progress in corporate governance along the lines suggested by the OECD code of corporate governance.

Conclusion

This chapter examined the underpinnings of the corporate governance system as it developed following mass privatization in Russia under conditions of highly volatile business environment when institutional deficiency was combined with an overall economic crisis. Although initially it was designed to resemble the so-called Anglo-Saxon model, in reality it emerged as a system based on the concentrated ownership of insiders. Research findings indicate that, in the Russian context, concentrated ownership is likely to have a negative impact on firm performance (Kuznetsov *et al.*, 2008). But Russian corporation does not only feature concentrated ownership, they are insiders-dominant as well. Some studies on the companies' performance supremacy in respect to the dominance of either insiders or outsiders indicate possible advantage of the latter, but not when propensity to restructure is considered (Filatochev *et al.*, 2001, 2003). In Russia, however, improvement in performance depends heavily on restructuring. All in all, performance-related implications of the Russian model of corporate governance are not entirely clear and might need further studies. What is clear though is that insiders' dominance slow down restructuring process and corresponding firms suffer from the syndrome of long-term commitment avoidance. Furthermore, concentrated ownership in Russian corporations makes them have many features typical of family firms with the only difference that they are not family firms by their origin: this feature seemingly has been acquired in response to the pressures of the business environment. This performance model offers no advantages to the Russian companies as it might be susceptible to governance failures. In addition, it might prevent firms from being dynamic and forward-looking. At the operational level, owner-managers sometimes fail to recognize business opportunities or pitfalls, in particular in times of change, where outsiders would see them and intervene, suggest Berglöf and von Thadden (2000). In such firms corporate governance also becomes an issue when there is a succession problem or when the firm decides to raise funds outside the family. In these important situations, the lack of links to the capital market may significantly reduce the value of the firm if outsiders are reluctant to buy assets of which they know little and over which they have little control. As recent research findings advocate, family businesses have positive impact in firm performance essentially due to lone-founder phenomenon. Outside of lone-founder firms, family-owned companies do not perform better than the non-family counterparts (Miller *et al.*, 2007).

The overall picture of the Russian corporate governance shows that it has absorbed all of the weakest components of various governance arrangements; it is not solving the conflicts but tends to leave them unsolved while creating numerous new. The situation in Russia fits well the theoretical model by Castaneda (2006) which suggests that when minority shareholders are not well protected, markets are not very liquid, share prices do not convey the information needed to improve efficiency in allocation, and legal and political institutions that protect the rights of all stakeholders are weak, ownership concentration will result in controlling owners choosing low-risk, low-productive projects if they feel that their position is threatened. A similar view is expressed by Desai and Goldberg (2000), who argue that the problem of corporate governance in countries like Russia is not limited to protecting minority shareholders or other financiers, rather it is the problem of insufficient incentives for owner-managers to restructure the firms and maximize their value over the long run. Desai and Goldberg (2000) relate this to two aspects of Russian reality. One is that firm performance reflects the insecurity of dominant shareholders as they feel threatened by the general instability and uncertainty regarding property rights, inheritance rights, contract law, judicial protection, personal safety, and so on.[7] Another is that the underdeveloped state of the Russian capital markets makes it difficult for owners to release value accumulated in shares. In fact, as Pappe (2005) maintains, the only legal way of doing this is by trading shares of Russian firms on international stock markets. This, of course, is not possible for the majority of Russian companies. As a consequence of these constraints, controlling owners are more likely to be engaged in "tunneling" and asset stripping than in increasing the long-term value of the firm. Obviously, Russian managers currently operate their firms under constraints and incentives that result in "bad" corporate governance defined by Fox and Heller (1999) as a failure to maximize residuals and make pro rata distributions to shareholders.

To summarize, the poor state of the institutional framework puts a pressure on large shareholders to keep increasing their stake. As a result, their control over the firm grows. However, institutional inadequacies make this category of shareholders feel insecure about the future of their holding. This undermines their commitment to the firm they own/control, and encourages them to "tunnel" wealth out of companies. Evidently, these are the signs of an unhealthy situation that endangers the long-term restructuring and growth of the Russian economy. The findings about Russia, in our opinion,

---

[7] The Russian legal system offers inadequate protection to legitimate owners, even if they hold majority stakes. In the West, hostile takeovers are feasible when shares of the target company are widely available and easily purchased. In Russia, hostile takeovers rely on the abuse of the rights of shareholders and the exploitation of legalistic hitches and corruption in the judicial system. One of the common tricks is to obtain a judicial decision that bans the current owners of the firm from using their right to vote in the shareholders general meeting, or to take a position on the board of directors. Another ploy is to make the court requisite the registry of shareholders, the only legal proof of ownership, and then replace it with an alternative registry with a different composition of shareholders (Sizov, 2004). One notorious incident involved Krasnoyarsk Aluminium, which deleted from its share register a 20% stake held by the British Trans World Group, effectively wiping out its holding (Mileusnic, 1996).

are relevant for corporations with concentrated shareholding operating in economies with a weak institutional environment in general. In this respect, they have implication for potential foreign investors considering doing business in transition, emerging, and developing economies.

References

Berglöf, E and E-L von Thadden (2000). The changing corporate governance paradigm: Implications for developing and transition economies. In: *Annual World Bank Conference on Development Economics 1999*, P Boris and N Stern (eds.), pp. 135–162. The World Bank.

Black, B (2001a). Does corporate governance matter? A crude test using Russian data. *University of Pennsylvania Law Review*, 149, 50–2131; http://papers.ssrn.com/paper.taf? abstract_id=252706, [17 July 2008].

Black, B (2001b). The corporate governance behavior and market value of the Russian firms. *Emerging Markets Review*, 2, 89–108.

Brada, JC (1996). Corporate governance in transitional economies: Lessons from recent developments in OECD members countries. OCDE/GD (96)100. *General Distribution*. OECD: Paris.

Burkart, M, F Panunzi, and A Shleifer (2003). Family firms. *Journal of Finance*, 58.5, 202–2167.

Castaneda, G (2006). Economic growth and concentrated ownership in stock markets. *Journal of Economic Behavior & Organization*, 59(2), 86–249.

Chubais, A and M Vishnevskaya (1997). Main Issues of Privatisation in Russia in *Russia's Economic Transformation in the 1990s*, Å Anders (ed.). London and Washington: Pinter.

Claessens, S and S Djankov (1999). Ownership concentration and corporate performance in the Czech republic. *Journal of Comparative Economics*, 27(3), 498–513.

Daily, CM and DR Dalton (1992). Financial performance of founder-managed versus professionally-managed small corporations. *Journal of Small Business Management*, 30, 25–34.

De Jong, HW (1997). The governance structure and performance of large European corporations. *The Journal of Management and Governance*, 1(1), 5–27.

DeMarzo, PM (1993). Majority voting and corporate control: The rule of the dominant shareholder. *Review of Economic Studies*, 60(3), 34–713.

Desai, RM and I Goldberg (2000). Stakeholders, governance, and the Russian enterprise dilemma. *Finance & Development*, 37(2), 14–18; http://www.imf.org/External/Pubs/Ft/ Fandd/2000/06/desai.htm [30 July 2008].

Dharwadkar, R, G Gerard, and P Brandes (2000). Privatization in emerging economies: An agency theory perspective. *Academy of Management Review*, 25, 69–650.

Dolgopyatova, T (2004). Corporate ownership and control in the Russian companies in the context of integration. *Russian Management Journal*, 2(2), 3–26.

Dolgopyatova, T (2002). *Corporate Control in Russian Companies: Models and Mechanisms*. Preprint WP1/2002/05. Moscow: Higher Economics School.

Dolgopyatova, T (2005). Evolution of corporate control models in the Russian companies: New trends and factors. *Working paper WP1/2005/04*. Moscow: State University, Higher School of Economics.

EBRD (1999). Transition Report 1999. European Bank for Reconstruction and Development, London.

Fama, EF and MC Jensen (1983). Separation of ownership and control. *Journal of Law and Economics*, 26(2), 25–301.

Filatochev, I, R Kapelyushnikov, N Dyomina, and S Aukutsionek (2001). The effects of ownership concentration on investment and performance in privatized forms in Russia. *Managerial and Decision Economics*, 22(6), 299–313.

Filatochev, I, W Mike, K Uhlenbruck, T Laszlo, and RE Hoskisson (2003). "Governance, organizational capabilities, and restructuribg in transition economies. *Journal of World Business*, 38(4), 47–331.

Fox, MB and MA Heller (1999). Lessons from fiascos in Russian corporate governance. University of Michigan Law School Working Paper 99–012.

Hart, OD (1995). Corporate governance: Some theory and implications. *The Economic Journal*, 105.430, 89–678.

Kuznetsov, A, R Kapelyushnikov, and N Dyomina (2008). Ownership concentration and firm performance in a transition economy: Evidence from Russia. In *Corporate Governance and International Business*, Strange, R and G Jackson (eds.), London: Palgrave.

Kuznetsov, A and O Kuznetsova (2005). "Business culture in modern Russia: Deterrents and influences. *Problems and Perspectives in Management*, 2(2), 25–31.

Kuznetsov, A and O Kuznetsova (2003a). Corporate governance: Does the concept work in transition countries? *Journal for East European Management Studies*, 8(3), 62–244.

Kuznetsov, A and O Kuznetsova (2004). Crisis of governance: Why market solutions to economic problems are not popular in Russia. *Journal of East-West Business*, 9(3–4), 11–25.

Kuznetsov, A, O Kuznetsova, and R Kapelyushnikov (2006). Ownnership structure and corporate governance in Russian firms. In *Corporate Governance and Finance in Poland and Russia*, Mickiewicz, T, New York: Palgrave Macmillan.

Kuznetsova, O and A Kuznetsov (1999). The state as a shareholder: Responsibilities and objectives. *Europe-Asia Studies*, 51(3), 46–433.

Kuznetsova, O and A Kuznetsov (2001). The virtues and weakness of insider shareholding. *Journal of East-West Business*, 6(4), 89–106.

La Porta, R, F Lopez-de-Salines, and A Shlefer (1999). Corporate ownership around the world. *Journal of Finance*, 54(2), 471–517.

La Porta, R, F Lopez-de-Silanes, A Shleifer, and RW Vishny (1998). Law and finance. *Journal of Political Economy*, 106(6), 55–1113.

La Porta, R, F Lopez-de-Silanes, A Shleifer, and RW Vishny (1997). Legal determinants of external finance. *Journal of Finance*, 52(3), 50–1131.

McCarthy, DJ and S Puffer (2003a). Corporate governance in Russia: A framework for analysis. *Journal of World Business*, 38, 397–415.

McCarthy, DJ and S Puffer (2003b). Corporate governance in Russia: Towards a European, U.S. or Russian model. *European Management Journal*, 20(6), 40–630.

Mileusnic, N (1996). The great boardroom revolution, *Moscow Times*, p. 1.

Milgrom, P and J Roberts (1992). *Economics, Organisation and Management*. Englewood Cliffs, NJ: Prentice Hall.

Miller, D, I Le Breton-Miller, RH Lester, and AA Cannella (2007). Are family firms really superior performers? *Journal of Corporate Finance*, 13(5), 58–829.

Moerland, PW (1995). Alternative disciplinary mechanisms in different corporate systems. *Journal of Economic Behavior & Organization*, 26(1), 17–34.

Pappe, Y (2005). *Rossiiskii krupnyi biznes: sobytiia i tendentsii v 2004 godu. Moscow: Tsentr Ekonomicheskogo Analiza.*

Pappe, Y (2002). Rossiiskii Krupnyi Biznes kak Ekonomicheskii Fenomen: Spetsificheskie Cherty Modeli ego Organizatsii. *Problemy Prognozirovaniya*, 2, 83–97.

Peng, MW (2004). Outside directors and firm performance during institutional transition. *Strategic Management Journal*, 25, 71–453.

Potthof, E (1996). Board-System versus duales System der Unternehmungsverwaltung. *Betriebswirtschftliche Forschung und Praxis*, 3, 68–253.

Puffer, S and D McCarthy (2003). The emergence of corporate governance in Russia. *Journal of World Business*, 38, 98–284.

Rozman, R (2000). The organizational function of governance. *Management*, 5(2), 99–115.

Shleifer, A and R Vishny (1997). A survey of corporate governance. *Journal of Finance*, 52(2), 83–737.

Sizov, Y (2004). Novyi Vitok Korporativnykh Konfliktov. Aktsionernoe obschestvo: voprosy korporativnogo upravleniia, November 2004; http://www.sovetnik.orc.ru/texts/sizov.htm [17 July 2008].

Sullivan, JD (2002). Democracy, governance and the market. Center for International Private Enterprise publications, 2002; http://www.cipe.org/publications/fs/articles/article3162. htm [09 June 2008].

Yakovlev, A (2004). Evolution of corporate governance in Russia: Government policy vs. real incentives of economic agents. *Post-Communist Economies*, 16(4), 387–403.

Yoshimori, M (1995). Whose company is it? The concept of the corporation in Japan and the West. *Long Range Planning*, 286(4), 33–44.

Young, MN, MW Peng, D Ahlstrom, GD Burton, and Y Jiang (2008). Corporate governance in emerging economies: A review of the principle–principle perspective. *Journal of Management Studies*, 45(1), 196–220.

Chapter 9

BRAND MANAGEMENT IN EMERGING MARKETS: PRIVATE LABELS IN CROATIAN GROCERY RETAILING AND THE CASE OF DONA TRGOVINA D.O.O.

MAJA MARTINOVIC AND JOHN BRANCH

Abstract

Brand management is a fundamental business practice of any company. In a globalizing world economy, however, brand management has become more challenging, especially in emerging markets which have attracted much attention from multinationals, and which have spawned their own internationally competitive companies. Private labels — sometimes called house branding — are a subform of brand management which have their own peculiarities and which, in emerging markets, are racing to catch up to that of the developed world. This chapter provides a brief overview of brand management and private labels in emerging markets. The evolution of private labels in Croatian grocery retailing is then outlined. Finally, the case of Dona Trgovina D.O.O., one of the leading Croatian manufacturers of private grocery labels, is presented.

Introduction

Globalization has been defined, especially in recent decades, as the international spread of capitalism across national boundaries, with minimal restrictions by governments. With globalization, therefore, has come the spread of brand management, especially in emerging markets, whose rapid growth rates have enamoured multinationals. Indeed, with stagnation in their domestic economies (Wilson and Purushotaman, 2003), these companies have been considering emerging markets with new interest (Keller and Moorthi, 2003), thereby suggesting the need for a brand management paradigm specifically for emerging markets (Sarkar and Singh, 2005; Xie and Boggs, 2006). At the same time, globalization has raised the aspirations of local companies in emerging markets to become multinationals themselves, as their international competitiveness grows. Consider Pollo Campero, for example, a fried chicken restaurant chain from Guatemala which has been successful in other Central American countries and in the United States, and which is now preparing to attack Asia, namely China.

Like both the nature and pace of economic development which differ dramatically from country to country, brand management progress and practice vary across emerging markets, not only vis-à-vis the developed world. Clifton (2007) reported that in Latin America, for example, brand management indeed lags behind that of the United States and Europe, but that wide discrepancies among Latin American countries also exist in the level of brand management expertise. This lag and these discrepancies, he argued, are due partly to the lack of competition which persists — privatization has been slower to take hold in Latin America, many economies are dominated by large "dynastic industrial families," and the forces of globalization have been felt (and responded to) differently in different nations. A notable exception in brand management maturity, he suggested, has been in tourism and, to a lesser extent, the quest for foreign direct investment, in which government-sponsored destination (or nation) branding has become both sophisticated and successful across almost the entirety of Latin America (Zerillo and Thomas, 2007).

In general, however, it is assumed by many that the growth of brand management in emerging markets is being driven in large measure by the demand (and therefore opportunity) for foreign — that is to say, "global" — brands. Some research concludes that a preference for imported, branded products prevails among consumers in emerging markets (Ettenson, 1993; Agbonifo and Elimimian, 1999; Marcoux *et al.*, 1997; Batra *et al.*, 2000; Klein *et al.*, 2006). To Essoussi and Merunka (2007), for example, these foreign products have greater appeal because of the symbolic meaning which they provide for consumers. To Okechuku and Onyemah (1999), they win out over domestic products simply because the quality from local producers is thought to be inferior.

Whatever the reason, a flurry of brand management activity by multinationals in emerging markets has been witnessed in the past decade. Likewise, brand management strategists have been eager to offer up frameworks and models for internationalization. Meyer and Tran (2006), for example, outlined market penetration and acquisition strategies for expansion to emerging markets. Xie and Boggs (2006) discussed the merits of corporate versus product-oriented branding in emerging markets.

Davar and Chattopadhyay (2002) suggested, however, that multinationals, despite the flurry of activity, are not doing particularly well in emerging markets. Indeed, they noted that there was a marked contrast between their high profit expectations and actual performance. The hoped-for treasures from "billions of new customers" had, instead, been weak market penetration, disappointing market shares and low profitability. These results, they argued, were due to strategies which relied on global platforms with little or no localization. Their conclusion for emerging markets ... global brands do not work.

This conclusion highlights the tension between global and local — between standardization and customization — which was initially raised by Theodore Levitt 1983 in his seminal piece *The Globalization of Markets*, but which apparently continues today in emerging markets, with perhaps even stronger force. Levitt's future of a standardized world never truly materialized, and, on the contrary, the pressure of globalization and the reality of localization have combined to make brand management in emerging markets extremely challenging. In China, for example, "global brands with Western associations and status can garner more interest, but that's still no guarantee of success" (Branding, 2007, p. 50). Some level of localization is absolutely fundamental, especially given the Chinese pride in language and history. But localizing in a culture which has variously been defined as mysterious, baffling, and impenetrable can prove difficult.

Additionally, as multinationals, responding to the tension between global and local, have attempted to appropriate "localness" and create global platforms with local adaptations, the distinction between global and local has become blurred. Indeed, foreign brands with adopted domesticity have led to a conflict between global and local images. And the result, according to Zhou (2005), is a high degree of brand confusion among consumers in emerging markets.

Consequently, Ger (1999) believed that local companies can win domestically by simply "out-localizing" the multinationals. Indeed, because of their abundant cultural resources, especially when economic resources are often lacking, these companies have an intrinsic advantage at home; knowledge of their own culture allows them to define that which is culturally "authentic," to create alternative strategies which conform to local economic systems, and to target and position, very precisely, products which resonate with their consumers. The challenge here is that the knowledge and skills of brand management in emerging markets are still at an infant stage.

Like brand management overall, private labels have also seen a surge in emerging markets. In general, however, their progress lags behind that of the developed world by several years which, according to AC Nielsen (2008), continues to increase year on year (15% to 17% of all retail sales during the period 2003–2005). The one exception is South Africa, where private labels can be found in 78% of all product categories (Product Focus, 2006). The average market share across these product categories, however, is only 10% — much lower than in France or Spain, for example, where one in three products in almost every product category is a private label (Reinhold, 2007), or in the United States, where, by the mid-1990s, a private label was the leader in 77 of 250 product categories and second or third in an additional 100 (Quelch and Harding, 1996).

As when private labels entered the United States and Europe, the initial appeal of private labels in emerging markets has tended to be the lower price; in some instances, private labels have been 30–50% less expensive than major brands, and even more for premium imported products. The lower price of private labels, however, has equated to perceptions of lower quality, and therefore, lower levels of consumer acceptance on the whole. Sales have also been volatile, paralleling economic changes which occur frequently. These perceptions, however, appear to be changing, albeit slowly. Some level of innovation in private labels has been seen, with multiple tiers of private labels which correspond to different quality levels, for example. And many consumers have become loyal to private labels, irrespective of the state of the economy. As an illustration of brand management in emerging markets — and private labels more specifically — the following section outlines the evolution of private labels in Croatian grocery retailing.

Private Labels in Croatian Grocery Retailing

The evolution of private labels in Croatian grocery retailing largely reflects the evolution of grocery retailing itself, which is logical, given that grocery retailing is often more advanced than other industries in emerging markets, and that grocery retailing chains and private label manufacturers work closely when developing private labels. Croatia only gained political independence in 1995, after four debilitating years of war with Serbia, which occurred within the larger series of conflicts which drew in all six of the former republics of

Yugoslavia. The war caused massive economic disruption and reduced Croatia to near poverty.

After the independence, however, the process of privatization and the introduction of the market economy took hold, and European style grocery retailing chains began to develop. Slowly, as in other parts of Europe and elsewhere, industry consolidation started, although in 2001, small "mom and pop" grocers still accounted for 74% of the market (Građani, 2005). Today, however, Croatian grocery retailing is among the most concentrated in Central and Eastern Europe, with these same small grocers reduced to only 38% by 2006. It is one of the most, if not the most, dynamic sectors in the Croatian economy, with the five leading grocery retailing chains comprising almost half of the retail market in 2007, dominated by the domestic chain *Konzum* (Trgovačke, 2007).

The introduction of private labels

Private labels were introduced in the late 1990s in the expanding Croatian grocery retailing chains. Consumers were definitely attracted to the new foreign brands which had appeared on the market, but prices for these products remained out of reach for all but the most affluent consumers. Most consumers were also accustomed to shopping with small local grocers or at farmers' markets. In hopes of attracting more and more consumers, therefore, the grocery retailing chains began to create private labels, realizing that they could be acquired at lower cost and therefore offered at lower prices.

At first, these private labels were created in product categories which required little specialized manufacturing techniques (The economic disruption of the war had left many companies in shambles.). Most were products which relied on Croatian manufacturers to perform basic processing or, even more elementarily, packaging of raw materials which were often imported. Coffee was one such product. In Croatia, as elsewhere, all coffee is imported, and the grocery retailing chains at that time contracted local manufacturers to roast and package coffee under private labels. Private label carbonated beverages and potato chips were also common in the early years as the grocery retailing chains experimented with private labels.

These grocery-retailing chains soon learned that they had the "power" to negotiate even lower prices for private labels. First, manufacturers could avoid the high costs which were associated with the development, promotion, and distribution of their own branded products. Second, unlike the small local grocers, the grocery retailing chains committed to purchasing fixed quantities over fixed periods, allowing manufacturers to plan their production. And third, grocery retailing chains paid their accounts on time and "in cash." As such, manufacturers were very eager to develop strong relationships with the chains. With both interest rates and inflation at astronomical levels, it could even be argued that private label contracts were at least partially responsible for the rebuilding of the Croatian food processing industry.

Lessons learned

Initial success of private labels prompted many grocery-retailing chains to expand their private labels to all product categories. The result was the seemingly absurd situation in which totally unrelated products shared the same private label. This lesson was soon learned, and some chains launched a premium private label under which they sold only specific product categories. More often, however, individual private labels were created for each product category. Consequently, despite the improved alignment between private label and product category, the chains incurred higher development and marketing costs, and profits suffered. In a sense, the successes of their private labels had become their own downfall. The grocery retailing chains resembled more and more the branded product manufacturers whose prices the private labels were intended to undercut.

As private labels continued growing in Croatia, and both industry consolidation and competition for consumers intensified, grocery retailing chains also applied more pressure on private label manufacturers to cut prices. Simultaneously, the once intimate relationships with these manufacturers grew more distant, and grocery-retailing chains lost control over product design and production. Wanting a piece of the growing private label pie, small entrepreneurial upstarts also began offering their services, promising lower prices than the established manufacturers.

The result of these factors, however, was a dramatic reduction in product quality. Indeed, feeling the pressure from the grocery retailing chains to match price demands, and exploiting the new product design and production freedom, manufacturers lowered their prices by lowering their costs — by changing recipes to use less expensive ingredients, by substituting lower quality vegetables or different vegetables altogether, by eliminating better but more costly manufacturing processes, etc. The small entrepreneurial upstarts had smaller investments and more flexible manufacturing processes, but the smaller economies of scale meant that their quality was inevitably inferior.

One example of this reduction of quality in Croatia at the time was particularly telling. The product category is known in Croatia as fruit and vegetable preserves. It is almost impossible to change the manufacturing quality of "fruit in a glass jar." But in order to cut costs and meet the lower price goal, both decreasing the quantity of fruit and increasing the quantity of sugar necessarily changed the recipe. At one particular private label manufacturer, a 720 ml jar which initially contained 400 g of fruit was first decreased to 350 g and finally to 300 g. At first glance, consumers could hardly notice the difference. But in the longer run, the reduction in quality was indeed noticeable, and sales of the private label preserves dropped significantly.

The overall consequence of lower quality, despite lower prices or perhaps even in concert with lower prices, was that consumers in Croatia developed an image of private labels as being low quality products for poor people. Even one low quality product could taint the image of all products under the label. For many grocery-retailing chains, the premium private labels were also demoted to the lowest levels in the minds of consumers.

Since this experience, however, grocery-retailing chains in Croatia have attempted to resurrect their premium private labels, complementing them with "B" (or "silver") level private labels. They have regained control over their product design and manufacturing, and now position premium private label products as those with the highest level of quality. Moreover, they are prepared not only to pay the price for this higher quality, but also to allocate more resources for their promotion. "B" level private label products are targeted at consumers with lower incomes, and are often distinguished by their lower quality packaging, and their shelving location by themselves, away from the remainder of the product assortment. In summary, the products which were initially developed by Croatian grocery retailing chains as private labels have become "B" private label products, and a new array of high quality, strictly controlled, and almost gourmet level products have been designed under new premium private labels.

The landscape of private labels

The first grocery retailing chain in Croatia to introduce private labels was the domestic company *Getro*. It was indeed the leader in recognizing the power of private labels, and in the late 1990s set about to develop a host of its own products, including fruit juices and syrups under the name *Fruta*, and pasteurized fruit and vegetable preserves under the name *Grandi*. At first, *Getro* aimed to capture only 5–10% of any product category with its private labels, but demand (and production capacity) for them has continued to grow and today they account for 60–70% in some categories. Early on, *Fruta* fruit juice succumbed to the low price-low quality spiral which then affected all products under the brand. Currently, *Getro* has 17 private

Table 9.1.   Getro private labels.

Getro food private labels	Getro non-food private labels
Cookie	Baby Star
Dominic	Blur
Frozen Land	Butterfly
Fruta	Chic Décor
Grand	Grandi
Grandi	Kitchenline
Gurman	Life
Gurman Mare	Master
Kristina	Nice
Luna	Ozone
Ole!	Perfect Kid
President's Choice	Personality
Sweet Star	Rubis
U Slast	
Vitafit	
Vita Milk	
Vau Mijau	

labels in food products, and an additional 13 private labels in other non-grocery categories (Table 9.1).

The private label *K plus* of *Konzum* has been exceptionally successful, with strong growth in a short period. Industry analysts even suggest that the success of *K plus* was instrumental in the rise of *Konzum* to its position as market leader. For consumers, *K plus* represents very high quality, and in many product categories, it outperforms branded products. *Konzum* has also introduced the private label *Rial* in its *Velpro* wholesaler subsidiary which supplies small grocers.

It is the success of *Konzum*'s private labels which has more or less influenced all other grocery retail chains in Croatia, especially the foreign companies which entered the Croatian market after 2000 when *K plus* was introduced. *Metro*, a German grocery retailing chain, for example, has developed a line of products (but not in all product categories) which share the same private label, *Aro*. *Metro* has expanded its private label sales by likewise supplying small grocers. Similar to *Konzum*, *Metro* demands that its *Aro* products meet or exceed the quality of branded products. Private label producers, who hope to supply *Metro*, compete in a public tender process in which the quality of both recipe and production, in addition to price, are assessed.

Billa, another grocery retailing chain, has followed the example of *Metro*, offering only those products under the *Clever* brand which it gauges to match the high quality standards of its private label. The Slovenian *Mercator*, with its self-titled private label, competes in a similar way. *Ultra* Group has *Ultra plus*, and CBS its own private label. NTL differs only slightly because, as a holding group of several grocery retailers with different names, it has developed a corporate level private label, but also unique private labels at the store level.

Finally, it is interesting that private labels have also found their way into Croatian wholesaling. The *Gastro Group*, for example, a strategic association comprised of about 35 wholesalers which supply about 40% of the hotels, restaurants, and bars in Croatia, has its own private labels for food stuffs. The breadth of its network and access to hotels, restaurants, and bars has meant that the *Gastro Group* has, in turn, had a significant influence on the Croatian grocery retailing industry.

Now and the future

Today, there are over 60 different private labels in Croatian grocery retailing, making it one of the leading countries in Central and Eastern Europe with respect to private labels. In certain product categories, they account for more than 30% of sales, sometimes exceeding the share of the "leading" branded products. Overall, growth of private labels has been steady: 5.4% share of total grocery sales in 2004, 6.4% in 2005, 7.4% in 2006, and 10.0% in 2007. Customers have a renewed faith in the quality of private labels, especially given that many are now produced by the same companies which supply the grocery retailing chains with branded products. Loyalty to private labels is rising, and not only among low income consumers. Private labels in Croatian grocery retailing, on the other hand, remain small in comparison to that of Western Europe. In Germany, for example, which has the widest grocery retailing in Europe, private labels make up 34% of all food and drink sales. In Britain, this number is 40% ... and increasing.

Fast growth of private labels in Croatian grocery retailing is projected for the future, however. Indeed, negotiations for Croatian accession to the European Union continue, with entry expected in 2010 or shortly thereafter. And accession means more competition from Western European giants like Tesco and Spar, which have very experienced private label managers and, perhaps more importantly, strong relationships with manufacturers.

Possibly foreshadowing the impending competition from an enlarged Europe which contains Croatia, the German hard discount grocery retailing chain *Lidl* entered the Croatian market in late 2006. Its strategy of ultralow prices is achieved largely through private labels, which account for 80% of its product assortment. *Lidl* has very well-established relationships with manufacturers which, combined with extremely large volume orders, yield incredibly low costs. Their control over product design and production is also very high, leading to products whose quality meets or exceeds that of branded products.

In order to defend themselves, several Croatian grocery retailing chains introduced new private labels shortly after *Lidl's* entry. *Konzum*, for example, created the *Standard* label, which is entirely void of any added value, and which is positioned as no frills but high quality products at low prices. *Lidl*, however, still has the upper hand, with a first mover advantage as pioneer of the high quality-low price private labels strategy, and because its company-managed distribution system has reduced costs even further. Additionally, *Lidl* has made it a company policy to settle accounts payable within 30 days; some Croatian grocery retailing chains take upwards of five months, and, in some instances, payment is made in kind rather than cash. Consequently, *Lidl* commands even lower prices from its manufacturers.

Lidl's strategy and corporate discipline have also had a spillover effect on manufacturers. The shorter payment periods have meant that they have more liquidity, and thereby requiring less operational financing. This, in turn, lowers the manufacturers' cost structure, and subsequently allows them to offer their products to *Lidl* at even lower prices. It can be expected, therefore, that additional consolidation will also occur in Croatian grocery retailing, as less financially astute chains are acquired.

Adding fuel to the fire, *Lidl's* grocery retailing arch enemy in Germany, *Aldi*, is also making motions toward Croatia. Started by Theo and Karl Albrecht in the 1960s, *Aldi* essentially defined the hard discount grocery retailing model, and all other hard discount chains are basically copycats, with varying degrees of success. Today, *Aldi* is known for its excellent product quality which, some industry analysts and many consumers believe, is superior to that of premium branded products. Undoubtedly, the presence of *Aldi* will cause additional changes to private labels in Croatian grocery retailing. In another twist, Slovenian grocery retailing chain *Mercator* has announced that it plans to expand its *Hura!* hard discount format to Croatia, Serbia, Montenegro, Bosnia, and Herzegovina in the coming year. It is no coincidence, therefore, that one Croatian grocery retailing chain recently launched a *Golden* private label which was touted as "the best quality at the lowest prices." Now, in order to see the supplier side of private labels in Croatian grocery retailing, the following section presents the case of Dona Trgovina D.O.O., one of the leading Croatian manufacturers of private grocery labels.

The Case of DONA Trgovina D.O.O.

DONA Trgovina D.O.O. is headquartered in Gornja Stubica, a small village in the continental part of Croatia about 11 km east of the capital city, Zagreb. Its main activity is fruit and vegetable processing. DONA employs 130 workers in seven departments: sales and marketing, supply, production, product quality control, transport, finance, and legal and personnel. All departments are housed at the headquarters in Gornja Stubica, although the sales and marketing department is comprised of several units which are located in larger regional centers of Croatia, such as Split, Osijek, and Rijeka.

DONA manufactures a wide range of products under its own brand, including fruit syrup, jams and marmalades, and fruit and vegetable preserves. Semi-finished products and concentrates have more recently become an important source of revenue; these are sold to leading Croatian and Slovenian manufacturers, such as *Lura Pića, Jamnica, Vindija*, and *Fructal*. DONA is also one of the leading Croatian manufacturers of private grocery labels, almost all of which are destined for Croatia. Indeed, it manufactures more than 50 products under the private labels *Rial, Rial-Standard, K plus, Frudela, Ultra Plus, P-Super, Mercator, Gasty, vitally, ideal, and others*.

Currently, the DONA brand generates 52.27% of the company's revenue. Semi-finished products and concentrates account for 22.30%. And private labels make up the remaining 26.43%. Within the DONA brand, fruit syrups dominate with 55.30% of all sales; jams and marmalades contribute 19.42%, fruit and vegetable preserves yield 25.28%. Private label breakdown is similarly syrup-dominated: fruit syrups 57.64%, jams and marmalades 19.22%, and fruit and vegetable preserves 23.61%.

History of DONA

DONA was founded in 1978 in the former Yugoslavia, the name itself an abbreviation for *DOmaći NApitak* (*domaći* meaning domestic and *napitak* meaning beverage). The slogan of the brand is *Bogatstvo Plodova Prirode*, which is translated as *The Richness of Nature's Fruits*. During the Yugoslav period, DONA was considered a guarantee of high quality. In the fruit syrups product category, DONA was the market leader for years across all of

Yugoslavia. Its success in fruit syrups contributed significantly to the development of other products under the DONA brand.

With the independence of Croatia in 1991, however, DONA suffered badly. The very profitable markets of the neighboring republics of the former Yugoslavia shut down completely, not only for DONA but also for all other local manufacturers. The company had problems sourcing raw materials; its suppliers were often located in war-torn areas in Croatia and elsewhere, and production capacity, therefore, decreased dramatically. The newly independent Croatia was also plagued with economic instability and a lack of financial market liquidity, which, naturally, took their toll.

Gradually, the Croatian market underwent a process of liberalization, with a commensurate increase in imported food products. The war had also been devastating on citizens, however, resulting in high unemployment and correspondingly low incomes. Consequently, there was a huge demand for inexpensive products, with quality pushed to the background. DONA continued to manufacture the same high quality products, and would not succumb to price competition. Sales fell dramatically and the company came close to bankruptcy.

A restructuring program, therefore, was initiated in the early 2000s in order to insure the future of DONA. It began with an analysis which explored the types of products and the prices which could be supported in the market. More specifically, it identified the range of products under the DONA brand which could be produced at prices which would be acceptable to grocery retailing chains, and, of course, which would be appealing to consumers, taking into account the grocers' margins. The conclusion, however, highlighted the fact that it was only possible to make a profit if production operated at near full capacity.

Further exploration of the competitive landscape of Croatian grocery retailing suggested that achieving this scale domestically, relying solely on the DONA brand, would be challenging. Exporting to neighboring republics in which the DONA brand had once achieved great status was one alternative to meet production objectives. Entering the European Union was also possible, although the competition was fierce and the company had little international experience.

The growth of private labels in Croatia had taken off in the late 1990s, however, and offered potential sales, seemingly without too much direct price competition with its own-branded products in the grocery retailing chains. The decision was taken at DONA, therefore, to "fight to win" in certain product categories with its DONA branded products, and pursue private label sales to grocery retailing chains, first domestically, then with great care internationally.

DONA branded products

DONA's competitors at the time varied, depending on the product category. With fruit syrups, for example, DONA faced several strong Croatian manufacturers (*Voćko, Maraska*, and *Lero*) and the Slovenian *Fructal*. In the jams and marmalades category, and the fruit and vegetable preserves category alike, the most significant competitor was *Podravka*, a leading Croatian manufacturer at that time. In general, however, DONA-branded products were higher quality than those of its competitors. Prices were sometimes higher and sometimes lower. Design of the competitors' brands, however, was considered more attractive.

DONA set out to target middle-aged women of average to higher income, whose main reason for purchasing products was price-quality ratio. In doing so, it hoped to exploit the high quality perception which DONA had nurtured among Croatian consumers, but underpriced the more expensive European and other foreign imports. More recently, however, another salient factor for these women has been health, which they largely gauge by the type, quality, and purity of a product's ingredients. A healthy lifestyle and quantity of fruit, for example, are nowadays being emphasized in DONA slogans and in promotional campaigns. In its most recent television advertisements, for example, DONA stressed the value of cranberries for treating urinary tract ailments, alongside a prominent display of DONA cranberry syrup.

In order to meet the target customers' price-quality ratio (and to adhere to EU packaging requirements which were on the horizon), DONA labels also needed to be addressed. The labels at the time, according to customers, were outdated and lackluster (Fig. 9.1). New labels, therefore, were implemented across the entire DONA product range (Fig. 9.2).

A new promotional program, using both push-and-pull tactics, was conducted, aimed specifically at increasing sales in grocery retailing chains.

Figure 9.1. DONA labels from 1980s, mid-1990s, and late 1990s. (From Company file. Printed with permission.)

Figure 9.2.   DONA labels today. (From Company file. Printed with permission.)

In one, for example, a customer would receive a free baseball cap, towel, umbrella, pair of sunglasses, key ring, T-shirt, or other gift which had been printed with the DONA logo, for any three DONA products which were purchased. The gifts were distributed at promotional desks which were located in the grocery store.

DONA also installed specially made DONA-branded shelves, on which its products were displayed. There were trolleys at which employees made fresh pancakes and offered DONA jams and marmalades as toppings. Some of the largest stores also had juice machines which provided fresh drinks with DONA fruit syrups.

More recently, DONA has also been active in developing new products, both to increase the breadth and depth of its offerings. As mentioned before, semi-finished products and concentrates have been added to the portfolio. And DONA is the only Croatian manufacturer with the following fruit syrup flavors: cranberry–apple, elderberry–apple, and grape. Similarly, in the jams and marmalades category, DONA has developed cranberry–apple and apple–cinnamon combinations.

The results of the restructuring program have been impressive. In 2006, DONA was the leading manufacturer of fruit syrups in Croatia in terms of production quantity, with almost one-third of the market (Table 9.2).

Indeed, it beat its closest competitor by a small margin, but almost doubled the production quantity of the number three players. Profitability has also risen steadily, with exports now comprising more than 15% of the profits of DONA-branded products (Table 9.3).

Table 9.2. Production quantity of fruit syrups in Croatia, 2006 (000 L). (From Company files).

Manufacturer	Production quantity
Lura	1,558
Maraska	843
Istravino	2,863
DONA	2,960
Dalmacijavino	154
Segestica	834
Unattributed	90
Total	9,302

Table 9.3. Profit on DONA-branded products, 2003–2006 (HRK). (From Company files.)

	2003	2004	2005	2006
Domestic market	8,451,719	16,382,481	28,070,033	59,939,691
International market	0	351,735	7,226,868	11,815,637
Total	8,451,719	16,734,216	35,296,901	71,755,327

Dona private label sales

Paralleling its efforts to regain the past glory of the brand, DONA also pursued private label sales to grocery retailing chains as part of the restructuring program. It first began manufacturing jams and marmalades for the *Getro* private label. Today, however, it supplies products across its entire range to Croatian grocery retailing (Table 9.4). Like with its own DONA-branded products, both the syrup and the jams and marmalade product categories dominate private label sales. The distinction between the two is usually only product depth; quality is equally high for both.

As mentioned previously, private label sales now generate more than 25% of DONA's revenues. The stability of these sales combined with the on-time and quick payment from the grocery retailing chains has also improved the financial situation of DONA. Contracts are now usually one year in length, and grocery-retailing chains are sometimes foregoing the lowest price private label manufacturer in favor of those companies (like DONA), which can supply the highest quality on a regular basis. Additionally, relationships with the grocery retailing chains have allowed DONA to negotiate better terms and

Table 9.4.   Examples of DONA private label sales. (From Company files.)

Private label	Product category
CBA International	Fruit syrups
Gastro Grupa	Jams and marmalades; fruit and vegetable preserves
Presoflex	Fruit syrups; jams and marmalades; fruit and vegetable preserves
Stridon Promet	Fruit syrups
Tommy	Fruit syrups; fruit and vegetable preserves

marketing-related conditions for its own-branded products, including better shelf location and wider promotional opportunities, for example.

DONA believes that there has been little cannibalization of its own-branded products. The relatively clear segmentation of the Croatian grocery market in which price-sensitive shoppers rarely move "up brand" has allowed DONA to compete with its branded products side-by-side with private labels. In some product categories, with customers who are actually aware of the provenance of the private label products, DONA has also benefitted from of a sort of halo effect.

The growth of private labels — especially high quality at low price private labels — which was outlined in the previous section, however, portends a threat to DONA-branded products. Indeed, more and more Croatian customers are questioning the value of big name brands (domestic and international), concluding that high quality can be had for lower prices. Croatian grocery retailing chains are also becoming savvy brand managers themselves, collaborating with private label manufacturers to launch new and exciting products under private labels, almost always at lower prices than the branded products.

The future of DONA

In the long term, it appears that DONA has good prospects due to the growth of private labels, especially as Croatian (and foreign) grocery retailing chains select private label manufacturers on more than just price — that is to say, on criteria such as production capacity, product quality, financial security, and industry reputation. DONA-branded products, however, will continue to be "attacked from inside" with the growth of its private label sales to grocery retailing chains. The strong relationships which it has with these grocery retailing chains will certainly help, but DONA's own ability to innovate — to create new and exciting branded products — will be key to survival of this component of the company.

Finally, accession to the European Union will surely result in more competition for DONA from both branded and private label manufacturers. On the other hand, it will also open new markets to DONA-branded products and private label manufacturing. Perhaps more critically in the short term, however, accession will also bring new manufacturing requirements. For example, the European Union has very strict rules of packaging and packaging waste, especially with respect to PVC and PET containers. With these rules come additional costs (machinery conversion costs, material costs, and taxes, for example), the effect of which DONA will need to address in order to maintain its competitiveness in both branded and private label manufacturing.

Conclusion

Emerging markets might be characterized by their dynamism. Indeed, the often double-digit growth, the skylines which arise seemingly overnight, and the incessant introduction of new goods and services, can sometimes, even for locals, be dizzying. It is this notion of dynamism which also appears to characterize brand management in emerging markets. Multinationals, racing to exploit a new cadre of customers, bring the latest brand management concepts, theories, and tools. Local companies, struggling not only to survive at home but also to compete as multinationals in their own right, discover swiftly how to employ these same brand management concepts, theories, and tools.

The evolution of private labels in Croatian grocery retailing provides an apt illustration of the dynamism of brand management in emerging markets. In less than a decade, with many lessons learned along the way, private labels have become an integral feature of Croatian grocery retailing. Accession to the European Union, however, will bring more change...and quickly. Companies like DONA Trgovina D.O.O. have adapted to change, and they will continue to adapt, as Croatia itself continues to adapt to the globalizing world economy.

Acknowledgments

The authors thank Ivan Goenawan, Christy Brandenburg, and Andrija Klaric and the Sales and Marketing Department of DONA Trgovina D.O.O.

References

Agbonifo, A and J Elimimian (1999). Attitudes of developing countries toward 'Country-of-Origin' products in an era of multiple brands. *Journal of International Consumer Marketing*, 11, 97–116.

Batra, R, V Ramaswamy, VD Alden, J Steenkamp, and S Ramachander (2007). Effects of brand local and no-local origin on consumer attitudes in developing countries. *Journal of Consumer Psychology*, 9, 83–95.

Clifton, D (5 November 2007). Branding in Latin America: Mas y Mejor for Latino Brands. *Brand Strategy*, 54.

Davar, N and A Cattopadhyay (2002). Rethining marketing programs for emerging markets. *Long Range Planning*, 35, 457–474.

Essoussi, L and D Merunka (2007). Consumers' product evaluations in emerging markets: Does country of design, country of manufacture, or brand image matter? *International Marketing Review*, 24, 409–426.

Ettenson, R (1993). Brand name and COO effects in the emerging market economies of Russia, Poland, and Hungary. *International Marketing Review*, 10, 14–36.

Ger, G (1999). Localizing in the global village: Local firms competing in global markets. *California Management Review*, 41, 64–83.

"Građani o Markama" (1 April 2005). http://www.gfk.hr/press/marke.htm.

Keller, K and Y Moorthi (2003). Branding in developing markets. *Business Horizons*, 49–59.

Klein, G, R Ettenson, and B Krishnan (2006). Extending the construct of consumer ethnocentrism: When foreign products are preferred. *International Marketing Review*, 23, 304–321.

Levitt, T (1983). The globalization of markets. *Harvard Business Review*, 92–102.

"Mamac za Potrošaće. "Kvaliteta Uz Nižu Cijenu" (23 May 2008). *Lider* — Special, 20–22.

Marcoux, J, P Filialtrault, and E Cheron (1997). The attitudes underlying preferences of young urban educated polish consumers toward products made in Western countries. *Journal of International Consumer Marketing*, 9, 5–29.

Meyer, K and Y Tran (2006). Market penetration and acquisition strategies for emerging economies. *Long Range Planning*, 39, 177–197.

Nielsen (2008). Private label brand assessment (Manufacturer View). Nielsen, 26 November 2008, http://en-us.nielsen.com/etc/medialib/nielsen_dotcom/en_us/documents/pdfcase_studies.pa.

Okechuku, C and V Onyemah (1999). Nigerian consumer attitudes toward foreign and domestic products. *Journal of International Business Studies*, 30, 611–622.

"Product Focus — Private Label Products in South Africa" (January/February 2006). *Market: Africa/Mid-East*, 2.

Quelch, J and D Harding (1996). Brands versus private labels: Fighting to win. *Harvard Business Review*, 74(1), 99–109.

Reinhold, E (2007). Trading up. *Soap, Perfumery, and Cosmetics*, 25–28.

Sarkar, A and J Singh (2005). New paradigm in evolving brand management strategy. *Journal of Management Research*, 5, 81–90.

Wilson, D and R Purushotaman (2003). "Dreaming with BRICs: The Path to 2050. *Global Economics Paper No. 99 Economic Research* from the GS Financial Workbench, Goldman Sachs 2003.

Xie, H and D Boggs (2006). Corporate branding versus product branding in emerging markets: A conceptual framework. *Marketing Intelligence and Planning*, 24, 347–364.

Zerillo, P and G Thomas (2007). Developing brands and emerging markets: An empirical application" *Place Branding and Public Diplomacy*, 3, 86–99.

Zhou, L (2005). Understanding consumer confusion on brand origin in a globalizing world. *Asia Pacific Advances in Consumer Research*, 6, 359–363.

Chapter 10

BALTIC TIGER OR WOUNDED LION — RETAIL TRADE AND SHOPPING BEHAVIOR IN ESTONIA, LATVIA, AND LITHUANIA

BRENT MCKENZIE

Abstract

This chapter focuses on the retail sector in the Baltic States of Estonia, Latvia, and Lithuania and examines this sector from an historic perspective, including a discussion of the role of retail trade in these countries during the Soviet communist period through re-independence in 1991, and accession to the European Union in 2004. This chapter also compares and contrasts the retail sector in the three countries, with extensive support provided through the analysis of empirical consumer shopping data collected in each country. The findings indicate that although retailers may wish to view the region as a single market, there are non-trivial differences in how consumers perceive retail service delivery, and that these drivers need to be accounted for in terms of successful retail performance.

Introduction

Transition economies[1] represent many of the fastest growing markets in the world and almost one-third of the world's population can be categorized as living in countries in transition (IMF, 2000). Transition economies

---

[1] The terms, transition, emerging, catching-up countries, and economies have all been used to describe former Republics of the Soviet Union during the last 10–15 years.

represent a significant opportunity for both domestic and international commercial activity (Arnold and Quelch, 1998; Gielens and Dekimpe, 2007) and play an increasingly larger role in international bodies such as the European Union, NATO, and the World Trade Organization (Michalopoulos, 2000; Baltas, 2001).

The focus of this chapter is to examine one economic sector, the retail sector, in three of the most dynamic transition economies, namely, the former Soviet Republics of Estonia, Latvia, and Lithuania. These Baltic States are an important region for the study of retail practice in transition as they arguably represent the most overt change from the Soviet planned economic system, to the free market, capitalist one. Furthermore, retailing and shopping behavior signified a meaningful change in social behavior by the people in these countries. As recently as 1993, in a popular tourist guide on the Baltic States (Williams, 1993), the section on shopping for all three countries contained such descriptions as "Shopping is not one of Estonia's major attractions. In fact, shopping can often be a totally fruitless experience (p. 409)." As will be demonstrated, this has certainly changed in the ensuing 15 years as the Baltic State retail sector has consistently led the European Union (EU) in terms of per capita retail growth.

The format of this review is based on a five-stage approach. First, a background to the area of study as well as a discussion of the relevance of such research utilizing the Baltic States as the region of interest is presented. The next section provides an overview of the retail history in these markets through three major periods, the period prior to incorporation into the Soviet Union (<1941); the Soviet period (1946–1991); and return to independence, transition, and EU accession (1991–2004). Included is an overview of the major discount/department/hypermarket store players currently operating in these markets. These reviews will highlight the significance of the retail sector to both the development of the countries themselves, but also the changing role of the consumer within these regions.

The fourth section of the chapter presents the findings of a major empirical consumer retail survey study conducted during the period of 2003–2008 that helps to highlight the major perceptions of Baltic retail shoppers in terms of retail metrics such as customer loyalty, service quality, pricing, merchandising, and brand development. The findings are discussed in terms of academic and practitioner research. This chapter concludes with suggestions and predictions as to the future of retail sector in this and other markets in transition.

The Baltic States

The Republics of Estonia, Latvia, and Lithuania are commonly referred to as the Baltic States, and are generally regarded as one single market, particularly by the West. Although this chapter links the three as a region, at many levels they represent distinct and separate markets, as will be demonstrated in terms of retail practice and shopping behavior findings. There are many reasons why the West views the Baltic States as one entity, including their geographic presence on the Baltic Sea; their recent joint history as Republics annexed into the Soviet Union in the 1940s; their return to independence in 1991 and simultaneous joining of the EU in 2004.

In contrast, as is the case for most independent nations, there are a number of differences between the three. In terms of the role of religion, Lithuania's main linkage has been to the Catholic Church, while in Estonia and Latvia, it is the Lutheran Church. In terms of the degree of Sovietization, or Russification, that each country experienced during the Soviet period, it was much greater in Estonia and Latvia in comparison to Lithuania. This was mainly a result of the higher degree of forced Russian emigration into Estonia and Latvia to grow the industrial sector, while Lithuania remained primarily an agricultural nation. Even today, approximately 26% of Estonians are ethnic Russians, 38% in Latvia, but less than 7% in Lithuania.

In terms of economic prosperity, Estonia has led the other two in economic growth since 1991, focusing on the financial and other value-added service industries. Latvia has attempted to also move in this direction, but due to the heavy industry legacy from the Soviet Union this has been more difficult. Furthermore, concerns with corruption and political instability have also had an impact (Raubiško, 2001). Lithuania, although arguably the first of the three to formally shed the communist planned economic model and transition to market economic growth in the early 1990s, now trails the other two in growth, partially attributed to a continued high economic concentration in the agricultural sector.

Beyond economic measures, there are a number of cultural and social resemblances and differences between the three countries. Each differs in terms of language, but it can be argued that the similarities between Estonia and Latvia, and its peoples, are extensive, but not interchangeable. Due to the geographic proximity of Estonia and Latvia, their relative size in terms of geography and population, and the similarity of their histories, particularly during the 20th century, has resulted in a high degree of commonality in their shopping and retail market environments

(Eesti Konjunktuurlinstituut, 2002). Both Estonia and Latvia have benefited from a continued growth of retail players and formats, with linkages in terms of logistics, product selection, and other retail drivers. In contrast, Lithuania, although larger than the other two in both geographic size and population, has a retail sector that represented less of a focus in terms of economic growth. This could be partially attributed to the presence of one main retail player, Maxima, and many smaller players (these differences will be discussed later in this chapter).

Finally, the significance of the Baltic States for retail study can be supported by the fact that these three have been the fastest growing retail markets in the EU, in terms of per capita sales (Baltic Business News, 2007). Although in absolute terms these markets are relatively small as their respective populations are just over 1.3 million in Estonia and 2.3 million in Latvia and 3.5 million in Lithuania, they nonetheless represent an important venue for theorizing and measuring the drivers of retail success. Reasons for this rapid growth of the Baltic States retail sector include the typical reasons of overall growth in a country's economy (i.e., GNP growth numbers) and a corresponding increase in worker's wages, and higher disposable incomes. A less common and arguably more region specific reason for this growth can be attributed to the changing social nature of these former Soviet states. One way in which Estonians, Latvians, and Lithuanians have been able to overtly demonstrate their full integration into the EU is an increased focus on Western concepts of shopping and consumerism, as these activities represent tangible links to their inter-war period of independence, and political and economic relations with Western Europe (Seitz, 1992).

Baltic Retail History

The origins of the retail sector before 1941

Retail trade in the Baltic States had a strong past due to the historic tradition of membership in the Hanseatic League and international east-west trade (Raun, 2001). This tradition managed to continue during the first period of independence of the three countries following World War I. The retail sector consisted mainly of small shopkeeper co-ops, which represented a strong sense of nationalism and beyond providing employment, were also a funding source of education goals (Palm, 1989). Although co-ops represented less than 10% of all retail outlets, they represented over one-third of Baltic retail trade.

Sovietization of Baltic retail trade

In the initial years of the Soviet Union, the economy was stimulated by permitting private retail trading, but like most industries, retail enterprises were soon encompassed in nationalization efforts. The retail sector, like most aspects of the Soviet economic system was depicted in official propaganda posters. Within the Soviet Union, the retail trade workers were celebrated, and even the concept of providing good customer service was highlighted, particularly in Soviet propaganda posters (Russian Posters: http://eng.plakaty.ru/). In the Baltic States themselves, their economies in general and Estonia's specifically were similar to other Scandinavian countries prior to 1940. With their forced annexation into the Soviet Union, their economies, as were other Soviet republics, were transformed into a centrally planned, communist, economic, political, and social system. The Soviet system went beyond physical occupation to encompass all aspects of social and economic life, starting with the banning of private ownership (Raun, 2001).

In terms of the retail sector, with the initial Soviet invasion of the Baltic States in 1940/41 the Soviet Union nationalized the co-ops which were now subordinate to the central government (Central Union of consumers' Societies in the USSR — "Centrosoyns"). State-owned retail outlets dominated the cities, but co-op stores continued to do well in rural areas. Under this initial period of Soviet power, retail outlets dropped in number up to four times. The forced industrialization of their economies required Baltic suppliers to now supply goods to the whole of the Soviet Union. Thus fewer consumer goods remained in the Baltic States (Kutt, 1968) but overall, Baltic consumers had access to better products, had better distribution systems, and a higher standard of living, compared to rest of USSR (Järvesoo, 1978).

In the latter years of the Soviet period, co-ops began moving to urban settings as they could now purchase inventories from co-op producers, state enterprises, or individuals. As consumer shortages began to occur, the regional governments tried to increase the flow of goods and services to consumers, but most co-ops continued to focus on serving state contracts for the same goods, as these provided bigger orders and would accept "poorer" quality. This compounded the shortages as goods that could be "semi-finished," those that could be used in further production such as zippers, electrical components, were bought up from retail establishments by co-ops to use in industrial (higher profit) items. In order to halt this process, local governments would limit (or in some cases ban) co-ops from buying these goods from State stores (Palm, 1989).

Although vastly secondary to industrial output, the retail sector did play a role in the Soviet political agenda. As early as 1935, the capital city of each Soviet Republic was charged with establishing a model department store to represent the success of the Soviet system (Hessler, 2004). This policy regained prominence under Khrushchev in the 1950s and 1960s as he saw the growth of consumer goods, and consumerism, "austere consumerism" as a way to demonstrate the Soviet Union's superiority to the West (Reid and Crowley, 2000). Each of the three Baltic States had a large central department store that occupied a prominent spot in the downtown of their capital cities, Tallinn, Estonia, Riga, Latvia, and Vilnius, Lithuania.[2]

The period of transition between 1991 and 2004

In contrast to developed markets, where the services sector represents the majority of economic output and growth (World Bank, 2003), as noted, prior to the transition to a market-based economy, economic output in countries/regions of the Soviet Union, and Central, and Eastern Europe were predicated on industrial production at the expense of the service sector. It has only been since the end of the communist period that the service sector began to flourish (Stearns, 2001; LeBaron, 2002).

In 1991, re-independence was re-established in the Baltic States, and since 1992, under new constitutions, private property, and economic market conditions were protected by law. The economies began to change dramatically, and by 1999, the GDP percentages had shifted more toward Western economic metric norms. The number of retail establishments increased rapidly as the planned economy period ended, although initially the vast majority of the retailers were small and competed mainly on price (Drtina, 1995; Robinson, 1998; Seminonoviene, 2003). As the economies began to grow, and the political and social environments changed, more modern, larger, and foreign-owned retailers entered. No longer was price the sole criterion for retail competition, thus there was a need for retailers to have a greater understanding of additional retail practices and drivers from a local perspective (Dunne *et al.*, 2002).

In all three markets, the most dominant form of retailing was the discount/department/hypermarket store format. This was a logical extension from the central department store and central open air markets that existed during the Soviet period. With the growth in the respective economies, the

---

[2] Although all three sites still exist today, and are involved in retail, only the one in Estonia, "Tallinna Kaubamaja" still operates as a department store.

number of retail brands began to increase. In Estonia, the central department store Tallinna Kaubamaja (www.kaubamaja.ee) was privatized and became a publicly traded company in 1994, and opened a supermarket/hypermarket brand, Selver (www.selver.ee) in 1995. The other major domestic Estonian retailer, Maksimarket (www.etk.ee), is a retail brand of the Estonian cooperatives, and was the first hypermarket to open in Estonia in 1994. In terms of foreign entrants, the Finnish department store Stockmann (www.stockmann.fi) opened their first foreign-based store in Tallinn, while the hypermarket Prisma, which is also a Finnish brand (www.prismamarket.ee), opened it first store in 2000.

In comparison to Estonia, the Latvian and Lithuanian retail sector has been slower to expand, particularly in terms of number of large format stores. In Latvia, the one major domestic retail brand, Rimi (www.rimi.lv), opened its first store in 1997 and has subsequently expanded into Lithuania. In contrast, in Lithuania, the domestic retailer originally known as VP Market, now known as Maxima (http://www.maximagrupe.eu), opened its first stores in 1992, and today is the largest retailer in Lithuania. Maxima now operates in Latvia and Estonia, and in addition to Rimi, two other hypermarkets, Iki and Norfa make up the discount/hypermarket/department store sector. Iki (http://old.iki.lt/en) is the oldest retail chain in Lithuania and has also expanded into Latvia. Norfa (www.norfa.lt), which opened its first store in Lithuania in 1997, continues to grow its operations in Lithuania.

The current retail market

Not all retail brands have been successful in the Baltics. The large Finnish retailer SOKOS (www.sokos.fi) operated and then closed a department store in Tallinn in the late 1990s (although Prisma is also a SOKOS brand), and more recently the large German discount chain Lidl (www.lidl.de) purchased numerous retail sites in all three countries only to terminate their plans to enter the markets (BBN, 2006). What has been constant in all three countries is the continued shrinkage of market share by the small independent shops which has resulted in various degrees of involvement by local governments to address these issues.

What the Baltic retail sector has done is shown remarkable resilience to withstand the transition from the Soviet period, accession to the EU, and a continued blend of domestic and international competition. As noted in a report by retail consultants KOBA (2008), with wages in the Baltic States continuing to outpace inflation, the retail sector has been a major benefactor, and the premium on prime retail space will be the biggest challenge moving ahead. In another study, the Baltic States appear to have a healthy retail future in the coming years. The expectation is that if strong economic growth continues, then the growing youth population that continues to aspire to their brethren in Western Europe will drive the retail marketplace (PWC, 2008).

Empirical Research Study

In contrast to the focus on retail practice in the Baltic States, there continues to be a limited amount of academic research in the field. Part of the reason for this can be attributed to the increased complexities that researchers face in studying phenomena within transition economies that do not exist in studying the same phenomena within developed markets (Lascu *et al.*, 1993). For instance, one of the principal tenets of international economies is the theory of Purchasing Power Parity (PPP), which is based on the premise that a common basket of goods, when quoted in the same currency, should cost the same in two countries (Kotabe and Helsen, 2004). One of the assumptions of the theory is that all goods are identical in both countries, and that transportation costs and trade barriers are low. In transition economies these assumptions have been questioned due to the strong monetary shocks that occurred during the transition from a planned to a market economy that meaningfully altered prices, exchange rates, and trade patterns (Halpern and Wyplosz, 1997).

Therefore, the remainder of this chapter attempts to contribute to this field of study by presenting the findings of empirical research of Baltic shoppers' perceptions of shopping behavior. The data presented here examines how Baltic consumers perceive retail performance in terms of shopping behavior variables such as price, location, merchandise, and retail service. These are typical retailing metrics, which historically have been used to help explain retail store loyalty. An additional factor, labeled "attitude to the retail brand" is also included as a mediating variable to account for the fact that for each country sample, multiple retail brands have been used. The focus of the study is to provide a cross cultural, or Baltic perspective, of retail shopping behavior. This perspective of retail shopping behavior has previously been supported in the research literature (Merrilees *et al.*, 2007). The relationship of the factors is depicted in Fig. 10.1.

In terms of the constructs for analysis, they are stated as follows:

- $L = f(B; \text{Loc})$
- $B = f(P; PA; PI; M)$.

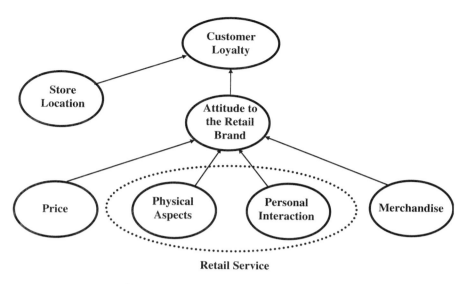

Figure 10.1. Model of shopping behavior.

Store loyalty is "*L*", "*B*" is the customers' attitude toward the store brand, "*Loc*" is the store location variable, "*P*" is product price, "*PA*" is the physical aspects of service; "*PI*" is the personal interaction variables of service, and "*M*" is merchandise selection.

A number of previous studies have used customer loyalty as the predictive validity of the shopping behavior factors as measured by the correlations of the constructs to store loyalty measures: such as intention to shop; and intention to recommend (Dabholkar *et al.*, 1996; Lewison, 1997; Levy and Weitz, 2004). For this study, it is suggested that a more sophisticated assessment of predictive validity is proposed that places the drivers of shopping behavior into a broader model that explains patronage loyalty behavior (i.e., customer loyalty) and store brand attitudes in relation to the retailer (i.e., attitude to the retail brand).

As such, shopper intentions are mediated through their attitude to the retail brand (Low and Lamb, 2000). Merchandise, retail service, and pricing factors are placed into a broader model of the formation attitude to the retail brand, and then to customer store loyalty. The suggestion is that if a retailer delivers a certain level of retail service, products, and price, then a level of trust will develop by the consumer that the store's performance will continue in the future (Morgan and Hunt, 1994). This view is that trust captures an attitude from the present and carries it over to the future (Merrilees and

Fry, 2002). In addition, as in most retailing research the store location can influence the willingness of a customer to revisit a store. However, the store location is not likely to influence brand attitudes about the store. Different locations would be valued differently so there would not be a constant relation to brand attitude.

The testing of these equations uses path analysis (Kline, 1998), which can attest to the variance in customers' attitude to the retail brand, and in turn customers' attitude to the retail brand as the main determinant of customer store loyalty, with support from the location attribute. When taken together, the indirect effects of merchandise, retail service, and price on customer store loyalty and thus shopping behavior can be established. Therefore, the research design incorporates the development of a survey instrument and administration methods to take into account the collection of data in the three Baltic countries.

Survey Instrument

The scale items were drawn from a number of sources, and reflect the items used in previous shopping behavior studies (Lindquist, 1975; Mazursky and Jacoby, 1985; Rinne and Swinyard, 1995; Berman and Evans, 2001). Each item was asked in terms of a rating on a one to nine scale, with nine the highest perceived performance, and one the lowest. The items were in different groupings, namely location (one item), price (two items), personal interaction (six items), physical aspects (six items), and merchandise selection (two items). Summative scales were included for brand attitude (four items) and loyalty (four items). The items and the mean customer perception scores are found in Table 10.1.

Data Collection

As this research involved a multicountry, multilanguage study, different approaches to data collection were employed, although all incorporated convenience samples in order to provide a consistent approach. For each country, the source stores were those mentioned in the previous section, and, as stated, represented the leading discount/department/hypermarket retailers in their respective markets. For the Estonian sample, the stores were Tallinna Kaubamaja, Selver, Prisma, Stockmann, and Maksimarket. For the Latvian sample, there were three stores, Stockmann, Rimi and Maxima, and for the Lithuanian sample, four stores Rimi, Maxima, Iki, and Norfa.

Table 10.1.   Scale items.

	Estonia	Latvia	Lithuania
Physical aspects of service items			
This store is clean and tidy	3.06	3.32	4.85
The merchandise displays at this store look good visually	3.14	3.65	4.90
This store is rarely out of stock on items	3.88	4.33	4.76
This store has a modern look about it	3.48	3.67	4.76
The displays have plenty of helpful information about the merchandise	4.11	4.44	4.98
Self-selection at this store is easy and well guided	3.64	3.89	4.97
Personal interaction service items			
The employees at this store give you confidence for your shopping	4.03	5.20	5.14
Selling staff at this store give prompt service	3.58	4.84	5.32
This store has knowledgeable staff who can answer customer queries	3.76	4.87	5.22
Selling staff are always courteous with customers	3.17	4.37	5.08
The selling staff at this store treat me with respect	3.53	4.50	5.18
Selling staff at this store show appreciation for my business	3.77	4.88	5.13
Price items			
This store's "sales" and specials are real bargains	3.77	3.94	4.92
This store has reasonable prices (value for money)	4.19	4.38	5.29
Location item			
The store location is convenient for me	4.23	4.03	5.16
Merchandise items			
The merchandise at this store is of high quality	4.04	4.77	5.06
This store has clothing of the latest trends and styles	4.37	5.08	4.58
The product brands in this store are really good	4.27	4.87	4.90
Attitude to the retail brand items			
There is something special about this store	4.57	5.31	4.67
I really admire this store	4.66	5.38	4.71
This store has a good reputation among customers	3.44	4.34	4.79
This store is consistently good in all that it does	4.19	4.85	5.00
Customer loyalty items			
I plan to shop at this store (again) in the next six months	3.39	3.88	4.87
I plan to recommend this store to others in the next six months	4.10	4.98	4.66
My next purchase is likely to be from this store	4.68	5.24	4.66
I am likely to spend the same (or more) amount of money in this store in the next six months compared to the last six months	4.49	4.70	4.76

Table 10.2.   Sample characteristics.

	Estonia (%)	Latvia (%)	Lithuania (%)
Male Shoppers	38	40	35
Female Shoppers	62	60	65
Age: <25	50	45	28
Age: 26–40	28	28	44
Age: 41–55	17	21	24
Age: >55	5	6	4

All data collection was conducted in the respective capital cities of Tallinn, Riga, and Vilnius, as these cities represent the dominate retail market for each country.

As stated, convenience samples were used, and although there was no way of knowing how representative the samples were in comparison to the general population of the country, screening questions were asked to ensure that the subjects had visited the store in recent months. The profile of the respondents based on age and gender questions is found in Table 10.2. The age distribution tended to a more youthful shopper, as approximately three-quarters of the sample respondents in each country were under 40 years of age. The relative youthfulness of the typical Baltic discount/department store/hypermarket consumer was noticed and confirmed by the author, based on direct observations made during several visits to each store. Furthermore, to test for potential age bias in responses based on years shopping as an adult pre- and post-communist period, a chi-squared test comparing the responses of younger (<40) and older (>40) respondents to the question "is this your favorite store" indicated no statistically significant difference (Estonia: $\chi^2 = 0.552$; $p = 0.457$; Latvia: $\chi^2 = 1.63$; $p = 0.201$; Lithuania: $\chi^2 = 0.029$; $p = 0.866$).

Reliability of Constructs

Each shopping behavior construct was tested for reliability, using Cronbach alpha values. All scores were above the accepted level of 0.60 indicating the interrelatedness of the set of items. The results were as follows, with the order being, Estonia, Latvia, Lithuania for the each construct:

- Overall brand attitude toward the retailer (four items): 0.84, 0.84, 0.86
- Future intention to shop/store loyalty (four items): 0.87, 0.82, 0.81

- Price (two items): 0.72, 0.64, 0.67
- Physical aspects (six items): 0.90, 0.86, 0.93
- Personal interaction (six items): 0.93, 0.89, 0.89
- Merchandise (three items): 0.86, 0.76, 0.74
- Location (one item): NA.

Path Analysis

In order to determine the magnitude of each of the constructs on customer loyalty, and/or attitude toward the retail brand, path analysis was conducted. Table 10.3 summarizes the path estimates for each country. For example, one of the key relationships is that of brand attitude to store loyalty. For each country, the relationship, as measured by a t-value, confirms the position that for Baltic consumers their brand attitude toward the store is a major influence of store loyalty. Location was also important in all countries, as expected for this retail category. Price, merchandise, and both physical aspects, and personal interaction indicators of service were also important influences of the attitude toward the brand.

A key finding in Table 10.3 reflects the influences of brand attitudes. There were noticeable differences in the leading variable for each country. For Estonia, it was the personal interaction factor, or staff impact on service, while for Latvia and Lithuania it was the merchandise factor. The second most important influence on the formation of a retail brand attitude also varied by country. In Estonia, it was the store merchandise, while in Latvia it was price, and in Lithuania it was physical aspects of service. In terms of influence on customer loyalty, for all three countries the attitude toward the brand was strongest. The next section provides some input as to the potential basis for these findings.

Discussion

When the actual average ratings for each of the shopping behavior variables are examined (Table 10.1), some interesting patterns emerge. For all Estonian ratings, except store location, the subjects rated the Estonian retailers the highest. The most pronounced differences were in the areas of price, personal service, and attitudes toward the brand. These findings may be attributed to the relatively more advanced retail sector in Estonia, and the fact that Estonian consumers have had a greater history and knowledge of Western retailing even during the Soviet period due to the their proximity, and ability to watch TV and listen to radio broadcasts from Finland. In contrast, the findings for

Table 10.3. Path analysis findings.

PATH	Averages		
	Estonia	Latvia	Lithuania
Attitude toward the Brand ⟹	4.22	4.97	7.80
Price ⟹	3.98	4.16	5.10
Location ⟹	4.23	4.03	4.74
Personal interaction ⟹	3.64	4.78	5.18
Physical aspects ⟹	3.55	3.88	4.87
Merchandise ⟹	4.23	4.91	4.85
Customer loyalty ⟹	4.16	4.70	4.74

PATH	Customer loyalty		
	Estonia	Latvia	Lithuania
Attitude toward the Brand ⟹	0.59 (18.59)**	0.49 (13.88)**	0.56 (20.43)**
Location ⟹	0.29 (9.32)**	0.31 (8.67)**	0.39 (14.14)**

PATH	Attitude to the brand		
	Estonia	Latvia	Lithuania
Personal interaction ⟹	0.37 (8.51)**	0.14 (3.07)**	0.16 (4.59)**
Price ⟹	0.24 (7.61)**	0.22 (5.71)**	0.14 (7.74)**
Merchandise ⟹	0.32 (9.77)**	0.36 (8.65)**	0.48 (16.51)**
Physical aspects ⟹	0.08 (1.93)#	0.12 (2.49)*	0.31 (9.31)**

A score of 1 if you strongly agree with the statement and 9 if you strongly disagree.
(t-values in parentheses) *Significance $p < 0.05$ **Significance $p < 0.01$ *Significance $p < 0.10$.

Lithuania may be attributed to the fact that unlike in Tallinn (Tallinna Kaubamaja and Stockmann) and Riga (Stockmann) there is no traditional department store currently operating in Vilnius, and thus a lower expectation and perception of personalized service are expected from discount and hyper-market stores. When the individual item scores are examined, the level of retail service is less easy to compare because the system is somewhat different and so Estonians and Latvians may have been slightly less harsh in judging the stan-dards of service received. Notwithstanding some differences across store attributes, transition economies will need time to develop their retail systems to levels found in the West. Observations by the author in visits to all three countries has indicated that the Estonian retail sector has progressed in a more rapid fashion, but that since entry into the EU the three markets may be expe-riencing a greater degree of convergence.

These findings suggest that opportunities continue to exist for foreign retailers to invest in these markets, but they should not be complacent in set-ting retail service norms. Even though the broad factor pattern was roughly similar for all three countries, retailers must not consider this as one market. It is suggested that cross-cultural differences seem to be in the detail of the various constructs. The purpose of including these research findings in this chapter is intended to provide insight into inter-country differences in the way that consumers form brand attitudes to the retailer and store loyalties in the discount/department/hypermarket store category. In addition, different retail categories might call for a different perspective, so the results are conditional on that context.

In terms of brand attitude formation, for all three countries, the average scores were middling at best. This may indicate that Baltic consumers do form an attitude about the store brand, but that their attitude is not strongly oriented one way or the other. This finding may be of interest to retailers with a more established brand image when thinking of entering these markets, as it appears that it may be difficult to shape that attitude once established. For existing retailers wishing to enhance their brands may require focusing on the individual drivers of brand attitude rather than an overall brand image.

In a similar vein, the average rating for store loyalty mirrored those of attitude toward the brand, although slightly higher for each country. Again this may indicate a hesitation on the behalf of the Baltic consumer to overtly express their loyalty to a store, or that they continue to shop most stores in the discount/department/hypermarket category. This may be the result of a continued ease of access to each store brand in the capital city regions.

Shopping Behavior

Although the research presented provides a solid grounding in the area of Baltic consumer perceptions of retail performance and a greater understanding of the significance of various retail shopping drivers, one limitation of the findings was that the questions asked did not fully account for how Baltic consumers rank the importance of retail drivers. In order to acquire a better understanding of this, the survey included a question where respondents could list the top two reasons they had for selecting a store. The categories were retail service, store location, prices, and products. These results are of interest in light of the findings based on specific perceptions of measures of the individual factor items. The findings by country are found in Table 10.4.

As indicated, for Estonian shoppers, the product themselves and the retail service provided by the store are the leading reasons for selecting a store. Location and price, although not trivial, trail the other two. In contrast, for Latvian shoppers, the location of the store is the leading reason for selecting a store, followed by products. Service and price are similarly rated, and trail the other two. The findings of Lithuanian shoppers differ significantly from the other two countries. Location is by far the most dominant factor, seconded by products. The price of the products is third, with the role of retail service a distant fourth.

Management Implications

These findings provide some interesting opportunities for Baltic retailers. For instance, in continuation of the findings in Table 10.3, Estonian consumers appear to be looking for a more balanced blend of the four factors of service, products, price, and location, which is not dissimilar to consumer shopping expectations in the West. In comparison to their Baltic neighbors, a much higher focus is placed on service than for Latvian and Lithuanian shoppers. This could be attributed to the more advanced (i.e., richer) economy in Estonia compared to the others, as well as a more developed knowledge of

Table 10.4.   Number one reason for choosing to shop a store.

	Estonia (%)	Latvia (%)	Lithuania (%)
Retail service	27	21	11
Location	23	30	42
Prices	20	20	17
Products	29	29	30

retail service, which as noted, can be attributed to the leading role that Estonia played historically in retail trade during the Soviet period as their greater window to the West in comparison to the other two countries. For retailers looking to succeed in this market, there is the opportunity to provide greater levels of service to distinguish their store, and have the added advantage of having some flexibility in pricing if needed to provide this service as Estonian shoppers place less importance on store choice based on the price of the products.

For Latvian shoppers, store choice is more a question of the dual factors of products and location, and price and service. One implication for retailers would be that Latvian shoppers may be like most shoppers, in that they would prefer "good" versus "poor" service, but they see this as a trade-off to price. Therefore, the consumer interprets the fact that since greater service is provided then the store must be charging greater prices in order to provide that service (and vice versa). With this being the case, retailers should make a concerted effort to instill a service orientation in Latvia (i.e., consumers must learn to expect improvements in service without corresponding increases in price), but until this happens, they must be able to deliver service in an efficient manner that does not directly translate into higher product prices.

In Lithuania, the traditional retail adage of "location, location, location" still appears to hold. The Lithuanian culture, particularly in comparison to Estonian and Latvian culture, continues to be linked to its agrarian economy, the role of the church, with the result being a more collectivist society. This collectivist orientation leads to retail patronage being a way to support local businesses (Baltrimiene, 2005). Retailers must be able to emphasize the community and thus be seen as a "local" retailer. This helps to explain the vast market share gained by the only Lithuanian-based retailer in the study, Maxima, having such as large market share in Lithuania (Graham, 2007). These findings indicate that for a retailer to be successful in Lithuania, they should attempt to be viewed as "Lithuanian," which could be reinforced by carrying "Lithuanian" products as products is the second highest rating for store selection. This finding also highlights the limited focus Lithuanian discount/hypermarket shoppers place on service, and thus greater attention on those drivers that aid in self-service should be paid.

Conclusions

In conclusion, the aim of this chapter was to provide both a brief historical and current view of the retail sector in the little studied countries of Estonia,

Latvia, and Lithuania. Through the use of secondary and primary data, a stronger awareness of how retailers should make strategic and operational decisions in these markets was made. These findings have important managerial implications in terms of retailing practice, employee development, and east/west business opportunities (Smith, 1990; Lempert, 1996; Cyr, 1997). The research findings of this study, using the Baltic States as a proxy for other transition economies, is expected to be of interest to both foreign retailers looking at expanding operations into these and similar countries in transition, as well as to domestic retailers who would have historically had less experience and access to retailing research of this type.

In brief, the retail sector in Estonia, Latvia, and Lithuania will continue to represent an interesting area of study from a number of viewpoints. The first is to determine to what degree the retail perspectives in transition economies will drift toward Westernized or developed economy views that focus on the marketing concept and meeting the needs of the consumer (de Mooij, 2004). A second question to address is what are the legacies of the former Soviet period that will continue to have an impact on consumer behavior in these markets? The final question that both retail researchers and practitioners must address is what are the similarities across the three countries, and what are the differences, and thus what retail drivers must be localized and what can be regionalized. The findings of the study helps to highlight these issues, and the suggestion is that future research may want to examine additional retail formats, and additional retail variables (i.e., temporary discounts, loyalty programs, etc.) and retail perceptions in additional markets in transition to better understand these points.

References

Arnold, DJ and JA Quelch (1998). New strategies in emerging markets. *Sloan Management Review*, 40(1), 7–20.

Baltas, NC (2001). European Union enlargement: An historic milestone in the process of European integration. *Atlantic Economic Journal*, 29(3), 254–265.

Baltrimiene, R (2005). Cultural dimensions of Lithuania and its relative position in the context with other European countries. http://www.klsmk.lt/galery/_klsmk/mokslas/karjera/renata_baltrimiene.pdf [21st January 2008].

Baltic Business News (BBN) (12 July 2006). Lidl allegedly won't open a chain in the Baltic's. *Newsletter*, July 12.

Baltic Business News (BBN) (6 June 2007). Latvia reports the steepest retail trade growth in EU. *Newsletter*, p. 4.

Berman, B and JR Evans (2001). *Retail Management: A Strategic Approach*, 8th edn. Englewood Cliffs, NJ: Prentice Hall.

Cyr, DJ (1997). Culture and control: The tale of east–west joint ventures. *Management International Review*, 37(1), 127–144.

Dabholkar, PA, DI Thorpe, and JO Rentz (1996). A measure of service quality for retail stores: Scale development and validation. *Journal of the Academy of Marketing Science*, 24(1), 3–16.

de Mooij, M (2004). *Consumer Behavior and Culture: Consequences for Global Marketing and Advertising*. London, UK: Sage Publications.

Drtina, T (1995). The internationalisation of retailing in the Czech and Slovak Republics. *Service Industries Journal*, 15(4), 191–203.

Dunne, PM, RF Lusch, and DA Griffith (2002). *Retailing*, 4th edn. Orlando, FL: Harcourt Inc.

Eesti Konjunktuurlinstituut (2002). *Baltic Facts 2002: Economic and Social Indicators*. CD-Rom.

Gielens, K and MG Dekimpe (2007). The entry strategy of retail firms in transition economies. *Journal of Marketing*, 71, 196–217.

Graham, T (2007). Is maxima a wal-mart in sheep's clothing? *The Baltic Times*. http://www.baltictimes.com/news/articles/17168/ [15th July 2008].

Halpern, L and C Wyplosz (1997). Equilibrium exchange rates in transition economies. *International Monetary Fund Staff Papers*, 44(4), 430–461.

Hessler, J (2004). *A Social History of Soviet Trade*. New Jersey, Princeton University Press.

Iki (http://old.iki.lt/en) [10th March 2008].

International Monetary Fund (2000). Transition: Experience and policy issues. *World Economic Outlook: Focus on Transition Economies*, 84–137.

Järvesoo, E (1978). The postwar economic transformation. In *A Case Study of a Soviet Republic: The Estonian ESSR*, Parming, T and E Järvesoo (eds.), pp. 131–190. Boulder, CO: Westview Press.

KOBA (2008). *Commercial Property Market Report: Baltic States 2008*, Vilnius, LT.

Kline, RB (1998). *Principles and Practices of Structural Equation Modeling*. New York: Guilford Press.

Kotabe, M and K Helsen (2004). *Global Marketing Management*, 3rd edn. New Jersey: John Wiley and Sons Inc.

Kutt, A (1968). Reflections on Baltic economies under Soviet management. *The Baltic Review*, 35, 18–26.

Lascu, D, LA Manrai, and AK Manrai (1993). Marketing in Romania: The challenges of the transition from a planned to a market economy. *European Journal of Marketing*, 27(11/12), 102–120.

LeBaron, D (2002). *Mao, Marx and the Market*. New York: John Wiley and Sons, Inc.

Lempert, DH (1996). *Daily Life in a Crumbling Empire: The Absorption of Russia*, Volume 1. New York: Columbia University Press.

Levy, M and BA Weitz (2004). *Retail Management*, 5th edn. New York: McGraw Hill.

Lewison, DM (1997). *Retailing*, 6th edn. *US: Prentice Hall International Inc.*

Lidl (www.lidl.de) [10th March 2008].

Lindquist, JD (1975). Meaning of image: A survey of empirical and hypothetical evidence. *Journal of Retailing*, 50, 29–38.

Low, G and C Lamb (2000). The measurement and dimensionality of brand associations. *Journal of Product and Brand Management*, 9(6), 350–368.

Maksimarket (www.etk.ee) [10th March 2008].

Maxima (http://www.maximagrupe.eu) [10th March 2008].

Mazursky, D and J Jacoby (1985). Forming impressions of merchandise and service quality. In *Perceived Quality: How Consumers View Stores and Merchandise*, Jacoby, J and J Olson (eds.), Lexington, pp. 139–153. MA: Lexington Books.

Merrilees, B and M Fry (2002). Corporate branding: A framework for E-retailers. *Corporate Reputation Review*, 5(2/3), 213–225.

Merrilees, B, B McKenzie, and D Miller (2007). Culture and marketing strategy in discount retailing. *Journal of Business Research*, 60, 215–221.

Michalopoulos, C (2000). World trade organization accession for transition economies. *Russian & East European Finance and Trade*, 36(2), 63–86.

Morgan, R and S Hunt (1994). The commitment-trust theory of relationship marketing. *Journal of Marketing*, 58, 20–38.

Norfa (www.norfa.lt) [10th March 2008].

Palm, T (1989). Perestroika in Estonia: The cooperatives. *Journal of Baltic Studies*, 20(2), 127–148.

PriceWaterhouseCoopers (PWC) (2008). *Baltic Property Market Report*. Vilnius, LT.

Prisma (www.prismamarket.ee) [10th March 2008].

Raubiško, I (2001). Letting in the Sunshine: Latvia fights publics perception of corruption. *Central Europe Review*, 3(15), http://www.ce-review.org/01/15/raubisko15.html, [1st June 2008].

Raun, T (2001). *Estonia and the Estonians*. California: Hoover Institution Press.

Reid, SE and D Crowley (2000). Style and socialism: Modernity and material culture in post-war eastern Europe. In *Style and Socialism: Modernity and Material Culture in Post-War Eastern Europe*, Reid, SE and D Crowley (eds.), pp. 1–24. UK: Oxford.

Rimi (www.rimi.lv) [10th March 2008].

Rinne, H and WR Swinyard (1995). Segmenting the discount store market: the domination of the 'difficult discounter core.' *International Review of Retail, Distribution and Consumer Research*, 5(2), 123–145.

Robinson, T (1998). The role of retailing in a Russian consumer society. *European Business Review*, 98(5), 276–281.

Seitz, H (1992). Retailing in Eastern Europe: An overview. *International Journal of Retail & Distribution Management*, 20(6), 4–10.

Selver (www.selver.ee) [10th March 2008].

Semionoviene, A (2003). Emerging markets of the Baltics: Getting bigger, quicker. *The European Retail Digest*, 40, 41–42.

Smith, H (1990). *The new Russians*. New York: Random House.

SOKOS (www.sokos.fi) [10th March 2008].

Stearns, PN (2001). *Consumerism in World History*. London: Routledge.

Stockmann (www.stockmann.fi) [10th March 2008].

Tallinna Kaubamaja (www.kaubamaja.ee) [10th March 2008].

Williams, R (1993). *Insight Guides: Baltic States*. Boston, MA: Houghton Mifflin.

World Bank (2003). Selected world development indicators. *World Development Report*, 186–189.

Part III

LATIN AMERICA

Chapter 11

DATA MINING AS A DECISION TOOL FOR MATERIALS PROCUREMENT IN A MULTINATIONAL COMPANY HEADQUARTERED 1N BRAZIL

DENISE CHAVES CARVALHO BARBOSA,
WALTER GASSENFERTH,
AND MARIA AUGUSTA SOARES MACHADO

Abstract

This chapter relates to how managers can improve their decision-making quality through the concept of data warehousing and data mining. By using a practical application of data mining in information technology (IT) purchase database and by analyzing the results, it is demonstrated that data mining could be used to obtain information, support the decision-making process, and formulate strategies in the procurement area. This chapter is particularly useful for procurement managers as they often are confronted with a large data set.

Introduction

The use of information technology (IT) has been undergoing several changes regarding data access and analysis. Such information has shaped a new paradigm based upon the storage, treatment, and analysis of the large amount of data. This new paradigm involves the use of systems specifically designed for handling the data and generating knowledge in a flexible and timely manner so as to allow for analysis by the managers of the companies. Applying data mining techniques in the search for knowledge in this new reality of the various departments within the organization is an issue of interest for large companies. It is quite common to find these techniques being applied in the fields of finance, sales, and especially, marketing. Nonetheless, the procurement department of any organization also has a huge amount of data and we believe a study on the application of data mining techniques for generating and analyzing valuable information for specific decision making in this area is of great importance, especially for the managers of the procurement area.

The objective of this chapter is to introduce the application of a data mining analysis tool to the information of the procurement area of a large company in the Brazilian market, thus demonstrating that the use of the analyses of such information is greatly important for the organization's future purchases. This chapter also aims to show that in emerging markets of countries such as Brazil this type of tool provides the company with a competitive advantage as the quality of decision making is improved. This chapter is organized in the following section: Material procurement, Decision making and supporting systems, Online analytical processing, Data warehouse, Data mining, Methodology, Results, and Conclusions.

Materials Procurement

According to Costa (2000), the term "purchase" in the organizations tends to be outdated and being replaced by "supply management" or procurement. The author defines the purchasing activity as an administrative job within the organization, while being accountable for coordinating a system of information and control that can buy from external suppliers in order to guarantee the flow of the materials required for achieving the organization's mission, the goods and services in the right amount, the right quality, the right source, the right moment, and at the right price.

The acquisition of raw materials, supplies, and components accounts for a decisive factor in the activities of an organization. According to Ballou (2001), those purchase-related activities comprise a series of factors such as selecting suppliers, qualifying services, setting sales deadlines, predicting prices, services and changes in demand, among others. Because most of the money from sales is paid to suppliers for the materials purchased, minor reductions in the purchase of materials can bring about considerable improvements in profits. Thus, it can be said that procurement is of utmost importance for the success of a company. According to Gaither and Frazier (2001), the purchase department plays a key role in the company's achieving its goals. The mission of this department is to perceive the competitive necessities of the products and services, and thus becoming accountable for timely delivery, costs, quality, and other elements within the strategy of operations. The procurement managers are required to be involved in several activities such as keeping a database and selecting suppliers, negotiating contracts with such suppliers, and acting as an intermediate between the suppliers and the company. In a general sense, procurement is a fundamental tool for the performance of the company as a whole that has to be analyzed, strategically studied and modified according to marketing requirements. In order to adjust the purchases with market necessities, the procurement manager must be prepared for decision making, which must be precise and based upon consistent data.

Decision Making and Supporting Systems

The survival of the companies as well as the situation of the people who are either directly or indirectly linked to it, whether employees, suppliers, customers or shareholders, are directly affected by management decisions. Thus, the decision maker is struck by several factors of influence, including the demands from the people involved toward attaining a successful result. Each of these people requests differentiated and, possibly, antagonistic solutions, as a solution for a problem. Therefore, it is necessary that priorities are established when managers are faced with different, antagonistic positions and goals or disputes of information and resources. It is necessary to transform the objectives of the organization into general objectives for all the members of the company, and thus seeking to share the participation and the vision for the future, the satisfaction of the users and customers, not neglecting, though, the other groups of interests — shareholders and employees.

According to Pereira and Fonseca (1997), on a daily basis, rendering this process feasible, which involves conflicts of interests, requires leadership, permanent negotiation ability, shared objectives as well as effective communication. It is through information that one can better support the decision making process, and it is the duty of the several tools that will provide support for the process to obtain the information required in a reliable, timely way and show it in a comprehensible manner. According to Power (2002), the concept of decision-oriented computing support arises from the development of two sources of research; namely, theoretical studies on organizational decision making process, conducted during the 1950s and 1960s at the Carnegie Institute of Technology, and the works performed with Interactive Computer Systems during the 1960s at the Massachusetts Institute of Technology.

According to Fisher (1996) and Pearson and Shim (1995), the pioneering SADs (Decision Support Systems) appeared in 1960 and 1970 to provide support to decision makers on the solution for unstructured management problems. However, there was no possibility that, with such system, a good support to the decision making process was attained because it is a dynamic process whereby the supply of information needs to take place at the right time. For Weldon (2006), the CASE tools and the 4th Generation Language appeared in the early 1980s promising to solve the problems of the users who needed information quickly and could not afford a waste of time on specific development for their needs. Over the time, there occurred the necessity of growth of data analysis, of fast, reliable and adaptable responses to the new forms of management of companies and businesses. New business management methods were prepared such as reengineering (Hammer, 1994) and the total quality management (Deming and Scherkenbach, 1991). According to Fisher (1996), whenever the needs for technological progress and market needs converge, they bring about basic changes in business practices, and the evolution of IT have enabled many companies to face an even more competitive environment. Bispo and Cazarini (1998) stated that in the 1990s several company-oriented decision-supporting systems were created. Among these new tools is the enterprise resource planning (ERP) which is an integrated management tool used for management in the operating environment as well as a new generation of systems; namely, *Data Warehouse*, OLAP and *Data Mining,* which have been used for managing the administering environment. By means of the *Data Warehouse* and OLAP tools, the reports and queries are now made by the actual users of the systems, who no longer need some deep knowledge of the computer technologies to obtain the data required in the analyses, the making of these reports being cost effective, quick, reliable, and adaptable to the various business models. By using these tools, the managers make use of a much shorter time manipulating the data and building models according to their needs, and thus better using the time for the analyses and problem solving required.

Objectives of the Decision-Supporting Systems

The applications of Data Bank Systems can be classified into on-line transaction processing systems (OLTP) and decision-supporting systems including the on-line analytical processing (OLAP) (Silberschatz *et al.*, 1999). The transaction processing systems are common in companies, because these systems handle information made up by name and identifier, and generate a large amount of data that need to be stored (Silberschatz *et al.*, 1999). The data bank technology, by itself, fulfills the transaction processing applications.

As for the decision-supporting systems, they are interactive and their main goal is to help people with decision power in a business, their end users, how to use data and models in order to identify and solve problems as well as defining decisions (Cabral, 2001). The large data bank resulting from the transaction processing systems is a real source of information for the decision making process even though some key points in data recovery for decision-supporting applications demonstrate that the database technology alone is not appropriate for its specific necessities (Silberschatz *et al.*, 1999). Various aspects can be mentioned such as (1) some decision-supporting queries cannot be expressed or are not easily expressed in structured query language (SQL); (2) large companies have several sources of data stored under different schemas and, many times, some parts of the company have no access to them either for performance or security reasons or because in order to consult such sparse data — each of these sources has to be accessed — individually, which is not so efficient and (3) from a large amount of data, such activities as extracting relevant information, classify and associate them, which are indispensable for the decision making process, become hard and laborious to be carried out.

In order to provide for these and other demands of the database systems in helping with decision making and to meet the needs of business analysts and of those professionals with decision power, in general, the companies began to build the data warehouses — unified data warehouses, as will be seen in the following section.

Online Analytical Processing

The term OLAP was described by Codd *et al.* (2007) in 1992 through 12 rules used to identify the functionalities that those products specified as such should contain. OLAP (on-line analytical processing) is a category of applications and technologies used to group, manage, process, and present multidimensional data aimed at analysis and management. Codd *et al.* (2007) rules are as follows: (1) multidimensional vision concept, (2) transparence, (3) accessibility, (4) consistent report performance, (5) client/server architecture, (6) generic dimensioning, (7) dynamic treatment of sparse templates, (8) multiuser support, (9) unrestricted dimensional crossing operations, (10) intuitive data manipulation, (11) flexible reports, and (12) unlimited levels of dimensions and aggregations.

In addition to these 12 rules, the Gartner Group (Codd *et al.*, 2007) added nine more rules; namely: (1) multiple arrays data, (2) OLAP joint, (3) tools to manage the database, (4) store objects, (5) subsets selection, (6) drill-down line-level detail, (7) local data support, (8) incremental refresh of the database, and (9) SQL interface.

In the OLAP, the replies are not automatic; it is a more interactive process whereby the user asks the questions, gets the information, verifies a specific datum and makes comparisons. The OLAP provides organizations with a method for accessing, viewing, and analyzing the corporate data with high flexibility and performance. In today's globalized world, companies are facing more competition and expanding their presence to new markets. Therefore, how fast executives get information and make decisions determines the competitiveness of a company and its long-term success. The OLAP presents information to users through a natural and intuitive data model. By means of a simple type of browsing and searching, end users can quickly analyze countless scenarios, generate "ad-hoc" reports, and find out relevant trends and facts irrespective of size, complexity and source of the corporate data. Indeed, inputting information in corporate data banks has always been easier than retrieving them. The OLAP technology puts an end to these difficulties and takes information closer to the user in need of it. Therefore, the OLAP is frequently used to integrate and make available management information contained in operating databases, ERP systems and CRM, accounting systems, and data warehouses. These features have rendered it an essential technology in several types of decision-supporting applications and systems for business executives.

OLAP × OLTP

A comparison between OLAP and OLTP is made below. Basically, the difference is that the OLTP is an operating model for data bank transactions, and the OLAP is an analytical model for the information contained in a data bank.

Typical operation

In the OLTP model, transactions are carried out that can be, for instance, the updating of a registry, a removal, recovery, or creation. As for the OLAP model, the data are useful for being analyzed; for example, finding out what product has been sold for two months.

Speckle

In the OLTP model, the data are treated with a maximum of detail; as for the OLAP, the data are aggregated, that is, there is a summary of the data. Such summary is required so that analyses can be carried out.

Data temporality

In the OLTP, what matters are the current data; for example, if the price of a product rises from "*x*" to "*y*", then "*x*" is deleted and replaced by "*y*". In the OLAP, the past does matter. Because the data are utilized for future analysis and predictions, both activities need information from the past. Then, the OLAP model considers both the current and previous information, which could no longer exist in the OLTP.

Recovery

In the OLTP model, usually few registries are recovered in an inquiry; for example, the price of a product, a customer's data. In the OLAP, various registries are recovered such as the amount sold of a given product in each of the latest seven months grouped by city.

Users

In the OLTP model, there are many users using the system at the same time; however, with simpler queries in the OLAP, there are fewer users with more complex queries.

Orientation

The OLTP model is registry-oriented; a term which is very common in computing and generally means a line in a table of a relational data bank. The OLAP model uses arrays, which are good for representing dimensions like; for example, time dimension or site dimension.

Query

In the OLTP model, the types of queries that can be made are pre-defined; for example, querying the price of a product or the debt of a customer. In the OLAP, the queries are "ad-hoc," which means that they are defined in accordance with the interests of who is doing the query; for example, what is the total amount of sales of a given product in each of the late three months by city.

Data Warehouse

Large companies have a huge amount of data that are spread over various different systems, and thus not making it possible to search for information that allows for making decisions based on a description of the data, which would allow for identifying trends and strategically positioning the companies for competition and maximization of profits. Due to this, a new concept was introduced in the market that allows for regrouping such data spread over the various systems and reorganizing them strategically. According to Inmon (2005), this tool was defined as "a set of data that are based upon issues, integrated, non-volatile and variable in relation with time, which provides support to management decisions." Further, according to Singh (2001), "a decision-supporting environment that leverages the data stored in different sources and organizes and delivers them to the company's decision makers, irrespective of the platform they use or their level of technical qualification." Data warehouse arose from the acknowledgment of how important the value of information is in the organizations. It is such an environment that is extensible and is planned for the analysis of non-volatile data. These data are physically and logically transformed and stem from multiple applications; they are updated and kept over a long period, and are expressed in terms of the business and summarized for an efficient analysis. Thus, a data warehouse is a platform with integrated data and improved quality to support various DSS (decision-supporting system), EIS (executive information system) applications and business processes. In technological terms, a data warehouse is a combination of several technologies, and its primary objective is to integrate effectively the operating databases in such an environment that enables the strategic utilization of the data. These technologies include the multidimensional and relational data bank managing systems, client/server architecture, metadata and repository modeling, graphic interfaces for user, etc. In short, this concept (Fig. 11.1) consists of organizing corporate data in the best possible way to provide the managers and directors of the companies with information for decision making in a data bank that is parallel to the operational systems.

According to Taurion (1998), a simple way of knowing whether a DW will be useful to the company is by replying to a small number of questions. The higher the number of "yes" answers, the greater the potential of use of DW by the company: (1) is the company based upon information for making decisions? For example, if the knowledge of the market or of the behavior of its customers is required for a decision, the answer should be "yes." The "no" answer would be for a company whose decision-making culture is strongly based upon intuition; (2) is the business segment of the company characterized by a strong competition and rapid changes? A typical example is the finance segment. In this case, the "yes" answer is unquestionable. A "no"

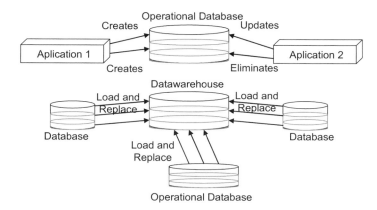

Figure 11.1. A typical operational database in comparison to data warehouse. (From Update models: Database × Data Warehouse (SIMON, 1995)).

answer would correspond to a stable segment with little competition; (3) is the customers' base large and diversified? An example of "yes" refers to the customers' base of a supermarket or of an insurance company. The "no" answer would come from a company that supplies products such as petroleum platforms for a single customer; (4) are the data stored in several places? In practice, "yes" would come from companies that use several technologies with several applications spread over several platforms. The "no" answer shall be a rare case of few companies that have only one technology; (5) are the data duplicated and spread over several systems? "Yes" shall be the majority of companies; (6) are the data in different format and specifications? One figures out a data bank where "customer's address" appears in half a dozen different places with different content and (7) is the company sharing the decision making process with an aim at greater agility and dispatch? Definitely, those are not yet changing, but soon will. It is a requirement for business survival in most business segments where competition is intense.

Having these questions answered, the company can decide with certain safety whether to use the technology or not. The items below aim at guiding this decision by relating the steps to be followed toward a safe and correct implementation of DW in the organization. According to Amaral (1999), the possible DW modes are as follows: *Corporate Data Warehouse* is the most robust mode; these are the solutions that are generally adopted to be large corporations for which the combination of the competition, business volume, and information variables justifies this type of solution. Its main characteristics are greater robustness in terms of volume of data to be stored (about 100 GB to TB of data); highly unpredictable utilization, non-structured, analytical applications; response time: from seconds to some minutes; relational data, non-volatile, quite non-standard; information organized by area of analysis, historical (5–10 years); End users: management, information consumers.

Operational data store (ODS)

It is not a DW; it is a production data bank replicated with error adjustment. The ODS is primarily used to generate standard reports and provides details of transactions for analysis. Depending on the reporting necessities of a corporation, an ODS can be updated, either monthly, weekly, or more often in real time. Its main advantage is that it improves the performance of the production system, because the results of the processing sessions are transferred from the OLTP to the ODS. Its main characteristics are predictability, partially structured, partially analytical utilization; response time: from seconds to some minutes; relational data, volatile or current, non-standard; information organized by area of analysis, historical (30–60 days); and end users: information consumers.

Data mart

It is a solution that is suitable to large and medium corporations, because it represents a less complex type of data warehouse in terms of implementation, and is simpler to manage because it has less complex requirements in terms of infrastructure and functional coverage. It is generally used in the main areas of the company such as the human resources, finance, and marketing. It is faster to implement and costs less. Its characteristics are type of DW where the data are closer to the user; easier management since it is smaller; decision making permission at department level; relational or multidimensional data, non-volatile; fast development (3–6 months); low cost ($50,000–500,000); politically more manageable project in terms of sponsoring and budget; personalization — meets the needs of a specific department or groups of users; smaller data volume storage, since it assists a single department. These modes of data warehouse implementation are not excluding among themselves. Each organization shall choose those modes that are most suitable for them in order to attain the competitive targeted advantages. This varies among the various market segments, in different levels of economic competitiveness of each country or region.

Data Mining

Much knowledge is hidden in the vast amount of data available in the data banks of the companies, and it is with via data mining that these raw data can be changed into valuable information in order to assist the decision making process. The difference between the data mining and the statistical techniques lies on the utilization of the actual data for discovering the patterns and not on the verification of hypothetical patterns. The databases store knowledge that can help us improve business and the traditional techniques only allow for verifying hypotheses which are approximately only 5% of all relations found by these methods. Data mining can discover the other unknown relations — the remaining 95%. That is, it can be said that the conventional techniques "speak" to the database, while data mining "listens" to the database.

Data mining has not come to replace the traditional statistical techniques; it is an extension of the statistical methods that, in part, result from a considerable change in the statistical community. The ever-growing power of computers, in conjunction with lower costs and the growing necessity to analyze huge sets of data with millions of lines, has allowed for developing techniques based upon the exploration of possible solutions through brute force (Thearling *et al.*, 2000). The main objective of data mining is to extract valuable information from the data, and discover the "hidden gold." This "gold" is the valuable information contained in the data. Small changes in the strategies resulting from the discoveries of the data mining tools can change into significant differences for the company's cash. With the expansion in the use of the data warehouses, the data mining tools became fundamental. Nevertheless, it is important to remember that a data warehouse is not required for the application of a data mining tool. It is enough to have the data. Several data analysis tools such as report generators or statistical analysis use the term data mining in their computer software. Artificial intelligence-based products also are called data mining tools. However, what is real data mining called? The main objective of data mining is to discover knowledge. Through its methodology, data mining extracts predictive information from the database. Data mining is a field that currently involves many important branches. Each type of technology has its own advantages and disadvantages, in the same way as no tool manages to meet all the needs in all applications. The implementation of a data mining system can be divided into six interdependent phases so that it meets its end objectives, namely: (1) understanding the problem — the initial phase of the project must aim at identifying the targets and needs starting from a perspective of the problem and then converting them into a data mining application and an initial plan to "attack" the problem; (2) understanding the data — the main activity of this phase is to collect a sample of the data to be used and assess the environment where they are located; (3) preparation of the data — creation of programs to collect, clean, and transform the data to be used by the data mining algorithms. In this phase, the data are adapted so they can be inserted in the algorithm selected for processing; (4) problem modeling — selection of the algorithms(s) from those presented for use and actual processing of the model. Some algorithms need the data in specific formats, and thus bringing about several returns to the data preparation phase; (5) model assessment — at the end of the modeling phase, several models must be assessed under the perspective of the analyst accountable. Then, the objective becomes to assess the models through the viewpoint of the problem, and making sure there are no faults or contradictions regarding the rules of the problem; (6) disclosure or publication of the model — the creation and validation of the model allow for moving one step ahead toward rendering the information generated. This can be done in several ways, from the creation of a specific software to the publication of an in-company report.

Methodology

For a practical demonstration of this utilization, we collected the data for applying the technique in a large multinational company based in Brazil. In order to make it easy, we shall call it "Alfa Company" — using the ERP system of the SAP supplier, which has been producing for approximately two years, as well as the Data Warehouse software, SAP *Business Warehouse* — BW, the specific environment of which, apart from the transactional environment, stores information that is structured to facilitate the query and analysis, and thus supporting the decision making process and management of the company. The study was conducted in the decentralized structure of small low-cost IT items (pen drives, printers, scanners, mouse, etc.) made up of five buyers who requested a minimum of 3 (three) quotes for each purchase order from 77 (seventy-seven) suppliers. The period of analysis was between October 2004 and March 2006. This study will be limited to the task of finding affinities among the data under analysis using the data mining technique called "association rules." Other limitations concern restrictions imposed by the code of ethics and the rules of the company being researched as to the use of the purchase database in its entirety due to strategic information safety issues.

Figure 11.2 summarizes the model used from the source of the primary data going through the stages of preparation and data mining, to the discovery of knowledge as an end product.

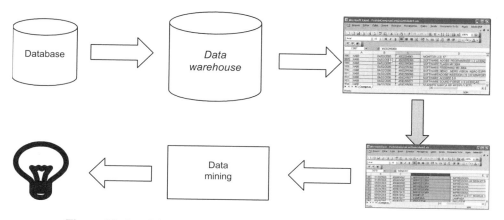

Figure 11.2. Diagram of the model used for discovery of knowledge.

Initially, the data generated by the SAP R/3 transactional system on a daily basis are periodically copied to other databases, which have the historical records of the purchases made (data warehouse). These data were collected by using the SP tool called BW, which stores the data in a structured manner, and thus facilitating both query and analysis, and adding value to the decision making. The outcome of this stage was a Microsoft Excel spreadsheet with all the attributes and values available in the original database. Eventually, cleansing, coding, and enrichment of the data (in details in the following subtitle) were performed manually by eliminating the lines and columns and creating new attributes. This new spreadsheet was then converted into Microsoft Access in such a way that it could be read by the data mining software *WizRule* (Wizsoft, 2006). Finally, the software processed the data and the association rules were generated in report format, and thus allowing for the discovery of knowledge.

The Preparation of the Data

This stage was of utmost importance for the data mining process to generate the association rules. More than 50% of the overall research time was spent in this preparation stage. (1) elimination of unnecessary items, fields (columns) and instances (lines) for the analysis: at this stage, some data of the spreadsheet generated by the BW query were eliminated in order to reduce the quantity and enhance the quality of processing. The following were excluded: all of the items that did not include the purchase of IT products, the columns carrying data regarded as unnecessary to any type of analysis, and the lines that showed inconsistencies. (2) filling out of blank fields: Some fields, as they migrate from the data warehouse, appear in the spreadsheet with zero values, and thus prompting a case-to-case analysis with the respective suitable action. Either the item was eliminated or identical values were attributed to the other identical values. (3) coding and standardization of the description of items: In order to ensure impartiality in the analyses of the associations presented after the application of the association rules, two tables were prepared; the buyers and suppliers were coded and next the names of the buyers and companies were replaced with their respective codes. (4) data enrichment: At the first data enrichment phase, the diversity of forms of description existing in the database for the same product was observed. This could not guarantee significant results after the application of the rules by *WizRule* (Wizsoft, 2006). To have this issue resolved, a column was inserted before the products description column and called "Type of Product." This column was eventually fed manually with the first word of the Description of the Product (e.g., Notebook), and thus maintaining the detailed description only in the 'Description of the Products' column (e.g., *NOTEBOOK HP COMPAQ NX5000* — ABNT KEYBOARD).

The Software Used

The software used in the analysis of the database was the 4.05 demo version of *WizRule* (Wizsoft, 2006). This software is easy to use and configure, which required very little learning time on the part of the user in order to use it effectively. It has some configuration parameters related to the level of reliability of the rules, and thus allowing for making the necessary adjustments according to each case being analyzed. The standard "*for Windows*" interface of the product and the reading capacity of input files generated by other tools in various possible formats (dbase/foxbase, access, and text files) make the product even more versatile. The demo version of this software is free and has a limitation of use related to the maximum number of lines (1,000) that can be analyzed. Nevertheless, this version was chosen because there is no need for using the full version, because after the pre-processing stage, the final database had less than 1,000 lines. The final result of the analysis is presented in an on-screen report showing the rules generated and the possible deviations (exceptions to the rules) of the data. The generated rules are numbered and are presented as follows:

If Fornecedor (Provider) is F45
Then
Tipo do produto (Product Type) is SOFTWARE

Rule's probability: 1000
The rule exists in 30 records
Significance level: Error probability is almost 0

This rule indicates that when the supplier is F45 (code), the product sold is a software. The rule has a probability equal to 1; it exists in 30 registries and the probability for exceptions to this rule exist is low.

Results

The software analyzed 935 purchase registries and 52 association rules were generated. They were configured in such a way that only the rules with a 90% probability and at least 20 occurrences were to be considered. Table 11.1 shows the consolidation of the first 15 rules generated.

After analyzing Table 11.1 with all the rules generated and cross-referencing the information among the rules, the following conclusions were drawn: (1) despite the large number of suppliers that already supply at least 1 item, most of the purchases (in registries) is concentrated in few suppliers; (2) this concentration also occurs in the buyer × supplier relation and in the supplier × item relation; (3) some vendors supply only one type of product; and (4) such products as printers and scanners (among others) are purchased, in most cases, per unit.

Table 11.1. Consolidation of the first 15 rules generated by *WizRule* (Wizsoft, 2008).

Rule	If	And	Then	Registries	Deviations
1	F03		C1	83	5
2	F45		SOFTWARE	30	0
3	F30		0–324 (VP)	50	0
4	F06		C1	46	2
5	F04		C4	85	4
6	C4	F09	0–329	49	2
7	F09		0–329	53	4
8	F11	1–5 (Q)	0–88 (VP)	46	2
9	F01		C1	26	0
10	MONITOR	F03	C1	25	0
11	F09	0–329	C4	49	3
12	MEMORY	1–5 (Q)	C4	39	1
13	PRINTER		1–5 (Q)	245	9
14	F45		C4	30	0
15	MEMORY	0–329	C4	32	2

Still as a result of the analysis, it was possible to establish a range of values for a large amount of the IT items that were bought. These ranges may be used as parameters for the analysis of future purchases.

Conclusions

After the application of the data mining analysis tool, valuable information was obtained which certainly demonstrate that the utilization of data mining in the database of purchases not only is possible, but also is recommended for decision making of future purchases. The benefits resulting from the information generated were evident. Such results may be used in procurement, in those management actions aimed at concentrating the purchase of some items to achieve economics of scale, in the implementation of measures to minimize the identified weaknesses, in the broadening of suppliers choice in order to prevent harmful monopolies as well as in other actions that add to attaining the targets of the strategic planning of the business.

Direction for Future Studies

The future studies may include other typical tasks of the data mining process such as the classification and analysis of groups. These tasks will be able to greatly augment this study. By means of classification, the stratification of the purchased items could be searched for in a degree based upon the value of the purchase. The decision for batch buying can be adjusted according to the values engaged by the market and the buyers. Through group analysis, it would be possible to obtain knowledge regarding the groups of items, identifying the items and suppliers that could be subject to supply contracts instead of being recurrent to spot purchases.

We recommend, however, for future works that data mining is applied to the entire purchase database and also the full version of the software, so that the results are the most complete possible and that they enrich the decision making process for the entire procurement area of the company.

Implications for Managers

Considering that this study is aimed at introducing a tool made up of methodology and methodology-supporting software to help procurement area managers in their making decisions, it can be asserted that one of its implications is a shift in paradigm and behavior on the part of such managers in the way they manage their work routines, and thus culminating in their making decisions as per the following recommendations that: (1) the periodic follow-up of the reports and analyses of the data mining tool be inserted in the management routine of the procurement activities; (2) the stratification of the items purchased according to a rank of purchase value be at all times carried out by the manager, who make decisions on more cost-effective purchases in moments/processes other than those of more investment-significant acquisitions; (3) the matching of the information contained in the purchases database be thoroughly examined with a view to better understand the possibilities of suppliers as well as the company's most critical requirements, thus using this better understanding to enhance the procurement decision making process and improving the cost–benefit ratio upon purchasing inputs for the company's end product and (4) the experiences and results achieved by the managers using this type of work/decision making be recorded, and thus intending to verify through facts and data the improved performance of the process as well as of the KPI (key performance indicators) of the procurement area.

References

Amaral, A (1999). Desmistificando definitivamente o Data. Warehousing. *Developer's Magazine*, São Paulo, fev. 14–17.

Ballou, RH (2001). *Gerenciamento da Cadeia de Suprimentos*, 4 edn. Porto Alegre: Bookmann.

Bispo, CAF and EW Cazarini (1998). A evolução do processo decisório, (CD-ROM). *Paper Presented at Encontro Nacional da Engenharia de Produção*, Niterói, RJ, *Anais*. Niterói, TEP-UFF, artigo 94.doc.

Cabral, Pedro da Costa Brito. *Sistemas Espaciais de Apoio à Decisão. O Sistema de Apoio ao Licenciamento da Direção Regional do Ambiente do Alentejo*, In Dissertação (Mestrado em Sistemas de Informação Geográfica) — Universidade Técnica de Lisboa, Lisboa: 2001. Available in <http://www.isegi.unl.pt/labnt/tese/TeseMaio2001_pedrocabral.pdf> [December 2007].

Codd, EF, SB Codd, and CT Salley (2007). *Providing OLAP (On-Line Analytical Processing) to Users–Analysts: An IT mandate*. http://dev.hyperion.com/resource_library/white_papers/providing_olap_to_user_analysts.pdf [June 2007].

Costa, AL (2000). Sistemas de Compras Provadas e Públicas no Brasil. *Revista de Administração*, 35(4), October/December 2000, pp. 119–128.

Deming, WE and WW Scherkenbach (1991). *The Deming Route to Quality and Productivity*, Cirencester: Management Books 2000 Ltd.

Fisher, LM (2006). Along the infobahn: Data warehouses. *Strategy & Business*, Third Quarter, 1996. Available in: http://www.strategy-business.com/press/article/17747?pg=0 [August 2006].

Gaither, N and G Frazier (2001). *Administração da Produção e Operações*, 8 ed., São Paulo: Pioneira.

Hammer, M (1994). *Reengenharia: Revolucionando a Empresa em função dos Clientes, da Concorrência e das Grandes Mudanças da Gerência*, Rio de Janeiro: Campos.

Inmon, WH (2005). *Building the Data Warehouse*, 4th edn. Indianapolis. Wiley Publishing, Inc.

Pearson, JM and JP Shim (1995). An empirical investigation into DSS structures and environments, Decision Support Systems, 13, 141–158.

Pereira, MJLB and JGM Fonseca (1997). *Faces da decisão: As mudanças de paradigmas e o poder da decisão*. São Paulo: Makron Books.

Power, D (2002). *Decision Support Systems: Concepts and Resources of Managers* (text book binding). Quorum Books.

Silberchatz, A, H Korth, and S Sudarshan (1999). *Sistemas de Banco de Dados*, 3 edn. São Paulo: Makron Books.

Simon, AR (1995). *Strategic Database Technology: Management for the Year 2000*. Morgan Kaufmann Publishers, Inc.

Singh, HS (2001). *Data Warehouse: Conceitos, Tecnologias, Implementação e Gerenciamento*. São Paulo: Makron Books.

Taurion (1998). O Data Warehouse Será Útil para a sua Organização. *Developer's Magazine*, São Paulo, Feb. 1998, 26–27.

Thearling, K, A Berson, and S Smith (2000). *Building Data Mining Appllications for CRM*, McGraw Hill.

Weldon, JL (2006). A Career in data modeling, *Byte*, Jun. 1997. Available in: http://www.byte.com/art/9706/sec7/art3.htm. Accessed in August 2006.

Wizsoft (2006). WizRule, Available in: http://www.wizsoft.com/default.asp?win=8&winsub=8. Accessed in [August 2006].

Chapter 12

THE IMPORTANCE OF NATURAL RESOURCES-BASED INDUSTRY CLUSTERS IN LATIN AMERICA: THE CASE OF CHILE

CHRISTIAN FELZENSZTEIN

Abstract

This chapter explores the role of marketing externalities and practices in clusters of three key natural resources-based industries in Chile, a region in Latin America where limited research has been conducted. The influence of regional clusters and networks in the growth of firms has been a key research theme in the literature. However, it has been mainly concentrated taking an economic geography perspective. One of the objectives of this chapter is to bring a management, marketing, and strategy perspectives to the topic. Following a review of some of the key literature related to geographic colocation, social networking, and regional innovation lessons from a Latin American perspective and especially for the new Chilean cluster-oriented local economic strategy will be analyzed.

Introduction

Many economic geographers, regional economists, and nowadays more international business and strategy scholars have seen agglomeration economies theories as a starting point for contemporary academic research. However, the concept of agglomeration economies is far from recent. Authors like Von Thünen (1842), Marshall (1842–1924), and Weber (1868–1958) are noteworthy for their roles in the development of theories of

221

agglomeration economies. Marshall (1920) introduced the early concepts of co-partnerships, social elements of proximity, and cooperation among industries. They combined the concepts of industrial districts, town development, and marketing. These indicate that the "soft" elements of personal contact between traders, customers and producers, as well as the exchange of information, the circulation of new ideas and the diffusion of innovation were among the main ideas considered to be Marshall's contribution to agglomeration theories. Marshall also introduced the concept of external economies or externalities[1] as the economies of scale benefits derived from industrial location. In other words, this explains that the economies of scale are not internal to the firm, their occurrence lies outside their control, yet they have a clear impact on the firm's internal production or performance (Brown and McNaughton, 2002).

Today it is well known that inter-firm interaction or networks in localized clusters cannot be seen in isolation. This is especially relevant in collectivistic-driven micro-regions (Felzensztein and Gimmon, 2007). Therefore, companies need to consider aspects of social structures (Ahuja, 2000), social capital, referring to the social structures that determine who is going to interact, as well as the notions of embeddedness (Granovetter, 1985), which is the mechanism whereby an entrepreneur, firm, or organization becomes part of the local structure involving the creation of social ties with the local environment.

Unlike colocated clusters, networks do not have to be geographically concentrated (Brown and McNaughton, 2002). As soon as trust among players has been established and the strategic direction agreed, the operational dialog and communication can then be made possible through electronic means. However, it has been suggested that the social process of learning in inter-firm cooperation works best when partners involved are sufficiently physically close to allow frequent interaction and effective exchange of information (Maskell, 2001). This can be achieved in a social process that is embedded in regional communities that share a common knowledge base and culture being a facilitator for inter-firm collaboration (Cooke, 1998). This leads to the creation of regional institutions that help reinforce the right environments for inter-firm interaction (Wolfe, 2003).

Buyer and seller relationships, as part of wider and complex social structures, have become an integral part of business-to-business strategies over the last two decades. Because the focus of this chapter is primarily on industrial marketing relationships, these interactions are likely to be developed in high

---

[1] Economies that depend on the general development of the industry providing general benefits to individual firms (Marshall, 1920).

impact areas of business associations with strategic partners. This may lead to better forms of interactions among firms and then to cooperation, which is defined as complementary actions taken by firms in inter-dependent relationships to achieve mutual outcomes over time (Anderson and Narus, 1990). This, of course, requires not only a proactive attitude toward cooperation and commitment, but also the construction of social capital among the participant of a cooperative network.

The concept of social capital in clusters

According to Wolfe (2003), the concept of systems of innovation is used to analyze the network of relationships among firms and the broader institutional settings that support their innovative process. Knowledge among institutions, both public and private, comprises this innovation system. Furthermore, several factors such as access to support service for local industry, the establishment of trust relations among networks of suppliers and buyers, and the interactive learning in geographically concentrated areas, among others, contribute to stressing the importance of local agglomeration effects and social interdependencies.

Close proximity at regional level facilitates frequent face-to-face interaction at both, formal, and informal settings (Fig. 12.1). This process creates a common language or code of communication through repeated interaction over time, which leads to the creation of regional institutions that helps reinforce the right environments for inter-firm interaction (McKelvey *et al.*, 2002; Wolfe, 2003). Figure 12.1 shows the "soft" elements of interaction — trust, commitment, mutual knowledge, communication, and similarity among partners — that build the social capital, which may lead to a greater cooperation among firms. Furthermore, these elements combined with the historical and cultural embeddedness of specific local regions, as well as colocation factors with interaction in the value chain activities, may lead to the result of networking and inter-firm cooperation in geographical regions.

Wolfe (2003) argues that the concept of *learning regions*[2] and its social components are seen as different in the North American context compared to the European one. In the former, learning regions are associated with the presence of a dense network of research institutions and the broader set of social as well as environmental amenities that attract resources to specific geographic locations. In a European context, the analysis of learning regions focuses more

---

[2] *Learning regions* are seen as the territorial and institutional embeddedness of learning organizations and interactive learning (Asheim, 1998).

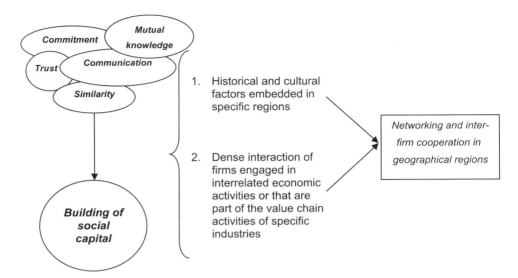

Figure 12.1.   The elements of social capital in the inter-firm cooperation. [From Author, derived from Stopper (1996) and Wolfe (2003).]

on the contributions that *social capital*[3] and *trust* make to support dense networks of inter-firms relationships and the process of interactive learning. This latter context is the one that this study takes as reference, as in some ways this is the kind of cluster strategy that some Latin American economies may use.

It is important to stress that not only SMEs are part of this learning process and social relationships in geographical clusters. Multinational firms are learning to exploit the richness and benefits of those geographically concentrated regions. They contribute, but also absorb, part of these local capabilities through research and development (R&D) activities in both their home base and those overseas center. Large firms, and subsidiaries of multinational companies, are willing to invest more in those places providing the best prospects for learning and innovation (Enright, 2000).

Clusters' externalities: Development and implications for firm's networks

During the last few decades, the increasing importance of networks and co-operation in a competitive environment as a part of territorial externalities has

---

[3] *Social capital* refers to the various features of the social organization of a region, such as the presence of shared norms and values that facilitates the cooperation of individuals and firms (Wolfe, 2003).

been seen as a tool for survival, a complement to skills and resources, as well as growth capacity among small- and medium-sized companies. Furthermore, inter-firm linkages have been subject of greatest attention within the small business and entrepreneurship literature (Freel, 2005). At the same time, horizontal linkages have been extensively analyzed in the literature on regional clusters and industrial districts (Becattini, 1990). Consequently, this analysis has re-emerged investigating the way in which SMEs, within industrial clusters, cooperate and compete, benefiting from the geographic proximity, local infrastructure, and spillover of knowledge as sources of positive externalities of cooperation.

According to Oughton and Whittam (1997), it is possible to distinguish four types of external economies of scale that affect SMEs: (1) internal economies, (2) competitive external economies, (3) technological external economies, and (4) collective external economies. The last one arises when firms cooperate over inputs activities, which includes marketing, export promotion, and other business services. Furthermore, internal economies arise at the firm level, while external economies are available to all firms within an industry, and therefore accrue at the industry, local, or regional levels. External economies play an important role in the economic development of regions. Thereafter, they can be seen as an important component of the Marshallian concept of "*industrial atmospheres*" used to describe the influence of "local environments" in industrial districts.

Other stream of the literature has explained the role played by agglomeration economies and industrial districts in influencing the location of foreign investment (Zander and Sölvell, 2000). However, for the most part, this research has concentrated on developing economies and has lacked comparative analysis with countries with different levels of economic development. Furthermore, there is a lack of attention on the positive externalities that multinational companies (MNEs) create in cooperative activities within regional clusters and how they "interact" with the embedded SMEs in the marketing activities at both local and international levels.

All the above elements combined with the historical and cultural embeddedness of specific local regions, as well as colocation factors with interaction in the value chain activities, may lead to improved networking and inter-firm cooperation in geographical regions, such as the ones found in natural resources-based clusters in Latin American and specially in Chile.

Regional Clusters in Chile: Competing Globally?

The Latin American context for studying regional clusters and inter-firm networks in an academic perspective is quite new. There are only very few publications related to natural resources-based clusters in the Latin American context and to public policies for inter-firm cooperation. The Chilean cluster context has traditionally been based on a "bottom-up" approach. This means that mainly the local companies with minimal or no governmental intervention have led the cluster strategy. This occurs under the most neo-liberal economic policies of any Latin American country. Thereafter, this model of cluster strategy differs to other international cases with a more "top-down" approach, as for example the case of the Scottish industry clusters, which is led by the Scottish Executive, the developmental agency for Scotland. However, only few significant differences were found between clusters from the salmon farming industry in Chile and Scotland, suggesting the international context of clusters in Chile (Felzensztein and Gimmon, 2007).

The previous clusters approach is currently under review in the Chilean economy, as the central government is trying to implement a new "cluster strategy" using the experience of more developed economies like the United Kingdom or Norway, as the country wants to achieve international competitiveness and compete in some natural resources-based industries with countries like Canada and Finland (in the forestry industry), Australia (in the wine and mining industry), Norway and Scotland (in the aquaculture sector), and New Zealand (in the agri-business-related industries, like milk production and fresh fruit exports to Europe).

It is clear that universities are important contributors to cluster development by providing trained people, advanced knowledge for the future and technical problem solving. But perhaps its most important role, one that is hardly practiced yet, is networking to encourage industry and government to work with the university to build clusters (Tiffin, 2008). Universities can play such a strong social capital building role that a cluster can be catalyzed into existence, if the industrial actors are already present and government support follows. For resource industry development, it is critical that small peripheral universities, like the ones located close to the natural-resources areas in northern and southern Chile, become aware of their potential to link with industrial clusters on multiple levels and be supported by the central government to do so. These issues are crucial if a country like Chile likes to compete with well-developed industry sectors in developed economies.

Methodology and Specific Study Area

The present study and lessons are based on three key natural resources-based clusters in Chile, namely the Salmon, Dairy, and Forest industries. These three industry sectors rank among the most important ones inside the economic activity in the country, generating a high percentage of job positions outside the metropolitan areas and exporting to foreign markets with high levels of international competitiveness.

The first part of research on these industries involved non-structured personal interviews with general managers from the selected industries during 2007. This data collection allowed a socially constructed learning process of the industry sectors. Later, the study was carried out based on data obtained through the application of a self-administrated questionnaire to managers from companies registered in the Chilean directory records of Aquaculture and Fishing (Salmon Industry), database from the Forestry Institute (2007) and the Milk Producers Association, 2006 (Diary Industry). The final sampling corresponded to 85 firms: 39 firms from Salmon Industry (43% response rate); 33 from Forestry Industry (44% response rate); and 13 from diary industry (100% response rate). A high level of item response was found in the usable questionnaires, as well as a high internal consistency of the responses.

The main objectives of this study were to (1) compare inter-firm cooperation among three key regional clusters industries, which have different levels of development; (2) explore perceived benefits and areas where inter-firm cooperation may be established and (3) gain managerial and public policy lessons from the results of this research applicable to the Latin American and Chilean context.

Description of Key Industry Sectors in Southern Chile

The salmon industry

The accelerated development of the Chilean aquaculture, at national and international levels, has supported population in southern areas to get economical stability by producing the most interesting number of job positions (55,000 approx.). Presently, there are about 90 companies, 70% of which are located in *Los Lagos Region*. The industry is export oriented, selling more than 90% of the production in foreign countries, being the main export markets the United States (37%), Japan (30%), the European Union (14%), Latin America, (7%) and other markets (12%). The farmed salmon has become the second export product in Chile, just after copper.

The Salmon farming industry has been defined as a "strategic cluster" for the current economic development and competitive strategy of Chile (Eyzaguirre, 2008). This industry sector possesses the following characteristics: they have a specific territorial concentration in *Los Lagos Region*, according to former political-administrative division, concentrating approximately 87% of salmon production in this region, external economies and all strategic links of value chain are found in the territory. Other characteristics are the importance of associative and public support, such as those coming from CORFO — the governmental agency for economic development.

The industry has been evolving from a commodity into a differentiated product, characterized by new elaboration degrees and high quality standards, thus reaching better prices and new consumers located in competitive international markets.

The forestry industry

Due to its sustained growth during the last few years, this industry is considered as highly important inside Chilean economy. The industry contribution to national GDP grew almost 30% during the period 1998–2006. There are over 75 forestry companies dedicated to exporting, located in central and southern Chile. The main export markets in 2006 were the Unites States (28%), China (9.4%), Mexico (8.5%) and Japan (8.1%). The main products from the primary industry were chips, pulp and paper, sawn wood, boards, veneers, and poles; while the products from secondary industry were elaborated wood, picture frames, furniture, crating, pre-made houses, parts, and pieces of furniture. This industry created about 34,000 direct jobs and presents an annual growth of 10.3% for 2007. The exporting firms in this industry show high dependence on few clients and high concentration of their products, mainly in the United States market.

The dairy products industry

The milk industry in Chile has undergone great changes during the last 30 years: a large number of artisan industries disappeared during this time, while multinational companies have been incorporated into this industry. New industry trends and new firms coming from New Zealand as well as mergers and acquisitions are taking strong place since 2007 in southern Chile, which concentrates 91% of the country milk production. There are 13 companies located in 27 plants producing milk, yogurt, cheese, condensed milk, butter, and *manjar* (a kind of milk jam) for the local (70%) and international markets (30%), exporting to countries such as Mexico, Venezuela, Peru, and Costa Rica. The total value of these exports was about US$200 million.

The southern area is mainly characterized by its rainy weather, privileged for agropecuarian activities. In this area, there are over 1.4 million hectares of meadows of which 45% are natural and 41% have undergone improvements. Therefore, grazing conditions together with livestock and critical mass of companies confer an important competitive advantage to this industry. On the other hand, this area shows good sanitary conditions, as it is free from *aphthous fever*, becoming part of a selected group of countries presenting this condition. Meadows showing the highest productive potential are in the southern area of Chile. Diary products composed by 13 companies are responsible for 97% of the Chilean dairy local consumption and export.

Results

Demographic characteristics

The participating companies of this sample are mainly concentrated in southern Chile and specifically 65% of them in the *Región de los Lagos*. Most of these companies have been in the market for 11 to over 30 years, and in the well-established diary industry 60% of the firms exist for over 30 years in the market. The most internationalized companies are those belonging to salmon and forestry industries; generating international sales level of 81%, and 75%, respectively. Their sales come from products exported to the European Union, Asia, and the United States. The dairy industry has 44% of sales in the local market; nevertheless, it shows relatively low foreign sales percentage (contrasted with the other two industries), 14% of its sales correspond to the European Union and approximately 26% to Asian countries. This reflects not only previous low export levels of its products, but also low experience in international markets. Direct competitors for these three industries are principally located in the same local area. Furthermore, in salmon industry, 75% of competitors have a mix of national and international investments. This is mainly due to the predominantly Foreign Direct Investment (FDI), strong subsidiaries of multinational firms and internationalization activities of this industry.

Most of the companies agreed in considering cooperation in marketing as highly important not only for the development of industrial sector they belong to, but also for new business development. From the total participating companies, the dairy industry is doing the hardest work toward future cooperation (37.5%), compared to the salmon (25%) and forestry (20%). This is due to higher expectations of the dairy industry concerning cooperation and pretensions to expand to more international markets in the long run, in addition to a current strategy of new product development based on technological cooperation with producers from New Zealand and France.

These developments are expected to have a future influence on the international marketing approach of the industry. Moreover, the Trade Association is also playing a more strategic role for the improvement of competitiveness in this industry.

Positive externalities and inter-firm cooperation

Over 50% of the sampled firms in each analyzed industry recognized access to specialized workers as a positive externality due to their location in *Los Lagos Region*. This region and mainly its capital city — Puerto Montt — generates qualified labor required for their activities, mainly by the universities which offer programs adapted to the needs of the local natural resources-based industries. Another positive externality found is access to specialized providers: 30% of the diary industry favored this factor since it enables them easiness of access to intermediate products; the same is expressed by salmon industry (50%). Whereas in the forestry industry, 32% of the respondents indicated the most important positive externality has been the improvement in reputation of their products.

Companies from the salmon and forestry industries recognize that inter-firm cooperation in marketing, and with the respective Trade Associations, would mainly permit them joint participation in commercial fairs and market research. Thus, the opportunity to generate commercial missions for new markets appears to be beneficial. However, firms from the dairy sector recognize only slightly the benefits given by participating in commercial fairs and market delegations.

All the three industries agreed about the importance of trying to attract new clients as result of cooperation among them. Keeping their present clients and increasing sales in their respective sectors in the long run as ultimate goals of cooperation was indicated by 100% of the salmon and dairy industries. Concerning the forestry industry, new clients (85%) and raising their sales in the short and long run (64%) are fundamental to their long-term strategy.

Most participants (94% of the salmon and dairy industries and 66% of forestry) indicated having informal contacts and regular talks concerning marketing activities with people from other firms belonging to their industry. This suggests that social networks do exist in these industries, at formal and informal levels. Concerning contact frequency among firms, interviewed enterprises from the salmon industry recognized the highest meeting frequency, reaching 13% of enterprises that stated frequent meetings with other firms, followed by the forestry industry (only 5%). No surveyed firms from the dairy sector admitted frequent social meetings. This may be related to the degree of competition and different roles of the trade association in each industry sector.

Finally, geographical colocation is considered to be crucial for marketing cooperation by firms of the salmon industry (63%), which is well reflected in the strength of industry cluster and their trade association *Salmon Chile*. Much lower percentage of firms that considered the issue of geographical colocation to be crucial was found in the forestry industry (38%), and even lower rate was found in the diary industry (10%). These variations may be due to differences on industry cluster development.

Implications for Academics, Public Policy, and Managers

This research suggests that the elements of networking are important for inter-firm cooperation. Among the social elements of networking, the importance of communication and trust between partners and managing directors are highlighted. Companies also recognized the difficulties of discussing strategic topics, as marketing collaboration with competitors. The use of face-to-face interaction between individuals is a key element in the discussion of strategic topics among managers. Respondent companies also specified the importance of informal relationships in the development of inter-firm co-operation. Informal contacts play a key role for collaborative marketing activities. Then, the importance of the social exchange process may become even more important than simply geographical colocation.

The current situation of clusters in Chile suggests that the concept of milieu characterizes the salmon industry (Camagni, 1991). This is due to the majority of firms being in close geographical proximity operating in one dominating industry, together with auxiliary industries that form the regional cluster, building horizontal and vertical relations. The other two industries under study seem to be only industry sectors and not real industry clusters, unless they are in a premature development.

In this chapter, it can also be recognized that the traditional transactional cost approach has largely ignored issues of social inter-dependencies. Then, managers and public policy officials developing regional cluster strategies need to take special attention in the study and analysis of the social networking aspects on inter-firm collaboration. Consequently, the concept of social capital needs to be seen much more than only social contracts, but more about social relations and strong mutual knowledge among firms that pretend to belong to a real regional cluster.

Future Directions for Research

It is clear that more work in Chile and Latin America is required on the differences between and the relative influence of other actors such as the local public sector and regional councils among collaborative firms. Future research needs to consider in depth and across a wide spectrum, *inter alia* issues of supply chain and horizontal collaboration. This naturally implies a more detailed analysis of subnational and subregional disparities influencing inter-firm cooperation; as well as the strategic importance of inter-firm communication and governance within inter-firm alliances and regional clusters, including several types of institutional mechanisms or facilitators, such as diverse social ties and information technologies.

Individual companies, participating industries, and regional policy bodies may largely benefit from this kind of studies. Specially, managers may benefit of new knowledge about the best opportunities and areas that inter-firm cooperation brings. Public policy and regional development bodies may benefit of this research for achieving better regional clusters strategies, as well as specific incentives for companies participating in these regional industries. Cooperation may be fostered in the context where a new national and regional cluster strategy in Chile as well in some Latin American countries is being currently implemented. Changing their traditional "top-down" approach to a more structured "bottom-up."

It is clear that more Latin American and Chilean key industries and regions need to be studied. This can be the mining industry, located in northern Chile, the fresh products industries located in Peru and Brazil. This can be done exploring industry and regional specificity in the Chilean and Latin American context. Further research also may consider other cohorts located in different countries and continents, to enhance validity and reliable comparisons. Nevertheless, this study may provide a contribution for the cluster policy discussion in the specific Chilean context and serve as an example for other developing economics seeking better levels and coordination of their local economic strategy through clusters development policies.

Acknowledgments

The author thanks the Science & Technology Commission of the Chilean Government-Conicyt and its programmes Fondecyt 11060185 & PBCT-SOC30 for funding this research.

References

Ahuja, G (2000). The duality of collaboration: Inducements and opportunities in the Formation of Inter-firm Linkages. *Strategic Management Journal*, 21(3), 317–343.

Anderson, J and J Narus (1990). A model of distributor firm and manufacturer firm working partnerships. *Journal of Marketing*, 54, 42–58.

Asheim, B (1998). Industrial districts as 'Learning regions: A condition for prosperity. *European Planning Studies*, 4(4), 379–400.

Becattini, G (1990). The Marshallian industrial districts as a socio-economic notion. In *Industrial Districts and Inter-Firm Co-operation in Italy*, Pyke, F, G Becattini, and W Sengenberger (eds.), pp. 37–51. Geneva: International Institute for Labor Studies.

Brown, P and R McNaughton (2002). Global competitiveness and local networks: A review of the literature. In *Global Competition and Local Networks*, McNaughton, R and M Green (eds.), pp. 3–37. Albershot: Ashgate Publishing.

Camagni, R (1991). *Local Milieu, Uncertainty and Innovation Networks: Towards a New Dynamic Theory of Economic Space. Innovation Networks, Spatial Perspective*. London: Belhaven Press.

Cooke, P (1998). Introduction: Origins of the concept. In *Regional Innovation Systems, The Role of Governance in a Globalized World Braczyky*, Cooke, P and M Heidenreich (eds.), pp. 6–19. London: UCL Press.

Enright, M (2000). Regional clusters and multinational enterprises; Independence, dependence, or interdependence? *International Studies of Management and Organization*, 30(2), 114–138.

Eyzaguirre, N (2008). Hacia una Estrategia Nacional de Innovación para la Competitividad. *Consejo Nacional de Innovación para la Competitividad*. Santiago, Chile.

Felzensztein, C and E Gimmon (2007). The influence of culture and size upon inter-firm marketing cooperation: A case study of the salmon farming industry. *Marketing Intelligence and Planning*, 25(4), 337–393.

Freel, M (2005). Patterns of innovation and skills in small firms. *Technovation*, 25, 123–134.

Granovetter, M (1985). Economic action and social structure: The problem of embeddedness. *American Journal of Sociology*, 91(3), 481–510.

Marshall, A (1920). *Principles of Economics*. London: Macmillan.

Maskell, P (2001). Towards a knowledge-based theory of the geographic cluster. *Industrial and Corporate Change*, 10(4), 921.

McKelvey, M, H Alm, and M Riccaboni (2002). Does co-location matter for formal knowledge collaboration in the Swedish biotechnology-pharmaceutical sector? *Research Policy*, 13(4), 1–19.

Oughton, C and G Whittam (1997). Competition and cooperation in the small firm sector. *Scottish Journal of Political Economy*, 44(1), 1–29.

Stopper, M (1996). Institutions of the knowledge-based economy. *Employment and Growth in the Knowledge-Based Economy*. Paris: OECD.

Tiffin, S (2008). Measuring university involvement with industrial clusters: A comparison of natural resource sectors in Chile and Canada. In *Working Paper, School of Business, Universidad Adolfo Ibáñez*, Santiago, Chile.

Von Thünen, J (1842) (1996). *Isolated Stated,* 1st edn. (English translation of *"Der Isolierte Staat"* by Carla Wartenberg and edited by Petter Hall, Pergamon Press Ltd.).

Weber, A (1929). *Theory of the Location of Industries.* Chicago & London: The University of Chicago Press (English translation by Carl J. Friedrich of "Ueber den Standort der Industrien").

Wolfe, D (2003). Social capital and cluster development in learning regions. In *Knowledge, Clusters and Learning Regions,* Holbrook, JA and D Wolfe (eds.), Kingstson: School of policy studies, Queen's University, pp. 11–38.

Zander, I and Ö Sölvell (2000). Cross-border innovation in the multinational corporation: A research agenda. *International studies of Management and Organization,* 30(2), 44–67.

Chapter 13

INSERTING SMALL HOLDERS INTO SUSTAINABLE VALUE CHAINS

MARCOS FAVA NEVES
AND LUCIANO THOMÉ E CASTRO

Abstract

An interesting opportunity exists to discuss sustainable agribusiness projects to be implemented in poor regions. This chapter presents a method that suggests four fundamental dimensions to be inserted in agribusiness projects and to be used by governments and development agencies for attracting the right investments. The first dimension is related to the technical and economical viability; the second one is related to organizational aspects, the players' ability to efficiently coordinate their transactions. The third one relates to business competitiveness and the fourth dimension is environment sustainability. Emblematic cases leading to the proposed method are presented. Finally, results from implementing the method through project done by PENSA (Agribusiness Intelligence Center) together with CODEVASF (Sao Francisco and Parnaíba Rivers Valleys Development Agency) are presented and discussed.

Introduction

There is a worldwide discussion, particularly in developing countries, about the conflict between small holders (entrepreneurs) and agribusiness corporations. According to some critics, the first will be "exterminated" by the unequal competition for areas and resources represented by the second. Agribusiness is defined as the sum of all production and distribution of agricultural inputs, production operation within farms, warehousing, stocking and processing of agricultural products, and byproducts (Davis and Goldberg, 1957).

The authors do not ever differentiate between large or small firms, family or independently owned firms. What was first conceptualized as agribusiness does not deserve the critics. Maybe, the point is a model that, in real practice, leaves no market for small and mainly poor growers. Buying and selling efficiently in the long term in a global scale is a game for well-prepared businesses in any industry.

Many researchers claim that small holders' biggest challenge is their ability to add value to premium products to niche markets, where scale gains are not critical for success. Being the small producer, a Swiss dairy farmer or an Ethiopian coffee grower, the success would come from premium or special products targeted to particular group of costumers willing to pay more for a particular product feature. Organics and more recently fair trade products have a good fit to this philosophy. Certainly, regardless of the product, the challenge for targeting niches will be the small holder's financial and mainly marketing capabilities. Interestingly, when large firms or professionally organized non-profit organizations (like *Rain Forest* or *Agro Fair*) opened their eyes for these niches, they started to grow faster.

Especially in developing countries, governments have spent significant resources to structure small growers' production areas, transferring land ownership rights to them and providing farms with agriculture investments and training. There are successful cases, but unfortunately a much larger portion of failed cases do exist, mainly when support turns out to be of no use. It can be concluded for instance from interesting World Bank reports of Public Irrigation Projects in Brazil (Banco Mundial, 2004). It clearly showed that growers were being strongly encouraged to grow traditional products like bananas and mangos in markets, lacking the desired upstream and downstream coordination, where product supply was higher than existent demand.

It is appealing the idea of maintaining people in rural areas with good life conditions, instead of large monocultures pushing rural population to large cities, particularly when raw material for biofuels may occupy large portions of arable areas in the world. The logic of economic efficiency and specialization challenges it tough. It is not possible however to stop discussing new business models that try to accommodate the expectation of the society.

A valid debate deals with the insertion of small holders into strictly coordinated agribusiness systems (Giordano, 1997; Saes *et al.*, 2001). It means the small holders will not produce just for subsistence or local markets, but also for industrialization or *in natura* consumption in any attractive market in the globe.

This view is more recognized by the growing concern on social sustainability. For a firm that, for instance, is involved in fruit juice production, buying from small holders may represent an opportunity for marketing appeal, an opportunity to use its scarce resources in downstream marketing activities, an opportunity to focus on juice production instead of agricultural production. All these benefits may be counterbalanced by additional transaction costs.

In the above discussion, a business plan for an agribusiness firm or a strictly coordinated system must take into account the sustainability concern. Many different public agents place this dimension on the top of a project analysis for its political acceptance and for the attainment of financial resources from state official sources (Mundial, 2004). The business plan models are well known in the literature. There are models which emphasize the financial aspect (Bernardi, 2003; Clemente, 2002), as well as others which emphasize the strategic view (Lambin, 2000; Chiavenatto and Sapiro, 2003). There are also farm management frameworks and crops viability analysis, well known in classic agricultural economics.

Regarding transaction cost economics, these plans when they are seen individually may represent a small part of the whole investment viability analysis (Zylbersztajn and Farina, 1999). Frequently, individual plans do not consider existent aspects of upstream and downstream in the chain and even with a positive financial analysis, organizational inconsistencies related to transaction costs may not be obvious. Zylbersztajn (2005) discusses the insufficient classic economic analysis for maximizing profits. Therefore, an important question is how to insert coordinated subsystems analysis in business plans as well. Cook and Chaddad (2000) highlight recent changes in agro-industrialization regarding the increasing importance of agricultural inputs, industrialization, and distribution related to agricultural production and the changes related to farming activities with non-farming activities. In fact, non-farming activities must be as viable as farming activities.

A business project with different viability dimensions and social considerations is interesting to public agents. They may attract firms to a specific region, aiming to develop this region. The benefits may not be limited to the generated taxes and jobs, but also to the positive externalities that might be brought by coordinated and sustainable transactions among all chain participants — upstream and downstream the focal firm. Clearly, it is also interesting to the private agents who have a systemic and long-term view. This comprehension facilitates the talks with politicians once positive externalities are clearer. Also, it is interesting to negotiate incentives for the organization to be installed in a specific location.

This chapter intends to introduce a method of integrated and sustainable agribusiness projects, and show directions for enriching business plans models at existing agro-industrial systems, inserting the contributions from different agribusiness, governments, and development agencies when dealing with economic development.

Objectives and Method

The objective of this chapter is to present and discuss a method to be used by governments and development agencies to implement sustainable and integrated agribusiness projects. The method for developing this chapter is first a theoretical essay, bringing aspects from the literature of business plans development. Aspects of general business administration are brought, as well as, marketing and transaction cost economics. Secondly, a multicase studies approach is used to bring examples of companies using a model suggested by Yin (2001). Also, some grounded theory is implemented, deriving frameworks by directly studying and interacting with the phenomenon of interest (Glaser and Strauss, 1967; Strauss and Corbin, 1990). This chapter gives brief information about the implementation of the method in public irrigated areas, where there are plenty of small growers having all kinds of difficulties in their activities. This project was sponsored by CODEVASF and implemented by PENSA researchers.

These are five agribusiness projects all based in the Brazilian northeastern, the poorest region in the country. These case reports are structured as following. Information was collected regarding the products they were producing, the time of the relationship, small growers responsibilities, firm responsibility, the farmer's income, the size of the farms, among other information.

It consisted of attracting agricultural processing firms to source part of their supply needs from public irrigated areas in a sustainable form. We formed a group of 27 researchers worked in nine project teams grouped by food product (orange, lemon, bioenergy products, dried fruits, among others). This project took 12 months to complete, from January 2007 to January 2008 and involved about 20 firms that contributed to the developed models. Those firms were also potential investors for the region. Timely and accurate information on business opportunities, in areas considered in this project, was the advantage the firms had in supplying the researcher specific information about their business. In another words, several firms were offered the opportunity to actively participate in a business opportunity analysis conducted primarily by PENSA researchers. Before reporting the case and the implementation phase, we explore the framework in the next section.

Integrated and Sustainable Agribusiness Projects Method

The process of developing an integrated and sustainable agribusiness project is composed of a sequence of steps and some dimensions. These are showed in Figs. 13.1 and 13.2, respectively. The final goal is to have the right investor, coordinating a food processing investment in a chosen region. This investor is called "an anchor firm" and will coordinate its supply chain with different sources such as local small holders, vertically integrated producers or large growers.

Figure 13.2 shows the idealized food chain built with the proposed method. Also, the four fundamental dimensions are highlighted.

We explore the aspects shown in Figs. 13.1 and 13.2 in the next section.

The project management dimension

In order to attract an agribusiness firm, it is important to think in terms of viability project and attractiveness. First, we need to analyze the technical

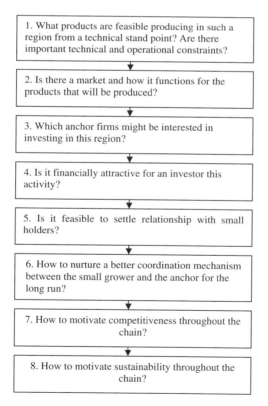

Figure 13.1. Steps toward building a sustainable and integrated agribusiness project. (From authors.)

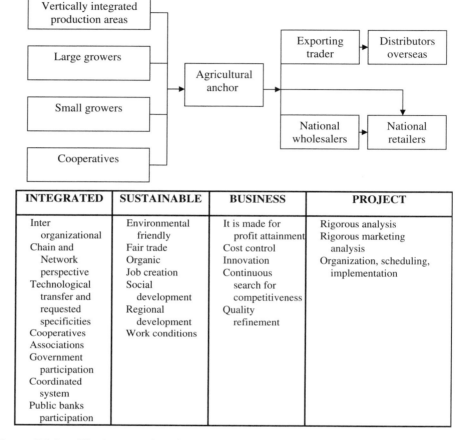

Figure 13.2. The integrated and sustainable agribusiness framework. (Elaborated by the authors.)

feasibility about the activity that one intends to attract to a specific region. Food processing depends of variety and environmental adaptation. Frequently it requires different models of estimating agricultural and industrial investments and costs. The first question to be answered is, what food and fiber may be technically produced in such a region? Are there important technical and operational constraints? Viability analysis was conducted in the Brazilian Semi Arid region — a dried, warm, and irrigation-dependent region. Embraba Semi Arido (Brazilian Agricultural Research Centre) to bring different cultures in order to diversify economic activities (Embrapa, 2006).

The second question is related to the market condition of the product to be produced. Insisting into products with many competitors and no clear competitive advantage is clearly a mistake. It is important to understand the demand behavior, quantitatively and qualitatively. Therefore, the second question is, is there a market and how it functions for the products we may produce? It is important at this point to have a diagnosis of the existent chain; where it is located in the country and how it has performed.

The third question has to do with which anchor firms might be interested in investing in this region? What defines an anchor firm is its status of residual rights owner. In a certain coordinated system, firm leads production. It has the control over the demand information and it drives business throughout the whole chain (Verhallen *et al.*, 2003); for example, Chiquita. This multinational firm places its supply sources globally with relatively lower investments on fruit production but high on distribution and commercialization assets and capabilities. It seizes marketing opportunities and suppliers' production seasons and matches them efficiently. Chiquita has clearly a leading position among players involved in its business. This firm is an example of a potential anchor firm that indeed participated in the project.

In fact, an anchor firm has considerable brand image or superior costumer contact. According to Sauvel (2001) discussing the roles of two leading semi-processed vegetables firms in France, these companies compose the "strategic center." Their role is to create value for their partners, define rules, and build competences while they establish a network structure and strategy. These roles help identify strategic center or agricultural anchor in certain network. Firms like this should be primarily the candidates for being invited to the analysis of this "new business opportunity" and join the preparation phase.

If there are investment opportunities that are technically viable and show a market need and feasibility, then nothing is better to an investor than a good simulation of an enterprise. This information will facilitate for attracting the firm. Thus the fourth question is, is this activity financially attractive for an investory? For example, Neves (2007) showed that a citrus project could be feasible in a new citrus frontier in Brazil. To answer this question, the chosen potential anchor firms could use the information to enhance the analytical accuracy.

The integration dimension

Many enterprises fail, not for the right answers for the questions placed above, but for a lack of a holistic view, considering chain coordination and integration aspects. There are other fundamental questions which must be answered that have little to do with technical, market, or financial analysis.

A firm when is based in one region must competitively buy from suppliers and sell to distributors and final consumers. The way the firm will govern the relationships with these agents will be fundamental for its development. Brazilian agribusinesses have shown countless examples of conflicts among chain participants, and companies and even whole industries disappearing from a region as a result. According to Farina *et al.* (1997), the governance structure is the form a firm chooses to govern a transaction with another part. This may range from vertical integration, contractual arrangements, and spot market. Talking about sustainability, it is expected that the model has a long run orientation searching for ongoing relationships and wealthy distribution.

The challenge for the anchor firm must be to coordinate transactions with small holders. It is clear that different governance modes, when seen from a social perspective, have different consequences. Vertical integration creates jobs, salaries, taxes, exports and might transfer knowledge from the firm to the employees by means of training programs, which, in fact, employees may become entrepreneurs later on. As an example of this strategy in regions in question is Del Monte in Assu, State of Rio Grande do Norte in Brazil.

Buying from large growers based in the region also generates the benefits listed above, except for the quicker technological transfer due to the fact that there are some independent producers and more employees linked to them. As an example of this strategy, there is *Intermellon at Mossoro, which* exports melons, also in the Rio Grande do Norte State. Buying from small holders and cooperatives may be even better in terms of wealth distribution and development, once there are a larger number of rural families involved in the production activities. As an example of this strategy is Caliman. This firm coordinated the insertion of people from "movimento dos sem terra" (an organization that aggregates landless people and fight for land redistribution in the country). These producers have access to special credit conditions from the Brazilian government (PRONAF — Familiar Agriculture National Program) and the firm takes advantage of it.

We also advance the discussion that a governance model is feasible considering existing or estimated transaction costs. If we ignore relationship conflicts, transaction costs, information asymmetry and opportunistic behavior following the basic transaction dimensions from Williamson (1985), we can say that the best for a processing firm is to concentrate in its core business. For instance a fruit juice producer has to concentrate on juice production instead of growing fruits. But it is well known that real market characteristics force firms to try to better control supply activities. The idea of inserting small holders into the business model has to be carefully evaluated.

Therefore, we may add a fifth question to our method: considering estimated transaction costs, is it feasible to settle relationships with existent small holders? If it is too costly dealing with small holders, if they are not trustable, there will be a trend for consolidation and later to vertical integration clearly (Azevedom, 1996).

A possible form and a key research agenda are the public incentives and advantages for the projects that insert the larger number of producers. It is interesting to learn as to how it may affect the efficiency and competitiveness of the whole system against social benefits created by the incentive.

This will not be sustainable if this is an artificial incentive that will end up hiding operational and transaction inefficiencies. Therefore, carefully made contractual models are a good viable case. Interesting quasi-integration contracts, as the ones used in the poultry and pork chains in Brazil, are good examples of vertical and horizontal firms that despite contextual problems seem to survive and succeed in the international markets. Now we answer the sixth question, how to nurture a better coordination mechanism between the small grower and the agricultural anchor, avoiding a future vertical integration as a future supplying strategy? Neves (2003) suggested a framework for contract building and revision with risk simulation aspects. Contract theory has given several contributions to the design of contracts with relationship incentives and a cooperative equilibrium (Barzel, 2001).

The business dimension

In response to previous questions, several pre-requisites were placed for the implementation of an agribusiness project; for example, the agents have to generate profits. Regarding small holders, their income must be high enough to keep them motivated and committed to the activity. This is the basis for the long-term orientation of the chain and economic sustainability. Important issues to be considered regarding economic viability are farm size and product prices. One of the Brazilian Government's mistakes at redistributing land ownership in the country was the size of the farms. This was too small to fit a competitive production and generate money sufficiently to keep people employed; for instance, farms of around four hectares in certain regions would just allow subsistence agriculture (Codevasf, 2006). Clearly, a chain should strive for innovation and quality improvements. The seventh question to the public agent is, how to motivate competitiveness throughout the chain? The simultaneous attraction of research centers, universities, technical consultants are some of the important initiatives.

The sustainable dimension

Giordano (2003) writes on the broadness of the concept of sustainable: "The most interesting of all is that it will not focus just products, but environmental friendly production systems. Another phenomenon occurred in the last four years focused only on environment to a wider concept, more subjective and more complicated, in which environment is part of it. According to Giordano (2003), sustainable is defined as a capacity of sustainability or support, determined by a group of factors. Further, sustainability comprehends three different components: the environment, the economic development, and the equal wealthy distribution for everyone. For the United Nations: (1) sustainable development is the improvement of life quality of the humanity respecting the support capacity (sustainability) of ecosystems; (2) the sustainable economy is the product of sustainable development with the maintenance of the natural resource production base; and (3) the sustainable society is the one that could "continue to develop, adapt and increase knowledge, organization, technical efficiency, and wisdom. Filho and Zylberstajn (2003) showed that socially responsible organizations and corporative governance are closely related for the creation of value for the organizations themselves. Therefore, the final question is, how to incentive the sustainable development at the proposed chain? It is important to motivate national and international environmental certification processes because they help prepare the firm and the region to attend environmental criteria and later on to open markets. The government agent must act like a facilitator in this process. It is important for the company to invest in poor communities where investments will be made to promote social insertion.

Cases of Integrated and Sustainable Agribusiness Projects

Table 13.1 lists firms that have competitive business models and insert smallholder into their supply chain. These firms help us understand the challenges for implementing a diverse supply chain and refine the proposed method. The cases are Agropalma, Brasil Ecodiesel, Calimaan, Intemellon, and Pindorama Cooperative. Information was collected regarding the products they are producing, the time of the relationship, small growers responsibilities, firm responsibility, the familiar payouts, the size of the farms, among other information.

The following are the key aspects of the cases that could be used to design a framework for replicating the model elsewhere: (1) different concomitant governance modes and one of them is composed of small growers: the firms

Table 13.1. List of smallholders.

Case	Product	Farm size and familiar payouts	Grower responsibilities	Anchor responsibilities
Agropalma	Palm oil, Biodiesel	10 ha R$ 15 a 20 thousand per year per family (about US$8 thousand)	Produce Make available the land Access to special funding	Technical assistance Buying commitment of all production in the long run at a agreed price
Brasil ecodiesel	Biodiesel from castor plant Biodiesel from soy beans	For the castor plant: 25 ha, being just 8 h a for the castor plant. The rest used for subsistence R$ 18 thousand per family (about US$ 10 thousand)	Produce Make available the land Access to special funding	Offers services center (healthy care, education, cultural, and recreational center) Offers land property for production Committed to buy all small grower production Seeds Basic inputs Basic agricultural equipments Technical assistance for the small growers

(Continued)

Table 13.1. (*Continued*)

Case	Product	Farm size and familiar payouts	Grower responsibilities	Anchor responsibilities
Calimann	Papaya	27 families share 48 ha Between R$ 600 e R$ 1.200 per adult per month (about US$ 250 per adult)	Land (small grower from the "MST — Movimento Sem Terra) Money Workforce There is a incentive system for following the required agricultural procedures	Technological package Technical assistance Control and supervision Basic input
Intermellon	Watermelon Melons	Producer of 8 ha It reaches R$ 7 thous./month (around US$ 4 thous.)	Land Production	Technological package Technical assistance Finances agricultural inputs
Pindorama	Sugar cane Coconuts Passion fruit Pineapple Acerola Milk	From 5 to 30 ha Payouts are around US$ 400 per hectare per month	Produce in the farm for at east two years the products the cooperative is interested in and if everything is all right renew the contract	Land with "renting free contract" since the land is explored following the cooperative criteria

have a vertically integrated area but slowly increase the small growers contracting proportion according to the acquired experience; (2) most of them make use directly or indirectly of cheaper interest rates given to small growers by official banks in the country. Interest rate, when used smartly, has made a difference; (3) a long-term perspective is present; (4) strong presence of the firm at coordinating contracts and monitoring the small holders area with some of them establishing contracts with quality incentives was observed; (5) strong social vision is present in the projects. It is important to notice that the social appeal is not just a nice speech. These companies are proud to have these projects, and their organization culture supports these activities; (6) in cases where small holders own the land, there is clearly an advantage to the anchor firm related to less fixed capital invested in land; (7) training and technical assistance are strong in all cases. The absence of it is actually the main reason why the critics say governmental programs for land distribution fails. The lack of grower capabilities and the insufficient governmental support has been critical for the failure. In this case, the private agent brings to them these responsibilities, and surely they are in a better position to offer those since they are in the same market and have the experience following market requirements for food products; (8) long-term contracts with some characteristics of quasi-integration contracts are present and (9) one of the biggest challenges for small holder is the obtainment of credit for financing investments and production. In this case, the presence of a well-known agribusiness firm in the arrangement makes much easier for them to obtain credit. In some cases, the firm acts like an intermediary for giving the credit and it is paid when production is shipped. It decreases interest rates for the small growers. When giving credit directly to the small holder, experience has shown that in general there is a high chance of going bankrupt.

These insights from existing private initiatives helped PENSA work together with Codevasf to attract agribusiness firms to base their production in some of the irrigation projects managed by Codevasf manages.

The Project for Implementing the Method Together with Codevasf

Codevasf (Development Agency of São Francisco and Parnaiba Rivers Valleys) is a State-owned agency associated to the Brazilian Ministry of National Integration. Its influence area represents 640 thousand km² in Brazil. One of its main development strategies is providing irrigation for the Brazilian Semi-Arid region. The total potential irrigation area accounts for 360 thousand hectares, and it has implemented about 110,000 hectares so far, in 25 irrigation

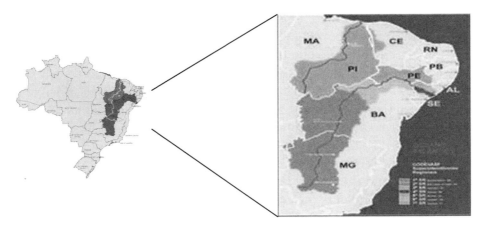

Figure 13.3.   Location of São Francisco (red) and Parnaíba (green) Rivers valleys. (From Codevasf, 2008.)

perimeters. Another 100,000 hectares is going to be implemented in 2008 (Rabobank, 2005). Figure 13.3 shows the location of São Francisco (red) and Parnaíba (green) Rivers Valleys.

Public Private Partnerships (PPP) will be used by Codevasf to implement new irrigation perimeters. This resulted in a new business model. Private firms will do the operation and maintenance of common irrigation facilities. The agricultural area inside the perimeter will be subjected to public bidding for agricultural anchor firms, which will lead production inside the perimeter, either producing or renting the land for contracted small holders, and will coordinate the agricultural chain toward insertion into agribusiness. On the other hand, the Brazilian government will assign the right for exploring the land for renewable periods that ranges from 25 to 50 years, and will offer several alternatives for financing the project.

PENSA (The Agribusiness Intelligence Center of University of São Paulo) and Codevasf established a partnership for the development of Integrated and Sustainable Agribusiness Projects, in which nine business opportunities were analyzed at the São Francisco and Parnaíba Rivers Valleys containing full agricultural and processing financial analysis, logistics analysis as well as financial evaluation. The elicited chains and a summary of their results are showed in Table 13.2. The team prospected about US$ 500 million for the considered area, being about 40% of it for industrial investments (Juice, Ethanol, Slaughterhouses, etc.) and 60% agricultural and animal production. The higher investments in the agricultural and animal production related to industrial plants are justified by the size of the areas and mainly the need to

Table 13.2. Potential results of the implementation of the method.

Chain	Agribusiness participating firms	Job creation	# of integrated small holders	Total tax generation\ (thous. R$ yearly, industrial and agricultural)*	Extra revenues for ag.-inputs and logistic firms (thous. R$ yearly)*
Banana	Chiquita Inc. (USA), Noboa Inc. (USA).	1,550	13	R$ 1,053	R$ 7,100
Pinneaple	Itaueueira (BRA)	1,600	16	R$ 1,086	R$ 4,200
Ovines	Agrosavana (BRA)	1,535	152	R$ 1,600	
Dried fruits	Bauducco (BRA)	1,570	Nd	R$ 216	R$ 642
Processed vegetables	Green Way (USA), Itochu (JAP)	3,580	156	R$ 3,600	R$ 27,000
Palm trees	Agropalma (BRA)	9,100	340	R$ 24,100	R$ 5,000
Jatropha	FMC (USA)/ Ateon (USA)	20,000	1,250	R$ 51,300	R$ 20,000
Poultry	Mauriceia (BRA), Seara-Cargill (USA), Frango de Ouro (BRA)	700	40	R$ 9,700	R$ 1,200
Lemon	Itacitrus (BRA), Cutrale (BRA)	1,200	108	R$ 4,380	R$ 24,000
Total		40,835	2,075	R$ 92,655	R$ 89,842

Source: Elaborated by the authors. *US$ 1,00 was worth R$1,80.

irrigate them using drip systems. The projects considered about 150 thousand hectares of production areas.

Once the products were defined by the technical and market analysis, the researchers of each of the nine project teams prepared business proposals, estimating investments, costs, revenues, and financial analysis with several scenario analysis. Concomitantly potential investors were contacted to support the analysis, confirming data and contributing with refined and current information. The way to get their commitment was to promise them prompt access to all the information we would be preparing and show them this would help analyze a new business opportunity. There were confidential agreements that specific firm information would not go public. However, if they at the end did not implement the project, we would be free to offer it to any interested firm (without releasing the firm confidential information). Table 13.2 shows the results of the project. These are prospected numbers. The investments are under implementation with some companies still taking the final decisions.

An interesting part of the project was to define a business model for the small holder that met all the criteria discussed above. It included a technological package, a farm size and mainly an estimated income (with some range of variation) that the family will take out of it. Table 13.3 reports the size of the farm and the approximate level of expected income. Other crops were included in this analysis as well.

It is important to mention that for the implementation of the projects, firms had an option to vertically integrate some of the areas (this was calculated for each case) and it was by "right to use the land for 20 years, automatically renewable if everything goes right.

Implications for Managers

This chapter brings several implications for managers in food chains and governmental leaders. Four will be highlighted here. Inserting small holders into food value chains is a way of building sustainability around the world. This is an important global concern and although image might not be the main firm's concern, there are important positive image implications. In addition, staff morale increases since they belong to the firm's sustainable initiatives. Hence, the project should be communicated properly.

Second, managers of private firms have to insert the dimensions discussed in this chapter when presenting to government decision makers to negotiate important incentives for their investments or important joint actions in areas like educational programs for training small holders. It is important for managers to fully understand the government concern on

Table 13.3.   Farm size and small holder income.

Products	Size of the farm (ha)	Estimated mensal income for small holders family (in Reais)*
Banana	19	1,508.75
Pineapple	17	1,558.33
Lemon	37	1,513.00
Sugar cane	33*	1,523.00
Citrus	35	1,537.00
Cotton	20	1,586.00
Semi processed vegetables	7	1,585.00
Palm oil	25	1,548.48
Jatropha	28	1,582.76
Poultry	1	1,378.00
Ovines	3 (irrigated)/50 (for pastures without irrigation)	1,666.00

Source: Elaborated by the authors *US$1,00 is worth R$1,80.

development and think of how to integrate their efforts with existing governmental efforts.

Third, more specifically for government leaders, this chapter has shown a project for investment attraction using a different methodology. It hired a consulting group to prepare a first business plan for potential investors in the region is a way to motivate investors to invest in the region. This is a superior method than just highlighting generally local comparative advantages related to some competing locations and use communication tools like advertising. Particularly for Codevasf, it is a more active form of interacting with businesspeople and with better results.

Fourth, the proposed method may enhance business-planning activities of a firm. Using these questions as a checklist will improve the business plan and give the managers a holistic perspective.

Conclusions

This chapter has presented a method for improving business plans for development agencies and governments for attracting agribusiness firms. Some emblematic cases were presented in order to show how they contributed to the ideas for the project implementation. The experience in trying to implement these "designed chain" was rich. It gave the project teams the real notion of what are the difficulties in working with agribusiness and small holders. Especially in developing countries, projects like this are fundamental because they bring small and poor holders' options to improve their activities. Agribusiness firms need to develop and diversify their suppliers globally. Especially, for Brazil, a country that has witnessed the increase of large-scale monocultures like sugar cane or soybeans. This kind of project may alleviate unemployment and migration from traditional cultures which were pushed by expansion of large scale commercial crops. There is a need for inclusion, without any ideological view, but with a sustainable and competitive reasoning. It impossible to ignore it and not to think of how small holders may prosper in countries like Brazil.

An interesting research agenda is what should be the role of the State in motivating the creation of such arrangements. Some will say that the role of the State is simply guaranteeing good institutions for market development. Other, however, will say that there is a need to motivate more inclusive models with more assertive policies. Particularly, it is a good research topic in Brazil when biofuels are booming.

References

Azevedom, PF (1996). Integração Vertical e Barganha. São Paulo: USP, 1996. Tese de Doutorado em Economia na Faculdade de Economia, Administração e Contabilidade.

Barzel, Y (2001). A theory of organizations to supersede the theory of the firm, *Working Paper*.

Bernardi, LA (2003). *Manual de Empreendedorismo e Gestão*, p. 314. São Paulo: Atlas, 1ª ed.

Chiavento, I and A Sapiro (2003). *Planejamento Estratégico: Fundamentos e Aplicações*. Rio de Jeneiro: Elsevier.

Clemente, A (2002). *Projetos Empresariais e Públicos*, p. 341. São Paulo: Atlas, 2ª. ed.

CODEVASF (2006, 2008). *Companhia de Desenvolvimento dos Vanes do São Francisco e Parnaíba*: www.Codevasf.gov.br.

Cook, M and FR Chadda (2000). *Agroindustralizaton of the Global Agrifood Economy: Bridging Development Economics and Agribusiness Research, Forthcoming in Agricultural Economics*.

Davis, J and R Goldberg (1957). *A Concept of Agribusiness*, p. 167. Harvard University.

EMBRAPA (2006). Empresa Brasileira de Pesquisa Agropecuária: available at http//:www.embrapa.gov.br.

Farina, EMMQ, PF Azevedo, and MSM SAES (1997). *Competitividade: Mercado, Estado e Organizações*, p. 285. São Paulo: Singular.

Giordano, SR (1997). *O Sistema Agroindustrial dos Frutos do Cerrado: O Agribusiness do Pequeno Produtor*, p. 21. São Paulo: Série Estudos Temáticos 003/97.

Giordano, S (2003). Marketing e Meio Ambiente. *Marketing e Estratégia em Agronegócios e Desenvolvimento*. MF Neves and LT Castro (eds.), Atlas, p. 369.

Glaser, BG and AL Strauss (1967). *The Discovery of Grounded Theory: Strategies for Qualitative Research*. Chicago: Aldine-Atherton.

Lambin, JJ (2000). *Marketing Estratégico*. Portugal: McGraw-Hill. 4a. ed.

Machado Filho, CAP and D Zylbersztajn (2003). *Responsabilidade Social Corporativa e a Criação de Valor Para as Organizações.* Working Paper No 03.024.

Mundial, B (2004). Brasil: Agricultura Irrigada na Região do Semi-Árido Brasileiro: Impactos Sociais e Externalidades, abril de 2004.

Neves, MF (2003). Marketing and network contracts (agreements). *Journal on Chain and Network Science*, 3(1).

Rabobank (2005). São Francisco valley integrated fruit production an interesting alternative for new investments.

Saes, MSM, MCM Souza, and MN Otani (2001). *Actions to Promote Sustainable Development: The Case of Baturité Shaded Coffee, State of Ceará, Brazil*, p. 36. São Paulo: FAO (Food and Agriculture Organization of the United Nations).

Sauvee, L (2001). Strategic interdependence and governance: Empirical evidence with two agri-food networks in the fresh and processed vegetable sectors in France. *V Congresso Internacional de Economia e Gestão de Redes Agroalimentares*, Ribeirão Preto.

Strauss, AL and J Cobrim (1990). *Basics of Qualitative Research: Grounded Theory Procedures and Techniques.* Newbury Park, NJ: Sage Publications.

Trobin, VG and MF Neves (2007). Proposição de um Método Para Analisar a Viabilidade da Implantação de uma Cadeia Produtiva em um Novo Local: O Caso da Citricultura no Pólo Petrolina-Juazeiro. Dissertação de Mestrado Faculdade de Economia Administração e Contabilidade de Ribeirão Preto, Universidade de São Paulo.

Verhallen, T *et al.* (2003). *Demand Driven Chains and Networks, in Camps, t. et al. The Emerging World of Chains and Networks*, p. 467. Amsterdam: Reed Business Information.

Williamson, OE (1985). *The Economic Institutions of Capitalism*, p. 450. USA: Macmillan.

Yin, RK (2001). *Estudo de Caso: Planejamento e Métodos*, 2a ed. p. 205. Porto Alegre: Bookman.

Zylbersztajn, D (2005). Papel dos Contratos na Coordenação Agro-industrial: Um Olhar Além dos Mercados. *XLII Congresso Brasileiro de Economia Rural*, Ribeirão Preto.

Zylbersztajn, D and EMMQ Farina (1999). Strictly coordinated food-systems: Exploring the limits of the Coasian firm. *International Food and Agribusiness Management Review*, 2, 249–226.

Chapter 14

FRANCHISE AS AN EFFICIENT MODE OF ENTRY IN EMERGING MARKETS: A DISCUSSION FROM THE LEGITIMACY POINT OF VIEW

CLAIRE GAUZENTE AND RÉGIS DUMOULIN

Abstract

The entry mode choice on a new market is always a hot issue for both practitioners and academics. One of the most widely used solutions is franchising. This chapter explains why in emerging market this option can be interesting. It also delineates the different suboptions within the franchise option. It reviews success criteria as identified in franchise literature and introduces the concept of legitimacy as a key factor to entry success. Grounding on the new institutionalism theoretical framework, the different types of legitimacy — coercive, normative, and cognitive — are exposed and discussed in light of emerging markets characteristics.

Introduction

Emerging markets apparently offer opportunities for growth and profits for Western firms operating in saturated domestic markets. Choosing markets and identifying adequate entry mode both represent a challenge to managers. Literature relating to international economics, international strategy, and international marketing suggests relevant decision criteria. Among entry modes, franchising stands out as a relatively straightforward technique (Duniach-Smith, 2004). Indeed, international franchising is one of the most dynamic entry modes with a high rate of development (Michael, 2003; Welsh *et al.*, 2006). Franchise can be defined as a mode of organization chosen by one franchiser and several franchisees in order to compete successfully, generally in the retail industry. The franchiser who owns a trademark and a technology or specific know-how grants to the franchisee the right to use the trademark/technology/know-how package in a definite territory. In exchange, the franchisee pays royalty on sales and/or franchise fees. Franchisees are typically local independent entrepreneurs and are supposed to possess a better knowledge of the local market than the franchiser. The association is supposed to represent a win-win solution: the franchisor gains a fast-growing coverage of the targeted territory with minimal investment and franchisees get a successful business recipe.

From the franchisers' point of view, several advantages are attached to this form of development, not only do they transfer the entrepreneurial (mainly financial) risk to franchisees but they also gain indirect knowledge of the market and coverage, therefore limiting the pioneer failure risk. This is probably why a certain number of firms adopt the franchise strategy for their expansion in foreign markets even if they do not operate on a franchise basis in their domestic market.

This chapter examines the potentials of franchise as an adequate form of organization when investing in new markets, especially in emerging ones. It tries to identify decision criteria in the light of the potential risks and drawbacks of franchise. In particular, the importance of the legitimacy is underlined. The chapter is organized in two parts. First, strategic interests of emerging markets are discussed in relation to franchise entry modes and franchising decision criteria. Second, the value of the legitimacy concept for entering EM is discussed in terms of normative, cognitive, and coercive aspects.

An Analysis of the Opportunity to Franchise in Emerging Markets

Emerging markets: A strategic analysis

From an economic point of view, the world is divided into three kinds of countries. Advanced economies (AE) are post-industrial countries (Kanter, 1991), shifting from manufacturing to service-based development, because of deindustrialization to the benefit of low-wages areas. The main characteristics of AE are a capitalist economic system, a high gross domestic product (GDP) per capita, highly competitive industries, and trade. Countries characterized by weak incomes, stagnant growth, and weak industrialization are called developing economies (DE). Emerging market economies (also called emerging markets or EM) stand between theses two types of economies. They are rapidly evolving toward AE. They are highly industrialized countries, with high growth rates. According to the International Monetary Fund,[1] the average real GDP growth in the EM was about 6% in 2007, and will rise to 6.3% in 2008, even if GDP per capita remains lower than in AE. These markets nevertheless exhibit important financial risks.

An EM is actually a country in a transitional phase moving from a centrally planned economy to a liberalized one and from an agricultural society to an industrial one. International business scholars unanimously consider that EM, from a demographic and economic standpoint, are well fitted to franchising. Saturation of post-industrial markets largely explains franchise development in EM. These countries, China, India, Turkey, among others, are new markets in which AE wish to develop business. EMs are characterized by population size and growth. The size of the middle class is another aspect to be taken into account. In China, the middle class is estimated to be 30 million households; in India, it is about 300 million people. This growing middle class is aspiring for higher standards of living. Due to massive and rapid urbanization, people move from rural area and concentrate in big cities. In China, for example, population concentrates in the East/South-East coast of large cities. In Russia, urbanization level is about 75% (Anttonnen *et al.*, 2005). Workforce that includes a great proportion of young people and female labor is increasing.

As a result, there is a growing demand of Western-like goods and services such as high technology products, equipments, automobile, insurance, health care, and leisure and tourism infrastructures. According to the US Department of Commerce, EM Economies will represent more than 75% of the expected growth of the world trade in the next two decades. Not only EMs has an increasing per capita income, a large consumer market, and a growing middle class with a high purchasing power, but also firms and governments have important needs. As they become industrialized, firms require manufactured technology (e.g., machine tools, etc.) to develop industrial and agricultural potential. Governments need infrastructure-related products and services in order to modernize their countries such as communication routes, water management, and real estate, among others. The lack of retail infrastructure is also a major issue. A synthetic view of the opportunities and threats associated with entering EM is summarized in Table 14.1.

---

[1] http://www.imf.org/ (accessed July 23rd 2008).

Table 14.1.   Opportunities and threats of emerging markets.

Opportunities

From the consumers' standpoint:

> A large consumer market, an increasing income rate, and a growing middle class with
> a high purchasing power.
> A strong need and interest in quality Western products.
> A rather centralized population, in large towns.

From the governments' standpoint:

> Globalization and deregulation have been the major reasons of the development of
> international franchising, especially in EM. Globalization involves reduction of
> entry barriers.
> Political reforms to secure economic environment.
> Support from local governments, development of organizations promoting franchising,
> securing entrepreneurship.

From the firms' standpoint:

> Factories producing the Western goods are often located in the EM, facilitating carriage
> at low costs.
> The number of educated and skilled labor force is plentiful.

Threats

Political instability, covering black economy, corruption, and crime and generating economic
instability.
Legal instability: in some EM legislation and taxation can still be rather complicated and
discouraging for entrepreneurship or for a franchisor–franchisee relationship.
EM have poor infrastructures, especially distribution infrastructure.
Protecting intellectual property can be challenging.
The availability of financing can be rather poor. Franchisees must be supported by local
banks, whose decision process can be slower than market development opportunities.
Furthermore, franchisees may face high establishment costs.

Source: Anttonnen *et al.* (2005).

The Identification of Success Factors: Classical Decision Criteria

Decision criteria can be divided into two types: external one pertaining to the analysis of the target market, and internal one covering the firm's preoccupations. Among external criteria, one of the most prevalent concerns is the size of the market. In line with this, Alon (2006) underlines that big Emerging Markets (BEM such as China and India) are not necessarily the most attractive ones. Indeed, economic factors should be considered in the light of other environmental factors. These additional environmental factors entail public opinion (Paswan and Kantamneni, 2004), cultural distance, and geographical distance, as well as political uncertainty (Sashi and Karuppur, 2002). Another important aspect is the availability of managerial talent in host country (Dev *et al.*, 2002).

From an intra-organizational point of view, chief considerations stem from the strategic motives of the firms, and especially franchisers' (Pak, 2002). While international franchisers are often equated with market seekers, Pak (2002) shows that strategic asset or capability seekers who decide to franchise abroad are more successful than growth or market seekers. In addition to this, Sashi and Karuppur (2002) underline the importance of prior experience in global markets. Firms with such an experience will franchise more easily in foreign markets, including emerging ones, as they are accustomed to dealing with foreign cultures and countries. A reputable brand name will also constitute strength when entering a new market with franchise (Sashi and Karuppur, 2002). It is also important to examine why franchise could be preferred to alternative entry modes. Table 14.2 focuses on the strengths and weaknesses of developing franchise in EM.

Table 14.2. Strengths and weaknesses of franchise in emrging markets.

Strengths

Franchising represents a less risky and costly entry mode. Sharing the economic risk is essential when entering into an unstable business environment.

Franchising enables a faster entry and growth because various resources will be acquired from franchisees.

Franchising is regarded as an effective business method because independent entrepreneurs are assumed to be more motivated than salaried employees.

International franchising may be better accepted in a host country because most of the revenues will stay in the country.

Weaknesses

Since franchising is not very popular or common business method in some EM, franchisee recruitment procedures can be rather time and resource consuming. As mentioned by Noor *et al.* (2002), the majority of people in Malaysia prefer to wait and see the economic performance of franchise before committing to be a franchisee.

Training and control of franchisees may require more efforts than normally. For example, post-communist countries may suffer from a lack of entrepreneurial behavior.

Some countries may develop resistance against privatization and market economy, etc.

EM culture and language create conditions that require changes in the business concepts and operations. The Cyrillic alphabet and the feminine culture in Russia (Anttonen *et al.*, 2005), but also Ideograms and multiple local languages in China, where culture is family oriented. India has a serious competitive advantage given by the English colonization.

Franchisee selection criteria must select real entrepreneurs and avoid financial investors.

Source: Anttonnen *et al.* (2005).

Franchising in Foreign Markets: Modes, Pros and Cons

It is important to underline that franchising as an entry mode is not necessarily adopted by firms that are operating through franchise in their domestic market (Quinn and Alexander, 2002). Firms that are operating through organic growth or acquisitions in their domestic market can choose franchise as a mode of entry in foreign markets. Marks & Spencer is an example of it. In contrast, Carrefour and Ahold are counterexamples: these firms operate on a franchise basis in their domestic market but choose to hold their units when expanding abroad.

From a theoretical standpoint, the franchiser–franchisee relationship can be conceived as an agency relationship where the franchiser (the principal) grants to the franchisee (the agent) a decision power (Jensen and Meckling, 1976). Grounding on the individual profit maximization principle, several studies dedicated research efforts to the study of franchisees' free rider behaviors (Caves and Murphy, 1976; Brickley and Dark, 1987; Lafontaine, 1999; Michael, 2000). For the head of a retail network, the choice is between franchise and self-owned outlets. Both solutions generate agency costs if individuals' goals are not aligned (Rubin, 1978). Two types of agency problems are emphasized: vertical agency problems and horizontal agency ones. Vertical issues pertain to the comparison of costs linked to, on one hand, internal management that is costly in terms of behavioral control and to, on the other hand, franchised outlets that are more profitable given that franchisees possess their outlet and dedicate their efforts to it. These are topics that Lafontaine and Kaufmann (1994) examined thoroughly. The co-alignment of individual interests is more easily obtained *via* the franchise system. Horizontal issues concern free-rider behaviors that stem from brand and image utilization (Klein, 1995) and from geographical dispersion of franchised outlets (Rubin, 1978; Brickley and Dark, 1987). Combs *et al.* (2004) consider that vertical agency costs rather than horizontal ones justify the choice of franchise as an organization mode for retail networks.

In addition to these considerations, it is important to note that there exist several types of franchising arrangements in order to get involved in foreign markets, whether emerging or not. One can distinguish two main options: direct franchising (DF) and indirect franchising (Burton *et al.*, 2000). The latter can be implemented through either master franchising (MF) or area development franchising (ADF). Besides these classical forms of franchising, the emergence of micro-franchising (mF) constitutes an interesting avenue for economic development in developing countries.

DF is an arrangement where the franchiser directly establishes franchise contracts with individuals in the target market. The functioning mode is then the same as in its domestic market but requires a dedicated department in order to deal with foreign franchisees. From a transaction cost perspective, this option is adapted only when the franchiser already has a global experience in international franchising, has a certain size, engages in franchise relations with markets that are culturally and geographically close. In other cases, indirect franchising should be preferred. Master franchising is an arrangement where the franchiser grants to a master franchisee the right (1) to establish franchise units but also (2) to recruit franchisees. The master franchisee will, hence, act in place of the franchiser with subfranchisees. This option is potentially preferred in cases of low local commercial infrastructure and high political uncertainty (Sashi and Karuppur, 2002). Area Development Franchising (ADF) is also an indirect type of franchising where the franchiser grants to an area developer the right to operate its own units in the target market. The AD franchisee is, hence, a multiunit franchisee in a specific area; an employee paid by the ADF can manage each unit. This option can be adopted in small markets or can help to cover a market by cutting it in several areas with a minimum of AD franchisees to deal with. Depending on how it is implemented, ADF can be considered as an intermediate option between direct franchising (multiple franchisees per market) and MF (one master franchisee per market).

The case of micro franchising

Taking a sustainability stance at franchising, Fairbourne (2006) suggest that franchising can stand as a new tool for creating economic self-reliance. mF uses the basic principles of franchising in order to set up micro-businesses with individual entrepreneurs in developing countries. It is designed to fit the conditions of economic poverty but aims at developing sustainable micro-businesses from which people can live, and contribute to social and economic welfare. It usually targets development issues such as health, sanitation, or energy; for example, Cellular City in the Philippines (cellular phones and accessories retail), EasyTeva in Sri Lanka (wifi access) or Fan Milk in Ghana (dairy products) illustrate how the model of franchising can be applicable not only in EM, but also in poorer ones. It also proves that for-profit businesses can successfully combine sustainability/accountability and profit.

Table 14.3. Characteristics of different franchising mode.

	Brief definition	Degree of control	Adaptation to distant cultures	Monitoring costs
DF	Franchisor directly contracts with foreign franchisees	++	−	++
MF	Franchisor contracts with one master franchisee per country. The master franchisee then contracts with local franchisees	−	+	=
ADF	Franchisor contracts with a limited number of area development franchisees who own and operate several outlets	+	+	+
mF	Franchisors directly contracts with individuals on an adapted economic basis, in developing countries	+	++	+

Legend: +: high; −: low.

Table 14.3 summarizes the main characteristics of each different franchising mode.

Previous strategic criteria and franchising options are important for the choice of franchise when entering EM. However, we suggest that firms considering entering EM should examine the kind and extent of legitimacy they will have. At least, they should be conscious of the following underlying processes in order to maneuver adequately.

Franchising in EM: The Importance of Legitimacy

Theoretical framework

The concept of legitimacy has been particularly analyzed in new institutionalism where the isomorphic concept is a key process through which legitimacy is obtained. Isomorphic processes pertain to the adoption by organizations of similar structures, strategies, and process. An organization is isomorphic when it resembles to other organizations in its organizational field. (Tolbert and Zucker, 1983). Institutional isomorphism enhances organizational legitimacy in its acceptance by external environment (Meyer and Rowan, 1977; Deephouse, 1996). "Legitimacy is a generalized perception or assumption that the actions of an entity are desirable, proper, or appropriate within some socially constructed system of norms, values, beliefs and definitions" (Suchman, 1995, p. 574). The legitimacy concept is at the heart of new institutionalism analyses (Powell and DiMaggio, 1991). We use this theoretical perspective in order to examine organizational choices, and in particular the choice of franchise as a mode of entry in EM. New institutionalism posits that norms, values and rules present in the environment are determinants in strategic choices (Oliver, 1997). Imitation and conformity seeking (i.e., isomorphism) behavior guides the development of structures. Conformity to institutional environment's expectations help acquire legitimacy and resources and attain higher performance (Deephouse, 1996). Powell and DiMaggio (1991) emphasize the role of coercive, normative, and cognitive mechanisms in the emergence of isomorphism. Legitimacy has then three sources: coercive, normative, and cognitive. In short, the coercive source stems from stakeholders' scrutiny, the normative one from peers' one, and the cognitive one from one's own.

Further, coercive legitimacy results from isomorphism implemented in response to "both formal and informal pressures exerted on organization by other organizations upon which they are dependent" (Powell and DiMaggio, 1991). They underline the significance of legal environment of organizations. In this perspective, new political and legislative rules tend to favor organizational change. Then, the role of potential positive or negative sanctions is important in organizational compliance. Normative legitimacy mainly originates from professionalization. It is the collective struggle of members of an occupation to define the conditions and methods of their work, to control the production of producers (Larson, 1977). Contrary to coercive legitimacy, the aim of these efforts is to guide and promote certain preferred behaviors. Professionalization maintains uniformity and self-reproduction. Members of the profession decide and act in order to exhibit conformity to social norms and expectations rather than economic requirements.

Cognitive legitimacy stems from the fact that certain ideas are taken-for-granted by the different actors of the environment. This taken-for-grantedness property can be linked to the concept of dominant logic developed by Bettis and Prahalad (1995). Uncertainty is an explanation of why cognitive isomorphism happens. As firm managers face great environmental uncertainty, they seek practical and successful solutions in their neighborhood. Imitation of successful recipes hence becomes a rationale. In addition, the fact that the

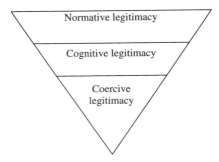

Figure 14.1. Sources of legitimacy.

different actors of a given field share a common vision about the environment and the range of acceptable solutions reinforces isomorphism.

We hold the view that in the case of franchising in EM, the importance of each source of legitimacy follows the descending order: normative, cognitive, and coercive (see Fig. 14.1). The importance of normative legitimacy in EM is prominent compared to cognitive and coercive legitimacy.

Normative Legitimacy

As mentioned above, normative legitimacy derives from the compliance to norms the profession itself prescribes. The central role of professional association is linked to three aspects (Greenwood *et al.*, 2002). First, professional associations play a role of self-representation that reinforces internal cohesion and comfort the spirit of the time. Second, professional associations negotiate with their political and economic environment. This activity allows them to disseminate norms outside the circle of professionals and elaborate and refine "best practices" that will be spread to their members. Third, professional associations scan their environment in order to anticipate significant changes. This helps the community adapt more tightly to legal, technological and economic evolutions. All in all, professional associations are normalization sources as well as information and norm's dissemination sources for their members. The normative pressure of professional associations can be traced in their behaviors, history, codification power, and legislation. For instance, the French franchise federation initiated a code of ethics that has been partly reproduced in the European franchise federation; this code has been adopted in 1972 and is regularly updated.

The Moroccan Franchise Federation code of ethics: An illustration of institutional proximity

The Moroccan Franchise Federation was created in 2002. As other franchise federation, its role is to promote franchise and disseminate best practices information. The official web site of the MFF conveys different information about franchised networks development recruitment and code of ethics.

Looking carefully at this code, it appears as a transposition of the French and European code of ethics with very minor amendments. The history of Morocco is strongly linked to France due to the French protectorate from 1912 to 1956. Moroccan institutions have been exactly copied on French ones. This common history and institutional proximity is still irrigating Moroccan functioning, and this is illustrated in the formation of the MFF and its code of ethics.

Governments are also a source of normative pressure. Indeed, certain governments even help the creation of franchise regulation bodies. For instance, a Franchise Development Body was created in Malaysia in 1992, under the execution Coordination Unit, department of Prime Minister. Then the Malaysian Franchise Association was established in 1994 to promote entrepreneurship through franchise (see Noor *et al.*, 2002). The Russian Franchise Association was established in 1997 (Anttonen *et al.*, 2005). In several Central European countries, local governments have promoted franchise as a way to rapidly develop economy, employment, incomes, and managerial skills especially in small- and medium-sized firms.

Local normative can explain franchising development and spreading pressures to introduce standardized and globally shared organization modes in spite of potential local opposition (Coller, 1996; Ferrer and Quintamilla, 1998; Paswan and Kantamneni, 2004). The action of governments in promoting franchise through the creation of franchise federations can be explained in two ways. First, one of the aspects of globalization is the diffusion of standardized organizational structures and norms. As a result, strategic and organizational globalization is enhanced by internationally shared thoughts and practices that create rational myths (Meyer and Rowan, 1977). Legitimacy comes with the development of an internationally shared organization mode, sponsored by EM governments, even if it may require local adaptations (Meyer *et al.*, 1997). Franchising can be seen as a way of

promoting local entrepreneurship and there is poor hostility toward this form
of organization. No other entry mode receives such a government support
because it protects local economy. In addition to this, created value remains
in the country, which helps safeguard EM's autonomy. Second explanation is
the tendency to follow the herd. Franchising is a capitalist mode of organization that proved to be successful in advanced economies. The development of
local franchise federations gives a strong positive signal to international economic and political actors. Hence, the adoption of franchise at a country level
is a means that helps reassure international partners.

Cognitive Legitimacy

Cognitive legitimacy relates to the notion of taken-for-granted and cognitive
blindness. Firms that are franchising in their domestic market gain expertise
in franchise development. This expertise can obviously be used at profit when
going abroad. Prior experience with recruiting, training, and managing franchisees can be redeployed in new EM at no additional costs in terms of
organizational learning. This rationale can be reinforced by the idea that franchising is the right way to do things and that no other reliable alternative
exists. In fact, the dissemination of a specific norm (i.e., choosing franchise as
an entry mode in EM) is associated with the fact that it is taken for granted
and that it guides managerial decisions and actions. Meyer and Rowan
(1981) suggest that institutionalization is the process by which actors to
accept norms as if they were intangible rules. This leads to a strongly shared
social reality that raises no questions for actors themselves. A commonly
shared view of what is appropriate is created (Zucker, 1983). These taken-
for-granted views irrigate practices and behaviors (Berger and Luckman,
1967). A parent idea is developed in the work of Prahalad and Bettis (1986)
and Bettis and Prahalad (1995) who advance the notion of "dominant
logic." A dominant logic represents a sort of informational genetic code
that has been built from the firm's observation of environment. It predis-
poses one specific organization to analyze and act in a specific direction (or
a specific set of directions).

   The interiorization of one specific view of the world restrains the number
of strategic options managers will consider (Fligstein, 1990; Greenwood and
Hinings, 1996). This process is strengthened by the limited rationality of
individuals (Cyert and March, 1963) who judge strategic and organization
options through a satisfaction process, and not an optimizing one. All this
leads to entry mode choices that are mimetic by nature as managers use
heuristics that favor easy, already known or already observed solutions that

appear to be successful. In this simplified heuristic process, the role of leaders and pioneers is foremost. These represent examples of what should be done to be successful and their recipe tends to be copied.

Ryans *et al.* (1999, p. 34) stresses that much of the global interest in franchising, and US franchisors in particular, has resulted from the success of pioneer companies like McDonald's Corp. and Midas Inc. They also suggest that franchising overseas is not always that easy. More specifically, master franchising is stigmatized as a mode of entry that leaves very little control to the franchisor and that can provoke serious damages to the brand reputation and name abroad. Indeed, although recipes tend to be copied, their very interest may be questionable. Several studies adopting a population ecology view examine franchise survival and growth. The results obtained by Lafontaine and Shaw (1998) and Shane (1996) exhibit that 70–75% of new franchise systems fail in their first years, a mortality rate that is not significantly different from new ventures in general. In addition, a good franchisees' recruitment, an efficient support system and a clear division of local locations are fundamental factors for reducing failure probability (Azoulay and Shane, 2001).

Coercive Legitimacy

Coercive legitimacy can be analyzed from two different lenses. As explained previously coercive process is linked to the possibility of a sanction, whether positive (reward) or negative (punishment). Sanction can stem from either economic world or from laws and governments. First, economic sanction takes shape at least in survival and at best in performance. As mentioned previously, an analysis of franchise systems' survival showed that they do not necessarily differ from other types of businesses. However, success of franchise in foreign markets is significantly linked to survival in domestic markets. Perrigot (2008) demonstrates this on a large sample of 912 networks observed on a time period ranging from 1992 to 2002. It gives the firm, in its domestic market, the advantage of first movers (Julian and Castrogiovanni, 1995). These two points represent positive sanction of franchising internationally, and especially in EM. However, negative sanctions are also possible when public opinion (Paswan and Kantamneni, 2004) does not accept the brand and considers certain franchise names installing as an aggressive maneuver against their country and culture. This can be linked to what is called, in marketing literature, the country-of-origin effect (Teegen, 2000). This effect can be either positive or negative and corresponds to the positive halo effect of a country's reputation on consumers' evaluations of products and brands (e.g., French cosmetics and perfumes are supposed to be sophisticated and *chic*, whatever the brand).

Second, governments also exert sanction toward economic forms. As emerging countries open their markets to foreign private investors, they try to attract them with government support, low capital cost, specific legislations on foreign property or compliance to international rules on copyright and intellectual property. All these represent positive sanctions.

There exist some drawbacks, however. One of the most important threats in developing international business in the EM is the weakness of the regulatory environment associated with political risk. Political instability directly affects the development of franchising through the general business environment. When governance is weak or non-reliable, when governments are not recognized, when authority is not embodied by the legitimate power, business costs and risks increase as well as uncertainty. All this reduces managers' ability to predict business evolution. Political risk or instability refers to corruption, organized crime, and weak legal structure that discourage investments. One of the difficulties of using franchise on EM countries lies on poor venture capital monitoring which may inhibit the return of fees and royalties at the expense of the franchisor.[2]

Lack of transparency in the public sector as well as bureaucracy may promote local firms against foreign investors. Transparency International[3] (2007) highlights the linkage between corruption and legal system, "An independent and professional judicial system is critical to ending impunity and enforcing the impartial rule of law, to promoting public, donor, and investor confidence. If courts cannot be relied upon to pursue corrupt officials or to assist in tracing and returning illicit wealth, progress against corruption is unlikely." The absence of a strong legal framework prevents prosecution and makes litigations long, hazardous, difficult and costly to resolve conflicts COFACE,[4] one of the world's most important credit insurance company, whose mission is to facilitate trade between companies worldwide, notes for instance that in African and Middle East countries, in spite of a strong economic and financial dynamism, the business environment nevertheless is weak (weak

---

[2] Franchise may nevertheless be useful to the franchisor as it helps develop a business in emerging countries while promoting local entrepreneurship and thereby avoiding the phenomena of corruption sometimes in use against foreign firms in the EP (Meschi, 2007). Franchise may be seen as a way of avoiding liability of foreignness. (Zaheer and Mosakowski, 1997) and thereby gaining local legitimacy (Yiu and Makino, 2002; Rodriguez *et al.*, 2005).

[3] See http://www.transparency.org/ consulted July 19th, 2008.

[4] http://www.trading-safely.com/sitecwp/cefr.nsf/vwNL/2172A8717BB60863C12573-BF0064E2F5, consulted July 21st, 2008.

enforcement of laws making recoveries random, lack of transparency of company accounts, widespread corruption). Hence, paradoxically, because of good economic performance, certain governments may not be urged to strengthen institutions. Economic performance does not always contribute to improving business environment.

In Russia, business is affected by weak enforcement of law. Law enforcement and legal environment are not safe for foreign business. Financial transparency remains very inadequate. In China, financial information is often not available or reliable. Legal environment does not protect foreign investors. In India, financial information is available for large companies, but not for smaller ones. It is also difficult to obtain financial information from groups. The legal environment is satisfactory even if Indian laws are sometimes not in favor of foreign business. Procedures are time consuming. In Brazil, COFACE notes that business information is highly available and that legal environment respects international business. Coercive legitimacy related to the establishment and development of franchise in emerging countries is still not very strong, except in countries that meet international expectations of legislation (e.g., Brazil). Whether for franchise in particular or for international business in general, international trade, due to the gap between their legal framework and protections, explains this weakness. The strengthening of a specific legislation would reduce uncertainty both for franchisers and franchisees.

EM legislation is in constant change. Between new laws and old ones EM need legislative reforms to revise confusing, insufficient, and partially contradictory laws (Anttonen *et al.*, 2005, p. 9). In advanced countries, laws on franchise fight against opportunism. In emerging countries, legal framework first has to secure the relationship between franchise stakeholders by securing the economic environment.

Conclusion

The aim of this chapter was not only to analyze the opportunity of franchising in EM, but also to introduce an additional view — institutionalism and the concept of legitimacy. This leads to several theoretical and managerial implications. From a managerial point of view, managers can be inspired by Oliver's recommendations about how to manage institutional environment. Oliver (1991) identified five main strategies that can be used to manage all three types of legitimacy, and this also holds true in EM. Five potential categories of strategic responses can be distinguished: acquiescence, compromise, avoidance, defiance, and manipulation. *Acquiescence* corresponds to conformism. This is less-risky strategy in order to get legitimacy. It entails three distinct tactics. *Habit* corresponds to an unconscious conformism. This is the case where *taken-for-grantedness* applies fully. Actors blindly apply rules and norms. *Imitation* is a mimetic acquiescence response. Preferred dominant models are consciously or unconsciously adopted. *Compliance* is a deliberate process through which actors decide to conform to the dominant model.

Other strategies involve decoupling between the firm and norms. Legitimacy is then obtained using potentially more risky strategies such as adopting certain normative aspects (compromise), disguising non-conformity (avoidance), ignoring or contesting norms (defiance), and shaping norms (manipulation, which is only available to powerful firms in economic, relational, or institutional terms). In EM, given the flexibility or simply lack of rules and legislation, some powerful pioneer franchisers may exert their influence in order to enforce their model and build their own legitimacy.

From a research standpoint, the idea according to which franchisers should assess the target market, only in economic terms, is undermined. Institutional and social dimensions are important but gaining legitimacy is even more important in emerging markets. This leads to several research avenues. Considering that legitimacy is an important factor for resource access, it should lead to higher performance or, at least, better survival. Performance of franchise systems can no longer be interpreted in terms of technical economic performance. Franchise as an efficient entry mode cannot be examined in these terms either. This offers new research opportunities where entry modes are analyzed taking into account the three types of legitimacy firms can gather and develop in EM. More specifically, comparative studies of legitimacy building between the three main types of franchise entry (direct, master, area development) could significantly advance our knowledge and help practical recommendations.

References

Alon, I (2006). Executive insight: Evaluating the market size for service franchising in emerging markets. *International Journal of Emerging Markets*, 1(1), 9–20.

Alon, I and R Perrigot (2003). Marks & Spencer et son échec à l'international. *Décisions Marketing*, 30, 41–50.

Anttonnen, N, M Tuunanen, and I Alon (2005). The international business environments of franchising in Russia. *Academy of Marketing Science Review*, 5, 1–18.

Azoulay, P and S Shane (2001). Entrepreneurs, contracts and the failure of young firms. *Management Science*, 47(3), 331–358.

Bettis, RA and CK Prahalad (1995). The dominant logic: Retrospective and extension. *Strategic Management Journal*, 16, 5–14.

Brickley, JA and FH Dark (1987). The choice of organizational form: The case of franchise. *Journal of Financial Economics*, 18, 401–420.

Burton, F, AR Cross, and M Rhodes (2000). Foreign market servicing strategies of UK franchisors: An empirical enquiry from a transaction cost perspective. *Management International Review*, 40(4), 373–400.

Caves, RE and WF Murphy II (1976). Franchising: Firms, markets and intangible assets. *Southern Economic Journal*, 42, 572–586.

Comb, JG, SC Michael, and GJ Castrogiovani (2004). Franchising: A review and avenues to greater theoretical diversity. *Journal of Management*, 30(6), 907–931.

Deephouse, DL (1996). Does isomorphism legitimate? *Academy of Management Journal*, 39, 1024–1039.

Dev, CS, M Krishna Erramilli, and S Agarwal (2002). Brands across borders. Determining factors in choosing franchising or management contracts for entering international markets. *Cornell Hotel and Restaurant Management*, 43(6), 5–16.

Duniach-Smith, K (2004). Entry mode choice: The case of franchising. In *18th International Conference of ISOF*.

Fairbourne, JS (2006). Micro franchising: A new tool for creating economic self-reliance. *ESR Review*, 8(1), 18–23.

Greenwood, R, R Suddaby, and CR Hinings (2002). Theorizing change: The role of professional associations in the transformation of institutionalized fields. *Academy of Management Journal*, 45(1), 58–80.

Jensen, MC and WH Meckling (1976). Theory of the firm: Managerial behavior, agency costs and ownership structure. *Journal of Financial Economics*, 3, 305–360.

Julian, SD and GJ Castrogiovanni (1995). Franchisor geographic expansion. *Journal of Small Business Management*, 33(2), 1–10.

Kanter, RM (1991). *When Giants Learn to Dance*. London: Simon and Schuster.

Klein, B (1995). The Economics of franchise contracts. *Journal of Corporate Finance*, 2, 9–37.

Lafontaine, F (1999). Franchising vs. corporate ownership: The effect on price dispersion. *Journal of Business Venturing*, 14, 17–34.

Lafontaine, F and PJ Kaufmann (1994). The evolution of ownership patterns in franchise systems. *Journal of Retailing*, 70(2), 97–113.

Lafontaine, F and KL Shaw (1998). Franchising growth and franchisor entry and exit in the US market: Myths and reality. *Journal of Business Venturing*, 13, 95–112.

Meschi, P-X (2007). Firmes Etrangères et Corruption d'état dans les Pays Emergents. Analyse Transactionnelle de la Survie de la Participation des Partenaires Européens dans les Coentreprises Internationales entre 1996 et 2006. In *16th Association Internationale de Management Stratégique Conference*, Montreal.

Meyer, J and B Rowan (1981). Institutionalized organizations, formal structure as myth and ceremony. *American Journal of Sociology*, 83(1), 340–367.

Michael, SC (2000). The effect of organizational form on quality: The case of franchising. *Journal of Economic Behavior and Organization*, 43, 295–318.

Michael, SC (2003). First mover advantage through franchising. *Journal of Business Venturing*, 18, 61–80.

Michael, SC (2003). Determinants of the rate of franchising among nations. *Management International Review*, 43(3), 267–290.

Noor, SM, N Mokhtar, IA Rahman, and JA Moen (2002). Franchise development program: Progress, opportunities and challenges in the development of bumiputera entrepreneurs in Malaysia. *Journal of American Academy of Business*, 2(1), 272–278.

Oliver, C (1997). Sustainable competitive advantage: Combining institutional and resource-based views. *Strategic Management Journal*, 18(9), 687–713.

Pak, YS (2002). The effect of strategic motives on the choice of entry modes: An empirical test of international franchisers. *Multinational Business Review*, 10(1), 28–36.

Paswan, AK and P Kantamneni (2004). Public opinion and franchising in an emerging market. *Asia Pacific Journal of Marketing and Logistics*, 16(2), 46–61.

Perrigot, R (2008). La Pérennité des Réseaux de Points de Vente: Une Approche par L'écologie des Populations et les Analyses de Survie. *Recherche et Applications en Marketing*, 23(1), 21–37.

Powell, WW and PJ DiMaggio (1991). *The New Institutionalism in Organizational Analysis*. Chicago: The University of Chicago Press.

Prahalad, CK and RA Bettis (1986). The dominant logic: A new linkage between diversity and performance. *Strategic Management Journal*, 7(6), 485–501.

Quinn, B and N Alexander (2002). Franchising activity in international retail operations. *International Journal of Retail and Distribution Management*, 30(5), 264–276.

Rodriguez, P, DS Siegel, A Hillman, and L Eden (2006). Three lenses on the multinational enterprise: Politics, corruption and corporate social responsibility. *Journal of International Business Studies*, 37(6), 733–746.

Rubin, PH (1978). The theory of the firm and the structure of the franchise contract. *Journal of Law and Economics*, 21, 223–233.

Ryans, JK Jr, S Lotz, and R Krampf (1999). Do master franchisors drive global franchising? *Marketing Management*, 8(2), 32–37.

Sashi, CM and DP Karuppur (2002). Franchising in global markets: Towards a conceptual framework. *International Marketing Review*, 19, 499–524.

Shane, S (1996). Hybrid organizational arrangements and their implications for firms growth and survival: A study of new franchisors. *Academy of Management Journal*, 39(1), 216–233.

Teegen, H (2000). Examining strategic and economic development implications of globalizing through franchising. *International Business Review*, 9, 497–521.

Welsh, DHB, I Alon, and CM Falbe (2006). An examination of international retail franchising in emerging markets. *Journal of Small Business Management*, 44(1), 130–149.

Yiu, D and S Makino (2002). The choice between joint venture and wholly owned subsidiary: An institutional perspective. *Organization Science*, 13(6), 667–683.

Zaheer, S and E Mosakowski (1997). The dynamics of the liability of foreignness: A global study of survival in financial services. *Strategic Management Journal*, 18(6), 439–464.

Part IV

AFRICA

Chapter 15

PUBLIC PROCUREMENT REFORM IN EMERGING ECONOMIES: A CASE STUDY OF KENYA

PETER M. LEWA AND SUSAN K. LEWA

Abstract

This chapter examines the reform of public procurement in emerging economies using public procurement reform in Kenya as a case study. Primary data were obtained from interviews of knowledgeable individuals. Secondary data were mostly collected through review of available literature on public procurement in emerging economies, the UNCITRAL Model Law and the WTO literature on public procurement. Based on the findings relating to procurement reform, this chapter study recommends that institutional and regulatory frameworks need to be revised and harmonized with other laws; suppliers need to be empowered; training of procurement staff must be given priority as well as better systems of remuneration be developed; political and other interests need to be addressed, and key stakeholders must be allowed to play an increased role in public procurement.

Introduction

Governments engage in procurement to support their activities. Government or what might generally be described as public or national procurement refers to the purchasing by government bodies from external providers of the products and services these bodies need in order to carry out their public service mission (Arrowsmith, 2003). Recent years have witnessed increased worldwide concern about the critical role of public procurement in development, and this has led to reform measures in many countries. The concerns have also led to extraordinary growth in procurement regulation at both national and international level (Trepte, 2004). In developed, emerging, and developing countries, public procurement reform has been initiated resulting in new procurement systems being born at an increasing rate. This raises issues about their appropriateness and compatibility as well as their governance (Trepte, 2004). For emerging economies and developing countries, both the process of national procurement and the use of legal rules to achieve this reform have been promoted by regional and international institutions, and by individual developed countries with an interest in the reform process (Arrowsmith, 2003). Reform of public procurement is expected to bring about "good governance" in the process of development. Governance has been defined by the World Bank as "the manner in which power is exercised in the management of a country's economic and social resources for development," whilst good governance is indicated by predictable, open, and enlightened policy making..., a bureaucracy imbued with a professional ethos; an executive arm of government accountable for its actions; ...and all behaving under the rule of law (World Bank, 1994). The Asian Development Bank (2005) defines governance in similar terms. In many African countries, governance is a key issue of concern (Olowa, 2002). Reforms to address problems in public procurement have been attempted in African countries and in many others as part of a wider economic reform program.

Scope of Public Procurement

Governments engage in the economy as a provider of essential services such as defense, clean water, health, education, and infrastructure. For the purposes of both national regulation and international treaties, it is common to categorize public procurement transactions into three: construction services (works), supplies, and (non-construction) services. Examples of construction procurement include construction of administrative buildings, bridges, highways, and schools. Supplies procurement includes simple as well as complex projects such as purchase of office stationery and acquisition of power generation plants, respectively. Services procurement involves the acquisition or purchase of services to support government activities. Examples of services include legal advice and ICT advice (Arrowsmith, 2003). These essential government services cannot adequately be provided by the private sector as they are mostly public goods whose provision cannot be left entirely to the private sector, which has the capacity to exclude some consumers due to a variety of reasons including inability to pay.

Public procurement is an important part of any economy as it claims a large percent of a country's budget. In spite of the significance of public procurement in an economy, it has, until recently, received little attention by academic researchers and policy makers, because it was considered an administrative function too mundane to worry about (Wittig, 1998).

The value of the contestable government procurement market was estimated at over $2,000 billion between 1998 and 2000. This is equivalent to about 7% of world GDP and 30% of world merchandises trade at the time. The size of public procurement varies between 5% and 8% of GDP in industrialized countries. In most European Union (EU) Member States, procurement purchases are estimated at 10% to 15% of GNP, or some 25%–30% of public expenditure, representing many billions of Euro (Sigma Policy Brief No. 3). For the Middle East and Africa, the magnitude of central government purchases ranges between 9% and 13%. In Kenya, public procurement consumes 45% of the budget, excluding local government procurement (APNAC, 2003). The figure is quite huge as to have an important bearing on economic development. It is easy, therefore, to see that there is a close relationship between development and sound public procurement (Waiganjo, 2006). Consequently, there are concerns in many emerging economies about what options are available for improving the management of public procurement.

Theoretical and Conceptual Framework

Meaning and scope of public procurement

Procurement is a common function carried out in both the public and private sectors, and is a part of the discipline of purchasing and supply. Purchasing and supply is concerned with the acquisition of resources, including goods and services, for use in the productive process. The process of purchasing involves planning and determining requirements, specifications to meet needs, advertising for supplies, selection of suppliers, preparation of purchase orders, receipt and storage of goods, issuance of materials and goods to users and the movement and or disposal of materials. It also includes managing relationships between buyers and suppliers (IPAR, 2006). Considering the total cost of purchased material, it can emphasize the importance of procurement as a key function in the management of business. For instance, the average manufacturing company disposes of more than 50% of its income on materials, supplies, and services. Government markets constitute an important part of the economy — more than 10% in most countries (Baily and Farmer, 1977; Arrowsmith, 2003; Lewa, 2006). The total cost of material includes the specification being purchased. In turn, this may involve marketing and the desire to have an acceptable product to sell, production and the need to ensure smooth operations without disruptions, disposal of waste, scrap, and transportation (IPAR, 2006).

Public procurement is different from private procurement, because in public procurement the economic results must be measured against more complex and long-term criteria. The volume of government purchases and the complexity of products and services take significant time of management. Also the range of purchases is extremely wide, involving items from food and clothing to highly sophisticated construction works and equipment such as battleships and satellites. The management task in public procurement is complicated by influences, which do not apply in the private sector. Public procurement must be transacted with other considerations in mind, besides the economy (IPAR, 2006). These considerations include openness, account-ability, non-discrimination among potential suppliers and respect for international obligations. For these reasons, public procurement is subjected, in all countries, to enacted regulations in order to protect the public interest. It is important to note that unlike private procurement, public procurement is a business process within a political system engendering significant consid-eration of integrity, accountability, national interest, and effectiveness (Wittig, 2002). The process of public procurement requires improved visibility of expenditure, more time afforded to planning, data and information manage-ment, and staffing and controlling activity in order to make the process more effective and efficient. There are certain generally established objectives of purchasing or procurement. A well-known definition of purchasing or pro-curement objectives is to purchase the right quality of material, at the right time in the right quantity from the right source, at the right price (Baily and Farmer, 1977).

Right quality means what exactly it is that is required for the intended application (specification), ensuring that the chosen supplier has the capacity to comply with the specification, and the monitoring of physical supply.

Right time means goods and services are received at the time when they are expected to be ready for use as and when required. Right time could mean at the time of use (just in time), a few days or weeks or even months before the time of use in the productive process depending on their nature, deter-mined lead times, and other considerations.

Right quantity means the amount required at the time it is required. In most cases, the right quantity is the amount or quantity of order that gives the least-cost result. The ordering policy in place largely determines the order quantities. For example, calculating the economic order quantity (EOQ) gives the least-cost result while pursuing a materials requirements planning (MRP) policy. This is particularly suitable for procurement of parts and material required for batch production of complicated manufactured goods.

The right source means a vendor or vendors with the capacity to meet the stated needs. According to Baily and Farmer (1977), sourcing is comprised of the identification or development of suitable sources of supply; the systematic investigation and comparison of such sources; the sourcing decisions: which suppliers to patronize, how many to use for a given item, how to allocate available business, what terms to do business on; the continuing relationship, both with preferred sources which are actually supplying goods and services, and with potential sources which are still in the running although they have been passed over for the moment.

The right price is the value of what the vendor offers or what is negotiated between the buyer and the vendor.

According to Baily and Farmer (1977, p. 13), the objectives of procurement can be summarized in a statement of objectives as follows: (1) to supply the organization with a steady flow of materials and services to meet its needs; (2) to ensure continuity of supply by maintaining effective relationships with existing sources and by developing other sources of supply either as alternatives or to meet emerging or planned needs; (3) to buy efficiently and wisely, obtaining by any ethical means the best value for every pound spent; (4) to manage to give the best possible service to users at lowest cost; (5) to maintain cooperative relationships with other departments, providing information and advice as necessary to ensure the effective operation of the organization as a whole and (6) to develop staff, policies, procedures, and organization to ensure the achievement of the foregoing objectives.

Regulating Public Procurement

The reform of public procurement systems largely aims at establishing the nature and extent of regulation in order to pursue public procurement objectives in an efficient, economic, and effective manner and in line with government's social, economic, and political objectives. Regulation aims at establishing how the underlying objectives of procurement are to be achieved in such a way that government is able to fulfill its tasks in providing public services in a transparent manner (IPAR, 2006). Regulation is based on the principles of economic efficiency, transparency, equality of treatment, non-discrimination, contestability, and value for money.

In an undistorted economic world, the workings of the market lead to allocative efficiency. Where there are no distortions, competition leads to economically efficient outcomes. Distortions arise from public goods or externalities and presence of inequalities in the flow of information. Public procurement discloses market failures due to the above distortions. Regulation is aimed at correcting such distortions (Trepte, 2004; IPAR, 2006).

In the free market economy, there are infinite number of economically efficient outcomes that depend on individual abilities and consumption preferences based on free choice. Under the circumstances, what is efficient will depend on production or technical efficiency of the supplier and on the preferences of the consumer. In the case of government, these preferences will reflect the value judgment of the government as well as of the society, which has put it in power. In making decisions as to how it will act in the market place, it indicates its purchasing preferences that will reflect and incorporate aspects of social welfare. In exercising its choice to promote social welfare gains the government is no longer seeking to correct market failure but to compensate for the efficient operation of the market by assisting those who are left badly off through its workings (Trepte, 2004, p. 389). This is a choice based on equity considerations and is thus informed by political considerations. Economic efficiency is harder to achieve under the circumstances and the regulation is thus inefficient but is aimed at welfare gains that the market is unable to deal with.

Where the market is the sole means of allocating resources, all purchasing decisions made by individual consumers will be made with the aim of maximizing their own welfare. The consumers make their choices on the basis of costs and benefits. They thus make their purchases on the basis of gain from a particular purchase above the costs of making the purchase. In this way, "value for money" may be used to express the reasons, which prompt an individual consumer to prefer the purchase of a given buy at a certain price to another. The price paid matches the value the consumer attaches to the benefits to be gained from the buy. In the case of the government procurement, the preferences will reflect the political as well as social aspirations. Thus, the value for money in this case will need to consider the range of political and social policies in question. In the case of international procurement, what the government might consider as value for money may be at variance with the rules and regulations applied by the international economic arrangement in question.

Equality of treatment, generally speaking, presupposes equality before the law. It plays an important role in enforcement proceedings and is supposed to guarantee all bidders the same rights in enforcing procurement regulation. In an international contest, however, equal treatment may not always be guaranteed because access to national procurement markets is usually the privilege accorded only to members of the market or the relevant international organization (Trepte, 2004). Equality of treatment can also be looked at in terms of "substantive" equal treatment. In this case, the general rule is that identical situations should be treated in same way. This means that suppliers' bids will be considered on the basis of the advertised specifications and bias will not be introduced by considering other factors. Where the purchaser is the government, political and social considerations may lead to the promotion of positive discrimination, which is in effect, unequal treatment.

In the case of international procurement, the concept of equal treatment is based on the nationality or origin of goods, such that all tenderers of whatever nationality and all bids including goods of whatever origin must be treated equally. This implies that any condition of eligibility or origin will automatically lead to unequal treatment since those conditions will, by definition, discriminate against foreign tenderers (Trepte, 2004, p. 391). In international procurement, foreign bidders are most likely to be discriminated against because they do not belong to the procurement clubs inherent in such systems.

Transparency implies that all parties in the procurement process have all the information needed to make informed choices and decisions. There are three main parties in the public procurement process: the government or public authority, the procurement agent and the tenderers. Procurement regulation applies different conditions to the parties. The government or public authority does not stand in a direct relationship with the tenderers but operates by way of agents (individual procurement officers and tender committees). The authority is at a disadvantage since it is the agents who generally possess all the relevant information and make decisions on behalf of the principal (government or public authority). The principal's objective is that the agent operates in the best interests of the principal and not in his or her own interests. The principal must develop a way of verifying the actions of its agents in the procurement process (Trepte, 2004). The procurement agents and the bidders, on the other hand, are not always at par in terms of information. The bidders, generally speaking, have much more information in terms of the market, products or services, costs, transport, price levels, etc. Transparency in the procurement process is meant to encourage tenderers to provide all the relevant information to the agents so that they can be able to make informed decisions. The agent must have all the relevant information in order to be able to impose transparency on the tenderers.

The procurement agents and the tenderers are expected to promote transparency in the procurement process. Tenderers will only be prepared to be transparent if they have faith in the procurement process, that is, if they believe that their bids will be treated fairly and will be kept in the picture in terms of the procedures inherent in the procurement process. Tenderers require confidence in the implementation of procurement procedures and in their ability to enforce them in case of deviation (Trepte, 2004).

Effective competition enables different suppliers to communicate prices and terms on which products or services are available. It is prices that will most accurately communicate scarcity and hence reflect the true cost of production. Determining the equilibrium market prices is a function of information availability. The government and its agents rarely possess such information. In order to help deal with the problem, the government and its agents must ensure a level playing field for all bidders in any procurement effort. Tenderers will only be prepared to be transparent if they have faith in the procurement procedures and believe that the best tenderers have the best chance of winning the tender awards.

Regulation of procurement in the private sector does not happen. In the sector, procurement is a practical function, which has little to do with the strict rules and regulations found in public procurement but has every thing to do with the efficiency of purchasing and hence value for money (Trepte, 2004). On the other hand, public sector procurement is the subject of strict mandatory administrative rules and procedures due to the unique place of public bodies in the economic, political, and social spheres. The concern in public procurement is "why" rather than "how" procurement is regulated. The issues, which arise in the regulation of procurement, are complex and therefore invite a multidisciplinary approach. To begin with, procurement is primarily an economic activity involving the relationship between suppliers and purchasers of goods and services. The laws of the market determine their relationship. Another fundamental consideration concerns the identity of the purchaser. Public procurement refers to the economic relationship between suppliers or vendors and the government as the purchaser or buyer of goods and services. The sheer size of the government and its operating complexities mean that it cannot be treated just like the other actors in the market. The government has the potential to create distortions through its public procurement actions in the market. Under the circumstances, regulation makes sense (IPAR, 2006). At the international level, the ability of the government to apply discriminatory or protectionist procurement policies may raise trade barriers and undermine the international economic order (Trepte, 2004). This is most likely to engender conflicts and cause unnecessary misunderstandings between the various actors in international trade.

Factors Influencing Effective and Efficient Operations

Efficient and effective operations of the public procurement system can be considered in terms of (1) the institutional framework; (2) the professional-ism of procurement staff; (3) the participation of suppliers; (4) the types of procurement processes and (5) the legal and regulatory framework.

These factors are depicted in Fig. 15.1.

Legal and regulatory framework

A comprehensive, adequate, and enforceable legal and regulatory framework is indispensable for the effective and efficient practice of public procurement. That is, the legal framework must be clear and comprehensive.

Institutional framework

The public procurement institutions should be adequate in number, inde-pendent, and powerful enough to formulate procurement rules and regulations and enforce them (Nzai and Chitere, 2006). These authors state that the institutional framework must have the following features: (1) have autonomy decision making; (2) provide a conducive working environment

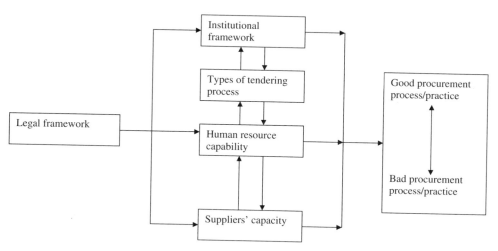

Figure 15.1.   Factors influencing procurement process. (From Nzai and Chitere, 2006.)

for its staff; (3) permit adequate representation of key stakeholders; (4) provide a working environment that has performance targets and (5) operate on the basis of strategic planning, work plans, and budgets.

Human and other resources

The personnel must have competencies, they must be well trained, motivated, and must be technologically sound.

Suppliers' capability and participation

The suppliers must have requisite capacity. Nzai and Chitere (2007) outline the capability issues as (1) they must be legally registered; (2) must meet qualifications specified in procurement law and regulations; (3) need to participate at all stages of the process to ensure ownership and control; (4) suppliers from the SME sector need to be facilitated through an enabling environment, e.g., ready access to low-cost credit and (5) vendors must have ready access to information.

Involvement in procurement

Stages involved in each type should be clear to tenderers and should be less time consuming, and adequate information needs to be continuously availed to suppliers.

Methodology

Research design, sampling procedures, and analysis

This study was undertaken by combining both secondary and primary data. Secondary data were mostly collected through review of available literature on public procurement including the UNCITRAL Model Law, WTO literature on public procurement, the reform instruments in Kenya: Public Procurement and Disposal Act, 2005 and the Public Procurement and Disposal Regulations of 2001 and 2006. Other sources of secondary data included Kenya's Supplies Guide of 1978, draft policy papers and Gazette notices, policy documents and legislative laws of Kenya, Research findings and policy documents from other countries including the works by Lewa (1984, 2006) and IPAR (2006).

Because of dearth of data, the author relied more on primary data and anecdotal evidence. Primary data were collected through fieldwork in Nairobi and several districts for a period of 10 weeks in the months of February, March, and April 2008. Data were collected through consultations, focus group interviews, and discussions conducted with professionals in the procurement discipline; some selected international agencies, some contractors selected at random on the basis of availably in the city of Nairobi, districts, provinces and other stakeholders from the Kenya Institute of Supplies Management (KISM). Altogether 200 knowledgeable individuals were interviewed at different times. The number was considered representative for the purposes of the research. Primary data were qualitative and mostly reflected the opinions of the various respondents interviewed. The data were thus descriptive.

Reforming Public Procurement in Emerging Economies

The need to reform public procurement in emerging economies became more urgent from mid-1980s due to a growing scrutiny and pressure to reform the public procurement processes with a view to improving efficiency and effectiveness. In Kenya and in the other two East African countries, there was growing pressure from within and without the countries to make changes to the public procurement systems due to their inefficiencies (IPAR, 2006). Various stakeholders in the three countries generally expressed dissatisfaction with the public procurement system because of issues considered critical impediments in the operations of the public procurement system. These issues included corruption, misallocation of resources, inadequate infrastructure, inefficient services, high taxes, growing indebtedness, and high risks. These issues were common in the three East African countries. They were also the key issues of concern in other emerging economies (Sigma Policy Brief No. 3). These concerns that generally translate to the need for improved governance have been summarized by Nzai and Chitere (2006) as (1) corruption and waste within public procurement entities; (2) lack of a comprehensive and well-articulated public procurement policy; (3) loose institutional arrangements for processing procurement and collective decision making in awarding contracts; (4) weak capacity of procurement staff; (5) lack of a unified system of procurement practices; (6) absence of or inadequate independent disputes resolving bodies and (7) lack of an independent procurement auditing function.

Sigma Policy Brief No. 3 outlines the key issues in public procurement in Central and Eastern European countries as the need to design a legal and administrative framework that facilitates the integration of myriad procurement entities throughout the public sector into a functional and coherent network with high professional standards. That is consistent with the international obligations, ensuring that government purchasing entities employ trained personnel who understand the need for efficient procurement systems; invest heavily in systems which provide adequate access to data and information which facilitate professional networking within the public sector; give suppliers access to training and information that promote their competitiveness which in turn strengthens the market economy; and design and implement effective mechanisms to curb fraud, waste, abuse, and corruption which impede competition and threaten public procurement systems in all countries.

In reaction to the concerns expressed above, many governments in emerging economies recognized the need for reviewing public procurement. External pressures from donors and multilateral organizations also played an important role in pushing for procurement reform in these economies. In the 1980s, the UN General Assembly played an important role in pushing for reform of public procurement through the enactment of the UNCITRAL model law. The external agencies and organizations, since the era of structural adjustment, had made public procurement reforms a condition for budgetary support to many emerging economies including the East African countries. For example, in 2005 the EU delayed the release of Kshs. 4.5 billion budgetary support to Kenya until the government of Kenya passed a new public procurement law (IPAR, 2006).

Like in many emerging economies, the process and the speed of public procurement reforms in the three East African countries have been fairly varied. Public procurement reforms in Uganda were perceived as part of a policy package focusing on strategies to eradicate poverty, through creation of an appropriate policy framework and the reorientation of government spending in crucial sectors. This approach helped speed up the process. In Tanzania, public procurement reforms were carried out on the basis of a study conducted in 1995 by the Crown Agents. A key recommendation by the Crown Agents was to establish an independent and autonomous body to control public procurement in the country. The study by Crown Agents recommended the delinking of the Central Tender Board from the Ministry of Finance.

In Kenya, commitment to public procurement reform has been patchy and intermittent (IDS, 2004). Kenya's public procurement system demonstrates the common issues in reform of public procurement in emerging economies. It is generally known that in most emerging economies the governments played a central role in public procurement through the creation and management of public procurement bodies at different levels in the economy.

Public Procurement in Kenya

Brief history of public procurement in Kenya

Since independence in 1963 until the early 1970s, the Crown Agents, a British firm, largely undertook public procurement in Kenya because local supplies or goods and services were inadequate and in short supply in the local market. Thus, most of the needs of the newly independent country could only be met from external sources (IPAR, 2006). Thereafter, the government of Kenya established supplies offices within its ministries and departments, and appointed supplies officers to take responsibility for procurement. The appointees were not formally and professionally qualified in the discipline of purchasing and supply. They had to learn through practice. The Crown Agents initially took the responsibility of training government supplies officers. The Ministry of Finance regulated public procurement through issuance of regulations and guidelines, in the form of circulars and directives, to ministries and other public agencies from time to time. However, there remained no uniform law governing public procurement in Kenya (IPAR, 2006).

Kenya's public procurement system has always had serious deficiencies, many of which related to poor governance (Lewa, 2006; Mwangi, 2006; Nzai and Chitere, 2006; Oanda, 2006; Wanyande, 2006; Waiganjo, 2006). The system was poorly managed, unethical decisions were common and it lacked sanctions against government officers and politicians who breached the regulations. It was thus vulnerable to glaring abuses. The government of Kenya dismissed 500 supplies officers in 2003, accusing them of mismanagement of the system (Nzai and Chitere, 2006; IPAR, 2006). This indicated how serious corruption had crept into the system. Moreover, the public procurement policies and procedures were scattered in various government documents. It was difficult to comprehend existing financial regulations without the benefit of the Treasury circulars that were subject to different interpretations. There existed poor information management. There were no standardized procedures. The system lacked transparency in all its processes (Government of Kenya, 1999; Lewa, 2006; Nzai and Chitere, 2006).

In addition to the above problems, dissatisfied suppliers and indeed the general public had no recourse to appeal against the procurement decisions of the various tender boards. There were many deficiencies including over-spending, which was attributed to poor planning and alleged interference of procurement contracts by heads of ministries and departments (accounting officers) to favor certain suppliers. Also their lacked supervision and poor monitoring of project implementation was the order of the day. It was also common practice to vary contracts upwards from the originally quoted prices, often with the connivance of accounting officers and other senior govern-ment officers and powerful politicians including Cabinet Ministers (Oanda, 2006; Waiganjo, 2006; Wanyande, 2006).

Kibisu and Haji (2006) outlined the historical deficiencies of Kenya's pub-lic procurement as follows: (1) first, there were no sanctions against government officers who breached regulations. The system was thus vulnera-ble to abuse. The officers could get away with wrong doing because they had protection in the law. Kenya's Government Contract Act provides that "pub-lic officers" cannot be sued personally upon any contracts, which they make in that capacity. Thus, the incentive for public officers to engage in corrupt pro-curement deals was quite strong; (2) procurement policies and procedures were scattered in various government documents. This necessitated issuance of Treasury circulars to interpret the rules and regulations governing public pro-curement. The circulars were always subject to different interpretations. There was massive abuse and manipulation of the system by procurement officers for personal gain or that of their politically well-connected friends and politicians due to the above; (3) corrupt public procurement officers allegedly favored certain firms in the award of tenders under the influence of powerful politi-cians. This state of affairs was exacerbated by the fact that mostly junior officers who were powerless in the sense that they could easily be manipulated by sen-ior officers and powerful politicians manned the procurement system. Most senior officers and politicians owned firms that tendered for government pro-curement and allegedly always won tenders. The existing law did not prohibit public officers from participating in tenders. The participation of public offi-cials in private enterprise has always been a key source of corruption in Kenya's public procurement system and (4) further, there was no provision for dissat-isfied bidders or the general public to appeal against the procurement decisions of the various tender boards in case of what they considered as irregularities in the process. The system only allowed appeals by accounting officers. The judiciary played no role in the system.

The above deficiencies in the public procurement system contributed to huge losses of public funds (Fee, 2005). Transparency International estimated that Kenya lost about Kshs. 459 billion to shoddy public procurement deals between 1998 and 2005 (IPAR, 2006).

Organization and Management of Public Procurement in Kenya

The government of Kenya organized and managed public procurement through a system of tender boards at various levels of government. There existed a central tender board, ministerial tender boards at ministries' level, district tender boards at district level, and other tender boards as indicated in the figure below which shows the historical structure of Kenya's procurement system from 1963 to 2001 when changes began to be implemented in the system. Figure 15.2 shows the structure of the procurement system for the period 1963 until 2001.

The Central Tender Board (CTB) was responsible for handling all public procurement valued at above Kshs. two million. Until it was dismantled in 2001, the CTB acted as the judge and jury in adjudicating tenders without reference to anyone. Below the CTB was the Ministerial Tender Board (MTB) comprising of the accounting officers (permanent secretaries) and responsible for procurement of up to Kshs. two million. District Tender Boards were established to cater for procurement at the district level. Other state entities were more or less left on their own to decide the procurement systems and processes to follow under the general direction of

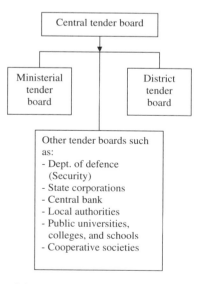

Figure 15.2. Structure of the procurement system, 1963–2001. (From IPAR, 2006.)

the procurement guidelines (Wanyande, 2006). The public procurement system was thus not synchronized and managed for economy, efficiency, and effectiveness.

Kenya's Public Procurement Reform Efforts

In 1986, a study was conducted by SGS Consultants to evaluate the public procurement system in Kenya. The key finding of the study was that Kenya's public procurement system was extremely inefficient leading to loss of large sums of money and resources. Another study commissioned by the Kenya government and the World Bank in 1997 reached the same conclusion as the SGS study. Both studies called for a comprehensive review of the public procurement system in Kenya. The World Bank study confirmed what had always been known about the lack of governance in the procurement system but specifically called for reform in terms of fairness and creation of a level playing field in the system, transparency, training of staff, and professionalization of the system, and better management of information (Government of Kenya, 1999; Kibisu and Haji, 2006).

The World Bank (WB), the African Development Bank (ADB), and the International Trade Centre (ITC), in conjunction with the government of Kenya, initiated the public procurement reform process in the late 1990s. The reform process was meant to achieve certain objectives: creation of a system that allowed; a proper delegation of responsibility and authority; incentives; procurement thresholds; planning; development of procurement manuals; new legislation to guide public procurement; establishment of procurement institutions; and, improvement of governance in the system. A taskforce charged with the work presented its recommendations to Parliament. Upon the receipt of the recommendations, a draft bill was prepared for approval by Parliament. However, there was a delay in approving the bill. In response to this, the Minister for Finance proposed the approval of Public Procurement Regulations in 2001 to guide public procurement.

The public procurement regulation changes introduced in 2001 included the passing of the Exchequer and Audit (Procurement) Regulations of 2001 (revised in 2006), and the subsequent enactment of the Public Procurement and Disposal Act in 2005 that abolished the Central Tender Board and decentralized the procurement process by allowing public entities to set up tender committees responsible for all procurements within each entity. These changes led to the setting up of a monitoring and supervisory body, the Directorate of Public Procurement (DPP), which was subsequently replaced by the Public Procurement Oversight Authority (PPOA). The changes were aimed at streamlining public procurement operations.

The regulations and the Act were meant to address the deficiencies in the public procurement system. They addressed the following aspects: (1) capacity to manage the system; (2) procurement thresholds; (3) quality of human resources given the responsibility to manage public procurement; (4) procurement procedures and controls; (5) disposal procedures for obsolete, obsolescent, and redundant stocks; (6) complaint review procedures; (7) inclusion of procurement for the department of defense and security and making them open to public scrutiny and (8) role of stakeholders in public procurement.

Findings and Analysis

Legal and institutional frameworks

There is consensus in many quarters that Kenya's Public Procurement and Disposal Act, 2005 and the Draft Regulations of 2001 and 2006 have met the basic requirements of a public procurement system that is in tune with agreed international standards (Nzai and Chitere, 2006; Mwangi, 2006; Lewa, 2006). The baseline indictors met by the legal frameworks are outlined below.

Scope of application and coverage of the act: (1) Contracting entities at all levels including government authorities, municipalities, regional authorities, and utilities/state-owned enterprise are covered (Section 3 of the Act); (2) all areas of procurement: works, goods, and consulting services are included (Section 3 of the Act); (3) procurement using public funds, irrespective of contract value, is included (Section 3 of the Act) and (4) the Act is structured, consistent, and accessible to users and all interested stakeholders.

Procurement methods: Stated preference for the use of open, competitive procurement unless otherwise justified in accordance with the Act (Part IV Section 29); (1) international competitive tendering methods have been defined for specified contracts (e.g., where monetary thresholds exist) that are consistent with international standards (Part IV Section 29); (2) defined basis for the procurement method, if other than open competition. (Part VI Section 72); (3) negotiated procedures and direct purchasing only under well defined and justified and (4) circumstance, subject to controls (Section 74).

Advertising Rules and Time Limits (Section 54): (1) mandatory and accessible publication of opportunities for competitive procurement

(Section 46); (2) mandatory publication of result information on contract awards based on defined thresholds (Section 46) and (3) minimum time limits for submission of tenders and applications, which should be consistent with method of procurement, national conditions and, when applicable, international requirements.

Rules on participation and qualitative selection: (1) fair, predictable, and defined rules for participation that rely on qualifications and ability to perform the requirement are defined (Section 31); (2) limited and controlled use of preferential clauses is stated (Sections 31 and 39); (3) debarment process is covered by the Act, on defined basis, and allows for due process and appeal.

Tender documentation and technical specifications (Section 34): (1) the minimum content of the tender documentation is specified (Section 52); (2) neutral technical specification with reference to international standards where possible have been included (Section 31(4)); and (3) content of tender documentation that is relevant to meeting requirement and implementing the process is outlined.

Tender evaluation and award criteria (Section 66): (1) objective, fair, and pre-disclosed criteria for evaluation and award of contracts are outlined (Section 31(3)); (2) clear methodology for evaluation of tenders based on price and other fully disclosed factors leading to award of contracts is outlined; and (3) requirement to maintain confidentiality during the evaluation process is established (Section 44).

Submission, receipt and opening of tenders (Section 58): (1) public opening of tenders in a defined manner that ensures the regularity of the proceedings is provided for (Section 60); (2) clear requirement to maintain records of proceedings and process that are available for review/audit is stated (Section 45); (3) requirement to maintain security and confidentiality of tenders prior to bid opening is outlined (Section 58); (4) submission and receipt modalities of tender documents are well defined (Section 58); (5) complaint review procedures (Part VII Section 93); and (6) inclusion of complaint and remedy procedures that provide for fair, independent, and timely implementation is provided for.

However, the regulations suffer from certain weaknesses that must be addressed urgently if reform is to occur as intended. IPAR (2006) identified these weaknesses. The key weaknesses are outlined below: (1) few technical terms are not clearly defined. These terms are subject to different interpretations and different application of the rules. This would result in lack of effective competition, transparency, fair treatment, and efficiency; (2) The Regulations and the Act contradict each other in some regards. This means that practitioners can ignore either of the instruments at times when it suits them to do so. This is likely to lead to different interpretations of the regulations resulting in different applications; (3) The Act and the Regulations do not adequately address the issue of separating the authorization of procurement initiation, selection, and commitment. This creates a situation where it may be difficult to apply checks, controls and balances (Lewa, 2006; IPAR, 2006); (4) the instruments are silent on procurement audits that would ensure that the activities of the different parties are under check. Audits are important activities in ensuring governance in the procurement process; (5) As IPAR (2006) observes, the Public Procurement and Disposal Act 2005, and the Regulations, do not provide security of tenure for the Chief Executive Officer of the Public Procurement function, i.e., the Director General of procurement. As a result, the Board has the powers, under Sections 15(a) to discharge the director from his/her duties on the basis of incompetence, which is not even clearly elaborated in the Act. This provides opportunity for the Board to misuse or even misapply its powers in firing a Director General; (6) the Public Procurement and Disposal Board (PPDB) is constituted in such a way that it has some executive appointees. These executive appointees can easily manipulate the procurement process given that in the past such appointees interfered with the process of procurement. There is no reason to believe that they cannot interfere again. Executive interference dilutes the effectiveness of Public Procurement. APNAC (2003) contents that the main issue here is bid rigging by executive appointees, a common problem in the past operations of Kenya's public procurement system; (7) Section 22 of the Act states that the Minister shall appoint the members of the PPAB and such appointments will be approved by Parliament from persons nominated by the prescribed organizations. The Act and the Regulations are silent about the qualifications of such appointees, other than technical qualifications as implied in the Regulations. What this implies is that the minister can easily appoint persons attuned to particular political interests (Waiganjo, 2006). In the past, the discretion given to Ministers was abused and there is no reason to believe that it cannot be misused under the Act (IPAR, 2006); (8) There is no clear definition of administrative compliance criteria within the standard bidding documents pertaining to legality of the vendor that should be met by vendors before being allowed to participate in the public tender process. Absence of a clear administrative compliance creates vagueness and affords ample opportunity to supplies officers and other vested interests to abuse the procurement system through such acts as discrimination of some players and favoritism to others (IPAR, 2006); and (9) The Act and the Regulations have not addressed all the key issues in the procurement cycle. The Regulations are completely silent on the aspects of warehousing, inventory management, and audit. This omission of important facets of procurement can easily become a breeding ground for corruption as it creates weaknesses and or gaps in the process (Lewa, 2006; IPAR, 2006).

Institutional Framework

Procurement entities are provided for by both the 2001 and 2006 regulations and the Act (Government of Kenya, 2006). The entities include the central government ministries/departments, local authorities, state corporations, universities, schools, and other institutions that procure using public funds. Each entity is required to establish a procurement unit staffed by professional supplies personnel. The main function of the unit is to procure for the entity.

A Tender Committee (TC) is established by each procuring entity. Within any one central government ministry, the accounting officer who is the Permanent Secretary (PS) chairs the TC, and the Chief Finance Officer is the alternate chairperson. The function of the TC is to implement the tendering process within the entity by holding opening and evaluation sessions and awarding contracts to successful bidders. Table 15.1 shows the composition of the TCs in both the central government ministry and other selected entities.

- Advisory Board members are to be nominated by unspecified organizations and approved by the Minister and Parliament. This implies that the Minister will be in a position to control the Board.
- Within procuring entities, the accounting officers are given much responsibility by the new Act, especially in establishing the tender committees. This will likely create situations of conflicts of interests and vested interests in the procuring process.
- Treasury will also control the PPOA through annual financial allocations for both recurrent and development expenditures.
- Whereas the Advisory Board may have some members from the private sector, professional associations and civil society, its membership will also include senior civil servants — PS, Treasury; PS, Provincial Administration; Solicitor-General; and DG as its secretary, implying that the government will dominate the Board.
- The District Commissioner will chair TCs in the districts. The membership of TCs includes many government officials with non-government officials being the minority. This does not auger well for good governance.

Table 15.1. Composition of selected tender committees.

Composition	Ministerial/departmental	District	Local authorities	Schools
Chairpersons	Accounting officer	District commissioner	Clerk to local authority	Principal/head
Alternate chairperson	Chief finance officer	District officer I	Chair-finance committee	Deputy principal
Members	— Deputy secretary (Adm.), head of accounting division — 4 Departmental heads	— Chair, county council — District development officer — District accountant — Heads of ministries/departments	— All heads of departments	— 2 members of BoG — Chairman, PTA — 2 Teachers — 1 member of PTA — Matron/official in-charge of boarding
Secretary	Officer heading the procurement unit/department	Supplies officer	— Supplies/procurement officer	Officer responsible for procurement

Types of Tendering Procedures

Both the 2001 regulations and the Act provide for open tendering that is transacted through four stages of invitation, opening, evaluation, and award. Tenderers are expected to meet specified requirements including their qualifications as well as providing an amount of money for security where necessary. The Act provides more detail about conditions under which security may be forfeited, or modifications made to the tender documents before the expiry date for their submission. It further safeguards the process by providing that each of the members of the opening committee must sign all tender documents and initial against the quoted price, any modifications made to the documents as well as the minutes of the opening committee meeting. Where the expiry date is extended, the tenderers are notified about it, as well as about conditions related to the extension. The Act also provides that, where the procuring entity finds that none of the tenderers is "responsive;" that is, does not meet the specified qualifications; it has to notify them (Nzai and Chitere, 2006).

Both the 2001 regulations and the Act provide for alternative tendering procedures — restricted and direct tendering. Restricted tendering is used in situations of complex or specialized goods, works or services or where there are only a few known suppliers of the items. In this case, a limited number of qualified candidates that may have been pre-qualified by being listed by the entity are invited to tender — the tender will also be open to other candidates. The Act provides for circumstances under which direct tendering is used: (1) those where there is only one person who can supply the items; that is, single sourcing; and (2) where there is urgent need for the items owing to unforeseeable circumstances.

The 2001 regulations provide for open international tendering procedure, which is transacted along the lines of national open tendering but adheres to international standards and is based on reliable foreign currency. The Act provides for international tendering by including a clause within the open national tendering to cater for circumstances under which the process could require overseas competition, such as where there may be no adequate local competition and where there is no reliable local supplier of the needed goods and services.

Other procedures outlined by the Act are (1) request for proposals in situations where services are being procured; (2) request for quotations in situations where items to be procured are readily available in the market; (3) low-value procurements that are used in situations where the established value of items being procured is specified by the regulations and (4) other procedures permitted by the PPOA including "concessioning" that helps mobilize resources from the private sector, for example, for building or rehabilitation of public facilities such as the railway system and "design competition" that covers bids for creative services.

Human and Other Resources

Procurement personnel link the procurement agency with the supplier system. Their level of professionalism and the environment in which they work determines the effectiveness with which they perform this linkage role. As professionals, their success depends on their ability to effectively enforce the procurement law and regulations in spite of pressures from the two systems.

Whereas the 2001 regulations and the new Act forbid procurement officers from having vested interests in the procurement process, their level of remuneration, especially within the civil service is low and likely to make them vulnerable to temptations such as vested interests, canvassing, and being given bribes. The relationship between the PPOA and the procurement staff within the procuring entities is important. So long as the staff in the entities will not be part of the PPOA and remain underpaid within the mainstream civil service, they will either sabotage the functioning of the PPOA or will collude with administrators for their personal gain. Supplies officers are dispersed, that is, located in different entities so that they do not report directly to the Public Procurement Directorate (PPD).

Suppliers' Capacity

Firms to be contracted are supposed to meet qualification criteria specified in the 2001 regulations and the Act. One criterion is that the firm must possess the necessary technical and professional qualifications, financial resources, equipment, physical facilities, management capability, and experience. Another criterion is that the firm must have legal capacity to enter a contract and must not be solvent, in receivership, bankrupt, being wound up, suspended or subject to legal proceedings.

Both the 2001 regulations and the Act provide that after submitting bid documents, suppliers or their representatives can participate at the opening session or at a meeting where a successful bidder is announced. Whereas overseas firms and governments post their tender invitations in their web sites, this practice is not common in Kenya owing to lack of well-developed Internet facilities. This means that information to tenderers is availed to them mainly through newspapers and notice boards.

Conclusions

The objective of this study was to examine the reform of public procurement in emerging economies using Kenya as a case study. The intention was to bring out the key issues of concern in the reform of public procurement.

Recommendations for Policy Makers/Managers

Legal framework

(1) The key gaps identified including conceptual ambiguity should be addressed. There is need for harmonization of the legal framework with other similar frames within the central government, for example, the Trade and Company Acts. (2) There is need for clarification about certain provisions of the Act that are in conflict with a foreign Act, especially considering WTO's Government Procurement Agreement (GPA) that Kenya might one day accent to.

Institutional aspects

To: (1) understand the magnitude of vested interests and canvassing, their causes, and what could be done to reduce them; (2) clarify the link between PPOA and procurement personnel located in various entities in terms of technical matters and (3) address the issue of remuneration.

Human and other resources

(1) Qualifications of procurement personnel, committee members, their education and training are matters that must be addressed urgently; (2) facilities such as the Internet and web hosting need immediate attention and (3) a career development plan and policy for government procurement officers needs immediate development.

Suppliers' capacity

(1) Participation of suppliers is restricted to bidding and presenting themselves at opening sessions. Whereas they may not be directly involved at evaluation

and adjudication, these processes are currently opaque and especially as practiced by the central government in that they are monopolized by the staff of the procuring entities. It is important that these stages of procurement be made transparent through professional, civil society or private sector or some form of supplier representation (Nzai and Chitere, 2006); (2) there is need for suppliers to be empowered to make demands through lobbying and other forms of affirmative action. This can be achieved through awareness programs that enlighten them about various aspects of public procurement including their rights and obligations; (3) training of suppliers, especially those from the Small and Micro Enterprise (SME) sector, information should be made a priority to increase their capacity and (4) there is need for recognition of supplier organizations as a means for mediating between the procuring entities and their member suppliers as well as professional organizations such as the Kenya Institute of Supplies management (KISM).

Types of procurement and timing

Timing — following the deadline for closing of a tender, bids are opened about two hours after the closing hour. The time taken from announcement of award to signing has been shortened from the current 21 to 14 days. If the time taken for evaluation and adjudication were shorter (e.g., 14–21 days), then the process would be timely.

Key Survey Results

Various stakeholders expressed their views on various aspects of the Public Procurement and Disposal Act and the Public procurement Regulations. All the 200 respondents interviewed expressed optimism in regard to reform of the public procurement sector in Kenya. They welcomed the reforms but called on the government to revise the legal instruments by addressing the various gaps to make them more relevant. Respondents expressed the need for dissemination in order to educate the public on what had been reformed. Ninety-five percent of the respondents called for a more active role of stakeholders, particularly key industry players. Such stakeholders would be expected to beef up the efforts of the public sector in making public procurement more efficient. Ninety percent of the respondents expressed the need for professionalization of the public procurement function. All the respondents recommended training for all actors in the procurement process. Ninety-seven percent of the respondents called for the immediate application of IT in the tendering process. They urged for the creation of web sites where tenders advertisements can be placed.

References

Akech, JMM (2005). Development partners and governance of public procurement in Kenya: Enhancing democracy in the administration of Aid. *Research Paper*, NYU School of Law, Institute for International Law and Justice.

APNAC (2003). New challenges in the fight against corruption. *Proceedings of the 1st Regional Conference of the African Parliamentarians Network against Corruption (APNAC)*, November 3–4, Grand Regency Hotel, Nairobi, Kenya.

Arrowsmith, S (2003). *Government Procurement in the WTO.* Kluwer Law International.

Asian Development Bank (2005). *Elements of Governance.* http://www.adb.org/Governance/gov_elements.asp.

Fee, D (17 June 2005). Procurement reforms will improve efficiency. *The Standard*.

Government of Kenya (1978). *The Supplies Manual (Guide).* Nairobi: Government Printer.

Government of Kenya (1999). *Kenya Public Procurement Reform and Enhanced Capacity project.* Nairobi: Ministry of Finance.

Government of Kenya (2001). *Exchequer and Audit (Public Procurement) Regulations, Legal Notice* 51. Nairobi: Government Printer.

Government of Kenya (2005). *The Public Procurement and Disposal Act.* Nairobi: Government Printer.

Government of Kenya (2006). *Public Procurement Regulations (Draft).* Nairobi: Public Procurement Directorate (Ministry of Finance).

IPAR (2006). *Public Procurement Reforms: Redressing the Governance Concerns.* Policy View 2.

Kibisu, AG and AA Haji (2006). A study on public procurement in Kenya: Investigating the policy options within the public procurement system. Unpublished Undergraduate research project, United States International University, Summer Semester.

Kihikah, P (2005). Towards a sustainable fight against corruption in public procurement. *Adili*, Transparency International News service publication, Nairobi.

Lewa, PM (2007). Management and organization of public procurement in Kenya: A review of proposed changes. Discussion Paper No. 092/2007. IPAR Discussion Paper Series. *Institute of Policy Analysis & Research (IPAR)*.

Lewa, PM (1984). Management and organization of the supplies branch. Unpublished paper written in partial requirements for the award of a Diploma in Supplies management, Kenya Institute of Administration.

Lewa, PM (2006). Discussion notes on professionalizing public procurement in Kenya. IPAR/DPP/KISM Stakeholder forum, Nairobi.

Mwangi, M (2006). Highlights of the Public Procurement and Disposal Act, 2005 and the Draft Regulations 2006, Nairobi.

Nzai, C and P Chitere (2006). *Public Procurement in Kenya: A Study of Factors Influencing its Effectiveness.* Nairobi: Institute of Policy and Research.

Oanda, C (2006). *Professionalising Public Procurement in Kenya.* Nairobi: Kenya Institute of Supplies Management.

Odhiambo, W and P Kamau (2003). Public procurement: Lessons from Kenya, Uganda and Tanzania. *Working Paper No. 208*, Organization for Economic Co-operation and Development (OECD) Centre.

Olowa, D (2002). Introduction: Governance and policy management capacity in Africa. In *Better Governance and Public Policy: Capacity Building and Democratic Renewal in Africa*, Olowa, D and S Sako (eds.), Bloomfield: Kumarian Press.

The United Nations Commission on International Trade Law (UNCITRAL). Model Law on Procurement of Goods, Construction and Services. Official Records of the United Nations General Assembly, Forty-Ninth Session, Supplement No. 17 (A/49/17).

Transparency International Report (2005). Report on Kenya public procurement system.

Trepte, P (2004). *Regulating Procurement: Understanding the Ends and Means of Public Procurement Regulations*. Oxford University Press.

Waiganjo, K (2006). *The Legal and Institutional Framework for Effective Implementation of the Public Procurement and Disposal Act*. Nairobi: IPAR/DPP/KISM Stakeholder forum.

Wamugo, J (2005). Tackling graft in public procurement. *Adili*, Transparency International News service publication, Nairobi.

Wanyande, P (2006). The Socio-Political Context of Public Procurement in Kenya. *Draft Paper Presented at the Stakeholder Forum on Public Procurement Reforms in Kenya*, Nairobi.

Wittig, WA (2002). A framework for balancing business and accountability within a public procurement system. (2002) in www.wto.org/Englsh/tratop_e/gpro_e.

Wittig, WA (1998). Building value through public procurement: A focus on Africa. 3.

World Bank (1994). *Governance: The World Bank's Experience, 1998*.

Chapter 16

RURAL TOURISM IN SOUTH AFRICA: THE CASE OF DAMDORYN AND BUFFLESPOORT

KOFI POKU QUAN-BAFFOUR

Abstract

Rural tourism may be described as voluntary visits people make to the countryside, usually motivated by socioeconomic reasons. South Africa is naturally endowed with beautiful geographical features, game parks and historical sites, which attract both local and foreign visitors. Most of these attractive tourism sites were, however, exclusive to the white South Africans (descendents of settlers before the democratic dispensation of 1994. The dawn of democracy has made all public places in the country accessible to people of all races. This equal opportunity has made millions of people from all walks of life to visit all places of interest to them. This chapter focuses on two countryside destinations that have become important tourism-based markets in the country. The rapid growth of these tourist destinations and their implications for managers is the focus of this case study.

Introduction

Tourism is an activity concerned with the temporary movement of people to destinations outside the places they normally live and work, and their activities during the stay at these places (Bennet, 2000). This temporary or short-term movement of people to various destinations in the world could be domestic or international. Tourism has always been part of humankind, but in the contemporary world, this activity is on the rise. This rapid increase in tourists' movement in recent times has made tourism a booming and perhaps the most popular industry in the contemporary modern world. It is argued that if its potentialities are adequately exploited, tourism could create jobs for the unemployed, assist in rural development, and contribute immensely to foreign exchange earnings, especially, in the developing world. Further, travel and tourism might contribute to the growth of allied industries such as agriculture, sports, transport, communication, and entrepreneurship in rural areas. Boucher (1999), for example, reports that tourism accounts for 11.5% of the world's Gross Domestic Product (GDP) and 12.5% of its employment. Considering its potential, World Tourism Organization (1997) predicts that by the year 2020, 1.5 billion people will visit foreign countries annually and spend more than five billion US dollars everyday.

Whatever might be the motives of tourists, the main factors that influence their movement to certain destinations may include the image or perception of places, price in terms of money, attraction of such places, existence of good facilities, and accessibility to the destinations. The most common factors however might relate to education, health (medical treatment), sight seeing (i.e., adventure), entertainment, business, and religion. Keyser (2002) confirms that tourism consists of the following types: adventure tourism, business tourism (including MICE-meetings, incentives, conference, and exhibitions tourism), coastal tourism, cultural tourism, (including heritage and ethnic tourism), educational tourism, events tourism, cruise tourism, health tourism, rural tourism, nature tourism (including eco-tourism), sports tourism, and urban tourism. In reality, many of the above-mentioned forms of tourism coexist in the same area, region, or country. For example, rural tourism can take the form of education, agriculture, events, nature-based, adventure, cultural, heritage, or ethnic tourism.

The popularity of tourism in recent times is the direct result of democratization (which has made public places accessible to all people), advancement in technology and globalization. These modern realities have made travel and tourism not only a fast expanding industry, but also perhaps the most popular human activity and a growing industry. According to World Travel and Tourism Council (WTTC), tourism generated a significant number of jobs, making the industry the world's largest employer. By 2011, jobs in travel and tourism is expected to be 53 million and the tourism economy will represent 11% of global employment — one in eleven jobs (Keyser, 2002).

South Africa

South Africa is a large country, which occupies the most sourthern part of the African continent. Its population is over 45 million people made up of Africans, whites (settlers), and the others. Africans, the country's indigenous people, form the majority and mostly live in the countryside. Before 1994, the country was under the British rule, which relegated the Africans to the fringes of socioeconomic and political activities in the country. The consequences are enormous — unemployment, poverty, diseases, and violent crime. The apartheid policy of discrimination is largely blamed for these socioeconomic problems. The segregation of people based on race did not provide the Africans with the opportunity to learn relevant knowledge and skills which would prepare them to participate in socioeconomic and even political development of the country.

During the era of apartheid, many places of interest such as holiday resorts and tourism sites were reserved for the country's white population. The Africans were not allowed to visit such places because of the color of their skin. With the inception of non-racial democratic dispensation in 1994, all places in the country are now open to all races and consequently the country has been accepted back into family of nations. There are many interesting and beautiful places of historical or recreational nature in the rural areas of South Africa, which attract both domestic and international tourists. Two such places which have become very popular tourists' destinations are Damdoryn (near Haartebeespoort) and Bufflespoort dams in the North West province. The rapid growth of these rural tourists' destinations and the implications they may have for managers motivated this investigation.

Damdoryn and Bufflespoort dams

The two rural tourists' destinations selected for an exploratory investigation are Damdoryn and Bufflespoort dam. These rural tourism sites are about 20 km apart and record an average of over 5,000 visitors a week. Damdoryn as a tourists' destination emerged from the Hartbeespoort dam, which is about 1.5 km away. It is an area where tourists go to rest, entertain and buy suvinoirs (African beads, artifacts, and clothes) food, drinks or enjoy camel riding. Damdoryn is a beautiful area within the vicinity of the stunning Magalisburg Mountains. It is about 45 and 80 km from Pretoria and Johannesburg, respectively. Damdoryn is just far enough from the hustle and bustle of the three cities — Pretoria, Johannesburg, and Rustenburg — with a good road network. Accommodation for visitors is readily available. The area boasts of two petrol filling stations, a large super market, modern restaurants, over 30 lodges, Bed and Breakfast (B&B), guest houses, residential accommodation (houses and apartments) for both visitors and business owners.

Bufflespoort dam is an eco park, which is less than 30 km from Rustenburg. The place is an hour and half drive from Pretoria and is near to the stunning Magalisburg Mountains. This destination offers visitors with outdoor experience in the form of bird and animal watching, skiing, and canoeing. The faclities witin the vicinity of the eco park include a shopping center, club house, tennis courts, swimming pools, caravan park, over 15 Bed and Breakfast, guest houses, conference rooms, and modern houses.

The two dams coupled with nearby wildlife parks and beautiful scenery have turned an otherwise quite countryside area into a bubbling tourists' destination. Travel and tourism at the two destinations is fast growing and perhaps it is an unanticipated profitable by-product of the dams, which were most probably constructed to conserve water for irrigation, industrial, and domestic purposes. The area has added advantages of cool temperate climate, peaceful countryside environment, safe haven for holiday makers, existence of a host of growing small-scale businesses which provide social services like water-sport (e.g., canoeing, water-skiing, board sailing), guest houses, motels, hotels, restaurants, fresh, vegetables, fruits, and fresh meat from the nearby game park.

Rural Tourism and Socioeconomic Development in an Emerging Society

It is difficult to define rural tourism due to the fact that not all visitors to the rural areas are tourists and not all activities in the countryside can be regarded as tourist activities. Sharpely and Sharpely (1997) contend that a definition of tourism may vary particularly within the context of the countryside. For example, the distinction between activities which are strictly forms of tourism, leisure, or sport can often be blurred. At the same time, it is equally difficult to define what is meant by "countryside" or "rural areas." What compounds the problem even more is the fact that very often rural tourism is used as synonymous to eco-tourism, green, or nature tourism. In some cases, rural tourism is equated with specific activities or locations as a means of describing a more general and broader approach to development and promotion of tourism. Different criteria are used by many people in referring to which area could be seen as rural or urban. The term *RURAL*, in most cases, is defined geographically and culturally. In short, a variety of meanings or definitions may be attached to rural tourism and it is unlikely therefore that a single, satisfactory answer to the question: what is rural tourism? could be found (Sharpely and Sharpely, 1997).

In spite of the difficulty in providing an appropiriate definition, some descriptions of the concept have been suggested by some authorities in the field. For example, rural tourism is described by Sharpley and Sharpley (1997) as the type of tourism that occurs in rural areas. This definition could imply that rural areas encompass all areas, both land and water that lie beyond towns and cities. In Killion's (2001) view, rural tourism is the type of tourism which takes place outside heavily urbanized or concentrated areas, and which offers the tourist the experiences of society and heritage (indigenous and or settlers), open space and contact with nature. The experiences offered by rural tourism to visitors can be various — covering all aspects of activities of the countryside. The experiences could get the visitor closer to nature because they are authentic. Rural tourism may be more than farm tourism, or agritourism. It may include all tourist activities in rural areas. Rural tourists may take part in an array of interests and activities at the destinations. These activities may include horse riding, cycling, touring, cultural activities, fishing, swimming, sailing, visit to monument or heritage sites, friends relatives, farm tours, pony trekking, or mountaineering. The array of activities in which rural tourists participate might have motivated Keyser (2002) to describe rural tourism as "the planned use of resources of countryside areas that will lead to an increase in the general welfare of the environment, the community, and visitors."

The definitions outlined in this discussion point out that the main characteristics of rural tourism are closeness to nature, quietness, absence of crowds, a non-urbanized environment, personal contact with nature and or people, a sense of stability and retention of individual identity. The distinguishing feature of rural tourism is the wish to give visitors personalized contact, a taste of the physical and human environment of the countryside, and as far as possible, allow them to participate in the activities, traditions, and lifestyles of local people (Keyser, 2002). The countryside, in particular, has much resources to attract people, and this is perhaps the reason why it has become an important and popular destination for tourists. Peine (1998) affirms that many tourist areas are anchored by natural resource attractions such as lakes, beaches, waterfalls, canyons/gorges, and mountains. Forests, prairies, deserts, and wetlands support wildlife that attract people in their search for renewal. Rural tourism is thus becoming an important countryside activity because of the latter's multiresources for tourism.

Factors Contributing to the Development and Popularity of Rural Tourism

Rural tourism is relatively a new industry and activity. Before the mid 1800s, it was unthinkable for many people (even in the developed world) to visit the countryside because of poverty, insecurity, inadequate roads, and general lack of inclination for such a venture. Mass tourism is a recent phenomenon, and has developed since World War II to become one of the most important global economic activities of current times (Keyser, 2002). Advancement in technology and good communication network however changed people's perception about the countryside. The construction of railway lines through-out Europe and North America in the 1840s opened up more remote and beautiful rural areas to the traveling public. During the same period, indus-trialization brought in its trail employment, higher income, and leisure for many people in the developed world. These higher levels of income and more free time motivated people in industrial towns and cities to visit the country-side (Sharpely and Sharpely, 1997). This made rural areas to benefit from a thriving tourism industry.

In the modern world, many urban dwellers participate in and enjoy rural tourism. To some people, it may be only occasional visits which last few hours; however, there are others who see the rural areas as their regular holiday destinations. Many affluent and well-educated urban dwellers may often want to get out of the noisy, crowded, polluted, and insecure urban areas to spend quality time with their loved ones in a quiet, unpolluted, and safe countryside environment. Keyser (2002) affirms that many tourists spend their holidays in the countryside, seeking peace and relaxation that a rural environment can offer, experiencing being close to nature. Rural tourism thus appeals to urban residents who want to escape from the modern urban and suburban environment to less spoilt and less developed areas of the country-side where they can obtain the ideal alternative. Thus, as modern urban life becomes faster, expensive, insecure, less authentic, and more stressful, the countryside is seen by many as a rural "utopia," a natural and pleasant area where people can escape from the present into a nostalgic past.

The factors that attract tourists to the rural areas may include natural fea-tures (e.g., rivers, lakes, and forest) and cultural features such as picturesque villages, folkways, and festivals. The core elements of tourism — attractions — are based on the natural and cultural resources of the destination. The images and positive perceptions that people have of places draw tourists from tourist-generating areas or markets along certain routes (Keyser, 2002). Attractions of destinations are therefore powerful elements of the supply aspect of tourism. Word of mouth recommendations by people who have had the rural tourism experience, for example, can attract both domestic and international visitors to rural destinations. For an instance, recommendations regarding the beauty of the scenery, safety of visitors, warmness or politeness of the local people, cheaper cost of destinations can motivate tourists to visit rural destinations. Beeton (1999) adds that a motivating factor for tourists to visit rural areas is to experience the "rural idyll." Thus, the search for the roots of long-standing folkways may remain a powerful motive for both domestic and international visitors to destinations at the countryside. Killion (2001) contends that the growth in demand for REAL travel (tourism that is Rewarding, Enriching, Adventuresome and provides an opportunity to Learn) provides further opportunity for the development of rural tourism products as contemporary tourists become better educated and more discerning in their demands for a satisfying travel experience. Both myth and reality attract tourists who in many cases have been motivated by rural images presented by the media of popular culture and in others by a search for a rural idyll. The youth in particular are mostly attracted by the Western consumption patterns and lifestyles in tourist areas. While poverty and the lack of economic opportunity are the reasons to leave one's community, the promise of quick money and a better future pull back local people to tourist areas.

Physical Environment as a Major Attraction

The success of rural tourism depends upon attractive environmental features and attributes. Holden (2000) states, inter alia, the following as very important environmental conditions that attract tourists to rural destinations: (1) beautiful landscape, (2) relaxed atmosphere, (3) cleanliness of the environment, (4) healthy climate, (5) quietness with little traffic, (6) typical country surroundings, and (7) attractive places for excursions.

In most cases what motivates many visitors to the countryside is its rural natural beautiful environment. Rural tourism, no doubt, depends on the environment. Images of "unspoilt" physical and cultural environment, for example, can attract tourists to rural destinations. Tourists may prefer to spend a portion of their leisure time getting away from the day-to-day urban/suburban lifestyle and reconnecting with the natural environment. Some tourists visit a particular destination because of its scenic attraction and may not like to visit a destination where the environment is polluted, filthy, congested or does not posses good facilities such as accommodation and entertainment. The physical environment is thus the focus of tourist activity.

This is why, to many people, environmental protection should be broadened to cover the conservation of the countryside and not only the urban areas. Tourism authorities in many rural destinations have now realized that the conservation of the "townscape" is crucial to rural tourism development. This realization has resulted in an increased restoration and renovation of historical and even dilapidated buildings and villages. The crux of the matter is that tourists may not like to visit a destination, which has nothing to offer in terms of attraction or appearance. Attractive features such as clean beaches, the sea, mountains, lakes and forests form the natural resource base for rural tourism. Environmental quality, scenic and unique landscapes, pleasant climate, unique historical buildings and cultures, etc., have an important influence on the popularity of specific localities, regions, or countries. These environmental features and qualities attract tourists directly. There is, therefore, an intimate relationship between environment and tourism. Tourists to rural areas particularly seek a more intimate experience with nature and/or indigenous culture closely tied to the natural environment. Keyser (2002) refers to the paradox between rural tourism and the environment and notes, "tourism cannot exist without the environment, yet the relationship between tourism and environment is often one of destructions of the very foundation on which it is built." This is a true observation of the dilemma that faces the rural tourism industry. The relationship between tourism and the environment is thus a double-edge sword — it can be beneficial and at the same time destructive. Rural conservation must, therefore, include the protection of physical environment as a means of attracting tourists to the countryside for the realization of socio-economic regeneration.

The Socioeconomic Benefits of Rural Tourism

The over riding purpose of rural tourism is its potential to uplift the countryside socially, economically, and environmentally. Although rural tourism is relatively new and small (as compared to the total world market for tourism), it still makes important contributions to rural social life and economies. In England, for example, rural tourism generates about nine billion pounds annually, and in some parts of the country, it is the dominant source of employment (Sharpely and Sharpely, 1997).

Social benefits

Rural tourism contributes to social development of countryside communities. Killion (2001) argues that rural tourism is among the most polymorphous of all forms of special interest tourism. The diversity of attractions included in rural tourism embrace indigenous and European heritage sites and aspects of culture. For example, the folkways of rural communities reflected in festivals and cultural displays bring rural communities together in a common identity and as people with rich culture worthy of seeing by outsiders. Thus, the various activities of rural communities do not only attract tourists, but also provide them with the opportunity to exhibit (show case) their cultural values and identity.

An important point about rural tourism is its influence on provision of social services at the countryside. Rural tourism can contribute to the support and maintenance of social services such as transport, accommodation, health care, education, and entertainment. The frequent visit to rural tourism destinations by both domestic and international tourists motivate local governments to improve social services like roads, telephones, opening up clinics, and building sports facilities at the countryside. The provision of such infrastructure for the rural communities are some of the indirect social benefits the countryside residents may recieve from rural tourism. The availability of visitors in rural communities also provides a market that motivates the local people to establish hospitality industry such as restaurants, motels, guest houses, and bed and breakfast. These local initiatives could provide employment for people and contribute to the social regeneration of rural communities. Rural tourism thus can contribute significantly to improved quality of social life of rural community residents.

One major characteristic of the countryside is its sparse population mainly due to lack of employment opportunities and amenities such as clean and safe water, electricity, good houses, schools, shops, health facilities, etc. These harsh conditions make rural residents migrate to towns and cities in search of better life and thereby create "ghost towns" at the countryside. Killion (2001) affirms that rural communities face a future of socioeconomic readjustment or become ghost towns. However, rural tourism can assist in reversing the trend by repopulating rural areas through vibrant tourist activities. The tourist attractions and renewed opportunities at the countryside can change this bleak situation when local residents voluntarily move back to their roots. Dahles (2000) adds that tourism is a catalyst of population movements. Young men in particular are attracted by the Western consumption patterns and lifestyles in tourist areas.

Rural tourism could lead to the regeneration of local customs, crafts and cultural identities of otherwise "margianalized" tribes and communities. In South Africa, for example, the Ndebele crafts and beads loved by both local and foriegn tourists alike are often sold by indigenous women at rural tourist sites. Colourful beads and crafts symbolizing cultural values of the local communities are usually displayed at tourist destinations. Most tourists buy some of these crafts as souvenirs or gifts to friends and relatives. The social benefit here is the marketing of local crafts and customs and the exhibition of African identity to international visitors. Thus, increased social contact with rural communities offer greater opportunities for cultural exchange between visitors and residents. In South Africa, for example, rural tourism assists the agricultural sector to introduce domestic and international tourists to the country's agricultural heritage. Rural tourism, therefore, supports and maintains farming in marginal areas of the countryside.

Economic benefits

The economic benefits of rural tourism are numerous. In many developing countries including South Africa, governments alone cannot provide jobs for all the unemployed citizens and therefore encourage people to engage in self-employment activities to reduce unemployment and poverty. This motivation has resulted in the emergence of many small, medium and macro-scale businesses such as street vendors, restaurants, transport (bicycles, horses, taxis, and motor bikes), accommodation (bed and breakfast, hotels, and guest houses) and entertainment palaces along side the rural tourism industry. Dahles (2000) agrees with this writer that the small-scale enterprises are a vigorous and visible element in the tourism sector, employing a large proportion of the labor force. Several opportunities for informal employment are emerging within the industry and should be considered when examining the economic impact of tourism. Rural tourism and its concomitant development of small-scale businesses are the means by which the rural community residents can adjust themselves economically to the new global environment.

The existing employment opportunities in the rural areas such as transport, tuck shop, medical care, catering, crafts, and entertainment facilities could be safeguarded and expanded because of market created by tourists. Dauglas *et al.* (2001) affirm that opportunities for new businesses are enhanced by the swarms of tourists and day trippers who provide an accessible market. This helps put more money into the local rural economy in addition to employment creation.

Rural tourism also encourages diversification of local economy and offers a broader and a more stable economic base for local communities. Local entrepreneurs may respond to the needs of tourists and thereby diversify their goods and services to cater for the diverse needs of visitors. New businesses and services may be attracted to the area, further diversifying and strength-ening the local economy whilst reducing the need for state subsidy of farming (Sharpely and Sharpely, 1997). Agricultural tourism, for example, can contribute to the income of farmers as supplementary activity. Diversification of goods and services can therefore broaden the economic base of rural communities.

Rural areas in most developing countries face the double challenge of decreasing agricultural production and the continued migration of the youth to urban centers. Rural tourism can reverse this situation because it is a sig-nificant means of sustaining rural economies and societies. It is a resource that can be exploited for financial gain by both individuals and communities as a whole. In fact, in the face of the declining role of agriculture and the increas-ing marginalization of many rural areas, tourism can become the "new cash crop" in the countryside. By attracting higher numbers of visitors, rural tourism is capable of strengthening the economic structure and base of rural areas. The more tourists visit the countryside, the more money gets into the local economy. And as the local economy improves, many people who migrated away to the cities could go back to their roots to engage in eco-nomic activities.

In sum, Killion (2001) mentions that rural tourism is designed to (1) sus-tain and create local incomes, employment and growth, (2) contribute to the costs of providing economic and social infrastructure, (3) encourage the development of other industrial sectors, and (4) achieve sustainable tourism.

Research Design and Methodology

This study was undertaken to explore the factors that attract tourists to rural tourists sites of Damdoryn and Bufflespoort. The study was an exploratory investigation which involved a survey and literature study. Thus, both primary and secondary sources were used in the investigation. Hundred visitors at the two destinations (Damdoryn 50 and Bufflespoort 50) and 25 business owners/managers were randomly selected to participate in the investigation. In view of the nature of the investigation, the researcher used a qualitative research method for data collection. The choice of qualitative-survey method was informed by the fact that the investigation of this nature involves direct interaction between the researcher and the participants. Such per-sonal interaction can assist in acquiring the data needed to meet the objectives of the study. Leedy (1992) points out that a qualitative research project requires descriptive and survey method, where data are obtained by verbal means. In view of this, the researcher employed the conventional qualitative research tool in the form of interview to collect data for this study.

Interview

The participants in this investigation were both men and women, local, foriegn, and from all races. This was done to make the selection of participants all inclusive (by taking into consideration the demographic realities of the country) in order to get views that cut across all cultural and population groups in South Africa as well as those of international visitors. The interviews were unstructured and the researcher used the participant-observation approach. This was done deliberately to avoid any suspicion that might arise and perhaps jeopardize the research; for example, tourists could be indifferent and refuse to be interviewed. By using the participant-observation approach, the researcher concealed his identity and managed to talk to the tourists. He visited the two tourist destinations six consecutive times. On each occasion, he spent three hours at each destination. The researcher chose summer time, weekends, and public holidays when many families visit the destinations. At each visit, the researcher took part in various tourists activities and siezed the opportunity to engage the visitors in purposeful conversations based on the information being solicited. The purposeful conversation focused on where visitors have come from, why they chose the particular destinations, the impression of the guests about the sites, the hosts, facilities and services, how many times they have visited, whether they would visit again, safety concerns, what they do not like about the place and suggestions for improvement.

The researcher used the same approach to interview 25 facility managers/owners at the two destinations. These included tour guides, owners of bottle stores, restaurants, handicrafts, coffee shops, hotels, guest houses, bed and breakfasts, supermarkets, sellers of bilton (dry meat from antelop, springbok, and zebra), fresh fruit (avacados, mangoes, and oranges) and vegetable sellers along the road, boat, cycle, camels and taxi services, entertainers and entertainment centers, caravan park, safari braai, kentucky fried chicken, and steers. The interviews which took the form of normal conversations focused on the number of clients per day/week, specific period of the year they receive more customers; when they receive less clients; why they think many people come to this particular place; which visitors patronize their businesses; how they advertise their goods and services; number of people employed and the implications of the above for the management of their businesses. The inclusion of the 25 non-tourists made up of tourism and conservation personnel and small- and medium-scale business owners/managers was pertinent because as owners of tourism related businesses they have direct contacts with the tourists on daily basis. Their views were used to validate those provided by the tourists.

Results and Discussion

This study specifically investigates the factors that have made the two countryside (Damdoryn and Bufflespoort) destinations so popular that large number of visitors congregate there on daily basis. The main objective of the investigation was the search for and gathering of data aimed at explaining what attracts visitors to the otherwise quiet and rustic rural area. As an exploratory study, the researcher employed the qualitative research tool of interview in order to get the personal and candid views of randomly selected visitors and small- and medium-scale business owners/managers operating at the two destinations. Two sets of interviews were conducted. The first focused on visitors attracted to the destinations, and the second on managers or owners of small- and medium-scale tourism-related businesses that have sprung up at the tourist sites.

Results from interviewing of visitors

The interview of the visitors comprised eight unstructured items which sought information on issues related to where visitors come from; how far from their place homes; how they got to know about the destinations; what makes them to come there; number of times they have visited; their impression of the destinations (the product); the people; facilities, and services offered; whether they intend coming to visit again and suggestions they have for the improvement of the tourism product. Hundred visitors were randomly selected and interviewed through informal normal conversation. Out of the 100 visitors interviewed, 69 of them live in South Africa with 49 (of the 69) being the Westerners and people of European and Asian origin. The other 20 visitors (out of the 69) were the Africans and other nationals. The visitors come from all the nine provinces of South Africa. Over 35 of the local visitors come from as far as Cape Town, George, Stellenbusch, Durban, Petermarisburg, RichardsBay, Port Elizabeth, East London, Grahamstown, Bloemfontein, Kimberley, Klerksdorp, Welkom, Mafikeng, Lightenburg, Johannesburg, Rustenburg, and Pretoria. The higher number of white South Africans among the tourists has some historical and socioeconomic significance. Historically, untill 1994, the Africans were not allowed at public facilities. Although every public facility is now open to all races, the Africans, in general do not patronize them perhaps due to economic reasons. The Westeners, on the other hand, have the means and the tradition of taking families out on holidays.

The interview confirmed that the few South Africans of European origin vistors are educated and well-to-do middle and upper class or petite bourgiousees who have the means and can afford taking their families for holidays. These are either senior civil servants, politicians or business men, and women. One lady, accompanied by her two kids and husband, confirmed that she is a chief director of a parastatal in the Western Cape Province. The reality is that it is unconcievable for the poor, unemployed or very low income black South Africans to visit rural tourism sites which are far from their places of residence or pay for accommodation and other entertainments. Out of the 20 Africans interviewed, 15 of them live in Gauteng (i.e., Pretoria, Johannesburg and their surrounding towns). These are well-to-do black families who perhaps take advantage of the proximity of the area to their homes and visit the areas (during the day without sleeping over) for recreational purposes.

The remaining 31 visitors interviewed were white people from outside South Africa. Twenty-one of them come from Europe and America and 10 from neighboring countries such as Botswana, Malawi, Zimbabwe, Lesotho, Moxambique, and Mauritius. These are perhaps expatriates who live and work in other African countries and choose to spend some of their holidays at Damdoryn and Bufflespoort. The figures mentioned above indicate that the highest number of patronage for the rural tourism product comes from non-indigenous African people who are more adventurous, have the means, the tradition, and inclination to travel.

Regarding how the visitors got to know about the two rural tourism destinations, 56 of the visitors said they learnt about the area through word of mouth and 44 said they got it from the media. The indication is that most visitors talk to their friends about their experiences of the area and this form of advertisement serves as a motivation for those who have never seen the place to come and experience things for themselves. The word of mouth is therefore the most single important advertising mechanism for the rural tourism product. The 44 visitors represent visitors who, with the availability of various media (e.g., electronic and print), search for information about unspoilt countryside destinations where they can pass time with their loved ones.

When asked the number of times they have visited, 87 of the 100 visitors affirmed that they have been there for more than once and love to come again any time they are on holidays. Thirteen of them said that it was their first time but they might visit again. The above responses motivated the researcher to find out what really pulls many visitors to the rural tourism destinations. Sixty of the visitors say the area is idyllic, unspoilt and quiet where people in the cities can visit and escape from the bustling, huzzling, and congested urban life. The indication is that a majority of visitors to the rural tourism destinations visit the places to take a break away from noisy, over crowded, and insecured urban life, at least for a short time.

Twenty-eight of the visitors come to the destinations because of the beautiful scenery, vegetation, clean environment, and nearby sourrounding mountains. These are town and city folks who love to get closer to nature either to watch birds, wild animals, do skiing, boating or interact with the forests and trees. There are also 12 of the participants who see their visit to the destinations as an adventure. These visitors said they want to learn and know more about the countryside. This group might consist of people who grew up in the cities and towns and might have heard about the safety, simplicity, and less expensive rural life but have never experienced it. They might be adventurous city folks who, perhaps, like to experience how rural life is and compare it to urban one they know.

All the participants agreed that the two sites are accessible to visitors from all places. They mentioned good road network that connects the destinations to Johannesburg international airport, Pretoria, Rustenburg (Sun City tourist resort), Magalisburg, Brits, and Harteespoort dam. There are various means of transport (e.g., tour buses, mini-buses, taxis, and cars) that can be hired by visitors from these cities and towns to the tourist destinations. They added that this accessibility coupled with availability of good accommodation, security, and good services at the site makes them feel at home and always want to stay for more days.

Results from the Interviewing of Business Owners/Managers

Twenty-five managers of rural tourism-related businesses at the two tourists' destinations were interviewed. These included private tour guides, small- to medium-scale business owners such as restaurant, bottle store, petrol stations, supermarkets, bed and breakfast, guesthouses, hotels, boat owners, sellers of bilton (dry meat), vegetables, fruits, artifacts, beads, traditional dresses, and tuckshops. The unstructured interview in a normal conversation sought information on their gender; the type of business or services they render, motivation for particular small business; who form the bulk of the customers for the businesses; time of the year when the small businesses receive the highest patronage; how the tourism sites have contributed to the growth of their businesses and the implications of visitor arrivals on the management of the small- and medium-scale businesses.

Gender of business managers

The first issue related to the gender of the tourism-related business owners. About 60% of the small- to medium-scale business owners interviewed were males and 40% females. Although the information indicates that there are more men owning tourism-related businesses, women have made significant progress in the area too. The positive implication is that more women have taken advantage of the market created by visitors to initiate self-employment and entrepreneurial projects. This is a challenge to men who have dominated the business in many areas. It also indicates the awareness among rural women about the need to start and manage their own businesses. The self-employment initiative by these women might inspire many women in other rural tourism destinations to start self-employment projects. As one of them put it "with the coming of 2010 to South Africa we are going to take advantage to make a living through self-employment." It is interesting to note that four of the 10 women own and manage telephone, coffee shops, B&Bs (Bed & Breakfasts), and a restaurant.

Types of tourism related businesses

The discussion touched on the type of rural tourism-related businesses owned by the 25 people interviewed. The responses indicated that the type of rural tourism business owned by the interviewees range from small- to medium-scale entreprieses. It was also revealed that the small businesses included fruit and vegetable sales, public phones, tour guide services, selling of artifacts while the medium size included hotels, guest houses, B&Bs, supermarket and restaurants. The small businesses are operated by the owners themselves or their relatives. The medium size businesses on the other hand employ an average of eight people.

Motivation for staring a small- and medium-size business

As regard the motive for establishing a particular small business around the rural tourism sites, various reasons were given by the respondents such as self-employed, availaibility of market, job creation, and independence. The respondents added that formal employment opportunities are very limited, particularly in the rural areas and the best way to earn a living is for them to start their own small businesses. Thus, self-employment is a major motive for the emergence of small businesses in the area. An improtant reason for starting tourism-related businesses is to cater for the demand for goods and services created by the number of visitors who frequent the tourism destinations. Out of 25 business managers interviewed, 24 of them constituting 96% of the total respondents confirmed that demand and supply issues are the factors that motivated them to establish tourism-related businesses. This response is important because without a market it would be unconceivable for any entrepreneur to produce goods and services. Market, created by visitors, is therefore a major motivating factor for people to start B&Bs, guesthouses, restuarants, super-market, boat, telephone shops, bottle stores, tour guide, and services in the area.

Twenty-two of the business owners also mentioned that they started small businesses in order to create jobs for the people in the rural areas. This response is laudable because unemployment is very high in rural communities and to create jobs means reducing poverty. Some of the owners of tourism-related businesses employ local people to assist them in the running of their businesses. This means that the establishment of many small- and medium-scale businesses in the area could reduce unemployment and its concomitant social vices such as house breaking, mugging, snatching of handbags or cell phones, prostitution, and drug peddling. Nineteen respondents indicated that they started small businesses in order to be independent. These are the people who might have experienced some mistreatment from their former employers and therefore resolved to work for themselves.

Regarding the time of the year that rural tourism-related business booms, all the interviewees concurred that summer time (especially, weekends and public holidays) is always the period when many people visit and therefore patronize their businesses. The respondents added that the bulk of their customers are visitors from afar.

Bulk of customers for small-scale businesses

The majority of customers patronizing small-scale businesses at the tourism sites are visitors and travelers who frequent the rural tourism destinations. These visitors and travelers constitute 96% of the customers of the small-scale businesses. Although local residents buy goods and services, their patronage is only 4% compared to that of travelers and visitors to the area. This response is significant in the light of the fact that naturally visitors and travelers to places outside their homes may be in need of refreshments, accommodation, food, fuel, and other social services more than local residents.

When the interviewees were asked about the implications of the increased number of visitor arrivals for their businesses, 17 of the participants conceded that management has become more complex as a result of increased demand for goods and services by the ever-increasing number of visitors to the destinations. They added that it is sometimes difficult for them to cope with accounting and management aspects of their businesses and that it could be costly to engage the services of professionals bacause they do not have much income. Like most parts of the developing world, rural-tourism-related business entreprises in South Africa are small- to medium-scale and are found in the informal sector where generally the managers or owners have low educational background and therefore lack managerial and accounting skills to sustain the businesses.

The participants also mentioned that as businesses thrive, they sometimes lack funds to expand them. This is because banks have problems in lending out loans to owners of small business entreprises. Banks always need collateral security before granting loans, a condition which most of the emerging rural tourism-related entrepreneurs cannot meet. The lack of knowledge, skills, and funds to expand and manage businesses may affect growth and sustainability of the tourism-related microbusinesses.

One of the small business owners mentioned three different unintended results of increased number of visitors to the rural tourism destinations. She mentioned how rich and powerful business people (mostly white South Africans) have used their financial power to push out poor African people who have created an informal market for African clothes, artifacts, and fruits for their livelihood. These were the people who started selling things in the area to visitors long before the arrival of big businesses but now they have been ejected from the place with an excuse that new development structures are to be put there. The small business woman manager (of European origin) who wanted to remain anonymous added that with the increased number of visitors, the area has become a *haven* for drug peddlers, prostitutes, and robbers. These activities are done openly but the police are not acting against the perpetrators. Business managers therefore have to be extra vigilant or spend extra money to hire people to protect their goods from thieves.

Conclusion

This exploratory study was undertaken to find out what motivates people to visit rural tourism destinations of Damdoryn and Bufflespoort dam in the rural areas of the North West province. This investigation has revealed that several factors motivate both local and foreign holiday makers to congregate at the two rural tourism sites. The major reasons given by visitors are as follows: (1) idyllic, unspoilt quiet places that provide hide out and entertainment for urban dwellers who like to (temporarily) escape from the hustle and huzzle of overcrowed city life; (2) enjoyment of beautiful scenery made up of forests, mountains and the African sun; (3) adventure for people who want to be nearer to nature, watch birds, wild animals, enjoy boating, skiing and simplicity of rural life and (4) accessibility of the destinations because of proximity to cities and towns, international airport, good road network, and transport. The investigation also revealed that although the desire to be self-employed motivated the local people to initiate rural tourism-related businesses, the majority of the managers especially Africans have very little formal education, management and accounting skills to cope with the rapid expansion of their businesses as a result of increase in visitor arrivals.

In conclusion, the chapter recommends that (1) to boost local economic development initiatives through the establishment of small- and medium-scale tourism-related businesses, the local government must assist the emerging local entrepreneurs financially in order to expand their businesses and get them space where they can operate such businesses; (2) the department of tourism and labor must conduct a survey on the small business owners to find out their training needs, provide them with training in basic managerial and accounting skills which may empower them to manage and expand their businesses and (3) law enforcement agents must assist small- and medium-scale business managers in the area to stamp out crime, especially drug peddling, stealing, and prostitution.

The above-mentioned measures may not only assist local business owners to create more jobs and to reduce unemploymemt in the rural areas; it may also bring about sustainability of small businesses and reduction of poverty, especially among the most vulnerables in the rural communities.

References

Beeton, S (1999). Rural (Tourism) policy: Cross-sectoral land use regulation and government policy in Australia. In *Proceedings of Sustaining Rural Environment: Issues in Globalisation, Migration and Tourism*, Daugherty, CM (ed.), North Arizona University: Department of Geography/Planning.

Bennet, JA (2000). *Managing Tourism Services*. Pretoria: Van Schalk.

Boucher, C (1999). No island is an island. In *Our planet*, UNDP Magazine for Environmentally Sustainable Development 10.

Dahles, H (2000). Tourism, small enterprises and community development. In *Tourism and Sustainable Community Development*, Richards, G and D Hall (eds.), London: Routledge.

Dauglas, N, N Dauglas, and R Derret (2001). *Special Interest Tourism*. Brisbane: John Willy & Sons Ltd.

Holden, A (2000). *Environment and Tourism*. London: Routledge.

Keyser, H (2002). *Tourism Development*. Cape Town: Oxford University Press, Southern Africa.

Killion, L (2001). Rural tourism. In *Special Interest Tourism*, Dauglas, N, N Dauglas, and R Derret (eds.), Brisbane: John Willey and Sons Ltd.

Leedy, PD (1992). *Practical Research, Planning and Design*. New York: Prentice Hall Ltd.

Peine, JD (1998). *Ecosystem Management for Sustainability; Principles and Practices Illustrated by a Regional Biosphere Reserve Co-operative*. London: Lewis Publishers Ltd.

Sharpely, R and J Sharpley (1997). *Rural Tourism; An Introduction*. London: International Thomson Business Press.

World Tourism Organisation (1997). *Tourist Safety and Security*.

Chapter 17

AN INSTITUTIONAL NETWORK APPROACH OF PARTNERSHIP MODE OF INTEREST-FREE MICROFINANCE AND ISLAMIC BANKING: A CASE STUDY

MOHAMMED N. ALAM
AND MOSTAQ M. HUSSAIN

Abstract

Interest-free banking has been expanding its operation in many countries. On the other hand, micro-credit has been increasingly becoming effective in different parts of the world. In the mean time, interest-free banks have started rendering micro-credit to the rural-based micro entrepreneurs in different developing nations. However, the effectiveness of partnership between interest-free banking and micro-credit finance has not been explored though there are similarities exist in both modes of operation. This chapter attempts to explore the "partnership mode" of Islamic banking; that is, how and to what extent Islamic banking finance contributes to eliminating rural poverty and creating job opportunities for unemployed people in rural areas. This exploratory case study is carried out within "Institutional-Network" theoretical approach with a particular reference to Omdruman, a suburb nearby Khartoum, Sudan. Face-to-face interview method was used to the collect the data. The empirical findings demonstrate that the "Partnership Mode" Islamic banking finance may work effectively in developing and developed countries for some reasons such as lenders and borrowers joint interest in a particular venture, and a unique lender–borrower network relationship.

Introduction

Anderson and Khambata (1982) and Macuja (1981) observed that the rural-based micro enterprises (MEs) play a predominant role in solving a nation's economic problems through the generation of employment opportunities for rural people. Further, the ability of MEs to generate greater employment opportunities at a low cost particularly suits those developing countries confronted with a rapidly growing population (Farooque, 1958). MEs play significant roles in the elimination of the unemployment problem, which remains a serious impediment to a nation's economic growth in least developed countries and also in developing countries. Although the large-scale industries are involved in mass production and invest large amounts of capital, these industries are mostly urban based. However, large-scale industries fail to play a significant role in solving unemployment problems particularly in the rural areas. This is exactly where micro entrepreneurs succeed better (Macuja, 1981; Anderson and Khambata, 1982). Several studies highlight the issue as to how and to what extent MEs contribute toward the development of a particular economy (Little *et al.*, 1987; Little, 1988; Ashe and Corselet, 1989).

The most important economic role that the ME sector plays is the creation of job opportunities for unemployed people in the rural as well as in urban areas. A report published by the United Nation Development Program (UNDP, 1993) shows that the MEs in the informal sector expanded about 7% during the period of 1980 and 1989. The MEs, which are mainly run by family members, for micro entrepreneurs do not observe any formal procedures to initiate their business activities. Ashe and Corselet (1989) observe that in rural areas, in addition to the legion of subsistence and small farmers, there is a growing percentage of individuals whose primary source of income is trading, cottage industries and a wide range of services, generally categorized as off-farm activities: the figure ranges from 19% to 23% in countries like India, Sierra Leone, and Colombia; from 28% to 38% in Indonesia, Pakistan, Kenya and Philippines, and as high as 49% in Malaysia.

Not only do MEs create job opportunities, but they also contribute to a considerable extent to economic solvency among the resource-poor class in the rural areas. In almost all least developed countries under the phase of rapid population growth, MEs may thus play a unique role in the development of a nation's economy. Due to various problems, such as the lack of sufficient funds caused by inadequate infrastructural and institutional arrangements and shortcomings in the area of marketing and distribution, the growth of the MEs in the rural areas is less pronounced than could be expected. The slow growth of MEs, in turn, results in the migration of manpower from rural to the urban areas, which ultimately increase problems, such as overcrowding, increased competition for fewer jobs, etc., in the urban areas. Moreover, due to the limited job opportunities such urbanization additionally hampers the nation's economy (Myrdal, 1968). Under the auspices of the United Nations Economic Commission for Asia and the Far East (ECAFE), UNIDO and Asian Development Bank (ADB), many studies were conducted on small-scale industry in the ECAFE region. Among these, a number of studies[1] highlight the root causes of the impediments to the development of MEs and also make suggestions for solving these problems.

Theoretical Framework

The concept of an institutional network is based on "Business System" institutional approach and "Network Institutional Model" (Jansson's, 2002; Alam, 2002), which is designed to study business organizations, inter alia in Asian countries. Whitley (1992b) in his comparative study of Business Systems in East Asian countries; for example, Chinese family business units in Taiwan and Hong Kong, Japanese Kaisha and Korean chaebol, the author tried to find how firms are constituted as relatively distinct economic actors in different market societies and how they organize economic activities in the form of dominant hierarchy-market configurations. The comparative analysis of business system is the study of these configurations (Whitley, 1992b). The author argues that a key task concerning the comparative study of business systems is to analyze how distinctive patterns of economic organizations become established and effective in different societies and how they change in relation to their institutional context. Whitley (1992a) observed that these patterns concern the nature of economic activities that are coordinated through managerial hierarchies, and how these

---

[1] For example, in Bangladesh, Nepal and India (ESCAP Secretariat, 1984), Sudan (Siddiqi, 1992), China (Sit, 1991; Wang, 1992), China, Japan, India (Vepa, 1984), Ceylon (Abeyasingha, 1982), Hong Kong (Tam, 1984), Korea (Ouh, 1984; UNIDO, 1988), India (Rooseboom, 1971, 1972; Bhende, 1978; Brodribb, 1981; Singh, 1982; Vepa, 1982; Venkataraman, 1986; Sury, 1987; Agrawal, 1988; Ganguly, 1988; Bhattacharyya, 1988; Brodribb, 1991; Kundra, 1991; Solanki and Qureshi, 1991), Indonesia, Philippines, Malaysia (ESCAP/UNIDO, 1984; Suhardi, 1991), India, Pakistan, and Sri Lanka (Subramanian, 1992), Japan (Aburtani, 1964), Malaysia (Jordon, 1972; Hoong, 1989), Pakistan (Syed, 1984), Philippines (Rossario, 1964; Macuja, 1981; Tan, 1987; Alonzo *et al.*, 1992), Philippines and Thailand (UNIDO, 1988), and Singapore (Yue, 1992).

hierarchies organize their cooperative and competitive relations through markets.

Because one of the objectives of the research relates to the finding as — how the interest-free micro-credit (by Islamic banks) contributes to establishing the lender–borrower network relationships, apart from Whitley's (1992a, b) institutional concept in the Institutional-Network theoretical framework, we also used the network concepts of Jansson's (2002) "Networks Institutions" model, where the author integrated network with institutions and viewed the network from an institutional perspective. According to Jansson (2002), institutions also concern different types of habitual or recognized behavior such as habits, rules, and procedures, implying that institutions are characterized by a rule-like or governing nature, an ability to facilitate and constrain inter-human and inter-social relations, and by predictive behavior. Veblen (1919) observed that institutions themselves are comprised of settled habits of thought common to generality of men. And to study the relationships between multinational corporations (MNCs) and their commercial partners, the author used a network approach and developed a theory to analyze such linkages. In order to study the network relationships between and within organizations belonging to the two-focused institutions; for example, MEs and major financing systems (MFS) and their relationships with other economic actors in the organizational fields. We used the concept of Jansson's (2002) Trans-organizational Network theory while developing the analytical framework. As the networks are looked upon from different angles, this study also used the network concepts as defined by different authors (Anderson and Carlos, 1976; Aldrich and Whetten, 1981; Emerson and Cook, 1984; Rasmussen, 1988; Kuklinski and Knoke, 1988; Easton and Araujo, 1991; Elg and Johansson, 1992; Easton, 1992; Håkansson, 1993).

To study the impact and influence of "Interest-free micro-credit" to the rural-based micro entrepreneurs, based on Whitley's Business System model, we developed the concept of four components of different ME and Financing Systems. These components, for example, are the nature of organization, market organization, employment systems, and authority and control systems. Accordingly to Whitley (1992b), a comparative analysis of the Business System is the systematic study of these configurations and as how they become established in markets. Like Whitley's (1992b), the Islamic Financing System is seen as a Financing Business System of its own, with a foundation based on religion, having its own rules governed by the Islamic laws. These rules differ from those of other financial systems. Different financial systems; for example, market-based financing system such as conventional banks, cooperative financing system, and traditional money lending system and viewed as particular arrangements of hierarchy-market relations that become institutionalized and relatively successful in a particular context. A similar arrangement is also done to institutionalize different rural-based MEs. Various MEs of similar nature are thus grouped into three different ME Systems such as grass-root level, season-based, and semi-mechanized ME Systems. Financing organizations and MEs under different Financing Systems and ME systems are regarded as economic actors acting within these organizational fields.

Islamic Banking Finance

Islamic banking finance toward ME sector

One of the major aims of Islamic banks under Islamic Financing System is to render financial services to the rural-based ME sector. In many ways, Islamic banks are similar to other privately owned formal financial intermediaries. The main difference is that an Islamic bank neither accepts deposits nor invests funds to its customers on interest. Instead, the bank shares profit or loss. Nienhaus (1983, 1988, 1993) observes that the rural-based micro entrepreneurs are not being benefited much either by the state-owned or the privately owned financial organizations. One might therefore find it interesting to observe how an Islamic bank acts as "bank for rural micro entrepreneurs"; for example, how far an Islamic bank, with its motive of investing funds on a "profit and loss sharing" basis may contribute toward financing and promoting rural-based ME sector.

The Islamic financing systems: An institutionalized form

The Islamic Financing System includes different financing organizations that are guided by *shariah* (Islamic law) based on financing principles. These organizations use different financing techniques and lending procedures than those in the other Financing Systems. The IFS is a mix of market-based and non-market-based Financing Systems. Although many exchange functions in organizations within the IFS are similar to those of Western inspired commercial banks, they are also based on non-market rules and regulations, which are based on religious ethics. The organizations in the IFS functions beyond the market-based economy, because the exchange relations of this system are mainly ethics-based, originating from religious beliefs, trust and faith (Alam, 2002)

Concept of partnership financing mode of Islamic banking

The word "Musharaka" (partnership) means a profit-sharing joint venture, designed to limited production or commercial activities of long duration. In this case, the bank and the customer contribute capital jointly. They also contribute managerial expertise and other essential services at agreed proportions. Profit or losses are shared according to the contract agreed upon. An individual partner does not become liable for the losses caused by others. Due to this joint venture, this technique is also known as equity participation mode of investment. Profit is distributed according to a predetermined ratio and loss, if any is also shared according to the capital ratio. Both the bank and the customer take part in the management and control of the entrepreneurial activities.

Features of profit sharing investment

The following are some of the salient features of the Musharaka mode of investment: (1) the bank invests under this mode in commerce, industry, agriculture, and other sectors for productive purposes; (2) fund provided by the bank and the client jointly constitutes the capital of the business; (3) ratio for distribution is determined at the time of entering into the agreement between the bank and the client; (4) the bank participates in policy decision and ensures correct accounting of the business transaction. The client manages the business project; if necessary, the bank may appoint representatives at the cost of the client; (5) because the client takes responsibility of the management, the bank usually allows a higher ratio of profit to the client than his share of capital; (6) according to the Islamic Shariah (law), losses if any are borne by the bank and the client as per contribution ratio; and (7) the bank dose not bear any loss caused due to the mismanagement, breach of contract, breach of trust, etc. In such a case, the client has to bear all losses. (Ahmad, 1981, 1994; Alam, 2003, 2006).

Sudanese Islamic bank: A bank for poor people in Sudan

Sudanese Islamic Bank (SIB) started giving credit in early 1988 to small farmers and rural MEs on a "Musharaka" (partnership financing) mode of investment. To assist rural-based small farmers and Mes, SIB started pilot projects based on "Musharaka" financing principle of Islamic banking. One of these projects is called "The productive family project." The SIB provides credit to these rural based MEs on a partnership mode of investment.

Respondents interviewed were clienteles of the SIB who took loans under the "Productive Family Project" program of the bank.

Sudanese economy is based on agriculture; however, to develop this sector of economy, the government did not take sufficient initiatives. The Agricultural Bank of Sudan (SAB) is the only government agency that supplies capital to farmers. Small farmers normally are deprived of using facilities from this bank. They traditionally get their financing from private and family sources. The SAB failed to succeed in rendering its proper services to small farmers in rural Sudan. The failure was due to reasons such as lack of providing comprehensive financing, small farmers inability to afford to provide garantor, slow procedure of giving loan, high cost of credit, and interest on loan that religious farmers reject to pay. While highlighting on the role of conventional banks in Sudan, Khalifa and Hassan (1992) argue that the formal financial market failed to function efficiently and to reach the small farmers in the agrarian sector. It is basically due to the failure to accommodate the risk aversion attitude of the small farmers in their finance model. Consequently, the small farmers resort to the informal financial markets (village merchants). The informal market is characterized by quick response to the small farmers credit needs, in addition to collateral-less requirement. However, the informal financial markets charge externally high monopoly rents amounting to over 300%, thus defeating the sole purpose of credit objectives. To overcome this problem, the SIB started giving loan to agricultural and other small manufacturer on a "Musharaka" mode of Islamic financing system (Khalifa and Shazali, 1988; Khalifa, 1992).

Micro-Credit Procedures of Islamic Bank in Sudan

The procedure of giving loans initiate soon after the bank select a particular family as a prospective customer. SIB normally follows the following procedures while lending funds on "Partnership Mode" of Islamic financing: (1) The bank selects potential customers through informal communication; (2) customers visit bank officials called "Musharak" manger in charge of funding to the clienteles under Productive family projects; (3) the customer provides 10% of the required capital to buy equipments; (4) the bank pays the remaining 90% of the capital; (5) the bank buys necessary materials for the microentrepreneurs as they need; (6) the "Musharaka Manager" visits every customer at least once in a week and inquires about the progress of the work; (7) once the production is complete the finished goods are sold to the local customers; (8) the bank maintains a big show room in the bank premises where produced goods of different customers are kept for demonstration; (9) the bank takes initiatives in marketing for the clienteles and keeps samples of the products of their customers in the bank show room; (10) the "Musharaka Manager" assists in promoting clienteles business and also assists in marketing their products; (11) the customer pays visit to the bank premises time to time and demonstrates their new products in bank's show room and collects orders from different sources; (12) the Musharaka Manager prepares accounts for the customers at regular intervals; (13) a profit or loss is determined after deducting all expenses; (14) profits are shared according to the agreed proportion; (15) the clienteles start repaying the loan from the amount of profit; (16) once the business is expanded the bank extends more credit; (17) once loans are paid and the family is self-sufficient, the bank concentrates on other customers; and (18) there is no specific term for the repayment time of loans. However, the more the clienteles repay the loans the higher the share of profits they own. This policy encourages the customer to repay the loans quickly from the earned profit.

Research Methodology

This case study of lender–borrower network relationships between rural-based MEs and Islamic banks has been conducted in three different time periods. The data have been directly collected from the field; that is, face-to-face in-depth interviews in 1994. The follow-up was made in 1997, and subsequently the last communications over the phone took place in 2002–2003. This study is qualitative in nature (Jick, 1979; Patton 1985; Merriam, 1998; Sherman and Webb, 1988). Based on Merriam's (1998), *Interview Structure Continuum* idea, we used structured, semi structured, and unstructured interviews in order to adapt with different interview circumstances. A multiple explanatory case study (Yin, 1994) method was adopted as a research strategy in order to focus on contemporary phenomenon within the real life context of different rural-based micro entrepreneurs under various ME Systems and their relationships with financing organizations within the Islamic Financing Systems.

To collect data, owners of different micro entrepreneurs in different ME System (Alam, 2002) were grouped together in the following order: (1) Both formal and informal interview methods were used; (2) questions were asked to respondents based on questionnaires depending on the circumstances and the qualifications of the respondents; (3) different micro entrepreneurs are taken as a different individual case while interviewing respondents in order to receive the benefits of multiples case study (Yin, 1994); (4) tape recorder used to record respondents answers, and subsequently interview data were recorded in the spread sheet; (5) twenty respondents were interviewed during the field studies. All of them are clienteles of the Sudanese Islamic Bank under its "Productive Family Project." Respondents belong to different professions like, tailoring, handicraft, soap making and oil producing, etc. These MEs are categorized as grass-root level micro entrepreneurs under GLME System; and (6) the interview period for each respondents ranged to an average of three to four hours.

Direct contact with customers: An example of Sudan Islamic Bank

In the case of SIB, when various formalities regarding credit to a customer end, the SIB enters into a partnership agreement with the customers, where various terms and conditions of profit or loss sharing and conditions for the repayment of loans are mentioned. As the loan is given on a "Musharaka" (participating) mode of financing, the bank agrees with customers about the percentage of profit or loss to be shared with them. Thus, through the agreement, as mentioned above, the bank establishes a direct contact with customers. From the following excerpt, the bank's customer relationship can be understood.

> The SIB gave loan to me for buying a sewing machine and materials for making dresses. According to the condition of the contract, I had to show a deposit in the bank that equals to 10 percent of the machine and material costs. A portion of loan amount is still remaining with the bank. The 'Musharaka' (partnership) manager of the bank buys materials for me. When I use the lot and prepare men and women dress, I sell it to the local market. Sometimes the 'Musharaka manager' also assists me in finding customers for me. After I sell dresses, made the bank officer prepare a rough account and finds profit derived from the sale. As per agreement, 30 percent of the profit derived so is deposited in the bank. This amount is the part repayment of my loan. From the remaining 70 percent profit the bank takes 60 percent and I keep for myself 40 percent. Determination of profit is made after deducting all expenditure. The bank again releases portion of loan amount to buy raw material and the same procedure is followed as mentioned. It is one year since I took loan from the local SIB branch and with the profit money; I have bought one more machine recently. The loan of the first machine has already been paid back after six months, and now I have owned the machine. In the same way, I have got the loan for the second machine. While I shall finish the repayment of the loan for the second machine, I shall be free from liability. That means I shall not have to depend on Bank loan.

The agreement also includes what is the allowable expenditure to be deducted before determining the profit, the mode of repayment of loan, etc. From the experience of the "Productive Family Project" program, the SIB noted that with the sincere help and good contact with a customer, the bank may make a family self-sufficient and can solve unemployment easily.

Contribution of Musharaka Mode of Financing to the Society

A unique administration of borrowed funds

The loan giving procedure of the Islamic bank in Sudan is unique. The bank staff are assigned duty to contact customers and to observe their activities in order to be sure that they are properly using their borrowed funds and eager to repay the loan in time.

No securities required to borrow funds

SIB normally does not impose any burden of securities on its customers. Due to the partnership mode of financing, a close supervision of loans is given more importance than the any collateral for loans. In order to develop customers' position and to make use of borrowed funds in a profitable way, the bank takes various steps such as reliance on personal network to deal with the rural-based micro entrepreneurs and potential customers.

Developing and maintaining relationships with customers

The medium of communications is not as developed in Sudan as other developed countries of the world. Moreover, due to the nature of Islamic banking, "Musharaka" mode of finance used in investing funds, the bank prefers to communicate customers directly to contact through other means; however, the banks may communicate with customers through local influential persons and religious leaders of the society.

Islamic banks' concerned about their customers: Unique services of the PRD

Officials of the SIB in Sudan are concerned about welfare of customers and their interest. The Public Relation Department (PRD) of every Islamic bank is responsible for dealing with customers' affairs. The bank management ensures that every individual customer receives proper attention by the dealing officers. In order to develop public relations, banks give training to their staffs.

Customers' easy access to the bank: Develop a close bank-customer relationship

The SIB encourages micro entrepreneurs and welcomes them to discuss issues of their business concern. As the "Family Productive Project" program is a new project introduced by the SIB, the bank opened various departments for its customers such as department for women customers. Women micro entrepreneurs directly visit women staff of the bank responsible for discussing issues about "Musharaka" financing and give necessary advice to customers in their project work. Clienteles of the bank — mostly illiterate — are assisted by bank staff from the inception of loan application to marketing of products. Also, they have easy access to the bank to discuss issues relating to business.

Personal assistance to a customer: Creates closer ties and reduces middleperson's interferences

As officers at various levels help rural-based MEs, they need not to take any assistance from middlemen. Thus, a direct assistance to customers by the SIB staff reduces the possibilities of any middleperson's interference. It is the duty of the Musharak manager to look after different aspects of members of the "Productive Family Project" in the area. The manager with his subordinates visits different customers on different days of the week and helps translate views of customers who mostly speak Arabic.

Developing customers relationships through other services

To improve the bank–customer relationship, the SIB renders various other services to their customers: (1) sometimes bank staff visit customers' business place; (2) in order not to lose its potential customers, problems of customers are taken care of; (3) customers are encouraged to inform about any difficulties they face with banking activities; (4) customers are allowed to place complaints about the management and administration if they are not satisfied or of any staff of the bank with whom they are not satisfied; (5) customers can contact to senior officials in case of emergency; and (6) bank staff voluntarily advice customers regarding their business.

Regarding the role of a "Musharaka Manager" in the SIB, one of the MEs reported:

> My daughter and son who are going to school note down the daily income and expenditure of our business on a rough paper. The bank staff when come to our house to supervise record, it is in the books of accounts maintained by him. When

the lot of materials that the bank supplied is finished, the total products prepared from that lot and the finished products sold, etc., are calculated. By this way, the Musharaka manager finds profit figure, which later on is divided according to the pre-determined P/L ratio. The visit of bank officers encourages my children to take active part in my work. My daughter and son help me much to make dress and to get more customers. As the bank showed them a very simple way of keeping record of various transactions, they have learnt by now how to maintain books of accounts.

These sorts of services by bank normally develop bank customer relationships and give bank staff chance not only to know a customers' behavior from a close range, but also to known members of the customer' family.

SIB's policies to assist customers in marketing their products

Micro entrepreneurs normally receive order for their products from local customers. A few MEs informed that customers like home made products as one can buy these good at a cheaper rate than the market. The products are also of better quality. One of the respondents who make dresses for women and children reported, "People in my area like to buy clothes from me and I get lots of order from them. I have noted that prices of clothes, which we supply to the people, are much cheaper than those sold in the market." The women also reported that before she started taking loan from the SIB she used to take loan from local moneylenders. As per agreement, she had to repay the loan not in cash but in kind. She used to give the lender ready-made clothes instead of loan money. By that the lady would not get proper price for her products. After she started taking loan from the SIB she received direct order from local people. The SIB knows most of her buyers. Her products are placed in the show room of the SIB office. When other customers of the bank visit the show room of the bank, a women publication officer of the bank introduces various ME products to bank customers, where her products were also demonstrated. Thus the women got many customers who directly give order to her for dresses and she was able to get a good market of her products.

When one of the staff of the SIB was asked as to how they assist customers to promote the marketing of their products, the respondent of the bank took the interviewer around their showroom where different clienteles' products were kept for demonstration. They informed:

Once, the bank gives loan to a customer for any project, the 'Musharaka' manager along with the subordinate staff supervise the loan till products are ready for sale. Before selling these products in the market, the bank buys some of the products and put it in bank's show room. The bank sells these goods to public at a cheaper rate than the local market price and also informs about particular producer who is producing the particular products. In this way, we make an arrangement of advertising our customers' products and also help them in finding profitable customers for them. Various types of products we sell from our bank as a sample and at the same time we introduce the producers of the same.

Provision for women customers in the SIB

The SIB encourages poor women in the society to take loan. There are special arrangements in the bank for women customers. Normally, women in the locality feel very shy to go to a man officer and to discuss anything about their family affairs. The bank employed many women staff and they take care of the women section. Almost half of the MEs of the "Productive Family Project" in Omdruman are women. The bank officer reported that women are found more organized and active than their male customers. Most of the projects run by the women MEs were found to be successful. They arrange their work jointly with other members of the family. They are most sincere and utilize their time and money in a proper way. The bank increased various facilities for women and the manager of the bank want to ensure that the bank officer neglects no women customers in any way.

A deposit of 10% of the borrowed funds is a must in SIB

It is must for a customer of the SIB to open a savings account with the bank before they take loan. The bank does not give loan to a customer under "Musharaka" mode until the balance of deposit comes to the 10% of the loan that the customer applies for. It makes customers interested in raising savings to borrow funds from the bank. From the banks' perspective, it does not take much time in sanctioning loan; it is the time that a customer takes in accumulating a saving of 10% of the loan applied for. This policy of the bank helps poor farmers and MEs to be saving-minded and utilize their savings toward productive purposes. One of the respondents in SIB told that through the introduction of the "Productive Family Project," the bank attracted a large amount of deposits from public. The bank succeeded in utilizing these savings in productive ways. The respondent reported that people in this area are satisfied with a minimum need. They lead a very simple life. The main problem with them was they had no guide to show them as to how to make their money and efforts productive. The SIB has succeeded in giving a new life to many distress and needy people in the locality.

The SIB's Exceptional Investment Policies

The SIB has taken a revolutionary step to eliminate problems of finance among small farmers and rural-based MEs by providing fund under "Musharaka" mode of investment in which bank takes the responsibility to make a project successful. The only condition to implement the system in a proper way is that the bank management must be well organized and customers must be sincere and honest in their activities. Regarding the success of Musharaka financing, Al-Harran (1992, p. 369) states:

> The Sudanese Islamic Bank, in spite of being a young institution, has taken the initiative in *'musharaka'* financing and paved the way for other Islamic banks in the Sudan and elsewhere. It has demonstrated that *musharaka* financing is workable and profitable. The banks' experience has broken the inertia of banker who thought that *musharaka* financing is a risky venture and should be avoided by concentrating on short- and medium-term investment (*through mudaraba and murabaha*), rather than a long-term investment through *musharaka*. Needless to say that the continued success of *musharaka* financing will depend on the quality of management.

Regards toward social and religious status of a customer

Respondents of the SIB expressed different views with regard to customers' religious and social status. When Islamic banking finance operates on a "Musharaka" mode, then besides security, one should carefully study the habit, behavior, social, and religious status of a customer. All these qualities lead a customer to utilize the borrowed funds in a profitable way. Those who borrow funds under "Musharaka" mode are active partners, rather than mere customers of the bank. According to the information of the senior officials in SIB, the bank ensures that their customers should have both material and spiritual qualities in order to share a business with them. In Sudan, Islamic banks also give due consideration to these qualities even though these banks do not restrict their financing activities only for Muslim customers.

Influence of Societal Sector Institutions

Different societal sector institutions such as country culture, political systems or the government, religious beliefs and faith and habits, etc. influence lending and borrowing activities of financial organizations. Influences of these institutions on financial activities differ from country to country (Alam, 2006).

Political systems and the government

The government supports activities of SIBs. The only problem faced by SIB is the political unrest and unstable political systems of the country.

Country culture, norms, and habits

Islamic banking activities are influenced by country culture, norms, and habits of the people in different societies. In Sudan, these societal sector institutions have high influence on the Islamic banking functions. Islamic banking idea is a new innovation in the money market of these countries. People are not much aware of these systems and Islamic banks have taken very negligible steps to educate the general mass. It is reported by some senior of Islamic banks in Sudan that when they deal with rural-based MES, sometimes they find it difficult to divert customers from their cultural beliefs and norms which really do not bring any financial gains, rather take time, money, and energy. Further, the habits of people like food, clothing, accommodation, etc., influence the activities of both lenders and borrowers. Due to the change in the habit of people in different seasons, the demand of certain ME products increases and MEs find these projects profitable.

Religious faith and beliefs

An Islamic bank is based on certain Islamic principles and its financing systems works well, where customers are religiously developed. Although the bank follows Islamic principles, it does not mean that customers should be Muslims. Many customers of Islamic banks are from other religion. Regardless of religion, the bank only inquires about the honesty and faith of customers.

The lending procedure makes grass-root level entrepreneurs more organized

The study found that most of the customers of the SIB are not well educated and consists of rural poor. They need guidance to utilize a little savings that they have in a productive way. The very micro-credit policy of Islamic banks not only educates them regarding interest free loans but also organizes their activities through close supervision so that they might contribute to the society. Besides, the entire lending activities of the banks are organized in such a way that the borrowers are benefited from the beginning to the final stage of their projects.

Contributes to developing different types of network relationships

Islamic banks normally collect information about their customers from several sources before they start an exchange relationship with their clients. They use both formal and informal means of collecting such information. When financing, organizations in the market-based financing system and the cooperative financing system mostly use formal means. Islamic banks go beyond the formal means in order to procure information about their prospective customers. To collect information about the rural-based micro entrepreneurs, they sometimes contact local political leaders, influential religious leaders; for example Imams (priests) of mosques, other well-known religious leaders, seniors, and other key social figures. They also contact their customers in certain locality before initiating loans to any new client. The MEs belonging to different MES spend a great deal of time developing their network relationships with such people in order to have a good reputation or to have easy access to the financing organizations for a loan. Thus, this lending technique of the Islamic banks widens the scope of network relations not only with borrowers but also with different economic actors in the organizational fields.

The close ties among workers within the organization promote the intra-organizational network relationships, and because the individual savings are organized and managed through group savings, an individual develops a close ties with other members in the group which ultimately contributes in promoting inter-organizational network relationships with members in the group (Aldrich, 1979). Further, because the entire saving activity and accumulation of required customers' deposits are supervised by the financing organizations within IFS, their external network relationships are extended to different organizational units at the grass-root level ME System. Thus, the micro entrepreneurs not only extend their network relationships with the lending organizations within IFS, but also with different entrepreneurs within the grass-root level ME System. This in return develops and intensifies *intra and inter-organizational* network relationships.

It may also be concluded that the long-term lending policy of the organizations in the Islamic financing system increases the interdependency between exchange partners. This results in the deepening of lender–borrower relationships and also helps exchange partners to get to know each other better. A continuous and long-term exchange relationship contributes to developing trustful financial ties between the lenders and borrowers. When the long-term lending policy increases interdependency, the commitment to exchange partners also increases.

Conclusion

Interest-free micro-credit is gaining its importance these days in almost all the developing countries. It was noted from the study that the "Partnership Mode" Islamic banking finance may work perfectly in almost all developing and well as developed countries. Due to the lenders and borrowers joint interest in a particular venture, the very lending process develops a unique lender–borrower network relationship. It is also noted that various micro entrepreneurs regardless of cast creed and religions show their keen interest in borrowing funds from Islamic banks. It is due to the banks' close contact with customers and advice they give to their clienteles. Because the micro-credit is based on "Partnership Financing Mode" of Islamic financing, the lending institutions ensure that micro types of credit given to the needy and experienced rural entrepreneurs are being properly utilized. It can be concluded that once Islamic banks show their interest in investing in a partnership mode of finance, it will not only eliminate the rural poverty, but also be successful in establishing just and balanced social order, free from all kinds of exploitations in the society.

References

Abeyasingha, AIG (1982). Role of appropriate technology and marketing in modernization and improvement of efficiency of small-scale industries. *Small Industry Bulletin for Asia and Pacific*, Vol. 18, pp. 8–10. New York: United Nations.

Aburtani, S (1964). Marketing of small industry products in Asian countries: A re-appraisal of the role of markets. *Small Industry Bulletin for Asia and Pacific*, Vol. 4, pp. 27–29. New York: United Nations.

Agrawal, C (1988). Human resources development for small industries promotion. *Small Industry Bulletin for Asia and Pacific*, Vol. 23, pp. 100–104. New York: United Nations.

Ahmad, K (1981). Economic development in an Islamic framework. In *Islamic Foundation*, Ahmad, K (ed.), pp. 171–188. Leicester:

Ahmad, K (1994). Elimination of RIBA from the economy: Concept and problems. In *Institute of Policy Studies*, Ahmad, K (ed.), pp. 33–53. Islamabad:

Alam, MN (2006). The influences of 'Societal Sector Institutions' in Promoting Lender–Borrower Network Relationships between Islamic Banks and Small and Cottage Industry Owners. *Humanomics*, 22(1/2), 67–83.

Alam, MN (2003). Institutionalization and development of saving habits through Bai-Muajjal Mode of Islamic Banking Finance — A unique means of mobilizing rural savings towards productive sources. *Managerial Finance (UK)*, 29(2/3), 3–22.

Alam, MN (2002). *Financing Small and Cottage Industries in Sudan by Islamic Banks: An Institutional-Network Approach*. Lund, Sweden: University Press.

Alonzo, RP, ES De Dios, and GR Tecson (1992). Role of small and medium scale enterprises in industrial restructuring in The Philippines. *Small Industry Bulletin for Asia and Pacific*, Vol. 26/27, pp. 33–40. New York: United Nations.

Aldrich, HE (1979). *Organizations and Environments.* Englewood Cliffs, NJ: Prentice Hall.

Aldrich, H and DA Whetten (1981). Organisation-set, action sets and network. Making the most of simplicity. In *Handbook of Organizational Design*, Nystrom, PC and WH Starbuk (eds.), Vol. 1, pp. 385–408. Oxford University Press.

AL-Harran, SAS (1992). *Islamic Finance: Partnership Financing.* Kualalampur, Malaysia: Pelanduk Publication.

Anderson, D and F Khambata (1982). Financing small-scale industries and agriculture in developing countries, the merits and limitations of commercial policies. *World Bank Staff Working Paper*, p. 518. Washington, DC: World Bank.

Anderson, BO and ML Carlos (1976). What is social network? Power and control, social structures and their transformation. *Studies in International Sociology.* SAGE.

Ashe, J and CE Corselet (1989). Credit for the poor past activities and future directions for the United Nations development programme. *UNDP Policy Discussion Paper.* New York: United Nations Publications.

Bhende, NM (1978). Small industries development, a tool for social transformation. *Small Industry Bulletin for Asia and Pacific*, Vol. 15, pp. 75–79. New York: United Nations.

Bhattacharyya, M (1988). Planning and development of small-scale industries in India. *Small Industry Bulletin for Asia and Pacific*, No. 23, pp. 88–99. New York: United Nations.

Brodribb, L (1991). Financing for small business. *Small Industry Bulletin for Asia and Pacific*, Vol. 25, pp. 12–15. New York: United Nations.

Brodribb, M (1982). Modernization and improvement of efficiency of small-scale industries. *Small Industry Bulletin for Asia and Pacific*, Vol. 18, pp. 1–3. New York: United Nations.

Easton, G (1992). Industrial networks: A review. In *Industrial Networks. A New View of Reality*, Axelsson, B and G Easton (eds.), pp. 1–36. London: Routhledge.

Easton, G and L Araujo (1991). Language, metaphors and networks. In *Paper presented at the 7th I.M.P. Conference; International Business networks; Evaluation, Structure and management, Uppsala, Sweden.*

ESCAP (1984). On some aspects of the strategies, policies and measures for the development of small-scale industries in Bangladesh, Nepal, and India. *Small Industry Bulletin for Asia and Pacific*, Vol. 19, 37–40. New York: United Nations.

Elg, U and U Johansson (1992). *Dagligföretags Strategiska Agerande: En Analysis or ett Interorganisatoriskt Nätverkperspective.* Lund, Sweden: Lund University Press.

Emerson, RM and SK Cook (1984). Exchange network and the analysis of complex organisation. *Research in the Sociology of Organisation*, 3, 1–30.

Farooque, QH (1958). *Small-Scale and Cottage Industries as a Means of Providing Better Opportunities for Labour in India.* Aligarh, India: Aligarh Muslim University Publication.

Ganguly, AK (1988). Export promotion in the small-scale industry: India. *Small Industry Bulletin for Asia and Pacific*, No. 23, pp. 3–14. New York: United Nations.

Hoong, SS (1989). Action plan for the development of small and medium-scale industries — Malaysia. *Small Industry Bulletin for Asia and Pacific*, Vol. 24, pp. 65–67. New York: United Nations.

Håkansson, H (1993). *Industrial Network and Technological Innovation.* Sweden: Uppsala University (Anders Lundgren), Stockholm School of Economics.

Jansson, H (2002). International business management in emerging markets. Global Institutions and networks. *Book Manuscript.* Sweden: Baltic Business School, University of Kalmar.

Jordon, D (1972). Small scale production — Which way? *Small Industry Bulletin for Asia and Pacific*, Vol. 9, pp. 39–42. New York: United Nations.

Jick, TD (1979). Mixing qualitative and quantitative methods, triangulation in action. *Administrative Science Quarterly*, 24, 602–611.

Khalifa, MU and S Shazali (1988). The experience of Sudanese Islamic Bank in Musharaka Financing. Khartoum, Sudan: SIB Publication.

Khalifa, MU (1992). The bank run alternative to classical modes of finance. In *Paper Presented at the UNDP/ADS –Rural Credit Seminar*, 28–29.

Khalifa, MU and D Hassan (1992). Musharaka finance: An alternative approach to human resource development. In *Paper Prepared for the 4th International Islamic Economic Conference*, Washington DC, pp. 15–17.

Khalifa, MU (1992). Musharaka finance: An optimum risk management approach to small farmers. In *A Paper Prepared for the Risk Management Workshop*, Damascus, Syria, pp. 24–27.

Kundra, JP (1991). Financing small-scale industries in India. *Small Industry Bulletin for Asia and Pacific*, Vol. 25, pp. 3–8. New York: United Nations.

Kuklinski, JH and D Knoke (1988). *Network Analysis Series, Qualitative Application in the Social Sciences*. Beverly Hills: SAGE University Press.

Little, MD (1988). Small manufacturing enterprises and employment in developing countries. *Asian Development Review* 6(2).

Little, MDI, D Mazumdar, and M John Page Jr (1987). Small manufacturing enterprise. New York: Oxford University Press.

Macuja, PC (1981). Small scale industry development in The Philippines. *Small Industry Bulletin for Asia and Pacific*, Vol. 1(21), pp. 182–189. New York: United Nations.

Merriam, SB (1998). *Qualitative Research and Case Study Applications in Education, Revised and Expanded from Case Study Research*. San Francisco: Jossey-Bass Publishers.

Myrdal, G (1968). Asian drama. *An Inquiry into the Poverty of Nations*, p. 537. New York: Pantheon, A Division of Random House.

Nienhaus, V (1983). Profitability of Islamic PLS banks competing with the interest based banks: Problems and prospects. *Journal of Research in Islamic Economics*, 1(1), 38.

Nienhaus, V (1988). The performance of Islamic banks trend and cases. In *Islamic Law and Finance*, Millat, C (ed.), London: Center of Near and Middle Eastern Studies.

Nienhaus, V (1993). Conceptual and economic foundations of Islamic banking. In *Banche islamiche in contesto nonislamico (Islamic Banks in a non Islamic Framework)*. Piccinelli, GM (ed.), Rome: Instituto per l'Oriente.

Ouh, YB (1984). Major policies and measures for promotion of export by small-scale enterprises in The Republic of Korea. *Small Industry Bulletin for Asia and Pacific*, Vol. 19, pp. 29–35. New York: United Nations.

Patton, MQ (1985). Quality in qualitative research: Methodological principles and recent development. *Invited Address to Division of the American Educational Research Association*, Chicago, April.

Rasmussen, J (1988). Goodbye theory — Hello reality? Recent trend in social and regional theory its consequences for network studies in Africa. *Working Paper*, Centre for Development Research (CDR) 88(3), 8(2).

Rooseboom, HJB (1971). Marketing for developing countries. *Small Industry Bulletin for Asia and Pacific*, Vol. 8, pp. 120–121. New York: United Nations.

Rooseboom, HJB (1972). Role of government in promotion of employment in small scale industries. *Small Industry Bulletin for Asia and Pacific*, Vol. 9, pp. 70–72. New York: United Nations.

Rosario, ATD (1964). Problems of marketing in the cottage industries. *Small Industry Bulletin for Asia and Pacific*, Vol. 4, pp. 35–40. New York: United Nations.

Sherman, RR and RB Webb (1988). Qualitative research in education: A focus. In *Qualitative Research in Education: Focus and Methods*, Sherman, RR and RB Webb (eds.), Bristol, PA: Falmer Press.

Siddiqi, GAH (1992). Role of small- and medium-scale enterprises in industrial restructuring in Bangladesh. *Small Industry Bulletin for Asia and Pacific*, Vols. 26/27, pp. 35–40. New York: United Nations.

Singh, BN (1982). Standardization and development of small-scale industries. *Small Industry Bulletin for Asia and Pacific*, Vol. 18, pp. 11–13. New York: United Nations.

Sit, VFS (1991). Export-oriented industrialization of Macau and the role of small and medium size industries. *Small Industry Bulletin for Asia and Pacific*, Vol. 25, pp. 41–50. New York: United Nations.

Solanki, SS and MA Qureshi (1991). Promotion of commercialization of indigenous technology by small entrepreneurs: Role of financial institutions in India. *Small Industry Bulletin for Asia and Pacific*, Vol. 25, pp. 28–40. New York: United Nations.

Subramanian, SK (1992). Role of small- and medium-scale enterprises in industrial restructuring in South Asia. *Small Industry Bulletin for Asia and Pacific*, Vols. 26/27, pp. 59–65. New York: United Nations.

Suhardi, T (1991). Financing small and medium-scale industries in Indonesia. *Small Industry Bulletin for Asia and Pacific*, Vol. 25, pp. 9–11. New York: United Nations.

Sury, MM (1987). Excise concessions to small-scale industries in India: Some issues. *Small Industry Bulletin for Asia and Pacific*, Vol. 22, pp. 92–96. New York: United Nations.

Syed, HR (1984) Development of small-scale industries sector in Pakistan. *Small Industry Bulletin for Asia and Pacific*, Vol. 19, pp. 10–12. New York: United Nations.

Tam, E (1984). The role of joint-venture in the development of small industries in Hong Kong. *Small Industry Bulletin for Asia and Pacific*, Vol. 19, pp. 71–74. New York: United Nations.

Tan, QG (1987). Success stories in small industries: Case studies. *Small Industry Bulletin for Asia and Pacific*, Vol. 22, pp. 85–91. New York: United Nations.

UNIDO (1988). Promotion of small- and medium-scale industries in The Republic of Korea. *Small Industry Bulletin for Asia and Pacific*, Vol. 23, pp. 18–30. New York: UNIDO, United Nations.

UNIDO (1988). Promoting small-scale industry in South-East Asia: Selected support scheme in Malaysia, The Philippines and Thailand. *Small Industry Bulletin for Asia and Pacific*, Vol. 23, pp. 31–40. New York: UNIDO, United Nations.

UNDP (1993). *Human Development Report*, p. 41. New York: Oxford University Press, UNDP.

Veblen, TB (1919). *The place of Science in Modern Civilisation and other Essays*. Huebsch: New York.

Venkataraman, G (1986). Development of small industries in India: Policies, programmes and perspectives. *Small Industry Bulletin for Asia and Pacific*, Vol. 21, pp. 40–49. New York: United Nations.

Vepa, RK (1982). Modernization of small industry with special reference to India. *Small Industry Bulletin for Asia and Pacific*, Vol. 18, pp. 6–7. New York: United Nations.

Vepa, RK (1984). Strategies for small industry development in Japan, China, and India. A comparative study. *Small Industry Bulletin for Asia and Pacific*, Vol. 19, pp. 3–9. New York: United Nations.

Wang, H (1992). Role of small- and medium-scale enterprises in industrial restructuring in China. *Small Industry Bulletin for Asia and Pacific*, Vols. 26/27, pp. 41–45. New York: United Nations.

Whitley, RD (1992a). The comparative analysis of business systems, societies, firms and markets: The social structuring of business systems. *European Business Systems*. Whitley, R (ed.), SAGE.

Whitley, RD (1992b). *Business System in Asia: Firms Markets and Societies*. London: SAGE.

Yin, RK (1994). *Case Study Research, Design and Methods*. Beverly Hills: SAGE Publication.

Yue, CS (1992). Role of small- and medium-scale enterprises in industrial restructuring in Singapore. *Small Industry Bulletin for Asia and Pacific*, Vols. 26/27, pp. 55–58. New York: United Nations.

Chapter 18

CHALLENGES OF INTERNET ADOPTION OF BANKS IN GHANA

NNAMDI O. MADICHIE, ROBERT HINSON,
AND ZUBEIRU SALIFU

Abstract

In recent years, information technology (IT) — notably the Internet — has been largely adopted on a commercial basis by businesses across the globe. This has been the case in both developed and emerging markets spanning various sectors including education (e-learning); retail (e-commerce); and financial services (e-banking). This chapter highlights the opportunities offered by the deployment of IT for the competitiveness of banks — taken from an emerging market perspective.

Introduction

The financial services industry globally is undergoing a rapid transformation mainly on account of increasing deployment of electronic technology in delivering financial services. The rapid adoption of technology has precipitated a host of e-developments such as e-finance, e-money, e-banking, e-brokering, e-insurance, e-exchanges, and even e-supervision in several areas of the financial intermediation process. In the banking industry, especially, the increased use of new information technology (IT) to support the service delivery channels has resulted in increased benefits to both banks and their customers. To the banks, the use of electronic banking technology has greatly influenced their marketing and business strategies. Many banks now consider technology as a route for improving service quality while others consider it as a cost-effective expansion strategy. In addition to these, banks that apply the state-of-the-art technologies in their operations also tend to derive competitive advantages through enhanced brand image and market share, customer satisfaction, and overall business performance.

The numerous advances in Internet technology have brought considerable changes to banking operations in Ghana. A host of banks in the country have introduced a number of technologically backed products and service offerings onto the market in recent years. In addition, almost all the banks in Ghana have invested in expanding and improving their IT systems, which has provided them with the platform for delivering a wide range of value-added products and services — having transformed from manual to automated systems. But does merely having an online presence ensure competitiveness? Is it enough to use e-banking for information dissemination purposes? Should e-banking be more transaction-based in order to affirm the true meaning of online banking?

This chapter addresses these bugging questions in the Ghanaian context by exploring the online activities of "banks in Ghana" (both indigenous and foreign-owned) with the view to gauging their e-banking posture. This is primarily in order to determine the level of Web presence of banks in Ghana and the nature of e-commerce activities dependent on the web site. The rest of the paper is structured as follows. While section two reviews the extant literature on e-commerce, section three provides an overview of the banking industry and electronic banking in Ghana. Section four describes the conceptual framework and the methodology. The findings and analysis are discussed in section five whilst the final section draws the conclusions as well as presents the implications of the study.

Growth of E-Banking in Emerging Markets

There is no consensus on the definition of e-commerce (Kendall *et al.*, 2001; Daniel *et al.*, 2002; Grandon and Pearson, 2004). It depends on what the researchers are investigating. Some authors define e-commerce broadly as any business activities carried out over any electronic media (see, e.g., Wigand, 1997; Timmers, 1999), whereas others (Zwass; 1996; Kalakota and Whinston, 1997; Tassabehji, 2003) see e-commerce as being focused narrowly on certain activities or technological means.

The extant literature on e-commerce documents at least three ways in which e-commerce is perceived. E-commerce is first perceived in terms of Internet application (see, e.g., Mehrtens *et al.*, 2001; Quayle, 2002; Lawson *et al.*, 2003; Brown and Lockett, 2004). Secondly, it is perceived in terms of business activities (Stern and Weitz, 1998; Raymond, 2001; Daniel and Wilson, 2002; Daniel *et al.*, 2002; Daniel, 2003); and finally the mix of

Internet applications and business activities (e.g., Kendall *et al.*, 2001; Beveren and Thomson, 2002; Fillis *et al.*, 2004). Recently, however, the most dominant definition of e-commerce is basically conducting business activities over the Internet (see Fig. 18.1). This study adopts Zwass's (1996) definition of e-commerce as "...sharing of business information, maintaining business relationships, and conducting business transactions by means of Internet-based technology."

The term "internet banking" can also be used to describe a situation, where banks' customers conduct their banking transactions on the Internet. In the contemporary context, this mainly not only implies usage of personal computers or laptops, but also allows for other possible devices such as mobile phones and digital TVs amongst others — for accessing Internet branches — a platform where the transactions are made (Sayar and Wolfe, 2007, p. 123). Internet banking is attractive for customers as it makes it possible to conduct banking transactions anytime and anywhere, faster and with lower fees compared to using traditional bank branches. Despite all the apparent advantages for customers, adoption rates vary across countries. In general, it can be said that not as many customers as banks would desire use Internet banking services — with the exception of the Scandinavian countries.

Core Day-to-Day Banking Needs	Nineteen Products and Services
Account Management	• Current account • Online banking • Call centre
Cash Utilisation	• Deposit at desk (counter services) • Deposit at ATM • Withdrawal at desk • Withdrawal at bank's ATM • Withdrawal at other banks' ATM networks
Exceptions Handling	• Debit card stop payment • Cheque stop payment • Document search • Banker's draft
Payments	• Cheque • Debit card • Credit card • Internal wire transfer • External wire transfer • Standing order (fixed amount transfer) • Direct debit

Figure 18.1. E-commerce in the retail banking.

Source: Adapted from *World Retail Banking Report* (2006, p. 6).

According to a Euro barometer survey (2002), Internet banking is the sixth application in order of importance of use, preceded by e-mail and online searches for information on news/topics, travel, training/education and health (see Sayar and Wolfe, 2007, pp. 123, 124).

Based on research of Turkish Internet banking users, Akinci *et al.* (2004) found that the selection of an Internet banking service provider is effected by security, reliability, and privacy. They identify three segments underlying the selection of the bank (Sayar and Wolfe, 2007, p. 125): first, speed seekers — who view download speed, transaction speed, user-friendliness of the site, and privacy; second, cautious users — who value the reliability of the bank, security of the Internet branch, variety of services offered and loyalty; and finally, exposure users — who are more open to influence of external factors like advertising and suggestions of others.

Functionality refers to the range of online services offered. Functions provided through Internet branches have been increasing in number over time in all countries. Moreover, the Internet enables new functions that are unique to Internet branches, like personalized financial information menus, e-mail alerts, electronic commerce, real-time brokerage and third-party services like management of utility bills and tax payments (Centeno, 2004). Diniz *et al.* (2005) evaluate functionality of a web site by categorizing it along the lines outlined in Table 18.1.

Turkish banks offer a wider range of services from their internet branches compared to British banks, despite the fact that the United Kingdom has a more favorable environment for Internet banking in terms of its banking sector

Table 18.1.   Diniz model of functionality.

Functionality	Subdimensions of functionality		
	Basic	Intermediate	Advanced
1. Dissemination	News Institutional Promotion Publications	Search tool Downloadable documents and forms Links	Information customizing Use of audio-visual resources
2. Transaction	Requests Sign up	Inquiries Payments	Online services delivery New payment means
3. Relationship	E-mail forms	Cookies calculators	Chat forum

Source: Adapted from Sayar and Wolfe (2007, pp. 129, 130).

and technological infrastructure. Second, the main reasons for this are advanced to be the different banking cultures of two countries and the technology appetite of Turkish banks. Finally, a difference is observed in the approaches of banks toward the issue of "security," where Turkish banks rely on technology to avoid fraud and British banks prefer more conventional methods to discourage it. They concluded that "despite all the advantages a bank enjoys by offering Internet banking services, the decision of customers to use these services depends primarily on their perceptions, especially those related to security and ease-of-use issues". Figure 18.1 shows E-commerce activities in the banking sector.

In his survey of US banks web sites also, Diniz (1998) split the functionality of the web sites in such a way as to provide some insight on three different opportunities that the technology could bring to banks, namely: (1) information delivery, (2) transaction, and (3) customer relationship. With 121 banks selected from across the United States that were running a web site, the study revealed that bigger banks were doing better at the basic and intermediary levels, and many banks were offering transaction services at the advanced level. He noted that banks have improved in their web sites and that they are only in the beginning in terms of functionality.

According to Shuman (1998), the Federal Reserve documented more than 63 billion consumer and commercial paper cheques to have been written in 1996 in the United States alone. He argues further that, assuming there were 1.5 additional back office transactions per cheque, a total of more than 157 billion non-cash paper-based transactions took place in 1996. This presents the web Banking advocates with compelling evidence as to its potentials and viability. Kurtas (2000) reported that the United States used their web sites not only for the provision of classical operations such as fund transfer or account details, but also to provide stock trading in the world markets, financial calculators, investment advice, and bill payments. US banks are now using very high technology in encryption in order to provide safety and privacy. They have reached a stage where a number of banks are operating entirely online without any need for physical location or branches. He therefore attributed a set of factors as hindering web-banking applications. These included computer piracy and general security issues, telecommunication infrastructure, and possible social implications, such as downsizing and lay offs.

Corbitt and Thanasankit (2002) argued that if e-commerce is crucial for economic success, businesses not involved in e-commerce would be left behind in the global marketplace. Through the adoption of e-commerce, small companies can rival large organizations because of the equal access provided by the Internet. Chung and Paynter (2002) surveyed the state of Internet banking in New Zealand by examining the web sites of seven online banks using a tailored electronic-commerce model. The results revealed that most of the banks had up-to-date information on their web sites and identified security and complication of Internet banking as some of the inhibiting factors. Ovia (2003) also argued that the hype of e-commerce, e-banking, and e-everything is gradually being embraced by Nigerian financial institutions who are poised to be in the vanguard of narrowing the digital divide.

According to Ezeoha (2005), the Central Bank of Nigeria (CBN) in its survey on the extent of e-banking adoption by Nigerian banks in September 2002, a period prior to the consolidation of the sector, found that of the 89 licensed banks in the country, only 17 offered Internet banking, 24 offered basic telephone banking, seven had automated teller machines (ATM) services while 13 of the banks were offered other forms of e-banking. This implies that as of then, 19.1% of the banks were offering Internet banking, signifying that Internet banking was yet to take center stage despite its widely acclaimed benefits against the traditional branch banking practice. Madichie (2007) argued, however, that post-consolidation of the Nigerian banking industry had not yet resulted in the provision of expected service improvements if Internet banking provision was used as a yardstick.

Taking the position of financial services of South African firms, Okeahalam (2007, p. 923) observed that "the level of access to services is inadequate, does not meet the needs of consumers, and is a symptom of market power and the absence of a competitive market in retail banking." His findings suggest that there is a need for greater regulatory attention on the enhancement of consumer welfare in the retail-banking sector in South Africa (Okeahalam, 2007, p. 938). The role of proactive e-banking in assuring enhanced consumer welfare cannot, therefore, be overemphasized.

From the Arab world perspective, Jarrah (1999) reported that Arab electronic shoppers spent approximately 95 million US dollars in April 1998 making payments mainly by credit cards (82%), followed by bank transfers (11%), cash upon delivery (9%), and cheques (3%). Seventy-eight percent of online shoppers said they believed fax transmission of private financial information was secure enough, versus telephone at 70%, and e-mail at confidence of 50%. The evidence presented in his study suggests that opportunities are available to banks to strengthen their online presence and assure both security and privacy of their operations to customers.

However, Al-Sabbagh and Molla (2004) explored the drivers and inhibitors of customers' Internet banking adoption in the Sultanate of Oman and found only two banks offering Internet banking services. They however noted that members of banks in Oman were considering going online, as online banking was still reportedly in its infancy at the time. In a related study on the United Arab Emirates (UAE), Awamleh and Fernandes (2005) adopted the Diniz model in their evaluation of the web sites of both domestic and foreign banks. The study analyzed the web sites of banks on the UAE using the Diniz model to access the extent of adoption of Internet banking. The results revealed that Internet banking in the UAE was also very much in its infancy. They therefore emphasized the need for proper development in the design, infrastructure, and interface of Internet banking in the UAE to be established in order for customers to be encouraged to take full advantage of this technology.

Blankson *et al.* (2007) investigated bank choice/selection criteria in a range of cultural settings using the United States, Taiwan, and Ghana in order to understand international consumers' selection criteria of banks. In their paper, they noted "...the scarce stream of empirical studies dealing with consumers' selection of banks in liberalized developing nations despite the fact that several governments in these economies were encouraging bank savings, channelling college students' loans through bank accounts and proactively attracting global banks to establish branches in their countries."

While they argued that their study complemented the extant literature dealing with consumers' selection of banks, Blankson *et al.* (2007) admitted that their study was limited by the fact that it was "...based on the college student cohort and thus the results do not represent the public. This poses generalizability questions without further replications and validations. This study did not examine whether there were consumers' switching behaviours involving banks."

Tang *et al.* (2007) on a separate level examined the sociodemographic and economic variables impact on the probability of purchasing financial products in a generic sense. They argued that there was relatively little empirical research to demonstrate an understanding of how the underlying economy affected customers' subsequent financial product purchase behaviors. The results show that the external economic environment was an extremely important influence in driving customers' financial products purchasing behaviors. This external environment is consistent with allusions to industry norm, which include nature of competition and the consumer perception of quality financial service offering. However, their study suffers some limitations as it essentially considered economic conditions and sociodemographic variables in modeling the long-run purchase behavior of customers for insurance and savings products (taken from a large dataset of a major insurance company.) It is also one of the first papers to make a detailed comparison between the semi-parametric and parametric proportional hazard models in the bank marketing area (Tang *et al.*, 2007).

From the brief review of the literature, it has become rather clear that banks the world over have made major strides on the adoption of e-banking or online banking to varying degrees of success. This confirms the trend in the global financial services industry, a place where Ghanaian banks should be a key part.

The Banking Industry in Ghana

The banking industry is a segment of Ghana's overall financial system, which comprises commercial banks, insurance companies, discount houses, leasing companies, savings and loans associations, credit unions, and a stock exchange. The banking system is by far the largest component of the financial system. It is the engine around which the whole financial system revolves. Ghana's banking system consists of the Central Bank, which has overall supervisory and regulatory authority of the sector. Commercial banks are the major players in the sector and rural banks account for just about 5% of assets of the banking system. There are currently 23 banks operating in Ghana. Out of which six are publicly held and traded on the Ghana Stock Exchange whilst the remaining are unlisted (Table 18.2). The banking industry in Ghana has undergone several structural changes as a result of a series of reforms introduced by the Central Bank. These reforms have not only brought some efficiency and vibrancy into the sector, but have also rekindled competition in the sector.

Some of the key reforms that were implemented in the sector include the abolition of the secondary reserves requirement in 2006 by the Central Bank, which was intended to free more resources to the private sector; the replacement of the Bank of Ghana Law of 1992 (PNDCL 291) by the Banking Act 2004 (Act 673), which has strengthened the Bank of Ghana in its regulatory and supervisory functions as well as introduction of the Universal Banking Business License (UBBL) in 2003 which has deepened competition within the industry. For instance, to operate under the UBBL, existing banks must have a minimum net worth (excluding statutory reserves) of ¢70 billion or US$714,000 (based on December 2007 Interbank rate of 1353US$ = ¢9,797.74) — and new banks should have a paid-up capital of ¢70 billion before they commence operations. The introduction of the UBBL concept by the Central Bank has removed the segmentation of banks into

Table 18.2.   Banks in Ghana.

Bank name	2007 ranking*	Availability of online banking transaction	Indigenous or multinational
1. Ghana Commercial Bank^c	1	N	I
2. Standard Chartered Bank (Ghana) Ltd.^c	2	N	M
3. Barclays Bank (Ghana) Ltd.	3	N	M
4. Agricultural Development Bank	4	Y	I
5. Cuban Ghana	5	Y	M
6. Social Security Bank (SG-SSB) Ltd.^c	6	N	M
7. Merchant Bank (Ghana) Ltd.	7	N	I
8. National Investment Bank	8	N	I
9. Cal Bank (Ghana) Ltd.^c	9	N	I
10. Prudential Bank (Ghana) Ltd.	10	N	I
11. The Trust Bank Ltd.^c	11	Y	I
12. First Atlantic Merchant Bank Ltd.	12	N	I
13. HFC Bank Ghana	13	N	I
14. Stanbic	14	N	M
15. International Commercial Bank (Ghana) Ltd.	15	N	M
16. Amalgamated Bank	16	N	M
17. Unibank	17	N	I
18. BPI Bank	18	N	M
19. Zenith Bank	19	N	M
20. Guaranty Trust Bank (Ghana) Ltd.	20	N	M
21. Fidelity Bank	**U	N	I
22. Intercontinental Bank	**U	Y	M
23. UBA	**U	N	M

*The ranking. *Ranking based* in terms of the overall industry — *PWC Banking Survey 2007*.
** U-Bank did not participate in the survey by PWC.
^cListed on the Ghana Stock Exchange.
Source: Author's compilation.

commercial, development, and merchant banks. With the removal of these delineations, a bank can compete in any segment of the market after securing the license.

The Central Bank in Ghana also recently proposed an increase in the minimum capitalization threshold from ¢70 billion to between ¢500 billion and ¢600 billion (US$51 and US$61.2 million) within the next 1 year. Under the new proposition, banks are required to submit their capitalization plans to the Central Bank by June 2008. The increase in the stated capital is intended to position financial institutions adequately to support an expansion in banking activities and its attendant increase in exposures and other risks. The higher capital base is also to support the remarkable increase in credit creation and hence the loan book in the banking system. These reforms have contributed variously to strengthening structured competition in the sector. Other factors that have accentuated this intense competition among the banks for banking business include the squeezing margins in the industry in a period of a stable macroeconomic environment and the influx of foreign banks especially from Nigeria to Ghana.

The cumulative impact of all these factors is that banks in Ghana can no longer afford to be complacent with their market share. Most of them are beginning to shift their attention to non-price variables such as differentiating their product and service offerings in order to charge premium rates; increasing their deployment of electronic banking technology in order to meet the growing sophistication of their clientele as well as creating value for their shareholders. The change in strategic focus in the industry is expected to further intensify ccompetition within the industry.

Internet Adoption Levels of Banks in Ghana

Methodology

This methodology is based on a survey of web sites of banks in Ghana as a proxy for their e-commerce readiness. In this study, content analyses of the web site message itself, not the communicator or the audience was employed (Salam *et al.*, 1998). This method is useful for examining trends and patterns in web sites (Steve, 2001). It involves identifying and counting certain activities or attributes in the web sites (Riley *et al.*, 2000), which provide room for inferences and subsequently enables data corroboration using other methods of analysis (Holsti, 1969).

In addition, we adopted other approaches from previous studies, particularly on locating company web site addresses, determining web site operability, and identifying types of e-commerce activities (Soh *et al.*, 1997; Salam *et al.*, 1998; Laudon and Traver, 2002; Adham and Ahmad, 2005). It is important to emphasize that this study looked only at the web sites of banks operating in Ghana (informational sense) and commerce activities dependent on the web sites (i.e., real transactions). We considered all the 23 banks currently operating in Ghana. First, all web sites were checked to ensure the address indicated in the database of banks in Ghana was correct or really belonged to the bank. The web sites of the selected banks were then identified and tested several times for operability (whether they had downloading problems, etc.).

In locating the web site addresses of the banks as well as determining their operability, we adopted some of the steps of Adham and Ahmad (2005), which included: (1) clicking on the hyperlinks provided on the database of the Ghana Association of Bankers; and (2) using the search function on Web sites such as Google (www.google.com); click Afrique (http://www.clickafrique.com), and click-on-Ghana (http://clickonghana.com) to confirm the banks' web presence.

The contents of all operable web sites were then examined for evidence of e-commerce activities. If a listing of the bank was not found through any of these approaches, the conclusion was that the bank did not operate a web site.

Discussion

From our investigation of the 23 commercial banks currently operating in Ghana, we noticed that only one bank (a subsidiary of a foreign bank) did not seem to maintain a specialized and functioning web site for its local operations. The remaining 22 banks maintained specialized and seemingly well functioning web sites (Table 18.3). This clearly indicates that nearly 96% of banks in Ghana maintain a web site for their operations. The result is not surprising given that a majority of the banks consider having an online presence — a form of abolishing geographic and time barriers, improving communication with customers, investors and employees as well as creating new ways of doing business. But is it enough to just have an online presence without any real commercial/ business activity?

All functioning web sites of the selected banks were analyzed to determine their e-commerce activities (Table 18.3). It is clear that there is a 100% record for banks (i.e., all banks evaluated) having a web presence and providing company and product information, branch location details, and contact addresses on their websites (i.e., using their online presence for information dissemination purposes only). However, when it came to transactional e-banking, only a few banks seemed to conduct transactions such as processing letters of credit and funds transfer — online. For the limited number that offered some form of this notable online banking, customers were only able to view their accounts, access account(s) from any location, view and verify transactions on account(s), check their account balances, reconcile entries in account with their own records, track inflows and outflows, as well as monitor uncredited and unpresented cheques.

Although such access gave customers' real-time access to their accounts enabling them to remain up-to-date with their accounts, they are not

Table 18.3.   Website features.

Web site features	Number of banks	Percent of total
Company address and location	22	100
Phone number and other contact details	22	100
Branch locations	22	100
Details of products and services	22	100
Corporate news (Annual Reports, new branches, etc.)	22	100
Document downloads	17	77.3
Cash machine locations	16	72.7
Web master e-mail	15	68.2
Site search facility	15	68.2
Customer feedback	11	50.0
Online requests for statement of accounts	9	40.9
Online account opening services	8	36.4
Online enquiries (exchange rate and loans)	8	36.4
Online investment application service	3	13.6
Electronic card request	3	13.6
Utilities (loan calculator, currency converter)	2	9.1
Letters of credit	0	0
Funds transfer	0	0
Any interactive communication	0	0

Source: Authors' compilation.

transactional services (Diniz *et al.*, 2005), as customers are still unable to do transactions from the comfort of their homes and offices. Indeed, no Ghanaian bank offers any form of transactional e-banking whether its electronic funds transfer, processing letters of credit or transacting other forms of e-banking. It is persuasive to argue, therefore, that most banks in Ghana, despite their online presence, merely use this e-presence to disseminate corporate information as well as information on products and services as highlighted in Table 18.1. These findings are similar to those in other studies on the variation IT adoption for business activities (Beveren and Thomson, 2002; Drew, 2003; Brown and Lockett, 2004; Fillis *et al.*, 2004).

Another common feature on the web site of banks in Ghana is document downloads, where various application forms or documents are posted. However, the banks do not make adequate provision for these application forms to be completed and submitted online. In most cases, customers are only able to download and manually complete these forms for onward submission to the banks. Indeed, one important point to note from this study is the shocking revelation that no Ghanaian bank seems to conduct any banking transactions whether it is fund transfer, processing letters of credit, or trans-acting other forms of banking business online. Only a limited number of the banks allowed their customers to undertake core day-to-day banking services which include account management (e.g., online banking) and means of payment such as wire transfer (Capgemini, ING and EFMA, 2006).

Implications for Managers

The results from our study are quite revealing. Even though banks in other developed countries are increasingly viewing e-banking as a viable option for their international competitiveness, banks in Ghana are still "toying with the possibilities". The ability of banks to capitalize on the opportunities being offered by e-banking will not only enhance their bottom line, but also help in making their financial services cost effective, competitive, and more accessible for customers. This would allow the banks to satisfy the needs of their customers (irrespective of their networth), reduce the need for "manned" branches, and thus curtail costs associated with branch expansion. There is therefore the need for banks in Ghana to leverage their online presence from an "information platform" to a more robust 'transactional medium' — considering the growth in number of Internet users as well as the vast opportunities associated with this "real" e-banking activity.

Further, all the major banks have emphasized e-business as the core strategy that would underlie their future plans. The adoption of state-of-the-art technology to deliver banking services represents a significant departure from the manual processes that were in operation in the 1980s. This apparent shift in strategic focus is aimed at enabling them catch up with global developments and improve the quality of their service delivery. Some of the notable e-banking delivery channels banks have deployed in Ghana include e-banking, use of Automated Teller Machines (ATMs), Telephone banking, Points of sale terminals, electronic funds transfer, and lately mobile banking. Each of these delivery channels has its advantages. Web banking has proven to be a very attractive choice. It is fast, economical, and flexible. Through the web, both corporate and retail customers of a bank are able to manage their accounts and do their banking operations. Web banking can also allow a relatively small company to structure and issue basic financial tools such as letters of credit. Other companies are attracted to online banking because it enables them to monitor their accounts on a 24-h basis.

In addition, some banks allow their corporate clients to invest overnight funds through the web. This can generate substantial profits for a company that has significant, but temporarily idle cash funds (Martin, 1998). According to

Peffers (1991), banks that were early adopters of ATMs gained significantly more than later adopters, and that the use of even a single information technology application could affect a wide range of performance variables. IT also impacts organizations in other ways, such as changing the decision structure of banks to better deal with competition (Clark, 1989). Future research should focus on the barriers to e-commerce adoption by banks in Ghana.

References

Adham, KA and M Ahmad (2005). Adoption of website and e-commerce technology among Malaysian public companies. *Industrial Management and Data Systems*, 105(9), 1172–1187.

Al-Sabbagh, I and A Molla (2004). Adoption and use of Internet banking in the Sultanate of Oman: An exploratory study. *Journal of Internet Banking and Commerce*, 2.

Awamleh, R and C Fernandes (2005). Internet banking: An empirical investigation into the extent of adoption by banks and the determinants of customer satisfaction in the United Arab Emirates. *Journal of Internet Banking and Commerce*, 10(1).

Beveren, JV and H Thomson (2002). The use of electronic commerce by SMEs in Victoria, Australia. *Journal of Small Business Management*, 40(3), 250–254.

Blankson, C, J Cheng, and N Spears (2007). Determinants of banks selection in USA, Taiwan and Ghana. *International Journal of Bank Marketing*, 25(7), 469–489.

Brown, DH and D Lockett (2004). Potential of critical e-applications for engaging SMEs in e-business: A provider perspective. *European Journal of Information Systems*, 13, 21–34.

Capgemini, ING and EFMA (2006). World retail banking report. *Joint report by the Capgemini Group, The ING global financial services group, and the European Financial Management & Marketing Association (EFMA)*.

Centeno, C (2004). Adoption of Internet services in the acceding and candidate countries, lessons from the Internet banking case. *Telematics and Informatics*, 21(4), 293–315.

Chung, W and J Paynter (2002). An evaluation of Internet banking in New Zealand. *Proceedings of the 35th Hawaii International Conference in System Sciences. IEEE Hawaii*, pp. 1–9.

Clark, R (1989). Congruence between strategy, IT, and decision making at the unit level: A comparison of U.S.A and Canadian Retail Banks. *Unpublished dissertation, University of Massachusetts*.

Corbitt, BJ and T Thanasankit (2002). Acceptance and leadership: Hegemonies of e-commerce policy perspectives. *Prometheus*, 20(1), 39–57.

Daniel, E (2003). An exploration of the inside-out model: E-commerce integration in UK SMEs. *Journal of Small Business and Enterprise Development*, 10(3), 233–249.

Daniel, E and H Wilson (2002). Adoption intentions and benefits realised: A study of e-commerce in UK SMEs. *Journal of Small Business and Enterprise Development*, 9(4), 331–348.

Daniel, E, H Wilson, and A Myers (2002). Adoption of e-commerce by SMEs in the UK. *International Small Business Journal*, 20(3), 253–270.

Diniz, E, RM Poro, and A Tomi (2005). Internet banking in Brazil: Evaluation of functionality, reliability and usability. *The Electronic Journal of Information Systems Evaluation*, 8(1), 41–50.

Diniz, E (1998). Web banking in USA. *Journal of Internet Banking and Commerce*, 3(2).

Drew, S (2003). Strategic uses of e-commerce in the East of England. *European Management Journal*, 21(1), 79–88.

Durkin, M (2007). On the role of bank staff in online customer purchase. *Marketing Intelligence & Planning*, 25(1), 82–97.

Ezeoha, AE (2005). Regulating Internet banking in Nigeria, problem and challenges — Part 1. *Journal of Internet Banking and Commerce*, 10(3).

Fillis, I, U Johansson, and B Wagner (2004). Factors impacting on e-business adoption and development in the smaller firm. *International Journal of Entrepreneurial Behavior & Research*, 10(3), 178–191.

Grandon, EE and JM Pearson (2004). Electronic commerce adoption: An empirical study of small and medium US businesses. *Information and Management*, 42(1), 197–216.

Holsti, OR (1969). *Content Analysis for the Social Sciences and Humanities*. Reading, MA: Addison-Wesley.

Jarrah, F (1999). Internet shoppers in the Arab world spend US$ 95 million. www.dit.net/itnews/newsjune99/newsjune22.html.

Kalakota, R and AB Whinston (1997). *Electronic Commerce: A Manager's Guide'*. Upper Saddle River, NJ.: Addison-Wesley.

Kendall, JD, LL Tung, KH Chua, CHD Ng, and SM Tan (2001). Receptivity of Singapore's SMEs to electronic commerce adoption. *Journal of Strategic Information Systems*, 10, 223–242.

Kurtas, A (2000). Analytical study of investment opportunities in direct and Internet banking (Translated). Arab Banks Union Magazine, June 2000, 35.

Laudon, KC and CG Traver (2002). *E-Commerce: Business, Technology and Society*. Boston: Addison-Wesley Books.

Lawson, R, C Alcock, J Cooper, and L Burgess (2003). Factor affecting adoption of electronic Commerce by SMEs: An Australian study. *Journal of Small Business and Enterprise Development*, 10(3), 265–276.

Madichie, N (2007). The Nigerian banking recapitalisation experiment: Corporate governance faux pas? In *Competitive paper presented at the Academy of International Business (AIB) Conference*. UK & Ireland: King's College London, April 13–15.

Martin, J (1998). Say goodbye to bankers' hours. *Management Review*, 87(1), 33.

Mehrtens, J, PB Cragg, and AM Mills (2001). A model of Internet adoption by SMEs. *Information & Management*, 39(3), 165–176.

Okeahalam, C (2007). Economics of access in a developing country: An analysis of firm-conduct in financial services. *International Journal of Social Economics*, 34(12), 923–942.

Ovia, J (2003). Internet banking: Practices and potentials in Nigeria. In *A Paper at the Conference Organized by the Institute of Chartered Accountants of Nigeria (ICAN)*. Lagos, September 5.

Peffers, KG (1991). IT impact on performance: An investigation on investment and ATMs. Unpublished dissertation, Purdue University, USA.

Quayle, M (2002). E-commerce: The challenge for UK SMEs in the twenty-first century. *International Journal of Operations and Production Management*, 22(10), 1148–1161.

Raymond, L (2001). Determinants of Web site implementation in small businesses. *Internet Research: Electronic Networking Applications and Policy*, 11(5), 411–422.

Riley, M, RC Wood, MA Clark, E Wilkie, and E Szivas (2000). *Researching and Writing Dissertations in Business Management*. Croatia: Thomson Learning.

Salam, AF, HR Rao, and CC Pegels (1998). Content of corporate Web pages as advertising media. *Communication of the ACM*, 41(3), 76–77.

Sayar, C and S Wolfe (2007). Internet banking market performance: Turkey versus the UK. *International Journal of Bank Marketing*, 25(3), 122–141.

Shuman, JR (1998). Banking services harness technology and come up with a wining business strategy which continues to serve public interest. *Business America*, 119(1), 27.

Soh, C, M Quee, G Fong, D Chew, and E Reid (1997). The use of the Internet for business: The experience of early adopters in Singapore. *Internet Research: Electronic Network Application and Policy*, 7(3), 217–228.

Stern, LW and BA Weitz (1998). The revolution in distribution: Challenges and opportunities. *Long Range Planning*, 4(6), 813–821.

Steve, S (2001). An overview of content analysis. *Practical Assessment, Research and Evaluation*, 7(17).

Tang, L, L Thomas, S Thomas, and JF Bozzetto (2007). It's the economy stupid: Modelling financial product purchases. *International Journal of Bank Marketing*, 25(1), 22–38.

Tassabehji, R (2003). *Applying E-Commerce in Business*. London: SAGE Publication Ltd.

Timmers, P (1999). *Electronic Commerce: Strategies and Models for B2B Trading*. New York: Wiley.

Wigand, RT (1997). Electronic commerce: Definition, theory and context. *The Information Society*, 13(1), 1–16.

Zwass, V (1996). Electronic commerce: Structures and issues. *International Journal of Electronic Commerce*, 1(1), 1–23.

Part V

MIDDLE EAST

Chapter 19

DOES THE RELIGIOUS NATURE OF ORGANIZATIONS AFFECT PERFORMANCE MEASUREMENT? A CASE OF GCC BANKS

EHAB K. A. MOHAMED AND MOSTAQ M. HUSSAIN

Abstract

Management accounting performance measurement (PM) practices in manufacturing industry are well reported, but little is known about PM practices in financial services industry (FSI) and almost nothing is reported regarding Islamic FSI. This research attempts to study the multidimensional PM practices in Islamic FSI. Several Islamic financial institutions have been studied in the Gulf Cooperation Council (GCC) countries in order to explore the effect of the nature of organization in PM practices. Special emphasis is given on non-financial PM practices that conform the principles of Shariah in different type and size of Islamic FSI in different macroenvironment in GCC countries. As it is known that the objective of Islamic FSI is not only to maximize profit, but also to improve the socioeconomic condition of the community in order to conform the principles of Shariah, which actively advocates non-profit activities that make a positive contribution toward the needy and poor, and promote welfare programs that may or may not be financially viable. This study reveals that management accounting plays a moderate role in measuring both financial and non-financial performances in the Islamic FSI in GCC countries. However, research results indicate that the nature and characteristics of organization (Islamic FSI) do not have great impact on PM practices though it is generally held belief that Islamic FSI should conform the principles of Shariah.

According to research findings, some research directions are given at the end of this chapter.

Introduction

Multidimensional aspects of management accounting (MA) measures are gaining increasing importance in both academic and practitioner literature and in real-life situations. Much has been written about the need for multidimensional performance measures, but comparatively little is known about the role of MA in non-financial performance measurement (PM) in services, specially in financial services industry (FSI) and even very little is known about such practices in emerging markets. There has been so far not any single report available on the practices of non-financial PM in Islamic FSI though Islamic FSI has been growing its size and has reached to a considerable maturity in the FSI in many countries. This study aims to investigate multidimensional PM practices, in particular, nature and occurrence of Islamic FSI in some Gulf Cooperation Council (GCC) countries.

This chapter is organized as follows: the next section briefly reviews the literature as a means of stating the importance of multidimensional PM and its current problem in Islamic FSI, followed by the research methodology. The final section reports on the practices of MA in multidimensional PM practices in Islamic FSI in GCC countries along with summary and conclusion.

Background to the Study

The PM has traditionally been used as a control means to assess whether organizations have met their financial goals in hierarchical manufacturing organizations (Nanni *et al.*, 1990). However, contemporary business environments have led organizations to change their traditional management control patterns (Otley, 1994). The rapid globalization, intense competition, growth of the financial industry, and a heightened need for consistent accounting information systems have been of an increasing interest in the development of alternative approaches to MA and PM systems. The dynamically changing environment, in which organizations operate, has rendered it essential for organizations to modify their strategies in order to respond to the rapidly changing environment. A growing realization of the limitations of traditional MA systems has led to the examinations of multidimensional PM practices such as non-financial techniques. One of the major developments in the area of PM during this period was Kaplan and Norton's (1992) Balanced Scorecard that concentrates not only on financial performance measures, but also on non-financial measures.

MA helps firms enhance cross-functional communication, integration, and cooperation in order to help organizations' management face the deep competitive changes that have occurred in the last decades and carry out the customer orientation needed. In such a need, the scope of MA has widened toward effectiveness, control, market analysis, quality assessment, customer satisfaction empowerment, and competitive status management (Ostinelli and Toscano, 1994; Nanni *et al.*, 1992), among many others.

Several studies have found that traditional financial-orientated PM models were becoming increasingly inadequate in meeting the complex and competitive nature of the new business environment (Kaplan, 1983, 1984; Bromwich and Bhimani, 1989; Nanni *et al.*, 1990; Govindarajan and Shank, 1992; Lee, 1992; Kaplan and Norton, 1992; Neely *et al.*, 1995; Shields, 1997; Sim and Koh, 2001; Anderson and McAdam, 2004; Neely, 2005; Gomes *et al.*, 2006). The needs for multidimensional performance measures that focus on different dimensions, both financial and non-financial, have been demonstrated in several studies (Johnson and Kaplan, 1987; Fitzgerald *et al.*, 1991; Eccles *et al.*, 1992; Govindarajan and Shank, 1992; Kaplan and Norton, 1992; Euske *et al.*, 1993; Gregory, 1993; Henri, 2004; Powell, 2004; Najmi *et al.*, 2005). Few studies have examined management's experience regarding the success of using PM initiatives (Bourne *et al.*, 2002; Halachmi, 2002; Tangen, 2004; Cinquini and Mitchell, 2005). It was suggested that the use of traditional performance measures such as return on investment or net earning distracts from non-financial factors such as efficiency and effectiveness, productivity, product quality, market share, customer satisfaction, employee satisfaction, and so on. At the same time the inadequacy of the performance measures based on traditional MA methods has highlighted the need for more advanced PM systems. Hence, it was recommended by Lynch and Cross (1991), Kaplan and Norton (1996, 2001) and Otely (1999) that multidimensional performance measures should lead to appropriate actions in supplementing or replacing the traditional techniques.

Therefore, non-financial PM has received considerable attention from contemporary MA scholars. There is a view that non-financial measures are needed as a predictor of an organization's long-term performance as they help managers monitor and assess their firm's progress toward strategic goals and objectives (Kaplan and Norton, 1996, 2001). There are several studies .

that have dealt with non-financial performance measures without discussing the critical issues of the actual practices of non-financial PM (Hiromoto, 1988; Turney, 1991; Ezzamel, 1992; Scapens, 1997). Other studies recognize the impact of organizational and strategic change on MA and PM (Neely *et al.*, 2000; Kennerley and Neely, 2002; Rouse and Putterill, 2003; Anderson and McAdam, 2005; Hassan, 2005).

Furthermore, according to Acton and Cotton (1997), there should be no fundamental difference between analyzing the costs for manufacturing support departments and the costs for the support activities of service organizations. However, Modell (1996) investigates the accounting control implications of various characteristically perceived organizations, based on the framework of Ansari (1977), in order to distinguish services from manufacturing. Modell also constitutes a framework for further research into the relative balance between formal and informal control and how this relates to the various service characteristics. Euske *et al.* (1993) provide a comprehensive approach for developing and applying activity-based PM system to different services processes within organizations; they discuss the different applicability of services processes, support as well as operational, from manufacturing organizations. Likewise, other studies (Hussain and Kock, 1994; Hussain and Gunasekaran, 2001) discuss the need for ABC in service organizations and, particularly, in the financial industry.

The nature and characteristics of the business, that is, size, kind and type, determine the range of possible change and adaptation to the economic climate (Thompson, 1967; Long, 1995; Karimi *et al.*, 1996). Fitzgerald *et al.* (1991) classify three service process types. According to Miles and Sweeting (1988), service costing differs from one type to another. Brignall *et al.* (1991) found that cost traceability varies systematically, as does the PM system, in the three different service process/types (mass, shop, and professional). Brignall (1997) argues that, on the basis of the Process Type Theory of Silvestro *et al.* (1992) and Fitzgerald *et al.* (1991), business strategy should link with effective PM systems. Moreover, some studies drew relationships between external environmental factors and managers' need for financial and non-financial information (Modell 1995, 1996; Brignall *et al.*, 1992; Brignall and Modell 2000; Cobb *et al.*, 1995).

The service production process of banks differs from other service types and substantially diverges from manufacturing organizations because of obvious factors such as the indispensability of customers to the organizations' production process (Milles and Morris, 1986), strict governing by the central bank (CB), the size of the organization, and the exact line of business they are in, among others. Hence, it is more difficult to identify non-financial indicators in services organizations as opposed to their manufacturing counterparts. Thus, many service organizations especially banks find it harder to incorporate customer opinions — non-financial Indicators — into service production process in order to enhance the quality due to its intangible and transistor nature. Moreover, although it is harder to incorporate non-financial MA measures in service companies, Cobb *et al.* (1995) demonstrated that activities, like the monitoring of bad loans, initiated significant changes in MA systems.

Considering the strong competition faced by banks and the uncertain economic conditions that slow down banks' operation faster than other business management are forced to direct their attention more to improve and measure financial performance than to non-financial performance. Thus, the business kind, or say the nature of organization, has to be taken into account. Such organizational characteristical impact has also been demonstrated in some studies; notable one is Hussain and Hoque (2002). In a turmoil of economic conditions, banks are not only affected by the Central Bank's regulation but also by the amount of deposit as well as pay back from borrowers that fall down by adverse economic conditions, because these are the major inputs and outputs of banks. The results of such slow down affect banks more quickly than other business organizations that could keep producing the tangible products by making use of its human and other resources in the future. Garnaut (1998) stated "Recession turns good banks into bad banks." It was found that all financial performance measures (interest margin, expense/income, return on assets, and capital adequacy) are positively correlated with customer service quality scores among Australian financial institutions (Duncan and Elliott, 2004). While Nielsen *et al.* (2000) show that financial institutions are increasingly integrating MA systems with customer-related activities thus enabling customer profitability analysis, other studies examined MA practices in financial institutions (Oldenboom and Abratt, 2000; Hussain *et al.*, 2002; Hussain, 2005; Wei and Nair, 2006).

Moreover, it is established that strategy is closely linked with the long-term plans of top management, and in this case, the kind of business has effect on long-term planning. The possible strategy that management can establish in a given time, the objectives to carry them out until the fulfilment of chosen strategies, all have significant impact on non-financial PM. Tapinos and Dyson (2005) indicate that PM stands as one of the four main factors characterizing the current practice of strategic planning. It was found that the great majority of banks responded to changes in growth opportunities through diversification moves but no clear link to core capabilities (Batiz-Lazo and Wood, 2001).

Banks have to function under the regulation of central banks, which determine their policy in order to stabilize financial market and strengthen economic condition. As a result, banks encounter difficulties in making long-term plan for PM. Considering the difficulty with long-term plan and strategy, the objective of non-financial PM is jeopardized, and accordingly, the PM practice is hampered. When organizations are not able to make long-term plans, then it is hard to enhance non-financial PM, because non-financial indicators are meant to achieve competitive advantages of business and that depends on the long-term strategy and vision of organizations.

According to service process type, banks are considered one type. Therefore, the importance of "type" does not hold particular significance. However, the special nature and characteristics of Islamic banking may result in the type of business having an effect on MA practices. Therefore, this study starts with the notion that nature and type of business (i.e., Islamic banking) are the biggest influencing factors on PM practice.

The above literature also reveals that a fewer number of studies concentrate on PM in service industry (Fitzgerald *et al.*, 1991; Brignall, 1997; Ballantine *et al.*, 1998; Hassan, 2005; Mohamed and Hussain; 2005; Mukherjee and Nath, 2005). Comparatively little is known about the role of MA in PM in practice in developing countries, particularly in the Islamic banking sector. Thus, this study examines PM practices in growing (particular kind) Islamic FSI with a reference to some GCC countries.

Research Methodology

Considering the importance of MA and PM in ensuring the successful implementation of an organization's strategy and the little research of these practices in emerging economies, the objective of this chapter is to study the PM practices in one emerging markets, namely GCC countries, and particularly in the ever-growing sector of Islamic banking. The research methodology employed to accomplish this aim is presented in this section. To meet the objective of this study, the following issues were addressed: (1) what (financial and non-financial performances) are being measured, and how? (2) the importance banks place on measuring both financial and non-financial performance and (3) problems encountered in measuring performance.

To answer the above-stated questions, the research methods relied on semi-structured interviews that took place in the corporate offices of five Islamic banks in three GCC countries, namely Bahrain, UAE, and Kuwait in the period January–October, 2004. The interviewees were with senior management. Each bank was visited twice and the average time for interviews per bank was about 1–3 h. The questions covered an introduction to the organization, MA practices within the organization, and PM — both financial and non-financial.

Hence, this study applied descriptive multiple case studies rather than explanatory single case study. This was due to the unavailability of detailed information that permits explanatory study, also because multiple cases better replicate the findings than does the evidence from one or two cases (Yin, 1991). Multiple cases enable us to carry out cross-case (comparative) analysis. Thus, it could be used to predict similar results (a literal replication); produces contrary results but for predictable reasons (a theoretical replication); or both literal and theoretical replication (Hussain and Hoque, 2002).

The Case Studies: Performance Measurement in Islamic Banks

This section provides the results of the analysis of the data collected. (Commitment not to disclose information does not permit detailed description about the banks studied.)

Bank Alfa (a large Islamic bank)

At the time of the study, Bank Alfa employed 1,070 employees, its average rate of return was 5% during the last 4 years and its average growth rate was 7%. Table 19.1 summarizes our key findings about Alfa.

Managers of bank Alfa acknowledged the importance of both financial and non-financial measures noting they were both important for the growth

Table 19.1.   Bank Alfa.

Description	Financial PM	Non-financial PM
Importance (of)	Very important	Important
Practice (of)	Every division of the bank	Regularly
Model/method that is used	Benchmarking and activity-based cost management	Questionnaires and surveys
Problem/contentment with	Lack of standards	Lack of benchmarks
Opinion/suggestions to improve the method of PM systems	Developing a set of standards	Developing benchmarking model

and profitability of the bank. They use a mix of benchmarking process and activity-based cost management (ABCM) to measure financial performance. Although management admits having difficulty in evaluating the results achieved due to the lack of accounting standards that are tailored especially to meet the special nature of operations in Islamic banking, they also point out that the size of the bank is an important factor when performance is measured. A senior executive of the bank stated, "PM is affected by the size of the bank. Since the bigger we are, the more diverse to offer our services. However, that is not a problem in itself. That is the nature of our bank. The bigger you are, the more investors trust you, and the more transaction you have." Thus, it was observed that management of Alfa are experiencing problems with measuring financial performance accurately. They emphasized the need to modify standards used to make the use of benchmarking and ABCM more meaningful. However, they failed to point out exact ways to modify the standards and methods used.

Alfa's management stated that non-financial performance is measured regularly and it is important to top management. Many aspects of non-financial performance are considered for measurement, customer satisfaction and quality of services are in high priority. Quick response and on-time services are also important factors to managers. Managers in Alfa use questionnaires and customer surveys to measure non-financial performance. An executive of the bank has pointed out that "We regularly measure non-financial performance and we aim to satisfy our customers by providing quality service." Though, they emphasized the fact that top management views financial performance to be of more important than non-financial. They mentioned that the well-being of the bank which is non-financial is directly related to the banks ability to strengthen its financial position in the highly competitive market in order to provide better services to its customers. It was noted that while managers are well satisfied with and do not have any problems with the methods being used to measure non-financial performance, they are trying to improve their non-financial PM by developing a system that allows them to benchmark non-financial performance. A senior executive pointed out "management is currently focusing on building a database that would allow us to use benchmarking to measure both financial and non-financial performance."

Bank Bravo (a small Islamic bank)

At the time of the study, Bank Bravo employed around 130 staff. During the last 5 years, its growth rate was approximately 4% and had an average rate of return of 5%. Key findings are summarized in Table 19.2.

Table 19.2. Bank Bravo.

Description	Financial PM	Non-financial PM
Importance (of)	Important	Very important
Practice (of)	Every division of the bank	Monthly
Model/method that is used	Budgeting and ratio analysis	Questionnaires and surveys and direct interviews
Problem/contentment with	A bit problematic (lack of accuracy)	None
Opinion/suggestions to improve the method of PM systems	None	None

Management of Bank Bravo focus their attention on non-financial performance measures; hence, it is measured on monthly basis and measures used include quality control, customer satisfaction, social well-being, and quick response. Financial measures are seen as less important and measured semi-annually using benchmarking and ratio analysis. The reason financial and non-financial ones in Bravo overshadow measures is management's belief that as a service organization they should be more oriented toward customers' satisfaction rather than profit. They also highlighted that the nature of Islamic banking necessitates the good service of customers rather than profit making. They also emphasized that their utmost priority is maintaining their reputation. It was observed from the actions and words of top managers at bank Bravo that their attitudes were different from their counterparts in the other four banks. The CEO of Bravo has mentioned, "financial performance is derived by non-financial performance." They believe that the bank's aim should be to attain good reputation as a bank that cares about its social well-being. He stated, "when customers are satisfied with our services and contribution to the Islamic world, we stand to gain financially." Managers believe that their financial position will be strengthened by the fact that they have a reputation for charging fair prices for their services. The bank's CEO stated, "we have to provide other services in the time necessary, in other words, we have to keep up with our competitors. We had to offer services that do not bring fees revenues in order to satisfy our clients. For instance, we provided paying bills, e-banking, and phone banking features in order to fight competitiveness from other banks."

Managers of Bank Bravo are satisfied with the accuracy of the present non-financial performance measures models. They emphasized the fact that several reports show the bank as one of the top organizations in the country when it comes to customer service. They view this as a testimony to the success of the measures used to measure non-financial performance. Hence, they stated that there was no need to change anything. Though, it was stated that the accuracy of financial measures might not be so accurate. The financial controller of the bank said, "the issue of PM gets complicated when more subjective matters are involved. In the case of the budget, the actual figures from last year are easily incorporated, but when it comes to the forecasts of next year, we may have a problem here since they may not be 100% correct." He elaborated further by stating "The problem is not in the budget system itself. The problem is more with getting accurate reliable financial information." When the issue was discussed with top management, they stated their intention to improve the way FP is measured, though they point out that the nature of Islamic banking makes accurate measurement of financial performance "a bit problematic." Still the bank seems to focus more on non-financial PM as means of sustaining its current position.

Bank Charlie (a medium-sized Islamic Bank)

At the time of the study, Charlie employed approx. 207 employees, its average growth rate for the last three years was 5.3%, and its average rate of return for the last four years was 4.2%. Table 19.3 summarizes key findings about Bank Charlie.

As revealed in Table 19.3, Bank Charlie's top management recognizes the need of financial performance; they give high priority to measuring financial performance in every department of their bank. They believe that doing so will allow them to keep their place in the business and survive. They rely on

Table 19.3. Bank Charlie.

Description	Financial PM	Non-financial PM
Importance (of)	Very important	Low importance
Practice (of)	Every section of the bank	Rarely
Model/method that is used	Financial statements and master budget	None
Problem/contentment with	Somewhat problematic (wrong estimates)	None
Opinion/suggestions to improve the method of PM systems	Develop evaluation model	Develop evaluation model

analyzing financial statements with particular emphasis on income statement; their main concern is to measure profit and assets growth. They also measure their financial performance is by comparing the budgeted results with the actual ones, through the master budget. However management finds the budgeting method "somewhat problematic," due to the possibility of wrong estimation. The financial controller of the bank stated, "we focus on income statement and balance sheet. Our focus is on the measurement of profit and losses and the growth rate of assets. Hence, PM in the bank is primarily financial."

Non-financial performance has hardly been given any importance by the top management of Bank Charlie. Even though management admits that customer satisfaction and on time quality services are essential to keep their customers, they admit that non-financial performance is not measured. Managements hope to develop a system that could be used to measure non-financial performance in the future. The CEO stated, "we are in the process of improving the way we measure our financial and non-financial aspects. We are in the process of coming up with a system that will facilitate the input of data and output of all reports required. This system is hoped to be a reliable system."

Bank Delta (a medium-sized Islamic bank)

At the time of the study, Delta employed between 195 and 210 staff. During the last five years, its growth rate was approximately 6% and with an average rate of return of 8.7%. Table 19.4 summarizes key findings.

Management of Bank Delta puts high emphasis on measuring financial performance in each division of the bank. The method that they usually use to measure their financial performance is by using ratio analysis that is used

Table 19.4. Bank Delta.

Description	Financial PM	Non-financial PM
Importance (of)	Very important	Somewhat important
Practice (of)	Every section of the organization	Regularly
Model/method that is used	Benchmarking and ratio analysis	Questionnaires
Problem/contentment with	Lack of standards	None
Opinion/suggestions to improve the method of PMS	Establish Islamic banking standards	Training employees

to compare results against predetermined benchmarks. Managements do not have any difficulty or problems with the models that they use, and they are satisfied with the results achieved. The CFO of the bank said, "we use the benchmarking model. In the sense, we set a budget and evaluate things based on it. This is mainly used for financial performance aspects." Moreover, they emphasized the problems encountered in the Islamic banking sector by saying "The major problem for financial performance in Islamic banks is the fact that we do not have a coherent accounting standards framework. This is very confusing because we have to revert to International Accounting Standard in dealing with transactions that are not covered by the Islamic accounting standards issued by the Accounting and Auditing Organization of Islamic financial Institutions (AAOIFI)."

The non-financial performance of Delta is seen as important but somehow less important than as the financial performance. Many aspects of non-financial performance are measured regularly; customer satisfaction and quality of services are in high priority. Managers in Delta use questionnaires to measure non-financial performance. An executive of the bank stated that "customer satisfaction, commitment, on time quality services are essential in the services provided by the commercial branches. If a customer is not satisfied, they will withdraw deposits which will decrease our mudarabah fees." Although managements are satisfied with the methods used and do not have any problems, they are trying to improve their non-financial performance by providing further training to their employees.

Bank Echo (a large Islamic bank)

At the time of the study, Echo employed 1,300 employees, its average rate of return during the last five years was in the range of 7 to 8%, and the average growth rate was between 10 and 11% during that time. Table 19.5 summarizes key findings about bank Echo.

Management of Bank Echo places almost equal emphasis on both financial and non-financial PM. However, they admitted their primary concern was financial rather than non-financial measures. That was due to putting more emphasis on profit as it was seen to reflect the success of the bank in increasingly competitive sector. A senior executive of the bank, "Our main concern is income statement. Profit measurement is an essential in measuring financial performance. We need to maintain our position in the increasingly competitive market and we can only do so if we maintain our levels of profitability and improve on it." He admitted that the only problem they encounter in measuring financial performance is the comparison drawn with conventional

Table 19.5.   Bank Echo.

Description	Financial PM	Non-financial PM
Importance (of)	Very important	Very important
Practice (of)	Every division of the bank	Regularly
Model/method that is used	Benchmarking and ratio analysis	Monthly performance appraisals and surveys
Problem/contentment with	None	None
Opinion/suggestions to improve the method of PM systems	None	None

(non-Islamic) banks due to the different nature of the two types of banks. He further stated, "The problem is not the input and the building of a model to help measure performance; the problem is the difference in accounting standards between banks due to the nature of Islamic banking. In fact, the comparison between the financials of Islamic banks and conventional ones may not be accurate because of the aforementioned differences."

Meanwhile, non-financial performance is measured through customer satisfaction, quality control, and quick response. They reported that non-financial performance is measured on regular basis in order to maintain high standard of customer service that enables Echo to maintain its leading share in the Islamic banking sector. An executive of the bank stated, "Quick reposes is a basic issue, we must meet the deadlines given. We consider we have failed if we do not provide the quick response necessary." He further emphasized "customer satisfaction is a very important factor in our success in a highly competitive market." It was noted that management of the bank uses customer survey to measure customer satisfaction as it is viewed as an easy tool to use to measure non-financial performance. Management of Echo appeared to be well satisfied with the accuracy of their PM models both financial and non-financial. However, it was observed that though management of Echo appeared to be concerned with the social well-being aspect of non-financial performance, there was no defined model or measure that was used to measure such aspect of performance.

Comparative Analysis

Findings of this study, as summarized in Tables 19.6 and 19.7, reveal that all of the five banks acknowledged the importance of measuring financial

Table 19.6. Comparative analysis.

	Case 1 Bank Alfa	Case 2 Bank Bravo	Case 3 Bank Charlie	Case 4 Bank Delta	Case 5 Bank Echo
Importance of financial PM	Very important	Very important	Very Important	Very important	Important
Practice of financial PM	Every division of the bank	Every division of the bank	Every division of the bank	Every division of the bank	Every division of the bank
Model that is used	Benchmarking and ratios analysis	Master budget and financial statements	Benchmarking and ratios analysis	Benchmarking and ABCM	Budgeting and ratios analysis
Problems faced	Lack of standards	Somewhat problematic (wrong estimation)	None	Lack of standards	A bit problematic (lack of accuracy)
Suggestions to improve the financial PM systems/model	Developing set of standards for Islamic banking	Develop evaluation model	None	Developing set of standards for Islamic banking	None

Table 19.7. Comparative analysis based on non-financial PM practices.

	Case 1 Bank Alfa	Case 2 Bank Bravo	Case 3 Bank Charlie	Case 4 Bank Delta	Case 5 Bank Echo
Importance of non-financial PM practices	Somewhat important	Low importance	Very important	Important	Very important
Practice of non-financial PM	Regularly	Rarely	Regularly	Regularly	Monthly
Model that is used	Questionnaires	Questionnaires and direct interviews	Monthly appraisal/ surveys	Questionnaires/ surveys	Questionnaires, surveys, and direct interviews
Problems faced	None	None	None	Lack of benchmarks	None
Suggestions to improve non-financial PM	Training employees	Develop evaluation model	None	Developing benchmarking model	None

performance. While only one of the five stated that measuring non-financial performance was of more importance to them than measuring financial performance. Benchmarking and ratio analysis are used in three out of the five banks for measuring financial performance. While budgeting is used in two of the banks, ABCM and financial statements are used to measure financial performance in only one of the banks. It is important to note that the two banks that are using budgets reported problems with the model in terms of wrong estimates, and instead of trying to use different models, they resort to finding the cause of variances and deal with it. Moreover, the concept of benchmarking with best practice organization seems to be problematic in all banks due to the lack of clearly set of standards for Islamic banking. Management thinks that comparing the bank's performance with that of a more conventional bank is not appropriate due to the difference in nature and objectives of both types of banks.

This study found that all but one of the banks studied realizes the importance of measuring non-financial performance. Only one of banks indicated that non-financial performance was of more importance than financial performance. While one other bank sees non-financial performance of equal importance to financial performance, the remaining banks place it at lesser importance than financial performance. Still four banks reported using some models to measure the non-financial aspects of their performance. Quality control and customer satisfaction seem to be the most important factors in measuring non-financial performance. Banks seem to relate these two factors to financial performance; hence, the attention paid to them. The organization's well-being and social reputation seem to be an important aspect to all these four banks.

All but one of these four banks stressed their satisfaction with the models used, and only that firm expressed interest in trying to train their staff and finding better models for measuring non-financial performance. There seem to be a great deal of contention with traditional methods and a lack of interest in trying to apply more advanced MA systems.

On the other hand, only one of the five banks studied revealed that non-financial PM is of insignificant importance to them. Management of that bank seemed only interested in financial performance measures. They view financial performance as the key for their existence and fighting competition. Nevertheless, it is interesting to note that management of that bank realise the importance of customer satisfaction in keeping customers. Therefore, they emphasised their hope to be able to use non-financial performance measures in the future.

Summary and Recommendations for Managers

The main objective of this chapter was to study MA practices performance measures in the particular domain/nature of Islamic FSI in GCC countries. Results from this multiple-case study suggest that MA play a role in measuring both financial and non-financial performances in the Islamic FSI. However, the significance of the role played by these measures is subject to scrutiny, as there seems to be no institutionalized perspective of the equal importance of both financial and non-financial performance measures. There seems to be a tendency to think that financial PM is more significant. The significant importance of using either or both types of measures is left to management views and discretion. Also, there appears to be a gap between the perception of the best practice that should take place and the actual practice taking place, particularly in the case of non-financial PM. Also, the size of the bank does not seem have to a significant effect on PM practice.

It is demonstrated earlier that the nature of business that is, FSI has an effect on its service function and performance. Good banks management like to provide quality services but the intangibility of the service creates difficulty for them (like other service organizations) to measure it. The characteristics of FSI also create impact on the quality of services, as Smith (1998) argues that quality measurement in services is notoriously difficult.

Furthermore, considering the economic conditions, banks have faced more difficulty during last recession than other business organizations (Niemelä, 1999). The result of such uncertain economic conditions forced management to direct their attention more to improve and measure financial performance than to non-financial performance. In a turmoil of economic conditions, banks are not only affected by the central bank's regulation but also by the amount of deposit as well as pay back from borrowers that fall down by adverse economic conditions, because these are the major inputs and outputs of banks. The results of such slow down affect banks more quickly than other business organizations that could keep producing the tangible products by making use of its human and other resources in the future. In this respect, Garnaut (1998) states, "Recession turns good banks into bad banks" is worth restating. As it is known that strategy is closely linked with the long-term plans of top management, the kind of business also has an effect on long-term planning. The possible strategy that management can establish in a given time, the objectives to carry them out until the fulfilment of chosen strategies, all have significant impact on non-financial performance measurement. However, empirical evidences suggest that the particular kind or nature of Islamic principles does not have remarkable impact on PM in all studied Islamic FSI. Two Islamic banks committed to consider the well-being of society, irrespective their profitability, in order to conform the principles of Shariah.

Adaptation to economic pressures can also influence service processes. In considering the adverse effect of economic conditions on the FSI, where economic survival becomes the burning question for BFI, NFP and its measurement is jeopardized, Islamic FSI is no exception. In this regard, the moderating effects of the characteristics or the nature of Islamic FSI on PM should be acknowledged.

Further, it is found that the nature of Islamic FSI does not have a remarkable impact on PM; however, studied banks put higher emphasis on financial performance due to the need of competing with counterparts (most of them are conventional banks). One bank clearly demonstrates its objective to put higher importance on non-financial performance because of its own principles (to consider the well-being of society as Shariah advocates). Another bank's management also tuned the same but not so provocative. However, the nature itself does not demonstrate the sole reason for managing and measuring non-financial performance because three banks management like to think more about competition rather than the conformity principles of Shariah. One may argue that if all banks would be Islamic in a particular economy, Islamic banks may get an opportunity to conform their principles. However, such a notion cannot be validated or avoided in the absence of such a state of economy.

The data in this study came from five Islamic banks operating in the GCC countries; therefore, any generalization of its results to the GCC Islamic or general banking sector or beyond cannot be made without considerable caution. However, due to the limited number of Islamic banks operating in the region, the results of this study can give us an indication of the trends that help formulate some hypotheses. Applying the common mode of analysis in a cross-case comparison means that this study was able to make a meaningful comparison of the role of MA in both financial and non-financial PM practices. Consequently, lessons were learned about organizational factor; that is, the nature of organization moderately influences the choice of PM practices. This leads to several directions for further research. Other banks could then be studied to verify the practices in the Islamic banking sector and other sectors.

Other issues in multidimensional PM remain to be studied. This study was conducted in a single sector; a cross-sector research would be worth considering for the exploration on PM practices in different environments.

Considering the dynamics of micro- and macroenvironments, it would be interesting to demonstrate the changing attitude of management in measuring multidimensional aspects of performance in different time horizon in different kind of FSI.

References

Acton, D and W Cotton (1997). Activity-based costing in a university setting. *Journal of Cost Management*, 32–38.

Anderson, K and R McAdam (2004). A critique of benchmarking and performance measurement: Lead or lag? *Benchmarking: An International Journal*, 11(5), 465–483.

Anderson, K and R McAdam (2005). An empirical analysis of lead benchmarking and performance measurement: Guidance for qualitative research. *International Journal of Quality & Reliability Management*, 22(4), 354–375.

Ansari, S (1977). An integrated approach to control system design. Accounting Organization and Society, 2, 101–112.

Ballantine, J, S Brignall, and S Modell (1998). Performance measurement and management in public health services: A comparison of UK and Swedish practice. *Management Accounting Research*, 9, 71–94.

Batiz-Lazo, B and D Wood (2001). Management of core capabilities in Mexican and European Banks. *International Journal of Bank Marketing*, 19(2), 89–100.

Brignall, T, L Fitzgerald, R Johnston, and R Silvestro (1991). Product costing in service organizations. *Management Accounting Research*, 2, 227–248.

Brignall, T, L Fitzgerald, R Johnston, R Silvestro, and C Voss (1992). Linking performance measures and competitive strategy in service businesses: Three case studies. In *Management Accounting Handbook*, Drury, C (ed.), pp. 196–216. London: Butterworth-Heinemann — in conjunction with CIMA.

Brignall, S (1997). A contingent rationale for cost system design in services. *Management Accounting Research*, 8(3), 325–346.

Brignall, S and S Modell (2000). An institutional perspective on performance measurement and management in the new public sector. *Management Accounting Research*, 11(3), 281–306.

Bromwich, M and A Bhimani (1989). *Management Accounting: Evolution not Revolution*. London: CIMA Publications.

Bourne, M, A Neely, K Platts, and J Mills (2002). The success and failure of performance measurement initiatives: Perceptions of participating managers. *International Journal of Operations & Production Management*, 22(11), 1288–1310.

Cobb, I, C Heller, and J Innes (1995). Management accounting change in a bank. *Management Accounting Research*, 6, 155–175.

Cinquini, L and F Mitchell (2005). Success in management accounting: Lessons from the activity-based costing/management experience. *Journal of Accounting and Organisational Change*, 1(2), 63–77.

Duncan, E and G Elliott (2004). Efficiency, customer service and financial performance among Australian financial institutions. *International Journal of Bank Marketing*, 22(5), 319–342.

Eccles, R, P Pyburn, and A Creating (1992). Comprehensive system to measure performance. *Management Accounting* (USA), 74(4), 41–44.

Euske, R, M Lebes, and C McNair (1993). Performance management in an international setting. *Management Accounting Research*, 4, 275–299.

Ezzamel, M (1992). *Business Unit & Divisional Performance Measurement*. London: CIMA Publications.

Fitzgerald, L, R Johanston, T Brignall, R Silvestro, and C Voss (1991). *Performance Measures in Service Businesses*. London: CIMA.

Garnaut, R (1998). The financial crisis: A watershed in economic thought about East Asia. *Asian-Pacific Economic Literature*, 12(1), 1–11.

Gomes, C, M Yasin, and J Lisboa (2006). Performance measurement practices in manufacturing firms, an empirical investigation. *Journal of Manufacturing Technology Management*, 17(2), 144–167.

Govindarajan, V and J Shank (1992). Strategic cost management: Tailoring controls to strategies. *Journal of Cost Management*, 6(3), 14–25.

Gregory, M (1993). Integrated performance measurement: A review of current practice and emerging trends. *International Journal of Production Economics*, 30/31, 281–296.

Halachmi, A (2002). Performance measurement: A look at some possible dysfunctions. *Work Study*, 51(5), 230–239.

Hassan, M (2005). Management accounting and organisational change: An institutional perspective. *Journal of Accounting and Organisational Change*, 1(2), 125–140.

Henri, J (2004). Performance measurement and organizational effectiveness: Bridging the gap. *Managerial Finance*, 30(6), 93–123.

Hiromoto, T (1988). Another hidden edge–Japanese accounting data in performance evaluation. *Harvard Business Review*, 67–77.

Hussain, M and S Kock (1994). Activity based costing in service management. In *Managing Service Quality*, Kunst, P and J Lemmink (eds.), p. 1. London: Paul Chapman Publishing Ltd.

Hussain, M and A Gunasekaran (2001). Activity-based cost management in financial services industry. *Managing Service Quality*, 11(3), 213–223.

Hussain, M and Z Hoque (2002). Understanding non-financial performance measurement practices in Japanese banks: A new institutional sociology perspective. *Accounting, Auditing & Accountability*, 15(2), 162–123.

Hussain, M, A Gunasekaran, and M Islam (2002). Implications of non-financial performance measures in Finnish banks. *Managerial Auditing Journal*, 17(8), 452–463.

Hussain, M (2005). Management accounting performance measurement systems in Swedish banks. *European Business Review*, 17(6), 566–589.

Johnson, H and R Kaplan (1987). *Relevance Lost — The Rise and Fall of Management Accounting*. Boston, MA: Harvard Business School Press.

Kaplan, R (1983). Measuring manufacturing performance: A new challenge for managerial accounting research. *The Accounting Review*, 686–703.

Kaplan, R (1984). The evaluation of management accounting. *The Accounting Review*, 390–418.

Kaplan, R and D Norton (1992). The balanced scorecard — measures that drive performance. *Harvard Business Review*, 70(1), 79–80.

Kaplan, R and D Norton (1996). *The Balanced Scorecard — Translating Strategy into Action*. Boston, MA: Harvard Business Press.

Kaplan, R and D Norton (2001). Transforming the balanced scorecard from performance measurement to strategic management, Part I. *Accounting Horizons*, 15(1), 87–104.

Karimi, J, Y Gupta, and T Somers (1996). Impact of competitive strategy and information technology maturity on firms' strategic response to globalization. *Journal of Management Information Systems*, 12(4), 55–88.

Kennerley, M and A Neely (2002). A framework of the factors affecting the evolution of performance measurement systems. *International Journal of Operations & Production Management*, 22(11), 1222–1245.

Lee, J (1992). How to make financial and non-financial data add up. *Journal of Accountancy*, 62–73.

Long, B (1995). Global competition: The environmental dimension. *Business Economics*, 30(2) 45–50.

Lynch, R and K Cross (1991). *Measure Up! Yardsticks for Continuous Improvement*. London: Blackwell.

Miles, R and C Sweeting (1988). *Pricing Decision in Practice*. London: CIMA.

Milles, P and J Morris (1986). Clients as "Partial" employees of service organisations: Role of development in client participation. *Academy of Management Review*, 11, 726–735.

Modell, S (1996). Management accounting and control in services: Structural and behavioral perspectives. *International Journal of Service Industry Management*, 7(2), 57–80.

Modell, S (1995). A three-dimensional approach to management control systems. *Journal of Business and Management*, 35–73.

Mohamed, E and M Hussain (2005). Management accounting and performance measurement practices in service sector in Oman. *International Journal of Management and Decision Making*, 6(2), 101–111.

Mukherjee, A and P Nath (2005). An empirical assessment of comparative approaches to service quality measurement. *Journal of Services Marketing*, 19(3), 174–184.

Najmi, M, J Rigas, and L Fan (2005). A framework to review performance measurement systems. *Business Process Management Journal*, 11(2), 109–122.

Nanni, AJ, JR Dixon, and TE Vollman (1992). Integrated performance measurement: management accounting to support the new manufacturing realities. *Journal of Management Accounting Research*, 1–19.

Nanni, A, R Dixon, and T Vollmann (1990). Strategic control and performance measurement. *Journal of Cost Management*, 4(2), 33–43.

Neely, A, M Gregory, and K Platts (1995). Performance measurement system design — a literature review and research agendas. *International Journal of Operations and Production Management*, 15(4), 80–116.

Neely, A, J Mills, K Platts, H Richards, M Gregory, M Bourne, and M Kennerley (2000). Performance measurement system design: Developing and testing a process-based approach. *International Journal of Operations & Production Management*, 20(10), 1119–1145.

Neely, A (2005). The evolution of performance measurement research: Developments in the last decade and a research agenda for the next. *International Journal of Operations & Production Management*, 25(12), 1264–1277.

Nielsen, J, P Bukh, and N Mols (2000). Barriers to customer-oriented management accounting in financial services. *International Journal of Service Industry Management*, 11(3), 269–286.

Oldenboom, N and R Abratt (2000). Success and failure factors in developing new banking and insurance services in South Africa. *International Journal of Bank Marketing*, 18(5), 233–245.

Ostinelli, C and G Toscano (1994). Putting quality to work in banking through management accounting systems: Three Italian banks' alternative approaches. *Paper Prepared for the 17th Annual Congress of European Accounting Association*, 6–8 April, Venice, 1994.

Otely, D (1994). Management control in contemporary organizations: Towards a wider framework. *Management Accounting Research*, 5(3/4), 289–299.

Otely, D (1999). Performance management: A framework for management control systems research. *Management Accounting Research*, 10, 363–382.

Powell, S (2004). The challenges of performance measurement. *Management Decision*, 42(8), 1017–1023.

Rouse, P and M Putterill (2003). An integral framework for performance measurement. *Management Decision*, 41(8), 791–805.

Scapens, RW (1997). Management accounting and strategic control: The implications for management accounting research. *Paper presented at the EIASM Third International Seminar on Manufacturing Accounting Research*, 11–13 June, Edinburgh, 1997.

Silvestro, R, L Fitzgerald, R Johnston, and C Voss (1992). Towards a classification of service processes. *International Journal of Service Industry Management*, 3(3), 62–75.

Sim, K and H Koh (2001). Balanced scorecard: A rising trend in strategic performance measurement. *Measuring Business Excellence*, 5(2), 18–27.

Shields, M (1997). Research in management accounting by North Americans in the 1990s. *Journal of Management Accounting Research*, 9, 3–62.

Tangen, S (2004). Performance measurement: From philosophy to practice. *International Journal of Productivity and Performance Management*, 53(8), 726–737.

Tapinos, R and M Dyson (2005). The impact of performance measurement in strategic planning. *International Journal of Productivity and Performance Management*, 54(5/6), 370–384.

Thompson, J (1967). *Organisation in Action*. New York: MacGraw-Hill.

Turney, PBB (1991). *Common Cents: The ABC Performance Breakthrough*. Hillsboro, OR: Cost Technologies Inc.

Wei, K and M Nair (2006). The effects of customer service management on business performance in Malaysian banking industry: An empirical analysis. *Asia Pacific Journal of Marketing and Logistics*, 18(2), 111–128.

Yin, R (1991). *Case Study Research, Design and Methods*. Beverly Hills: Sage Publications.

Chapter 20

CHALLENGES AND OPPORTUNITIES FOR INTERNATIONAL MARKETERS IN KUWAIT

C. P. RAO

Abstract

Kuwait is an affluent developing Gulf Arab country. Endowed with oil wealth, which is increasing at an accelerated rate in recent years, Kuwait offers excellent business opportunities and poses challenges of a developing country market. With the implementation of WTO regime in 2005, the country provides many opportunities for international businesses. The Kuwait government policy initiatives in liberalizing and privatizing the country are creative, very conducive, and attractive business environment. This chapter presents an overview of the country's business environment. Growth trends of the country's gross domestic product (GDP) and the overall contributions of oil and non-oil sectors of the economy were detailed. The Kuwait business environment in terms of trends in demographics and marketing conditions was detailed and discussed.

Introduction

Kuwait is a small but affluent country in the gulf cooperation council (GCC) region. Kuwait economy is dominated by oil industry with 10% of the world reserves. With ever-increasing oil prices, the Kuwait economy is booming in recent years. The increased oil income boosted economic activity in the country. The business growth and expansion are further facilitated by the liberal economic policies of the Kuwait government. Kuwait started implementing the World Trade Organization (WTO) regime in 2005. This opened up the service industries to outside competition. In addition, other economic policy goals, such as the need for diversifying the predominantly oil depended economy and the need to generate employment opportunities for increasing Kuwaiti population are also providing the necessary impetus to expand the private sector in the country. In recent years, Kuwait government started implementing active privatization policies to achieve the national goals. Other national goals, such as the desire to develop Kuwait into a regional financial services hub, develop tourism industry with major projects and create new townships to alleviate the housing problems for nationals; have the same effect of expanding the business activity. The traditional non-profit services sectors such as higher education and health care are being opened up for private sectors. These macro-economic developments are creating many business opportunities not only to Kuwaiti nationals, but also to international business enterprises. In order to profitably participate in the Kuwait economic development, it behooves international businesses to become fully familiar with the emerging business opportunities and challenges in the context of Kuwait economy. Hence, the major purpose of this chapter is to identify and discuss in detail the business opportunities and challenges in Kuwait to international businesses. The rest of the chapter is presented under the following sections in terms of Kuwait business environmental trends. These trends have significant implications for assessing business opportunities and challenges by international businesses. Business environmental trends included in this study are (1) macro-economic; (2) demographic; (3) employment; (4) external trade; (5) major development projects; (6) political and legal; (7) social and cultural; and, (8) technological.

Macro-Economic Trends

The Kuwaiti economy is witnessing its best performance in years, as nominal gross domestic product (GDP) growth soared to 35% in 2005, following 20% plus growth in each of the previous two years. The oil sector continued to lead growth with soaring oil prices, which contributed 59% to GDP. In real terms, the non-oil sector also did equally well. Real GDP went up more than 10% in each of the past two years (2006 and 2007), with the growth in non-oil activities matching the oil sector on the average. Higher government expenditures, accompanied by increased public and private sector investment, boosted domestic spending. With continued strong domestic demand and oil prices reaching new record highs in 2006, it is expected that nominal GDP will increase by more than 12% and real growth to be around 5%.

Kuwait is currently experiencing its first oil-price-driven economic boom in three decades. The current rise in oil prices can only be compared with the soaring prices in the early 1970s, which also fueled rapid economic growth. However, the current economic expansion differs notably from the one that followed the 1974 jump in oil prices. Then, government spending with capital spending on infrastructure playing an important role largely led growth. In contrast, the current boom has seen the private sector play a far more pivotal role with private investment leading growth, although public spending continued to play a key role as well.

"Analyzing GDP by type of expenditure revealed the fact that Kuwait economy was primarily a consumption led economy up to the end of 2005. Through the period 2001–2005, final consumption — both private and public — continued to account for the major share of GDP followed by net exports. By the end of 2005, they formed 32.2% and 15.7%, respectively of GDP. However, it is important to note that over years final consumption's contribution to GDP continued to decline in favor of the increasing share of net exports. As a result, net exports accounted for the highest contribution in GDP for the first time during 2006." — AlWatan Daily (May 26, 2008). Table 20.1 reports GDP for the period 2001–2007.

Oil sector

Oil portion of GDP rose to KD 13.83 billion in 2005, which was more than 60% following the previous two years of strong growth. Crude oil, which accounted for 93% of oil GDP, generated most of the sector's growth as oil prices rose significantly. The price of Kuwait export crude averaged $46.8 per barrel, up 48% on the previous year's average. Oil production was also higher, increasing 12.4% to 2.57 million barrels per day. Value added by petroleum refining, which accounted for the remaining 7.2% of oil GDP, also saw rapid growth of 26%, although this was slower than the previous year's growth of 39%. The increase was primarily driven by higher refining margins that averaged $10.5 per barrel. The value added by the oil sector should rise by about 13% in 2006.

Non-oil sector

Growth in the non-oil sector was solid at 10.7%, with non-oil GDP rising to KD 10.4 billion. Growth was slower than in the previous two years

Table 20.1. Gross domestic product.

	2001	2002	2003	2004	2005	2006	2007
Nominal GDP (KD billion)	10.7	11.6	14.3	17.5	23.6	28.6	34.4
Nominal GDP (US$ billion)	37.5	40.8	50.1	61.6	83.0	100.8	120.9
Nominal GDP growth rate (%)	−7.5	8.3	23.0	22.9	34.7	21.4	20.0
Real GDP (KD billion)	11.6	11.9	14.0	15.5	17.3	18.4	19.6
Real GDP (US$ billion)	40.8	42.0	49.3	54.6	60.8	64.6	68.9
Real GDP growth rate (%)	0.2	3.0	17.3	10.7	11.4	6.3	6.6
Per capita GDP (KD)	4,633.8	4,789.5	5,596.9	6,361.3	7,887.6	8,999.2	10,110.8
Per capita GDP (US$)	16,299.1	16,846.5	19,686.4	22,375.1	27,743.8	31,654.0	35,563.8
Crude oil production (million b/d)	1.95	1.75	2.17	2.34	2.50	2.52	2.46
Avg. Kuwait crude export prices (US$/b)	21.4	23.6	26.9	34.1	48.7	58.9	66.4

Source: Central Bank of Kuwait (2008).

Note: At the Current exchange rate 1 KD = US$3.7.

(2005–2007), when it had benefited from a boost in trade and business activity following the end of war in Iraq. This trend, which saw Kuwait, become a base for foreign companies doing business in the Iraqi market and a conduit for a large part of Iraq's imports has continued though at a slower pace. The sectors that benefited the most from the trend were transport, storage, communications, and business services.

In 2005, these sectors continued to grow, at a slower pace as the trend matured and the security situation in Iraq worsened resulting in limited growth in business activities between the two countries. Nevertheless, transport and storage remained the fastest-growing non-oil activity, with its contribution to GDP rising by 25%. Their growth was driven in large part by the rise in oil shipments, but also by growth in re-exports and logistics services related to Iraq. Communications ranked second with a rapid growth of 22% compared with last year's (2006) 25% rate. The much-smaller business services sector also saw rapid growth of 16%.

Financial institutions, which continued to be the leading non-oil sector in the economy in terms of contribution to non-oil GDP, saw rapid growth of 20%. At 17.2% of non-oil GDP, their size has surpassed public administration and defense in the last two years. The solid performance of banks and investment companies raised their importance in the economy, though most of the value added by this sector is from profits, a big part of which is investment related. Table 20.2 reports GDP by economic activity.

Real estate services are second in importance among activities led by the private sector. However, this sector's growth was disappointing at 3.8%, although it was slightly higher in the previous year's 3.1%. Real estate services' contribution to non-oil GDP decreased from 13.4% in 2002 to 10.9% in 2005. Wholesale and retail trade, whose share of non-oil GDP was slightly lower than real estate, also saw moderate and slowing growth of 4.2% compared with 8.2% and 6.7% registered in the previous two years (2005–2007), respectively. This may come as a surprise given that growth in imports nearly doubled and that much of the wholesale trade activities are import related. These suggested substantial revisions could be made to this sector's figures in the future.

Construction, which represented nearly 5% of non-oil activities, registered strong growth of 13% following double-digit growth in the previous two years. In the manufacturing sector, chemicals and chemical products, which included petrochemicals, saw a third year of strong growth. However, at 23.5%, that growth was slower than in the previous two years. Strong global demand helped lift prices of commodities and related industries in general. Fabricated metals also performed well because this subsector tended to be correlated with construction activity.

Table 20.2. GDP by economic activity (in current prices).

	Million KD			Percent change		
	2003	2004	2005	2003	2004	2005
Agriculture and Fishing	65	71	78	8.3	9.2	10.6
Mining and Quarrying	5,815	7,845	12,853	31.5	34.9	63.8
Petroleum refining	572	796	1,004	32.9	39.0	26.2
Manufacturing (excl. refining)	555	660	753	16.3	19.1	14.0
Electricity, gas, and Water	299	307	317	8.8	2.5	3.2
Construction	349	402	455	12.0	15.1	13.3
Trade, hotels and restaurants	1,064	1,108	1,155	12.5	4.1	4.3
Transport, storage, and communication	800	1,045	1,294	34.6	30.7	23.8
Finance, real estate, and business services	2,485	2,871	3,256	29.1	15.5	13.4
Community, social, and personal services	2,726	2,925	3,086	7.3	7.3	5.5
Subtotal	14,731	18,029	24,250	22.9	22.4	34.5
Less: imputed bank services	613	724	811	23.7	18.2	11.9
GDP at producer prices	14,118	17,305	23,440	22.9	22.6	35.5
Plus: import duties	135	162	148	39.4	19.5	-8.2
GDP at purchaser prices	14,254	17,466	23,588	23.0	22.5	35.1

Source: Ministry of Planning (www.mop.gov.kw), 2006.

GDP by type of expenditure

Strong growth in fixed investment spending and private consumption fueled a rapid 19% increase in domestic demand, contributing to 41% of the growth in total expenditure on GDP. However, the primary engine behind the strong economic performance remained exports, specifically oil exports. Meanwhile, imports rose more than 26%, the strongest increase since liberation in 1991.

Investment, which has seen strong growth in recent years, soared still higher. Gross capital formation rose 49% following increases of 19% and 32% in the previous two years (2005–2007), respectively. The growth reflected strong private sector investment, particularly in the real estate sector, in addition to the rapid growth in capital spending by the government on development and maintenance projects. Accordingly, investment's share of domestic demand surged to 30%, or 20% of GDP.

Private consumption, which represented almost half of domestic demand, also increased at a rapid 13% rate. Higher transfers to households fueled growth and salary increases for government employees and Kuwaiti nationals. Consumer spending also benefited from the boom in real estate and equity markets, with wealth effect on consumer wallets. In contrast, government consumption spending continued to moderate for a third consecutive year, and thus rising a more modest 4.6%. Table 20.3 reports the aggregate expenditure on GDP.

Inflation, measured by consumer price index (CPI), has gone up to unprecedented level of 7.1% in the 4th quarter of 2007 standing at 122.2 points. Such inflation level came on top of 3.03% reported by the end of 2006. It is important to note that inflation rates went through an increasing trend over the last four quarters. More important was the higher inflation rates reported during the year 2007. On a monthly basis, inflation picked up even much more rapidly to hit new records above 7.54% up to the end of December 2007 to stand at 124.1 points. Entering the year 2008, figures from Central Statistics Office revealed inflation picking up even more too unprecedented record levels of 9.53% by the end of January 2008. According to the data, CPI hit 126.4 points by the end of January 2008 as compared with 115.4 points a year ago. Table 20.4 reports constituents of CPI.

Demographic Trends

The total population of Kuwait by the end of 2005 was 2.99 million. This was an increase of 8.63% over 2004. The growth rate of Kuwaiti population was 3.76% in 2005; this rate of growth was more than in 2004. The growth rate of non-Kuwaiti population in 2005 was 11.2%, which was almost the same as

Table 20.3.   Aggregate expenditures on GDP (in current prices).

	Million KD			Percent change		
	2003	2004	2005	2003	2004	2005
Total expenditures on GDP	14,254	17,466	23,588	23.0	22.5	35.1
Government consumption	3,281	3,478	3,637	12.0	6.0	4.6
Private consumption	6,098	6,574	7,395	6.1	7.8	12.5
Gross capital formation	2,359	3,116	4,656	19.2	32.1	49.4
Net exports	2,515	4,298	7,900	171.0	70.9	83.8
Exports	7,432	9,970	15,059	43.7	34.1	51.0
Imports	4,917	5,672	7,159	15.9	15.4	26.2
Domestic Demand*	11,739	13,168	15,688	10.2	12.2	19.1

*"Domestic Demand" is defined as government and private consumption and gross capital formation.
Source: Ministry of Planning (www.mop.gov.kw), 2006.

the rate of growth in 2004. The Kuwaiti population is growing at an increasing rate, while the non-Kuwaiti population is growing at a constant rate. The Kuwaiti population by the end of 2005 was 33.2% of the total population as compared to 34.7% in 2004, 36.4% in 2003. Non-Kuwaiti population was 66.8% of the total population by the end of 2005 as compared to 65.3% in 2004. In general, the number of Kuwaiti females exceeded the number of males (51% females and 49% males by the end of 2005). This ratio was almost the same as in 2004. However, the percentage of non-Kuwaiti males was significantly more than the percentage of non-Kuwaiti females (69.6% in 2005). Percentage of females in non-Kuwaiti population was only 30.4% in 2005.

The distribution of population according to age groups indicates the dominance of young Kuwaiti population. By the end of 2005, the percentage of young Kuwaiti people in the age groups less than 15 years was 40% of total Kuwaiti population, as compared to 40.5% in 2004. The percentage of Kuwaiti population less than 30 years of age was 67.9% in 2005, as compared to 68.3% in 2004. The majority of non-Kuwaiti population is concentrated in the age group of 25–49 years (66.4% in 2005). The young non-Kuwaiti population (less than 15 years) accounted for only 12.4% in 2005.

The percentage off illiteracy among the Kuwaiti population continued to fall. It was 5.7% by the end of 2005 as compared to 6% in 2004, 6.8% in 2002, and 8% in 1999. The educational status of Kuwaiti population in 2005 was as following: Illiterates (5.7%), Just read and write (11.5%), primary school (20.9%), intermediate school (27.9%), high school (15.9%), diploma (7.5%) and university and higher education (10.7%). Table 20.5

Table 20.4.   Constituents of CPI (2000 = 100).

Categories	2001	2002	2003	2004	2005	2006	1Q07	2Q07	3Q07	4Q07
Food	103.1	104.5	106.6	110	119.4	124	129.6	127.4	128.6	133.9
Beverages and tobacco	101.5	105.8	107.5	111.2	112.2	114.3	119.3	118.5	122.6	128.9
Clothing and footwear	103.2	105.9	108	111	118.1	122.8	126.6	128	128	131.9
Housing services	101.1	102.1	103.8	104.6	105.3	108	110.4	113.4	117.6	123.3
Household goods, and services	96.9	99.1	100.3	96	99.5	102.2	103.7	105.1	106.1	108.2
Transport and communications	99.1	95	93.8	99.8	100.7	102.6	109.6	110	110.2	111.1
Education and medical care	103.9	106.6	112.4	116.6	123.2	126.2	126	126.4	134.7	140.8
Other goods and services	106.2	108.5	105.7	102	110	115.3	117.4	117	119.3	119
General index	101.3	102.2	103.2	104.5	108.8	112.1	115.7	116.5	118.7	122.2
Y-o-Y change	1.30%	.89%	.98%	1.26%	4.11%	3.03%	4.33%	5.05%	5.32%	7.10%

Source: Central Bank of Kuwait (2008).

Table 20.5. Total population (Kuwaiti and non-Kuwaiti) according to age groups and gender.

Age groups	Kuwaiti			Non-Kuwaiti			Total population		
	Male	Female	Total	Male	Female	Total	Male	Female	Total
Less than 5	72317	70591	142908	46447	43465	89912	118764	114056	232820
5–9	67556	64267	131823	43764	41244	85008	111320	105511	216831
10–14	61973	59659	121632	38935	33390	72325	100908	93049	193957
15–19	54506	53253	107759	41126	34286	75412	95632	87539	183171
20–24	45589	45818	91407	113585	62607	176192	159174	108425	267599
25–29	38051	40005	78056	249828	96579	346407	287879	136584	424463
30–34	33183	36467	69650	235967	86213	322180	269150	122680	391830
35–39	28900	32343	61243	215764	77304	293068	244664	109647	354311
40–44	23836	27315	51151	157793	55910	213703	181629	83225	264854
45–49	17230	22027	39257	115139	35740	150879	132369	57767	190136
50–54	13023	17023	30046	69066	18700	87766	72089	35723	117812
55–59	8606	12611	21217	36511	9897	46408	45117	22508	67628
60–64	7184	9425	16609	15482	4990	20472	22666	14415	37081
65–69	6376	6754	13130	7321	3172	10493	13697	9926	23623
70–74	3728	4253	7981	2875	1896	4771	6603	6149	12752
75–79	2268	2302	4570	1057	1177	2234	3325	3479	6804
80–84	1036	1212	2248	385	583	968	1421	1795	3216
85 or more	727	803	1530	277	497	774	1004	1300	2304
Total	486089	506128	992217	1391322	607650	1998972	1877411	1113778	2991189

Source: Public Authority of Civil Information (2006).

reports total population — Kuwaiti and non-Kuwaiti — according to age groups and gender.

Kuwait's population is witnessing its third year of rapid growth in 2006. Statistics by the Public Authority for Civil Information (PACI) show that total population rose to 3.05 by June 2006, growing at a 6.5% rate over the previous 12 months. Rapid growth, which has characterized Kuwait's population since 2001, has been driven in large part by the inflow of expatriate workers into the country to meet growing demand for labor in a buoyant economic environment. Table 20.6 reports percentage growth in population.

The expatriate population has grown at an average annual rate of 6.5% since 2001. The growth had accelerated until a year ago, peaking at 11.3% in the 12 months ending June 2005, before dropping to a still rapid 7.9% rate in the last 12 month period. The number of non- Kuwaitis reached 2.04 million to represent 67% of the total population, 86% of whom participate in the labor force. The expatriate population is heavily skewed toward males, who account for almost 70% of non-Kuwaitis. To adjust such imbalances, the government eased residency requirements for family members in 2005, by reducing the minimum monthly income needed for applicants to issue a residency permit for a relative.

The population of Kuwaiti nationals continued to grow at a relatively steady pace rising by 3.6% during the past year 2006. The rate was slightly higher than in recent years, as the population grew at an annual average of 3.3% in the previous four years. Though the Kuwaiti population is relatively young, it is slowly maturing. The percentage of nationals under the age of 19 has fallen from 55% a decade ago to under 51% in June 2006. This is taking place as Kuwaitis are marrying at a later age, and as the fertility rate declines. Despite this maturing trend, the population of Kuwaiti nationals remains a very young one.

Table 20.6.   Percentage growth in population (at mid-year).

	Population ('000)			Percent growth		
	Kuwaiti	Non-Kuwaiti	Total	Kuwaiti	Non-Kuwaiti	Total
2003	913.5	1570.8	2484.3	3.3	6.2	5.1
2004	942.9	1701.9	2644.8	3.2	8.3	6.5
2005	973.3	1893.6	1866.9	3.2	11.3	8.4
2006	1008.1	2043.8	3051.8	3.6	7.9	6.5

Source: Public Authority of Civil Information (2007).

Educational profile of the adult population

Kuwait's adult population — over 20 years of age or older — reached 2.2 million, constituting 73% of the total population. Kuwaiti adults number 498,000; making up 22.5% of the total, while expatriates number 1.7 million. Table 20.7 reports population by educational attainment.

About 212,000 adult Kuwaitis — representing 42% of nationals — have some education, but have not completed high school. Men account for a disproportionate 55% of this segment. About 15.5% of the Kuwaiti adult population is college educated or has professional training, up from 14.4% five years ago. These figures reflect the rise in the level of education and career expectations in parallel to the economic growth. The government has made tangible efforts to improve the accessibility and quality of education. Kuwaiti women are more likely to have a university education than Kuwaiti men, and constitute almost 64% of total nationals with college education.

Expatriates with at least a high school diploma represent 19% of non-Kuwaiti adults. Although only 5.2% of expatriates hold a university degree, Kuwait still relies on the expatriate labor force to fill a significant number of professional jobs. By June 2006, more than half of adults with professional training or college degrees were expatriates. The percentage of expatriates who have not completed high school but had some schooling is significant,

Table 20.7.   Population by educational attainment.

	Kuwaiti			Non-Kuwaiti			Grand total
	Male	Female	Total	Male	Female	Total	
Adult population ('000)	234	264	498	1257	463	1720	2217
No education	6	34	41	79	38	117	157
Can read and write	11	15	26	632	228	860	886
With some schooling	107	80	186	314	99	413	599
High school	56	52	108	130	57	187	296
Diploma	25	33	58	37	14	51	109
University or professional	29	49	78	65	27	92	170
Adult population (%)	100	100	100	100	100	100	100
No education	3	13	8	6	8	7	7
Can read and write	5	6	5	50	49	50	40
With some schooling	45	30	37	25	21	24	27
High School	24	20	22	10	12	11	13
Diploma	11	13	12	3	3	3	5
University or professional	12	19	16	5	6	5	8

Source: Public Authority for Civil Information (www.paci.gov.kw) (June 2006).

representing as much as 74% of non-Kuwaitis adults. Illiteracy is high among expatriates reaching up to 7% of total non-Kuwaiti adults, with a heavy skew toward men.

Employment trends

Table 20.8 reports the force by gender, nationality, and employment status.

The total number of employees in 2001 was 79617 of which 8.4% were in mining and oil sector and 91.6% in manufacturing. Value added in the industrial sector in 2001 was KD 5265.8 million of which 87.1% was in mining and oil sector and 12.9% in manufacturing. The total output in the industrial was KD 7709.3 million in 2001, divided between 60.7% from oil andÿmining sector and 39.3% from manufacturing sector. Table 20.9 reports selected indicators of industrial activities and employment in Kuwait.

External Trade Trends

Trade

Kuwait's merchandise trade surplus continued to widen, rising from KD 4.7 billion in 2004 to KD 8.0 billion in 2005, and KD 8.9 billion in the first nine months of 2006. In 2005, the surplus amounted to 34% of GDP, up from 27% in the previous year and a 22% average during the previous five years. The rise in oil exports was the main factor behind the improvement.

Table 20.8. Labor force by gender, nationality and employment status.

Nationality	Gender	Unemployed			Employed		
		2003	2004	2005	2003	2004	2005
Kuwaiti	Male	3990	5020	5692	167545	174617	183378
	Female	5614	6612	6666	102207	113027	124775
	Total	9604	11632	12358	269752	287644	308153
Non-Kuwaiti	Male	5586	6581	6700	917800	1045462	1181577
	Female	2650	4992	5439	260700	278004	301865
	Total	8236	11573	12139	1178500	1323466	1483442
Total	Male	9576	11601	12392	1085345	1220079	1364955
	Female	8264	11604	12105	362907	391031	426640
	Total	17840	23205	24497	1448252	1611110	179595

Source: Public Authority of Civil Information (2006).

Table 20.9.   Selected indicators of industrial activities and employment in Kuwait.

Industrial activity		Gross addition to fixed assets	Total value added	Gross output	Compensation of employees	No. of persons engaged	No. of establishments
Mining and quarrying; crude	1999	233.6	3327.7	3391.8	110.5	6273	3
	2000	176.5	5543.9	5622.3	120.4	6529	3
Oil and natural gas	2001	188.8	4586.5	4676.3	129.2	6558	3
Total mining and	1999	233.7	3328.6	3393.8	110.8	6431	7
quarrying	2000	176.6	5544.4	5623.1	120.6	6683	6
	2001	188.8	4587	4677.2	129.4	6718	6
Total manufacturing	1999	89.3	1015.6	3037.2	243.2	71678	4104
industries	2000	68.4	801.7	3437	226.2	70463	4109
	2001	186.1	678.8	3032.1	257.2	72899	4130
Total mining and	1999	323	4344.2	6431.1	354	78109	4111
manufacturing	2000	244.9	6346.1	9060.1	346.8	77146	4115
	2001	374.9	5265.8	7709.3	386.6	79617	4136

Source: Public Authority of Civil Information (2006).

Oil exports, which account for 95% of Kuwait's total exports, increased 29% in the first nine months of 2006 following a 58% increase in 2005 and an average 35% rise in the previous two years. Soaring prices for crude oil and refined products were the main driver behind this growth. While a 12.4 percent production increase contributed to export growth last year, it was much smaller in 2006 as production neared full capacity. Growth in non-oil exports was also strong, mainly in ethylene products and fertilizers. Petrochemicals dominated non-oil exports of Kuwaiti origin and constituted more than half of the total. Other exports included rubber, plastics, and base metals. Re-exports constituted 25% of the total since the resumption of trade with Iraq. Table 20.10 reports summary of foreign trade.

After growing by 37% in 2005, imports dropped 13% in the first nine months of 2006. An exceptionally large increase in 1Q05 accounted for the drop in imports this year. A comparison of the second and third quarters with the same period in 2005 reveals growth of 10%. Rapid growth in domestic demand was the main factor behind the rise in imports. Consumer products constitute the largest share of the import bill, although, since the resumption of trade with Iraq and the surge in construction activity, imports of capital goods have increased substantially, making up a larger share of total imports. According to the latest 2004 data, the European Union, the United States, and Japan remain Kuwait's main trading partners. Trade with these countries increased strongly during the three years through 2004, although at a slower rate than trade with developing Asian economies (mainly China and India). Trade with Iraq and inter-GCC trade also saw rapid growth since 2003, when

Table 20.10.   Summary of foreign trade (million KD).

	2001	2002	2003	2004	2005	9M06
Exports	4,969.7	4,666.2	6,162.1	8,428.1	13,101.6	12,371.5
Oil	4,590.8	4,272.8	5,663.5	7,861.1	12,392.6	11,822.5
Non-oil	378.9	393.4	498.5	567.0	709.0	549.0
Ethylene Products	190.3	191.0	188.4	229.1	311.0	261.0
Fertilizers	21.5	15.5	31.6	41.1	56.0	47.5
Other	104.8	121.2	153.3	156.9	162.0	102.5
Re-exports	62.3	65.7	125.3	140.0	180.0	138.0
Imports	2,413.3	2,735.8	3,274.1	3,722.2	5,106.4	3,442.1
Balance of Trade	2,556.5	1,930.5	2,888.0	4,705.8	7,995.2	8,929.4

Source: Central Bank of Kuwait (www.cbk.gov.kw), 2007.

Note: Imports are stated on c.i.f. basis.

the GCC customs union and resumption of trade with Iraq provided a strong boost.

Kuwait has made efforts to strengthen trade relations with partners in the region as well as internationally. Starting January 2005, Kuwait began enforcing a zero-tariff regime on exports originating from members of the Greater Arab Free Trade Area. The same year also witnessed the signing of a number of bilateral trade agreements for the promotion of bilateral investment and the avoidance of double taxation, including with South Africa, South Korea, Singapore, Malaysia, and Honk Kong. Additionally, Kuwait signed a trade and investment framework agreement with the United States as a first step toward a free trade agreement. Within the GCC framework, the country is taking part in negotiations that will lead to free trade agreements with the European Union, China, Japan, and Turkey. Table 20.11 reports top trade partners.

Kuwait trade surplus continued to grow for the fifth year in a row up to the end of 2007. Trade surplus grew rapidly by 29.7% over the period 2001–2007. Increasing exports over the year surpassing the growth in imports of 23.6% and 14.8%, respectively supported such growth. By the end of 2007, trade surplus budged to a new landmark of 12.2 billion Kuwaiti dinars over last year's peak of KD 11.5 billion. Such increase translates into a growth rate of 5.6% on top of 35.9% of growth reported last year. As a result of its declining growth rate in 2007, trade surplus represented 35.4% of the GDP down from 40.3% in 2006. Tables 20.12 and 20.13 show non-oil exports by origin, and balance of trade, respectively.

Table 20.11. Top trade partners (million KD).

| | Exports | | | | Imports | | | |
| | | Percent change | | | | Percent change | | |
	2004	2002	2003	2004	2004	2002	2003	2004
Total trade	7,380	−3	18	34	3,860	13	30	15
The United States and Canada	931	−7	21	38	512	13	47	1
Japan	1,542	−5	8	26	304	31	22	−11
European Union	726	−20	24	26	1,427	11	27	24
West Asia	197	−12	11	25	624	3	13	2
Gulf co-operation council	145	7	22	−1	499	3	13	2
Developing Asia	3,851	8	20	40	697	11	63	16
Other	132	−37	65	−1	697	11	63	16

Source: United Nations Conference on Trade and Development (www.unctad.org), 2005.

Table 20.12.   Non-oil exports by origin.

Year	Exports of Kuwait origin			Re-exports	Total
	Manufactured fertilizers	Ethylene products	Other		
2001	21.5	190.3	104.8	62.3	378.9
2002	15.5	191.0	121.2	65.7	393.4
2003	31.6	188.4	153.3	125.2	498.5
2004	41.1	229.0	156.9	140.0	567.0
2005	56.0	311.0	162.0	180.0	709.0
2006	63.5	348.0	138.5	186.0	736.0
2007	76.0	400.0	160.0	207.0	843.0
Growth rate	23.4%	13.2%	7.3%	22.2%	14.3%

Source: Central Bank of Kuwait (2008).

Table 20.13.   Balance of trade.

KD million	2001	2002	2003	2004	2005	2006	2007	Growth rate (01–07)
Total exports	4,970	4,666	6,162	8,428	13,102	16,167	17,689	23.6%
Oil exports	4,591	4,273	5,664	7,861	12,393	15,431	16,846	24.2%
Non-oil exports	379	393	499	567	709	736	843	14.3%
Total imports	2,413	2,736	3,274	3,722	4,614	4,629	5,510	14.8%
Balance of trade	2,556	1,930	2,888	4,706	8,488	11,538	12,179	29.7%

Source: Central Bank of Kuwait (2008).

Major Development Projects

Construction activity

Government spending on development and maintenance projects has seen solid growth for five consecutive years, giving rise to a boom in construction activity. The fiscal accounts for 2005/2006 show capital spending reaching KD 750 million, or 11% of total government spending, compared with KD 570 million two years earlier. Table 20.14 reports selected construction projects.

The bulk of the increase in spending was at the Ministry of Public Works (MPW), which also accounted for a third of capital expenditures. MPW also accounts for a list of government-sponsored projects with schemes worth KD 1 billion (US$ 3.4 billion) including the development of Boubyan and Failaka

Table 20.14.   Selected construction projects (million KD).

Project	Value	Status	Project start	Project end
Silk city (Tamdeen/Ajial)	24,820	Planned		
Subiya urban development (PAHC)	5,840	Planned	2008	2012
Arifjan/Sabah Al-Ahmad Urban housing (PAHC)	2,920	Design	2007	2012
Mutlaa township (PAHC)	2,920	Planned	2008	2012
Fahd Al-Abdullah township (PAHC)	2,920	Planned	2008	2012
Bubiyan island (MPW)	1,752	Planned	2007	2011
Khabary city (Al-Dar First Holdong)	1,606	Design	2007	2012
Failaka island resort (MPW)	972	ITB	2006	2014
New Kuwait university campus	876	Planned	2007	2013
Ahmadi township development (KOC)	584	FS	2008	2013
Kuwait city metro (MOC)	526	Planned	2007	2011
Jahra house project (PAHC)	500	ITB	2007	2010
Subiya causeway (MPW)	438	FS	2006	2010
Bubiyan seaport (MPW)	350	ITB	2006	2016
Kuwait airport expansion (DGCA)	292	Planned	2007	2010
Iraqi-Saudi border road (MPW)	146	Planned	2007	2010
Ardiya business & education colleges (PAAET)	128	ITB	2006	2008
Media city (Al-Mal Investment Co.)	117	Planned	2007	2010
Mahabella complex (CRC)	93	Design	2006	2009
Al-Asima tower (Salhiya Real Estate)	91	Planned	2006	2008

Source: MEED Projects (www.meedprojects.com), 2006.
Notes: PAHC, Public Authority for Housing Care; MPW, Ministry of Public Works; KOC, Kuwait Oil Company; DGCA, Director General of Civil Aviation, PAAET, Public Authority for Applied.
Education and Training; CRC, Commercial Real Estate Co.; ITB, invitation to bid released; FS, feasibility study. Table includes projects valued at more than KD 90 million.

islands. The Public Authority for Housing Care, with its independent budget, has a still more sizable portfolio, including multimillion-dinar housing projects and township developments. In total, government and affiliated institutions are sole sponsors on roughly KD 10 billion in projects, awarded or under way.

Although government spending has played a key role in the current construction boom, increased private investment has also contributed to the sector's growth. Roughly KD 2.5 billion in private investments has been earmarked to real estate projects since 2005, encouraged by amendments to the building code that lifted the maximum permitted built area to 210% of a plot's surface area for residential plots, and to 270% for investment plots. Rapidly rising rents across commercial, residential, and investment sectors have also helped boost private investment. In the future, the government is expected to contribute further to the growth in private investment through planned public–private–partnership (PPP) initiatives, including the proposed multibillion-dinar developments at Failaka and Boubyan islands.

In line with the increase in construction activity, commercial loans for the construction sector increased 30% in 2005 and an additional 27% in the first three quarters of 2006 to reach KD 974 million. Commercial loans to the real estate sector also increased 25% and 17% in the two periods, respectively, reaching almost KD three billion. Bank loans extended to the construction and real estate sectors constituted 28.5% of local banks' total loans to residents at the end of September 2006.

Building permits

Buoyant construction activity ought to be reflected in a rise in the number of building permits issued; however, data are not yet available for 2006. The Kuwait Municipality reported issuing around 9,700 permits in 2005, 6% more than in the previous year. Although permits issued for additions and renovations accounted for 60% of this growth, the rise in permits issued for new construction was solid compared with the previous year. Table 20.15 shows number of building permits issued for the period 2002–2005.

Permits for new construction were mainly issued for residential properties. The number of industrial permits also increased significantly during the year, but they constituted only a small part of permits. Meanwhile, permits for the construction of investment properties, primarily multistory residential

Table 20.15. Building permits.

	Permits issued				% change		% of total	
	2002	2003	2004	2005	2004	2005	2004	2005
New construction	5,560	5,629	3,640	3,907	−35.3	7.3	40	40
Commercial	46	154	55	52	−64.3	−5.5	1	1
Investment	524	868	913	712	5.2	−22.0	10	7
Industrial	103	162	55	85	−66.0	54.5	1	1
Residential	4,887	4,445	2,617	3,058	−41.1	16.9	28	32
Additions	6,949	6,432	4,566	4,921	−29.0	7.8	50	51
Renovations	1,584	2,320	977	876	−57.9	−10.3	11	9
Total	14,093	14,381	9,183	9,704	−36.1	5.7	100	100

Source: Kuwait Municipality (www.municipality.gov.kw), 2006.

apartment buildings, experienced a significant drop, possibly as a result of an increase in interest rates and the rapid growth experienced by this sector in prior years.

Infrastructure

Transportation

Kuwait's road system links Kuwait city to every population center within the country as well as to the Saudi Arabia and Iraq borders. Kuwait has no railroads. Kuwait has three commercial ports. The largest port is located at Shuwaikh (near Kuwait City) and has a total of 21 berths. Shuaibia, 50 km south of Kuwait City, is mainly used for the import of heavy equipment and materials. The smallest port is located at Doha and has 20 small berths. Mina al-Ahmadi, 40 km south of Kuwait City, is Kuwait's oil port and is capable of loading over two million barrels of oil per day. Kuwait has four airports with permanent-surface runways all between 2,440 and 3,659 m length. The country's primary airport is Kuwait International in Kuwait City.

Communications

Kuwait's civil network suffered extensive damage as a result of the Gulf war and reconstruction is still under way with some restored international and domestic capabilities. The country's communications capability is comprised of the following: (1) 3 AM, 0 FM, 3 TV broadcast stations; (2) satellite earth stations; (3) destroyed during Gulf war and not yet rebuilt; temporary mobile satellite ground stations provide international telecommunications; and, (4) coaxial cable and microwave radio relay to Saudi Arabia.

Roads

An extensive network of mostly well-surfaced roads covers the country. There are 5,749 km of bituminous roads and another 1,000 km of road surfaced with earth, sand, or gravel. Buoyed by high income from oil in three decades, Kuwait announced a number of road infrastructure projects in the second half of 2005 including a 25 km causeway linking the northern area of Subbiya with Kuwait City at a cost of US $1.5 billion as well as two main road projects linking Iraq to the Kuwaiti port of Bubiyan and to Saudi Arabia for an additional 250 km. There are also plans to upgrade the country's system of seven ring roads with the addition of an eighth ring road to divert traffic away from the suburbs of Kuwait city.

Railways

There is no railway network in Kuwait but discussions are underway regarding the development of a domestic rail network as part of an overall US $5 billion Gulf rail link and the building of an underground metro system. During the visit of the then German chancellor, Gerhard Schröder, in March 2005, the possibility of the sale of a magnetic above-the-ground railway option was also discussed. This would link into the regional plan to provide a railway link between Kuwait and Muscat. The exact route of the Metro has yet to be defined but it is likely to consist of a 32 km section from Ardiya to Salmiya as part of the first phase, with two further phases to extend the line, southwards to Fintas and Fahaheel and westwards to Shuwaikh. The network would include both surface and underground rails and is projected to carry an average of 8,000 passengers an hour.

Ports

Kuwait exports its oil and refined hydrocarbon products through the ports of Mina Ahmadi, Mina Abdullah, Mina Az-Zoor, and Shuaiba. Kuwait also has two commercial sea-ports, in Shuwaikh and Shuaiba, for imports and non-oil exports. These ports handle bulk, containerized, refrigerated and general cargoes and they also have Ro-Ro (roll-on roll-off) facilities. A third commercial port in Doha is used by dhows and barges carrying light cargoes between Kuwait and Iran and ports lower down in the Gulf.

The country is also developing its logistics infrastructure, especially with the Kuwait Free Trade Zone (KFTZ), which is located in Shuwaikh Port, close to the international airport. Operational since 2000, it offers a range of business-friendly incentives, including 100% foreign ownership, tax exemption, and full repatriation of capital and profits. Backed by established infrastructure and advanced telecommunication systems, the free zone has already proved a valuable asset to the country's logistics industry, although simplifying the current procedures could boost activities further. "The free zone is strategically located in Shuwaikh Port providing access to these big potential markets in northern Iran, Iraq, Turkey, the Commonwealth of Independent States or the CIS," says DHL's Parker. "However, it is currently at an early stage in terms of capacity and operations. The procedures are not very user friendly as it could take up to three days to process a Kuwait inbound or outbound clearance process." Indeed, the local government's ability to simplify procedures and further develop its infrastructure will naturally play an important role in transforming Kuwait into a logistical superhub. (The Arabian Business.com, February 1, 2007).

Political and Legal Trends

The political system

Kuwait votes in a parliamentary election on Saturday (May 17, 2008), two months after its ruler dissolved parliament to end a crisis within the government. Following are some facts about the Gulf Arab state's political system: (1) Kuwait gained independence from Britain in 1961 and its first fully elected parliament was voted in 1963; (2) Kuwait has a 50-seat parliament with a history of challenging the government, unusual for a region dominated by families. Deputies have to approve the state budget and all major laws. They often exercise their right to question ministers, sometimes prompting them to resign under pressure; (3) Kuwait's ruler, Emir Sheikh Sabah al-Ahmad al-Sabah, has the last say in policy. He can dissolve the assembly and appoint new governments. Key cabinet portfolios such as defense, interior, and foreign affairs are held by members of the ruling al-Sabah family, none of whom have ever held a parliament seat; (4) Emir or his predecessors have dissolved parliament five times since its establishment — in 2008, 2006, 1999, 1986, and 1976. According to Kuwaiti law, elections must be held within 60 days of the assembly being dissolved, but rulers have ignored this rule before, suspending the assembly for five years from 1976 and six years from 1986; (5) Kuwait does not allow political parties but tolerates informal political groups. These include the hardline Islamist Salafist movement, the liberal Democratic Forum Bloc, the Shi'ite Muslim-led National Islamic Coalition, the Islamist Ummah Party, the Islamic Constitutional Movement and the liberal Popular Action Bloc; (6) Parliament passed a law in May 2005 giving women the right to vote and run in elections for the National Assembly. No woman was elected in the last election in 2006; (7) Emir is the 15th ruler in a dynasty which has ruled Kuwait for 250 years since part of the Anaiza tribe, to which the al-Sabah belong, migrated from the Arabian hinterland; (8) Since the US-led invasion of neighboring Iraq in 2003 and US calls for change in the Middle East, the ruling family has come under pressure from both Islamists and pro-Western liberals to loosen its grip on government and share power; (9) In July 2003, Emir issued a landmark decree separating the post of Prime Minister from the crown prince for the first time since Kuwait's independence; (10) Kuwait passed a new election law in 2006 cutting the number of constituencies from 25 to five in the hope that it would increase competition and reduce vote-buying that has long marred polls; (11) some 361,685 Kuwaitis, over half of them women, are eligible to vote in the 2008 election. Members of the security forces are not allowed to vote, nor are expatriates, who form almost 2.2 million of Kuwait's 3.2 million population; (12) Over 270 candidates, including 27 women, contested in 2008 election; and (13) changes of the oil minister usually do not have an impact on the energy policy of the major OPEC producer (Factbox, 2008). Table 20.16 reports the nature of companies that can be formed in Kuwait.

Legal framework for doing business

The right to carry on business

Any Kuwaiti or GCC national over 21 years of age may carry on commercial activities in Kuwait provided he or she is not affected by any personal restrictions (such as bankruptcy) or by the nature of the transactions undertaken (such as dealing in contraband goods). However, non-GCC nationals may not, as a general rule (Article 23(1) of the Commercial Code), carry on a trade in Kuwait unless they have one or more Kuwaiti partners and the capital owned by the Kuwaiti partner(s) in the joint business is not less than 51% of the total capital (60% in case of financial institutions such as banks, investment houses, and insurance companies). And a foreign company (including a partnership) may not set up a branch in Kuwait and may not perform any business activities in the country except through a Kuwaiti agent (part 24 of the Commercial Code). In addition, foreign individuals and corporations may not acquire commercial licenses in their own name, nor may they own real estate in Kuwait.

In the past few years, the above general rules have been modified to enable Kuwait to join the World Trade Organization (WTO). Foreigners (non-GCC nationals) may now establish businesses in the Free Trade Zone, in Shuwaikh, and retain 100% ownership of their businesses. The new foreign direct investment (FDI) law allows wholly foreign-owned businesses to be established in Kuwait. And foreigners may invest directly on the Kuwait Stock Exchange, rather than being restricted to mutual funds as in the past.

Recent business laws

The three main laws regulating business in Kuwait, which have been amended several times since they were first issued are (1) The Civil Code (Law 67 of 1980); (2) The Commercial Code (Law 68 of 1980); (3) The Commercial Companies Law (Law 15 of 1960) and (4) The rules of commerce in Kuwait are, in general, similar to West European practice.

Table 20.16. Legal forms of companies.

Form	Number of partners/ shareholders	Minimum and/or maximum capital	Liability	Registration fee	Release of financial documents
The close shareholding company	Minimum five partners.	KWD 7,500 minimum capital.	Partners' liability is limited to the amount contributed.	About KWD 3,000.	Yes
Limited liability company (WLL's)	Minimum two partners. Maximum 30 partners.	KWD 7,500 minimum capital.	Partners' liability is limited to the amount contributed.	About KWD 1,500.	Yes
General partnership	Minimum 2 partners.	No minimum capital.	Partners' liability is limited to the amount contributed.	About KWD 500.	No
Limited Partnership	Minimum 2 partners. Two types of partners: sleeping partners and active partners.	No minimum capital.	Liability of active partners is unlimited. The liability of sleeping partners is limited to the amount contributed.	About KWD 500.	No

Source: The Federation for International Trade Associates, 2007.

Intellectual property rights protection

The protection of intellectual property rights in Kuwait is quite good in theory. Trademarks are well protected provided they have been registered. A law protecting intellectual property, such as the rights of publishing or reproducing literary, artistic, musical, computer software, and other intellectual works, issued on the last day of 1999 is comprehensive. However, pirated copies of software, and audio and visual CDs and cassettes, are freely available on the streets in Kuwait and in many shops, notably in Hawally area. However, in recent years, especially after the implementation of WTO regime in 2005, Kuwait government clamped down on violations of intellectual property rights.

The state of Kuwait is a signatory to the WTO agreement on the protection of intellectual property rights (TRIPIS) and is a party to the Arab Convention for Copyright Protection. It is affiliated to the World Intellectual Property Organization. A trademark is anything that takes a distinctive shape and that is used or intended to be used to distinguish products for the purpose of indicating that they belong to the owner of the mark because he or she, makes them, selects them, trades in them or displays them for sale. Articles 61 to 85 of the Commercial Code provide for the registration and protection of trademarks. A patent is the sole right to the proceeds of an invention, including the right to exclude others from making, using or selling an invented product during specified time. Law 64 of 1999 is designed to provide comprehensive protection to the authors of all forms of intellectual works in letters, arts, and the sciences including: (1) literary works (written and oral); (2) theoretical shows; (3) musical works (with or without lyrics); (4) choreographic works; (5) motion pictures; (6) audio, video, radio, and TV works; (7) artistic works (paintings, sculptures, carvings and architectural, and decorative works); (8) photographs; (9) works of applied art (craft and industrial designs); (10) illustrations and maps; (11) designs and models; (12) computer works (software and databases); and (13) translated works. Protection, however, is not limited to the above types of work and the legislation has been framed so that new types of works will be protected. The title to a work is also protected provided this has been created and it is not a common expression.

Extent of modernization of the society

Kuwait's democracy has experienced ups and downs, and more are probably in the offing as the country takes up such problems as women and naturalized citizens (along with their descendants) claim their political rights as well as allowing political parties to organize. It is critical that democracy does not fragment Kuwaiti society along tribal, sectarian, and religious lines. Intellectuals and opinion leaders in Kuwait commonly object not to democracy but to the way that it is practiced in their country. Khalifa al-Luqayan, a leading Kuwaiti poet and writer, recently expressed this sentiment.

Democracy, as we understand it, is a way of citizen participation in the affairs of society. But unfortunately it brings us inexcusable behavior by awakening tribal and sectarian fanaticism. What we saw in the 1992 elections for the Assembly, municipal council, and cooperatives — voting for tribal and sectarian reasons — will fragment our society rather than uniting it.[1] Conditions in Kuwait have reached near maturity, yet it should always be remembered that such a process is by nature slow, and that maturation depends, internally, on the development of social and economic factors, and externally, on a more peaceful coexistence in the region, with progressive economic and political development. If Kuwait can take these steps forward, it may have an immense impact not just on Kuwait itself, but also on developments in the entire region. Only time will tell.

Social and Cultural Trends

Islamic culture

Arab culture and traditions, anchored by Islam, are the secure foundations upon which the modern State of Kuwait is built. The metamorphosis in lifestyle brought about by the discovery of oil did not efface the identity of the people of Kuwait. The ravages brought by the Iraqi aggression also did not stifle the spirit of the Kuwaitis as they rebuilt their country in record time. The State of Kuwait has always paid special attention to the preservation of its culture and heritage by maintaining monuments and preserving artifacts and historical documents. The National Museum is one of the 50 locations where these are housed. The destruction caused by the Iraqi troops created a heightened awareness among the people about the need to preserve and resurrect the arts and crafts of Kuwait. The new architecture of the city, which combines modern design with traditional, reflects this awareness.

Kuwait has a large variety of customs and traditions, and this gives rise to a colorful and extensive culture, reflected in the Diwaniya, the Bedouin traditions, and Al Sadu weaving. The people of Kuwait also have special love for the arts, be it literature, theatre, music, dance, films, or contemporary art. The National Council of Culture, Arts and Literature (NCCAL); The Free Art Studio and The Kuwaiti Society of Formative Artists are promoting the visual arts in Kuwait. Most aspects of the business culture are conservative. Dress should be formal and conservative (particularly for women) and greetings should be between same sexes only. There is often accompanying small talk when meeting someone for the first time. Be sure to adhere to local customs. Affection between opposite sexes is not shown in public. Most business is conducted in English, although using a few words of Arabic (particularly for titles) will be appreciated. It can be difficult to conduct business in Kuwait as the working week runs from Sunday to Thursday. Business hours vary, but are usually from 7 a.m. to 1 p.m. and 4 p.m. to 10 p.m. Government offices and banks are usually open from 8 a.m. to 2 p.m. (Arabian business.com, 2008).

Importance of working with Kuwaiti partners

In order to do business in Kuwait, an expatriate entrepreneur or company needs an agent, sponsor or equity partner, unless he is investing under the direct foreign investment rules. Choosing a Kuwaiti associate wisely is one of the critical factors for success. Because locally there is no such thing as a pure business relationship, the reliability and depth of the personal relationship are very important when choosing a Kuwaiti associate. Other factors that must be considered are the associate's financial resources, his overall business experience, the extent of his current operations, and his experience in the proposed products or services. Practical issues such as the availability of the licenses needed to carry on the particular business and how to control over day-to-day management and business assets is to be shared should never be overlooked. One of the most important criteria in choosing a Kuwaiti associate is his standing in the local business community and in government circles. If a foreign firm's products or services are directed to a particular ministry or business area, then a potential associate's personal connections with the main decision makers in that field require thorough evaluation. However, an overseas businessman will soon discover that many individuals and firms habitually present themselves as having more influence than they do in fact have in a particular area and caution needs to be exercised in evaluating offers of sponsorship. A foreigner is strongly advised to refrain from signing with an agent until he has made several trips to the country, knows some of the main decision makers in the areas in which he is interested, and is fully satisfied as to the suitability of a particular associate.

Large and growing youth market

Kuwait's Census Bureau has called on authorities to establish training programs and incentives to start small businesses in order to stem rising youth unemployment. Hessa Al-Janahi, acting director of the bureau, also suggested curbs on the number of foreign workers entering Kuwait. The latest unemployment data show that 19,250 Kuwaitis are unemployed; 5.5% of the national work force. Over 80% of those unemployed are women. Only 16% are men. Kuwait's rising youth population is struggling to find work. Half of the total unemployed are under the age of 30, and three-quarters are under 40. Education appeared to be key to cutting long-term jobless rates, Al-Janahi said. Over half of the unemployed in Kuwait do not hold "below high school credentials," according to the Census Bureau. 12.8% hold no formal education (Arabian business.com, 2008).

Technological Trends

Telecom and IT

Kuwait's mobile telecommunication segment is regarded as one of the strongest and most advanced in the world. Current penetration rate rests at 90%, but is expected to reach 100% by 2008. The country's two operators, Zain and Wataniya, continually roll out advancements of their products and services such as 3.5 G, and 3.8 G, respectively, with the goal of providing greater download speeds and the use of TV and online services, as well as increasing the ease of user accessibility. Both operators have also become involved in a rampant spate of merger and acquisition activity in recent years. Such activity is allowing both companies to expand their operations abroad — Zain now has operations in 20 countries and close to 30 m subscribers, with further growth expected in the years to come. A third operator, however, is expected to enter the market in the coming months, although bids have yet to be formally tendered. The introduction of a third operator will increase competition, resulting in a price reduction for mobile users, which will be much welcomed by consumers, who currently pay some of the highest rates in the region. The fixed-line segment, however, is not doing so well, having long been superseded by the mobile segment. The Ministry of Communications' (MoC) monopoly on fixed lines is at the root of the problem, with international call rates the highest among Gulf countries, thus discouraging the use of landlines. Many now argue the MoC should relinquish its control on regulatory matters to an independent telecommunications regulatory authority or privatize its landlines, as taking on the role of both regulator and operator impedes further expansion. Despite an impressive IT history that includes the distinction of being the first country in the Middle East to have widespread Internet access, Kuwait's prominence among its Gulf Cooperation Council neighbors in terms of IT has slightly fallen over the past five years. Liberal import laws for IT hardware and a relatively high GDP per capita, some $29,000 per citizen, will serve to bolster desire for the latest technologies, with 15%–30% growth expected for the PC market in 2008. While the hardware segment will continue to grow, software piracy in Kuwait remains one of the biggest hindrances to overall growth in the IT sector, with the rate of piracy in 2006 resting at 64%, down from the previous year, yet still the highest in the region. Broadband penetration, at only 28% in 2006, is also facing problems. A lack of infrastructure, particularly in newly developed areas, along with high prices for Internet, services has been the key inhibiting factor to further penetration. New initiatives and reforms are currently being implemented in a joint effort by the private sector and the government to increase penetration, but these efforts may prove irrelevant, as mobile operators are now offering faster-than-ADSL internet speeds to mobile subscribers. Meanwhile, new projects and organizations are currently being set up with the hope of diversifying Kuwait's economy through the widespread transfer of IT knowledge and the creation of more IT jobs, thus spurring the development of IT software and services.

Development of IT

The State of Kuwait has a long history of active use of physical development planning. It is now more than 40 years since the first Kuwait Master Plan, 1952 laid down the essential principles that have been followed ever since. These principles and a succession of master plans and reviews have helped guide the development of Kuwait from a small mud brick town of 75,000 persons to today's contemporary metropolis of three million persons.

Before the review of the Kuwait Master Plan in 1989–1990, the need to establish a systematic database using computer technology was recognized by Kuwait Municipality. At that time, a utility and data management project (KUDAMS — Kuwait Utility and data Management System) was nearing completion. This had been conceived as a large-scale utility management project derived from field survey and aerial photography, implemented on Intergraph equipment basically as a CAD system for access to public utility data. Disruption caused by the Iraqi occupation and its aftermath has been a prime factor in aborting many projects. Among them include the Kuwait Master Plan Review and the KUDAMS projects.

In post-liberation Kuwait Municipality recognized that it was no longer sensible to carry out a further review of the Master Plan. Instead, a new comprehensive development planning project was required in view of the transformation in Kuwait, principally in terms of demographic composition and economic structures. Following a short initial assessment study in 1992, to identify and prepare data needed for the new Master Plan, Kuwait Municipality formed a team associated with a local consultants (SSH — Salem Al-Marzouk & Sabah Abi-Hanna) to prepare a wholly new Third Kuwait Master Plan (3KMP). This furnished an opportunity to embody GIS technology as an integral part of the new master plan. In recent years, Kuwaiti government is placing major emphasis on developing and implementing e-government development programs.

Internet access and use

The *.kw* is managed by the Ministry of Communications, which entered into a contract with GulfNet Kuwait Computer Company (now Gulfnet International Company) in 1994 to offer Internet connections on an exclusive basis to the public and government agencies for two years, with the contract being renewable for additional two-year terms. The contract remains in force today, although, in early 1996, the Ministry announced that a second ISP was to be licensed, in order to "improve the Internet service" and lower prices; no second license has been forthcoming. The service is marketed as the Kuwait Electronics Messaging Services (KEMS) (www.moc.kw). KEMS is connected to the Internet in the United States via a satellite circuit leased from SprintLink, operating originally with one Class C network (196.1.69) registered with the InterNIC and now with a complete Class B network (168.187). Services offered include dial-up shell (UNIX) and SLIP/PPP accounts, and leased lines. At the time that it was granted the ISP contract, the Ministry of Communications had already registered and connected more than 200 Internet hosts, principally at government agencies. An affiliated company, Gulfnet Kuwait (www.kuwait.net), offers identical services, although most government agencies and public companies are connected to the Internet via KEMS. Gulfnet has been assigned 64 Class C blocks of IP numbers (194.54.192-194.54.255) by UUNet Gulf (Dubai), and is connected to a UUNet Technologies Internet port in the United States by a satellite link.

Kuwait hosts the most Internet sites in the Persian Gulf region, almost half of the total. A large number of domains are registered with the InterNIC, however, rather than the Ministry of Communications. Some of these registrations pre-date the existence of the Internet in Kuwait, but many companies today continue to prefer a domain name without a country identifier. Of passing note, the Kuwait Ministry of Information has its own Web site (www.info-kuwait.org), which includes among the ministry's responsibilities "censorship," but the domain is not only registered with the InterNIC, but the server is located in North Carolina. At least several Kuwaiti companies also use servers located in the United States.

An Internet service provider, ZakSat, was established in Kuwait in 1997 and started offering public Internet access in 1997. The company uses satellite technology similar to Hughes Network System's "PC Direct" Internet service, whereby subscriber-to-ISP transmissions are carried via leased or dial-up telephone lines but ISP-to-subscriber communications (i.e., the bulk of the data) are transmitted via satellite. ZakSat is connected to the Subic Bay Satellite Systems Inc. teleport in the Philippines, which is in turn connected to the Internet in the United States via a 7.7 Mbps satellite link which will be increased to 45 Mbps in the near future. The teleport's network operations center also hosts proxy servers that locally cache frequently requested Web pages. Subscriber communications are carried on AsiaSat 2 (100.5°E), with a footprint reaching from Egypt to New Zealand, wherein resides two-thirds of the earth's population. Tables 20.17 and 20.18 show mobile research rates in GCC, and share in total mobile telecom subscriber base, respectively.

Table 20.17. Mobile research rates in GCC — 2007.

Country	Percent
Oman	93
Saudi Arabia	101
Kuwait	111
Qatar	140
UAE	142
Bahrain	113

Source: Global research.

Table 20.18. Share in total mobile telecom subscriber base (2007).

Subscriber	Percent
Zain	56.8
Wataniya	43.2

Source: Zain & Wataniya Telecom.

Conclusion

International business enterprises intending to enter Kuwait market should become familiar with the overall business environments and its emerging trends. This chapter attempts at providing an overview of the Kuwait business environmental dimensions. An understanding of the emerging Kuwait business environmental trends would enable international business to become aware of both opportunities and challenges of doing business in Kuwait. As the Kuwait economy is expected to grow with the increased oil revenues in the foreseeable future, it is logical to expect that many business opportunities will be available to international businesses. The globalization, privatization, and liberalization forces shopping the Kuwait economy and society provide business opportunities. The opening up of business opportunities is enhanced by the following key characteristics of the Kuwait business environment: (1) Kuwait is a highly import-dependent country. The imports of various products and services from different parts of the world are continuously increasing facilitated by increased favorable balance of trade; (2) the capital intensive country with the national goal of diversifying the predominantly oil dependent economy is resulting in the initiation of a variety of industrial, infrastructural, and tourism development projects. The technological and human needs of such projects offer many business opportunities to international businesses. Business opportunities will be especially attractive in the area of developing upstream petrochemical industries; (3) participation of foreign enterprises in retailing field is progressively increasing. Given the Kuwaiti consumer preferences for quality foreign products and services, many well established US and Western European franchises; (4) recent legislation by Kuwait government aimed at attracting foreign direct investment will also facilitate entry of foreign enterprises; (5) many leading trading companies in Kuwait have long experience in dealing with foreign businesses which should help the new entrants to function effectively in the Kuwait market and (6) one of the national goals of Kuwait governments is to develop the country to develop into a regional business hub, which provides foreign businesses a regional alternative to Dubai when the costs of operating business operations are escalating.

The international businesses should become aware of some of the challenges of operating businesses in Kuwait. The following are some of such challenges: (1) first and foremost, effective business functioning would require a Kuwaiti partner. Both legal and practical aspects of doing business in Kuwait would require finding a suitable Kuwaiti partner; (2) given the rising unemployment problem with Kuwaiti population, Kuwait government follows an active Kuwaitization policy. This policy requires the private sector businesses to employ certain proportion of their human resource requirements with Kuwaitis. Given the general paucity of qualified and experienced Kuwaitis, the foreign businesses may have to develop programs to recruit, train, and employ Kuwaitis; (3) for the bulk of the technically qualified and experienced human resource needs, foreign companies have to depend on expatriates from other Arab and Asian countries. This situation poses two types of challenges. First, given the global demand exceeding the supply for such skilled personnel, it becomes progressively more difficult to recruit and retain the qualified expatriate skilled employees. Second, the need to assemble the human resources from diverse cultures results in facing the problems of effectively managing multicultural work forces; (4) adapting to cultural values, traditions, and norms of Islamic Arab society becomes imperative when doing business in Kuwait. Although Kuwait is more modernized society by Arab regional standards, the core cultural aspects of Kuwait confirm to Islamic Arab cultural environment and (5) finally, it is important to emphasize that competitiveness in Kuwait is progressively becoming more intense. For many imported consumer goods and services, the intensity of competition is ever increasing as Kuwait imports from many countries. In recent years, imports from emerging Asian countries have vastly increased the intensity of competition. In manufacturing sector in the past several companies enjoyed monopoly conditions since the government policy was not to license additional manufacturing companies, if some companies already exist in that product field. However, this policy seems to have been relaxed. Hence, one can expect increasing competition in non-oil manufacturing industries.

Finally, It is no doubt that major challenges facing the Kuwait economy as well as other GCC members in the future would mainly be economic diversification, employment generation, and increasing inflation. This is especially in the current scenarios of tumbling dollar as well as high population growth rates and skewness toward young population.

References

http://www.meed.com/databank/2008/04/major_tourism_projects_in_the_gcc.html
http://in.reuters.com/article/oilRpt/idINL1741566820080517
http://www.oxfordbusinessgroup.com/publication.asp?country=33
http://fita.org/countries/kuwait.html?ma_rubrique=investissement
FACTBOX (17 May 2008) Some facts about Kuwait's political system, *Reuters India*.
The Gulf Monarchies: Kuwait's Real Elections (1996). *The Middle East Quarterly*, 3(4).
http://www.arabianbusiness.com/520573-kuwaits-youth-struggle-to-find-work.html

http://www.meforum.org/article/150 Kuwait: Oasis of liberalism, Mohammed Al Rumaihi (1994). *The Middle East Quarterly*, 1(3).

http://www.gisqatar.org.qa/conf97/links/e3.html. Dynamic planning using GIS: The Kuwait Experience, Waleed Khalifa Al Jassim, Kuwait Municipality.

http://www.emeraldinsight.com/Insight/ViewContentServlet?Filename=Published/Emeral dFullTextArticle/Articles/2630240606.html

Annual Statistical Abstract 2006 Edition, 43, Ministry of Planning, Kuwait.

Economic and financial review of Kuwait, 2006, National Bank of Kuwait. Global Investment House (29 May 2008). Trade surplus bulged to a new landmark of KD 12.2 Billion by the end of 2007. *AlWatan Daily*, p. 19.

Global Investment House (28 May 2008). BOP Surplus Reaches KD1.04 Billion by the End of 2006. *AlWatan Daily*, p. 19.

Global Investment House (30 May 2008). Telecom revenues more than doubled to KD 571.5 Million by the end of 2007. *AlWatan Daily*, p. 18.

Global Investment House (26 May 2008). Kuwaiti economy reports stellar performance for the fifth year in a row. *AlWatan Daily*, p. 18.

Global Investment House (27 May 2008). Inflation reaches 9.53% by the end of January 2008. *AlWatan Daily*, p. 19.

Global Investment House (13 May 2008). Kuwaiti economy reports stellar performance for the fifth year in a row. *AlWatan Daily*, p. 23.

Global Investment House (6 June 2008). Local residential sales up by 23.9% in 2007, apartments and commercial sector sales up by 39.2%. *AlWatan Daily*, p. 18.

Global Investment House (4 June 2008). Kuwaiti insurance market witnessed declining loss ratios over years. *AlWatan Daily*, p. 18.

Kennedy, PD. *Doing Business with Kuwait*, 2nd edn.

The National Bank of Kuwait (12 June 2008). Kuwait inflation to rise further after hitting a record 10.1% in February. *AlWatan Daily*, p. 18.

U.S. Commercial Services (2007). "Doing business in Kuwait: A country commercial guide for U.S. Companies 2007. International Copyright, U.S. and Foreign Commercial Service and U.S. Department of State, 2007.

Chapter 21

GLIMPSES AT SOCIETY AND MANAGEMENT IN IRAN

HAMID YEGANEH

Abstract

This chapter aims to shed light on main aspects of society and management in Iran. Iran represents a major regional player that has gained a growing geopolitical and economic importance over the course of past decade. Understanding Iranian business requires a holistic approach as in Iran religion, society, culture, economy, politics, and family are intimately intertwined.

Introduction

To managers, Iran appears an important country. Iran represents a large regional economy with a strategic location in the Persian Gulf and Central Asia, a large consumer market, tremendous natural resources and numerous petrochemical/manufacturing industries which require heavy investment. Politically, historically, and culturally, Iran is a unique and complex country that necessitates in-depth investigation. Indeed, most Westerners tend to think of Iran in clichés or bizarre caricatures that they get from CNN. Therefore, the current chapter is an attempt to shed light on some aspects of society and management in Iran. The discussion might be of potential interest for multinationals, NGOs, international negotiators, businessmen/women, expatriated managers, diplomats, and investors. This chapter is organized in two major parts. In the first part, the Iranian social context is described and demographic, economic, religious, political, and cultural factors are examined. In the second part, management practices in Iranian organizations are analyzed and practical recommendations are provided.

Iranian Social Context

A ruler who described his empire as Iranshahr and himself as the "king of kings" of Iran used the name "Iran" as early as the third century B.C. This word is derived from Aryan that means noble or of good birth. Aryans were a branch of Indo-European peoples who appeared around 2500 B.C. and gradually migrated to India and southwest Asia. These people and their empire were known Persians or Persia. Therefore, Iran and Persia were used interchangeably. Iran is located in southwest Asia. It shares borders with Turkey, Iraq, Armenia, Azerbaijan, Turkmenistan, Afghanistan, and Pakistan. It has coastlines along the Persian Gulf and the Sea of Oman in south, and the Caspian Sea in north. Iran has an area of 636,296 sq. miles (1.6 million sq. km) making it the 16th largest country in the world. The country is highly diverse from every point of view, especially in topography and climate. The climates can be extreme and vary in different regions of the country. The geopolitical importance of Iran is influenced by its location in the Middle East and Central Asia. Indeed, Iran is considered a bridge between the landlocked central Asian republics and the Indian Ocean.

Demography and ethnicities

Shortly after the Islamic Revolution (1979), the government abolished family planning programs. As a result, the population of Iran grew at an average annual rate of about 4% per year between 1976 and 1986 (Abbasi-Shavazi, 2000). Faced with the grave social consequences of population growth, the government was obliged to adopt new family planning programs and subsequently, fertility has declined dramatically since 1988 (Abbasi-Shavazi, 2000). Currently, the population of Iran is estimated at some 66 million (CIA Factbook, 2008).

The official language of Iran is Persian (Farsi). Persian is an Indo-European language derived from Sanskrit and it is taught and practiced in all schools from the first grade across the country. Other local languages that are spoken include mainly Turkish and Kurdish. The country has one of the world's most diverse ethnic groups ever assembled in one country. The major ethnic groups are Persian (56%), Turk (Azari) (24%), Gilaki (8%), Kurd (8%), Arab, Lur, Baluch, and Turkaman. The religious groups in descending order are Shiite Muslim, Sunni Muslim, Zoroastrian, Jewish,

Christian, and Bahaii. Over the course of past two decades, rapid urbanization and migration have narrowed the gap between rural areas and large cities. This trend has resulted in emergence of a new middle class culture and the prevalence of Persian (Farsi) language among other ethnic minorities (Kian-Thiebaut, 1999).

Political environment

For over 2500 years, monarchy was the norm of political life in Iran. By one account, 46 such dynasties and over 400 *Shahs* (kings) ruled in Iran (Daniel, 2001). This long and old monarchical tradition was interrupted in 1979 with proclamation of Islamic Republic and adoption of a new constitution. The Shiite clergy assumed control of the state and reversed shah's pro-Western policies. This led to interruption of diplomatic relations between Iran and the United States. For the moment, Iran is an Islamic republic ruled according to a constitution providing for executive, legislative, and judicial branches. The president is elected every four years by popular vote, although the Guardian Council must approve all presidential candidates. Contrary to what happens in many other Muslim countries, once candidates have been approved, the election is left to take its own course, and the results seem not to be falsified (Andersen and Seeberg, 1999). Therefore, the political system in Iran can be considered an indigenous democracy that relies on both public opinion and nominated authorities. The past 25 years of Iranian political environment are characterized by chaos, instability, eight-year war, blood shed, US hostility, and strife over the nuclear program.

Economic environment

With a relatively large population and the world's largest oil and gas reserves, Iran is an important regional economy. Iran is OPEC's second largest oil producer. It has approximately 9% of world oil reserves and is believed to have the second largest reserves of natural gas (OPEC, 2005). Iran might be described as a "rentier economy" receiving substantial amounts of oil revenues (80% of GDP) from the outside world. The high reliance on oil revenues may be linked to unaccountable/autocratic governments and economic/administrative inefficiency (Mahdavi, 1970).

According to Iranian constitution, "the economy of the Islamic Republic of Iran is to consist of three sectors: state, cooperative, and private, and is to be based on systematic and sound planning" (Article 44, Iranian Constitution). In practice, Iran economy is a mixture of central planning, state ownership of large enterprises, village agriculture, and small private firms (Khajehpour, 2000). The state sector includes all large-scale and mother industries such as foreign trade, radio and television, telephone services, and aviation. Some major industries are run by revolutionary foundations, which own about 20% of the country's assets but are generally mismanaged (Khajehpour, 2000). The private sector consists of small- and medium-size companies concerned with production and services that supplement the economic activities of the state. The cooperative sector is practically insignificant and includes enterprises offering limited number of products and services. While the first decade of the Islamic government (1980–1990) was marked by socialist plans, the second decade (1991–1999) witnessed a trend toward market economy (Kian-Thiebaut, 1999).

Another unofficial but powerful part of Iranian economy is "Bazaar" or an ultraconservative and religious trading community, which has no equivalent in any part of the Western world (Husain, 1995; Schramm-Nielsen and Faradonbeh, 2002). Traditionally, the religious clerics and the "Bazaar" community have been interdependent. The bazaar is not only a place for exchanging commodities, but also a place where religious norms and cultural values could be discussed and exchanged. The bazaar played an active role in the revolution, helping to organize it and being the major financial supporter. After the establishment of the Islamic Republic, the Bazaar has managed to enforce its role in society and has made efforts to become part of the new regime (Mozzafari, 1991).

Societal culture

Based on Hofstede's findings (1980), Iran is classified in near Eastern cultural cluster including Turkey and Greece (Ronen and Shenkar, 1985). Another research conducted through GLOBE project found that Iran is part of the South Asian cultural cluster consisting of such countries as India, Thailand, and Malaysia (Gupta *et al.*, 2002; Javidan and Dastmalchian, 2003; House *et al.*, 2004). As a country situated in the Middle East, Iran has many commonalities with neighboring Arab/Muslim countries; however, due to its unique historical, linguistic, and racial identities, it has developed a different and unique culture (Ali and Amirshahi, 2002). It is possible to consider two distinct vectors in Iranian culture: nationalist and Islamist. The nationalist aspect of Iranian culture is related to Ancient Persian civilization and Zoroastrianism heritage, which date 3000–2000 B.C. but are still prevalent in different aspects of Iranian society such as Calendar and New Year Festivals (*Nowrooz*). On the other hand, Islamist and subsequently Shiism aspects are relatively younger and date seventh and sixteenth centuries, respectively. It has been suggested that besides Persian and Islamist influences, the effects of Western culture on Iranian society should be taken into consideration (Bani-Asadi, 1984).

Hofstede (1980) ranked Iran 41 for individualism orientation. Based on this score, Iran has a collectivistic culture. This feature has been confirmed by other studies (Javidan and Dastmalchian, 2003; Yeganeh and Su, 2007). Another feature of Iranian culture is high degree of hierarchical distance (Hofstede, 1980; Javidan and Dastmalchian, 2003; House *et al.*, 2004; Yeganeh and Su, 2007). This dimension concerns the extent to which the less powerful members of a society expect and accept that power is distributed unequally. Iranian culture tends to be past-oriented and future orientation receives very low emphasis (Dastmalchian *et al.*, 2001; Hoveyda, 2003; Shayegan, 2003; Yeganeh and Su, 2007). The past-orientation seems quite conceivable, since Iran represents a traditional country haunted by a long history. Hofstede (1980) described Iranian society as a relatively feminine culture (Hofstede, 1980). In fact, Iranians are believed to maintain harmonious relationships with their environment, and to attach importance to their being.

Religion

The majority of Iranians belong to the Shiaa branch of Islam, which represents only about 15% of the world community of Muslims. The Shiaa Muslims believe that the Prophet nominated Ali to be the first caliph of the Muslim community. Nevertheless, Iranians share many values with other Islamic countries. For Muslims, Islam is not a man-made institution; the Koran contains the words of God, revealed to the prophet some 1400 years ago and its commands are absolutely correct and practical even in modern times. Islam is generally viewed by some non-Muslims as being a fatalist creed; however, the position of the Prophet as reflected in the Koran is very shifty and equivocal. Unlike many other religions, Islam is an all-encompassing creed; it governs every aspect of life, public and private, political, and economic. This implies that Islam has its say in all areas of everyday life including business life. The good Muslim manager should be guided by his conscience and by God's written instructions and they are supposed to do the right thing for people. By studying traditional and modern Islamic texts, Latifi (1997) identified work-related values such as equality before God, individual responsibility, paternalism, fatalism mixed with personal choice, and consultation in decision making. Respect for seniority, loyalty, and obedience are other widespread Islamic work-related values (Namazie and Tayeb, 2003).

Management and Organization in Iran

In following sections, by referring to social factors, some aspects of human resource management and organizational behavior in Iran will be analyzed.

Labor and staffing

In recent years, economic growth has not kept pace with labor force increase, leading to an unemployment rate, which is estimated about 20%. Hence, the labor supply is abundant and the employers can choose among relatively well educated and young workers. It is estimated that there are over 800,000 entrants into job market per year (Khajehpour, 2000). In Iran, especially after the Islamic Revolution of 1979, it was believed that unemployment belonged to Western capitalistic economies. Consequently, the government put priority on reducing unemployment by hiring a large number of people especially war veterans and revolutionary guards. This trend led to overstaffed organizations in public sector, suffering from high operating costs and inefficiency. However, there are signs that after two decades, the government is abdicating its paternalistic role in providing secure jobs.

When opportunities arise to hire new personnel, most organizations advertise job vacancies and conduct professional interviews to select the best candidates, but the results are generally affected by networking and recommendations (Yeganeh and Su, 2008). During selection process, employers consider many credentials such as experience, professional skills, education, and personal conduct of the candidate in their previous positions. Among different criteria, education and university diploma receive a good deal of attention even if they are not directly related to job requirements. Iranians have a high regard for university diploma and generally they continue their education as far as possible even though sometimes they do not have clear objectives in continuation of their studies. Some state-owned organizations, depending on the nature of their activities, pay attention to what they have defined as compliance and code of conduct. According to what has been imposed shortly after the Islamic revolution (1979), only those who conform to Islamic/revolutionary criteria are employed by state-owned organizations. Verifying candidate's conformity is often a separate procedure, which takes long time and might be evaluated by those who are not concerned with candidates' capabilities. Such restrictions have underprivileged skillful workforce for more than two decades and have resulted in increasing inefficiency in public sector. In large organizations, especially in public sector, the criteria for promotion are not clearly defined. Mostly, promotions are based on a wide range of behavioral or implicit criteria, which are not related to performance or professional capabilities (Yeganeh and Su, 2008).

Compensation

An essential question regarding compensation is the extent to which it is related to performance. The compensation policies in most Iranian large organizations are not related to productivity, and therefore do not create enough motivation for workers (Yeganeh and Su, 2008). This may be related to "rentier" nature of Iranian economy that relies upon oil revenues rather than domestic production. The preference for fixed pay is a traditional view, which is common in large organizations. By contrast, variable pay is used rather in relatively young and small firms that are concerned with productivity and growth (Namazie and Frame, 2007; Yeganeh and Su, 2008). Performance and seniority are not mutually exclusive; however, most of the time, they reflect two different reward philosophies. Many Iranian organizations regard seniority as the major criterion for pay increase and promotion. This orientation is in conformity with traditional Iranian cultural values, cherishing past experience and elderly people. In Persian literature, the word "elder" is taken often as equivalent to savvy, experienced, and knowledgeable (Yeganeh and Su, 2008). Another criterion for pay increase is the level of education. People with higher education get more chances not only in recruitment, but also in promotion. Even in smaller firms, which attach importance to productivity, and where the measurement of performance is not always possible or accurate, pay increase is based ultimately on seniority and higher education. The structure of reward system in most Iranian organizations is hierarchical. In other words, there is considerable difference between compensation packages intended for people working at the top of organization and those working at entry levels. Top management mostly decides compensation policies and the employees have little involvement in negotiating their salaries. In large organizations, the remuneration package may include many non-financial rewards such as bonuses, subsidies, uniforms, daily shuttle services, a meal per day, food coupons, housing assistance, and day care. New Year bonuses are compulsory and they are paid at the beginning of Iranian New Year (March 21st). They may reach up to two or three times of monthly salary. Among non-financial subsidies, housing is a very important item. During 1980s and 1990s, workers in large organizations were given lifetime employment. It seems that lifetime employment was a reflection of paternalistic role of "allocation government" in creating secure jobs and distributing wealth. Over the course of past years, there has been a trend of privatization. As a result, most companies in public sector are closing their doors to unqualified workers and some are trying to get rid of unnecessary personnel.

Training and development and performance appraisal

One of the main objectives of training and development is to help employees achieve at their full potential in the organization (Schuster, 1985). Therefore, training and development lead ultimately to improve the overall functioning of human resources. While Iranian organizations have an easy access to young and relatively well-educated workers, the typical workforce is not specialized in demanded areas. In other words, a typical Iranian worker has a good base of theoretical knowledge, which is not functional to meet employers' requirements. The lack of experience and practical skills may be attributed to two major issues: Iranian education system and political/economic environment. On the one hand, Iranian education system is highly theoretical and on the other hand, two decades of political unrest have led the country and its workforce to economic isolation. Many large organizations have training centers to enhance employees' competence. The training programs cover a wide range of issues such as technical, managerial, and clerical skills.

An important issue regarding training is the extent to which it is related to productivity. In the case of Iranian human resource management, training programs seem to be related to employees' behavior rather than their productivity. This orientation toward quality of life may be understood in view of social, cultural, and economic factors. Iranian culture is relatively feminine (Hofstede, 1980) and has a tendency toward getting gratification from life. Moreover, affected by Islamic culture, Iranians tend to view the world as an ephemeral step, which is not worth hard work and should be considered as a transitional phase toward eternal life. High reliance on natural resources is another factor that decreases motivation for efficiency and economic productivity (Mahdavi, 1970; Yeganeh and Su, 2007).

While most of Iranian organizations recognize the importance of training and development programs, they do not take enough time for planning and preparation. Namazie and Tayeb (2003) reported that training programs in Iranian organizations were not designed systematically. Past orientation and two decades of political uncertainty/turmoil might be underlying such unsystematic approaches. Like compensation policies, training programs are designed generally with low level of employees' participation. Most of time, the top management decides about training programs and approaches.

The rationale behind any form of appraisal, especially in industrialized countries, is to improve the utilization of human resources in the organization. The data collected at appraisal phase can be used in other functions such as planning, recruitment, compensation, promotion, training, and layoff. Despite this importance, appraisal is not a common practice in Iranian HRM (Yeganeh and Su, 2008). Furthermore, managers involved in appraisal performance hardly rely on systematic approaches. An important issue in appraisal process is the extent to which criticism is accepted. In collectivistic cultures such as Iran, people attach too much importance to interpersonal relations and negative feedback can bring about many problems for both managers and subordinates.

Social networking

A very fundamental issue in every society is the priority given to interests of individuals versus those of collectivity. Hofstede (1980) views an individualistic society as one in which beliefs and the individual determine behaviors; whereas in a collectivistic society, the attitudes are determined by loyalty toward one's group. In that sense, collectivism and individualism correspond to traditional (*Gemeinschaft*) and modern societies (*Geselleschaft*) as described by Toennies (1963). In collectivistic societies, identity is based in the social system and group's interests invade private life, whereas in individualistic societies identity is based in the individuals and private life is protected (Hofstede, 1980). The collectivistic orientation of Iranian culture may be related to the importance of family in the society. For most Iranians, the primary building block of many social relationships is family (*Khanevadeh*). It is associated with honor, social status, and wealth, and therefore is well protected. Children are central to family; especially in middle classes, they receive a good deal of attention. For Iranians, the family is wife, children, and siblings; it includes a network of friends transcending regulations and leading to favoritism (Schramm-Nielsen and Faradonbeh, 2002).

The manifestations of collectivism and social networking are very prevalent in Iranian management. Personal connections and informal channels seem more practical, whereas formal systems, official institutions, and procedures are considered less efficient and even bothering (Faradonbeh, 2000). As a direct result, Iranian society tends to operate rather on the basis of personal relationships among people than on the basis of impersonal and dehumanized institutions. The use of informal channels may imply bending rules and taking advantages to which one is not formally entitled. The popular Persian term for this practice and other forms of nepotism and favoritism is *partibazi*, which is a common practice in Iranian organizations. For instance, it would not be unusual for Iranian managers to hire a relative or acquaintance for a job vacancy, even though they could easily employ a more competent but unknown worker (Yeganeh and Su, 2007). Generally, when favoritism does not imply any bribe, it is not regarded as corruption (Schramm-Nielsen and Faradonbeh, 2002). Under some circumstances, favoritism may be regarded as a positive or humane act toward friends, family, and acquaintance.

Leadership and authority

Iran can be considered as a country with high hierarchical distance (Dastmalchian *et al.*, 2001; Gupta *et al.*, 2002; Javidan and Dastmalchian, 2003; House *et al.*, 2004; Yeganeh and Su, 2007). The antecedents of high hierarchical distance are deeply rooted in many aspects of Iranian mythology, history, politics, religion, and family structure. The collection of Iranian mythology "*Shahnameh*" (Book of Kings) is marked by exaggerations about realizations of powerful kings and superheroes such as *Rostam, Jamshid*, and *Keykhosrow*. In his famous book *The Great Civilization*, former Shah of Iran maintained: "A king in Iran represents people… He is the teacher, the master, the father, in short he is everything" (Pahlavi, 1978). Not surprisingly, for over than 2500 years, monarchy and dynastic rules were the norms of political life in Iran. This long and old monarchical tradition was interrupted in 1979 with proclamation of Islamic Republic and the adoption of a new constitution. However, shortly after, a new similar hierarchical order of theocratic Guardianship was restored. As Hoveyda (2003) pointed it out, "the Iranian leader is a kind of two-faced father: compassionate on the one hand, but also stern and cruel on the other." The high degree of power distance in Iranian families is manifested in terms of patriarchy. The head of household is generally the husband and expects respect from the members of its family, but in return he is responsible to support them and satisfy all their social and material needs (Chapin Metz, 1989). Associated with hierarchical distance is a very strong sense of class culture. After Islamic revolution, although the old order of society changed and many revolutionary people from lower classes got important positions or amassed wealth, the class-based mentality remained almost intact.

Manifestations of high degree of hierarchical distance are various and numerous in Iranian management. Some examples include top-down management (Schramm-Nielsen and Faradonbeh, 2002), authoritarian decision making (Javidan and Dastmalchian, 2003), and hierarchical structure of reward systems (Yeganeh and Su, 2007). An outcome of hierarchical distance, combined with effects of collectivism and family orientation, is the dominance of paternalism in Iranian organizations, which is encouraged by Islamic teachings (Latifi, 1997). Paternalistic management can be considered as an authoritarian fatherliness in which the responsibility of managers extends into private lives of their employees (Schramm-Nielsen and Faradonbeh, 2002). Paternalistic managers consider in their function to protect and solve personal or familial difficulties of their employees inside and outside of the organization (Dastmalchian *et al.*, 2001). Schramm-Nielsen and Faradonbeh (2002) reported that Iranian employees expected superiors to help them in a variety of issues such as financial problems, wedding expenses, purchasing of new homes, illness in the family, education of children, and even marital disputes.

Communication and negotiation

In a collectivistic society such as Iran, group's interests determine one's attitudes and identity. As a result, the individual tends to be conformist by satisfying the group's expectations and restraining his direct messages. With this regard, Hofstede (1980) found a correlation between individualism dimension and press freedom. Similarly, Korac-Kakabadse *et al.* (2001) found an association between collectivism/individualism and the context of communication as described by Hall (1976). A high-context communication is one in which most of the meaning is in the context while very little is in the transmitted message. By contrast, "in low-context cultures most of the information must be in the transmitted message in order to make up for what is missing in the context" (Hall, 1976). An outcome of collectivism is the implicit and high-context communication in Iranian culture. Iranians from an early age learn to be careful about what they say and are advised to use an indirect language for expressing their intentions (Javidan and Dastmalchian, 2003). Persian language and literature are full of nuances and metaphors, which should be interpreted in their context and cannot be taken at face value. A particular and very common form of indirect language in Iranian culture is *Taarof*, which can be translated literally as politeness but has a much more profound significance. In fact, *Taarof* implies a wide range of complicated and highly polite expressions/behaviors that should not be interpreted literally. This kind of context-bound communication is very common in Iranian organizations in both written and oral forms.

Iranians like their neighbors in the Middle East are tough negotiators. The bargaining represents an old tradition that goes back thousands of years, and which has been maintained by the Bazar community (Schramm-Nielsen and Faradonbeh, 2002). In fact, negotiation is a game that entails some intrinsic pleasure. Obviously, trust plays a major role in all business relationships and merchants tend to deal with those whom they know and trust. This implies a long-term business strategy to gain trust and credibility.

Women in workplace

The traditional image in the West of Islam being repressive toward women cannot be confirmed (Schramm-Nielsen and Faradonbeh, 2002). In fact, social underdevelopment is the main reason of gender inequality around the world. It seems that all agrarian/underdeveloped economies are characterized by women's repression (Inglehart, 1997). Despite the political rhetoric of Western politicians, Iranian women enjoy more privileges than their counterparts in other Middle Eastern countries (Schramm-Nielsen and Faradonbeh, 2002; Ghorbani and Tung, 2007). Over the course of past years, many of women's restrictions have been relaxed (Mehran, 2003). Iranian women may hold offices and conduct business. There is nothing to prevent them from doing so on condition that they do not violate Islamic codes of conduct (Schramm-Nielsen and Faradonbeh, 2002). Women in Iran are present in most occupations of their choices including managerial and professional positions (Schramm-Nielsen and Faradonbeh, 2002; Ghorbani and Tung, 2007). In 2005, except for technical/engineering studies, women outnumbered men in all academic disciplines (Ghorbani and Tung, 2007). It may seem paradoxical, but imposing the Islamic dress (*hijab*) has led to growing presence of women in all spheres of the society. One explanation is that the Islamic dress (*hijab*) is in conformity with Iranian culture and arguably provides conservative women especially those working in rural areas with more flexibility. In 2004, women accounted for 33% of Iran's labor force (World Bank, 2004). In the same year, approximately 13% of senior officials, legislators, and managers were female (UNDP, 2005). These numbers are promising because they are the highest in the Middle East and they show steady progress after the Islamic Revolution (Afshar, 1997; Ghorbani and Tung, 2007).

Conclusion

This chapter aimed at providing a better understanding of contemporary society and management in Iran. With a young and energetic population, with a vibrant and evolving culture, and with a growing economy, Iran is undergoing substantial changes. Due to the complexity of the country, it is hard to predict the extent of these changes, but it is plausible to say that the current trend will lead to higher levels of economic, cultural, and political openness. Over the course of past five years, despite all harsh political sanctions, Iran has continued to attract foreign investments from a wide range of countries including China, France, Germany, Italy, and Russia. Therefore, from a business perspective, Iran offers a huge market opportunity that cannot be neglected. In fact, for international managers the question is not "whether," but "when" Iran will emerge as a global business player. The future will tell us, but only those who are prepared now will succeed later.

References

Abbasi-Shavazi, MJ (2000). National trends and social inclusion: Fertility trends and differentials in the islamic republic of Iran, 1972–1996. *Paper Presented at the IUSSP Conference on Family Planning in the 21st Century*, Dhaka, 16–21 January.

Afshar, H (1997). Women and work in Iran. *Political Studies*, 45(4), 755–767.

Ali, AJ and M Amirshahi (2002). The Iranian manager: Work values and orientations. *Journal of Business Ethics*, 40(2), 111–133.

Andersen, LL and P Seeberg (1999). *Iran, fra Revolution til Reform*. Copenhagen: Gyldendal uddannelse.

Bani-Asadi, H (1984). Interactive planning on the eve of the Iranian revolution. *PhD Dissertation, University of Pennsylvania*.

Chapin Metz, H (1989). *Iran: A Country Study*. Washington D.C.: Federal Research Division, Library of Congress.

Daniel, E (2001). *The History of Iran*. Westport, CT: Greenwood Press.

Dastmalchian, A, M Javidan, and K Alam (2001). Effective leadership and culture in Iran: An empirical study. *Applied Psychology*, 50(4), 532–558.

Faradonbeh, HA (2000). Management culture in Iran. Master thesis, Copenhagen Business School, Denmark.

Ghorbani, M and RL Tung (2007). Behind the veil: An exploratory study of the myths and realities of women in the Iranian workforce. *Human Resource Management Journal*, 17(4), 376–392.

Gupta, V, G Surie, M Javidan, and J Chhokar (2002). Southern Asia cluster: Where the old meets the new? *Journal of World Business*, 37, 16–27.

Hall, ET (1976). *Beyond Culture*. New York: Doubleday.

Hofstede, G (1980). *Culture's Consequences: International Differences in Work Related Values*. Beverly-Hills: Sage.

House, R, P Hanges, M Javidan, P Dorfman, and V Gupta (2004). *Culture, Leadership, and Organizations: The Globe Study of 62 Societies.* Thousand Oaks: Sage.

Hoveyda, F (2003). *The Shah and the Ayatollah: Iranian Mythology and Islamic Revolution.* Westport: Praeger.

Husain, MZ (1995). *Global Islamic Politics.* New York: HarperCollins College Publishers.

Inglehart, RF (1997). *Modernization and Post Modernization: Cultural, Economic and Political Change in 43 Societies.* Princeton, NJ: Princeton University Press.

Javidan, M and A Dastmalchian (2003). Culture and leadership in Iran: The land of individual achievers, strong family ties, and powerful elite. *Academy of Management Executive,* 17(4), 127–142.

Khajehpour, B (2000). Domestic political reforms and private sector activity in Iran. *Social Research,* 67(2), 577–609.

Kian-Thiebaut, A (1999). Political and social transformations in post-Islamist Iran. *Middle East Report,* 212, 12–16.

Korac-Kakabadse, N, A Kouzmin, A Korac-Kakabadse, and L Savery (2001). Low- and high-context communication patterns: Towards mapping cross-cultural encounters. *Cross-cultural Management,* 2(8), 3–24.

Latifi, F (1997). An expressive model to interpret multi-faceted cultures: An application for strategic planning in Iran. *Working Paper Series, Henley Management College.*

Mahdavi, H (1970). The patterns and problems of economic development in rentier states: The case of Iran. In *Studies in the Economic History of the Middle East,* Cook, MA (ed.), pp. 37–61. London: Oxford University Press.

Mehran, G (2003). The paradox of tradition and modernity in female education in the Islamic republic of Iran. *Comparative Education Review,* 47(3), 269–286.

Mozaffari, M (1991). Why the Bazar rebels. *Journal of Peace Research,* 28(4), 377–392.

Namazie, P and P Frame (2007). Developments in human resource management in Iran. *The International Journal of Human Resource Management,* 18(1), 159–171.

Namazie, P and M Tayeb (2003). The development of human resources management in Iran. *Paper Presented at First HR Conference in Tehran.*

Pahlavi, MR (1978). *Toward the Great Civilization.* Tehran (in Persian).

Ronen, S and O Shenkar (1985). Clustering countries on attitudinal dimensions: A review and synthesis. *Academy of Management Journal,* 10(3), 435–454.

Schramm-Nielsen, J and HA Faradonbeh (2002). Society and management in Iran. *Working Paper.* Denmark: Copenhagen Business School.

Schuster, M (1985). Models of cooperation and change in union settings. *Industrial Relations,* 24(3), 382–394.

Shayegan, D (2003). Le regard mutilé: Schizophrénie culturelle: Pays traditionnels face à la modernité, La Tour d'Aigues, France: Éditions de l'Aube.

Yeganeh, H and Z Su (2008). An examination of human resource management practices in Iranian public sector. *Personnel Review,* 37(3), 203–221.

Yeganeh, H and Z Su (2007). Comprehending core cultural orientations of Iranian managers. *Cross Cultural Management: An International Journal,* 4(4).

Chapter 22

INTERNET CONSUMER BEHAVIOR IN CYPRUS

ALKIS THRASSOU, DEMETRIS VRONTIS,
AND ANGELIKA KOKKINAKI

Abstract

This chapter aims to investigate the relationship of Cypriots with the Internet and to comprehend their corresponding consumer behavior, constructing in parallel a set of critical factors influencing this behavior and ultimately drawing explicit and prescriptive conclusions on the subject. The methodology is based primarily on quantitative primary data and secondarily on qualitative primary and secondary data. The research methods employed include: a questionnaire survey of 750 interviewees used to obtain generic Internet usage and related information on Cyprus; 10 experts' semi-structured in-depth interviews; and a second questionnaire survey of 130 interviewees used to obtain behavior-specific data. The results are largely consistent with similar researches in other developed countries in terms of this new technology adoption and with similar demographic patterns such as greater penetration among the young and the more educated. The motivators underlying Internet shopping behavior are also similar and include speed, convenience, and information. Critical factors affecting Internet purchase are found to include predominantly product variety, quality, and price. In terms of "negative motivators", again consistent with existing international patterns, "security" and "protection of private data" are found to dominate Internet shoppers' concerns. The results are finally interrelated and developed to reach conclusions regarding both online and "brick-and-mortar" business in Cyprus.

Introduction

With the effort for gaining competitive advantage shifted toward non-price factors, new electronic forms of communication and distribution channels are invaluable since they provide the opportunity for raising quality or cutting costs without diminishing existing standards. According to Colum Joyce, the Global Electronic Business Strategy Manager, DHL, "No-one is ever going to move to a channel or service that is harder to use or less beneficial." Whether a company should use a single or a multiple channel strategy is not the question anymore. The future of customer service is multichannel but, as Hobmeier (2001) supports, it is expensive and inefficient to offer all available options, and most companies must choose. Electronic Business, or e-commerce is the process of buying, selling, transferring or exchanging products services and/or information via computer networks and the Internet. Similarly, e-business is a broader definition of e-commerce that goes beyond the process of buying and selling goods and services. E-business serves customers, collaborates with business partners, and conducts e-learning and electronic transactions within an organization (Turban *et al.*, 2004). Information technology (IT), and the use of Internet in various industries, has benefited both consumers and companies as it allows a faster, easier, convenient, and flexible provision of goods and services.

Research objectives

The chapter aims to investigate the relationship of Cypriots with the Internet and to comprehend their corresponding consumer behavior, constructing in parallel a set of critical factors influencing this behavior. Toward this aim five specific research objectives have been set: to (1) undertake a literature review that will set the theoretical foundation on which the research will be conducted; (2) undertake primary research that will identify the relationship of Cypriots with IT in terms of usage frequency, abilities, and other factors; (3) undertake primary research that will allow the construction of the profile of Cypriots as consumers on the Internet; (4) identify the critical factors underlying this behavior; and (5) draw explicit descriptive and prescriptive conclusions on the subject.

The value of the research lies primarily in its findings, which expand beyond what existing researches have accomplished in Cyprus. Specifically, further to recording simple factual statistics such as Internet usage and frequency, it has expanded the research and interrelated the results to investigate preferences, attitudes, beliefs, and factors underlying behavior. Additionally, this research profiles the Cypriot Internet consumer in a scientific academic context, but ultimately offers substantial explicit, prescriptive, and practical advise to businesses; both online ones and "brick-and-mortar" ones.

The methodology employed by this research is based primarily on quantitative primary data and secondarily on qualitative primary and secondary data. Quantitative primary research included two questionnaire surveys. The first was used to obtain generic data regarding general Internet knowledge; the nature and frequency of Internet usage; IT infrastructure and access; and Internet training, knowledge, and attitudes, as described in the results section of the chapter. A sample of 750 long, fully completed survey questionnaires was received and analyzed. The sample was based on multistage random selection and is representative of the population residing within the geographical boundaries of government-controlled municipalities in Cyprus. The latter is based on the last official population census of 2001 (Cyprus Statistics Department, 2002). The final questionnaire completed was pilot-tested on 25 interviewees and two versions of questionnaires in Greek and English were used to address the issue of linguistic transparency. The second questionnaire survey included 130 personal interviews and the sample was chosen as above. The questionnaire used three techniques: the "Likert Scale," "rank order scaling," and "multiple choice questions" and was used to collect behavior-specific data such as product and retailer type preferences, factors underlying behavior, relative attribute importance, satisfaction, and others. The questionnaire was pilot-tested on a sample of 15 interviewees. Qualitative data were also collected through 10 experts' semi-structured in-depth interviews. These not only allowed both the understanding of some finer issues regarding the subject, but also assisted in the formation of the research methodology itself. Finally, the research utilized some existing secondary data on the subject, mostly in the form of statistical data, though to a limited extend.

Literature Review

This section satisfies objective one of the research through the presentation of the findings of a literature review on the subject of e-commerce. The subject is studied through different perspectives: in relation to businesses, in relation to consumers, as a value-adding phenomenon and as an alternative marketing channel. The review finally presents subject-related data specific to the case of Cyprus.

E-commerce: The business perspective

E-commerce has proven itself to be an essential medium for businesses to use for a variety of reasons. First, e-commerce manages to lower the number of intermediaries involved, thus reducing their production and logistics costs, including warehousing. This allows companies to compete better on price and/or to invest more in quality and marketing. Additionally, start-up costs are reduced and sometimes the need for physical premises is completely eliminated. Moreover, geographical barriers are largely eliminated and businesses can reach different international markets with minimal investment and risk (Thrassou and Vrontis, 2008).

E-commerce nevertheless also bears disadvantages. The first relates to the absence of personal contact. Further, the opportunity cost of further sales consequent to personal sales practices is lost. Furthermore, the lack-of-tangibility factor is a major setback owing to the inherent human need to make choices based on direct sensory experience. Finally, limited shipping coverage does impose physical restrictions to an otherwise and theoretically unlimited coverage.

E-commerce: The consumer perspective

Online shopping bears numerous advantages and disadvantages to the consumer (Berkeley, 2005; Thrassou, 2007; Thrassou and Lijo, 2007). In terms of the former, the most major ones relate to the consumers' potential to perform a thorough research and comparison that is practically impossible to do in physical stores. Also, the whole buying process takes place anywhere and anytime, thus offering a convenience which is much valued in the context of modern, time-pressured, and demanding lifestyles. Finally, owing to the factors presented above, prices are frequently much lower on the Internet.

In terms of disadvantages, *security and privacy of personal data* are foremost among the concerns of online shoppers; and though these issues are slowly fading, due to the higher security measures and certificates that exist today, they are still strong. Another disadvantage arises in the form of delivery time and charges which sometimes add both to the time and price costs of buyers; especially those living in location-wise disadvantaged positions. *Tangibility and trial/testing is also a* major issue as described above though this is also gradually partially overcome through technological advances such as 360° view images, three-dimensional models, detailed descriptions, etc. (Stockport *et al.*, 2001). In some cases, the consumers themselves solve the problem by modifying their buying process, e.g., some shoppers will visit a physical store, try the product, and then order it online. Finally, *return/refund policies* sometimes act as impediment to online shopping since shoppers need to be assured the right to return a faulty damages or unfit-for-purpose product.

According to Armstrong and Kotler (2000), a person's buying decision is influenced by four major psychological factors: motivation, perception, learning and beliefs, and attitude. These factors are not so easy to interpret as they are often formed through culture and experiences. Modahl (2000) suggests that race and gender are not the factors that affect online consumers, but their attitudes towards technology are. Mohdal (2000) differentiates his position from Hofstede's (2007) corresponding research (on national culture differences' dimensions) and focuses on technology as the sole basis of consumer attitudes toward online shopping. This appears to be a well-founded approach; nevertheless there is little doubt that a broader understanding of cultural influences would provide more accurate results.

Babin *et al.* (1994) in his research identified two main consumer motives and consequent shopping behaviors: the shopping experience that does not require the actual purchase of a product (hedonic) and shopping for a specific need/purpose (utilitarian). Utilitarian shoppers perceive shopping as "work" and therefore their behavior aims primarily at efficiency and effectiveness. Hedonic shoppers on the other hand perceive shopping as a "joyful ride," an adventure and will do this for their pleasure purposes that may not even result in an actual purchase. Hedonic shoppers are likely to visit a large number of web sites before actually conducting an online purchase, whereas utilitarians are more likely to a limited search on the web and focus on a number of web sites. This is applied to regular shoppers as well. Therefore, this emphasizes that the shopping environment online has many similarities in relation to online shopping. It is vital to differentiate hedonic and utilitarian shoppers, in order to serve a more appropriate-based audience.

An additional factor that influences customer choice is the very design of the web page. Vrontis *et al.* (2008) present an extended literature review and research findings that build the profile of a successful Internet site. Table 22.1 reports the summary.

Alba *et al.* (1997) state that in online shopping, the consumer's decision-making process is dramatically shortened due to the increasing variety of retailers, comparisons, reviews, and reliability reasons. There are thousands of e-tailers online, and millions of products to choose from. How can customers go about in finding the right product from the right e-tailer? Since e-commerce took consumers by storm, some decided to create web sites that their use would be that of comparison between products and online stores, to ensure the

Table 22.1.   Summary of proposals toward the creation of a successful Internet site.

Subject	Proposal
Strategic marketing	Clear definition of the site's objectives in the strategic context
Integrated marketing communications mix	Clear definition of the site's objectives within the
	Identification of the objectives by both the marketers and the web developers
	Other marcom tools to be complemented by e-marketing by directing customers to the web site and through site-address presence on all marcom material
	Inclusion of links to other web sites that also link back to the site
	Listing of the site in free directories and search engines found on the web
	Web advertisement of the site on other popular sites
Integrated site functions	Additional functions to be included, e.g., demos, electronic coupons, events registration
	Creation of multiple action options for visitors to give their contact information (ultimately creation of a database)
	Clear avenues for the expression of customers' needs and complaints
	Encouragement of consumers to make a purchase
	Action options such as newsletter registration
	Continuous update on product and other information
Confidentiality	Confidentiality assurance through privacy policy inclusion
Value orientation	True marketing orientation toward delivery of real value
	Maximization of delivered value through the application of "usability" practices that allow quick, enjoyable, secure, and easy action
	Verification of ideal usability through the determination of the profile of the intended users
	Consideration to load time, navigation, pages size, hierarchy, and links
	Simple design
	Optimization of graphically heavy pages
Site visitor activity	Tracking of the web site visitor activity and analysis of a site's traffic enables better identification of customer profiles and needs
	Utilization of analytics packages toward tracking data
	Adoption of an ongoing controlling system to monitor, evaluate, and review operations
Visibility	Maximization of online visibility through search engines
	Improvement of site ranking and therefore visibility through content writing strategies

Source: Vrontis *et al.* (2008).

customer's best choice online and also force online retailers to lower their prices according always to the competition (www.bizrate.com). These web sites are for all practical purposes acting as "shopping consultants" and their importance is proportional to the trust they can gain from the consumers, the latter itself being proportional to the degree of independence and impartiality they are perceived to hold.

Not all product categories though are sold equally easily online. Peterson *et al.* (1997) came up with a framework that illustrates products and services that are considered to be more suitable for electronic retailing. This framework can help companies to understand the possibilities of each product category and understand how to pursue the promotion and distribution of specific products in the online environment. This framework uses three dimensions: cost and frequency of purchase, value proposition, and degree of differentiation.

Multichanneling and Value Propositions

The benefits of a multichannel approach are many. Briefly, they cut costs, develop deeper relationships with customers, increase sales and risk is reduced by spreading over multiple channels (Hobmeier, 2001). In terms of customers' channel preferences, Skiera and Gensler (2003) outline the primary influencers as the nature of the product purchased, the stage of the transaction process, and the customer with all its characteristics. Relating to the nature of the product purchased, Peterson *et al.* (1997) conclude that customer preference over channel choice would depend on the level of outlay, frequency, the nature of its tangible aspects, and the physical/informational nature of the service. Finally, considering customer profiles, Rollo (2004) suggests that the demographics and psychographics of customers also matter in channel preferences, with younger, more educated techno-users having a natural inclination toward channels such as M-banking. The delivery of technology-based services appears to be correlated with satisfaction (Laforet and Li, 2005). This has been shown to be especially true where the services were highly important to customers (Joseph and Stone, 2003). Similarly, the literature suggests that consumers prefer a mix of rather than any one single delivery channel (Howcroft *et al.*, 2002) and that it would be highly important for service providers to understand and improve each channel within the overall service offering rather than concentrating efforts on improving one delivery channel in isolation (Patricio *et al.*, 2003). Multichannel service delivery not only has it enabled firms to broaden their service delivery system and achieve competitive service positioning, but it has also taken the commonplace wisdom of "listening to the voice of the customer" (Keen *et al.*, 2000).

According to Pousttchi and Schurig (2004), in the banking sector, which is usually a leader in the adoption of new technologies, the ever-increasing spread of Internet-enabled phones and personal digital assistants made the transformation of applications to mobile devices a logical development of electronic banking, leading to mobile banking. This paradigm shift takes place as the new technologies are increasingly being recognized as a cost-effective way to deliver services (Tae-Gyu, 2006), as well as to achieve visible differentiation (Thorton and White, 2001). Internet and mobile technologies provide true one-to-one business-to-consumer interaction, which enables a level of customer intimacy unforeseen in the past.

According to Clarke (2001), value propositions define the relationship between supplier offerings and consumer purchases by identifying how the supplier fulfils the customer's needs across different customer roles. Clarke further outlines that value propositions specify the interdependence between the performances attributes of a product or service and the fulfilment of needs and solidifies the relationship between the customer and various dimensions of product value. Similar conclusions are also reached by Vrontis and Thrassou (2007). Thus, customer satisfaction is merely a response to the value proposition offered by a specific product/service bundle. The value of the new technologies rises from the mobility of their media. From the service providers' point of view, Keen and Mackintosh (2001) explain that even though the demand side of e-commerce is a search for value, a pure transformation of services into mobile services does not necessarily make them value adding from a customer's point of view. Furthermore, Clarke (2001) emphasizes that the value-for-time derived from the factors of mobility should leverage advantages of superior value propositions, toward greater consumer satisfaction. Four value propositions in e-commerce identified by Clark are ubiquity, convenience, localization, and personalization. In their qualitative mobile banking study, Laukkanen and Lauronen (2005) found that customers perceive location-free access and the ability to react immediately to the service needed as important aspects of the creation of convenience and efficiency in service consumption.

Laforet and Li (2005) review the subject and conclude that younger consumers value the convenience or time-saving potential of online and mobile banking more than older consumers while younger consumers also regard the lack of face-to-face contact as less important than older consumers. The educational levels of their respondents did not affect their preference or not of mobile banking (Howcroft *et al.*, 2002). Sarel and Marmorstein (2003a,b) though, found that household income and education did have a significant effect on the adoption of electronic banking among users. Moreover, a number of studies also found that trust and perceived risks have a significant positive influence on commitment (Bhattacherjee, 2002; Mukherjee and Nath, 2003). Bhattacherjee (2002) theoretically conceptualized and empirically validated a scale to measure individual trust in online firms to find that one's willingness to transact with an online firm may be predicted by additional variables above, and beyond trust, such as perceived usefulness and perceived ease of use of such transactions.

The question of actual practical adoption of the new technologies, especially by the customers, is largely governed by "classical" theories. Rogers (1995) formulated the Theory of Diffusion of Innovations to explain the adoption of various types of innovations. The theory views adoption as "a process by which an innovation is communicated through certain channels over time among the members of a social system." It is determined by five innovation characteristics: relative advantage, complexity, compatibility, trialability, and observability. The Theory of Planned Behavior posits that actual, voluntary use of a technology is determined by the individual's behavioral intention, which, in turn, is determined by the individual's perceptions on the "presence or absence of requisite resources and opportunities" to perform the behavior (Ajzen, 1991).

The Internet in Cyprus

Cyprus, despite its small size, shows a positive adaptation to the technological advancements in business, in relation to other larger European countries. Companies are trying to find ways to expand their businesses and take advantage of all new opportunities and means. Online shopping in Cyprus is relatively low, as data records show (Eurostat, 2007) and some reasons for this are related to the lack of the promotion of online shopping, education, local access, etc.

Eurostat performs various surveys in the EU, and Cyprus as one of its members is part of their researches. In one such survey (Eurostat, 2007) concerning individuals, a sample size of 6062 with a response rate of 94% offered what is probably the most reliable data on the subject. On the percentage of individuals who accessed Internet on average at least once a week, on overall of all age groups, Cyprus had a 29% peak of use in 2006 and on the important age group of 16–24 years old, Cyprus had a 55% peak use. An evident decrease was recorded through each higher age group. Despite its smaller size and population, new technologies and innovations appeared to adapt well to the Cypriot culture and businesses. According to the International Telecommunications

Union, there were 326,000 active Internet users as of March 2007, almost half of the population. This has grown from 120,000 users in 2000, a noticeable 172% in user growth (Internet World Stats, 2007).

Data on Cyprus e-tailers is practically non-existent. The Cyprus Telecommunication Authority's offspring "Emporion Plaza" is the most distinguished online store available to the Cypriot audience. Emporion Plaza (www.eplaza.com.cy) has engaged with agreements with a lot of local-based stores to offer their products to this unique local online mall. Moreover, it offers international shipping to Cyprus and the United Kingdom and the chance to businesses to sell their products online through integrated personal web sites through the mall. SMEs are therefore offered the chance to promote their products online with minimum investment and risk. Though no reliable data have been found regarding the venture, peripheral data indicate a poor start for this Cypriot Internet-based retailer channel.

Research Results

IT usage by the public in cyprus

This study subsequently satisfies objective two through the presentation of primary research results that identify the relationship of Cypriots with IT in terms of usage frequency, abilities, and other factors.

The public and IT

More than half of men (54%) use the Internet, while for women the percentage is considerably lower (34%). The rates of Internet usage are inversely proportionally to age. Eight out of ten young individuals in the age of 20–24 use the Internet compared to one in ten of the individuals, who are older than 70-years old. For intermediary ages, there is a systematic reduction of usage percentages with increase of age. Education also constitutes an indicative factor of Internet usage. Only 6% of those who did not finish primary school are using the Internet compared to 92% among those with postgraduate university degrees. The reasons why many do not use the Internet vary with "not having a computer" and "not interested" relating to 60% of the interviewees (though the latter may really be a result of the other factors. Half of those that use the Internet do it daily in comparison to one in three people with visits at least once a week). Seventy-three percent search for information on the Internet at least once a week. Six in ten users never buy anything through the Internet while one in four buys at least once a year. Daily use of electronic post is made by one in four people while one in three at least uses it once a week.

This study views mobile marketing as a natural evolution and/or parallel channel to Internet marketing. It has therefore included some generic questions on mobile usage as well. More than eight in ten individuals are using mobile telephone. Men users exceed 90% while women 75%. Use of mobile telecommunications also decreases with age. Sixty-five percent of individuals over 70 years old make use of mobile phones in comparison to 97% users of ages 20–24 years. One in four users of mobile telephone does not know how to send or receive written messages. However, this lack of knowledge is similar between men and women.

Though consumer behavior usually refers to the behavior of individuals in relation to consumer goods, modern definitions of the term include the behavior in relation to all goods and services an individual receives. Since these include also a range of public and governmental services, some generic questions were also asked in relation to e-government. Eight in ten individuals have never heard of the term "E-Government." The rates of unawareness are slightly higher in women than men. Roughly the same percentage expressed interest in making use of e-mail services, while a greater percentage expressed interest in making use of mobile phones. Seventy-six percent of the individuals asked consider printing and completing forms and applications through the Internet more useful, while 40% consider Internet communications with municipality's employees more useful. All other services rate between the above. These percentages are similar to e-mail services. These numbers differ for mobile phone users.

Public's perceptions of IT issues

One in three people asked does not worry about the validity of information compared to one in ten that worries "very much." The rate of concern is particularly increased in Larnaka and Paphos compared to the other provinces. Twenty-five percent are not concerned about payments' security, while 17% are "very much," 14% "much," 24% "quite enough" and 17% "not at all." One in five is "very much" concerned about the speed of correspondence, while four in ten "not at all" or "little." The provinces of Paphos and Ammochostos present particularities in relation to the "speed of correspondence." Significant apprehension also appears to exist concerning the "privacy of personal data" with almost 50% of the interviewees stating that they worry "much" or "very much."

Internet Consumer Motivation and Preferences in Cyprus

The following presents the primary research results that construct the profile of Cypriots as consumers on the Internet, thus satisfying objective three of the research.

Spending patterns

The majority of online shoppers use online shopping for their personal use (96%) and a small percentage for professional reasons (4%). The largest percentage of the participants spends €175–850 per annum. The three following groups (€90–170, €1–85, and €855–1,700) are similar in terms of expenditure while the €1,700+ group is very small.

Product types, e-tailers, and reasons for shopping online

"What do online shoppers buy" is a critical question toward identifying product categories most/least appropriate for Internet selling. Table 22.2 lists the results of this research.

The most popular product categories among the respondents are Electronics, CD's/DVD's/games, books, and airline/concert tickets. Clothing has an unexpected 33%, which comes to contradict theory on the subject. Computers and services had a similar number of responses. Under the "Other" category, the products that were listed were comics, model cars, hotel bookings, car parts, toys, and cosmetics. Automobiles were the only category with no response.

The products shoppers mostly buy online are products that apparently allow maximum online savings, indirectly reconfirming "price" as a critical

Table 22.2.   Product types.

Types of products	Percentage (%)
CD's/DVD's/games	39.4
Electronics	43.6
Clothing and accessories	33
Services	22.3
Airline/concert tickets	36.2
Books	38.3
Automobiles	N/A
Computers	20.2
Paintings/posters	14.9
Others	14.9

factor. Moreover, these types of products are identical in physical stores and therefore bearing minimum risk. This indirectly also reconfirms the importance of "risk," in its quality sense, as a critical factor. The same products are also usually offered in greater variety online re-stressing the importance of this factor as well. Services have their portion of followers since companies and public services are now offering online support for payments or purchases online in an attempt to minimize the queues and waiting time of their customers. Though less developed than other EU countries, this dimension of Internet usage, including e-government, is gaining ground.

These results are valuable to "brick-and-mortar" businesses as they indicate a need for greater variety in shops to minimize the loss of customers to the Internet. This may also indicate a strategic shift to specialization. "Price" on the other hand although more obvious and direct as a factor is also one, which is more difficult to adapt to owing to the cost advantages of Internet businesses. It is noted that the "other" category included "availability," "convenience," "ease of use," and "time saving" as factors influencing their choice. These are more general factors related with online shopping and one would have expected higher results on these based on literature review findings.

Further, there are more generic reasons for shopping online. "Speed" is the most important reason for online shopping, with "convenience" coming second. "Avoiding shopping hassles" (traffic, parking, queues, weather, etc.) also surfaces as significant, as does "delivery." Under the "others" category came factors seen also in the previous figure, including "availability" and "variety," and "lower prices."

The research has furthermore investigated consumer online preferences in terms of cyberspace location and the underlying factors of the preferences. The results showed that the largest percentage of the respondents (54%) prefer already established and prominent e-tailers, such as Amazon.com, Play.com, and others. This is hardly surprising since these e-tailers have been "around" for a long time, bear good reputation, are well branded, are perceived as "risk-free" especially in terms of security, have effective pricing strategies, offer strong customer support, and receive positive word of mouth. At the end of the day, safety/security and reliability appear to be the driving forces of preference in this case, though the factors met above "variety," "prices" also greatly affect choice.

A relatively high percentage of users have no preference (40%), and this is probably related to the fact that most customers require searching for the product they need, and might not find it in already known e-tailers. This involves risk, which online shoppers are sometimes willing to take to acquire their product of choice. Customers first decide on their product of choice and then decide on the shop to buy it from rather than doing the opposite.

Auction marketplaces have taken online shopping by storm and the Cyprus results support the trend (34%). Online consumers are also looking to shop from official designer brand stores (19%), such as Adidas, Reebok, and Nike official e-shops. This is mainly due to authenticity reasons and perceived higher quality that will be received through these official stores. Moreover, these stores are able to offer customers the "real thing" straight from the manufacturer rather than obtaining from distributors. Regarding online shopping from local (Cyprus) online store, the results show minimal preference. This on the one hand may be interpreted as a "red light" for the sector/channel and on the other it may be viewed an opportunity, assuming of course it will be properly developed.

Critical Factors of Internet Consumer Behavior in Cyprus

The following presents the primary research results that identify the critical factors underlying Internet consumer behavior of Cypriots, thus satisfying objective four of the research. In an attempt to identify, in more detail, the most important factors influencing online shopping, the respondents were provided with a list of factors to rate on a scale of 1 to 5 ("1" being the most important factor and "5," the least important one). Table 22.3 shows the most important factors are largely in agreement with both the previous results and the literature review findings, and they are "protection of private data," "low price," "geographical delivery coverage," "quality" and "convenience." The least important factors are "testing/sampling," "fast transactions," "search tools," "policies," and "promotions/special offers/deals."

A separate survey question has shown that the majority of online shoppers are satisfied with online shopping (90%) whereas a minimal percentage is not (3%). When asked if they feel that there is room for improvements in online shopping, the respondents were positive. The major desired improvements include "lower prices," "greater delivery coverage," "greater security of data," and "faster transactions." In the "Others" category, shoppers included the wish for "24/7 free customer support" and "better return and refund policies."

Though scientifically inconclusive ($p < .05$), it is evident that online shopping is affected by the immediate environment as 80% of the respondents stated that people in their immediate environment are using online shopping. Whether this is a result of technology diffusion, social adaptation, group aspiration, cultural phenomena, or other factors is a matter of further research.

Table 22.3. Online shoppers' importance of factors.

Importance factors when shopping online	Most important (1)	Important (2)	OK (3)	Not important (4)	Less important (5)
Web site appearance and ease of use	25	19	19	9	7
Variety	32	17	17	9	7
Quality	37	15	22	6	1
Geographical delivery coverage	37	17	13	5	4
Low price	43	22	9	5	5
Product availability	26	24	18	9	3
Search tools	19	22	13	10	10
Convenience	35	24	13	3	3
Fast transactions (1-click shopping)	20	14	21	13	11
Testing/sampling	9	13	16	17	18
Policies (refunds, returns, etc.)	23	21	14	8	9
Good customer support	22	24	15	7	7
On-time delivery	33	18	15	7	4
Security certificates and awards	33	12	18	7	3
Promotions/special offers/ deals	14	18	20	12	9
Reliability in the business	29	21	12	10	3
Protection of private data	49	9	5	7	5
Handling of the product	18	27	17	10	3

The fact remains that indications show a relationship between online shopping by people in the individual's environment and the individual's probability of also shopping online.

Conclusions

This final section of the paper draws explicit conclusions on the subject of Internet consumer behavior in Cyprus and consequently satisfies the fifth and last research objective. The first part of this section presents the essence of the findings in relation to the subject and it is essentially descriptive of the profile of behavior and its underlying factors/causes. The second part is a rational extrapolation of the descriptive findings toward prescriptive conclusions on businesses.

Descriptive: Internet Consumer Behavior and Influencers

Following the analysis performed, a profile for the online shopper has been built. According to the results, the majority of online shoppers are male with women following closely. They range between 25–34 years old and the largest portion of them has a higher education degree. Moreover, the mass of the online shoppers comes from a specialized employment field and has an income ranging from €8,500 to €34,000 (statistically adjacent to the population sample). Most online shoppers have been using the Internet for more than four years and have an average use of more than 20 h per month. Online shoppers shop either occasionally (special occasions, holiday seasons, etc.) or frequently on a monthly basis. Concerning the purchases, they are made for personal use and the amount that the online shopper spends online is €175–850. The most popular products that the online shopper buys are electronics, CD's/DVD's/games, books, airline/concert tickets, and clothing/accessories. The reason for shopping for these products online is primarily "price." The online shopper shops from established e-tailers, or auction marketplaces and a large percentage does not have preference when choosing their shop of purchase. The most important factors affecting online shopping behavior and preferences are "protection of private data," "low price," "geographical delivery coverage," "quality," and "convenience." Online shoppers wish to see improvements in "cheaper prices," "larger shipping coverage," and "higher security and protection of private data."

Prescriptive: Business Applications

The research findings, further to their strict academic value, allow for explicit conclusions to be drawn in relation to business practice in Cyprus. The market of Cyprus is too small to affect the Internet marketing strategy of international businesses. The research findings nevertheless should interest immensely business for which Cyprus is a primary market, essentially that is Cypriot businesses. These include both the traditional "brick-and-mortar" type (i.e., those with a physical presence) and those which are strictly operating in cyberspace.

The most important finding that affects traditional businesses is the fact that Internet purchases are increasing among Cypriot consumers and have a threshold, that is a point where the loss of traditional business to the Internet cannot be ignored. Though the situation has still not reached "panic" levels, serious companies should act proactively and implement immediately a strategic marketing plan that either includes or at least considers Internet marketing as a primary factor influencing their business.

One possible response is to embrace Internet technologies and utilize the many advantages they offer, expanding the businesses' presence into the Internet as well. The need thus arises for a web site that not only informs, but also allows sales and customer support. The online business site of these companies must be such as to offer added value that is specific to Cypriot consumers, so that the latter will prefer the site to other potentially more attractive international ones. There are three possible key advantages in this situation: (a) the design of a site that fits the Cypriot consumer profile (language, style, etc.), (b) the offer of a marketing mix again specifically for the Cypriot buyer (product quality, variety, price, etc.), and (c) the elimination of the element of "risk" that overshadows Internet purchases, through the existence of a "brick-and-mortar" presence in Cyprus. The latter consequently signifies the importance of retaining a physical business not only as an end in itself, but as an enhancer of Internet business. Ironically perhaps it may be that in the longer term many businesses might retain a "brick-and-mortar" location to support Internet business instead of the opposite which dominates present marketing philosophies.

Furthermore and as seen in the literature review section, the Internet option should not be seen as a separate business. At least until consumer attitudes change substantially, the Internet should be viewed as an additional marketing channel that expands the choice of consumers not simply in terms of products, but rather in terms of shopping behavior. This is especially true for the utilitarian shoppers. The research findings have additionally provided some strong indications as to the nature of businesses which probabilistically stand the greatest chance of being affected by the Internet. These are naturally the ones for which the urgency to adapt their marketing strategy is the greatest.

The shift to Internet operation though, is not the only strategic option for businesses, even for those that are mostly threatened by this consumer behavior. Ultimately, shoppers do find value in "brick-and-mortar" businesses versus Internet ones. The former therefore need to research, identify, and isolate the true value offered to their customers and concentrate and enhance that value. This research has found that this value stems usually from the *tangibility* of "brick-and-mortar" selling, the *personal/human factor*, and the *shopping hedonism* element. Other current advantages such as the lower sense of risk have probably a limited life span and cannot be relied on for longer-term planning. "Brick-and-mortar" businesses consequently can enhance this value through the display of more tangibles, increased personal attention to the customers, and through enhancement of the overall pleasure of the shopping experience.

Final Thoughts

Irrespective of the great and many changes to be inevitably faced by businesses in the future, the fundamental marketing philosophy of identifying and satisfying customer needs remains true. Businesses therefore have to adopt a scientific approach to the matter (Thrassou and Vrontis, 2006), which combined with their knowledge, and experience will allow the identification and strengthening of the factors that offer customer value. Beyond quality, price, information, choice, and support lies one critical truth: buyers do not pay for the product, they pay for the *experience* of the product. Whether "brick-and-mortar" or cyberspace or both, businesses can succeed as long as they understand their consumers' behavior and they utilize this knowledge toward the development of clear, comprehensive, and research-based marketing strategies consistent with the times and situation. The Internet defines the times and the situation, and marketing strategies can include or exclude it, but they cannot ignore it.

References

Ajzen, I (1991). The theory of planned behaviour. *Organizational Behaviour and Human Decision Processes*, 50, 135–211.

Alba, J, J Lynch, B Weitz, C Janiszewski, R Lutz, A Sawyer, and S Wood (1997). Interactive home shopping: Consumer, retailer, and manufacturer incentives to participate in electronic marketplaces. *Journal of Marketing*, 61, 38–53.

Armstrong, G and P Kotler (2000). *Marketing*, 5th edn., Englewood Cliffs, NJ: Prentice-Hall pp. 153, 154.

Babin, BJ, WR Darden, and M Griffin (1994). Work and/or fun: Measuring hedonic and utilitarian shopping value. *The Journal of Consumer Research*, 20(4), 644–656.

Berkeley (2007). Online shopping 2005, Online Shopping, viewed 21 March 2007, www.ocf.berkeley.edu/~jinnie/index.html.

Bhattacherjee, A (2002). Individual trust in online firms: Scale development and initial test. *Journal of Management and Information Systems*, 19(1), 41–211.

Clarke, I (2001). Emerging value propositions for M-commerce. *Journal of Business Strategies*, 18(2).

Cyprus Statistics Department (2002).

Eurostat (2007). Population and social conditions: Information Society 2007, European Commission — Eurostat, viewed 21 March, <http://epp.eurostat.ec.europa.eu/pls/portal/#>

Hofstede, G (2007). A summary of my ideas about national culture differences 2007, Official Website, viewed 12 April 2007, <http://feweb.uvt.nl/center/hofstede/page3.htm>

Hobmeier, M (2001). Professional multichannel management. *CEO*, 3, 36–38.

Howcroft, B, R Hamilton, and P Hewer (2002). Consumer attitude and the usage and adoption of home-based banking in the United Kingdom. *International Journal of Bank Marketing*, 20(3), 21–111.

Internet World Stats (2007). Internet Usage in European Union: Internet User Statistics & Population for the 27 European Union member states 2007, viewed 17 March 2007, <www.internetworldstats.com/stats9.htm>

Joseph, M and G Stone (2003). An empirical evaluation of US bank customer perceptions of the impact of technology on service delivery in the banking sector. *International Journal of Retail & Distribution Management*, 31(4), 190–202.

Keen, C, K De Ruyter, M Wetzels, and RA Feinberg (2000). An empirical analysis of consumer preferences regarding alternative service delivery modes in emerging electronic service markets. *Quarterly Journal of Electronic Commerce*, 1(1), 31–47.

Keen, P and R Mackintosh (2001). *The Freedom Economy: Gaining the M-commerce Edge in the Era of the Wireless Internet*. Berkeley, CA: Osborne/McGraw-Hill.

Laforet, S and X Li (2005). Consumers' attitudes towards online and mobile banking in China. *International Journal of Bank Marketing*, 23(5).

Laukkanen, T and J Lauronen (2005). Consumer value creation in mobile banking services. *International Journal of Mobile Communications*, 3(4), 325–338.

Modahl, M (2000). *Now or Never: How Companies Must Change to Win the Battle for the Internet Consumer*. New York, NY: Harper Business.

Mukherjee, A and P Nath (2003). A model of trust in online relationship banking. *International Journal of Bank Marketing*, 21(1), 5–15.

Patricio, L, RP Fisk, and JF Cunha (2003). Improving satisfaction with bank service offerings: Measuring the contribution of each delivery channel. *Managing Service Quality*, 13(6), 471–482.

Peterson, RA, S Balasubramanian, and BJ Bronnenberg (1997). Exploring the implications of the Internet for consumer marketing. *Journal of the Academy of Marketing Science*, 25(4), 329–346.

Pousttchi, K and M Schurig (2004). Assessment of today's mobile banking applications from the view of customer requirements. In *Proceedings of the Thirty-Seventh Annual Hawaii International Conference on System Sciences 2004*. Hawaii 2004, pp. 1–10 [Online]. http://csdl2.computer.org/comp/proceedings/hicss/2004/2056/07/205670184a.pdf [4 February 2006].

Rogers, EM (1995). *Diffusion of Innovations*, 4th edn. New York: Free Press, pp. 212–251.

Rollo, C (2004). Seniors, teens, and everyone tween: Selecting service channels to fit customer demographics. In *Benefits of Using Multi-Channels as Drivers for Channel Selection* [Online]. http://www.the-dma.org/dmef/proceedings04/6-Schijns.pdf [2 February 2006].

Sarel, D and H Marmorstein (2003a). Marketing online banking services: The voice of the customer. *Journal of Financial Services Marketing*, 8(2), 18–106.

Sarel, D and H Marmorstein (2003b). Marketing online banking to the indifferent consumer: A longitudinal analysis of banks' actions. *Journal of Financial Services Marketing*, 8(3), 231–243.

Skiera, B and S Gensler (2003). *Multi-Channel Management and Its Impact on Customers Purchase Behavior in Managing Enterprises of the New Economy by Modern Concepts of the Theory of the Firm*. Heidelberg, pp. 122–138.

Stockport, GJ, G Kunnath, and R Sedick (2001). Boo.com: the path to failure. *Journal of Interactive Marketing*, 15(4), 56–70.

Tae-Gyu, K. Korea leads world in mobile banking, The Korea Times, Jan. 30, 2006 [Online]. http://times.hankooki.com/lpage/biz/200601/kt2006013013175911860.htm [8 February 2006].

Thorton, J and L White (2001). Customer orientations and usage of financial distribution channels. *Journal of Services Marketing*, 15(3), 168–185.

Thrassou, A (2007). Internet marketing by professional services SMEs — A strategic orientation perspective. In *Proceedings: First Global Conference on eCommerce & Internet Governance*. Sousse, Tunisia, October 19–20.

Thrassou, A and PR Lijo (2007). Customer perceptions regarding usage of mobile banking services — The case of Kuwait. *World Journal of Business Management*.

Thrassou, A and D Vrontis (2006). A small services firm marketing communications model for SME-dominated environments. *Journal of Marketing Communications*, 12(3), 183–202.

Thrassou, A and D Vrontis (2008). Internet marketing by SMEs — Towards enhanced competetiveness and internationalisation of professional services. *International Journal of Internet Marketing and Advertising*, 4(2–3).

Turban, E, D King, J Lee, and D Viehland (2004). *Electronic Commerce, A Managerial Perspective*, International Edition, New Jersey: Pearson Education.

Vrontis, D and A Thrassou (2007). A framework towards a new business-consumer relationship. *Marketing Intelligence and Planning*, 25(7), 789–806.

Vrontis, D, D Ktoridou, and Y Papadamou (2008). Website design and development as an effective and efficient promotional tool: A case study in the hotel industry in Cyprus. *Journal of Website Promotion*, 2(3–4), 125–139.

Part VI

ASIA

Chapter 23

CORPORATE SOCIAL PERFORMANCE OF INDONESIAN STATE-OWNED AND PRIVATE COMPANIES

HASAN FAUZI, AZHAR A. RAHMAN, MOSTAQ HUSSAIN, AND ADNAN A. PRIYANTO

Abstract

The objectives of this chapter are to analyze the difference of corporate social performance between state-owned companies (SOCs) and private-owned companies (POCs) in Indonesia, and to examine the correlation between the corporate social performance and the corporate financial performance. Using a purposive sample from state-owned and private owned firms between 2001 and 2004, the results of this study indicate no significant difference in corporate social performance between SOCs and POCs. Further, no association between corporate social performance (CSP) and financial performance both in SOCs and POCs was detected.

Introduction

Baron (2000) defines altruism as action of people or group to voluntarily help somebody else regardless of the motives of the action or vested interest. A company has a role and responsibility to its environment and stakeholders. The stakeholder model states that the success of a company depends on its ability to maintain a good relationship with stockholders in its decision making (Ullman, 1985). If a company fails to do so, it faces problems raised by the constituents of stakeholder. Coffrey and Wang (1998) use the term corporate altruism to call the action of pro-social behavior conducted by business entity. During the last three decades, corporate altruism has received significant attention. Some studies describe that pro-social behavior is about how a company behaves in different countries. Moir (2001) contended that the hope for a company to be more responsible for its community and environment became debatable recently. Morimoto *et al.* (2004) emphasized the increasing pressures on companies to be more socially responsible. Several studies have been conducted on corporate social performance (CSP) in the context of developed countries (e.g., Wardock and Grave, 1997; Preston and O'Bannon, 1997; Mahoney and Roberts, 2007); however, similar studies in developing countries setting are rare. The indexes for corporate social performance in developing countries are not available (Domini, 2008; Jantzi, 2008). Indonesia is no exception. Therefore, this research attempts to focus on Indonesian state-owned companies (SOCs) and private-owned companies (POCs).

According to Republic of Indonesia (Law No. 19) (2003) on SOC, companies in Indonesia can be classified into SOCs, POCs, and companies under cooperative scheme (COCs). In SOCs, all stakes come from separated state asset, and are the economic actors contributing to Indonesian economic system. In operationalizing the business, SOCs, POCs, and COCs support each other based on democratic economy system (Republic of Indonesia, 2003). Currently, SOCs have served any sector of business line. Therefore, most of Indonesian people use the SOC's products and services. As stipulated in the law, the SOCs are ordered by the government (owner) to conduct public service offering (SOP) at the expenses of government, especially for the products and services not offered by POCs and COCs for economy viability. Thus, the issue is raised about the role of stakeholders including shareholder in affecting the Indonesian companies' policy to conduct corporate social responsibility, and how the social responsibility is reported to stakeholders?

Since 1998, changes have occurred in SOCs in order to be more transparent and accountable. It has happened when Indonesian government created the Ministry of State-Owned Companies. According to Abeng (2004), the strategy of restructuring, profitability, and privatization was needed to manage the SOCs well. Restructuring strategy was implemented by setting the holding of SOCs. Among 150 SOCs, the companies are classified into 10–12 holding. The objective of such setting is to place a business focus based on certain business goals. The concept of Abeng (2004) is to set the super holding SOC, with Republic of Indonesian President as Chairman, under which the giant holding of SOCs was operated. The giant holdings will be then the world-class economic actors indicated by Fortune 500 list as one of the indicators. The idea almost succeeded in 1999 when team restructuring batch II, supported by some world class consultants, McKinsey, Booz Allen and Hamilton, Price Waterhouse & Coopers, Andersen, Ernst & Young, and AT Kienery completed a blue book for restructuring per industry sector (Nugroho and Siahaan, 2005). The Indonesian government had the concepts of restructuring and privatizing SOCs to make them the world-class companies, and thus to be profitable.

In short, it can be said that some endeavors to improve the SOCs had been conducted: blue print on SOCs reform had been set up in 1998–1999, and a master plan for SOCs had been developed during 2002–2006, and the law No. 19 (2003) had been approved by the lawmakers. The ultimate objective of the efforts is to transform the SOCs toward modern and professional business institutional. It should be noted that good corporate governance principles have been placed in order to manage the SOCs well (Soedjais, 2005); that is, considering the required condition and given situation, the SOCs have a role (as corporate and good citizen) in taking corporate social responsibility. Therefore, it is interesting to observe empirically how social responsibility (which is often called social performance) is practiced in SOCs in comparisons with POCs as well as to analyze the relationship between CSP and financial performance. This study focuses on POCs and SOCs as both of them have to follow the same legal system. Differentiating factor between them is ownership only. COCs have different legal system from SOCs and POCs. The legal system for SOCs and POCs is Corporation (called "Perseroan" in Indonesian term), whereas COCs, as stipulated in the Indonesian cooperative law (Republic of Indonesia, 1992), must use the cooperative legal system (called "Koperasi" in Indonesian term). Thus, the objectives of this chapter are to discover the difference of CSP in SOCs and POCs, and correlation between CSP and financial performance in SOCs and POCs.

Corporate Social Performance

Concept of CSP, in which environmental aspect is included, is synonymous with corporate social responsibility (CSR) and socially responsible behavior. They are used interchangeably in empirical research. Sometimes, concept of CSP is subsumed under the umbrella of CSR, and sometimes the reverse (Wood, 1991; Carroll, 1979, 1999; Barnett, 2007). Generally, the terms social and environment are covered in the concept of CSP including the aspect of environment in measurement construct. However, due to the growing importance of environmental issue, there was a need to separate the performance of environment from the social performance. The concept of performance measurement focuses on three Ps: profit (financial), people (social), and planet (environment).

Thus far, there have been four main models in understanding CSR construct: Carroll (1979), Wartick and Cochran (1985), Wood (1991), and Clarkson (1995). Carroll defined CSR as the intersection at a given moment in time of three dimensions: CSR principles should be apprehended at four separate levels (economic, legal, ethical, and discretionary); the sum of the social problems that a firm faces (i.e., racial discrimination, etc.); and the philosophy underlying its responses, which can range anywhere along a continuum going from the firm's anticipation of such problems to the outright denial. Wartick and Cochran (1985) adjusted this model, re-sculpting its final dimension by borrowing from the strategic management of social issues.

Wood (1991) proposed a renewed CSP model that soon became an omnipresent yardstick in the construct's theoretical development (Gerde, 2000). In line with earlier studies, the authors define CSP as a business organization's configuration of the principles of social responsibility, processes of social responsiveness, and policies, programs, and observable outcomes as they relate to the firm's societal relationship (Igalens and Gond, 2005). The second orientation was based on a more pragmatic observation of how hard it is to apprehend CSP using the preceding typologies, and applying Stakeholder Theory as a framework to model CSP, which would then be defined as a firm's ability to manage its stakeholders in a way that is satisfactory to them (Clarkson, 1995). Igalens and Gond (2005) summarize CSR models in Table 23.1.

Approach to Measuring CSP

There have been five approaches to measuring CSP: (1) measurement based on analysis of the contents of annual reports, (2) pollution indices, (3) perceptual measurements derived from questionnaire-based surveys, (4) corporate reputation indicators, and (5) data produced by measurement organizations (Igalens and Gond, 2005). In the first approach, CSR is measured using content of corporate annual report. This method of measuring CSR is focused on the disclosure in the annual report. According to the second approach, measurement of CSR is focused on one dimensions of CSR (i.e., environment). This method generally is concerned with external party. Corporate reputation indicator is an approach to measuring CSR using reputation indicators as perceived by external parties of company. Data produced by measurement organizations is a result of measurement approach of CSP

Table 23.1.   Models of CSP.

Authors	Definition of CSP	CSP dimensions
Carroll (1979)	The articulation and interaction between (a) different categories of social responsibilities; (b) specific issues relating to such responsibilities and (c) the philosophies of the answers	Definition of corporate social responsibility Levels: economic, legal, ethical, discretionary Philosophy of responsiveness stances: responsive, defensive, accommodative, proactive Social issues involved examples: consumerism; environment; discrimination; productsafety; safety at work; shareholding
Wartick and Cochran (1985)	"The underlying interaction among the principles of social responsibility, the process of social responsiveness, and the policies developed to address social issues" (p. 758)	Corporate social responsibilities levels: economic, legal, ethical, discretionary Corporate social responsiveness stances: responsive, defensive, accommodative, proactive social issues management approach: identification; analysis; response
Wood (1991)	"A Business organization's configuration of principles of social responsibility, processes of social responsiveness, and policies, programs, and observable outcomes as they relate to the firm's societal relationship" (p. 693)	Principles of corporate social responsibility levels: institutional, organizational, and individual Processes of corporate social responsiveness includes: environmental assessment and analysis; stakeholder managements; issues management Outcomes of corporate behavior combines: societal impacts; corporate social programs and policies
Clarkson (1995)	The ability to manage and satisfy the different corporate stakeholders	This model identifies specific problems for each of the main stakeholder categories it distinguishes: employees; owners/shareholders; consumers; suppliers; state; stakeholders; competitors.

Table 23.2. Approach to measuring CSP.

Type of measurement	Suitability in terms of the SP concept	Characteristics/ problems	Mode of production
Contents of annual reports	A measurement that is more symbolic than substantive (discourse) and which contains no reference to the construct's varying dimensions	Subjective measurement/that can be easily manipulated	By the company
Pollution indicators	Measures just one of the construct's dimensions (its environmental aspects)	A measurement that is objective but which does not apply to all firms	By an entity that is external to the company
Questionnaire-based surveys	Depends on what measurements have been suggested. Can be a very good fit with the concept but actors' perceptions remain a priority in such measurements	Perceptual measurement that can be manipulated depending on how it is administered	By a researcher who uses a questionnaire to gather info directly from the company
Corporate reputation indicators	Overlapped with corporate reputation. Enables a measurement of overall CSP but is still relatively ambiguous	Perceptual measurement. Halo effects	By an entity that is external to the company
Data produced by "measurement entities"	Multidimensional measurement, with the extent of a theoretical model's "fit" depending on the operational modes and benchmarks that agencies are using	Depends on the agencies' operational mode. Halo effects	By an entity that is external to the company

conducted by external agency using multidimensional measurement. Igalen and Gond (2005) summarize the approaches in Table 23.2.

The approach to CSP measurement classified by Igalen and Gond (2005) is not clear because this approach merely indicates source of data; that is, contents of annual report, questionnaires, and other classifications. To bring clarity to CSP measurement, Orlitzky *et al.* (2003) proposed four types of measurement strategy: (1) disclosure, (2) reputation rating, (3) social audit; CSP process; and observable outcome, and (4) managerial CSP principle and value. The disclosure approach uses content analysis method of documented materials such as annual report. The objective of this approach is to find certain attributes contained in the documents that are considered to reflect a company's socially responsible behavior. This approach has been used by the previous studies (see for example Andersson and Frankle, 1980; Freedman and Jaggi, 1982, 1986). The reputation rating approach to measuring CSP is based on the company's perception of one of the stakeholders using single or multi-dimensions of CSP. In this case, it is assumed that the perceived items represent a good reputation of the company. Previous studies using this approach are many (Cochran and Wood, 1984; Spencer and Taylor, 1987; McGuire *et al.*, 1988; Simerly, 1995; Sharfman, 1996; Belkaoui, 1976; Turban and Greening, 1997). The next category of measurement method for CSP is social audit, CSP process, and observable outcome. This is a systematic process in which the third party assesses a company's behavior of CSP, normally using multidimension measures to have a ranked index of CSP. The third party includes Kinder Lydenberg Domini (KLD) and Council on Economic Priorities (CEP). This approach has been used previously (Wartick, 1988; Turban and Greening, 1997; Russo and Fouts, 1997). Their approach of measuring CSP is using managerial CSP principle and value. Under this approach, survey has been carried out to assess a company's activities using values and principles of CSR developed initially by Caroll (1979) and extended by Aupperle *et al.* (1985). The values and principles of CSR include four dimensions: economy, legal, ethics, and discretionary. The previous studies adopting this approach include Ingram and Frazier (1980), Aupperle *et al.* (1985), Freedman and Jaggi (1986), Cowen *et al.* (1987); O'Neal *et al.* (1989), and Hansen and Wemerfelt, (1989). Cochran and Wood (1984) contended that there are two generally accepted methods to measure CSP: content analysis and reputation index. Based on their argument, the last three classifications of Orlitzky *et al.* (2003) fall in the reputation index method. In line with Cochran and Wood (1984), Margolis *et al.* (2003) use other term for the two generally accepted methods: (i) subjective and (ii) behavior indicators. Subjective indicators refer to reputation index method of Cochran and Wood (1984) and the last three classifications of Orlitzky *et al.* (2003), while the behavior indicators represent content analysis method of Cochran and Wood (1984) and disclosure strategy of Orlitzky *et al.* (2003). Furthermore, some measures for CSP have also been developed based on single or multidimensional measurement. The approaches include eight attributes of reputation (often called fortune measure); five aspects focusing on key stakeholders and three pressure variables (often called KLD measure); quantitative measure of environmental aspect (often called TRI measure); quantitative aspect of company philanthropy (often called Corporate philanthropy measure); and return of six social measure on customer, employee, community, environment, minority, and non-US stakeholder (often called best corporate citizen). For some approaches, it may be possible to use similar measurement but with different judgment or evaluation, the overall CSR measurement may result in different perspective. Itkonen (2003) summarizes different perspective of CSR in Table 23.3.

Table 23.3. Types of corporate social performance measure.

Measure	Dimensions	Judge	Source
Fortune	Eight attributes of reputation	Financial analyst, senior executives, and outside managers	Griffin and Mahon (1997)
KLD	Five attributes of CSR on focusing on key stakeholder relation, there on topics with which companies have recently experienced external pressures	External audiences	Waddock and Grave (1997)
TRI	Qualitative measure of companies' environmental discharge to water, air and landfill, and disposal of hazardous waste	No external judge needed, companies themselves give the data	Griffin and Mahon (1997)
Corporate philanthropy	Quantitative measure of companies philanthropy, how much	No external judge needed, companies themselves give the data	Griffin and Mahon (1997)
Best corporate citizen	3-year average shareholder return and six social measures: company's influence on customer, employee, community, environment, minorities, and non-US stakeholders	Social investment research firm	Murphy (2002)

Mahoney and Roberts (2007) used the measures of social performance, developed by Michael Jantzi Research Associate, Inc. (long partner with KLD), in their study on social and environment performance and their relation to financial and institutional ownership, and included the following variables: community and society, corporate governance, customer, employee, environment, human rights, and controversies business activities. Their modified measures of social performance are presented in Table 23.4.

Corporate Financial Performance

It is the responsibility of management to improve the financial performance, as stakeholders are, such as investor, creditor, and labor, concerned about the performance. The higher financial performance leads to the increase in wealth of the stakeholders. In addition, based on the slack resource theory, improving financial performance leads companies to improve social performance (Waddock and Graves, 1997). Three measures are common to use in the financial performance: ROA and ROE (Waddock and Graves, 1997; Mahoney and Roberts, 2002), profitability in absolute term (Stanwick and Stanwick, 1987), and multiple accounting-based measure with the overall index using the score of 0–10 (More, 2001).

Corporate financial performance (CFP) can also be measured using three alternative approaches: (1) market-based measure, (2) accounting-based measure, and (3) perceptual measure (Orlitzky *et al.*, 2003). Under the first approach, the market value of a company derived from stock price of the company is used to measure CFP. This approach reflects notion that primary stakeholder of the company is shareholder (Vance, 1975; Preston, 1978; Shane and Spicer, 1983; Cochran and Wood, 1984; Simerly, 1994). Accounting-based measure measures CFP derived from a company's competitive effectiveness, competitive internal efficiency, and optimal utilization of assets. Measures such as net income, ROA, and ROE are some examples of this approach (Simerly, 1994; Turban and Greening, 1997; Waddock and Grave, 1997; Russo and Fouts, 1997.)

The last approach to measure CFP is the perceptual method in which respondents provide subjective judgments on perspectives such as ROA, ROE, and financial position relative to other companies (Reimann, 1975; Wartick, 1988).

The Relationship Between CSP and CFP

Given the importance of the CRS in corporate decision making, the relationship between CSP and financial performance is an important topic

Table 23.4. Dimensions of CSP.

Dimension	Indicator	Micro level indicator
Community and society	— Public reporting — Charitable donation program — Community relation — Aboriginal relation — Impact on society	— Policy statement on community donation — Cash donations as a percentage of pre-tax profit — Policy statement on engagement/consultation — Benefit sharing agreement with local communities — Policy statement on aboriginal relation — Policy statement on bribery and corruption — Impact/initiatives related to marginalized groups
Corporate governance	— Management systems — Governance data	— Statement of social responsibility principles or values — Code of business conduct — Board independence — Separate chairman and chief executive officer — Share structure — Shareholder proposals
Customer	— Management system — Impact on customer	— Policy statement on safety of product/service — Policy statement on the treatment of customers — Systems/programs to ensure product safety or fair treatment of customers
Employee	— Employee data — Reporting — Employee program and benefit — Diversity — Health and safety — Union relation — Other data employee	— Total number of employee — Employee turnover — Public reporting on employee issues — Education and development — Ownership program — Policy on employee diversity — Public reporting on diversity issues — Policy on occupational health and safety — Employee wellness programs

(Continued)

Table 23.4. (*Continued*)

Dimension	Indicator	Micro level indicator
		— Description of relations
		— No. of strikes/lockouts in the last 5 years
		— Employee controversies
Environment	— Exposure to Environmental Issues	— Potential environmental impacts
	— Management systems	— Formal environmental management system
	— Public reporting	— Environmental policy
	— Impact and initiatives	— Systems to measure and monitor environmental performance
	— Regulatory compliance	— Audits
	— Other environmental Data	— Life-cycle analysis
		— The company's environmental reporting
		— Resource use
		— Pollution control
		— Environmental penalties over the last 5 years
		— Environmental liabilities
		— Total environmental expenditures
Human rights	— Exposure to human rights issues	— Exposure related to countries in which the company operates
	— Management systems	— Human rights policy/code of conduct
	— Impact and initiatives	— Systems/programs to manage human rights issues
		— Community engagement
		— Implication in the abuse of human rights
Controversies business activities	— Alcohol	— Level of involvement (% of annual revenues)
	— Gambling	— Nature of involvement
	— Genetic engineering	
	— Tobacco	
	— Use of animal	

(McGuire *et al.*, 1988). In practice, social performance requires some costs that may reduce financial performance. As a result, the question arises, which should come first — social performance or financial performance. Justification to explain the importance is thus needed by management.

There are two important issues in the relationship between CSP and CFP: direction and causality of the relationship (Preston and O'Bannon, 1997).

The direction of the relationship refers to positive, negative, or neutral. The positive direction of the relationship between CSP and CFP occurs when increase in CSP leads to the increases in CFP. The change in CSP leading to the change in CFP in different way is negative direction of the relationship. If a change in CSP does not affect the change in CFP, then neutral effect in the direction of the relationship occurs. The causality of the relationship denotes if CSP or CFP is independent or dependent variable. In this case, two possibilities exist: CSP as independent variable and CFP as independent variable. If CSP is an independent variable, it affects CFP. If CSP is a dependent variable, CFP affects CSP.

The positive link between CSP and CFP can be explained in three ways (Waddock and Grave, 1997). First, firms trying to lower its implicit cost by being socially irresponsible, its explicit cost will increase, and, in turn, will result in competitive disadvantage (decrease in profit). Second argument of Waddock and Graves (1997) is using the better management theory. According to this theory, socially responsible firms improve relationship with their stakeholders. This relationship improves competitive advantage and, in turn, increases financial performance. This argument is equivalent to the social impact and synergy hypothesis of Preston and O'Bannon (1997). The last argument used by Waddock and Graves (1997) for positive relationship is the slack resource theory. According to this theory, firm's financial resource will determine activities in social responsibility. Given the resources, the firm has more chances to invest in socially responsible activities.

Explanation of the negative CSP–CFP link is based on neoclassical economic theory, which states that socially responsible firms' costs are considered unnecessary, and thus can lead to a competitive disadvantage; that is, a decrease in companies' profit and shareholder wealth (Preston and O'Bannon, 1997; Waddock and Garve, 1997). Neutral link between CSP and CFP exists as the relationship is by coincidence (Waddock and Grave, 1997). Argument for this link is that a company acting socially responsibly to customer can have different demand curve as compared to less responsible companies. Therefore, the activities are the only way to attain differentiation, and thus do not impact on company's profit (McWilliam and Siegel, 2001). The relationships of CSP and CFP are summarized in Table 23.5.

Conclusion can now be drawn from the previous findings on the relationship between CSP and CFP, which is not positive and the same under all conditions. The use of contingency perspective is needed to understand under which condition the relationship will be valid (Hedesström and Biel, 2008). That is why Fauzi (2008b) proposes a proposition on corporate performance explaining that the relationship between CSP and CFP can be

Table 23.5.   Positive, negative, and neutral direction of the relationship of CSP and CFP.

Study	Sample	CSR measure	Control variables
Positive relationship			
Worrell *et al.* (1991)	Market's reactions to announcements of 194 layoffs studied		
Preston and O'Bannon (1997)	Multiple industries, 67 large US corporations	Fortune	
Waddock and Graves (1997)	Multiple industries, 469 companies	KLD	Firm size, risk, industry
Frooman (1997)	Meta-analysis of 27 event studies		
Roman *et al.* (1999)	Reconstruction the literature study of Griffin and Mahon (1997), 4 studies added		
Orlitzky (2001)	Meta-analysis of 20 studies		Firm size
Orlitzky and Benjamin (2001)	Meta-analysis on the relationship and risk		
Ruf *et al.* (2001)	Multiple industries 496 firms	KLD	Firm size, industry
Murphy (2002)	S&P 500	Best corporate citizens	
Simpson and Kohers (2002)	Banking industry, 385 banks	Community reinvestment act rating	Industry
Neutral relationship			
Griffin and Mahon (1997)	Chemical industry, 7 companies (includes also a wide literature study)	Fortune, KLD, TRI, philanthropy	Industry
McWilliams and Siegel (2000)	Multiple industries, 524 firms	KLD	Investment in R&D
McWilliams and Siegel (2001)	Theoretical study, outlining supply, and demand model of CSR		

(*Continued*)

Table 23.5.   (*Continued*)

Study	Sample	CSR measure	Control variables
More (2001)	UK supermarket industry, 8 companies	16 measures of soc. performance and disclosure	Industry
Negative relationship			
Wright and Ferris (1997)	Multiple industries, 116 divestments	Divestments of South African businesses = CSR	

contingent upon four variables: (1) business environment, (2) business strategy, (3) organization structure, and (4) control system.

Griffin and Mahon (1997) raised the issue of causality of the relationship between CSP and CFP. In an effort to meet the stakeholder's expectation, company should try to improve CSP from time to time in light of economic and financial conditions. However, the question of priority arises; that is, which one (CSP and financial performance) comes first. Waddock and Graves (1997) and Dean (1998) put forward two theories to answer the question: Slack resource theory and good management theory. Under the slack resource theory, a company should have a good financial position to contribute to the corporate social performance. Conducting the social performance needs some fund resulting from the success of financial performance. According to this theory, financial performance comes first. Therefore, CFP is independent variable to affect CSP. A good management theory holds that social performance comes first. Based on the theory, CSP is an independent variable resulting in CFP. A company perceived by its stakeholders as having a good reputation will make the company easier to get a good financial position through market mechanism.

Hypotheses Development
The difference of CSP between SOCs and POCs

Rudjito (2005) states that one of the problems resulting in SOCs to have inferior business performance in past was the drawback in the direction of SOC's policy. Since the ministry of SOCs had been set up, the direction of the SOCs policy is clear and it became clearer when the Law No. 19, 2003 (Republic of Indonesia, 2003) has been passed. One of the functions of the

Ministry of SOCs is to emphasize the role of the government as the owner of SOCs (different from the role of the government as the regulator). The Law No. 19 (Republic of Indonesia, 2003) firmly differentiates the role of owner, regulator, supervisor, and operator. With the different roles, political interventions in SOCs will be minimized. As a result, SOCs can work professionally based on the principles of good corporate governance. In addition, the increasing demand, resulting from global situation, for SOCs to be corporate citizen is also the condition the SOCs are facing (Soedjais, 2005). Given the positive direction in managing SOCs, it is expected that the factors can encourage the SOCs to improve their performance in different dimensions; that is social, environment, and financial. Therefore, it is hypothesized that:

H1: There are no differences in social performance of SCOs and POCs.

The relationship between CSP and CFP

Based on the literature review, the relationship between corporate social performance and corporate financial performance could be positive, negative, or neutral (Worrell *et al.*, 1991; Preston and O'Bannon, 1997; Roman *et al.*, 1999; McWilliam and Siegel, 2001; Orlitzky, 2001; Simpson *et al.*, 2002). Griffin and Mahon (1997) reviewed 51 studies discussing the relationship between CSP and CFP from the 1970s through the 1990s. They mapped the issue of direction of the relationship between CSP and CFP for the periods. In the 1970s and there were 16 studies reviewed with 12 of which had positive relationship. During the period of the 1980s and 1990s, the positive direction of the relationship accounted for 14 of 27 studies and seven of the eight studies, respectively. Negative results were supported by only one study in the 1970s, 17 studies in the 1980s, and three studies in the 1990s. Four studies in the 1970s and five studies in the 1980s found inconclusive findings. There are additional studies contributing to the direction of the association between CSP and CFP relationship in the 1990s. During this period, positive direction of the relationship has been supported (Worrell *et al.*, 1991; Frooman, 1997; Roman *et al.*, 1999). Wright and Ferris (1997) supported the negative results. Furthermore, there are studies on the link between CSP and CFP using different methodology. Positive results were supported (Orlitzky, 2001; Murphy, 2002; Simpson and Kohers, 2002; Orlitzky *et al.*, 2003; Mahoney and Roberts, 2007). Patten (2002) found a negative correlation. Researchers such as McWilliams and Siegel (2000, 2001) and More (2001) found inconclusive results. Fauzi (2004) using content analysis of annual reports of companies listed on the New York Stock Exchange for the period of 2004 also provided support for inconclusive results.

Given that discussion, it is expected to have concern that the relationship between corporate and financial performance is positive. Hence, it is proposed that:

H2: There is positive relationship between corporate social performance and financial performance.

There are other variables affecting corporate social performance such as company size and institutional ownership.

Company size

According to Waddock and Graves (1997) and Itkonen (2003), company size is related to corporate social performance; that is, bigger companies behave in a more socially responsible manner than smaller ones. In addition, company size can have a relationship with institutional ownership; that is, bigger companies get more attention from the external stakeholder groups than smaller companies, and so, they need to respond to them. Orlitzky (2001) demonstrates that size is a factor in the relationship. Further, CSP is related to the firm size, because, in the beginning, entrepreneurial strategies focus on the basic economic survival and not on ethical and philanthropic responsibilities. Based on the arguments, it is expected that the size of the company can be related to CFP, resulting from, for example, the economies of scale.

Institutional ownership

Institutional ownership is generally a large investment in a company, and so, the investor has less ability than individual investor to move quickly without affecting the company's share price (Pound, 1988). Therefore, it is related to company's financial as well as overall performances (Johnson and Greening, 1999; Mahoney and Robert, 2007). To have a company's stake, institutional investors normally consider return and risk. A company with low CSP faces high risk to be pressured, and in turn, will endanger their investment. Therefore, they prefer to look for a company with higher CSP as the choice improves their potential return. The higher the CSP companies have, the more institutional ownership in those companies. In that case, CSP is a means to reduce the risk of investment.

Methodology

Data and sample selection

Population of this study is SOCs and POCs. Sampling method used is purposive sampling. The sample was based on the following criteria: (1) POCs have been registered in Jakarta Stock Exchange (JSX) during 2001–2004; (2) SOCs, registered in JSX, are treated as SOCs, and those that are not registered are listed in the SOCs list; and (3) they have issued annual report in JSX and SOCs Ministry.

Measurement of CSP

CSP is measured and calculated through content analysis for each company following the approaches of both by Kinder, Lydenberg Domini (KLD), the United States-based independent rating company and by Michael Jantzi Research Associate (MJRA), an independent rating company in Canada. Both these companies measure several dimensions of the CSP to arrive at a total measure of CSP. These dimensions include community issues, diversity in the workplace, employee relations, environmental performance, international issues, product and business practices, and other variables concerning compensation, confidentiality, and ownership in other companies.

Both positive and negative social responsible information was collected through examining the Corporate annual report (CAR), company corporate social reports, along with information obtained from the capital market directory, Jakarta stock exchange web sites, other web sites and other electronic news of sampled companies. The CSP for each company was assessed on a scale of −2 to +2 for each rating. A −2 rating for any dimension indicates major concern, −1 indicates a notable concern, 0 indicates no notable or major strength and concern, +1 indicates a notable strength and +2 indicates a major strength. A composite CSP score was then calculated by summing the scores of each dimension for each company. Table 23.6 reports the dimensions of CSP.

Measurement of financial performance

Following the works of Waddock and Graves (1997) and Roman *et al.* (1999), return on assets (ROA) and return on equity (ROE) were used to measure a firm's financial performance. ROA is defined as the ratio of net income after tax to total assets, and ROE is defined as the ratio of net income

Table 23.6. Dimension of CSP.

Dimension	Strength	Concern
Community issues	• Generous giving • Innovating giving • Community consultation/engagement • Strong aboriginal relationship	• Lack of consultation/engagement • Breach of covenant • Weak aboriginal relation
Diversity in workplace	• Strong employment equity program • Woman on board of directors • Women in senior management • Work/family benefit • Minority/women contracting	• Lack of employment equity initiative • Employment equity controversies
Employee relations	• Positive union relation • Exceptional benefit • Workforce management policies • Cash profit sharing • Employee ownership/involvement	• Poor union relation • Safety problem • Workforce reduction • Inadequate benefits
Environmental performance	• Environmental management strength • Exceptional environment planning and impact assessment • Environmentally sound resource use • Environmental impact reduction • Beneficial product and service	• Environment management concern • Inadequate environmental planning impact assessment • Unsound resource use • Poor compliance record • Substantial emissions/discharges • Negative impact of operation • Negative impact of products
International	• Community relations • Employee relations • Environment • Sourcing practice	• Poor community relations • Poor employee relations • Poor environmental management/performance • Human rights • Burma • Sourcing practice

(*Continued*)

Table 23.6.   (*Continued*)

Dimension	Strength	Concern
Product and business practice	• Beneficial products and service • Ethical business practice	• Product safety • Pornography • Marketing practices • Illegal business practices
Other	• Limited compensation • Confidential proxy voting • Ownership in companies	• Excessive compensation • Dual-class share structure • Ownership in other companies

after tax to outstanding shares. Information on ROA and ROE was collected from the CAR.

Measurement of control variables

There are three approaches to measure company size in literature: (1) total asset (Tsoutsoura, 2004; Fauzi, 2004); (2) the number of people employed (Simerly and Li, 2001) and (3) annual sales of the firm (Simerly and Li, 2001; More, 2001; Tsoutsoura, 2004). The present study follows the measure used by Mahoney and Robert (2007) with the argument that total asset is "money machine" to generate sales and income. Based on the literature survey, the institutional ownership variable, as used by Mahoney and Roberts (2007), is measured by the number of institutions owning the company shares.

Sample Characteristics

Tables 23.7–23.10 report sample characteristics and descriptive data.

The number of annual report collected from SOCs is 47. Of the total samples, 10 (21%) annual reports are not eligible for reasons such as damaged files, too short contents, leaving the number of 37 samples (79%).

The numbers of POCs supplying annual report were 508. Among the samples, 84 (17%) annual reports are not eligible for sampling. As a result, total samples for both SOCs and POCs are 461 companies. Descriptive statistics are presented by computing mean and standard dev. of CSR, ROA, total asset, and institutional ownership between SOCs and POCs.

Table 23.7. The number of sample of SOCs.

Description	Number
Total annual reports provided by SOCs in 2001–2004	47
Annual report not eligible for samples	(10)
The number of annual reports eligible for samples	37

Table 23.8. The number of POCs' samples.

Description	Number
Total annual report provided by POCs in 2001–2004	508
Annual repors not eligible for samples	(84)
Number of annual report eligible for samples	424

Table 23.9. Statistics of descriptive for SOC.

Variable	Mean	Standard Dev.
CSP	4.11	1.76
ASSET (billion Rp)	22.38	38.54
ROA (%)	4.75	5.75
ROE (%)	12.50	14.75
IO	12.38	38.03

Notes: CSP = corporate social performance indicates score of SOCs' CSP measured by using the dimension of MJRA.
ASSET = total asset as stated in SOCs' balance sheet.
ROA = return on asset computed by dividing SOCs' net income by total asset.
ROE = return on equity computed by dividing SOCs' net income by total asset.
IO = institutional ownership indicated by the number of SOCs' shares owned by institutional owner.

Results

For H1, the *t*-test analyzed the differences between SOCs and POCs. Table 23.11 reports the statistics.

Table 23.11 shows no significant mean diferrence between social performance in SOCs and POCs. As result, the hypothesis (H1), stating that there is mean difference in social perfomance of SOCs and POCs, cannot be accepted.

Table 23.12 indicates the result of correlation test between social performance and financial performance at SOCs situation. It is found that (as shown

Table 23.10. Statistics of descriptive for POCs.

Variable	Mean	Standard dev.
CSP	4.62	2.24
ASSET	4.26	13.54
ROA	4.99	35.44
ROE	23.01	693.24
IO	3.00	2.25

Notes: CSP = corporate social performance indicates score of POCs' CSP measured by using the dimension of MJRA.
ASSET = total asset as stated in POCs' balance sheet.
ROA = return on asset computed by dividing POCs' net income by total asset.
ROE = return on equity computed by dividing POCs' net income by total asset.
IO = institutional ownership indicated by the number of POCs' shares owned by institutional owner.

Table 23.11. Testing mean difference of CSP/CSR's score.

Description	SOCs	POCs
CSP mean	4.11	4.62
Standard dev.	1.86	2.24
Sig.	0.37	0.37
Difference	0.37	0.37

Table 23.12. The correlation test between social performance and finacial performance at SOCs.

Description	Coefficient	Probablity
CSR-ROA	−0.0480	0.78
CSR-ROE	0.1300	0.46
CSR-ASET	−0.0116	0.94
CSR-IO	−0.0969	0.59

in the table, using the two control variables for both measures of financial performance) there is no a significant corelation between social performance and financial performance.

Table 23.13 shows the correlation test between corporate social performance and financial performance at POCs. As indicated in the table, it is found that there is no significant correlation between social performance and financial performance at POCs situation.

Table 23.13. Correlation test between social performance and financial at POCs.

Description	Coefficient	Probability
CSR-ROA	0.0364	0.45
CSR-ROE	−0.0386	0.42
CSR-ASSET	0.1572	0.00
CSR-OWN	0.0403	0.41

Comparisons are needed specially in developing countries. Al-Khadash (2003) included companies (34) that have annual reports during 1998–2000. Compared to that study, our study has a larger sample. In addition, the classification used in Al-Khadash (2003) is disclose and undisclose, while this study classifies the sample companies as the SOCs and POCs.

Conclusion

The objective of this chapter was to analyze the difference in social performance in SOCs and POCs and the relationship between CSP and financial performance at SOCs and at POCs using the control variables of company assets and institutional ownership. The score of CSP is determined using content analysis of annual reports of the sampled companies. The independent *t*-test is used to analyze the mean difference between CSP in SOCs and POCs, while the partial correlation technique is to test correlation between CSP and financial performance. The results indicate no significant mean difference between CSP in the SOCs and in the POCs. In addition, this study finds no significant correlation between CSP at SOCs and POCs situation. It is also found that only one variable (company size) has correlation with the SCP.

Recommendations for Managers

The CSR activities in the Indonesian economics do not seem to contribute to business performance. This study demonstrates that Indonesian companies are increasingly trying to accommodate CSR and emphasizing on CSR as costs than stakeholder relationship. This could be due to the companies' objection of the Indonesian Law No. 40 (2007) on Indonesian Corporation. One of the articles of the law stipulates that Indonesian companies are obliged to conduct CSR. The reason for the objection is their un-readiness to carry out CSR responsibilities.

This study recommends that the authority of SOCs and POCs need to issue the regulations for the companies to disclose the CSR activities in their annual report. The awareness to disclose the CSR activities is expected to encourage them to conduct the CSR. This effort is especially important as CSR activities in developing countries such as Indonesia. The neutrality of the relationship of this study finding may be due to the incompleteness of the annual reports used (as the key data in the content analysis approach) in measuring CSP/CSR.

Direction for Future Research

Further research should include other approaches to measuring the CSP and financial performance. The reputation approach to measuring CSP, for example, as suggested by Orlitzky *et al.* (2003) is an alternative to content analysis or disclosure approach. In addition, financial performance also needs to be extended, and not only should be based on accounting-based measure but also be based on market-based measure and perceptual approach. Longitudinal approach is important to be used as alternative to cross-sectional approach. That endeavors are meant to get good understanding of CSR in Indonesia as well as in other developing countries.

References

Abeng, T (2004). Reformasi BUMN. In *Paper Presented at the Seminar BUMN Executives Club*. Jakarta, Indonesia.

Al-Khadash, HA (2003). The accounting disclosure of social and environmental activities: A comparative study for the industrial Jordanian shareholding companies. *Abhath Al-Yarmouk Journal: Humanities and Social Sciences*.

Anderson, JC and AW Frankle (1980). Voluntary social reporting: An iso beta portfolio analysis. *The Accounting Review*, LV.3.

Aupperle, KE, AB Carroll, and AD Hatfield (1985). An empirical examination of the relationship between corporate social responsibility and Profitability. *Academy of Management Journal*, 28(2).

Barnett, ML (2007). Stakeholder influence capacity and the variability of financial returns to corporate social responsibility. *Academy of Management Review*, 32, 794–816.

Baron, RA and D Byrne (2000). *Social Psychology*, 9th edn. Allyn and Bacon Publisher.

Belkaoui, A (1976). The impact of the disclosure of the environmental effects of organizational behavior on the market. *Financial Management*, 5, 26–31.

Carroll, AB (ed) (1977). *Managing corporate social responsibility*. Boston Little Brown and Company.

Carroll, AB (1979). A Three-dimensional conceptual model of corporate social performance. *Academy of Management Review*, 4, 497–506.

Carroll, AB (1999). Corporate social responsibility. Evolution of a definitional construct. *Business and Society*, 38(3), 268–295.

Chan, CSH and P Kent (2003). Application of stakeholder theory to the quantity and quality of Australian voluntary corporate environmental disclosures. In *Paper Presented to the Accounting and Finance Association of Australia and New Zealand (AFAANZ)*, July, Brisbane.

Cochran, PL and RA Wood (1984). Corporate social performance and financial performance. *Academy of Management Journal*, 27(1), 42–56.

Cowen, SS, LB Ferreri, and LD Parker (1987). The impact of corporate characteristics on social responsibility disclosure: A typology and frequency-based analysis. *Accounting, Organisations and Society*, 12, 111–122.

Clarkson, MBE (1995a). A stakeholder theory of the corporation: Concepts, evidence, and implications. *The Academy of Management*, 20(1).

Clarkson, MBE (1995b). A stakeholder framework for analyzing and evaluating corporation social performance. *Academy of Management Review*, 20(1).

Dean, KL (1997). The chicken and the egg revisited: Ties between corporate social performance and the financial bottom line. *Journal of Applied Psychology*, 82.

Dean, KL (1998). The chicken and the egg revisited: Ties between corporate social performance and the financial bottom line. *The Academy of Management Executive*, 2, 99–100.

Donaldson, T and LE Preston (1995). The stakeholder theory of the corporation: Concept, evidence, and implications. *The Academy of Management Review*, 20(1), 65–91.

Donalson, T (1999). Making stakeholder theory whole. *Academy of Management Review*, 24(2).

Coffey, BS and GE Fryxell (1991). Institutional ownership of stock and dimensions of corporate social performance: An empirical examination. *Journal of Business Ethics*, 10(6), 437–444.

Coffey, BS and J Wang (1998). Board diversity and managerial control as predictor of corporate social performance. *Journal of Business Ethics*, 17, 1595–1603.

Davidson, WN III and DL Worrell (1992). Research notes and communications: The effect of product recalls announcements on shareholder wealth. *Strategic Management Journal*, 13, 467–473.

Fauzi, H (2004). Identifying and analyzing the level of practices of company's social responsibility in improving financial performance. *Journal of Business and Management*, 4(2).

Fauzi, H, L Mahoney, and AA Rahman (2007a). The link between corporate social performance and financial performance: Evidence from Indonesian companies. *Issues in Social and Environmental Accounting*, 1(1), 149–159.

Fauzi, H, L Mahoney, and AA Rahman (2007b). The ownership and corporate social performance. *Issues in Social and Environmental Accounting*, 1(2).

Fauzi, H (2008a). Corporate social and environmental performance: A comparative study of Indonesian companies and MNCs operating in Indonesia. *Journal of Global Knowledge*, 1(1).

Fauzi, H (2008b). The determinants of the relationship between corporate social performance and financial performance. *Accepted for Presentation in American Accounting Association Annual Meeting*, Anaheim, California.

Frederick, WC, EP James, and K Davis (1992). *Business and Society: Corporate Strategy, Public Policy, and Ethics*. McGraw-Hill International Edition.

Freedman, M and B Jaggi (1982). Pollution disclosures, pollution performance and economic performance. *Omega: The International Journal of Management Science*, 10, 167–176.

Freedman, M and B Jaggi (1986). An analysis of the impact of corporate pollution disclosures included in annual financial statements on investors' decisions. *Advances in Public Interest Accounting*, 1, 192–212.

Freeman, RE (1994). The politics of stakeholder theory: Some future directions. *Business Ethics Quarterly*, 4(4).

Frooman, J (1997). Socially irresponsible and illegal behavior and shareholder wealth. *Business & Society*, 3, 221–249.

Fry, FL and RI Hock (2001). Who claim corporate responsibility? The biggest and the worst. *Business and Society Review*.

Gerde, VW (2000). Stakeholder and organization design: An empirical test of corporate social performance. In *Research in Stakeholder Theory, 1997–1998, The Sloan Foundation Minigrant Project*, Toronto, Clarkson Center for Business Ethics, 2000.

Gray, RH, R Kouhy, and S Lavers (1995a). Corporate social and environmental reporting: A review of the literature and a longitudinal study of UK disclosure. *Accounting, Auditing, and Accountability Journal*, 8(2), 47–77.

Gray, RH, R Kouhy, and S Lavers (1995b). Constructing a research database of social and environmental reporting by UK companies: A methodological note. *Accounting, Auditing, and Accountability Journal*, 8(2), 47–77.

Graves, SB (1988). Institutional ownership and corporate R&D in the computer industry. *Academy of Management Journal*, 31, 417–428.

Graves and SA Waddock (1994). Institutional owners and corporate social performance. *Academy of Management Journal*, 37(4), 1034–1046.

Griffin, JJ and JF Mahon (1997). The corporate social performance and corporate financial performance debate: Twenty-five years of incomparable research. *Business and Society*, 36(1), 5–31.

Griffin, JJ and JF Mahon (1999). Painting a portrait. *Business and Society*, 38(1), 126–133.

Hansen, GS and B Wernerfelt (1989). Determinants of firm performance: The relative importance of economic and organisational factors. *Strategic Management Journal*, 10, 399–411.

Hedesström, TM and A Biel (2008). Evaluating companies' social and environmental performance: Current practice and some recommendations. Goteborgs Universitet: *Goteborg Psychological Report*, 30, 1.

Husted, BW (2000). Contingency theory of corporate social performance. *Business and Society*, 39(1).

Igalens, J and J Gond (2005). Measuring corporate social performance in France: A critical and empirical analysis of ARESE data. *Journal of Business Ethics*, 56(2), 131–148.

Itkonen, L (2003). Corporate social responsibility and financial performance. *Institute of Strategy and International Business*, Helsinki, Finland.

Johnson, RA and DW Greening (1999). The effects of corporate governance and institutional ownership types on corporate social performance. *Academy of Management Journal*, 42(5).

Jantzi Research Incorporated (2008). http://www.jantziresearch.com/index.asp?section=7&level_2=34.

Kinder Lydenberg Domini (KLD) (2008). http://www.kld.com/indexes/index.html.

Mahoney, LS and RW Roberts (2007). Corporate social performance, financial performance and institutional ownership in Canadian firms. *Accounting Forum*, 31(3), 233–253.

Mangos, N and P O'Brien (2000). Investigating social responsibility reporting practices of global Australian firms and how those practices enhance economic success. http://www.iipe.org.

Margolis, JD and JP Walsh (2003). Misery loves companies: Rethinking social initiatives by business. *Administrative Science Quarterly*, 48, 268–305.

McGuire, JB, A Sundgren, and T Schneeweis (1988). Corporate social responsibility and firm financial performance. *Academy of Management Journal*, 3(4), 854–872.

McWilliams, A and D Siegel (2000). Corporate social responsibility and financial performance: Correlation or misspecification? *Strategic Management Journal*, 21(5), 603–609.

McWilliams, A and D Siegel (2001). Corporate social responsibility: A theory of firm perspective. *Academy of Management Review*, 26(1), 117–127.

Moeljono, D and R Nugroho (2005). Kantor Kementrian BUMN. *BUMN Executives Club*, Jakarta, Indonesia.

Moir, L (2001). What do we mean by corporate social responsibility? *Journal of Corporate Governance*, 1(2), 16–22.

More, G (2001). Corporate social and financial performance: An investigation in the U.K. supermarket industry. *Journal of Business Ethics*, 34, 299–315.

Morimoto, R, J Ash, and dan C Hope (2004). Corporate social responsibility audit: From theory to practice. *Research Papers in Management Studies*. Judge Institute of Management, University of Cambridge.

Murphy, E (2002). Best corporate citizens have better financial performance. *Strategic Finance*, 83(7), 20–21.

Murray, A, D Sinclair, D Power, and R Gray (2006). Do financial markets care about social and environmental disclosure? Further evidence and exploration from the UK. *Accounting, Auditing & Accountability Journal*, 19(2), 228–255.

Murphy, E (2002). Best corporate citizens have better financial performance. *Strategic Finance*, 83(7), 20–21.

Neville, SJB and B Menguc (2005). Corporate reputation, stakeholders and the social performance-financial performance relationship. *European Journal of Marketing*, 39(9–10), 1184–1198.

Nugroho, R and R Siahaan (2005). *BUMN Indonesia: Isu, Kebijakan, dan Strategi, Elex Media Komputindo*, Jakarta, Indonesia.

Orlitzky, M (2001). Does firm size confound the relationship between corporate social performance and firm financial performance? *Journal of Business Ethics*, 33(2), 167–180.

Orlitzky, M and JD Benjamin (2001). Corporate social performance and firm risk: A meta-analytic review. *Business and Society*, 40(4), 369–396.

Orlitzky, M, FL Schmidt, and SL Rynes (2003). Corporate social and financial performance: A meta analysis. *Organization Studies*, 24(3), 403–441.

O'Donovan, G and K Gibson (2000). *Environmental Disclosures in the Corporate Annual Report: A Longitudinal Australian Study*. Http://www.ssrn.com.

O'Neill, HM, CB Saunders, and AD McCarthy (1989). Board members, corporate social responsiveness and profitability: Are tradeoffs necessary? *Journal of Business Ethics*, 8, 353–357.

Patten, DM (2002). The relation between environmental performance and environmental disclosure: A research note. *Accounting, Organisation and Society*, 27(8), 763–773.

Pound, J (1988). Proxy contests and the efficiency of shareholder oversight. *Journal of Financial Economics*, 20, 237–265.

Preston, LE (1978). Analyzing corporate social performance: Methods and results. *Journal of Contemporary Business*, 7, 135–150.

Preston, LE and DP O'Bannon (1997). The corporate social-financial performance relationship: A typology and analysis. *Business and Society*, 36(4), 419–429.

Rashid, MZA and I Saadiatul (2002). Executive and management attitudes towards corporate social responsibility in Malaysia. *Corporate Governance*, 2(4), 10–16.

Reimann, BC (1975). Organizational effectiveness and management's public values: A canonical analysis. *Academy of Management Journal*, 18, 224–241.

Republic of Indonesia (1992). *The Law No. 25, 1992 on Cooperative-based Economy and Its Explanations*. www.ri.go.id.

Republic of Indonesia (2003). *The Law No. 19, 2003 on State-owned Companies and Its Explanations*. www.ri.go.id.

Republic of Indonesia (2007). *The Law No. 40, 2007 on Indonesian Corporation and Its Explanations*. www.ri.go.id.

Rudjito (2005). *Restrukturisasi BUMN Pasca UU BUMN, BUMN Executive Club*, Jakarta, Indonesia.

Roman, RM, S Hayibor, and BR Agle (1999). The relationship between social and financial performance: Repainting a portrait. *Business and Society*, 38(1), 109–125.

Rowley, T and S Berman (2000). A brand new brand of corporate social performance. *Business and Society*, 39(4), 397–418.

Ruf, BM, K Muralidhar, RM Brown, JJ Janney, and K Paul (2001). An empirical investigation of the relationship between change in corporate social performance and financial performance: A stakeholder theory perspective. *Journal of Business Ethics*, 32(2), 143–156.

Russo, MV and PA Fouts (1997). A resource-based perspective on corporate environmental performance and profitability. *Academy of Management Journal*, 40, 534–559.

Shane, PB and BH Spicer (1983). Market response to environmental information produced outside the firm. *Accounting Review*, 58, 521–538.

Sharfman, M (1996). A concurrent validity study of the KLD social performance ratings data. *Journal of Business Ethics*, 15, 287–296.

Simatupang, M (2003). BUMN Pasca UU BUMN. In *Paper Presented at Workshop II BUMN di Era Globalisasi*, Jakarta.

Simerly, RL (1994). Corporate social performance and firms' financial performance: An alternative perspective. *Psychological Reports*, 75, 1091–1103.

Simerly, RL (1995). Institutional ownership, corporate social performance, and firms' financial performance. *Psychological Reports*, 77, 515–525.

Simerly, RL (2003). Empirical examination of the relationship between management and corporate social performance. *International Journal of Management*, 20(3), 353–359.

Simerly, RL and L Minfang (2001). *Corporate Social Performance and Multinationality, A Longitudinal Study*. http://www.westga.edu/~bquest/2000/corporate.html.

Simpson, WG and T Kohers (2002). The link between corporate social and financial performance: Evidence from the banking industry. *Journal of Business Ethics*, 35(2), 97–109.

Spencer, BA and SG Taylor (1987). A within and between analysis of the relationship between corporate social responsibility and financial performance. *Akron Business and Economic Review*, 18, 7–8.

Soedjais, Z (2005). BUMN Incorporated. In *Paper Presented at the Seminar BUMN Executives Club*, Jakarta.

Sugiharto (2005). Restrukturisasi, Profitisasi, Privatisasi. In *Paper Presented at CEO Breakfast & Briefing*, BUMN Executives Club, Jakarta.

Stanwick, PA and S Stanwick (1987). The relationship between corporate social performance, and organizational size, financial performance, and environmental performance: An empirical examination. *Journal of Business Ethics*, 17, 195–204.

Tsoutsoura, M (2004). Corporate social responsibility and financial performance. *Working Paper Series*, http://repositories.cdlib.org, University of California, Berkeley.

Ullman, AA (1985). Data in search of theory: A critical of examination of the relationship among social performance, social disclosure, and economics performance of U.S. firms. *Academy of Management Review*, 10(3).

Turban, DB and DW Greening (1997). Corporate social performance and organizational attractiveness to prospective employee. *Academy of Management Journal*, 40(3).

Vance, S (1975). Are socially responsible firms good investment risks? *Management Review*, 64, 18–24.

Waddock, SA and SB Graves (1997). The corporate social performance financial performance ling. *Strategic Management Journal*, 18(4).

Wagner, M (2001). *A Review of Empirical Studies Concerning the Relationship Between Environmental and Economic Performance*. Liineburg: Center for Sustainability Management, August.

Wartick, SL and PL Cochran (1985). The evolution of the corporate social performance model. *Academy of Management Review*, 10(4), 758–769.

Wartick, SL (1988). How issues management contributes to corporate performance. *Business Forum*, 13, 16–22.

Wartick, SL (2002). Measuring corporate reputations: Definition and data. *Business and Society*, 41(4), 371–391.

Wood, DJ (1991). Corporate social performance revisited. *Academy of Management Review*, 16, 691–718.

Worrell, DL, WN Davidson III, and VM Sharma (1991). Lay off announcements and stockholder wealth. *Academy of Management Journal*, 34(3), 662–678.

Wright, P and SP Ferris (1997). Agency conflict and corporate strategy: The effect of divestment on corporate value. *Strategic Management Journal*, 18(1), 77–83.

Chapter 24

DOES INDIVIDUAL STOCK FUTURES AFFECT STOCK MARKET VOLATILITY IN INDIA?

NALINIPRAVA TRIPATHY, S. V. RAMANA RAO, AND A. KANAGARAJ

Abstract

Presently, India's derivative market turnover is more than the cash market. The impact of derivatives on the cash market volatility is much debated and widely studied. Because derivatives play a significant role in the stock market for the development of economy, this chapter focuses on assessing the impact of the introduction of stock derivatives trading on the underlying stocks volatility in India by applying both generalized autoregressive conditional heteroskedasticity and autoregressive conditional heteroskedasticity model for a period of 7 years from June 1999 to July 2006. Prior studies on the effects of futures and options listing on the underlying cash market volatility suggest that introduction of stock futures do not lead to a change in the volatility. However, our study indicates that although stock future derivatives are not responsible for increase or decrease in spot market volatility, market factors may contribute to increases in stock market volatility.

Introduction

A decade of reform has brought about a radical transformation of the Indian stock market and it is considered as one of the developed markets of the world. The recent reforms in the Indian capital market have helped improve efficiency in dissemination of information, better transparency in operations, and prohibiting unfair trade practices. The most certain thing about the markets is uncertainty, which leads to risk. One of the risks is financial risk, which is caused by changes in stock market prices. To manage these risks, financial derivatives have been developed and introduced into the Indian capital markets over a period. The term derivative implies that it has no independent value. Its value is derived from the value of the other asset. The financial derivatives were introduced in India mainly as a risk management tool for both the institutional and retail investors. The basic purpose of introducing derivative products in the market was to provide the investors with some effective measures to hedge their risk-exposure in different markets. The two main functions of derivative market are price discovery and hedging. However, apart from being used as hedging tools, these products are also used by risk-taking investors for availing arbitrage and speculative opportunities. Such uses of derivative products are believed to be helpful in building a strong relationship between the cash and derivative market segments, leading to more efficient price discovery in both the markets. There are conflicting claims about the impact of derivative trading on the market volatility. Derivative markets are also known to have a stabilizing effect on the underlying stock market (Raju and Karnade, 2003). The available literature offers two different kinds of arguments. Some researchers (Thenmozhi, 2002; Gupta and Kumar, 2002; Nath, 2003; Shenbagaraman, 2003) found that the overall volatility of the underlying stock market has reduced after introduction of derivative contracts on indices in India. The other side of the argument is that the entry of new speculators in the market could constitute a negative factor that would increase the volatility of the spot market (Stein, 1987). Similarly Hodgson and Nicholls (1991) reaffirm that the volatility of the spot market could increase with the derivative products because of speculation and arbitrage strategies. Some researchers argue that derivative trading reduces volatility through better price discovery. On the other hand, other studies claim that volatility increases after the introduction of derivative trading due to increased speculative activities. Low trading cost and leveraged trading are major attractions for speculators in derivative market. Presently, India's derivative market turnover is more than the cash market and India is one of the largest single stock futures. The impact of derivatives on the cash market volatility is much debated and widely studied research topic. Derivative products such as futures and options have become important instruments for price discovery, portfolio diversification and risk hedging in the Indian stock market in recent years. The concern over how trading index futures and options affect the spot market has been an interesting subject for investors, academicians, regulators, and exchanges. This chapter attempts to study the impact of introduction of individual futures on the underlying stock's volatility. This chapter is structured as follows: the next section presents a brief survey of the literature followed by the data used in this study, the methodology, and the results. The final section concludes the chapter.

Literature Review

Numerous amount of research has been done in testing the impact of financial derivatives on the underlying spot market volatility. Different arguments have been developed over the years about this topic. In the past, the researchers have most commonly used statistical tools like simple analysis of variance, standard deviation measurement of volatility, linear regression, or advanced statistical models like Genaralized Autoregressive Conditional Heteroskedasticity (GARCH). Finglewski (1981) found that future markets are likely to attract uninformed traders and that the lower level of information of futures traders with respect to cash market traders is likely to increase the asset volatility. Kawaller *et al.* (1987) examined the intraday price relationship between the S&P 500 futures and index prices and concluded that the future markets served as a vehicle for price discovery. Harris (1989) examined the impact of introduction of index futures on the spot market volatility. The data period for the study was from 1975 to 1987 that considered S&P 500 and a non-S&P 500 group of stocks for analysis. The author found that volatility had increased after the introduction of index futures. Further, they compared daily return volatilities during the pre-futures and post-futures period and also other attributes like beta, price level, size, and trading frequency. It was concluded that increase in volatility was a common phenomenon in different markets; index futures by themselves might not bear the sole responsibility. Schwarz and Laatsch (1991) suggest that future markets are an important means of price discovery in spot markets. Some scholars examined the price discovery efficiency of currency future market in various economics such as Hong Kong, Indonesia, Japan, South Korea, Malaysia, the Philippines, Singapore, Thailand, Taiwan, and America and observed strong bilateral causality between both markets (Granger and Huang, 1998; Covrig and Melvin, 2001; Yan and Zivot, 2004). They also found that the futures market is efficient for underlying currencies, in the sense that it leads the cash market. Stoll and Whaley (1990) studied the intraday price relationship between S&P 500 and the Major Market Index (MMI) futures. The study reveals that there is a strong evidence of the futures market leading the stock market. Turkington and Walsh (1999) examined the high frequency causal relationship between share price index (SPI) futures and the all ordinaries index (AOI) in Australia. The study concludes a strong evidence of bidirectional causality between the two series. The impulse response functions support these results.

Stewart (2000) focused on how the introduction of derivative securities affected the underlying market. A wide variety of theoretical approaches applied to the question of how speculative trading, the introduction of futures, and options might affect the stability, liquidity, and price in formativeness of asset markets were reviewed. In most cases, the resulting models predicted that speculative trading and derivative markets stabilized the underlying market and make spot markets more liquid and more informationally efficient.

Gulen and Mayhew (2000)[i] studied the stock market volatility before and after introduction of index futures in 25 countries. They examined whether spot market volatility after the introduction was related to futures market volume and open interest. The period of analysis was from 1973 to 1997 and used the excess returns over the world market index. They used a variety of econometric models like GJR-GARCH, nonlinear GARCH (NGARCH), and exponential GARCH (EGARCH) to estimate the impact of futures introduction. To study the effect of trading activity, the authors segregated the data series of open interest and volume into expected and unexpected components using an ARIMA model. They found that futures' trading was related to an increase in conditional volatility in the United States and Japan, but for the rest of the countries they found no significant effect. It was further found that, except for the United States and Japan, volatility tended to be lower in periods when open interest was high.

Oliveora and Armada (2001) studied the impact of futures market's introduction on the Portuguese stock market. The study period was 31st December 1992–1998; the daily closing data related to PSI-20 index (Portuguese Stock Index) were considered for the study. They used GARCH model to measure the futures impact on spot market volatility. The study revealed that the introduction of the PSI-20 index futures increased the Portuguese stock market volatility and that there was no improvement on the market efficiency front. Interestingly, this argument is not consistent with the majority of the other international studies.

Darrant *et al.* (2002) examined the role of futures trading in spot market fluctuations. The exponential GARCH was used to measure volatility and relationship between volatility in the spot and futures markets for the period of November 1987–November 1997. They used monthly prices rather than daily closing prices and found that the volatility in the futures market was an outgrowth of turbulent cash market and concluded that index futures trading could not be blamed for the volatility in the spot market because it was excessively volatile cash market, and that the fear among investors motivated them to engage more in hedging activities in the futures market that caused excessive volatility.

Faff and McKenzie (2002) investigated the impact of the introduction of stock index futures trading on the daily returns seasonality of the underlying index for seven national markets. They used modified GARCH model to determine the present evidence on the effect of stock index future trading on daily returns seasonality for the Australia, German, Japanese, Spanish, Swiss, US and UK markets. It was found that the introduction of future trading is associated with a change in the degree of seasonal effect. The results of GRACH show a decrease in volatility after introduction of futures trading; the same is true even in the case of individual stocks. The author reasoned that the onset of futures trading had moved the speculators to the more leveraged futures trading and hence led to a decrease in volatility in the spot market. Shenbagaraman (2003) examined the impact of introduction of NSE nifty index futures and options on nifty. To remove the effects of economic factors like inflation rates, growth forecasts, exchange rates, etc., the author used nifty junior as a perfect control variable to isolate market wide factors and thereby focused on the nifty volatility. Further, the lagged S&P 500 index returns were also introduced into the conditional mean equation to remove the effects of worldwide price movements. The results indicated that derivatives introduction had no significant impact on spot market volatility.

Thenmozhi and Sony (2002) analyzed the volatility of spot market before and after introduction of the stock index futures and lead lag relationship between stock index futures and spot index returns. Standard deviation of the daily returns has been used to assess the impact of derivatives on spot market volatility. They concluded that the volatility in the post-futures period had been on the decline. The study proved that there was a possibility of increase in the information flow that has influenced the market returns in the post-futures period. The study captured the impact of the introduction of derivatives trading on the spot market volatility returns and the variation in liquidity. The data used were from June 1996 to May 2003 and consisted of S&PCNX nifty index, nifty junior index, and individual stock returns on five stocks: Asia Brown Boveri, Hero Honda, Hindalco,

Reliance, and Ranbaxy. The data were analyzed by using standard regression techniques of volatility measurement, GARCH model, and liquidity analysis. The results of GRACH show a decrease in volatility after introduction of futures trading; the same is true even in the case of individual stocks. The author reasoned that the onset of futures trading had moved the speculators to the more leveraged futures trading and hence led to a decrease in volatility in the spot market. Raju and Karande (2003) examined the price discovery between the S&PCNX nifty and its corresponding futures by using cointegration analysis. Cointegration analysis measures the extent to which two markets have achieved long-run equilibrium. They also examined the effect of introduction of S&PCNX nifty index futures on the underlying spot market by using the ARCH family of models to study volatility. They found that the markets — cash and futures — are integrated. Information flows from one market to another market. The results proved that the volatility has been reduced after the introduction of index futures. Shenbagaraman (2003) examined the impact of introduction of NSE nifty index futures and options on nifty. They considered daily closing prices for the period from 5th October 1995 to 31st December 2002 and used univariate GARCH (1,1) model to examine the impact of index futures and options contracts on volatility. To remove the effects of economic factors like inflation rates, growth forecasts, exchange rates, etc., the author used nifty junior as a perfect control variable to isolate market wide factors and thereby focused on the nifty volatility. Further, the lagged S&P 500 index returns were also introduced into the conditional mean equation to remove the effects of worldwide price movements. The results indicated that derivatives introduction had no significant impact on spot market volatility. Nath (2003) studied the behavior of stock market volatility after derivatives for indices as well as individual stocks. The study captured the impact of the introduction of derivatives trading by using the longer period data (i.e., from January 1999 to October 2003). They used two benchmark indices, S&PCNX Nifty, S&PCNX Nifty Junior and 20 selected stocks. Out of the 20 stocks, 13 had single stock futures and options while seven do not have the same. The study revealed that volatility, as measured by standard deviation, was higher before introduction of derivatives, and after derivatives, it had come down for most of the stocks. It was concluded that the changes in the microstructure, robust risk management practices to contain volatility and introduction of derivative products might have led to the reduction of volatility.

Nagaraju and Kotha (2004) did event study to test the impact of index futures trading on the spot market volatility. They tested the changes in the structure of spot market volatility due to futures trading activity; i.e., trading volume and open interest. Their GARCH model results indicated a significant change in volatility structure. Further, the relationship between futures trading activity and spot market volatility had strengthened. Furthermore, after the introduction of futures, the market had become more efficient in assimilating the information into its prices as an indication of the market efficiency.

Methodology

The time series data were used as a methodological tool. The required time series daily closing prices data of individual stocks, S&PCNX Nifty and S&P CNX 500, have been collected from the web site of National Stock Exchange for a period of seven years from June 1999 to July 2006. This study includes stock of 10 companies: Reliance, SBI, TISCO, ACC, MTNL, TATA Power, TATA Tea, BHEL, MAHINDRA & MAHINDRA, and ITC. Daily returns were calculated for Nifty, Nifty Junior, and S&P 500 index by using the following formula:

$$R_t = \ln\left(\frac{P}{P_{t-1}}\right) * 100$$

where P_t and P_{t-1} are the prices at time t, and $t-1$, respectively and R_t is the return for time t.

The data considered for the study are time series, which is non-stationary whereas the examination of first difference often reveals wide swings which are predominantly the volatility effect suggesting that the variance of the time series varies over time. Volatility of the stock markets is measured by using standard deviation or GARCH model. GARCH model has been a preferred measure of volatility by many researchers (Nath, 2003; Shenbagaraman, 2003; Raju and Karande 2003; Sony and Thenmozhi, 2003). The GARCH model provides for heteroscadasticity in the observed returns. It is a time series modeling technique that uses past variance and the past variance forecasts to forecast future variances. The ordinary regression model proved to be inefficient because of one of its key assumptions that the errors have the same variance throughout sample (homoscadasticity). If the error variance is not constant, the data are said to be heteroscadasticity. It is observed that the model that takes into account the changing variance can make more efficient use of the data (Shenbagaraman, 2003).

Financial time series usually exhibits a characteristic called volatility clustering, which means that large changes tend to follow large changes and small changes tend to follow small changes. In either case, the changes from one period to the next period are typically of unpredictable nature. GARCH model accounts for certain characteristics like fat tails and volatility clustering that are commonly associated with financial time series. Graphical analysis and computation of statistics such as kurtosis and skewness can help provide relevant empirical evidence of the presence of volatility clustering tendencies. The fat tail phenomena in the data are known as excess kurtosis. Time series data that exhibit a fat tail distribution are often referred to as leptokurtic. Generally, the presence of leptokurtic tendencies on the time series returns suggests the presence of volatility clustering; hence, the modeling of such phenomena is recommended through the adjustment of ARCH.

The GARCH model is a variation of the ARCH model developed by Engle in 1982. Bollerslev (1986) originally proposed the GARCH model. A distinguishing feature of this model was that the error variance might be correlated over time because of the phenomenon of volatility clustering. Following Antonion and Holmes (1995) and others, the return series is modeled as a univariate GARCH process. In analyzing the behavior of volatility due to derivative products, it is necessary to eliminate the influences of other factors. This is achieved by regressing the return series over its lags, over its exogenous variables, and over day-of-the-week (Pagan and Schwert; 1990; Engle and Nag, 1992; Shenbagaraman, 2003; Kiran and Nagaraj, 2003). This study used the methodology followed by Shenbagaraman (2003) and Nath (2003). The GARCH (1, 1) framework has been found to have the best specification in both the works. Hence, this study has been carried out with GARCH (1, 1) model with necessary modifications. In the ARCH model, variance is modeled as a linear combination of squared past errors of specific lag and the autocorrelation in volatility is modeled by allowing conditional variance of the error terms to depend on the immediate previous values of the squared errors. An ARCH (P) can be specified as

$$\frac{\Psi_{\Psi_{\varepsilon t}}}{\Psi_t} \sim (0, h_t) \qquad h_t = \alpha_0 + \alpha_1 \varepsilon_{t-1}^2 + \cdots + \alpha \varepsilon_{t-p}^2$$

The ARCH model was generalized by Bollerslev (1986) and it is called GARCH. GARCH model explains variance by two distributed lags: first, on past squared residuals to capture high frequency effects or news about volatility from the previous period, measured as lag of the squared residuals from mean equation, and, second, on lagged values of variance itself to capture long-term influences. A GARCH (p, q) model is given as follows:

$$Y_t = \alpha_0 + \alpha_1 X_i + \varepsilon_t$$

$$\frac{\varepsilon_t}{\Psi_t} \sim (0, h_t)$$

$$h_t^2 = \alpha_0 + \sum_{t=1}^{p} \alpha_1 \varepsilon_{t-1}^2 + \sum_{j=1}^{q} \beta_j h_{t-1} + v_t$$

In this case, p is the degree of ARCH, q is the degree of GARCH, and V_t is the error term with white noise process. The size of the parameters α_1 and β_1 determine the short-term dynamics of the resulting volatility time-series. Large coefficient of β_1 shows that shocks to conditional variance take a long time to cancel out, and so volatility is persistent. Secondly, the GARCH $(1, 1)$ is estimated for measuring volatility. The underlying stock is being influenced by factors like previous day's stock return, market index, and broad-based market index. Hence, to remove these factors influence lagged individual underlying stocks; Nifty returns and Nifty 500 returns are introduced into the conditional mean equation. Thereby, it can isolate the impact of individual stock futures on the underlying stock's volatility. To determine the impact of the same, GARCH $(1, 1)$ model has been used, which has a conditional mean and variance equations. The conditional mean equation for individual stocks is as follows:

$$R_s = \alpha_0 + \alpha_1 \text{ lag return} + \alpha_2 \text{ Nifty return} + \alpha_3 \text{ NSE 500 return} + \mu_t$$

where R_s is the individual stock's return, α is the coefficients, Lag return is the one day lag in stock individual return, Nifty return is the daily S&P CNX Nifty index return, NSE 500 return is the daily S&P CNX 500 index return, and μ_t is the errors term.

Apart from the above conditional mean equation, the conditional variance equation is also being used to find out the impact of old news and latest news on the market. The following is the variance equation used.

$$h_t = y_0 + y_1 \varepsilon_{t-1}^2 + y_2 h_{t-1} + y_3 D_t.$$

In the above conditional variance equation y_1 and y_2 are news coefficients. y_1 is related to the latest news about the market, industry, etc., and y_2 is old news coefficient and y_3 is dummy coefficient for individual stock futures, which take a value of "0" for pre-introduction period of individual stock futures and "1" for the post-introduction period. The individual stock futures dummy determines the impact of individual stock futures on the underlying stock's volatility.

Analysis

Table 24.1 presents the estimates of GARCH (1, 1) model with dummies for sample company stock futures. This analysis explains the results pertaining to the determination of the impact of different sample company stock futures on volatility of the underlying stock future market. It exhibits that SBI stock futures, Reliance stock futures, TISCO stock futures, ACC stock futures, TATA Power stock futures, TATA Tea stock futures, BHEL stock futures, MTNL stock futures, MAHINDER & MAHINDER stock futures, and ITC stock futures are influenced by Nifty returns and Nifty 500 returns. Their coefficients are statistically significant at 1%. So, it is inferred from the table that there is an impact of underlying stock future market on the Reliance stocks, SBI stocks, TISCO, ACC stocks, Tata Power, Tata Tea, BHEL, and MTNL Stocks volatility. In the conditional variance equation, y_1 and y_2 are recent and old news coefficients, respectively. Their coefficients are also statistically significant at 1% level. So, it is evident that the stock is absorbing the latest and old news about the market. If the coefficient of the stock futures dummy is significantly different from zero, it may be inferred that there is an impact of stock futures on the sample companies' stocks volatility. y_3 coefficients are for all sample companies, that is, Reliance stock, SBI, TISCO, ACC, Tata Tea, BHEL, Mahindra & Mahindra, MTNL, and ITC different from zero. Hence, it is concluded that there is an impact of all company's stock futures on the company's scrip volatility.

Apart from this, the measure of the effect due to the introduction of stock futures; that is, the value of the coefficient y_3 has a negative sign in case of Reliance, HCL, MTNL, suggesting that the onset of stock future resulted in diminished stock market volatility. This finding depicts that the introduction of stock futures has no effect on underling stock market volatility. Hence, it is concluded that stock future derivatives are not responsible for increase or decrease in spot market volatility. Further, as its coefficients are not statistically significant, it can be inferred that there could be other market factors that have helped the increase in Nifty volatility in Indian stock market.

Table 24.1. Estimates of GARCH $(1, 1)$ model with dummies for individual stock futures.

Particulars		Reliance		SBI		TISCO		ACC		Tata Power	
		Coefficient	t-Statistic	Coefficient	t-Statistic	Coefficient	t-Statistic	Coefficient	t-Statistic	Coefficient	t-Statistic
α_0	Intercept	0.0452	0.7621	0.01021	0.13882	−0.00049	−0.00525	0.09131	0.96362	−0.00049	−0.00525
α_1	Lag return	0.0064	0.35236	0.01370	0.69182	0.066592	3.59575*	−0.00175	−0.08882	0.066592	3.59575*
α_2	Nifty return	1.3780	26.5333*	0.84884	17.65001*	0.35979	3.83900*	0.70707	12.53096*	0.35979	3.83900*
α_3	NSE 500 return	−0.2988	−6.08983*	0.15475	3.48972*	0.70160	7.73369*	0.30396	6.31768*	0.70160	7.73369*
γ_0	Arch (0)	0.2413	8.00835*	0.08595	3.65643*	0.02161	2.67057*	0.06047	2.92158*	0.02161	2.67057*
γ_1	Arch (1)	0.1691	11.1877*	0.05861	6.36132*	0.04963	7.75970*	0.075438	7.57539*	0.04963	7.75970*
γ_2	GARCH (1)	0.7468	37.2797*	0.91582	64.50913*	0.94745	60.4939*	0.91421	85.96768	0.94745	60.4939*
γ_3	Stock futures dummy	−0.0468	−0.6129	0.04656	0.50173	0.03425	0.31111	−0.08139	−0.72985	0.03425	0.31111
R^2		0.4908		0.4378		0.3473		0.3361		0.3260	
Adjusted R^2		0.4879		0.4345		0.3436		0.3323		0.3222	
No. of observations		1,401		1,401		1,401		1,401		1,401	

(*Continued*)

Table 24.1. (*Continued*)

Particulars		Tata tea		BHEL		M&M		MTNL		ITC
		Coefficient	t-Statistic	Coefficient	t-Statistic	Coefficient	t-Statistic	Coefficient	t-Statistic	Coefficient	t-Statistic
α_0	Intercept	-0.06018	-0.74993	-0.65214	-0.52227	-0.03997	-0.56813	0.00817	0.07611	-0.14766	-1.36244
α_1	Lag return	0.08881	4.06282*	0.06938	2.91885**	0.02912	1.30843	0.02914	1.40887	0.09116	4.40521*
α_2	Nifty return	0.60411	10.72908*	0.64105	11.97683*	0.87357	12.7835*	0.78872	8.80069*	0.86070	9.41322*
α_3	NSE 500 return	0.29519	5.74757*	0.33220	6.27493*	-0.17582	-2.70289**	0.24518	2.94362*	0.19481	2.37373**
γ_0	Arch (0)	0.13918	4.80869*	0.46385	4.13178*	0.08067	3.93391*	0.05448	3.89779*	0.05846	4.12339*
γ_1	Arch (1)	0.08211	7.73766*	0.10260	5.86065*	0.07091	6.82597*	0.04922	6.73366*	0.05363	8.27448*
γ_2	GARCH (1)	0.89229	69.64832*	0.83047	28.8217*	0.90916	69.76028*	0.94252	28.8129*	0.93677	14.8458*
γ_3	Stock futures dummy	0.07876	0.75806	-0.08014	-0.61523	0.03530	0.38216	0.07900	0.61151	0.24450	1.85365***
	R^2	0.3096		0.2964		0.2852		0.2864		0.2713	
	Adjusted R^2	0.3056		0.2923		0.2811		0.2823		0.2671	
	No. of observations	1,401		1,401		1,401		1,401		1,401	

Note: *statistically significant at 1% level; **statistically significant at 5% level; ***statistically significant at 10% level.

Conclusion

The relationship between stock futures derivative and corresponding stock market has been analyzed by using the GARCH technique. The stock futures dummy coefficients of all sample companies; that is, Reliance stock, SBI, TISCO, ACC, TATA Tea, BHEL, MAHINDRA & MAHINDRA, MTNL, and ITC are different from zero. Hence, it is concluded that there is an impact of all company's stock futures on the company's scrip volatility. This study reported reduced volatility after the introduction of stock futures derivative. The GARCH model, incorporating the effects of introduction of derivative as a dummy variable exhibits that stock market volatility decreased in the post-derivative scenario, suggesting an increase in the market efficiency in Indian stock market.

Implications for Policy Makers

Economic growth is essential for quality of life of nation. Financial sector plays a crucial role for mobilizing resources for development of economy. In such a situation, financial stability is a major concern for not only to regulators, police makers, but also for business houses. There are two constants in the business; that is change and risk which are apparent in financial asset volatility. The study of financial assets volatility is important to policy makers and corporate business houses for several reasons. Prediction of financial asset volatility is now considerably improved due to the work of Engle (1992), which gave birth to ARCH model that are capable of predicting the unpredictable hetroscedastic residuals from the mean equations. Prediction of financial market is important to economic agents because it represents a measure of risk exposure in their investments. Second, pricing of derivatives is a function of volatility, so instability of stock market creates uncertainty that adversely affects growth prospects of business houses, and leads to a barrier of growth prospects of economy. Apart from this, stock market volatility hinders economic performance through consumer spending and business investment spending that lead to structural and regulatory changes. So, this is a matter of concern that should be realized by policy makers, regulators, business houses, and investors. Keeping this in view, our study employs ARCH and GARCH model to study the behavior of volatility in stock market for the formulation of economic policies for the best interest of the country.

References

Apte, PG (2004). Study of the impact of derivatives trading on volatility and liquidity in the spot market. *Unpublished Paper.*

Benilde, MD, NO, and MJR Armada (2001). The impact of the futures market's on portuguese stock market. *Finance India*, 15(4), 1251–1278.

Board, J, S Gleb, and S Charles (2001). The effect of futures market volume on spot market
volatility. *Journal of Business Finance and Accounting*, 28(7/8), 799–819.

Corridor, P and R Santamania. Does derivatives trading destabilise the underlying assets?
Evidence from the Spanish stock market.

Covrig, V and M Melvin (2001). Asymmetric information and price discovery in the FX market:
Does Tokyo know more about the Yen? *Journal of Empirical Finance*, 9, 271–285.

Cox, CC (1976). Futures trading and market information. *Journal of Political Economy*, 84,
1215–1237.

Darrant, A, S Rahman, and M Zhong (2002). On the role of futures trading in spot market
fluctuations: Perpetrator of volatility or victim of regret? *The Journal of Financial Research*,
xxv(3), 431–444.

Faff, R and MD McKenzie (2002). The impact of stock index futures trading on daily returns
seasonality: A multi-country study. *Journal of Business*, 75(1), 31, 95.

Figleewski, S (1981). Futures trading and volatility in the GNMA market. *Journal of Finance*,
36, 445–456.

Golaka, CN (2003). Behaviour of stock market volatility after derivatives. *NSE News Letter*.

Granger, CWJ and B Huang (1998). A bivariate causality between stock prices and exchange
rates: Evidence from recent Asia flu. *Quarterly Review of Economics and Finance*,
40, 337–354.

Gulen, H and S Mayhew (2000). *Stock Index Futures Trading and Volatility in International
Equity Markets*. www.terry.ugaedu/finance/research/workingpaper/infact.pdf.

Gupta, OP and M Kumar (2002). Impact of introduction of index Futureson stock market
volatility: The indian experience. *National Stock Exchange*, Mumbai, 25.

Haris, L (1989). The October 1987 S&P 500 stock-futures basis. *Journal of Finance*, 44,
77–99.

Kawaller, IG, PD Koch, and TW Koch (1987). The temporal price relationship between S&P
500 futures and the S&P 500 index. *Journal of Finance*, 42, 1309–1329.

Kotha, KK and Mukhopadhyay (2003). Impact of futures introduction on underlying NSE
nifty volatility. In *Proceedings of the International Conference on Business & Finance 2003*,
ICFAI University Press, Hyderabad, pp. 42–326.

Nagaraju, KS and KK Kotha (2004). Index futures trading and spot market volatility: Evidence
from an emerging market. *The ICFAI Journal of Applied Finance*, 10(8), 5–16.

Nupur, HS and SD Saikat (2003). Impact of index futures on Indian stock market volatility:
An application of GARCH model. In *Proceedings of the International Conference on Business
& Finance 2003*, ICFAI University Press, Hyderabad, pp. 291–306.

Raju, MT and K Karande (2003). Price discovery and volatility on NSE futures market *SEBI*.
Working Paper Series, 7.

Schwarz, TV and F Laatsch (1991). Price discovery and risk transfer in stock index cash and
future markets. *Journal of Futures Markets*, 11, 669–683.

Shenbagaraman, P (2003). Do futures and options trading increase stock market volatility?
NSE Research Initiative, Paper 71.

Singh, YP and S Bhatia (2006). Does futures trading impact spot market volatility? Evidence
from Indian financial markets. *Decision*, 33(2), 41–62.

Sony, H and M Thenmozhi (2003). Impact of index derivatives on S&P CNX nifty volatility, information efficiency, and expiration effects. In *Proceedings of the International Conference on Business and Finance*, ICFAI University Press, Hyderabad, pp. 264–290.

Stennis, EA, M Pinar, and AJ Allen (1983). The futures market and price discovery in the textile industry. *American Journal of Agricultural Economics*, 65(2), 308–310.

Stewart, M (2000). The impact of derivatives on cash markets: What we have learned. www.terry.ugaedu/finance/research/workingpaper/infact.pdf.

Stoll, HR and RE Whaley (1990). The dynamics of stock index and stock index futures return. *Journal of Financial and Quantitative Analysis*, 25, 441–467.

Thenmozhi, M (2002). Futures trading, information and spot price volatility of NSE-50 index futures contract. *NSE Research Initiative*, Paper 59.

Turkington, J and D Walsh (1999). Price discovery and causality in the Australian share price index future market. *Australian Journal of Management*, 24, 97–113.

Chapter 25

PHILIPPINES IN THE 21ST CENTURY: BUSINESS OPPORTUNITIES AND STRATEGIC MARKETING IMPLICATIONS

EDUARDO P. GARROVILLAS

Abstract

This is a descriptive-exploratory study of the Philippines — a vibrant emerging market of Asia. It contains a mosaic of the country's features — a dash of history, sociopolitical and cultural information, economic indicators, affiliation with the ASEAN and WTO, investment opportunities, and strategic marketing implications. Under the lens of innovation and imagination, the attributes and endowments of this country speak eloquently of the untapped business opportunities, let alone its rich natural and human resources. This chapter serves as a guide for business investors, marketers, and international business managers and scholars.

Introduction

This is a descriptive-exploratory study about the Philippines in the 21st century, as an attractive business investment destination, which approach is deemed suitable for the purpose (Yin, 1984; Elsenhardt, 1989). Likewise, said descriptive-exploratory method is particularly useful for exploring implicit assumptions and examining new relationships, abstract concepts and operational definitions (Bettis, 1991; Weick, 1996). In fact, the power of innovation and imagination, not necessarily electronic commerce, shall determine the winners in the 21st century economy (Hamel, 2000). Therefore, it is the innovation and imagination that should be analyzed for business opportunities as well as their strategic marketing implications in the emerging markets of Asia. One such vibrant emerging market is the Philippines, which was discovered in 1521 and colonized by Spain for three centuries, thereby transforming it as the only Roman Catholic country in a predominantly Buddhist Asian region. It was ceded by Spain to the United States of America in 1898, and remained as a colony of America for half a century. Christianity was its legacy from Spain; a republican government with three main branches — executive, legislative, and judiciary — and the public school system were the legacy from America. Amidst the colonization of most Asian countries by the Western power prior to the turn of the century, the Philippines was the first to be freed from the yoke of colonization. In fact, Philippines is the first country in the Asian region to get independence from the USA in 1946. Neo-historians, however, designated the real independence day of the nation from Spain in 1898. It has an area of 300,000 sq. km, almost as big as Malaysia and Vietnam. The country is a vast reservoir of investment opportunities in mining, energy (hydro, wind, solar, and geothermal), services, BPO, ICT, agri-business (livestock and poultry, high value tropical fruits and vegetables; for example, banana, mango, rambutan, durian, pineapple, cloves, and pepper), aquaculture and fisheries, tourism (e.g., ecotourism, health tourism, and wellness), and natural resource-based industries. It has significant untapped mineral resources across the country, making it to the top five mineral powers in the world because of its rich mineral deposits of gold, silver, copper, nickel, and chromite. It is the oldest democracy in Asia with a population of 90 million, spread over an archipelago of over 7,000 islands, divided under three major island groups (Luzon, Visayas, and Mindanao), and consisting of 79 provinces, 117 cities, 1,501 municipalities, over 41,900 villages (also known as *barangay*, the smallest political unit). Being an archipelago, its coastlines measure 235,973 km, which is even longer than the USA. It has a young population, with a population growth rate of 2.3% and almost equal male–female ratio. In the Philippines, people who are 15-years old already belong to the older half of the population. The voting age is 18-years old. Its people speak over 160 odd languages and dialects, and yet are acknowledged as the third largest English-speaking country in the world, primarily because of its being an American colony. It is hoped that through innovation and imagination, international business scholars and educators may be able to identify a common pattern or paradigm for businesses in the Philippines.

Philippines and the Association of South East Asian Nations (ASEAN)

Philippines is a member of the ASEAN, which was founded in 1967 to focus on regional security. However, in 1992, the serious effort toward economic cooperation began with the idea of ASEAN Free Trade Area (AFTA), which is then complemented by the ASEAN Framework Agreement on Services (AFAS) in 1995 and Framework Agreement on the ASEAN Investment Act (AIA) in 1999. The proposal to create AIA, which aims to attract more investment into the region, is believed as the most recent development in forming ASEAN as a "single investment region." The pace toward full implementation of AIA idea was accelerated from 2020 to 2010, and expected to generate more liberal and transparent investment environment within ASEAN.

Parallel to the ASEAN initiative on economic integration is the favorable prospect of FDI in the region, which is now viewed by economists and policy makers as main vehicle for economic growth and development. As compared to portfolio investment, which is proven flighty and unreliable, FDI is now treated more than ever as the capital flow of choice (Braunstein and Epstein, 2002). According to the neo-liberal vision, FDI is an agent for spreading capital, technology and management skills across the globe, and likewise, a crucial agent for economic growth and development (Crotty *et al.*, 1998). Table 25.1 shows ASEAN summit data.

Table 25.1. ASEAN summit data.

ASEAN	Population (July, 2006 est.)	Per capita GDP, US$ (2005 est.)	Land area (sq. km)
Brunei	379,000	23,600	5,770
Cambodia	13.9 million	2,500	181,040
Indonesia	245.5 million	3,600	1,919,440
Laos	6.4 million	2,000	236,800
Malaysia	24.4 million	12,000	329,750
Myanmar	47.4 million	1,700	678,500
The Philippines	89.5 million	4,700	300,000
Singapore	4.5 million	28,600	692.7
Thailand	64.6 million	8,600	514,000
Vietnam	84.4 million	2,800	329,560

Source: Philippine Daily Inquirer (PDI), January 13, 2007, 12th ASEAN Summit.

Religion

Philippines is the only predominantly Roman Catholic country in the ASEAN region, all the others are predominantly Buddhists. However, two of the three richest countries in the whole Asian region, Japan and Brunei, are neither Catholic nor Buddhist; Japan is predominantly Shintoist, while Brunei is predominantly Islamic. Singapore, which completes the triad of richest countries in Asia, is Buddhist. Every town in the Philippines has, at least, three easily recognizable landmarks — a Roman Catholic church, a municipal hall, and a public market. The country observes the longest Christmas season in the world, beginning with the *ber-months* (i.e., from September to December), climaxing on the 25th of December, the birthday of Jesus Christ and tapering off to January 6, which is Feast of the Three Kings. It is also a *fiesta* (Spanish for feast) country, where beginning January up to May, every town and city celebrates the feast for its church's Patron Saint. During town fiesta, every household prepares lavish food for friends and relatives from other places, virtually spending one year of their savings.

Catholic or Buddhist account for about 3.6 billion people in Asia, relatively high population growth rate in most Asian countries. Todaro (1997) has enumerated some negative consequences of run-away population to the economy and the delivery of social services like education, health and sanitation, peace and order, and the overall quality of life. However, these cultural diversity and population explosion in rural Asia present challenges and opportunities for marketers and business investors. Retailers and wholesalers thrive during the long Christmas season and the *fiesta* months. Clearly, the upbeat retail and wholesale business have a positive chain-reaction effect to the various firms and suppliers, and this to the consumers.

Philippines as an Emerging Country

Emerging country is a new label outside of less developed country (LDC) and developing economy; the latter euphemistically refers to a poor country in the globe, like those found in either rural Asia or Africa. The World Bank defines an emerging country as one having per capita gross national income (GNI) that would place it in the lower or middle-income category. In 2004, an emerging country had an annual per capita GNI of US$1,460 as compared to high-income country of US$32,040. Although emerging countries of the globe are home to about 85% of the world's population, they produce only about 20% of the world's GNI and have only about 11% of the world's stock market capitalization (World Development Indicator Database, 2005).

The World Bank classifies the following countries as developed and emerging countries; Example of some developed countries include Singapore, the United States, the United Kingdom, Japan, Hong Kong, Australia, New Zealand, Germany, France, Switzerland, and Canada. Some emerging countries of Asia are Malaysia, Thailand, the *Philippines*, Indonesia, Korea, Taiwan, India, Pakistan, and China.

Asia, the Next Economic Phenomenon of the 21st Century

Sachs (2006), a member of the Millennium Development Goals (MDG) team, wished to see the end of global poverty. Stiglitz (2002), a Nobel Prize-winning economist, emphasized that we can no longer ignore the growing discontent of the world's poor at the base of the economic pyramid. Asia has a fair share of the world's poor. However, the bright side of the picture tells us that Asia with 3.6 billion people or roughly 50% of the world's population is a huge reservoir of human capital. The region is a classic study of contrasts and harmony of the opposites. In Asia, diversity of culture, races, religion, and politics coexist. One can find two of the richest countries in the world, Japan with a per capita GDP of US$28,700, and Singapore with a per capita GDP of US$28,600. In this region, the poorest of the poor countries also exist; for example, Bangladesh, Bhutan, Laos, Burma, Cambodia, and a number of LDCs such as India, Indonesia, the Philippines, and China with annual purchasing power parity (PPP) of US$1,500 or less, but hidden, informal economies (unregistered in the official GNP) are significant. Globally, it has been estimated that the informal sector of the economy includes more than US$9 trillion in hidden (or unrecorded) assets, an amount nearly equivalent to the total value of all companies listed on the 20 most developed countries' main stock exchanges (de Soto, 2000). In addition to assets, the value of economic transactions in these markets may match or even exceed the formal economic sectors in developing countries (Henderson, 1999). With the developed world markets becoming increasingly saturated (London and Hart, 2004), Asia is the next key location for future growth; the emerging market of the future, with a huge reservoir of human resources for the global economy. With outward-looking development policies, aligned with the philosophy of globalization, Asia is all set to be the next economic phenomenon of the 21st century.

Economic Indicators

Following are some economic indicators of the Philippines.

Gross domestic product

According to the Central Bank of the Philippines, real GDP growth rate was 4.38% in 2000; 1.76% in 2001; 4.45% in 2002; 4.93% in 2003; 6.18% in 2004; 4.97% in 2005; 5.37% in 2006; and 6.9%, first half of 2007. The remarkable increasing trend is expected to continue in 2008 and beyond, *ceteris paribus*. In 2005, the real GDP growth rates for selected Asian neighbors were as follows: Malaysia, 5.26%; Indonesia, 5.6%; Thailand, 4.47%; Singapore, 5.33%; India, 8.24%; Korea, 3.92%; Taiwan, 9.68%; Sri Lanka, 6.29%; and China, 10.24%.

The remittances

BSP figures show that remittances totaled $6.05 billion in 2000; went down to $6.031 billion in 2001; up to $6.886 billion in 2002; $7.578 billion in 2003; $8.55 billion in 2004; $10.689 billion in 2005; and $12.761 billion in 2006 (estimated at $14.00 billion, to include remittances through "informal" means). The reported remittances have more than doubled since 2000 (a 111% increase). Unreported remittances will make this much higher. The primary driver of the economy is private consumption, which is fueled largely by remittances. Remittances have increased because of the global manpower sharing of Filipino talents and expertise. In 1997, during the financial crisis, the remittances saved the Philippine economy.

Unemployment rate

BSP data place unemployment in 1999 at 9.8%; 11.2% in 2000; 11.10% in 2001; 11.4% in 2002 and 2003; 11.8% in 2004; 11.35% in 2005; and 7.9% in 2006. It is expected that the country could maintain a single-digit unemployment rate.

Exchange rate

According to the BSP, the average Philippine peso to $ exchange rate was P44.19 to $1.00 in 2000; P50.99 in 2001; P51.60 in 2002; P54.20 in 2003; P56.04 in 2004; P55.80 in 2005; P51.31 in 2006; and P43.85 in 2007 due to strong overseas remittances and stock market inflows. The strengthening of the peso in 2006 was due to increased OFW remittances (the highest in history to date), and a weak US dollar. The Economist Intelligence Unit (EIU) adds other factors such as improving fiscal outlook, the ending of monetary policy tightening in the United States, and booming exports. However, the EIU also states that the peso "remains vulnerable to domestic political instability and the threat of higher interest rates in Japan." Although the peso strengthened in 2006, it still is much weaker than it was in 2000, when the average exchange rate was P44.19 to $1.

Budget deficit

Per BSP data, it was P134.212 billion in 2000; went up to P147.023 billion in 2001; P210.741 billion in 2002; went down to P199.868 billion in 2003; P187.057 billion in 2004; P146.778 billion in 2005; and P62.198 billion in 2006. Although the deficit has been going down since 2003, the fact remains that the highest deficits in the country incurred between 2001 and 2005. The EIU makes the following analysis of the budget deficit in 2006 from the 2005 level: "The difference was attributable to the fact that expenditure fell below target. The underspending was a result of lower-than-expected interest payments (the single largest expenditure category), as well as lower non-interest spending as a result of Congress failure to approve the full budgetary appropriations for 2006. Government revenue, meanwhile, was slightly above target. Although the rapid increase in revenue is welcome, below-target government spending is a worry."

Competitiveness rating

As reported by the World Economic Forum, competitiveness ranking of the country has fallen, starting from a ranking of 48 in 2000 to 71 in 2006. In comparison, other countries in the region ranked in 2006 were Singapore 5th, Malaysia 26th, Thailand 35th, and Indonesia 50th. World Competitiveness Report (2001), a Switzerland-based institute, monitors competitiveness ranking. The competitiveness ranking of the Philippines, out of 60 countries, was 35th in 2000, 49th in 2003, and 52nd in 2004. Countries that rose competitiveness were India, from rank 51st to 22nd; and Russia, from rank 52nd to rank 40th. The Philippines got low ratings on the following criteria: (1) economics (GDP per capita was ranked 57th out of 60 countries; 40% of our national budget went to debt servicing of interest and principal, both local and foreign debt), government efficiency (ranked 59th in political stability out of 60 countries, and rank 56th in management of public finances), and infrastructure (ranked 60th last in infrastructure). In overall business efficiency, Philippines was 49th; Taiwan was the most efficient in the Region, 7th; Malaysia, Thailand, and South Korea consistently hovered in the 20th rank.

India is 22nd. The Philippines's ranking in other areas: growing workforce, 7th; competence of services manager, 7th; low productivity of the Philippine business, 57th; image abroad, 57th; not good in finance, 54th; management practices, 41st; attributes and values, 44th. According to the World Competitiveness Report of Switzerland-based Institute for Management Development, conducted in collaboration with AIM, the competitiveness ranking was based on four parameters — economic performance, government efficiency, business efficiency, and infrastructure.

Philippines, a developing economy that is home to some amazing indigenous MNCs

It is only in the Philippines that Jollibee, a local fastfood company that serves burgers and fried chicken, beat the globally famous McDonald, a hamburger store chain, in sales. For a developing economy, with per capita GDP of US$4700, and with a pregnant Lorenz curve symbolizing the yawning gap and wide disparity between the very few rich at the apex of the socioeconomic pyramid and the bleeding poor at the bottom, it may be anachronistic and even unthinkable to be talking of companies with extensive international operations. However, the Philippines is home to at least a number of indigenous MNCs that operate in the ASEAN region and as far as the United States and some countries in the Middle East. Over the years, MNCs have been coming from rich countries (developed economies) of the world. So, MNCs coming from the poor countries (developing economies) are a phenomenal rarity. An indigenous MNC may be operationally defined as a homegrown, parent enterprise, and its foreign affiliates with a threshold of 10% of equity, and operates (with portfolio of assets) in at least six countries (UNCTAD, 2004). According to the World Bank (2005), there are 148 Third World countries (meaning poor), six oil capital-surplus countries, 20 industrialized countries, and 12 centrally planned economies. Until 1990, most MNCs came from 20 industrialized countries; for example, the United States, the United Kingdom, Germany, France, Japan, etc. A fairly recent phenomenon is the overseas expansion of MNCs from developing countries. From a negligible share in 1990, outward FDI from developing countries has increased to account for one-tenth of the world's total stock and 6% of the world's total flows in 2003. Business firms in developing countries have learned that to survive and flourish in a globalized world, they must be competitive internationally, which necessitates operating across national boundaries and holding a portfolio of assets in different countries. In the Philippines, five indigenous MNCs easily stand out, which can be a source of our national pride — San Miguel Corporation, Unilab, Jollibee Foods Corporation, Shoe Mart Investment Corporation, and JG Summit Holdings; all five meet the UNCTAD definition of MNCs; that is, they operate with portfolio of assets in at least six countries. (1) San Miguel Corporations is globally known in the beer business, although it has equally formidable presence in the food and beverage markets. (2) Unilab is the acknowledged leader in the pharmaceutical industry, capturing no less than 25% of the market and beating premium-priced multinational drug companies. (3) Jollibee is the leader in the foodservice industry, exceeding the market share of McDonald; the Philippines is the only place in the world where McDonald was beaten by a local company. (4) Shoe Mart (SM) is the leading corporate giant in the shopping malls business, with a humble beginning as a small shoe store; the company, otherwise dubbed as the malls king, is also into banking. SM is easily the Wal-Mart of the Philippines, and perhaps of Southeast Asia. (5) JG Summit Holdings is the most diversified company, among the five MNCs. Its portfolio of assets include strong presence in the food business, hotel, low-cost housing, poultry, supermarket and malls, fuel, and airline industries. Table 25.2 shows the profile of TOP Five indigenous MNCs in the Philippines.

Table 25.2. Profile of indigenous MNCs in the Philippines.

MNCs	Age in the market	Business portfolio	Countries/region
San Miguel corporation	Over 100 years	Food and Beverage; National Foods Ltd. of Australia is their latest acquisition	Asia, China, Australia, New Zealand, Indonesia
Unilab	Over 50 years	Medicines	Asia, Indonesia, Malaysia, Thailand
Jollibee foods corporation	+ 30 years	Food and beverage; Chow King and Red Ribbon are their latest acquisition	Asia, China, the Middle East, the United States, Canada
SM investments corporation	+ 45 years	Shopping Malls "Asia's mall king," the Philippine's biggest conglomerate	Asia, China
JG Summit holdings	+ 20 years	Food, shopping malls/ commercial centers, high-rise buildings for offices, hotel, housing, petroleum oil, airlines	Asia, China, Taiwan

Specifically, these indigenous MNCs gained footage in the Asian market by seizing the market-seeking opportunities, and transaction-cost advantages as defined by geographic proximity and cultural convergence confirming the evaluation of Rugman (2005) that most MNCs are primarily focused on their home region and will continue to be so in the foreseeable future, because most firms can capture adequate benefits of scope and scale within their own region. In fact, according to Rugman (2005), only nine of the Fortune Global 500 qualify as global firms in terms of their sales distribution. Profile of these indigenous MNCs (e.g., age in the market, product/service diversification, regional/international penetration) could serve as constructs for hypothesis testing by future investigators.

The Philippines as an Investment Destination

Following are some of the reasons as to why foreign business organizations should invest in the Philippines.

Educated human resource

Education (i.e., literacy) is integral to national development (Todaro, 1997; Villegas, 2006). The Philippines has literate, teachable, affordable, and committed labor force with a high literacy rate of over 95%, mainly because the government offers free access to primary and secondary education to its citizens, as mandated by the constitution. For higher education, there are about 2,000 colleges and universities spread all over the country, mostly being private institutions; only 112 are public or state institutions. Four Philippine universities are among the top 500 universities: UP, De La Salle University, Ateneo de Manila University, and University of Sto. Tomas (World University Rankings, 2006). A significant portion of the budget is reserved for the education sector, suggesting a significant pool of educated human resources that can be tapped to achieve business objectives.

English communications skills

English fluency on both oral and written by the majority of the population makes the country the third largest English-speaking country in the world. Implications for managers are that (1) marketing communications in the English language can be understood by the critical mass of the population; it does not need to be translated in the local dialect; (2) marketing technology-transfer and overall knowledge management would be more efficient and effective; and (3) there is no need to post expensive expatriate or foreign managers and personnel as there are qualified local experts who can take and deliver the marketing management tasks.

Business-friendly environment

The Philippines offers the sophisticated amenities of cosmopolitan living as well as the exotic culture and traditions of rural country life. Metro Manila, the seat of the national government, is the center of business and commerce, world-class hotels, large shopping malls, headquarters of big businesses, and the country's premier universities. Makati City is considered as the Wall Street of the Philippines, where international banks and financial institutions are located. The country has 12–14 million Internet users, 87% of which are based in Metro Manila (Lizardo, 2008). Rural Philippines, world-renowned for its hospitality and year-round festivities, is just a breath-away in the north and south off Metro Manila and could be reached by air, land, and water transportations.

Untapped agricultural and natural resources

The Philippines is one of the top five mineral powers in the world. Outward-looking development policies, in consonance with the requirements of globalization, crafted and adopted by the government, are quite evident. The recently enacted Mining Act relating to liberalizing the exploitation of its rich mineral resources to foreign mining investors is a case in point. It is a departure from the inward-looking protectionist policies of previous regimes. The new law is designed to tap the country's rich natural mineral resources. Out of 17 regions of the country, only 12 are endowed with rich mineral deposits of gold, silver, copper, nickel, and chromite.

International trade linkages

The Philippines is a member country of international institutions and organizations that embrace free-trade policies (e.g., ASEAN, APEC, AFTA, G20, and G23). The Philippines is also a member of the UN, and one of the 191 countries supporting the Millennium Development Goals of the UN (in pursuit of a world free of poverty), which was signed in September, 2000.

Excellent infrastructure

Given excellent infrastructure, the country has attracted significant investment such as the $1.6 billion shipbuilding facility of Hanjin in Subic (a former US-military base in Zambales, the Philippines), and the $1 billion expansion plant of Texas Instruments in Clark (a former US airbase in Pampanga, the Philippines). Subic is fast becoming a maritime center with the new shipyard and container port, grains and fertilizer bulk facilities, and dry dock for ship repair. The Philippine Airlines (PAL, the flag carrier of the Philippines) has expanded its operations to the Diosdado Macapagal Airport in Clark. This development, along with the completion of the Subic-Clark-Tarlac Expressway helped Texas Instruments choose Clark over China despite the more liberal terms the latter offered. Due to the country's geography, it has 256 airports scattered all over the Philippine archipelago, 83 with paved and 173 with unpaved runways; 19,804 km of paved roads, 897 km of railways and over 200 port gateway terminals and natural harbors. As an archipelago, with a coastline longer than the United States, the country needs bigger and more modern ports to transport goods and people around the country. Also given the Philippine's strategic location within the international trade routes, it has the potential to become a major trans-shipment point for world commerce; for example, Singapore and Hong Kong generate about $20 billion a year in trans-shipments. Given the country has several natural harbors, it has the potential to join the leagues in the international maritime business.

Agricultural and food products

The Philippines is a leading provider of coconut, virgin coconut oil, palm oil and by-products, timber and other wood products, tuna, seaweeds, livestock and poultry, fruits, and vegetables (e.g., banana, mango, rambutan, durian, pineapple, cloves, pepper, and industrial tree crops).

Opportunities for tourism development

Because of its vast natural resource endowments and rich biodiversity (suitable for tourism activities; for example, diving, snorkeling, trekking, mountain climbing, fishing, golf, and adventure sports), there has been significant progress in building the Philippines' brand image as a multidimensional tropical destination of 7,107 islands and experiences.

Investment opportunities

This country provides opportunities for investment in mining, electronics, business process outsourcing and call center, malls, factories, processing plants, hydro-projects, wind tunnels, solar energy, geothermal power, training and education, trading, aqua culture and fisheries, health tourism and wellness, and textiles and garments.

Investment Opportunities in Mining Industry

Philippines is in the top five mineral powers in the world. It has an estimated US$1 trillion worth of mineral reserves across the country. For example, the abundance of nickel in the country is likened to Saudi Arabia's rich oil reserves, making the Philippines the top nickel producer in the world. Businessmen are therefore encouraged to invest in the Philippine mining industry. The development of the Philippines' mineral resources is a vital development strategy for the country. Mining investors are assured of a fair regulatory environment and other incentives, as mining is a key sector under the Medium-Term Philippine Development Plan.

The world's major mining players — Australia, Canada and Japan — have expressed their interest in investing and conducting exploratory activities in the Philippines. Chinese companies, Jinchuan, CITIC, and Jilin Nickel, have also expressed their interest in nickel and other mining projects. With investments projected to reach US$10 billion by 2010 and with 30,000 new jobs expected to be created in the next three years from the mining sector, the Philippines is on the track of becoming an official *mining country* by 2010. The World Bank defines a mining country as one where the mining industry contributes at least 6% to total exports. The Philippine mineral exports have been recorded at 4.6% of total exports and are expected to be 8.6% by 2010.

Investment Opportunities in Outsourcing Industry

The high literacy and affordable labor cost serve as magnets to outsourcing companies. Business Processing Association (BPO) of the Philippines indicates that the BPO industry employs about 250,000 people and earns more than $3billion a year. The global dot.com bubble in 1995–2000 saw several technology stocks being crashed. The global recession that followed somehow discredited the *new economy* prophets. Nevertheless, global companies realized that they should focus on their core competencies and outsource the rest through the use of information technology. In the *new economy*, profits are supposed to come from company' intangibles such as brands, intellectual properties, technical capabilities, and reputation. Routine functions like back office operations, manufacturing, and customer care could be outsourced elsewhere, preferably at low-cost locations in the developing countries. For this reason, the Philippines attracted outsourcing companies. Their presence is expanding rapidly. Its new metamorphosis is the knowledge-process out-sourcing where local MBAs, engineers, and economists perform analytical risk analysis for global companies to maintain its competitiveness in this sector. Undoubtly, the private sector has mobilized the resources to meet the chal-lenges. The Ayalas, for instance, are investing significantly in the buildings needed by the BPO and KPO. Rockwell Land of the Lopezes is expected to follow the suit. The BPO segment of the Philippine economy has brought excitement and promise to young entrepreneurs and workers and begun to have a positive impact on other sectors of the economy such as real estate, wholesale, retail, food and beverage manufacturing, and so on. Nowhere is its impact more visible than in the property sector. Following the Asian financial crisis, office vacancy rates in the country's urban centers such as Makati and Ortigas went as high as 50%. As the new economy crept in, office vacancies went down so fast that even property developers were caught by surprise. The BPO sector of the economy is highly labor-intensive, contrary to earlier notions that machines will ultimately replace humans. Teletech, for instance, has more than 10,000 employees; Convergy has 11,000. Many others are employing close to these numbers, and the list of companies keeps growing.

Opportunities to Invest in Malls

The Philippines may be a Third World country, but in terms of mall facilities and services, its citizens get world-class experience. In fact, three of the ten largest malls in the world are in the Philippines. These are the SM Mall of Asia, SM Megamall, and SM City North Edsa. Included in the top 10 list are four malls in China, two in the United States, and one in Canada. These large shopping malls seem to hold the same fascination as the tallest skyscrapers, the longest bridge spans, and a host of similar extreme achievements in archi-tecture and engineering. They actively promote their size with pride, implying that they offer a greater variety of merchandise or a richer consumer experience in comparison with their smaller competitors. The world's largest mall is the South China Mall in Dongguan, just across the border from Hong Kong. It has 50% more floor space than the Pentagon, the world's largest office building. This mall prides itself with a 2.1 km artificial river and themed shopping areas, which opened in 2005. The art deco Golden Resources Mall, located at Beijing's west side, opened in October 2004, was briefly the largest shopping mall in the world. The South China Mall eclipsed it in 2005. This mall boasts of 230 escalators across six floors. The SM Mall of Asia which was opened in May 2006 ranks third. In one of Manila's newest malls, shoppers can jump on a tram to travel between stores. This mall boasts of the first IMAX Theater in the Philippines and the first mall undertaking by the beautiful and scenic Manila Bay. The two other SM malls in the top 10 lists are SM Mega mall and SM City North Edsa. SM Megamall, which is the fifth largest mall, is noted for its ice-skating rink, the first in the Philippines and which introduced to Filipinos a sport otherwise unknown in tropical countries. SM City North Edsa, the eighth largest, is the first shopping mall that dominated shopping in Manila. It started the Philippine *malling phenomenon* as we know it today. This mall opened in 1985. The West Edmonton Mall in Alberta, Canada, completed in 1985 at a cost of $750 million, remains the largest enclosed shopping mall in North America. It ranks fourth in the world. This mall encompasses 800 stores (including eight department stores), a 360-room hotel and 110 restaurants, and eating places. Its list of amusement places is also impressively large. There is a full-scale amusement park with 47 different rides, an ocean-wave swimming pool with sand beach, an aquarium, and a miniature golf course. In fact, one can enjoy some peace and meditation in the chapel, so long as a wedding is not in progress. Completing the top 10 list are Beijing Mall at No. 6, which is divided into eight districts since eight is a lucky number in China; the Grandview Mall in Guangzhou, China, seventh; the King of Prussia Mall in Pennsylvania, now the biggest mall in the United States at No. 9, and the South Coast Mall in California.

Asia accounts for 7 of the world's 10 largest malls, four of them are located in China and three in the Philippines. Because of the construction boom in China, it is estimated that more than 100 shopping malls of over 150,000 square feet will be built in China each year. Thus mall watchers predict that in two to three years time, seven out of 10 of the world's biggest malls would be in China.

Mall experts attribute this building of large malls in Asia to two factors: (1) the increase in purchasing power of its citizens, which is most notable in China, and (2) the boom in Asian tourism. Tourists wandering through shopping malls have the time and inspiration to buy things they are too busy to shop for at home — even items that could be readily obtained in their home country.

Rural Philippines and Its One-Town-One Product Concept

Every town in the Philippines has a treasure just waiting to be discovered. This is the philosophy behind the Department of Trade and Industry's one-town-one product (OTOP) program that kicked off countrywide in November 2004. Under the program, local government units are tasked to identify, develop, and promote specific products or service that they can sell to the local and international markets. It is expected that by developing micro, small- and medium-scale enterprises, more jobs will be created in the community. Budding entrepreneurs are supported in their endeavor through government and private sector-sponsored business counseling, skills and entrepreneurial training, product design and development, and marketing. About 190 local government units and companies from Luzon that benefited from the OTOP program got the chance to put their best products forward during the OTOP Luzon Island Fair at the Megatrade hall of SM Megamall. Some of the featured products include the traditional roasted coffee from Calabarzon, gifts and holiday décor from Pampanga, pili products from Bicol, wooden furniture from Isabela and processed meat products from Quezon. New products include arrowroot delicacies from Marinduque, citrus fruits and rootcrops from Nueva Vizcaya, handmade paper products from Batangas, ceramics from Albay and footwear from Nueva Ecija. The OTOP program was inspired by Japan's 20-year old One Village, One Product program, which was instrumental in developing over 300 new products from the countryside. The DTI expects to duplicate, if not surpass, the success of Japan's OVOP program and it believes that it is on the way to doing just that. Since 2004, OTOP has been able to develop 3,589 SMEs and has generated P3.27 billion in investments, $178 million in export sales, P3.1 billion in domestic sales and more importantly, employed 142,277. OTOP has the support of the Local Government Units (LGUs, composed of towns, cities, and provinces), and as more LGUs get into the program, the government would be on its way to fulfilling OTOP's aim of helping give birth to three million entrepreneurs and generate 6–10 million new jobs.

Summary

This study demonstrates that the Philippines, as one of the most vibrant emerging markets in Asia, has investment opportunities in mining, energy (hydro, geothermal, solar, and wind), services, BPO, agri-business (livestock and poultry, and high value tropical fruits like banana, mango, rambutan, durian, and pineapple), tourism (e.g., ecotourism), malls, and other natural resource-based industries.

There are five reasons as to why companies should invest in the Philippines: (1) literate, teachable, affordable, and committed labor force; (2) good communication skills of the population; (3) livable environment; (4) diverse and largely untapped agricultural and natural resources; and (5) established and expanding international trade linkages.

The world-class performance of all five indigenous MNCs featured in this chapter is a proof of a profitable investment climate in the Philippines; for example, these companies achieved leadership and dominant brand equity in their chosen markets/industries and expanded internationally world-class Philippine products and expertise.

Globally, the Philippines is in the top five mineral powers. It has an estimated US$1 trillion worth of mineral reserves across the country. The recently enacted Mining Act relating to liberalizing the exploiting its rich mineral resources to foreign mining investors is aligned with the outward-looking economic development policies of the government. Out of 17 regions of the country, 12 regions are endowed with rich mineral deposits of gold, silver, copper, nickel, and chromite.

The Philippines has world-class mall facilities and services; three of the top ten malls are located in Metro Manila. Further, the country's strategic location offers strong potentials for expanding export trade to ASEAN, North and South Asia, and the Middle East.

The country offers extensive opportunities for regionalization in the production and processing of a wide variety of tropical agricultural food products and other natural resource-based industries; for example, coconut and by-products like virgin coco oil, palm oil and by-products, timber and other wood products, livestock and poultry, high value tropical fruits, and vegetables. Given the Philippine's strategic location within the international trade routes, it has the potential to become a major trans-shipment point for world commerce.

References

Bettis, RA (1991). Strategic management and the straightjacket: An editorial essay. *Organization Science*, 2(3), 315–319.

Braunstein, E and G Epstein (2002). Bargaining power and foreign direct investment in China: Can 1.3 billion consumers tame the multinationals? *Center for Economic Policy Analysis (CEPA) Working Paper* 2002–13. New York: New School University.

Chen, S-FS (2005). Extending internalization theory: A new perspective on international technology transfer and its generalization. *Journal of International Business Studies*, 36(2), 231–245.

Crotty, J, G Epstein, and T Kelly (1998). *Multinational Corporations and the Neo-liberal Regime. Globalization and Progressive Economic Policy*. Cambridge: Cambridge University Press.

Deen, T (25 May 2006). The scariest predators in the corporate jungle. *Business Mirror*.

Dela Pena, ZB (11 May 2006). Jollibee posts 25% income growth in Q1. *The Philippine Star*.

De Soto, H (2000). *The Mystery of Capital: Why Capitalism Triumphs in the West and Fails Everywhere Else*. New York: Basic Books.

Dream product, service for fame and fortune (19 August 2007). *Philippine Daily Inquirer*, p. B1.

Eisenhardt, KM (1989). Building theories from case study research. *Academy of Management Review*, 14(4), 532–550.

Hamel, G (2000). *Leading the Revolution*. USA: Harvard Business School Press.

Henderson, H (1999). *Beyond Globalization: Shaping a Sustainable Global Economy*. West Hartford, CT: Kumarian Press.

Hitt, MA, RD Ireland, and RE Hoskisson (1999). *Strategic Management, Competitiveness and Globalization*. Cincinnati, Ohio: South-Western College Publishing.

Kotler, P and G Armstrong (2001). *Principles of Marketing*. New Jersey: Prentice-Hall Inc.

Lizardo, R (17 January 2008). Demystifying online marketing: New trends for the new age. *Unpublished Lecture was Presented in a Seminar Co-Sponsored by the Philippine Marketing Association and Philippine Association of Colleges and Schools of Business*, San Sebastian College, Manila, Philippines.

London, T and SL Hart (2004). Reinventing strategies for emerging markets: Beyond the transnational model. *Journal of International Business Studies*, 35(5).

Lopez, EH (26 May 2006). Profiles, Hans T. Sy. *Manila Bulletin*.

Loyola, JA (4 March 2006). SMC reaps Ps 9.15 — B profit on record sales of Ps226.9 B. *Manila Bulletin*.

Maitland, E, E Rose, and S Nicholas (2005). How firms grow: Clustering as a dynamic model of internationalization. *Journal of International Business Studies*, 36(4), 435–451.

Millennium Development Goals (2000).

Prahalad, CK and SL Hart (2002). The fortune at the bottom of the pyramid. *Strategy + Business*, First Quarter, 2–14.

Reyes, HM (25 May 2006). JFC to open China tea house. *Business Mirror*.

Rugman, AM (2005). *The Regional Multinationals: MNEs and 'Global' Strategic Management*. Cambridge: Cambridge University Press.

Sachs, JD (10 May 2006). Fighting poverty with the right aid. *Business Mirror*.

San Miguel Corp (29 September 2005). http://www.sanmiguel.com.

Stiglitz, JE (2002). *Globalization and its Discontent*. New York: W.W. Norton & Co.

Stoner, JAF, ER Freeman, and DR Gilbert (1999). *Management*, 6th edn. Singapore: Prentice-Hall.

Todaro, M (1997). *Economic Development*. U.K.: Pearson Education Limited.

UNCTAD World Investment Report (2004).

Villegas, BM (12 May 2006). JY and the good company. *Manila Bulletin*.

Weick, KE (1996). Drop your tools: Allegory for organizational studies. *Administrative Science Quarterly*, 41(2), 301–313.

World Competitiveness Yearbook (2001).

World Development Indicator Database (August 2005).

Yin, RK (1984). *Case Study Research*. Beverly Hills, CA: Sage Publications.

Chapter 26

PAPUA NEW GUINEA — AN EMERGING ECONOMY IN THE SOUTH PACIFIC: CHALLENGES AND PROSPECTS

RAVINDER RENA

Abstract

Papua New Guinea (PNG) is the largest and most populated of all the Pacific Island countries. It is a developing nation with 15% of the population engaged in market economy and the remaining 85% of people engaged in farming. A prudent macroeconomic policy and favorable terms of trade trends have helped PNG maintain macroeconomic stability, strong external balances, and solid economic growth over the past five years. The country, however, faces difficult development challenges, including weaknesses in governance, infrastructure, human development, the business climate, public financial management, security, and service delivery. Despite the challenges, the PNG economy has been performing well for the last few years. This chapter examines the challenges in the economy and explores the prospects that exist for the future development of countries economy. This chapter also delves into the recent economic trends of PNG.

Introduction

Papua New Guinea (PNG) is the largest and most populated of all the Pacific Island countries.[1] Topographically, it is one of the most diverse countries in the world, with an extraordinary range of ecosystems. However, its rural sector is not well served despite a well-developed infrastructure as it is not easily accessible. This creates major challenges in achieving development objectives in the country. Considering PNG's prospects for growth and development, the government is addressing these challenges through appropriate interventions detailed in its policies and plans.

PNG's economic problems have been attributed by many analysts to a combination of factors such as limited infrastructure, the inadequate supply, and high cost of skilled labor, natural disasters, and a weak institutional environment. In the late 1990s, PNG's economic problems were compounded by drought and the Asian economic crisis. An economic reform program, started in 1994 with International Monetary Fund and World Bank support, continues with an emphasis on public sector reform, governance, and privatization (WHO, 2006, p. 10).

Literature review

Hughes (2004, p. 1) proposes that economic reforms could put PNG on an annual growth path of 7% a year that would double its gross domestic product (GDP) every decade. That is certainly not an unreasonable ambition, because such rates have been and are being achieved by many countries in South-east Asia, including Malaysia, Singapore, and Thailand, not to mention China. Moreover, when PNG's total GDP growth rate, as measured in Australian dollars, has been nearly 6% per annum since 1975, 7% ought to be attainable (Curtin, 2004). But the ambition seems unlikely to be attained if the country follows Hughes' advice against relying on development either of mineral resources such as the Gas-to-Queensland project, because such projects "create only economic rents that provide revenues for a swollen government and public services" (Curtin, 2004).

Hughes (2004) and Chand (2004) emphasize the apparent zero growth of per capita income in 2003, but add the claim that "[mineral] resource revenues have also led to waste and corruption, subsidising a small political elite at the expense of investment in roads, health, and education."[2] Among many commentators following Chand in anticipating closure (because of reserve depletion) of all PNG's current mineral projects except Lihir Gold Ltd. by 2012, Hughes looks at land tenure reform and massive expansion of the oil palm plantation sector as both the source of compensatory export revenues and the drivers of her 7% growth rate target, suggesting that oil palm exports could grow at 30% a year and replace oil and mining as the country's biggest exports.[3]

Bourke's (2004) evaluation is that there is not enough suitable land to permit the massive expansion of oil palm production needed to replace revenue from oil, gold, and copper. However, Kenya's larger agricultural exports from a smaller area than is available in PNG, including US$1 billion per annum in horticultural exports, despite a much larger population needing to be fed, suggest that there is scope for significant increases in palm oil and other agricultural production, if not to the extent needed to replace mineral revenues. But it would be necessary to go beyond the present mix of subsistence agriculture and smallholder cash crop production (Bourke, 2004).

Country background

PNG is a developing nation with approximately 15% of the population engaged in the market economy and the remaining 85% of people engaged in the subsistence farming and mostly live in rural areas. It got independence on 16 September 1975 from Australia. It comprises the eastern half of the second largest island in the world and extends to an approximate land area of 476,000 sq. km. It is located just south of the Equator and north of the eastern tip of Australia. The country has over 600 islands with a population over 6.2 million people (2007). Administratively, the country has 20 provinces and 89 districts; PNG has made some progress in social development over the last 33 years. It is a country of enormous physical and social diversity (Wheeler and Murray, 1993; World Bank, 1997). It has many natural resources. Mining, forestry, and oil dominate the economy. In 2001, total external aid amounted to US$24 per capita (WHO, 2006; World Bank, 2007). Around 800 languages (not dialects) are spoken in PNG, one-third of the world's languages are spoken in PNG. This diversity underpins the challenges for effective land management.

PNG is classified as a low middle-income country with a GDP per capita of US$660 (2007 see Table 26.1). Although literacy rate has improved from

Table 26.1.   Key development indicators for PNG and the Pacific.

Country	GNI per capita[†] ($US)	Access to water (% of population)	Life expectancy (years)	Adult literacy rate (% of population)
PNG	660	39	56	57
Solomon Islands	590	70	63	77
Vanuatu	1600	60	69	74
Fiji	3280	47	68	n.a.
Tonga	2190	100	72	99
Samoa	2090	88	71	n.a.
Kiribati	1390	65	n.a.	n.a.

Sources: Human Development Report 2006, UNDP, and for [†]World Development Indicators Online, World Bank (2007).

32% to 65%, only half of all women aged 15 years and above and two-thirds of all men aged 15 years and older have ever attended school, and enrolment rates vary significantly across provinces. Life expectancy at birth has also increased from 43 to 57 years and Human Development Index from 0.43 to 0.54 and PNG ranked 145 (of 177 countries assessed). However, in recent years, progress has slowed. In short, PNG has a number of important achievements in its socioeconomic development but many challenges ahead such as poverty still remain. Currently, about 40% of the population live within or below the poverty line. About 90% of the poor live in rural areas. Subsistence farmers, fishermen, and hunters constitute the poorest segments of the population (UNDP, 2006; WHO, 2006).

This chapter is based on the secondary data, which have been collected from various reports such as AusAid, UN, World Bank, WHO, Government of PNG, etc. Despite various challenges, the economy has been performing better for the last few years. Thus, the PNG emerged as important market economy in South Pacific. This chapter examines challenges in the economy and explores the future prospects for the PNG economy. Further, it delves into the recent economic trends of PNG. This chapter has been divided into five parts. The second part deals with the challenges and prospects for development; the third part highlights recent developments in PNG economy; the fourth part of the paper provides the results and discussion and the last part provides summary and conclusion.

Challenges and Prospects for Development

Since PNG attained Independence in 1975, some developments have been achieved — increased life expectancy; a drop of infant mortality rates; and a drop in illiteracy rates and increased school participation rates. Nevertheless, major challenges remain. The challenges highlighted in the Government's Medium Term Development Strategy (2005–2010), the 1999 National Charter on Reconstruction and Development and successive National Budget statements.

The slow pace of economic growth combined with a high population growth rate of 2.4–2.7% per annum, for a population that already totals 6.2 million, has meant that per capita growth has averaged less than one percent per annum over the last decade. The impact of the growth on the population has also been uneven with rural dwellers, seeing little improvement in their living standards. Education and training have proceeded at a slow pace with the low level of skills, reducing employment opportunities. Further, the land tenure system is a serious impediment to rural and urban development. Efforts to introduce a land registration process have failed. At the village level, the lack of investment opportunities is a constraint. Poor infrastructure, remoteness from markets, the collapse of government extension services, and the high cost or lack of credit have all been highlighted as impeding the creation of business enterprise (UNDAF, 2002, p. 11; WHO, 2006).

A lack of accurate data as well as comprehensive research impacts on the development of policies and the formulation of strategies that will ensure their implementation. It also impacts on the understanding of the community. A lack of accurate data and information leads to an ill-informed public about a range of health and other issues, including HIV/AIDS, TB, etc. There is also a need in areas such as environmental conservation to find locally developed mechanisms that will work in PNG over long term. Issues of violence and human security are complex and differ between urban and rural settings. It is critical to shed light on the issues of crime, human security, and personal safety as these issues impact on all aspects of life in PNG and limit opportunities for development. Urgency of the problem cannot be over-emphasized (Hanson *et al.*, 2001; UNDAF, 2002). HIV/AIDS is now a generalized epidemic in PNG, having reached an estimated 2% prevalence with 59,000 HIV/AIDS cases. PNG has the highest level of HIV infection in the Pacific. Without an effective response, it has been estimated that HIV/AIDS will affect approximately 10% of the general population by 2025. Corruption is also a significant governance issue: PNG is ranked 130 (of 163 countries assessed) in a 2006 global corruption index (UNDP, 2006).

A considerable proportion of the population still lives in rural areas, many in isolated villages. Only 30% of the rural population has access to safe water and sanitation and many do not understand the relationship between water quality, environmental sanitation, and health (WHO, 2006). There is no dispute that youth unemployment is a pressing development challenge in PNG. Concerted action is overdue to address this issue and to acknowledge the value of youth as assets for social and economic development, with the need for political commitment to promote decent and productive work for young people. Further, gender inequality is widespread in the country and manifests itself in many areas, including in the home, in employment, in government, in access to education and health services, and in the enjoyment of human rights.

Poverty

Poverty in PNG is massive. Many rural dwellers do not earn cash income. The 1996 National Household Survey estimated that 37.5% of the population was living at or below the poverty line, with 93% of the poor living in rural areas (World Bank, 1999). Real per capita consumption of the wealthiest quartile is eight times that of the poorest quartile, one of the widest differentials within countries at a similar stage of development. Subsistence farmers, fishermen, and hunters constitute the poorest segments of the population. The households with uneducated or elderly heads suffer more from poverty (WHO, 2006). PNG has an extensive informal safety net system, called wantok.[4] Members of a wantok support one another in a variety of ways and transfer income to needy members. However, reports suggest that these traditional coping mechanisms do not make a significant impact on the depth or extent of rural poverty. To reduce the poverty, government of PNG has developed a poverty reduction strategy, which is focused in the existing national Medium Term Development Strategy (2005–2010). PNG is a signatory to the United Nations Millennium Development Declaration. Achieving the targets contained in the Millennium Development Goals (MDG) poses a real challenge (WHO, 2006).

With these challenges, a prudent macroeconomic policy mix together with favorable terms of trade trends has helped PNG maintain macroeconomic stability, strong external balances, and solid economic growth over the past five years. Formal employment, although very low as a share of the labor force, has also expanded. The country, however, faces difficult development challenges, including weaknesses in governance, infrastructure, human development, the business climate, public financial management, security, and service delivery. The PNG government has the strategies for Supporting Public Sector Reform 2003–2007 and the Public Expenditure Review and Rationalization process. Trade and financial services liberalization and a range of other reform initiatives aimed at reducing business impediments have created a more supportive environment for private sector growth.

PNG is rich in natural resources, particularly minerals, timber, fisheries, and potentially oil and gas. If these resources are effectively utilized, they hold tremendous promise, both in terms of economic growth as well as human development. However, poor natural resources management and failure to apply environmental good practices, particularly in the forestry, fisheries and mining sectors led to overexploitation and environmental degradation, with serious threats to long-term sustainability of these vital resources, as well as unemployment for an increasing population.

Development cooperation

In addition to its rich natural resources, the international development assistance also plays an important role in PNG's economy with a total estimated Official Development Assistance (ODA) in 2005 of 12.8 billion PNG Kina. Australia contributes a major share to ODA.

Australia's assistance to PNG

As the former colonial administrator and nearby neighbor, Australia has a long record of assistance to PNG — the Australian Government is PNG's largest development cooperation partner and has recently increased its financial support from approximately AUS$330 million to AUS$436 million per year. As well as Australian Government assistance, there is also considerable support to PNG from the Australian NGO sector, through engagement and relationships that extend back many years (AusAID, 2004).

Estimated ODA from Australia, the prominent donor in PNG for 2005–2006 was AUD$492.3 million, which represents about 18% of the PNG total annual budget (2006). Other major donors are Japan, the European Union (EU), the Asian Development Bank (ADB), the World Bank, and New Zealand. During 2006, the Australian Agency for International Development (AusAID), the New Zealand Agency for International Development (NZAID), the EU, and the ADB have been preparing their development cooperation strategies for their respective programming cycles (UNCP, 2007).

On its part, the UN system will have an estimated $117,765,000 mainly from UNDP, UNICEF, UNFPA, WHO, UNV, UNAIDS, UNHCR, FAO, UNESCO, ILO, and UN HABITAT over the period of 2008–2012. The bulk of UN support has been provided to governance, health, education, the environment, and HIV and AIDS. Non-governmental organizations (NGOs), both national and international, are important development partners in PNG and are involved in all sectors. Faith-based organizations (FBOs) (mainly church and mission organizations) are responsible for supporting about 50% of all health and education facilities, with partial funding from Government. Further, external assistance is provided largely in the form of technical assistance, with a relatively small proportion devoted to operational expenses and capital projects. Recently, there has been a shift to the provision of funds to national programs through sector-wide approach (SWAp) mechanisms. This has been the case with support to the Law and Justice Programme and the Health Sector Improvement Programme, whereby funds are channeled through and managed by the appropriate sectoral departments. A SWAp arrangement is planned for the education sector (UNCP, 2007).

Recent Trends in the Economy

The political situation in PNG has stabilized in recent years. The coalition government headed by Prime Minister Somare between 2002 and 2007 was the first since independence to serve a full term. The 2007 national elections returned PM Somare's coalition to power. Political stability and the resulting greater consistency of policies have contributed to the recent strong macro-economic performance.

As part of its development strategy, the PNG Government articulated second Medium Term Development Strategy (MTDS)[5] 2005–2010 as an integral component of the Government's overall economic and public sector reform program, which maps-out an appropriate development strategy for the period 2005–2010 and a matching policy framework that guides the Government's budgetary allocations and wider policy initiatives. The objectives of the MTDS are consistent with the Millennium Development Goals (GoPNG, 2003). In line with this, more attention is paid into priority areas of transport infrastructure, rehabilitation and maintenance, basic education, primary health care, law and justice, and programs that promote rural income earning opportunities (GoPNG, 2004).

In the past five years, PNG has seen the longest period of uninterrupted growth since independence. Real GDP growth in 2007 climbed to around 6%, the highest in a decade. Growth was led by construction, telecommunications and export-oriented agriculture (coffee, copra, and palm oil), and mining. For example, contributions came from construction, where expansion of 10% was stimulated by mining projects and public expenditure on infrastructure, and from oil and gas, where 13.7% growth reflected both the start of production at two new fields and improved extraction rates from existing fields. Climbing oil production was encouraged by the high world oil price.[6] Manufacturing and services also made contributions to growth. However, despite rising world prices for copper and gold and the start of two new mines, mining (excluding oil and gas) contracted by 4.9%. This reflected disruption of production by a landslide at the major Porgera gold mine. On the demand side, net exports were a major driver, supported by increases in private and public investment and in consumption formal employment across most sectors has grown by around 10% annually since 2005. Growth is expected to continue although structural constraints are likely to slow its pace over the medium term. Nonetheless, a major contribution came from the agriculture, forestry, and fisheries sector, which accounts for about one-third of GDP; it expanded by 2.9%. This rise primarily reflected increased production of logs for export and of palm oil. Global prices for both commodities, which were the country's two major agricultural export earners in 2006, trended upward through the year. Copra production also has risen in response to an improving world price, whereas cocoa production remained stable in the face of price volatility (ADB, 2007).

In 2007, the PNGs mining and petroleum industries have made huge stride in taking the country toward becoming a liquefied natural gas (LNG) producer,[7] the startup of a new mine at Siniwit and a number of other mining developments moving closer to adding to the country's golden riches. As stated earlier, this success was the result of the positive state of the country's financial position, and the economy is growing at the strongest rate in more than a decade (Industry Review, 2008).

Higher economic growth also fed through the private sector employment in agriculture, trade, manufacturing, construction, transportation, and finance and business services, which collectively increased by 4.6% in the 12 months to September 2006. Employment rose particularly fast in construction (13.3%). Over the same period, mineral sector employment (i.e., oil, gas, and mining) registered negligible growth (ADB, 2007).

Additionally, the fiscal position remains strong. Budget revenue is booming as world market prices for PNG's key exports (oil, copper, and gold) reach new heights. The government has prudently restrained expenditures, directing part of the windfall mineral revenues to public debt repayments and saving a part in trust accounts for one-off investment spending in the future. As a result, the central budget had a strong fiscal surplus (around 6% of GDP) in both 2006 and 2007. The non-mineral budget deficit, meanwhile, remained relatively steady over the past two years at around 7–8% of GDP, indicating that the injection of windfall revenues into the economy remains under control. By the end of 2007, the windfall revenues in trust accounts designated for future investment reached about 17% of GDP. The 2008 budget and the newly prepared medium-term fiscal framework envision continued fiscal restraint and expenditure smoothing over the commodity price cycle (Kanu, 2008).

The public sector debt burden has been substantially reduced in the past five years. Healthy growth, an appreciation of the real exchange rate, tighter external borrowing policy, and prepayment of public debt using a portion of windfall revenues have led to a fall in the public debt-to-GDP ratio from over 60% in 2003 to around 35% in 2007.

Inflation appears to remain subdued: consumer prices rose by an average of 0.9% in 2007 compared to 2.3% in 2006. But average consumer price inflation excluding seasonal products, goods subject to price controls, and changing excises was close to 7% in 2007. In the medium term, inflation is expected to pick up as the economy will have to cope with continued monetary expansion coming from accumulation of foreign exchange reserves, strong growth of credit to the private sector, and record low interest rates. In the first nine months of 2006, exports (in nominal US dollars) shot up by 33.2% on the year-earlier period, imports rose by 16%, and the trade surplus widened by 8.3%. Copper, gold, and oil were the main boosts to export earnings, supplemented by palm oil and logs. The transfer accounts also improved, but deficits on the net services and income accounts widened. The current account surplus picked up to an estimated 14.2% of GDP (ADB, 2007, p. 246).

BPNG's move was based on inflationary forecast of 9%, a continuing private sector credit growth and a 7.6% expansion in gross domestic product for the year 2008. One effect of the tightening move is an increase in the cost borrowing, which would reduce demand for loans from the business sector, resulting to a lower growth in bank lending for 2008.[8]

The current account surplus rose to over 4% of GDP in 2007, thanks to high commodity prices. In the medium term, it is expected to decline as import growth rises in line with per capita income, investment, and output. International reserves increased from US$1.4 billion at the end of 2006 to US$2.1 billion at the end of 2007, equivalent to about 4.5 months of imports of goods and services or about a year of non-mineral project-related imports. Reserves have stabilized in early 2008 as imports have been increasing. The kina has been fairly stable in recent years, appreciating against the US dollar by around 7% in 2007–2008.

Discussion

Notwithstanding PNG's comfortable macro-fiscal position, significant structural and policy challenges limit its long-term growth potential. Most notable among these is the institutional and policy framework for public financial management (EAU, 2008). Critical areas for improvement are the integrity of budget processes, intergovernmental financial arrangements, efficiency of sectoral expenditure and service delivery, performance of the civil service and parastatals, and transparency and accountability in budget management. To stimulate private sector investment, particularly outside mining, the critical priority is improvement in the business climate, especially by opening more markets to competition, reducing the regulatory and licensing burden, clarifying property rights (especially for land), and maintaining law and order.

In Western eyes "development" is often seen as a desirable and necessary progression toward a Western-style economic and political system, from some inferior state of "under-development," with *kastom* (custom) and culture often viewed as getting in the way. For many, PNGs "development" is seen differently. The introduction of the cash economy and the various pressures associated with past patterns of development are seen as part of the problem, leading to social dislocation, environmental degradation, divisions within society, and the new phenomenon of poverty. PNGs want better access to income earning opportunities, better education and health services, improved water supplies, and social cohesion and harmony. However, they do not want to become "westernised." A Melanesian approach sees the way forward as a blend of tradition and modernity, and emphasizes the need for integrated human development (World Bank, 1999).

The land tenure issue starkly demonstrates the tension between these different views of development. In PNG, land is vital to livelihoods and cultural identity — widespread community concerns about a possible shift from communal ownership to individual title have been flashpoints in past protests around donor-led structural reform programs. Some Australian commentators continue to call for the abandonment of communal land tenure. "Wiser heads" point to the possibility of enhancing land utilization for development purposes while maintaining traditional owner control.

The government noted in handing down its latest budget that the improved economic growth picture stems from a combination of the commodity price boom, improved political stability, prudent macroeconomic, and fiscal policies, together with low interest rates and inflation. And most outside viewers can agree that there is significant potential for that economic growth to continue on the back of the exciting LNG opportunities and a string of new mining developments (Industry Review, 2008).

Summary and Conclusion

PNG continues to experience economic growth and improved fiscal stability. Yet, significant development challenges need to be addressed to translate growth into improved living standards for PNGs. The PNG's national income would grow rapidly with its natural resources such as mining, petrol and natural gas, and forests. The proposed LNG project has the potential for boosting the virtues of PNG and its people.

This chapter reviews economic and social conditions of the PNG such as poor economic growth, increasing levels of poverty, unemployment, and environmental degradation. The poor economic performance in the PNG has been attributed to the lack of appropriate economic policies and rampant corruption. The international trade of PNG is unfavorable; hence, the Government has to adopt policies and programs that will support free trade, foreign investment, and export-led growth. This will eventually make the PNG economy robust in the South Pacific.

Notes

1. There are 14 Forum Island Countries: Cook Islands, Federated States of Micronesia, Fiji, Kiribati, Nauru, Niue, Palau, Papua New Guinea, Republic of the Marshall Islands, Samoa, Solomon Islands, Tonga, Tuvalu, and Vanuatu. The remaining two members (developed countries) are Australia and New Zealand. Both Australia and New Zealand are major donors to South Pacific Island Nations.
2. Curtin (2004, 2005) has shown how PNG's economic performance has not been as poor as Chand and Hughes have contended, with growth of per capita GDP in current Australian dollar terms having been faster than in Australia since 1975.
3. Chand and Hughes were both too pessimistic about the dates of depletion of reserves at mines and oilfields in PNG. The mines at Porgera and Ok Tedi have both extended their closure dates, and the Kutubu and adjacent oilfields are now expected to continue production until after 2020, without taking into account the proposed gas to Queensland project.
4. A wantok is an informal association based on kinship, ethnicity, language, and/or friendship.
5. The Government of PNG also has prepared the long-term development strategy for 2010–2030, which is expected to be launched in November 2008.
6. The crude oil price in the world market has reached over 140 USD per barrel in mid-2008.
7. Energy companies involved in the planned gas pipeline from the Southern Highlands to Australia project have indicated willingness instead to consider developing the gas fields for liquefied natural gas exports and petrochemical production.
8. As quoted by Kanu (2008), BPNG tightens fiscal policy, The National News paper. www.thenational.com.pg (5 August 2008).

References

Annual Papua New Guinea (2008). *Industry Review*. Western Australia: Energy Publications.
Asian Development Bank (ADB) (2007). *Outlook 2007*. Manila: Asian Development Bank. Retrieved from: www.adb.org/Documents/Books/ADO/2007/figs/f2-31-1.xls [30 June 2008].
Australian Agency for International Development (AusAID) (2004). *Poverty Reduction Analysis' Background Paper for PNG Law and Justice Sector Program*. Canberra: AusAID.
Australian Agency for International Development (AusAID) (2007). *Papua New Guinea — Australia Development Cooperation Strategy, 2006–2010*. Canberra: AusAID. Retrieved from www.ausaid.gov.au/publications [23 June 2008].
Bourke, RM (2004). *Agriculture in the Papua New Guinea Economy, Seminar Paper*.
Chand, S (2004). Papua new Guinea economic survey: Transforming good luck into policies for long-term growth. *Pacific Economic Bulletin*, 19(1), 1–19.

Curtin, T (2004). How poor is Papua New Guinea? how rich could it be?, *Working Paper 56, Resource Management in Asia-Pacific*. Canberra: Australian National University. Retrieved from www.rspas.anu.edu.au/rmap/workingpapers.php [27 June 2008].

Curtin, T (2005). Papua new Guinea economic survey: A comment. *Pacific Economic Bulletin*, 20(1), 137–142.

EAU — East Asia Update (2008).

Government of Papua New Guinea (GoPNG), (2003). *Medium Term Development Strategy (MTDS) 2003–2007*. Port Moresby: Government of Papua New Guinea.

Government of Papua New Guinea (GoPNG), (2004). *Medium Term Development Strategy (MTDS) 2005–2010, Our Plan for Economic and Social Advancement*, Port Moresby: Government of Papua New Guinea, November, 2004. Retrieved from http://www.aciar.gov.au/system/files/sites/aciar/files/node/777/PNG+medium+term+development+strategy+2005-2010.pdf [28 May 2008].

Hanson, LW, BJ Allen, RM Bourke, and TJ McCarthy (2001). *Papua New Guinea Rural Development Handbook, Research School of Pacific and Asian Studies, Department of Human Geography*. Canberra: Australian National University.

Hughes, H (2004). *Can Papua New Guinea Come Back from the Brink?* Sydney: Centre for Independent Studies.

United Nations Country Programme (UNCP), (2007). *Final Draft UNCP Papua New Guinea 2008–2012 — A Partnership for Nation Building*. Port Moresby: United Nations Country Programme.

United Nations Development Programme (UNDP), (2006). *Human Development Report 2006*. Washington, DC: United Nations Development Programme.

World Health Organization (WHO), (2006). *Country Cooperation Strategy (CCS) for Papua New Guinea over the Period 2005 to 2009*. Geneva: World Health Organization.

Wheeler, T and J Murray (1993). *Papua New Guinea — A Travel Survival Guide*, 5th edn. Hawthorn, Vic.: Lonely Planet Publications.

Wikipedia, the Free Online Encyclopaedia (2008). *Papua New Guinea*.

World Bank (1997). *Papua New Guinea — Accelerating Agricultural Growth: An Action Plan*. Washington, DC: World Bank.

World Bank (1999). *Papua New Guinea: Poverty and Access to Public Services*. Washington, DC: World Bank.

World Bank (2007). *World Development Indicators 2007*. Washington, DC: World Bank.

Chapter 27

CONCLUSION

SATYENDRA SINGH

Abstract

Clearly, significant business opportunities exist for managers and investors in emerging markets where they can expand production, market products, and generate revenues. Because managers are often unfamiliar with the structure, culture, and risks associated with emerging markets, these chapters provide an understanding of differences in business practices among diverse range of emerging markets — from Asia to Africa and from Eastern Europe to South America — by concentrating on the unique characteristics, opportunities, challenges, and business strategies for growth. The next section, based on the findings of the chapters, provides the experience, insights, and recommendations for business managers.

Part I: China

In Chapter 2, Grigoriou recommends that, to effectively compete in emerging markets, organizations must develop products that are targeted to the needs of the consumer. As the emerging market grows toward a more industrialized economy, these needs will change over time. To successfully compete in emerging markets, new product developers should consider multiple products for each emerging market. The reason for such a suggestion is that as emerging market economies grow, disparity among its consumers grows as well. Therefore, the organization should develop high-end products for the growing middle class consumers found in emerging markets. This enables the international marketing organization to peruse consistent brand-building strategies. A second *stripped down* product should also be developed for the middle class of consumer of tomorrow;

that is, consumers who cannot afford a high-end version of the product now may be able to do so in the future.

In Chapter 3, Xie and White find that Chinese latecomers were able to successfully enter handset industry because (1) barriers to entry were reduced; (2) they were able to acquire the resources and capabilities to operate in the industry; and (3) they initially entered markets ignored or underserved by the incumbents.

In Chapter 4, Liu and Wei recommend that effective and efficient usage of assets should be a part of corporate culture despite a possible low-cost advantage in natural resources or labor in some emerging markets. This strategic goal is especially important for emerging markets because financial resources are generally scarce. In addition, knowledge-based assets should not be ignored just because they take a long time to materialize and are often difficult to measure.

In Chapter 5, Lee and Chen demonstrate that knowledge codification and information system integration are important. Because the Chinese market is different from a multinational corporations' (MNC) home market, having a learning mechanism that can allow managers to understand and convert local knowledge into systems is crucial. Knowledge acquired without understanding of causal ambiguity is of no use to the MNC and its subsidiary, in particular. Alternatively, managers should establish an information system that is compatible with their operations in China. Integrative information system allows managers to share information and knowledge with other foreign operations easier and faster. With quicker responses to the market, superior firm performance is likely to follow.

In Chapter 6, Chong finds that even though some auditing reports seem to be vague in details, the National audit office (NAO) has made a right decision on exercising and projecting transparency in audit reporting and findings. Undoubtedly, the NAO intends to show its sense of authority, impartiality, and objectivity to the public and fund providers; however, these reports need to be much more robust, in particular those relating to follow-up responses from the addressees. The addressees seem to comply with the deadlines, but the responses remain vague and ambiguous.

Part II: Commonwealth of Independent States

In Chapter 7, Kuznetsova discovers that the attitude of Russian medium and large companies toward Corporate Social Responsibility (CSR) contradicts the picture that the government seeks to create; that is, the growth of CSR is a priority for both politicians and corporations. One explanation is that usually CSR in Russia is discussed in relation to the handful of super large firms, operating in lucrative industries. By contrast, the respondents represented the hardcore of industrial firms enjoy no exclusivity. Their attitude signals that the link between CSR, trust, and economic growth as a way out of poverty is not fully recognized in Russia. Deficit of CSR in Russia should not come as a surprise if looked at through the *strategic approach* lenses. If a strategy does not bring performance or competitive advantages, then we cannot expect that the company managed by rational individuals for implementation will select it. From this perspective, the near absence of CSR initiatives from the managerial practices in modern Russia is not surprising. Moreover, in a sense, it can be seen as an encouraging sign indicating that firms are now tuned up with the market signals and tend to abandon or disregard practices that do not bring adequate rewards even if there is a non-economic pressure to do otherwise. This is a welcome departure from the model of thinking and operating that prevailed during the period of central planning.

In Chapter 8, Kuznetsova further indicates that, in the Russian context, concentrated ownership is likely to have a negative impact on firm performance. But Russian corporation does not only feature concentrated ownership, they are insiders-dominant as well. Some studies on the companies' performance supremacy with respect to the dominance of either insiders or outsiders indicate possible advantage of the latter, but not when propensity to restructure is considered. In Russia, however, improvement in performance depends on restructuring. All in all, performance-related implications of the Russian model of corporate governance are not entirely clear. What is clear though is that insiders' dominance slows down restructuring process and corresponding firms suffer from the syndrome of long-term commitment avoidance.

In Chapter 9, Martinovic and Branch, in the evolution of private labels in Croatian grocery retailing, provide an apt illustration of the dynamism of brand management in emerging markets. In less than a decade, with many lessons learned along the way, private labels have become an integral feature of Croatian grocery retailing. Accession to the European Union, however, will bring more change and quickly. Companies like DONA Trgovina D.O.O. have adapted to change, and they will continue to adapt, as Croatia itself continues to adapt to the globalizing world economy.

In Chapter 10, McKenzie gives both an historical and current view of the retail sector in Estonia, Latvia, and Lithuania, and provides managerial implications in terms of retailing, practices, employee development, and business opportunities between the East and West. Using the Baltic States as a proxy for other transition economies, the findings should be of interest to both foreign retailers aiming at expanding operations into these or similar countries in transition, as well as to domestic retailers who historically had less experience and access to retailing research of this type.

Part III: Latin America

In Chapter 11, Barbosa, Gassenferth, and Machado recommend that (1) the periodic follow-up of the reports and analyses of the data mining tool be inserted in the management routine of the procurement activities; (2) the stratification of the items purchased according to a rank of purchase value be at all times carried out by the manager, who makes decisions on more cost-effective purchases in moments/processes than investment-significant acquisitions; (3) the matching of the information contained in the purchases database be thoroughly examined to understand the possibilities of suppliers as well as the company's most critical requirements, and thus better understanding to enhance the procurement decision-making process and improving the cost–benefit ratio upon purchasing inputs for the company's end product; and, (4) the experiences and results achieved by the managers using this type of work/decision making be recorded.

In Chapter 12, Felzensztein suggests that the concept of milieu characterizes the salmon industry. This is due to the majority of firms being in close geographical proximity operating in one dominating industry, together with auxiliary industries that form the regional cluster and build horizontal and vertical relations. The managers and public policy officials developing regional cluster strategies need to analyze the social networking aspects on inter-firm collaboration. The concept of social capital needs not to be seen as social contracts, but as social relations and strong mutual knowledge among firms.

In Chapter 13, Neves and Castro offer three implications for managers in food chain industry. First, inserting small holders into food value chains is a way of building sustainability around the world. This is an important global concern and although image might not be the main firm's concern, there are important positive image implications. Staff morale increases because they belong to the firm's sustainable initiatives. Second, agribusiness firms need to develop and diversify their suppliers globally. Especially, for Brazil, a country that has witnessed the increase of large-scale monocultures such as sugarcane or soybeans. This kind of project may alleviate unemployment and migration from traditional cultures that were pushed by expansion of large scale commercial crops. And finally, there is a need for inclusion, without any ideological view, but with a sustainable and competitive reasoning.

In Chapter 14, Gauzente and Dumoulin suggest that legitimacy is obtained using strategies such as adopting certain normative aspects (compromise), disguising non-conformity (avoidance), ignoring or contesting norms (defiance), and shaping norms (manipulation, which is only available to powerful firms in economic, relational, or institutional terms). In emerging markets, given the flexibility or simply lack of rules and legislation, some powerful pioneer franchisers may exert their influence in order to enforce their business model and build their own legitimacy.

Part IV: Africa

In Chapter 15, Lewa and Lewa identify a few key areas for improvent relating to public procurement in Kenya: the framework, instituitional aspects, human and other resourses, suppliers' capacity and types of procurement, and timing.

In Chapter 16, Quan-Baffour recommends that to boost local economic development initiatives through the establishment of small- and medium-scale tourism-related businesses in South Africa, (1) the local government must assist the emerging local entrepreneurs financially in order to expand their businesses and get them space where they can operate such businesses; (2) the department of tourism and labor must conduct a survey on the small business owners to find out their training needs, provide them with training in basic managerial and accounting skills, which may empower them to manage and expand their businesses; and (3) law enforcement agents must assist small and medium-scale business managers to stamp out crime, especially drug peddling, stealing and prostitution.

In Chapter 17, Alam and Hussain suggest that the partnership-financing mode (PFM) of Islamic banking finance should work perfectly in almost all developing countries. Due to the joint interest of lenders and borrowers in a particular venture, the lending process develops a unique lender–borrower network relationship. And various microentrepreneurs, regardless of cast creed, and religions, show their interest in borrowing funds from Islamic banks. It is due to the banks' close contact with customers and their advice to clienteles. Because the micro-credit is based on PFM of Islamic financing, the lending institutions ensure that microtypes of credits, given to the needy and experienced rural entrepreneurs, are being properly utilized. It can be concluded that once Islamic banks show their interest in investing in a partnership mode of finance, it will not only eliminate rural poverty, but also be successful in establishing just and balanced social order, free from all kinds of exploitations in the society.

In Chapter 18, Madichie, Hinson, and Salifu find that in Ghana, the adoption of state-of-the-art technology to deliver banking services represents a significant departure from the manual processes that were in operation in the 1980s. This apparent shift in strategic focus is aimed at enabling them catch up with global developments and improve the quality of their service delivery. Some of the notable e-banking delivery channels in Ghanian banks include e-banking, use of automated teller machines, telephone banking, points of sale terminals, electronic funds transfer, and lately mobile banking. Each of these delivery channels has its advantages. Web banking has proven to be an attractive choice. It is fast, economical, and flexible. Through the web, both corporate and retail customers of a bank are able to manage their accounts and do their banking operations, and monitor their accounts on a 24-h basis.

Part V: Middle East

In Chapter 19, Mohamed and Hussain suggest that management accounting plays an important role in measuring both financial and non-financial performances in the Islamic financial service industry. However, the significance of the role played by these measures is subject to scrutiny, as there seems to be no institutionalized perspective on the equal importance of both financial and non-financial performance measures. There seems to be a tendency to think that financial performance measurement is more significant. The significant importance of using either or both types of measures is left to management discretion. Also, there appears to be a gap between the perception of the *best practice* that should take place and the *actual practice* taking place, particularly in the case of non-financial performance measurement. Also, the size of the bank does not seem to have a significant effect on PM practice. Further, the nature of Islamic financial sector industry does not have a remarkable impact on performance measurement; however, banks put higher emphasis on financial performance due to the need for competing against their counterparts.

In Chapter 20, Rao provides the key characteristics of the Kuwait business environment: (1) Kuwait is an import-dependent country. The imports of various products and services from different parts of the world are continuously increasing, facilitated by increased favorable balance of trade; (2) the capital intensive country with the national goal of diversifying the predominantly oil-dependent economy is resulting in the initiation of a variety of industrial, infrastructural, and tourism development projects. The technological and human needs of such projects offer many business opportunities to international businesses. Business opportunities will be especially attractive in the area of developing upstream petrochemical industries; and (3) participation of foreign enterprises in retailing field is progressively increasing because of Kuwaiti consumers' preferences for quality foreign products and services.

In Chapter 21, Yeganeh provides an understanding of contemporary society and management in Iran. With a young and energetic population, with a vibrant and evolving culture, and with a growing economy, Iran is undergoing substantial changes. Due to the complexity of the country, it is hard to predict the extent of these changes; however, it is plausible that the current trend will lead to higher levels of economic, cultural, and political openness. Over the past five years, despite all harsh political sanctions, Iran has continued to attract foreign investments from a wide range of countries such as China, France, Germany, Italy, and Russia. Therefore, from a business perspective, Iran offers significant market opportunities that cannot be neglected. In fact, for international managers, the question is not "whether," but "when" Iran will emerge as a global business player.

In Chapter 22, Thrassou, Vrontis, and Kokkinaki suggest that Internet technology is more than a simple web site; it should offer sales and support as well. The Cypriot web site of companies must be such that it offers added value that is specific to Cypriot consumers, so that they will prefer the web site to other potentially more attractive international ones. There are three possible key advantages to this strategy: (1) the design of a web site that fits the Cypriot consumer profile (language, style, etc.); (2) the offer of a marketing mix specifically designed for the Cypriot buyer (product quality, variety, price, etc.); and (3) the elimination of the element of "risk" that overshadows Internet purchases posed by the existence of a "brick-and-mortar" presence in Cyprus.

Part VI: Asia

In Chapter 23, Fauzi, Rahman, Hussain, and Priyanto, find that activities relating to corpoarate social responsibility (CSR) in the Indonesian companies do not seem to contribute to business performance, and that Indonesian companies are increasingly trying to accommodate CSR and emphasizing on CSR as costs rather than as stakeholder relationship. This could be due to the companies' objection to the Law No. 40 on Indonesian Corporation. One of the articles of the law stipulates that Indonesian companies are obliged to conduct CSR. The reason for the objection is the unreadiness of companies to carry out the CSR responsibilities. It is recommended that the awareness to disclose the CSR activities would encourage companies to conduct the CSR.

In Chapter 24, Tripathy, Rao and Kanagaraj, find that pricing of derivatives is a function of volatility, so instability of stock market creates uncertainty that adversely affects growth prospects of business houses, and leads to a barrier of growth prospects of economy. Additionally, stock market volatility hinders economic performance through consumer spending and business investment spending that lead to structural and regulatory changes. These findings have recommendations for policy makers, regulators, business houses, and investors.

In Chapter 25, Garrovillas identifies five reasons for investing in the Philippines: (1) literate, teachable, affordable, and committed labor force; (2) good communication skills of the population; (3) liveable environment; (4) diverse and largely untapped agricultural and natural resources; and (5) established and expanding international trade linkages. Further, the Philippines offers extensive opportunities for regionalization in the production and processing of a wide variety of tropical agricultural food products and other natural resource-based industries such as coconut and by-products like virgin coco oil, palm oil and by-products, timber and other wood products, livestock and poultry, high value tropical fruits, and vegetables. Given the Philippine's strategic location within the international trade routes, it has the potential to become a major trans-shipment point for world commerce.

In the final Chapter 26, Rena predicts that Papua New Guinea's (PNG) national income would grow rapidly with its natural resources such as mining, petrol and natural gas, and forests. The proposed natural gas project has the potential for boosting the virtues of natural gas and its people. The poor economic performance in the PNG has been attributed to the lack of appropriate economic policies and rampant corruption. The international trade of PNG is unfavorable; hence, the Government has to adopt policies and programs that will support free trade, foreign investment, and export-led growth. This will eventually make the PNG economy robust in the South Pacific.

INDEX